Österreich

Einwohner (2009): 8,2 Mio

0   25   50 Meilen
0   25   50 Kilometer

DEUTSCHLAND

Bodensee

★ Bregenz
VORARLBERG
● Feldkirch
Arlberg ●
● Landeck
DIE
SCHWEIZ
SÜDTIROL
● Meran
● Bozen

● Reutte
Kufstein ● ● Sankt Johann in Tirol
● Wörgl
● Kitzbühel ● Zell am See
Innsbruck ★ Inn
TIROL
● Bruck
SALZBURG
Osttirol
(zu Tirol)
● Lienz ● Spittal an der Drau
Drau

ITALIEN

OBERÖSTERREICH
● Gmunden
★ Salzburg
● Bad Ischl
● Hallstatt ● Liezen
● Bischofshofen
● Radstadt
● Mauterndorf
● Sankt Georgen
Enns

KÄRNTEN
● Feldkirchen
● Klagenfurt
● Villach
Wörther See

★ Linz
● Melk ● Sankt Pölten
● Amstetten
NIEDERÖSTERREICH
● Mariazell
● Bruck an der Mur
STEIERMARK

Graz ★ Mur

SLOWENIEN

Donau WIEN
Wien ✪
● Baden
Neusiedler See
● Wiener Neustadt ● Eisenstadt
BURGENLAND
● Oberwart
● Güssing

UNGARN

Die Schweiz und Liechtenstein

Einwohner

Schweiz (2009): 7,6 Mio
Liechtenstein (2009): 35 000

0   25   50 Meilen
0   25   50 Kilometer

Rhein

FRANKREICH

BASEL
(STADT)
Basel ★
★ Liestal
BASEL
(LAND)
Delemont ★
JURA
SOLOTHURN
Solothurn ★
● Biel
NEUENBURG
● Neuchâtel
Neuenburger See
JURA
Bern ✪
WAADT
★ Fribourg
FREIBURG
● Thun
Thuner See
Lausanne ●
Montreux ● ● Gstaad
GENF
Genf ●
Genfer See
● Sion
WALLIS
● Zermatt
Matterhorn ▲

SCHAFFHAUSEN
Baden ●
AARGAU
Aarau ●
LUZERN
BERN
BERNER
OBERLAND
Sarnen ●
UNTERWALDEN
OBW.
Brienz ●
Interlaken ●
Brienzer See
Jungfrau ▲
Jungfraujoch ▲ ● Grindelwald
● Brig
Rhône

ITALIEN

★ Schaffhausen DEUTSCHLAND
● Kreuzlingen
THURGAU
★ Frauenfeld
Winterthur ● Thur Bodensee
ZÜRICH
★ Zürich St. Gallen ★ ● St. Margrethen
Herisau ● AUSSER-RHODEN
SANKT GALLEN APPENZELL
● Appenzell
INNER-RHODEN
Zürichsee
Zug ● ● Einsiedeln Vaduz ★
ZUG ● Glarus LIECHTENSTEIN ÖSTERREICH
SCHWYZ GLARUS
Vierwaldstätter See ★ Schwyz ● Braunwald
Luzern ★
Stans ★
NIDW. Rhein
★ Altdorf ● Chur
● Engelberg ● Klosters
URI ● Davos
● Andermatt ● Disentis GRAUBÜNDEN
Rhein
Tessin ● St. Moritz
Inn

TESSIN
★ Bellinzona
● Locarno
● Lugano
Langensee

NIDW = NIDWALDEN
OBW = OBWALDEN

Deutsch: Na klar!

Sixth Edition

Deutsch: Na klar!

An Introductory German Course

Robert Di Donato
Miami University
Oxford, Ohio

Monica D. Clyde

Jacqueline Vansant
University of Michigan, Dearborn

Published by McGraw-Hill, an imprint of The McGraw-Hill Companies, Inc., 1221 Avenue of the Americas, New York, NY 10020. Copyright © 2012, 2008, 2004, 1999, 1995, 1991. All rights reserved. No part of this publication may be reproduced or distributed in any form or by any means, or stored in a database or retrieval system, without the prior written consent of The McGraw-Hill Companies, Inc., including, but not limited to, in any network or other electronic storage or transmission, or broadcast for distance learning.

This book is printed on acid-free paper.

1 2 3 4 5 6 7 8 9 0 DOW / DOW 1 0 9 8 7 6 5 4 3 2 1

Student Edition

ISBN: 978-0-07-338633-1
MHID: 0-07-338633-2

Instructor's Edition

ISBN: 978-0-07-737845-5
MHID: 0-07-737845-8

Vice President and Editor in Chief: *Michael Ryan*
Editorial Director: *William R. Glass*
Director of Development: *Scott Tinetti*
Developmental Editor: *Paul Listen*
Executive Marketing Manager: *Hector Alvero*
Faculty Development Manager: *Jorge Arbujas*
Editorial Coordinator: *Laura Chiriboga*
Text Permissions Editor: *Veronica Oliva*
Production Editors: *Chris Schabow and Brett Coker*
Production Service: *The Left Coast Group, Inc.*
Manuscript Editor: *Marie Deer*
Interior Designers: *Maureen McCutcheon and Cassandra Chu*
Cover Designer: *Adrian Morgan*
Photo Research Coordinator: *Sonia Brown*
Photo Researcher: *Emily Tietz*
Buyer II: *Sherry Kane*
Media Project Manager: *Thomas Brierly*
Composition: *10/12 Melior by Aptara®, Inc.*
Printing: *45# Liberty Dull by R. R. Donnelley & Sons*

Credits: The credits section for this book begins on page C-1 and is considered an extension of the copyright page.

Library of Congress Cataloging-in-Publication Data

Di Donato, Robert
    Deutsch: na klar! : an introductory German course/Robert Di Donato, Monica D. Clyde, Jacqueline Vansant.—6th ed.
        p. cm.
    ISBN-13: 978-0-07-338633-1 (alk. paper)
    ISBN-10: 0-07-338633-2 (student ed. : alk. paper)
    ISBN-13: 978-0-07-737845-5 (alk. paper)
    ISBN-10: 0-07-737845-8 (instructor's ed.) : alk. paper)
    1. German language—Grammar.   2. German language—Textbooks for foreign speakers—English.   I. Clyde, Monica.   II. Vansant, Jacqueline, 1954– III. Title.
    PF3112.D48 2012
    438.2'421—dc22

2010040903

The Internet addresses listed in the text were accurate at the time of publication. The inclusion of a Web site does not indicate an endorsement by the authors or McGraw-Hill, and McGraw-Hill does not guarantee the accuracy of the information presented at these sites.

www.mhhe.com

Contents

	Wörter im Kontext	Grammatik im Kontext

	Wörter im Kontext	Grammatik im Kontext

Sprache im Kontext	Landeskunde- und Sprach-Info	Audio-Aktivitäten

	Wörter im Kontext	**Grammatik im Kontext**

Sprache im Kontext	Landeskunde- und Sprach-Info	Audio-Aktivitäten

	Wörter im Kontext	Grammatik im Kontext

Landeskunde zum Mitnehmen 430

Preface

Welcome to the exciting new Sixth Edition of ***Deutsch: Na klar!***, wrapped in a clean, beautiful new interior design. Those familiar with this textbook know that ***Deutsch: Na klar!*** offers a versatile, comprehensive, and colorful program for introductory German courses. The Sixth Edition continues to provide an innovative package designed to suit a wide variety of approaches, methodologies, and classrooms, while still preserving many standard pedagogical features that instructors have come to rely on. ***Deutsch: Na klar!*** is not a one-method program. Among its trusted and proven features you will recognize the following:

- engaging video interviews with native speakers of German on the chapter topics as well as broader cultural footage that focuses on particular aspects of the chapter themes.

- a rich array of authentic visual and textual materials with accompanying activities and exercises

- succinct grammar explanations

- a commitment to the balanced development of both receptive skills (listening and reading) and productive skills (speaking and writing)

- abundant communicative activities, as well as many form-focused activities and exercises

- the promotion of meaningful acquisition of vocabulary and structures with considerable attention to accuracy

Deutsch: Na klar! — Just the Facts!

If one theme characterizes ***Deutsch: Na klar!*** best, it's "Back to Basics" in German. ***Deutsch: Na klar!*** introduces students to the fundamentals of German language and cultures through a flexible approach that has wide appeal. ***Deutsch: Na klar!*** does not rely on gimmicks or tricks. It immerses students in German language and culture through a careful combination of authentic materials and targeted listening and speaking exercises, ranging from controlled to open-ended. They provide comprehensible input of vocabulary and grammar. It also offers a wide variety of cultural texts and activities, including a totally new section in the Sixth Edition called **Landeskunde zum Mitnehmen** (or *Culture to Go*). Along with all of this, ***Deutsch: Na klar!*** offers readings that elaborate on the chapter theme, podcasts in which the students are given opportunities to develop their presentational skills, and video segments that demonstrate how German works in everyday situations.

"***Deutsch: Na klar!*** – Just the Facts" addresses many of the questions you have about the changing world of teaching German and how the program responds to those changes to support instructors and students in teaching and learning German. The following are some questions instructors and students alike have posed about ***Deutsch: Na klar!***

- **Question 1: What outcomes do German instructors want their students to achieve and how does *Deutsch: Na klar!* help accomplish this?**
Answer: First and foremost, instructors want students to be able to communicate in German and make themselves understood to other German speakers. And they want them to do it with the appropriate degree of accuracy. Instructors want their students to be able to understand both spoken and written German with a certain amount of detail. They also want them to read German with a certain amount of ease and without having to look up every word. And they want them to be knowledgeable about the cultures of German-speaking countries. How does ***Deutsch: Na klar!*** support these goals? It engages students with authentic materials in print, audio, and video and puts them into the kinds of situations they would encounter in any German-speaking environment. It gets students to communicate, both in a controlled way at first, and then in an open-ended fashion, on a variety of topics that affect their own lives. ***Deutsch: Na klar!*** engages students in cross-cultural comparisons and analysis throughout the book—they state opinions, summarize and synthesize texts, and narrate events. At every turn, the program increases students' proficiency in German—they communicate, learn about the culture of German-speaking countries, make connections with other disciplines, and reach out to learn about communities of German speakers.

- **Question 2: How does *Deutsch: Na klar!* work as a German program?**
Answer: The program takes students from their personal world (talking about themselves, their likes, their dislikes, where they live, their families and friends) to the world of everyday living (buying a train ticket, shopping for groceries or clothes, staying fit and healthy, enjoying leisure

time) and ultimately culminates in the world of topics and issues (the media, environment, public opinion). Vocabulary and grammar are presented in a functional framework so students will associate forms with functions. It is a carefully crafted program that takes students from sentence-level language and gradually builds their skills and knowledge to engage them in more extensive conversation about particular topics.

▶ **Question 3: What sets *Deutsch: Na klar!* apart from other introductory German programs?**
Answer: It is unabashedly "authentic," using authentic texts and materials in a coordinated way and embedding them in content and in a context supported by a step-by-step grammar program to ensure accuracy. What do we mean by authentic materials? Sure we use lots of ads and brochure-type documents to present vocabulary, grammar, and culture. But we don't stop there. All of the authentic documents we use, from text-based to video-based, are contextualized. Students are encouraged to use background knowledge and context to aid comprehension. When students are learning about leisure-time activities, they encounter documents that present the topic to them and follow this with a wide variety of listening, speaking, and writing activities to reinforce the concept. Vocabulary is thus introduced in context in order to stimulate meaningful language. Unique among introductory German programs, ***Deutsch: Na klar!*** introduces students to types of materials they will encounter in German-speaking countries. Finally, it is all brought together in activities that connect vocabulary (**Wörter im Kontext**), grammar (**Grammatik im Kontext**), and readings and culture (**Sprache im Kontext**).

Those are "Just the Facts" about ***Deutsch: Na klar!***, a high-quality introductory German program that has been consistently praised for addressing students at the appropriate level and for engaging them intellectually in an adventurous language-learning experience.

In the Sixth Edition, the interview-based video (**Videoclips**), taped on location in Berlin with footage from Bonn and Cologne, provides authentic input directly related to the chapter theme, language functions, and cultural topics. The language the students hear in the interviews with native speakers is visually supported with vocabulary and phrases printed on-screen, so that students can directly relate what they see on the screen to what they hear. The comprehensible yet natural speech of the interviews, combined with the images, provides students with a window into the lives, habits, and customs of today's German speakers, so that they can develop both communicative skills and cultural awareness. There are also documentary-style snippets that complement and elaborate on the topics of the interviews.

ACTFL National Standards

The five Cs of the National Standards—Communication, Connections, Culture, Comparisons, and Communities—developed by ACTFL in collaboration with AATG, AATF, and AATSP (*Standards for Foreign Language Learning: Preparing for the 21st Century*) permeate the activities, exercises, readings, cultural and language features, and video of ***Deutsch: Na klar!*** Each chapter provides opportunities for students to communicate in German in real-life situations for real purposes. Authentic materials and the video, as well as the exercises based on them, stimulate students' thinking about their own language and culture in order to draw cross-cultural comparisons and connect their study of German language and culture with other disciplines. And finally, opportunities for students to reach out to German-speaking communities locally and globally are provided through Internet activities. Although all the activities in ***Deutsch: Na klar!*** relate in some way to the National Standards, in the Sixth Edition, an instructor annotation highlights each Standard at least once in each chapter.

In summary, through its authentic materials, cultural features, readings, listening texts, communicative activities, grammar exercises, and innovative technology, ***Deutsch: Na klar!*** teaches students how to use German effectively in real-life situations and how to communicate successfully in the German-speaking world.

Organization of the Text

The structure of ***Deutsch: Na klar!*** is simple yet effective. The program begins with a focus on the world of the learner, moves to the survival world, and culminates in the world of issues and ideas. This is accomplished in the following way: The **Einführung** and **Kapitel 1–4** focus on students and their world, following learners in their daily lives and teaching them to describe who they are and how they live and interact with friends and family. **Kapitel 5–10** concentrate on the survival world, helping students to navigate the world outside their most immediate surroundings. Here they learn to make purchases and order in restaurants, to talk about what they do in their leisure time, and how they keep fit and healthy, as well as where they go and what they do in the city and when they travel. The last four chapters, **Kapitel 11–14,** focus on the world of issues and ideas. Students learn how German speakers talk about the world of work and the use of technology. They also learn about the bigger picture of living in German-speaking countries and how German speakers entertain themselves and get their news and information.

Zu guter Letzt

Ein Podcast über Sehenswertes* an der Uni

During your German learning experience using *Deutsch: Na klar!* you will practice your German in presentational mode through a series of four podcasts. The first podcast deals with life at the university you are attending. Take the following steps to create your po...

Schritt 1: Work with two other students in...
interesting places to see or things to do at t...

Schritt 2: In your group, jot down wor...
describe these places or activities.

Schritt 3: Use the words and phrases to w...
of each point of interest. This will serve a...

Schritt 4: Using a digital video camera or...
visit the places you have chosen to prese...
group describing one place, using the scrip...
creative and go beyond the scripts, using...
Make it a creative tour in German. (If you...
digital camera, check with your language...

Schritt 5: Edit the podcast, adding titles, a...
want to highlight, and present it to the c...
longer than three minutes.

Schritt 6: Ask the class which site on ca...
most interesting to them, and why.

Zu guter Letzt

Ein Reisebericht

Haben Sie je eine interessante Reise gemacht? allein? mit Freunden oder mit Familie? Schreiben Sie einen Bericht darüber – so kreativ wie möglich. Wenn Sie wollen, können Sie einen fiktiven Reisebericht oder im Stil von Bernd Maresch schreiben.

Schritt 1: Beginnen Sie mit einem Zitat (*quote*), das den Ton und die Stimmung Ihres Berichts angibt, z.B. aus einem Roman, einer Geschichte oder einem Lied. Das Zitat darf auf Englisch oder auf Deutsch sein. Erklären Sie dann, warum Sie die Reise gemacht haben.

○ Freunde oder Familie besuchen?
○ etwas Exotisches erleben?
○ ein neues Land oder eine neue Stadt kennenlernen?
○ einen Ferienjob finden?
○ ??

Schritt 2: Schreiben Sie über zwei oder drei spezifische, interessante Erlebnisse auf der Reise. Geben Sie möglichst viele Details. Haben Sie interessante Leute kennengelernt oder ungewöhnliche Dinge gesehen oder erlebt? (Benutzen Sie bitte drei Adjektive in der Komparativform und drei in der Superlativform. Gebrauchen Sie auch mindestens zehn Verben im Imperfekt.)

Schritt 3: Beenden Sie Ihren Reisebericht mit einer Überraschung (*surprise*) oder einer interessanten Bemerkung (*comment*) für den Hörer oder den Leser. Seien Sie hier so kreativ wie möglich.

Schritt 4: In kleinen Gruppen zu viert lesen Sie Ihre Reiseberichte Ihren Mitstudenten und Mitstudentinnen vor. Sie sollen Ihnen Fragen über den Reisebericht stellen und raten, ob Ihre Geschichte wahr ist oder nicht.

Zu guter Letzt

A task-based culminating project at the end of each chapter integrates skills and competencies learned in multimodal group or class activities; in several of the chapters, students develop a podcast as part of the project.

Das kann ich nun!

Students check that they've learned the basic material presented by completing a short series of concise exercises at the close of each chapter.

Das kann ich nun!

1. Nennen Sie sechs Körperteile mit Artikel und Plural.
2. Beschreiben Sie Ihre Morgenroutine. Bilden Sie mindestens drei Sätze mit reflexiven Verben.
3. Sie telefonieren mit einem Freund. Er klingt krank, kann kaum sprechen und hustet. Was fragen Sie ihn? Was empfehlen Sie ihm? Was wünschen Sie ihm?
4. Was machen Sie, wenn Sie eine Erkältung haben?

   Wenn ich eine Erkältung habe, ...

5. Sie gehen zum Arzt, weil Sie sich hundsmiserabel fühlen. Der Arzt fragt: „Was fehlt Ihnen denn?" Was sagen Sie?
6. Was tun Sie für Fitness und Gesundheit? (Nennen Sie drei Dinge.) Wenn Sie nichts tun, sagen Sie bitte, warum Sie nichts tun.
7. Sie haben sich erkältet, aber Sie müssen unbedingt zur Arbeit. Sie reden mit einem Freund / einer Freundin über diese Situation. Was sagen Sie zu ihm/ihr?

   a. Ich weiß nicht, ob ...
   b. Ich kann heute nicht zu Hause bleiben, weil ...
   c. Ich glaube nicht, dass ...

Landeskunde zum Mitnehmen

Following the regular, numbered chapters, *Deutsch: Na klar!* now includes a section with six cultural topics that are new to this edition. Their purpose is to provide students with the opportunity for more in-depth interaction with the cultures of German-speaking countries and to learn by doing, i.e., to acquire culture through interaction with the materials. These cultural units can supplement any chapter and they can be assigned for individual or group work.

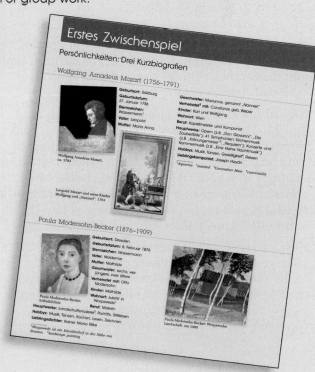

Zwischenspiel

Zwischenspiele are distributed throughout the book. These cultural "interludes," which appear after **Kapitel 3, 6, 9** and **12,** offer an opportunity to practice the vocabulary and grammar presented in previous chapters in the context of a cultural theme, as for instance in the **Erstes Zwischenspiel:** "**Persönlichkeiten: Drei Kurzbiografien.**"

Inspired by You to Enhance our Hallmarks

Our goal during the revision process for the Sixth Edition has been to retain the aspects of *Deutsch: Na klar!* that have set it apart from other texts while at the same time keeping it lively, contemporary, and up to date. We have responded directly to the feedback received on the previous edition. In the Sixth Edition, we have revised dialogues, added more cultural content and new readings with activities, and enriched the vocabulary program. We have expanded the Sixth Edition with several new and exciting features to make students' German-learning experience richer and more enjoyable. Major features appear in the visual Guided Tour Through *Deutsch: Na klar!*

The Sixth Edition has been improved through the following:

- A totally new section called **Landeskunde zum Mitnehmen,** focusing on six cultural topics in German-speaking countries. Rather than just reading about cultural topics, the **Landeskunde zum Mitnehmen** section allows students to interact with cultural materials in order to acquire cultural knowledge.

- Four new activities where students create podcasts, one per chapter in the **Zu guter Letzt** sections at the end of **Kapitel 4, 7, 12,** and **13.** These activites allow students to show their creative genius by incorporating their newly acquired knowledge, vocabulary, and grammar as they assemble a project reflective of some aspect of German-speaking cultures. The podcast activities should allow students to gain both cultural and linguistic insights into German.

- New questions in the **Landeskunde-Info** boxes that stimulate students to think about the cultural topic and draw cross-cultural comparisons with their own country or culture.

- The addition of new readings in **Kapitel 4, 5, 11,** and **12.** These new texts, accompanied by a bank of interesting new activities, extend the chapter topic and deepen students' knowledge of it. The readings in **Kapitel 8** and **13** were shortened to allow students greater accessibility. In **Kapitel 6, 8, 9, 10, 13,** and **14,** the reading activities have been substantially revised or replaced with new ones.

- New and updated authentic materials in each chapter to keep the textbook current and reflective of the contemporary cultures of German-speaking countries. Roughly 25% of all art in the textbook is new to this edition, including 40% new photographs. Around 20% of the realia, cartoons,

and other illustrations are completely new, and another 15% has been updated or modified.

- To keep abreast of the many changes in the German language, the new edition includes updated spelling and punctuation in order to adhere to the latest official spelling reform rules and recommendations as per *Duden: Die deutsche Rechtschreibung* (25th edition).

- The maps are now on the inside covers of the textbook where they are easier to find.

- Instructor annotations next to activities and exercises throughout the book highlight where and how specific ACTFL National Standards are addressed by *Deutsch: Na klar!*

Supplements

The following components of *Deutsch: Na klar!* Sixth Edition are designed to complement your instruction and to enhance your students' learning experience. Please contact your local McGraw-Hill sales representative for details concerning policies on, prices for, and availability of the supplementary materials, as some restrictions may apply.

Available to students and instructors:

- The *Student Text* includes a grammar appendix and German-English/English-German end vocabularies.

- The *Textbook Audio Program* contains material tied to the listening activities in the main text. This audio material is available free of charge at the *Deutsch: Na klar!* Online Learning Center (www.mhhe.com/dnk6).

- The *Workbook,* by Jeanine Briggs, includes additional form-focused vocabulary and grammar exercises as well as abundant guided writing practice.

- The Quia™ online *Workbook*, available through the **Centro** portal site, offers all the content of the print *Workbook* plus immediate feedback and a robust instructor gradebook feature.

- The *Laboratory Manual,* by Lida Daves-Schneider and Michael Büsges, contains engaging listening comprehension activities and pronunciation practice. Available on audio CD and free of charge at the *Online Learning Center* (www.mhhe.com/dnk6), the *Laboratory Audio Program* includes an audioscript for instructors.

- The Quia™ online *Laboratory Manual*, available through the **Centro** portal site, offers all the content of the print *Laboratory Manual,* integrated audio plus immediate feedback and a robust instructor gradebook feature.

- The **Deutsch: Na klar!** *Online Learning Center* (www.mhhe.com/dnk6) provides a variety of vocabulary and grammar self-quizzes as well as cultural activities and the complete *Laboratory Audio Program*. These quizzes, activities and the *Laboratory Audio Program* are available to students free of charge.

- The *Video to accompany* **Deutsch: Na Klar!** contains a wide variety of interviews with native speakers of German, enhanced with images that support the content and make it more accessible to students.

Available to instructors only:

- The *Annotated Instructor's Edition* of the main text includes marginal notes, answers, and an audioscript for the in-text listening comprehension activities.

- The *Instructor's Manual and Testing Program*, found at the Online Learning Center (www.mhhe.com/dnk6), provides theoretical background, practical guidance, and ideas for using **Deutsch: Na Klar!** It also contains tests and exams revised for the Sixth Edition by Liana McMillan and Mary Gell, both of the University of Michigan.

- The *Audioscript,* found at the Online Learning Center (www.mhhe.com/dnk6), contains the material found in the *Laboratory Audio Program.*

Acknowledgments

We would like to thank these instructors who participated in surveys and reviews that were indispensable to the development of **Deutsch: Na klar!** Sixth Edition. The appearance of their names does not necessarily constitute their endorsement of the text or its methodology.

Philip Adams, Bob Jones University
Christiane Baldus, Cabrillo College
Carol Bander, Saddleback College
Cornelia Becher, University of California, Santa Barbara
Perry Bennett, Moorpark College
Alison Beringer, Colgate University
Raymond Burt, University of North Carolina, Wilmington
Walter Campbell, University of California, Santa Cruz
Daniel Chaffey, Diablo Valley College
Kathryn Corl, The Ohio State University, Columbus
Katie Costa, Bob Jones University
Kathleen Demico, Cuyahoga Community College, Western Campus
Sandra Dillon, Idaho State University
Lara Ducate, University of South Carolina
Paul Dvorak, Virginia Commonwealth University

Jean Egbert, Bethel University
Sara Ferrar, The Ohio State University, Newark
Alfred Gay, St. Clair County Community College
Mary Gell, University of Michigan, Dearborn
Tatjana Goodman, East Carolina University
Barbara Greim, Black Hawk College
Katja Halle, Fullerton College
Tonya Hampton, University of Cincinnati
Brenda Hansen, Bob Jones University
Amelia Harris, University of Virginia College, Wise
Judith Harris-Frisk, University of California, Santa Cruz
Elke Hatch, University of Dayton
Olga Hiltunen, Oakland Community College, Auburn Hills
Kersten Horn, University of Missouri, St. Louis
Robin Huff, Georgia State University
Nicolas Humphrey, St. Norbert College
James Keller, Pasadena City College
Norgard Klages, Salem College
Edith H. Krause, Duquesne University
Danielle Lafata, Macomb Community College
Caralinda Lee, Saint Mary's College of California
Elfie Manning, College of Southern Nevada, West Charleston
Bettina Matthias, Middlebury College
Liana McMillan, University of Michigan, Dearborn
Eva-Maria Metcalf, University of Mississippi
Leslie Ortquist-Ahrens, Otterbein College
Lilian Ramos, Winona State University
Gisela Reid, University of North Carolina, Wilmington
Theodore Rippey, Bowling Green State University
Eckhard Rolz, South Dakota State University
Brigitte Rossbacher, University of Georgia
Christopher Sapp, University of Mississippi
Georg Schwarzmann, Lynchburg College
Rebecca Sibrian, Boise State University
Jane Sokolosky, Brown University
Oliver C. Speck, Virginia Commonwealth University
Saskia Stoessel, Tufts University
Wiebke Strehl, University of South Carolina
Lee Tatum, University of North Carolina, Wilmington
Olga Trokhimenko, University of North Carolina, Wilmington
Paul Truesdell, Old Dominion University
Jill Twark, East Carolina University
Nina Vyatkina, University of Kansas
Evelyn Wade, University of California, Santa Barbara
Cynthia Zurla, Coastal Carolina University

We would also like to thank the many people who worked on this book behind the scenes, beginning with Arden Smith, who painstakingly compiled the German-English/English-German vocabularies, and Veronica Oliva, who secured reprint permissions for the realia and texts. We would also like to acknowledge Wolfgang Horsch for his engaging line drawings and cartoons.

We would also like to thank Lida Daves-Schneider for her contributions to the Third Edition, some of which remain in this new edition. Likewise, we want to acknowledge and thank Michael Conner at Texas State University for the instructor annotations he wrote for the Fifth Edition, which remain in this edition as well.

The authors wish to express gratitude to Monika Rähse Weber, University of Freiburg, Germany, and Caralinda Lee, Saint Mary's College of California. Over the past few years, both of them have shared suggestions and made many useful comments regarding work on the new editions. We would also like to thank friends and colleagues at Miami University: Ruth Sanders, Mila Ganeva, and Nicole Thesz, who have used *Deutsch; Na klar!* and shared their experiences with it. Thanks go as well to Bettina Lülsdorf, Annette (Emmi) Unkelbach, Uta Kalwe, and Mike Meisner for their special assistance in matters of German *Landeskunde* and language. Our deep gratitude goes to Paul Listen, our development editor, whose tireless efforts and welcome inspiration kept us on track, provided us with the support we needed, and helped to make the Sixth Edition the best *Deutsch: Na klar!* yet. We also wish to acknowledge the editing, production, and art and design team at McGraw-Hill: Brett Coker, Chris Schabow, Cassandra Chu, Maureen McCutchen, Adrian Morgan, Emily Tietz, and Sherry Kane. Thanks also to Marie Deer for her wonderful copyediting and to Peggy Potter for her excellent proofreading, and to Jorge Arbujas, Hector Alvero, and Alexa Recio, and the rest of the McGraw-Hill marketing and sales staff, who have so actively promoted this book over the past five editions. Thanks to Aptara for their careful composition of the book. Finally, we would like to express our gratitude to the McGraw-Hill editorial staff: Bill Glass, our Editorial Director, Katie Stevens, our Publisher, Scott Tinetti, our Director of Development, and Laura Chiriboga and Margaret Young, our Editorial Coordinators. Special thanks are due to Thalia Dorwick, whose belief in the project originally made it a reality, and whose constant support helped bring it to completion, and Eirik Børve, whose vision made this book happen in the first place.

About the Authors

Robert Di Donato is Professor of German Studies at Miami University in Oxford, Ohio. He received his Ph.D. from The Ohio State University. He is the chief academic and series developer of *Fokus Deutsch,* a telecourse with accompanying texts and materials for teaching and learning German produced by WGBH Television and the Annenberg Foundation and coauthor of *The Big Yellow Book of German Verbs.* He has also edited two volumes for the Central States Conference, written articles about language teaching methodology, and has given numerous keynote speeches, workshops, and presentations on teaching methods and teacher education both in the United States and abroad. He has won a number of awards for his work in language teaching and learning including the Outstanding German Educator Award from the American Association of Teachers of German (AATG) and the Florence Steiner Award for Leadership in Foreign Language Education from the American Council on the Teaching of Foreign Languages (ACTFL). He was national president of AATG from 1986–1987. Presently he is serving as acting chair of the Department of Spanish and Portuguese at Miami University.

Monica D. Clyde is a native of Düsseldorf. She received her Ph.D. in German literature from the University of California at Berkeley. She has taught German language and literature at Mills College, Cañada College, the Defense Language Institute, and the College of San Mateo. She was Director of Faculty Development and Scholarship at Saint Mary's College of California until her retirement in 2003. She coauthored *Texte und Kontexte* and was a contributor to *Mosaik: Deutsche Kultur und Literatur,* Third Edition, both intermediate college-level German textbooks. Her scholarly work continues with a focus on the history of Germans who came to the San Francisco area from the time of of the Gold Rush up to World War I.

Jacqueline Vansant, who received her Ph.D. from the University of Texas at Austin with a dissertation on Austrian women writers, is Professor of German at the University of Michigan-Dearborn. Her particular interest in language pedagogy lies in reading and reading strategies. She has written widely on contemporary Austrian literature and culture, served as coeditor of *Modern Austrian Literature* from 2000–2005, and is presently working on a book entitled *Austria: Made in Hollywood.*

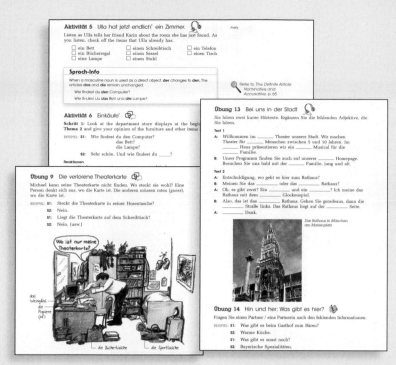

Aktivitäten und Übungen

A broad range of activities and exercises allows for structured communicative practice of vocabulary and grammatical structures. They progress from controlled and form-focused to open-ended and interactive. Some activities and exercises are tied to the audio program and provide receptive vocabulary and grammar practice. Some are designed to give students practice in noting details, while others encourage global comprehension.

Hier klicken!

At relevant locations throughout the text, this feature directs students to the **Deutsch: Na klar!** Online Learning Center (www. mhhe.com/dnk6), which contains additional vocabulary, grammar, and cultural activities.

Icons

Distinctive icons visually identify various types of activities, including listening, interactive-pair or small-group, writing, podcast, video, reading, and information-gap activities, as well as grammar section cross-references that alert students to where to find supporting grammar explanations. The listening icon appears next to activities with an audio component on the Textbook Audio Program. The video icon appears next to activities with a video component on the Video to accompany **Deutsch: Na klar!**

listening   interactive pair or small group   writing   podcast

video   reading   information gap   grammar section cross-reference

Sprach-Info

Expressions and "grammar for communication" are provided to assist students in carrying out a given activity. These points will be elaborated in the same or a later chapter.

Landeskunde-Info

Often enhanced with photos or other visuals, this feature expands on the cultural information presented in the **Themen,** activities and exercises, and readings. Follow-up discussion questions encourage cross-cultural connections.

Sprache im Kontext

This four-skills section is divided into three parts. **Videoclips** features interviews with German speakers on topics presented in each chapter and reflects the vocabulary and grammar presented. **Lesen** contains an authentic reading passage with pre- and post-reading activities: **Zum Thema**, **Auf den ersten Blick**, and **Zum Text**. **Zu guter Letzt**, consisting of interactive, task-oriented culminating activities, provides open-ended oral and written practice on the chapter theme.

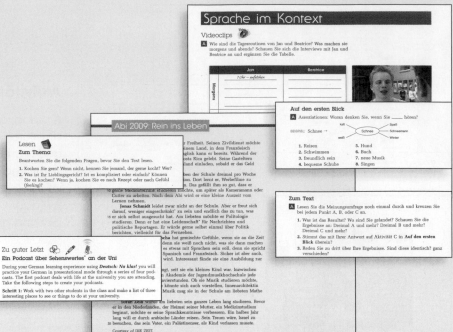

The *Deutsch: Na klar!* Vocabulary System

Vocabulary is presented by means of authentic materials, illustrations, descriptive texts, dialogues, and built-in activities. Students are encouraged to first "discover" the meaning of the new vocabulary, which is highlighted in the presentation, through contextual guessing. Less transparent new vocabulary is then reflected in the **Neue Wörter** lists, which students should use to verify their contextual guessing.

Analyse

Before completing many of the **Aktivitäten** or **Übungen,** students develop receptive skills by examining short authentic texts for specific vocabulary or grammatical structures.

A Guided Tour through
Deutsch: Na klar!

Wörter im Kontext

The vocabulary section, divided into two to three visual **Themen,** presents various aspects of the chapter theme. Each **Thema** is followed by activities (**Aktivitäten**) that encourage vocabulary learning in context.

Alles klar?

In the numbered chapters of **Deutsch: Na Klar!** the chapter opener introduces students to the chapter theme through a guided activity that involves a visual or an authentic text and a thematically related, global listening comprehension passage.

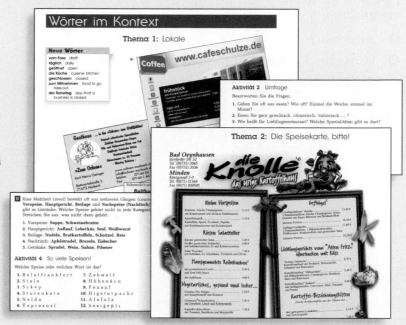

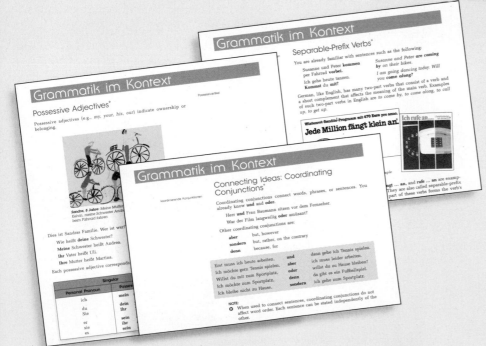

Grammatik im Kontext

Grammar is presented in succinct explanations with abundant charts and examples and, whenever possible, via authentic materials. Wherever useful, grammatical structures are contrasted with parallel structures in English. Some grammar explanations expand on points that are previewed in **Sprach-Info** boxes.

The Sixth Edition of the *Deutsch: Na klar!* textbook culminates in a new feature called **Landeskunde zum Mitnehmen.** This section presents students with six different cultural topics in German, ranging from geography through politics to legends and fairy tales—all accompanied by a variety of interactive activities. But students don't have to wait until they finish the book to engage with these materials; they can do so at any point while studying the various chapters. For a "culture break," they can dip into **Landeskunde zum Mitnehmen** and get some "culture to go."

Deutsch: Na klar! consists of a preliminary chapter (**Einführung**), fourteen regular chapters, and a closing chapter (**Landeskunde zum Mitnehmen,** described above). Each of the fourteen regular chapters is developed around a major theme and has the following organization:

- Alles klar?
- Wörter im Kontext
  Themen 1, 2, (3)

- Grammatik im Kontext
- Sprache im Kontext
  Videoclips
  Lesen
  Zu guter Letzt
- Wortschatz
- Das kann ich nun!

Cultural collages (**Zwischenspiele**), containing visuals and activities, appear after **Kapitel 3, 6, 9,** and **12** and give students the opportunity to review, consolidate, and apply what they have learned in previous chapters to cultural topics of German-speaking countries in new contexts.

Einführung

In diesem Kapitel

▶ **Themen:** Expressing greetings and farewells, getting acquainted, inquiring about someone's well-being, spelling in German, numbers, useful classroom expressions

▶ **Landeskunde:** Forms of address, postal codes and country abbreviations, German-speaking countries and their neighbors

—Grüß dich! Geht's gut?
—Na klar!

Wer ist das?

1

Hallo! Guten Tag! Herzlich willkommen!*

Internationale Studenten

Professor:	**Guten Tag! Herzlich willkommen! Mein Name ist** Pohle, Norbert Pohle. Und **wie ist Ihr Name?**
Sabine:	Sabine Zimmermann.
Professor:	Und Sie? **Wie heißen Sie?**
Antonio:	**Ich heiße** Antonio Coletti.
Safir:	Und **ich bin** Safir Youssef.

Auf einer Party

Peter:	**Grüß dich.** Ich heiße Peter Sedlmeier.
Katarina:	Mein Name ist Katarina Steinmetz.
Peter:	**Woher kommst du?**
Katarina:	**Aus** Dresden. Und du?
Peter:	Aus Rosenheim.

*New, active vocabulary is shown in bold print.

Herr Grote:	**Frau** Kühne, **das ist Herr** Yamamoto aus Tokio. Frau Kühne kommt aus Potsdam.
Herr Yamamoto:	**Freut mich.**
Frau Kühne:	Freut mich **auch.**

Ein Treffen (*meeting*) in Berlin

Landeskunde-Info

German speakers address one another as **Sie** or **du.** The formal **Sie** (*you*) is used with strangers and even co-workers and acquaintances. Family members and friends address one another with **du** (*you*), as do children and, generally, students. Close personal friends address one another with **du** and first names. Most adults address one another as **Herr** or **Frau** and use **Sie,** although some might use first names with **Sie. Frau** is the standard title for all women, regardless of marital status.

> ● Which form of address would German children use with their aunt: **du** or **Sie?**
> ● Which form of address would you use with your instructor?

STADT-
BIBLIOTHEK
GÖTTINGEN

>00946850

Herr/Frau

Weber, Melissa Alexandra

Benutzerausweis[1]   Bitte bei jedem Besuch mitbringen[2]

Aktivität 1   Wie ist der Name?

Introduce yourself to several people in your class.

S1: Mein Name ist _____.

S2: Ich heiße _____.

S1: Woher kommst du?

S2: Aus _____. Und du?

S1: Aus _____.

Aktivität 2   Darf ich vorstellen?°

Introduce a classmate to another.

May I introduce?

BEISPIEL: **Gina:** Paul, das ist Chris.

   Paul: Tag, Chris.

   Chris: Hallo, Paul.

Wie schreibt man das?°

When you introduce yourself or give information about yourself, you may have to spell out words for clarification. In contrast to English, German follows fairly predictable spelling and pronunciation rules. You will gradually learn these rules throughout the course.

The German alphabet has the same twenty-six letters as the English alphabet, plus four other letters of its own. The four special German letters are written as follows. Note that the letter **ß** has no capital; **SS** is used instead.

Ä	ä	a-Umlaut: **Bär, Käse**
Ö	ö	o-Umlaut: **böse, hören**
Ü	ü	u-Umlaut: **müde, Süden**
	ß	sz („ess tsett"): **süß, Straße**

A pair of dots above a German vowel is called an "umlaut." Although this book refers to these vowels as **a-, o-,** or **u-umlaut,** they are actually distinct letters. When spelling words, speakers of German refer to them as they are pronounced. Listen carefully to these vowels on the laboratory audio recordings and in your instructor's pronunciation of them.

The alphabet house (**Buchstabenhaus**) below shows how German schoolchildren learn to write the letters of the alphabet. In addition to displaying individual letters, the **Buchstabenhaus** also practices such frequently used combinations as **ch, sch,** and the diphthongs.

Aktivität 3 Das ABC

Repeat the letters of the German alphabet after your instructor.

Aktivität 4 B-E-R-L-I-N: So schreibt man das!°

That is how you spell it!

Listen as your instructor spells some common German words. Write the words as you hear them.

Aktivität 5 Wie bitte?°

I beg your pardon?

Introduce yourself to another student and spell your name.

BEISPIEL: S1: Mein Name ist _____.

S2: Wie bitte?

S1: (*repeat your name; then spell it in German*)

S2: Ah, so!

Aktivität 6 Buchstabieren Sie!°

Spell!

Think of three German words, names, products, or company names you already know or choose three items from the list below. Then close your book. Without saying the word, spell it in German (**auf Deutsch**) for a classmate, who writes it down and says the word back to you.

Frankfurt   Autobahn

Volkswagen

Hotel   Delikatessen

Radio   Kindergarten

Gesundheit   Einstein

Hallo! – Mach's gut!°

How do people in German-speaking countries greet one another and say good-bye? Look at the following expressions and illustrations, and see whether you can guess which ones are greetings and which ones are good-byes.

German speakers use various formal and informal hellos and good-byes, depending on the situation and the person with whom they are speaking. Saying hello:

Formal	Casual	Use
guten Morgen	Morgen	*until about 10:00 A.M.*
guten Tag	Tag	*generally between 10:00 A.M. and early evening*
guten Abend	'n Abend*	*from about 5:00 P.M. on*
grüß Gott†	grüß Gott	*southern German and Austrian for* **guten Tag**
grüß dich **hallo** **hi**		*greetings among young people any time*

Saying good-bye and good night:

Formal	Casual	Use
auf Wiedersehen	Wiederseh'n	*any time*
mach's gut **tschüss**		*among young people, friends, and family*
gute Nacht	Nacht	*only when going to bed at night*

Aktivität 7 Was sagt man?°

What do you say?

What would people say in the following circumstances?

1. _____ your German instructor entering the classroom
2. _____ two students saying good-bye
3. _____ a person from Vienna greeting an acquaintance
4. _____ two students meeting at a café
5. _____ a mother as she turns off the lights in her child's room at night
6. _____ a student leaving a professor's office
7. _____ family members greeting one another in the morning

a. Gute Nacht!
b. Grüß dich!
c. Tschüss!
d. Mach's gut!
e. Guten Tag!
f. (Auf) Wiedersehen!
g. (Guten) Morgen!
h. Grüß Gott!
i. Hallo!/Hi!
j. Guten Abend!

Aktivität 8 Minidialoge

Complete the following short dialogues with an appropriate greeting or leave-taking.

1. **A:** _____ _____! Ich heiße Stefan. Wie heißt du?
   B: Ich heiße Fusün.
2. **C:** _____ _____. Mein Name ist Eva Schrittmeier.
   D: Und mein Name ist Georg Stillweg. Woher kommen Sie?
   C: Aus Stuttgart.
3. **E:** Wiederseh'n und gute _____, Markus.
   F: _____, Johannes, mach's _____!

---

*The **'n** before **Abend** is short for **guten.**

†*Lit.* Greetings in the name of God.

So, how's it going?

NA, WIE GEHT'S?

ICH WEISS NICHT! ICH FÜHLE MICH HEUTE MORGEN SO ZERSCHLAGEN![1]

[1]Ich ... *I don't know! I feel so beat this morning!*

Na, wie geht's?°

So, how's it going?

German has several ways of asking *How are you?*

Wie geht es dir?
Wie geht's? } *a family member or friend*

Wie geht es Ihnen, Herr Lindemann? *an acquaintance*

You can respond in a number of different ways.

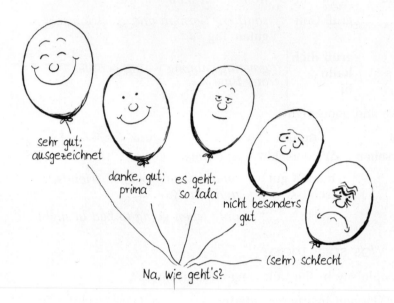

sehr gut; ausgezeichnet

danke, gut; prima

es geht; so lala

nicht besonders gut

(sehr) schlecht

Na, wie geht's?

Aktivität 9   Wie geht's?

Listen as three pairs of people greet each other and conduct brief conversations. Indicate whether the statements below match what you hear.

	Ja	Nein

Dialog 1
a. The conversation takes place in the morning.   ☐ ☐
b. The greetings are informal.   ☐ ☐
c. The man and the woman are both doing fine.   ☐ ☐

Dialog 2
a. The two speakers must be from southern Germany or Austria.   ☐ ☐
b. The speakers are close friends.   ☐ ☐
c. Both of them are doing fine.   ☐ ☐

Dialog 3
a. The two speakers know each other.   ☐ ☐
b. The man is feeling great.   ☐ ☐
c. They use a formal expression to say good-bye.   ☐ ☐

Aktivität 10   Und wie geht es dir?

Start a conversation chain by asking one classmate how he/she is.

BEISPIEL: **S1:**   Na, Peter, wie geht's?

S2:   So lala. Wie geht es dir, Kathy?

S3:   Ausgezeichnet! Und wie geht's dir, ...?

Landeskunde-Info

So zählt man auf Deutsch.°

This is how you count in German.

0 null	9 neun	18 achtzehn	90 neunzig
1 eins	10 zehn	19 neunzehn	100 (ein)hundert
2 zwei	11 elf	20 zwanzig	200 zweihundert
3 drei	12 zwölf	30 dreißig	300 dreihundert
4 vier	13 dreizehn	40 vierzig	1 000 (ein)tausend
5 fünf	14 vierzehn	50 fünfzig	2 000 zweitausend
6 sechs	15 fünfzehn	60 sechzig	3 000 dreitausend
7 sieben	16 sechzehn	70 siebzig	
8 acht	17 siebzehn	80 achtzig	

The numbers 21 through 99 are formed by combining the numbers 1–9 with 20–90.

21 einundzwanzig	24 vierundzwanzig	27 siebenundzwanzig
22 zweiundzwanzig	25 fünfundzwanzig	28 achtundzwanzig
23 dreiundzwanzig	26 sechsundzwanzig	29 neunundzwanzig

The numbers *one* and *seven* are written as follows: 1   7

German uses a period or a space where English uses a comma.

1.000   7 000

In German-speaking countries, telephone numbers generally have a varying number of digits and may be spoken as follows:

24 36 71 → zwei vier, drei sechs, sieben eins

[*or*] vierundzwanzig, sechsunddreißig, einundsiebzig

Hier klicken!
You'll find more about telephone numbers in **Deutsch: Na klar!** on the World Wide Web at **www.mhhe.com/dnk6.**

Aktivität 11 Wichtige Telefonnummern°

You need the phone numbers for the following items and services. Write the phone numbers you hear in the appropriate space.

Telefon-Ansagen	☎		Theater und Konzerte	
Polizei			Feuerwehr/ Rettungsleitstelle	
Kinoprogramme			Wetter	
Küchenrezepte			Zahlenlotto	
Sport			Zeit	

Analyse

Look over the examples of addresses (**Adressen**) from German-speaking countries. How do they differ from the way addresses are written in your country?

▶ Locate the name of the street (**Straße**) and the town (**Stadt**).

▶ Where is the house number (**Hausnummer**) placed? Where is the postal code (**Postleitzahl**) placed?

▶ Can you guess what the **A** before **9020 Klagenfurt** and the **CH** before **8050 Zürich-Oerlikon** represent?

▶ Now say each address out loud.

UNIVERSITÄT FÜR BILDUNGSWISSENSCHAFTEN KLAGENFURT

Universitätsstraße 65–67
A-9020 Klagenfurt

VERKEHRSMUSEUM **DRESDEN**
Augustusstraße 1, 01067 Dresden · Tel. 0351/ 864 40 · Fax 0351/ 8644110
http://www.verkehrsmuseum.sachsen.de
e-mail: verkehrsmuseum@verkehrsmuseum.sachsen.de

Gebecke
Buchhandlung & Antiquariat
Bücher · Musikalien · Graphik
seit 1881
☎ 2698
www.antiquariat-gebecke.de
Pölkenstraße 3 · 06484 Quedlinburg

Ferienträume?
Wir erfüllen sie!

TRAVELLER REISEN
Filiale Oerlikon
CH-8050 Zürich-Oerlikon, Ohmstrasse 14
Telefon 01- 312 10 14
Telex 823 221
Telegramm: Travellerag Zürich

Aktivität 12   Die Adresse und Telefonnummer, bitte!

You will hear three brief requests for addresses and telephone numbers. As you listen, mark the correct street numbers and jot down the postal codes and telephone numbers.

1. Professor Hausers Adresse ist …

Gartenstraße   9   12   19

_____ Ebenhausen/Isartal

Die Telefonnummer ist _____.

2. Die Adresse von Margas Fitnessstudio ist …

Bautzner Straße   5   15   14

_____ Dresden

Die Telefonnummer ist _____.

3. Die Adresse von Autohaus Becker ist …

Landstuhler Straße   54   44   45

_____ Zweibrücken-Ixheim

Die Telefonnummer ist _____.

> **Hier klicken!**
>
> You'll find more about the postal and country codes in **Deutsch: Na klar!** on the World Wide Web at **www.mhhe.com/dnk6.**

Landeskunde-Info

When mail is sent between countries in Europe, international abbreviations are used for the country names. Refer to the map and provide the missing country names and country codes.

_____	B	**Rumänien**	_____
Dänemark	_____	**Russland**	_____
_____	D		CH
Frankreich	_____	**die Slowakei**	_____
Griechenland	_____	_____	E
Großbritannien	_____	**Tschechien**	_____
Irland	_____	**Ungarn**	_____
Italien	_____		
_____	FL		
_____	L		
die Niederlande	_____		
_____	A		
Polen	_____		
Portugal	_____		

- ▶ What is the country code for Australia? Canada? The United States?
- ▶ Do vehicles in your country commonly display stickers with a country code?

Danke schön, Europa.

Aktivität 13   Hin und her°: Wie ist die Postleitzahl?

This is the first of many activities in which you will exchange information with a partner. Here, one of you uses the chart below; the other turns to the corresponding chart in Appendix A. Take turns asking each other for the postal codes of the persons living in the cities below.

BEISPIEL: **S1:** Wie ist Bettinas Postleitzahl in Hamburg?

   S2: D-21220. Wie ist Peters Postleitzahl in Salzburg?

Bettina		Hamburg
Peter	A-5020	Salzburg
Mathias		Zürich
Kathrin	D-01067	Dresden
Susanne		Wien
Felix	D-10825	Berlin
Marion		Vaduz
Michael	D-99817	Eisenach

Aktivität 14   Ein Interview

Schritt 1: Jot down answers to the following questions.

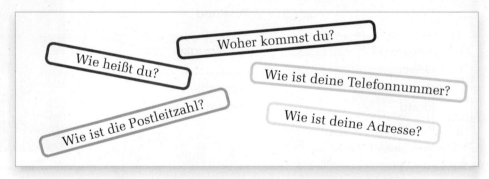

Wie heißt du?

Woher kommst du?

Wie ist deine Telefonnummer?

Wie ist die Postleitzahl?

Wie ist deine Adresse?

Schritt 2: Use the questions in **Schritt 1** to interview a partner and fill in the information in the grid below.

Name	
Stadt	
Straße und Hausnummer	
Postleitzahl	
Telefonnummer	

Ich weiß zwar nicht was ne Postleitzahl ist, aber Quelle hat 90750.[1]

1. Ich ... *I don't know what a*
(ne = eine)

Schritt 3: Now tell the class about the person you interviewed.

BEISPIEL: Das ist Kerstin aus Chicago. Die Adresse ist 678 Maple Street. Die Postleitzahl ist 60076. Die Telefonnummer ist 555-4797.

Sie können schon etwas Deutsch!°

You already know some German!

Even if you have never studied German before, you will soon find that you know more German than you think. For example, look at the ad.

▶ What is this ad for?

▶ Which words are *identical* in English?

▶ Which words in the ad look *similar* to words you use in English?

Words such as **Hotel, Restaurant,** and **Folklore** are borrowed from other languages: **Restaurant** and **Hotel** from French, and **Folklore** from English. These words are used internationally.

Some words in the ad look similar to English words, for example **Biergarten** and **Familie.** You may already have seen the word **Biergarten** in English language text. This word has been borrowed from German, along with some other German words commonly used in English, such as **Kindergarten** and **Delikatessen.** You may recognize the words *beer* and *garden* in **Biergarten. Bier** and *beer,* **Garten** and *garden* have the same meaning in both languages. These words are cognates. Cognates are descended from the same word or form. Since English and German are both Germanic languages, they share many cognates. This common linguistic ancestry will help you a great deal in understanding German. Recognizing cognates is an important skill stressed throughout this textbook.

Cognates such as **Bier** and **Garten** are easy to recognize. Understanding other words takes more imaginative guessing: for instance, what do you think **Blasmusik** means? Other words in the ad probably look completely unfamiliar, but often the meaning can be guessed from the context.

Now summarize what you have found out about the "Kur-Café." Add any additional information you were able to extract from the ad by guessing.

Hotel - Pension

Kur-Café
★★★
BAD SUDERODE · HARZ

Besitzer Familie Hofmann

Café – Restaurant – Wintergarten

Blasmusik
06.08.2005
und 20.08.2005
ab 15.00 Uhr

Tschechische Blasmusikanten
im Biergarten

Vorankündigung
Pfifferling und Waldpilzwochen

· täglich ab 7.00 Uhr geöffnet
ständig Veranstaltungen wie:
Folklore, Video- und Unterhaltungsabende

Kur-Café
★★★
BAD SUDERODE · HARZ

Hotel-Pension · Café
Restaurant · Wintergarten

06507 Bad Suderode Ellernstraße 12+14

Bad Suderode, Ellernstraße 12, 14 und 19
Tel. (03 94 85) 54 10, 5 00 52, 6 00 52, Fax (03 94 85) 54 11 19
e-mail: hofmanns-kur-cafe@web.de · Internet: www.hofmanns-kur-cafe.de

Aktivität 15 Sie verstehen schon etwas Deutsch!°

You have learned that you can use visual and verbal cues to understand a considerable amount of written German. Now you will hear some short radio announcements and news headlines. Listen for cognates and other verbal clues as you try to understand the gist of what is being said. As you hear each item, write its number in front of the topic(s) to which it corresponds. Not all the topics shown will be mentioned.

_____ Automobil   _____ Musik   _____ Sport

_____ Bank   _____ Politik   _____ Tanz

_____ Film   _____ Restaurant   _____ Theater

_____ Kinder

Aktivität 16 Informationen finden

An important first step in reading is identifying the type of text you have in front of you. Look for verbal as well as visual clues. Look at the texts below and on the next page. Write the letter of each text in front of the appropriate category in the list below (some categories will remain empty).

1. _____ ticket for an event
2. _____ short news item about crime
3. _____ concert announcement
4. _____ newspaper headline
5. _____ recipe
6. _____ section from a TV guide
7. _____ ad for a restaurant

Pfiffige Mischung aus Bistro, Café, Restaurant und Bar. Schlemmerfrühstück, großes Kaffeeangebot, kleine, leckere Gerichte, ausgesuchte Weine und Cocktails verlocken dazu, in einem Wiener Hauch von Caféhausatmosphäre zu genießen.

Täglich geöffnet
von 10.00 - 01.00 Uhr
Jüdenstr. 17 • 37073 Göttingen
Übrigens: Auch Sonntags geöffnet
Tel. 0551/ 4 72 08

a.

KABARETT
Leipziger Pfeffermühle

Kabarett Leipziger Pfeffermühle gGmbH
Thomaskirchhof 16 · 04109 Leipzig
Kartentelefon: 0341/9 60 31 96 · Fax: 0341/9 60 31 07
Internet: www.Kabarett-Leipziger-Pfeffermuehle.de
E-Mail: Kabarett.Pfeffermuehle@t-online.de

"Verkehrte Welt" mit Ute Loeck, Jan Gärtig, Marco Schiedt

Parkett Links / Reihe 05 / Sitz 05
Preisklasse 1 - 10.00 Euro
Mittwoch 11.08.2010 - 20:00 Uhr

b.

SYMPHONISCHES ORCHESTER BERLIN

Heute, 16 Uhr	**PHILHARMONIE**
Dirigent:	**László Kovács**
Solist:	**Boris Bloch**
Kodály:	Tänze aus Galanta
Tschaikowsky:	Konzert für Klavier und Orchester Nr. 2, G-Dur, op. 44
Rimsky-Korsakoff:	„Scheherazade" Symphonische Suite aus „Tausend und eine Nacht"

c.

20.15 KABEL 1

FILM **Lawrence von Arabien**

Kairo, 1916: Im Auftrag seiner Regierung vereint der britische Offizier Thomas E. Lawrence (Peter O'Toole, l., mit Anthony Quinn) die Wüstenstämme Arabiens zu einer schlagkräftigen Armee und führt sie in den Aufstand gegen die Türken.

d.

Frankfurter wird Lotto-Millionär

Mit den sechs richtigen Zahlen 33, 29, 58, 12, 11 und 90 hat ein Frankfurter am Samstag im Lotto 2 000 000 Euro gewonnen.

e.

Landeskunde-Info

Wo spricht man Deutsch? (*Where is German spoken?*)

Naturally, German is spoken in Germany, but it is also spoken in many other countries. The following countries have relatively large German-speaking populations.

Argentinien	Liechtenstein	Russland
Belgien	Luxemburg	die Schweiz
Bosnien	Österreich	die Slowakei
Brasilien	Polen	Tschechien
Italien	Rumänien	Ungarn

German is the official language of Germany (**Deutschland**), Austria (**Österreich**), and Liechtenstein. It is one of four official languages of Switzerland (**die Schweiz**) and one of three official languages of Luxembourg and Belgium. German is also spoken in regions of France, Denmark, Italy, the Czech Republic, Poland, Rumania, Bosnia and Herzegovina, Hungary, Latvia, Lithuania, Estonia, Russia, Slovakia, and Ukraine. Altogether, between 120 and 140 million Europeans speak German as their first language—more than the number of people in Europe who speak English as their first language.

German is also spoken by many people as a first language in other countries such as Brazil, Argentina, Canada, and the United States (Pennsylvania Dutch). In Namibia, German is spoken by a sizable minority. It is estimated that outside Europe, an additional 20 million people speak German as their first language. Another 50 million speak German as a foreign language.

According to U.S. census figures from 2000, over 40 million U.S. citizens claim German descent. In Canada, the figure is approximately 2.7 million.

○ In which areas of your country is German spoken?
○ Are there any German traditions, customs, or monuments in your area? If so, describe them.

Nützliche Ausdrücke im Sprachkurs°

Ihr **Deutschlehrer** / Ihre **Deutschlehrerin** sagt:

Bitte ...	*Please . . .*
Hören Sie zu.	*Listen.*
Schreiben Sie.	*Write.*
Machen Sie die Bücher auf Seite _____ auf.	*Open your books to page _____.*
Lesen Sie.	*Read.*
Machen Sie die Bücher zu.	*Close your books.*
Setzen Sie sich.	*Be seated.*
Wiederholen Sie.	*Repeat.*
Haben Sie Fragen?	*Do you have any questions?*
[Ist] Alles klar?	*Is everything clear?*
Noch einmal, bitte!	*Once more, please. / Could you say that again, please?*

Sie sagen:

Langsamer, bitte!	*Slower, please.*
Wie bitte?	*Pardon? What did you say?*
Wie schreibt man _____?	*How do you write _____?*
Ich habe eine Frage.	*I have a question.*
Wie sagt man _____ auf Deutsch?	*How do you say _____ in German?*
Was bedeutet _____?	*What does _____ mean?*
Das weiß ich nicht.	*I don't know.*
Ich verstehe das nicht.	*I don't understand.*
Alles klar.	*I get it.*
Ja.	*Yes.*
Nein.	*No.*
Danke [schön].	*Thank you.*

Aktivität 17   Wie sagt man das auf Deutsch?

Match the English expressions to their German equivalents.

1. _____ I have a question.
2. _____ I don't understand.
3. _____ Is everything clear?
4. _____ Be seated.
5. _____ How do you write _____?
6. _____ Open your books.
7. _____ What does _____ mean?
8. _____ Pardon, what did you say?
9. _____ Open your books to page _____.
10. _____ Once more, please. / Could you say that again, please?

a. Alles klar?
b. Machen Sie die Bücher auf.
c. Was bedeutet _____?
d. Machen Sie die Bücher auf Seite _____ auf.
e. Setzen Sie sich.
f. Ich verstehe das nicht.
g. Noch einmal, bitte.
h. Wie schreibt man _____?
i. Wie bitte?
j. Ich habe eine Frage.

Videoclips

A Michael, our moderator for the interviews throughout **Deutsch: Na klar!,** asks people their names in two different ways. Watch the video segment and complete the following questions.

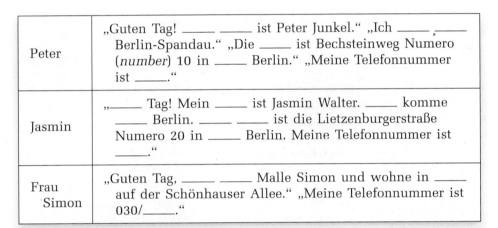

1. Using the informal form, he asks Dennis: "_____ _____ du?"
2. Using the formal form, he asks Herr Borowsky: "_____ _____ Sie?"

B Several people respond to the preceding questions in one of two ways. Watch and complete the following.

1. „Hallo! _____ Name _____ Dennis".
2. „Ich _____ Beatrice. Guten Morgen!"
3. „_____ _____ ist Kurt Borowsky".

C Now concentrate on the segments with Peter, Jasmin, and Frau Simon. Complete their profiles.

Peter	„Guten Tag! _____ _____ ist Peter Junkel." „Ich _____, _____ Berlin-Spandau." „Die _____ ist Bechsteinweg Numero (*number*) 10 in _____ Berlin." „Meine Telefonnummer ist _____."
Jasmin	„_____ Tag! Mein _____ ist Jasmin Walter. _____ komme _____ Berlin. _____ _____ ist die Lietzenburgerstraße Numero 20 in _____ Berlin. Meine Telefonnummer ist _____."
Frau Simon	„Guten Tag, _____ _____ Malle Simon und wohne in _____ auf der Schönhauser Allee." „Meine Telefonnummer ist 030/_____."

D Watch all the interviews again and listen for the following information. Select the correct response.

1. Oliver geht es ...
   a. glänzend.   **b.** sehr gut.   **c.** so lala.
2. Jan wohnt ...
   a. in Berlin.   **b.** in Hamburg.   **c.** in Hannover.
3. Harald kommt ursprünglich (*originally*) ...
   a. aus Hannover.   **b.** aus Berlin.   **c.** aus Leipzig.
4. Nicolettas Adresse ist ...
   a. Lietzenburgerstraße 13.   **b.** Pappelallee 35.   **c.** Schönhauser Allee 41.
5. Saras Postleitzahl ist ...
   a. 10557 Berlin.   **b.** 12203 Berlin.   **c.** 10437 Berlin.
6. Herr Borowsky kommt ...
   a. aus Hamburg.   **b.** aus Düsseldorf.   **c.** aus Berlin.
7. Michael fragt: „Wie heißt du?" Ali sagt: ...
   a. „Mein Name ist Ali."   **b.** „Ich bin der Ali."   **c.** „Ich heiße Ali."

Wortschatz

Zur Begrüßung	**Greetings**
grüß dich	hello, hi (*among friends and family*)
guten Abend	good evening
(guten) Morgen	good morning
(guten) Tag	hello, good day
hallo	hello (*among friends and family*)
herzlich willkommen	welcome
hi	hi

Beim Abschied	**Saying Good-bye**
(auf) Wiedersehen	good-bye
gute Nacht	good night
Mach's gut.	Take care, So long (*informal*)
tschüss	so long, 'bye (*informal*)

Bekannt werden	**Getting Acquainted**
Frau; die Frau	Mrs., Ms.; woman
Herr; der Herr	Mr.; gentleman
der Lehrer / die Lehrerin	teacher
Das ist …	This is …
Wie heißt du?	What's your name? (*informal*)
Wie ist dein Name?	What's your name? (*informal*)
Wie heißen Sie?	What's your name? (*formal*)
Wie ist Ihr Name?	What's your name? (*formal*)
Woher kommst du?	Where are you from? (*informal*)
Woher kommen Sie?	Where are you from? (*formal*)
Ich bin …	I'm …
Ich heiße …	My name is …
Ich komme aus …	I'm from …
Mein Name ist …	My name is …
bitte	please; you're welcome
danke	thanks
danke schön	thank you very much
Freut mich.	Pleased to meet you.
auch	also, too
und	and

Auskunft erfragen	**Asking for Information**
ja	yes
na klar	absolutely, of course
nein	no
Wie heißt …	What is the name of …
die Stadt?	the town; the city?
die Straße?	the street?
Wie ist …	What is …
deine/Ihre Telefonnummer?	your (*informal/formal*) telephone number?
die Adresse?	the address?

die Hausnummer?	the street address?
die Postleitzahl?	the postal code?

Nach dem Befinden fragen	**Asking About Someone's Well-being**
Geht's gut?	Are you doing well? (*informal*)
Na, wie geht's?	How are you? (*casual*)
Wie geht's?	How are you? (*informal*)
Wie geht's dir?	How are you? (*informal*)
Wie geht es Ihnen?	How are you? (*formal*)
ausgezeichnet	excellent
danke, gut	fine, thanks
nicht besonders gut	not particularly well
prima	great, super
schlecht	bad(ly), poor(ly)
sehr gut	very well; fine; good
so lala	O.K., so-so

Im Deutschunterricht	**In German Class**
Alles klar.	I get it.
Das weiß ich nicht.	I don't know.
Ich habe eine Frage.	I have a question.
Ich verstehe das nicht.	I don't understand.
Langsamer, bitte.	Slower, please.
Was bedeutet _____?	What does _____ mean?
Wie bitte?	Pardon? What did you say?
Wie sagt man _____ auf Deutsch?	How do you say _____ in German?
Wie schreibt man _____?	How do you write _____?

Zahlen (Numbers)

0	null	17	siebzehn
1	eins	18	achtzehn
2	zwei	19	neunzehn
3	drei	20	zwanzig
4	vier	30	dreißig
5	fünf	40	vierzig
6	sechs	50	fünfzig
7	sieben	60	sechzig
8	acht	70	siebzig
9	neun	80	achtzig
10	zehn	90	neunzig
11	elf	100	(ein)hundert
12	zwölf	200	zweihundert
13	dreizehn	300	dreihundert
14	vierzehn	1 000	(ein)tausend
15	fünfzehn	2 000	zweitausend
16	sechzehn	3 000	dreitausend

Deutschsprachige Länder und ihre Nachbarn	German-speaking Countries and Their Neighbors		
Belgien	Belgium	**Österreich**	Austria
Dänemark	Denmark	**Polen**	Poland
Deutschland	Germany	die **Schweiz**	Switzerland
Frankreich	France	die **Slowakei**	Slovakia
Italien	Italy	**Slowenien**	Slovenia
Liechtenstein	Liechtenstein	**Tschechien**	the Czech Republic
Luxemburg	Luxembourg	**Ungarn**	Hungary
die **Niederlande** (*pl.*)	the Netherlands		

Das kann ich nun!

Now that you have completed the **Einführung,** do the following in German to check what you have learned.

1. Formulate appropriate expressions to:
   a. Introduce yourself to a stranger.
   b. Introduce someone to another person.
   c. Greet a friend.
   d. Greet a stranger.
   e. Say good-bye to a friend.

2. Say the alphabet and spell your full name.

3. Ask a friend how he/she is doing and tell him/her how you are doing.

4. a. Give your phone number.
   b. Count from 1 to 100.

5. Formulate an appropriate statement or question for when . . .
   a. you don't understand something.
   b. you didn't hear what someone said.
   c. you want to know what something means.
   d. you want to know how to say something in German.

6. State five countries where German is spoken and give their official abbreviations.

Das bin ich

Was macht ihr hier?

In diesem Kapitel

- ▶ **Themen:** Giving personal information, describing yourself, inquiring about others, hobbies and interests

- ▶ **Grammatik:** Nouns, gender, and definite articles; personal pronouns; infinitives and present tense; the verb **sein;** word order; asking questions; interrogatives; **denn**

- ▶ **Lesen:** „Dialog" (Nasrin Siege)

- ▶ **Landeskunde: Einwohnermeldeamt,** multicultural society in Germany

- ▶ **Zu guter Letzt:** Einander kennenlernen

VIDEOCLIPS

Beruf, Studium und Hobbys

A One of the things you will learn to do in German is to give information about people in different contexts and situations. People give information about themselves in personal documents—documents they use in everyday life—as, for example, in personal IDs. Let's take a close look at one such ID.

Try to find the following information in the personal ID.

- ❯ What is the full name of the ID holder?
- ❯ When was he born?
- ❯ What is his nationality?
- ❯ Where does he live?
- ❯ What information is provided after the word **Größe?**
- ❯ What color are his eyes?
- ❯ What does the word **Unterschrift** refer to?

Vokabelsuche (*word search*). Find the German word for:

1. birthdate
2. nationality
3. color of eyes
4. height

PERSONALAUSWEIS

Nachname:
EMSLANDER

Vorname:
NIELS

Geburtstag:
24.05.90

Staatsangehörigkeit:
DEUTSCH

Gültig bis:
30.08.2015

Unterschrift:
Niels Emslander

Gegenwärtige Anschrift
Adresse:
OLDENBURG
AM TEICH 42

Größe:
183 cm

Augenfarbe:
BRAUN

B You will now hear five speakers introduce themselves. As you listen, see whether you can hear what cities they are from.

1. Berlin   Leipzig   München
2. Rostock   Köln   Luzern
3. Wien   Jena   Mainz
4. Düsseldorf   Graz   Leipzig
5. Erfurt   Zürich   Frankfurt

Wörter im Kontext

Information

Thema 1: Persönliche Angaben°

Wer sind diese Leute? Scan the information, then create a profile of each person.

Neue Wörter

bin ... geboren was born . . .
wohne (wohnen) live
jetzt now
ich bin ... von Beruf my profession is . . .
der Hochschullehrer university instructor
groß tall
arbeite (arbeiten) work

1. Mein Name ist Harald Lohmann. Ich **bin** 1970 in Dessau **geboren** und **wohne jetzt** in Magdeburg. **Ich bin Hochschullehrer von Beruf.** Meine Adresse ist Bahnhofstraße 20. Ich bin 1,82 Meter **groß**.

2. Mein **Nachname** ist Lercher und mein **Vorname** Daniela. Ich bin 1989 in Graz in Österreich geboren und wohne jetzt in Wien. Meine Adresse ist Mozartstraße 36. Ich bin 1,65 groß und bin Studentin.

3. Anton ist mein Vorname und Rütli mein Nachname. Ich komme aus der Schweiz. Ich bin 1980 in Luzern geboren und wohne und **arbeite** in Luzern. Meine Adresse ist Schulstrasse 8. Ich bin Architekt von Beruf. Ich bin 1,79 groß.

Schreiben Sie Steckbriefe (*profiles*) von diesen Personen:

1. Vorname:
   Nachname:
   geboren im Jahr:
   Geburtsort:
   Größe:
   Beruf:
   Wohnort:
   Straße und Hausnummer:
   Land:
2. Vorname:
   Nachname:
   geboren im Jahr:
   Geburtsort:
   Größe:
   Beruf:
   Wohnort:
   Straße und Hausnummer:
   Land:

3. Vorname:
   Nachname:
   geboren im Jahr:
   Geburtsort:
   Größe:
   Beruf:
   Wohnort:
   Straße und Hausnummer:
   Land:

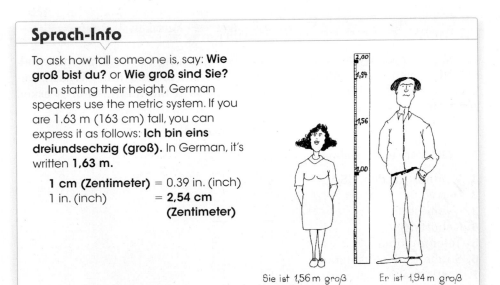

Sprach-Info

To ask how tall someone is, say: **Wie groß bist du?** or **Wie groß sind Sie?**

In stating their height, German speakers use the metric system. If you are 1.63 m (163 cm) tall, you can express it as follows: **Ich bin eins dreiundsechzig (groß).** In German, it's written **1,63 m.**

1 cm (Zentimeter) = 0.39 in. (inch)
1 in. (inch)   = **2,54 cm (Zentimeter)**

Sie ist 1,56 m groß   Er ist 1,94 m groß

Aktivität 1   Interessante Personen

Listen to the following statements about the people in the profiles and say whether they are true (**das stimmt**) or false (**das stimmt nicht**).

	Das stimmt	Das stimmt nicht		Das stimmt	Das stimmt nicht
1. a.	☐	☐	3. a.	☐	☐
b.	☐	☐	b.	☐	☐
c.	☐	☐	c.	☐	☐
d.	☐	☐	d.	☐	☐
e.	☐	☐	e.	☐	☐
f.	☐	☐			
2. a.	☐	☐			
b.	☐	☐			
c.	☐	☐			
d.	☐	☐			
e.	☐	☐			

Jetzt sind Sie dran! (Now it's your turn!)

   Mein Nachname ist _____.
   Mein Vorname ist _____.
   Ich komme aus _____.
   Ich wohne in _____.
   Meine Adresse ist _____.
   Ich bin ____,_____ groß.

Hier klicken!

You'll find more about the **Einwohnermeldeamt** in **Deutsch: Na klar!** on the World Wide Web at www.mhhe.com/dnk6.

Landeskunde-Info

Everyone who lives in Germany must register with the **Einwohnermeldeamt** (residents' registration office) within two weeks of moving to a new community. This applies to everyone, even students living in a community only temporarily. The **Einwohnermeldeamt** must also be notified when one moves from one place to another.

○ Do residents of your country have to register in their community?

○ What are some pros and cons of registering?

Aktivität 2   Eine neue Studentin

Julie, who recently arrived in Berlin, is registering at the **Einwohnermeldeamt.** Listen to the interview between the official and Julie. What information does the official ask her for? Check **ja** if the information is asked for, **nein** if it is not.

	Ja	Nein
BEISPIEL: Vor- und Nachname	☒	☐
1. Wohnort in den USA	☐	☐
2. Beruf	☐	☐
3. Geburtsort	☐	☐
4. Geburtstag	☐	☐
5. Telefonnummer	☐	☐
6. Straße und Hausnummer	☐	☐
7. Postleitzahl	☐	☐

Aktivität 3   Fragen Sie!°

Ask!

A Unscramble the following to form questions for a short interview.

1. dein / wie / Name / ist /, bitte / ?
2. Adresse / ist / deine / wie / ?
3. deine / Telefonnummer / wie / ist / ?
4. Geburtsort / was / dein / ist / ?
5. groß / bist / wie / du / ?

B Now use the questions to interview two people in your class.

C Tell the class what you've found out.

○ Das ist _____.

○ (Tims/Elizabeths) Adresse ist _____.

○ Seine/Ihre Telefonnummer ist _____.

○ Er/Sie ist in _____ geboren.

○ Er/Sie ist ___,_____ groß.

Aktivität 4   Wie groß bist du? Wie alt bist du?

Figure out your height in meters with the help of the conversion chart. Then exchange this information with one or two people in the class.

BEISPIEL: **S1:** Wie groß bist du?

　　　　S2: Ich bin 1,64 (eins vierundsechzig) groß.

　　　　S1: Wie alt bist du?

　　　　S2: Ich bin dreiundzwanzig.

Thema 2: Sich erkundigen°

„Info und Wissen": eine Quizshow

Inquiring

Ansager:	Guten Abend, meine Damen und Herren. Willkommen **heute** im Studio bei Info und Wissen. Und hier kommt Quizmaster Dieter Sielinsky.
Herr Sielinsky:	Guten Abend und herzlich willkommen. Und **wer** ist unsere Kandidatin? Wie ist Ihr Name, bitte?
Frau Lentz:	Lentz, Gabi Lentz.
Herr Sielinsky:	Woher kommen Sie, Frau Lentz?
Frau Lentz:	Aus München.
Herr Sielinsky:	Und **was machen** Sie denn in Berlin?
Frau Lentz:	Ich **besuche Freunde** hier.
Herr Sielinsky:	Na, und **wie finden Sie** Berlin denn?
Frau Lentz:	**Ganz toll,** faszinierend.
Herr Sielinsky:	Und was sind Sie von Beruf, Frau Lentz?
Frau Lentz:	Ich bin Web-Designerin.
Herr Sielinsky:	Und haben Sie Hobbys?
Frau Lentz:	**Aber natürlich! Lesen, Reisen, Wandern, Kochen,** und ich mache **Kreuzworträtsel.**
Herr Sielinsky:	So, na dann **viel Glück heute Abend.**
Frau Lentz:	**Danke sehr.**

Neue Wörter

heute today
wer who
was what
machen are doing
besuche (besuchen) am visiting
Freunde friends
wie finden Sie ...? how do you like ...?
ganz toll really great
aber but
natürlich of course
das Lesen reading
das Reisen traveling
das Wandern hiking
das Kochen cooking
das Kreuzworträtsel crossword puzzle
viel Glück good luck
heute Abend this evening
danke sehr thanks a lot

 Refer to *Personal Pronouns*, p. 34 and to *The Verb: Infinitive and Present Tense*, p. 36.

Neue Wörter

sag mal   tell me
hier   here
lerne (lernen)   am learning
das Deutsch   German
studiere (studieren)   am studying; am majoring in
echt (coll.)   really
die Universität   university
bleibst (bleiben)   are staying
nächstes Jahr   next year

Ein Gespräch an der Uni

Helmut:	Grüß Gott! Helmut Sachs.
Julie:	Guten Tag! Ich heiße Julie Harrison.
Helmut:	Woher kommst du, Julie?
Julie:	Ich komme aus Cincinnati.
Helmut:	Ah, aus den USA! Cincinnati? Ist das im Mittelwesten?
Julie:	Ja, im Bundesstaat Ohio.
Helmut:	**Sag mal,** was machst du jetzt **hier**?
Julie:	Ich **lerne Deutsch** am Sprachinstitut. Und du?
Helmut:	Ich **studiere** Physik an der T.U.
Julie:	**Echt?** Was ist die T.U. denn?
Helmut:	Die Technische **Universität.** Und wie lange **bleibst** du hier in München?
Julie:	Zwei Semester. **Nächstes Jahr** bin ich wieder in Ohio.
Helmut:	Ach so.

Sprach-Info

To convey strong curiosity or surprise, add the particle **denn** to your question.

> Was ist die T.U. **denn**?
> *What is the T.U.?* (strong curiosity)

> Arbeitest du **denn** heute?
> *Are you working today?* (surprise)

Analyse

Look at the dialogues again and locate the following information.

Info und Wissen

▶ How does the quizmaster ask his guest what her name is?
▶ What phrase does the quizmaster use to ask Frau Lentz where she is from?
▶ What does the quizmaster ask to find out Frau Lentz's profession?
▶ What question does he ask to find out about her hobbies?
▶ What question does he ask to find out if Frau Lentz likes Berlin?
▶ What pronoun does the quizmaster use to address Frau Lentz?

Ein Gespräch an der Uni

▶ How do Helmut and Julie greet each other?
▶ How does Helmut ask Julie where she is from? How does this differ from the same question asked by the quizmaster?
▶ What phrase does Helmut use to ask Julie what she is doing in Munich?
▶ Helmut doesn't know where Cincinnati is. What does he ask Julie to get that information?
▶ What pronoun do Julie and Helmut use to address each other?

Sprach-Info

To say that you are studying at a university or to state your major, use the verb **studieren**.

> Ich **studiere** in München.

> Ich **studiere** Physik.

To say you are studying specific material, such as for a test, use **arbeiten** or **lernen**.

> Ich **lerne** heute Abend für eine Chemieprüfung.

> Ich **arbeite** auch für die Matheprüfung.

To say that you are learning or taking a language, use the verb **lernen**.

> Ich **lerne** Deutsch.

Aktivität 5 Steht das im Dialog?

Mark whether the statements below are correct or incorrect, based on the information found in the dialogues in **Thema 2**.

	Das stimmt	Das stimmt nicht
1. Der Quizmaster heißt Dieter Sielinsky.	☐	☐
2. Gabi Lentz kommt aus Augsburg.	☐	☐
3. Frau Lentz ist Professorin von Beruf.	☐	☐
4. Tanzen ist ein Hobby von Frau Lentz.	☐	☐
5. Frau Lentz findet Berlin zu groß.	☐	☐
6. Julie kommt aus Cincinnati.	☐	☐
7. Julie lernt Deutsch in München.	☐	☐
8. Helmut studiert Mathematik.	☐	☐
9. Julie bleibt zwei Jahre in München.	☐	☐

Aktivität 6 Was sagen diese Leute zueinander?°

What do these people say to each other?

Determine whether the following phrases and questions would be used by two students addressing each other, by a professor and a student, or by both pairs of speakers.

	Zwei Studenten	Professor und Student
1. Was studierst du?	☐	☐
2. Grüß dich!	☐	☐
3. Auf Wiedersehen.	☐	☐
4. Wie heißt du?	☐	☐
5. Guten Tag!	☐	☐
6. Wie heißen Sie?	☐	☐
7. Was machst du hier?	☐	☐
8. Was studieren Sie?	☐	☐
9. Tschüss!	☐	☐
10. Mach's gut!	☐	☐

Aktivität 7 Fragen und Antworten°

Match each question in the left-hand column with a possible answer from the right-hand column. More than one answer is possible for some.

1. _____ Wie heißen Sie?
2. _____ Woher kommst du?
3. _____ Was machen Sie hier?
4. _____ Wo ist das?
5. _____ Wer ist das?

a. Ich studiere hier.
b. Das ist im Mittelwesten.
c. Mein Name ist Meier.
d. Ich heiße Keller.
e. Ich lerne Deutsch.
f. Ich komme aus Deutschland.
g. Das ist Peter.
h. Ich bin aus Kalifornien.

Aktivität 8 Kurzdialoge°

Listen to the brief conversational exchanges and indicate in each case whether the response to the first question or statement is logical (**logisch**) or illogical (**unlogisch**).

	Logisch	Unlogisch
1.	☐	☐
2.	☐	☐
3.	☐	☐
4.	☐	☐
5.	☐	☐
6.	☐	☐
7.	☐	☐
8.	☐	☐
9.	☐	☐
10.	☐	☐

Aktivität 9 Eine Konversation

Number the following sentences in order to form a short conversation between Herr Brinkmann and Frau Garcia, who are just getting acquainted. Then perform it with a partner.

_____ Wie bitte?

_____ Ich finde Hamburg interessant.

_1_ Guten Tag. Ich heiße Garcia.

_____ Woher kommen Sie?

_____ Ach so!

_____ Wie finden Sie Hamburg?

_____ Ich besuche Freunde.

_____ Ich komme aus Florida.

_____ Guten Tag. Mein Name ist Brinkmann.

_____ Brinkmann.

_____ Und was machen Sie hier?

Aktivität 10   Was studierst du?

Schritt 1: Find your major in the following list. Then, by asking questions, try to find at least one other classmate who has the same major as you.

BEISPIEL: **S1:**   Was studierst du?
S2:   Ich studiere Geschichte. Und du?
S1:   Ich studiere Informatik.

http://www.deutscheuni.de

VORLESUNGSVERZEICHNIS

Anthropologie
Betriebswirtschaft[1]
Biologie
Chemie
Deutsch/Germanistik
Englisch/Anglistik
Französisch/Romanistik
Geschichte[3]
Informatik
Jura
Kunst[4]
Marketing
Maschinenbau[6]

Mathematik
Medienwissenschaft[2]
Medizin
Musik
Pädagogik
Philosophie
Physik
Politik
Psychologie
Soziologie
Spanisch/Romanistik
Volkswirtschaft[5]

[1]*management*   [2]*media studies*   [3]*history*   [4]*art*   [5]*economics*   [6]*mechanical engineering*

Schritt 2: Now report back to the class. Does anyone have the same major as you?

BEISPIEL: Ich studiere Informatik. Candice und Ben studieren auch Informatik.

Neue Wörter

bestimmt no doubt
nie never
langweilig boring
immer always
ernst serious
ruhig quiet
Interessen interests
Musik hören listening to music
wirklich really
sportlich athletic
nicht not
die Zeitung newspaper
freundlich friendly
vielleicht perhaps
oft often
faul lazy
fleißig hardworking
lustig cheerful
nett nice
praktisch practical
sympathisch likable
Das macht Spaß. That's fun to do.
Das mache ich gern! I like doing that!
Bücher books
gehen to go/going
Computerspiele spielen to play/playing computer games
diskutieren to discuss/discussing
essen to eat/eating
Fahrrad fahren to ride/riding a bicycle
Karten spielen to play/playing cards
SMS schicken to send/sending text messages
tanzen to dance/dancing

Thema 3: Eigenschaften und Interessen°

Wir lernen Deutsch

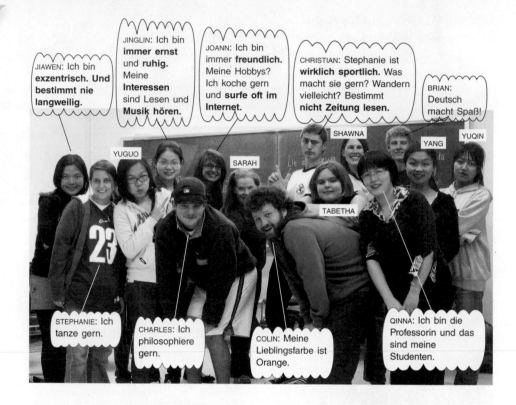

JIAWEN: Ich bin **exzentrisch. Und bestimmt nie langweilig.**

JINGLIN: Ich bin **immer ernst und ruhig.** Meine **Interessen** sind Lesen und **Musik hören.**

JOANN: Ich bin immer **freundlich.** Meine Hobbys? Ich koche gern und **surfe oft im Internet.**

CHRISTIAN: Stephanie ist **wirklich sportlich.** Was macht sie gern? Wandern vielleicht? Bestimmt **nicht Zeitung lesen.**

BRIAN: Deutsch macht Spaß!

SHAWNA

YUGUO

SARAH

YANG

YUQIN

TABETHA

STEPHANIE: Ich tanze gern.

CHARLES: Ich philosophiere gern.

COLIN: Meine Lieblingsfarbe ist Orange.

QINNA: Ich bin die Professorin und das sind meine Studenten.

So bin ich! (*That's me!*) Check the characteristics that apply to you.

- ☐ chaotisch
- ☐ dynamisch
- ☐ ernst
- ☐ exzentrisch
- ☐ **faul**
- ☐ **fleißig**
- ☐ freundlich
- ☐ interessant
- ☐ konservativ
- ☐ langweilig
- ☐ liberal
- ☐ **lustig**
- ☐ **nett**
- ☐ **praktisch**
- ☐ progressiv
- ☐ **romantisch**
- ☐ ruhig
- ☐ sportlich
- ☐ **sympathisch**
- ☐ tolerant

Das macht Spaß! Das mache ich gern! Check off your interests and hobbies.

- ☐ **Bücher** lesen
- ☐ ins Café **gehen**
- ☐ **Computerspiele spielen**
- ☐ **Diskutieren**
- ☐ **Essen**
- ☐ **Fahrrad fahren**
- ☐ Fotografieren
- ☐ im Internet surfen
- ☐ **Karten spielen**
- ☐ Kochen
- ☐ Musik
- ☐ Reisen
- ☐ **SMS schicken**
- ☐ Sport
- ☐ **Tanzen**
- ☐ Telefonieren
- ☐ Wandern
- ☐ Zeitung lesen

Aktivität 11 Gegenteile

Refer to the list of characteristics at the beginning of **Thema 3** and provide the opposite(s) of each of the following adjectives.

1. lustig ≠ _____
2. faul ≠ _____
3. konservativ ≠ _____
4. langweilig ≠ _____
5. dynamisch ≠ _____

Aktivität 12 Interessen und Hobbys

Provide the name of the activity represented by each drawing.

1. _____

2. _____

3. _____

4. _____

5. _____

6. _____

Aktivität 13   Ratespiel: Wie bin ich? Was mache ich gern?

Write down two adjectives that describe you, and one of your interests. Do not write your name. Your instructor will collect and distribute everyone's list. Then each class member will read a description out loud, while the others try to guess who the writer is.

BEISPIEL: Ich bin dynamisch und exzentrisch. Ich surfe gern im Internet.

Important

Aktivität 14   Wichtig° oder nicht?

1. Make a list of three characteristics and three interests that you consider important in a friend.
2. Tally the results on the board.

    Which characteristic is most important for the class?

    Which interest is most frequently mentioned?

Grammatik im Kontext

Nomen, Genus und bestimmte Artikel

Nouns, Gender, and Definite Articles°

Nouns in German can be easily recognized in print or writing because they are capitalized.

German nouns are classified by grammatical gender as either masculine, feminine, or neuter. The definite articles **der, die,** and **das** (all meaning *the* in German) signal the gender of nouns.

Masculine: der	Feminine: die	Neuter: das
der Mann	die Frau	das Haus
der Beruf	die Adresse	das Buch
der Name	die Straße	das Semester

The grammatical gender of a noun that refers to a human being generally matches biological gender; that is, most words for males are masculine, and words for females are feminine. Aside from this, though, the grammatical gender of German nouns is largely unpredictable.

> ### Sprach-Info
>
> The definite article in the plural is **die** for all nouns, regardless of gender.
>
> der Freund   **die** Freunde
> *the friend*   *the friends*
>
> You will learn how to form the plurals of nouns in **Kapitel 2.**

Even words borrowed from other languages have a grammatical gender in German, as you can see from the following newspaper headline.

Fußball ist der Hit

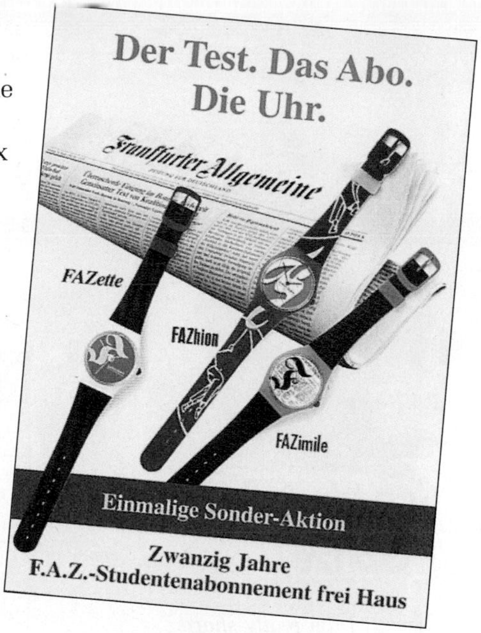

Since the gender of nouns is generally unpredictable, you should make it a habit to learn the definite article with each noun.

Sometimes gender is signaled by the ending of the noun. The suffix **-in,** for instance, signals a feminine noun.

der Amerikaner, die Amerikaner**in**

der Freund, die Freund**in**

der Professor, die Professor**in**

der Student, die Student**in**

Compound nouns (**Komposita**) are very common in German. They always take the gender of the final noun in the compound.

der Biergarten   = das Bier   + **der** Garten

das Telefonbuch   = das Telefon + **das** Buch

die Telefonnummer = das Telefon + **die** Nummer

Übung 1   Was hören Sie?

Circle the definite article you hear in each of the following questions and statements.

1. der die das
2. der die das
3. der die das
4. der die das

5. der die das
6. der die das
7. der die das
8. der die das

Übung 2   Hier fehlen die Artikel.

Complete each sentence with the missing article—**der, die,** or **das.**

1. ＿＿ Studentin aus Cincinnati lernt Deutsch am Sprachinstitut.
2. ＿＿ Student studiert Physik an der T.U.
3. ＿＿ Frau aus München findet Berlin ganz toll.
4. Was ist ＿＿ Hobby von Frau Lentz?
5. ＿＿ Adresse vom Hotel ist bestimmt im Telefonbuch.
6. Wo ist ＿＿ Telefonbuch?
7. Fußballtrainer? ＿＿ Beruf ist interessant, aber oft stressig.
8. ＿＿ Kreuzworträtsel ist sehr kompliziert.
9. ＿＿ Freund von Ute studiert Informatik.
10. ＿＿ Zeitung aus München heißt *Süddeutsche Zeitung.*

Übung 3   Wörter bilden°

Creating words

Create compound nouns using the words supplied.

BEISPIEL: der Garten + das Haus = das Gartenhaus

| das Bier | die Frau | das Haus | die Nummer |
| das Buch | der Garten | der Mann | das Telefon |

The advertisement reads:

Der Test. Das Abo. Die Uhr.

Frankfurter Allgemeine

FAZette

FAZhion

FAZimile

Einmalige Sonder-Aktion

Zwanzig Jahre F.A.Z.-Studentenabonnement frei Haus

Personal Pronouns°

A personal pronoun stands for a person or a noun.

Mein Name ist **Ebert. Ich** bin Architekt.
*My name is **Ebert. I** am an architect.*

Du bist immer so praktisch, **Gabi.**
You** are always so practical, **Gabi.

Der Wagen ist toll. Ist **er** neu?
***The car** is fabulous. Is **it** new?*

Ich bin rundum Spitze[1]
mit pan-ADRESS

[1]*Ich ... I am really sharp.*
(I am great in every way.)

	Singular		Plural	
1st person	ich	*I*	wir	*we*
2nd person	du	*you (informal)*	ihr	*you (informal)*
	Sie	*you (formal)*	Sie	*you (formal)*
3rd person	er	*he; it*	sie	*they*
	sie	*she; it*		
	es	*it*		

NOTE:

▶ The pronoun **ich** is not capitalized unless it is the first word in a sentence.

▶ German has three words to express *you:* **du, ihr,** and **Sie.** Use the familiar singular form **du** for a family member, close friend, fellow student, child, or animal. If speaking to two or more of these, use the familiar plural form **ihr.** Use the formal form **Sie** (always capitalized) for one or more acquaintances, strangers, or anyone with whom you would use **Herr** or **Frau.**

▶ The third-person singular pronouns **er, sie** (*she*), and **es** reflect the grammatical gender of the noun or person for which they stand (the antecedent).

Mark und Anja sind Studenten.	*Mark and Anja are students.*
Er kommt aus Bonn und **sie** kommt aus Wien.	*He comes from Bonn, and she comes from Vienna.*
—Wie ist **der Film?**	*How is the film?*
—**Er** ist wirklich lustig.	*It is really funny.*
—Wo ist **die Zeitung?**	*Where is the newspaper?*
—**Sie** ist hier.	*It is here.*
—Wo ist **das Buch?**	*Where is the book?*
—**Es** ist nicht hier.	*It is not here.*

Übung 4 Du, ihr oder Sie?

Would you address the following people with **du, ihr,** or **Sie?**

1. Frau Lentz aus München
2. Ute und Felix, zwei gute Freunde
3. Sebastian, ein guter Freund
4. Herr Professor Rauschenbach
5. Herr und Frau Zwiebel aus Stuttgart
6. eine Studentin in der Mensa
7. ein Tourist aus Kanada
8. Max, 10 Jahre alt

Übung 5 Herr und Frau Lentz

Working with a partner, take turns asking and answering questions, using a pronoun in each answer.

BEISPIEL: **S1:** Wie ist Frau Lentz?

S2: <u>Sie</u> ist nett und freundlich.

1. Wo wohnen Herr und Frau Lentz? _____ wohnen in München.
2. Was ist Frau Lentz von Beruf? _____ ist Web-Designerin.
3. Was ist Herr Lentz von Beruf? _____ ist Koch im Hofbräuhaus.
4. Wie groß ist Frau Lentz? _____ ist 1,63 m groß.
5. Und wie groß ist Herr Lentz? _____ ist 1,90 m groß.
6. Wie heißt Frau Lentz mit Vornamen? _____ heißt Gabi.
7. Was machen Herr und Frau Lentz in Berlin? _____ besuchen Freunde.

Übung 6 Informationen

Working with a partner, take turns asking a question and finding an appropriate answer among the ones provided. Complete each answer with the appropriate pronoun.

BEISPIEL: **S1:** Wo ist die Universität?

S2: <u>Sie</u> ist im Stadtzentrum.

Frage

_e_ 1. Wie heißt die schöne, alte Universitätsstadt im Schwarzwald?

_G_ 2. Wie ist das Leben (*life*) dort?

3. Wie alt ist die Universität in Freiburg?

_A_ 4. Im Filmklub spielt ein Film. Wie heißt der Film?

_H_ 5. Wo ist das Museum?

6. Wie findest du die Stadt?

_F_ 7. Wo wohnt der Student aus Hamburg?

_C_ 8. Was studiert die Studentin aus den USA?

Antwort

a. _Es_ heißt *Good bye, Lenin!*

b. _die_ ist über 500 Jahre alt.

c. _Sie_ studiert Deutsch am Sprachinstitut.

d. _____ ist sehr schön und nicht zu groß.

e. _sie_ heißt Freiburg im Breisgau.

f. _er_ wohnt im Studentenwohnheim.

g. _Es_ ist interessant und nie langweilig.

h. _sie_ ist im Stadtzentrum.

Im Stadtzentrum von Freiburg

The Verb: Infinitive and Present Tense°

In German, the basic form of the verb, the infinitive, consists of the verb stem plus the ending **-en** or, sometimes, just **-n**.

Infinitive	Verb Stem	Ending
kommen	komm	**-en**
wandern	wander	**-n**

The present tense is formed by adding different endings to the verb stem. These endings vary according to the subject of the sentence.

Here are the present-tense forms of three common verbs.

	kommen	**finden**	**heißen**
ich	komm**e**	find**e**	heiß**e**
du	komm**st**	find**est**	heiß**t**
er sie es	komm**t**	find**et**	heiß**t**
wir	komm**en**	find**en**	heiß**en**
ihr	komm**t**	find**et**	heiß**t**
sie/Sie	komm**en**	find**en**	heiß**en**

NOTE:

▶ German has four different endings to form the present tense: **-e, -(e)st, -(e)t,** and **-en**. English, in contrast, has only one ending, -(e)s, for the third-person singular (*comes, goes*).

▶ Verbs with stems ending in **-d** or **-t (finden, arbeiten)** add an **-e-** before the **-st** or **-t** ending **(du find<u>est</u>, er arbeit<u>et</u>)**.

▶ Verbs with stems ending in **-ß, -s,** or **-z (hei<u>ß</u>en, rei<u>s</u>en, tan<u>z</u>en)** add only a **-t** in the **du** form **(du hei<u>ß</u>t, reist, tanz<u>t</u>)**.

Use of the Present Tense

The present tense in German may express either something happening at the moment or a recurring or habitual action.

| Wolfgang spielt Karten. | *Wolfgang is playing cards.* |
| Antje arbeitet viel. | *Antje works a lot.* |

It can also express a future action or occurrence, particularly with an expression of time.

| Nächstes Jahr lerne ich Spanisch. | *Next year I'm going to learn Spanish.* |

German has only one form of the present tense, whereas English has three.

| Hans **tanzt** wirklich gut. | ⎰ *Hans **dances** really well.*
⎱ *Hans **is dancing** really well.*
⎱ *Hans **does dance** really well.* |

Analyse

▶ Identify the different verb endings in the illustrations.

▶ What is the subject in each sentence?
  Is it in the singular or in the plural?

▶ What is the infinitive form of each verb?

Ich lese das Journal, weil ...

Foto: Randy Kühn

MARS – WIR KOMMEN!

Hat den Flamenco in Berlin mitgeprägt: Amparo de Triana – heute zu erleben auf dem Pfefferberg

Berlin tanzt Flamenco

Ob[1] fünf oder zehn Jahre alt: „Schule macht Spaß"

Fußgänger[2] findet 10 000 Euro auf der Straße

Hier kommt Ihr Glück[3]!

Informationen zum Gewinnsparen

---

[1]Whether   [2]Pedestrian   [3]happiness

Übung 7　Zwei Freunde

Connect the matching sentence elements to create a profile of the two friends.

	studieren Mathematik in Zürich.
	tanzt wirklich gut.
	heiße Gisela.
Ich ...	macht gern Sport.
	wandern gern.
Mein Freund / Er ...	wohne in Zürich.
Wir ...	spiele gern Karten.
	fahren oft Fahrrad.
	wohnt auch in Zürich.
	finde die Stadt sehr schön.
	findet Karten spielen langweilig.
	koche gern.
	heißt Philipp.

Übung 8　Sabine und Michael in Österreich

Working with a partner, complete the following questions and answers by supplying the missing verb endings.

1. S1: Wie heiß**t** du?
   S2: Ich heiß**en** Sabine Keller.
2. S1: Woher komm**st** du?
   S2: Ich komm**e** aus den USA.
3. S1: Was mach**st** du im Internetcafé?
   S2: Na, ich surf**e** im Internet und spiel**e** Videogames.
4. S1: Wie find**st** du das Essen in der Mensa?
   S2: Ich find**e** das Essen da nicht gut.
5. S1: Woher komm**t** Michael?
   S2: Er komm**t** aus Kanada.
6. S1: Was mach**t** ihr in Graz?
   S2: Wir lern**en** Deutsch und wir studier**en** hier.
7. S1: Wie find**t** ihr die Professoren hier?
   S2: Wir find**en** die Professoren sehr gut.
8. S1: Wie lange bleib**t** ihr in Graz?
   S2: Ich bleib**e** zwei Semester hier. Michael bleib**e** ein Semester.

Übung 9 Kleine Szenen

Supply the missing verb endings and then role-play each scene.

Szene 1 (drei Personen)

A: Das ist Herr Witschewatsch. Er komm_____ aus Rosenheim.

B: Ah, guten Tag, Herr Wischewas.

C: Nein, nein, ich heiß_____ Witschewatsch.

B: Ach so, Sie heiß_____ Wischewasch?

C: Nein, Wit-sche-wat-sch.

B: Oh, Entschuldigung°, ich hör_____ nicht gut.   *excuse me*

Szene 2 (zwei Personen)

A: Ich hör_____, Sie komm_____ aus Rosenheim?

B: Nein, nein, ich komm_____ nicht aus Rosenheim. Ich komm_____ aus Rüdesheim, Rüdesheim am Rhein.

A: Ach, meine Freundin Antje komm_____ auch aus Rüdesheim.

Szene 3 (drei Personen)

A: Wie find_____ ihr Andreas?

B: Ich find_____ Andreas echt langweilig.

C: Ich auch.

A: Sabine find_____ Andreas super.

C: Na, und er find_____ Sabine total langweilig.

Szene 4 (zwei Personen)

A: Guten Morgen, meine Damen und Herren. Willkommen in Dresden. Heute besuch_____ wir das Verkehrsmuseum (*transport museum*).

B: Das Verkehrsmuseum? Ich bleib_____ im Hotel!

The Verb **sein**

The irregular verb **sein** (*to be*) is used to describe or identify someone or something.

> Marion **ist** Studentin.
>
> Sie **ist** sehr sympathisch.

sein			
ich	**bin**	wir	**sind**
du	**bist**	ihr	**seid**
er sie es	**ist**	sie	**sind**
Sie **sind**			

Übung 10 So ist das.°

Everyone is picking on Thomas. Complete the sentences with the appropriate form of **sein**.

1. Die Freundin von Thomas sagt: „Du _____ so konservativ, Thomas."
2. Thomas sagt: „Wie bitte? Das stimmt nicht. Ich _____ sehr progressiv."
3. Der Vater von Thomas sagt: „Thomas _____ so unpraktisch."
4. Thomas denkt: „Ihr _____ alle so unfair."
5. Die Mutter von Thomas sagt: „Wir _____ zu kritisch. Thomas _____ sehr intelligent und sensibel."
6. Der Chef von Thomas sagt zu Thomas: „Herr Berger, Sie _____ nicht sehr fleißig."
7. Thomas denkt: „Er _____ immer so unfreundlich und unfair." So _____ das Leben.

Sprach-Info

Some adjectives can combine with the prefix **un-** to indicate the opposite meaning.

praktisch	**un**praktisch
practical	*impractical*
freundlich	**un**freundlich
friendly	*unfriendly*

Word Order° in Sentences

One of the most important rules of German word order is the fixed position of the conjugated verb (the verb with the personal ending).

First Element (Subject, Adverb, etc.)	Second Element (Verb)	Other Elements
Ich	studiere	Informatik in Deutschland.
Nächstes Jahr	mache	ich ein Praktikum.
Heute	besuchen	wir das Verkehrsmuseum.

NOTE:

- The conjugated verb is always the second element in a sentence.
- The subject of the sentence can either precede or follow the verb.

Übung 11 Leas Freund

Restate the information in each sentence by starting with the boldfaced word or words.

BEISPIEL: Leas Freund heißt **Stefan.** →
Stefan heißt Leas Freund.

1. Stefan ist Musiker **von Beruf.**
2. Er wohnt **jetzt** in Berlin.
3. Er spielt **oft** im Jazzklub.
4. Er findet **Berlin** ganz fantastisch.
5. Stefans Hobby ist **Fahrrad fahren.**
6. Er arbeitet **nächstes Jahr** in Wien.

Übung 12 Wer macht was und wann?

Create two sentences for each group of words.

BEISPIEL: besuchen / das Museum / heute / wir →
Wir besuchen heute das Museum.
Heute besuchen wir das Museum.

1. Karten / wir / spielen / heute Abend
2. bei McDonald's / Peter / arbeitet / jetzt
3. ich / oft / mache / Kreuzworträtsel
4. spielen / wir / vielleicht / Tennis mit Boris
5. ein Praktikum in Dresden / Peter / nächstes Jahr / macht

Übung 13 Meine Pläne°

plans

Tell a partner two things you may do today and tomorrow (**morgen**), choosing from the list below or from your own plans. Then tell the class about your partner's plans.

BEISPIEL: Heute spiele ich Karten. Morgen spiele ich Tennis. →
Heute spielt Bob Karten. Morgen spielt er Tennis.

gar nicht arbeiten	Musik machen
viel arbeiten	SMS schicken
Freunde besuchen	Computerspiele/Karten/? spielen
tanzen gehen	im Internet surfen
Musik hören	???

Asking Questions°

Fragen stellen

There are two types of questions. We refer to them as *word questions* and *yes/no questions*.

Word Questions

Wann kommst du?	***When*** *are you coming?*
Was machst du?	***What*** *are you doing?*
Wer ist das?	***Who*** *is that?*
Wie findest du Berlin?	***How*** *do you like Berlin?*
Wo wohnst du?	***Where*** *do you live?*
Woher sind Sie?	***Where*** *are you from?*

[1]am ... *on the weekend*

NOTE:

- Word questions begin with an interrogative pronoun. They require specific information in the answer.

- The conjugated verb is the second element in a word question.

- German uses only one verb form to formulate a question, in contrast to English.

Wo **wohnst** du?   { *Where **do** you **live**?*
                      *Where **are** you **living**?*

Übung 14   Zwei Menschen

Read the two personal ads and answer the questions.

1. Wie heißt der Mann?
2. Wie heißt die Frau?
3. Wie alt ist die Frau?
4. Wie alt ist der Mann?
5. Wie groß ist der Mann?
6. Wie groß ist die Frau?
7. Wie ist Jürgen? (drei Adjektive)
8. Was macht Petra?

Übung 15   Ergänzen Sie.

Complete each question with an appropriate interrogative pronoun: **wann, was, wer, wie, woher,** or **wo.**

1. _____ heißt du?
2. _____ kommst du?
3. _____ studierst du denn?
4. _____ findest du Heidelberg?
5. _____ wohnst du denn?
6. _____ studiert Mathematik in Zürich?
7. _____ machst du denn hier?
8. _____ besuchst du das Verkehrsmuseum?

Übung 16   Formulieren Sie passende Fragen.

Formulate a word question for each answer.

BEISPIEL: _____*Woher kommst du*_____? Ich komme aus Kanada.

1. _____? Ich heiße Peter.
2. _____? Ich wohne in Essen.
3. _____? Ich studiere da Medizin.
4. _____? Ich komme aus Süddeutschland.
5. _____? Nächstes Jahr mache ich ein Praktikum.
6. _____? Meine Familie wohnt in Nürnberg.
7. _____? Ich finde Hamburg sehr schön.
8. _____? Das ist die Studentin aus Berlin.

Yes/No Questions

Kommst du?   *Are you coming?*

Studiert Lea in Berlin?   *Is Lea studying in Berlin?*

Heißt der Professor Kuhn?   *Is the professor's name Kuhn?*

NOTE:

○ A yes/no question begins with the conjugated verb and can be answered with either **ja** or **nein.**

○ The verb is immediately followed by the subject.

Übung 17   Ja und nein

What questions could trigger the following answers?

BEISPIEL: _Kommen Sie aus Hamburg_? Ja, ich komme aus Hamburg.

1. _Sind Sie Köln_____? Nein, ich bin nicht Frau Schlegel; ich bin Frau Weber.
2. _wohnen Sie in Köln_____? Ja, wir wohnen in Köln.
3. _Finen Sie Köln interessant_? Ja, ich finde Köln sehr interessant.
4. _Arbeiten Sie b.d.T._____? Nein, ich arbeite nicht bei der Telekom.
5. _Ist K. sehr groß_____? Ja, Köln ist sehr groß.
6. _Spielen wir Karten oft__? Ja, wir spielen oft Karten.

Übung 18   Zur Information

Take a survey and then share some of the results in class.

Schritt 1: Write down five informal yes/no questions using verbs and other words from the lists below or others if you like.

BEISPIELE: Wohnst du im Studentenwohnheim?

    Bist du immer freundlich?

arbeiten	nie	in der Disco
machen	manchmal (*sometimes*)	freundlich/unfreundlich/fleißig/?
schicken	oft	Karten/Fußball/Computerspiele/?
sein	immer	Kreuzworträtsel/Musik
spielen	gern	im Studentenwohnheim
surfen		klassische Musik / Rock / ?
tanzen		SMS/E-Mails
wohnen		im Internet
hören		

Schritt 2: Now move around the classroom asking these questions to find classmates who can answer yes. Your responses to one another need not be complete sentences.

BEISPIEL: **S1:**   Wohnst du im Studentenwohnheim?

    S2:   Ja. / Aber natürlich! / Na klar! / Nein.

Schritt 3: Now report back to the class on who does what.

BEISPIEL: Matt wohnt im Studentenwohnheim. Trudi ist immer freundlich. …

Übung 19 Wie bitte?

Schritt 1: Invent a fictitious person and fill in the blanks.

1. Ich heiße _____.
2. Ich komme aus _____.
3. Ich studiere _____. Das macht Spaß.

Schritt 2: Now take turns with a partner introducing your fictitious self. Your partner imagines that he/she has not clearly heard what you said and asks you to repeat. Follow the model.

BEISPIEL: **S1:** Ich heiße Fritz Fisch.

S2: Wie bitte? Wie heißt du?

S1: Fritz Fisch.

S2: Ach so!

S1: Ich komme aus Alaska.

S2: Wie bitte? Woher kommst du?

S1: Aus Alaska. ...

Student life

Übung 20 Das Studentenleben°

Schritt 1: You will hear some information about a German university student. Compare what you hear with the statements below. If a statement is incorrect, find the correct answer from among the choices in parentheses.

	Das stimmt	Das stimmt nicht
1. Die Studentin heißt Claudia. (_____ Katrin, ✓ Karin)	☐	☑
2. Sie kommt aus Göttingen. (✓ Dresden, _____ Bremen)	☐	☑
3. Der Familienname ist Renner. (✓ Reuter, _____ Reiser)	☐	☑
4. Sie studiert jetzt in Tübingen. (✓ Göttingen, _____ Dresden)	☐	☑
5. Sie studiert Mathematik. (_____ Jura, ✓ Informatik)	☐	☑
6. Sie wohnt bei einer Familie. (✓ im Studentenwohnheim, _____ allein)	☐	☑
7. Sie geht oft schwimmen. (_____ wandern, _____ Tennis spielen)	☑	☐
8. Sie geht oft ins Café. (_____ in die Disco, _____ ins Museum)	☑	☐

Schritt 2: Now formulate yes/no questions based on the statements given in **Schritt 1.** Ask another student in your class to verify the information.

BEISPIEL: **S1:** Heißt die Studentin Claudia?

S2: Nein, sie heißt Karin.

Sprache im Kontext

Videoclips

A Watch the interviews with Sara and Ali as they talk about what they are studying, their hobbies, and how their friends would describe them. Write **S** if the phrase or word applies to **Sara** or **A** if it applies to **Ali.**

_____ Medienwissenschaft   _____ Schwimmen

_____ Mathematik   _____ spontan

_____ Joggen   _____ zurückhaltend (*reserved*)

_____ Gitarre spielen   _____ lustig

_____ Zeichnen   _____ fröhlich

_____ Tanzen   _____ sehr aktiv

_____ Fahrrad fahren

B Who does what? Watch the interviews and match each person with a profession or job.

1. _____ Peter   **a.** ist Grafikdesigner
2. _____ Oliver   **b.** ist Pilot
3. _____ Alex   **c.** ist Bankkauffrau
4. _____ Jasmin   **d.** arbeitet bei KDW im Silbershop
5. _____ Frau Simon   **e.** ist Web-Designer

C Watch the interviews again and jot down notes about things you have in common with the interviewees. If you have anything in common, then write a few sentences that describe the commonalities. Follow the model.

BEISPIEL: Ali studiert Mathematik. Ich studiere auch Mathematik. Saras Hobby ist Tanzen. Mein Hobby ist auch Tanzen …

Lesen

Zum Thema°

About the topic

Where do the students in your German class come from? Were all students in the class born in the same country? What nationalities and ethnic groups are represented? How many students can speak more than one language? How many students have bilingual parents?

Auf den ersten Blick°

At first glance

1. Look at the title and the text itself. What type of text is this? What led you to your conclusions?
2. Label the exchanges in the dialogue with *S1 (Speaker 1)* and *S2 (Speaker 2)*.
3. Skim the text for references to geographical locations and references to a person's appearance.
4. From the context, what do you think **reden** and **aussehen (siehst … aus, sehe aus)** mean?

Sprach-Info

In spoken German, the question word **woher** is often split into two, with the **her** coming at the end of the sentence.

Woher kommst du? ⎫
Wo kommst du **her?** ⎬ *Where do you come from?*

Dialog

von *Nasrin Siege*

„Du redest so gut deutsch. Wo kommst du denn her?"
„Aus Hamburg."
„Wieso? Du siehst aber nicht so aus!"
„Wie sehe ich denn aus?"
5 „Na ja, so schwarzhaarig und dunkel …"
„Na und?"
„Wo bist du denn geboren?"
„In Hamburg."
„Und dein Vater?"
10 „In Hamburg."
„Deine Mutter?"
„Im Iran."
„Da haben wir's!"
„Was denn?"
not a 15 „Dass du keine° Deutsche bist!"
„Wer sagt das?"
„Na ich!"
„Warum?"

About the text

Zum Text°

1. What does the text tell you about the birthplace, place of residence, and citizenship of Speaker 2? What else can you determine about him or her?

2. Consider what you've learned about different forms of "you" in German. Speculate: How old are the two speakers? How well do they know each other? Where might this dialogue take place? How do you think it started?

3. Why is the nationality of Speaker 2 an issue for Speaker 1?

Hier klicken!

You'll find information about the topic of foreigners in Germany in **Deutsch: Na klar!** on the World Wide Web at **www.mhhe.com/dnk6.**

Zu guter Letzt

Getting to know one another

Einander kennenlernen°

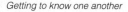

You are going to be working with other students in the class on various speaking and writing tasks in German. Some students you already know, others you don't. In this activity, you will interview three students you have not already met, tell someone else about one of them, and write a short profile of each of them.

Schritt 1: Before you ask the questions below, formulate them in German. Ask each student:

- ◐ his/her name _____
- ◐ where he/she comes from _____
- ◐ where he/she was born _____
- ◐ what he/she likes to do _____
- ◐ what he/she is studying _____
- ◐ how he/she likes the university here _____

Schritt 2: Now interview the three students and jot down their responses.

Schritt 3: Using your notes, tell another student about one of the persons you interviewed.

Schritt 4: Write a short profile of each student you interviewed, using complete sentences. Use the model below.

BEISPIEL: Eine Studentin heißt Stacey. Sie kommt aus …

Landeskunde-Info

Some 82 million people live in Germany. More than seven million are foreigners, who make up roughly 9% of Germany's population. In addition, 1.5 million "foreigners" have taken German citizenship, along with 4.5 million ethnic Germans from the former East Block. The poster below was one of many from a nationwide campaign in 1993 arguing for more tolerance. The author is unknown, but the poster often appears on personal websites and even on a T-shirt. At right is a new version, which appeared on a Swiss poster for the traveling exhibition "Jeder ist ein Fremder – fast überall" (*Everyone Is a Foreigner—Almost Everywhere*)."

- ◐ Can you find any differences between the two texts?
- ◐ Can you think of additional categories?

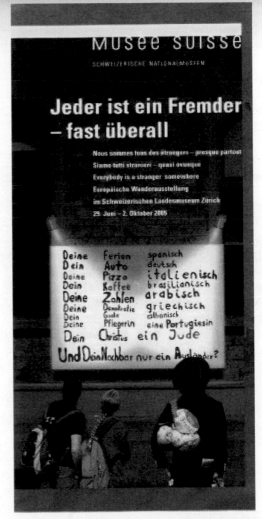

Dein Christus ein Jude
Dein Auto ein Japaner
Deine Pizza italienisch
Deine Demokratie griechisch
Dein Kaffee brasilianisch
Dein Urlaub türkisch
Deine Zahlen arabisch
Deine Schrift lateinisch

Und Dein Nachbar nur ein Ausländer?

Plakat gegen Rassismus und Ausländerfeindlichkeit (antiforeigner sentiments), gesehen in einer Hamburger U-Bahn Station

Plakat für die Wanderausstellung „Jeder ist ein Fremder – fast überall", hier im Musée Suisse ausgestellt.

Wortschatz

Eigenschaften	**Characteristics**
alt	old
ernst	serious
exzentrisch	eccentric
fantastisch	fantastic
faul	lazy
fleißig	hardworking, diligent
freundlich/unfreundlich	friendly/unfriendly
groß	tall
gut	good, well
Er tanzt gut.	He dances well.
interessant	interesting
kompliziert	complicated
konservativ	conservative
langweilig	boring
lustig	cheerful; fun-loving
nett	nice
praktisch/unpraktisch	practical/impractical
romantisch	romantic
ruhig	quiet
sportlich	athletic
stressig	stressful
sympathisch/	
unsympathisch	likable/unlikable
toll! (coll.)	super!
ganz toll!	super! great!

Substantive	**Nouns**
der **Amerikaner** / die **Amerikanerin**	American
der **Beruf**	profession, occupation
Was sind Sie von Beruf?	What do you do for a living?
das **Buch**	book
(das) **Deutsch**	German (language)
das **Essen**	food; eating
das **Fahrrad**	bicycle
der **Freund** / die **Freundin**	friend
der **Geburtsort**	birthplace
der **Geburtstag**	birthday, date of birth
das **Hobby**	hobby
der **Hochschullehrer** / die **Hochschullehrerin**	university instructor
das **Interesse**	interest
das **Jahr**	year
nächstes Jahr	next year
der **Journalist** / die **Journalistin**	journalist
der **Mann**	man
die **Mensa**	student cafeteria
die **Musik**	music
der **Name**	name
der **Nachname**	family name, surname
der **Vorname**	first name, given name

das **Praktikum**	internship
ein Praktikum machen	to do an internship
der **Professor** / die **Professorin**	professor
das **Semester**	semester
der **Spaß**	fun
der **Student** / die **Studentin**	student
die **Universität**	university
der **Wohnort**	place of residence
die **Zeitung**	newspaper

Verben	**Verbs**
arbeiten	to work
besuchen	to visit
bleiben	to stay, remain
diskutieren	to discuss
essen	to eat
fahren	to drive, ride
Fahrrad fahren	to ride a bicycle
finden	to find
Wie findest du ...?	How do you like ...?; What do you think of ...?
gehen	to go
heißen	to be called, be named
hören	to listen, hear
kochen	to cook
kommen	to come
lernen	to learn, study
lesen	to read
machen	to do; to make
Kreuzworträtsel machen	to do crossword puzzles
reisen	to travel
sagen	to say, tell
sag mal	tell me
schicken	to send
sein	to be
spielen	to play
Computerspiele spielen	to play computer games
Karten spielen	to play cards
studieren	to study
surfen	to surf
im Internet surfen	to surf the Internet
tanzen	to dance
telefonieren	to talk on the phone
wandern	to hike
wohnen	to reside, live

Personalpronomen	**Personal Pronouns**
ich	I
du	you (informal sing.)

er	he; it	echt (coll.)	really
sie	she; it; they	ganz	quite, very, really
es	it	gern	gladly
wir	we	gern + verb	to like doing something
ihr	you (informal pl.)	heute	today
Sie	you (formal sing./pl.)	heute Abend	this evening
		hier	here
		ich bin geboren	I was born

Interrogativpronomen — **Interrogative Pronouns**

wann	when	immer	always
was	what	jetzt	now
wer	who	natürlich	of course, natural(ly)
wie	how	nicht	not
wo	where	nie	never
woher	from where	oft	often
		sehr	very
		viel	a lot, much

Sonstiges — **Other**

aber	but	viel Glück!	good luck!
bestimmt	no doubt; definitely	viel Spaß!	have fun!
danke sehr	thanks a lot	vielleicht	maybe, perhaps
Das macht Spaß.	That's fun.	wirklich	really

Das kann ich nun!

1. Sagen Sie, wie Sie heißen und wo Sie wohnen. Sagen Sie auch Ihre Telefon-/Handynummer, wie groß Sie sind, und wo Sie geboren sind.

2. Was studieren/lernen Sie an der Universität? Nennen Sie zwei Fächer.

3. Beschreiben Sie einen Freund / eine Freundin. Drei Adjektive bitte.

   Mein Freund heißt … Er ist …

   Meine Freundin heißt … Sie ist …

4. Haben Sie Hobbys? Nennen Sie zwei.

5. Ergänzen Sie diese Sätze:
   a. Der Film _____ interessant.
   b. Ich _____ Berlin toll.
   c. Woher _____ Sie?
   d. Fotografieren _____ Spaß.

6. **Der, die** oder **das?**
   a. _____ Semester
   b. _____ Name
   c. _____ Zeitung

7. Sagen Sie **Sie, du,** oder **ihr?**
   a. ein Freund: _____
   b. Herr und Frau Lentz: _____
   c. dein Bruder und deine Schwester: _____

8. Wie fragt man auf Deutsch?
   a. *When are you coming?*
   b. *Where do you live?*
   c. *Is Susan studying in Munich?*
   d. *Who is visiting Berlin next year?*

9. Hier fehlt ein Wort.
   a. _____ heißen Sie?
   b. _____ kommen Sie?
   c. _____ kommt aus Berlin?
   d. _____ studierst du?

So wohnen diese Leute.

Kapitel 2

Wie ich wohne

Wie hoch ist die Miete? Hmm, ein Zimmer in einer WG?

In diesem Kapitel

▶ **Themen:** Talking about types of housing, furnishings, favorite activities

▶ **Grammatik:** The verb **haben;** nominative and accusative case of indefinite and definite articles; **dieser** and **welcher;** negation with **nicht** and **kein;** verbs with stem-vowel changes; the plural of nouns

▶ **Lesen:** „So wohne ich"

▶ **Landeskunde:** Living arrangements, history of the euro

▶ **Zu guter Letzt:** Wir suchen einen Mitbewohner / eine Mitbewohnerin

VIDEOCLIPS

A Just as in North America, flyers (**Anschlagzettel**) are a popular way to make announcements, advertise, or disseminate information in German-speaking countries. What do you think is the purpose of the flyer shown here? Once you've determined the purpose, answer the multiple-choice questions.

▶ Wo findet man (*one*) so einen Anschlagzettel?

    a. in einer Klinik

    b. an der Uni

    c. in einem Garten

▶ Die vier Studentinnen suchen _____.

    a. einen Regenschirm

    b. eine Wohnung

    c. ein Dach

▶ Sie brauchen _____ Zimmer.

    a. zwei bis (*to*) drei

    b. sechs bis sieben

    c. vier bis fünf

▶ Sie möchten (*would like*) eine Wohnung _____.

    a. im Stadtzentrum

    b. in einem Vorort (*suburb*)

    c. auf dem Lande (*in the country*)

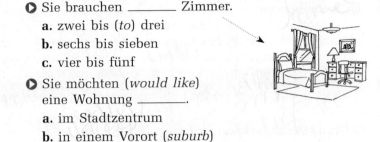

Vokabelsuche. Find the German word for:

1. kitchen

2. bath

3. central location

4. reward

B Listen to the following short conversations. Mark the kind of apartment the speakers are looking for.

1. a. eine Zweizimmerwohnung

    b. eine Dreizimmerwohnung

2. a. eine Zweizimmerwohnung mit Küche und Bad

    b. eine Dreizimmerwohnung in zentraler Lage

3. a. ein Zimmer bei einer Familie

    b. ein Zimmer in einem Studentenheim

Landeskunde-Info

In German-speaking countries, the kitchen and bathroom are not counted as "rooms" when describing the number of rooms in an apartment. Thus, a **Zwei-zimmerwohnung** has one bedroom and a living room, while a **Dreizimmerwoh-nung** has two bedrooms and a living room. An **Appartement** is a studio, or efficiency apartment.

Students either live in a **Studentenwohnheim** (residence hall) or share living accommodations such as an apartment to cut expenses. Many students prefer living in a **Wohngemeinschaft (WG),** a co-op in which each student has a private room while kitchen and bath facilities are shared.

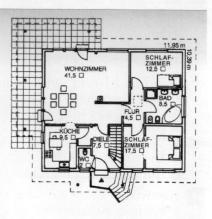

▶ Which rooms are included in a 1-bedroom / 2-bedroom apartment in your country?

▶ What kind of living arrangements do students have?

Wörter im Kontext

Neue Wörter

Was ist denn los? What's the matter?

suche (suchen) am looking for

dringend desperately

die Wohnung apartment

das Zimmer room

teuer expensive

nichts nothing

frei free, available

etwas something

da here; there

schönes (schön) beautiful

möbliertes (möbliert) furnished

der Nichtraucher (Nichtraucher, *pl.***)** nonsmoker

hoch high

die Miete rent

nur only

recht quite

preiswert reasonable

das Geld money

weit von der Uni far from the university

Da hast du recht. You're right.

gerade just, exactly

zentral gelegen centrally located

frage (fragen) ask

genau exactly

Thema 1: Auf Wohnungssuche

Ulla und Stefan treffen sich (meet) *vor der Mensa der Uni Freiburg. Ulla hat ein großes* **Problem.**

Stefan: Tag, Ulla! Wie geht's?

Ulla: Ach, nicht besonders.

Stefan: **Was ist denn los?**

Ulla: Ich **suche dringend** eine **Wohnung** oder ein **Zimmer.** Wohnungen sind aber **alle so teuer.**

Stefan: Ist denn **nichts frei** im **Studentenwohnheim?**

Ulla: Hier in Freiburg? Bestimmt nicht!

Stefan: Hier ist die Zeitung von heute. Ah, hier ist **etwas. Da,** schau mal: **schönes, möbliertes** Zimmer für **Nichtraucher.**

Ulla: Wie **hoch** ist die **Miete?**

Stefan: **Nur** 250 Euro.

Ulla: Das ist **recht preiswert.** Ich habe nicht viel **Geld** für Miete. Wo ist das Zimmer?

Stefan: In Gundelfingen.

Ulla: In Gundelfingen?! Das ist aber **weit von der Uni.**

Stefan: Na, **da hast du recht.** Preiswert ist es, aber Gundelfingen ist nicht **gerade zentral gelegen.**

Ulla: Naja, ich brauche dringend ein Zimmer. Ich **frage** mal, **genau** wie weit das bis zur Innenstadt ist.

A **Stimmt das oder stimmt das nicht?** Mark whether the following statements are correct (**das stimmt**) or incorrect (**das stimmt nicht**) based on the information in the dialogue.

	Das stimmt	Das stimmt nicht
1. Stefan sucht ein Zimmer.	☐	☑
2. Im Studentenwohnheim ist nichts frei.	☑	☐
3. Stefan findet ein Zimmer für Nichtraucher.	☑	☐
4. Das Zimmer ist nicht möbliert.	☑	☑
5. Die Miete ist nicht sehr hoch.	☑	☐
6. Gundelfingen ist nicht zentral gelegen.	☑	☐

B Wie wohnen Sie? Kreuzen Sie an.

☐ Appartement
☐ Haus
☐ Studentenwohnheim

☐ **Wohngemeinschaft (WG)**
☐ Wohnung
☐ Zimmer

C Ich wohne … / Meine Wohnung / Mein Zimmer / Mein Haus ist …

☐ allein (*alone*)
☐ bei den Eltern (*with my parents*)
☐ bei einer Familie

☐ weit von der Uni
☐ zentral gelegen

D Ich habe …

☐ einen Goldfisch
☐ ein **Handy**
☐ einen Hund (*dog*)
☐ eine Katze

☐ einen **Mitbewohner** / eine **Mitbewohnerin**
☐ ein Telefon

E Meine Wohnung / Mein Zimmer / Mein Haus hat …

☐ ein **Arbeitszimmer**
☐ eine schöne Aussicht (*view*)
☐ ein **Badezimmer** / **Bad**
☐ einen **Balkon**
☐ **Computeranschluss**
☐ ein **Esszimmer**
☐ ein (zwei/drei) **Fenster**

☐ eine **Garage**
☐ einen **Garten**
☐ eine **Küche**
☐ ein (zwei/drei) **Schlafzimmer**
☐ eine **Terrasse**
☐ ein **Wohnzimmer**

F Sie/Es ist …

☐ **groß**
☐ **klein**
☐ **dunkel**
☐ **hell**
☐ möbliert

☐ **unmöbliert**
☐ preiswert
☐ teuer
☐ schön
☐ **hässlich**

G Die Miete ist …

☐ hoch

☐ **niedrig**

Aktivität 1 Welches Zimmer ist das?

With which room do you associate the following?

1. wohnen: _____
2. kochen: _____
3. baden: _____
4. Auto: _____

5. lernen: _____
6. essen: _____
7. schlafen: _____

Neue Wörter

das Handy cell phone
der Mitbewohner / die Mitbewohnerin roommate, housemate
das Arbeitszimmer study
das Badezimmer/Bad bathroom
der Computeranschluss computer connection
das Esszimmer dining room
das Fenster window
die Küche kitchen
das Schlafzimmer bedroom
die Terrasse patio
das Wohnzimmer living room
groß big
klein small
dunkel dark
hell bright
unmöbliert unfurnished
hässlich ugly
niedrig low

Sprach-Info

Das ist **ein** Balkon.

Das ist **eine** Küche.

Das ist **ein** Badezimmer.

When a masculine noun is used as a direct object, **ein** changes to **einen**; however, feminine **eine** and neuter **ein** do not change:

Mein Haus hat **einen** Balkon, **eine** Küche und **ein** Badezimmer.

Refer to *The Indefinite Article: Nominative and Accusative*, p. 63.

Aktivität 2 Wir brauchen eine Wohnung / ein Zimmer.

Scan the five ads from people looking for housing. Label the ads from 1 to 5 in the order in which you hear them.

> Freundlicher junger 37-jähriger Englischlehrer sucht 1 Zimmer in WG um mit euch Deutsch zu sprechen und es besser zu lernen.
> ☎ 570 56 39

> Freundlicher Schauspieler[4] aus Hamburg sucht Zimmer in WG vom 1. Mai bis 1. August in München.
> ☎ 637 88 78, ♂ Manfred

> Musiker (24) sucht Zimmer oder Raum in WG zum 1.6. oder etwas früher. ☎ 040/439 84 20 Markus (rufe zurück[1]) PS.: Zahle[2] bis 250 Euro incl.[3]

> Fotodesignerin, 22, sucht preiswertes Zimmer in junger WG, möglichst zentral zum 1.7.07.
> ☎ 0170 123 45 678, Nichtraucherin.

---

[1]rufe … (*I'll*) *call back*   [2](*I'll*) *pay*   [3]incl. = inclusive *including utilities*   [4]*actor*

> Architekturstudentin (25) sucht zum 1. od. 15.5. ruhiges Zimmer bis 200 Euro inklusiv in WG ☎ 857 63 90 (oder 50 72 58)

Landeskunde-Info

The euro (€) is used in the countries of the European Union, including Germany. The currency has seven denominations of bills and eight different coins. The front side of each coin is the same in all countries, but for the reverse side each nation can choose motifs particular to that country.

Short History of the Euro

▶ January 1, 1999. The euro is born. The euro's exchange rate is established relative to other world currencies; however, people in Germany still use the **Deutsche Mark** (**D-Mark**) for everyday transactions.

▶ January 1, 2002. The euro coins and bills make their debut. The euro replaces the **D-Mark** as legal tender in Germany.

▶ March 1, 2002. In January and February of 2002, people can still exchange D-Marks for euros at any bank. After March 1, only the **Bundesbank** will exchange the D-Mark.

▶ June 30, 2002. While the new euro postage stamps make their appearance on January 1, 2002, stamps in **D-Mark** and **Pfennig** remain in circulation until June 30, 2002.

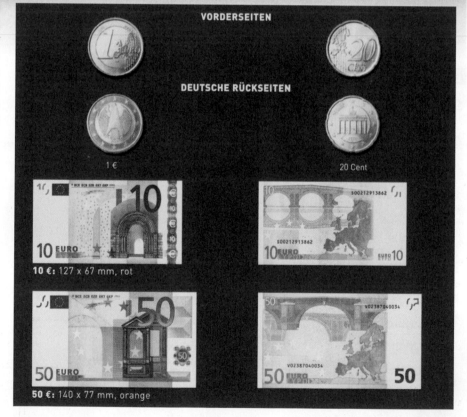

Fragen

▶ What symbols or images do the bills and coins of the currency in your country contain?

▶ Explain one of the symbols or images.

Aktivität 3   Wer braucht eine Wohnung?

Schritt 1: Look over the five ads from **Aktivität 2** and complete the following:

1. Der junge Englischlehrer sucht …
   a. eine Wohnung
   b. ein Zimmer in einer WG
   c. ein Appartement

2. Der Musiker braucht ein Zimmer …
   a. zum 1. Juli
   b. zum 1. Juni
   c. zum 1. August

3. Der Schauspieler sucht ein Zimmer …
   a. in München
   b. in Hamburg
   c. in Zürich

4. Die Fotodesignerin sucht …
   a. ein Zimmer
   b. eine Wohnung
   c. eine Nichtraucherin

5. Für das Zimmer zahlt die Architekturstudentin …
   a. bis 250 Euro
   b. bis 200 Euro
   c. bis 300 Euro

Schritt 2: Now look over the ads again and say as much as you can about each, giving more detailed information.

BEISPIEL: Ein Englischlehrer sucht ein Zimmer in einer WG.
       Er ist 37.
       Er ist freundlich und nett.

Aktivität 4   Eine Anzeige° schreiben

°ad

Using the newspaper ads on the previous page as models, create a simple ad in the following format. Trade ads with another person, who will read yours to the class.

| Student Studentin ?? | sucht | großes kleines ruhiges helles möbliertes unmöbliertes ?? | Zimmer mit | Telefon Bad Küche Garten Computeranschluss | in | einer WG einem Haus zentraler Lage ?? | bis zu Euro —. |

(handwritten note:) Freundliche Studentin sucht ruhiges Zimmer mit garten in einem Haus bis zu Euro

Thema 2: Auf Möbelsuche im Kaufhaus

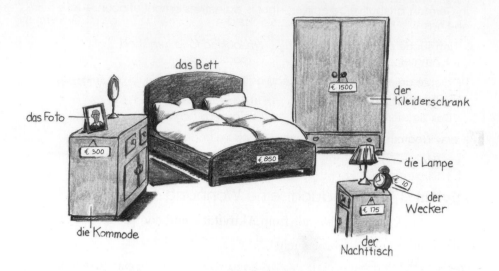

das Bett
das Foto
der Kleiderschrank
€ 1500
€ 300
€ 850
die Lampe
€ 10
€ 175
der Wecker
die Kommode
der Nachttisch

das Poster
das Bücherregal
die Wand
die Verkäuferin
die Tür
€ 1575
der Computer
€ 89
der Stuhl
€ 150
€ 850
der Kunde
der Schreibtisch
€ 25
das Telefon
der Papierkorb

das Regal
der Fernseher
der Sessel
die Zimmerpflanze
€ 1200
die Uhr
die Stereoanlage
das Radio
€ 70
das Sofa
der CD-Spieler
der Videorekorder
€ 225
€ 100
der DVD-Spieler
die Lampe
der Couchtisch
der Teppich

A Welche Möbel haben Sie **schon** in Ihrem Zimmer / in Ihrer Wohnung?

Ich habe …

- ☐ einen **Fernseher**
- ☐ eine **Lampe**
- ☐ ein **Radio**
- ☐ einen Computer
- ☐ einen **CD-Spieler**
- ☐ ??

Ich brauche noch …

- ☐ einen **DVD-Spieler**
- ☐ ein **Bücherregal**
- ☐ ein I-Pod mit Lautsprechern oder Boxen
- ☐ einen **Tisch**
- ☐ ??

Neue Wörter

das Kaufhaus department store
welche which
die Möbel (*pl.*) furniture
schon already
der Tisch table
dieser, diese, dieses this

B Was **kostet** das?

- ☐ **Dieser** DVD-Spieler kostet 100 Euro.
- ☐ **Diese** Lampe kostet 70 Euro
- ☐ **Dieses** Bett kostet 850 Euro.
- ☐ ??

🔍 Refer to *The **der**-Words **dieser** and **welcher**, p. 67.*

Aktivität 5 Ulla hat jetzt endlich° ein Zimmer. 🎧

finally

Listen as Ulla tells her friend Karin about the room she has just found. As you listen, check off the items that Ulla already has.

- ☑ ein Bett
- ☐ ein Bücherregal
- ☐ eine Lampe
- ☑ einen Schreibtisch
- ☑ einen Sessel
- ☑ einen Stuhl
- ☐ ein Telefon
- ☑ einen Tisch

Sprach-Info

When a masculine noun is used as a direct object, **der** changes to **den**. The articles **das** and **die** remain unchanged.

Wie findest du **den** Computer?

Wie findest du **das** Bett und **die** Lampe?

🔍 Refer to *The Definite Article: Nominative and Accusative, p. 65.*

Aktivität 6 Einkäufe° 💬

Purchases

Neue Wörter

bequem comfortable
billig inexpensive, cheap

Schritt 1: Look at the department store displays at the beginning of **Thema 2** and give your opinion of the furniture and other items shown.

BEISPIEL: **S1:** Wie findest du den Computer?
    das Bett?
    die Lampe?

S2: Sehr schön. Und wie findest du _____?

Reaktionen

zu (*too*) …	teuer	praktisch
sehr …	hässlich	(un)bequem
nicht …	schön	billig
	preiswert	toll

Schritt 2: Bring in several photos of pieces of furniture you have in your room, apartment, or house, or bring in several from magazines. Show them to a partner and, using the following model, ask them to react.

BEISPIEL: **S1:** Wie findest du diesen Fernseher?
    dieses Radio?
    diese Lampe?

S2: Nicht sehr preiswert. Und wie findest du _____?

Hier klicken!

You'll find more about home furnishings in German-speaking countries in **Deutsch: Na klar!** on the World Wide Web at www.mhhe.com/dnk6.

Aktivität 7 Ein Gespräch im Kaufhaus

Listen as Ulla talks with a salesperson. Then answer the true/false questions and correct any false statements.

	Das stimmt	Das stimmt nicht
1. Ulla braucht nur eine Lampe.	✓	☐
2. Ulla findet die italienische Lampe schön.	✓	☐
3. Die Lampe aus Italien ist nicht teuer.	☐	✓
4. Ulla kauft eine Lampe für 25 Euro.	✓	☐
5. Das Kaufhaus führt (*carries*) keine (*no*) Bücherregale.	✓	☐

Thema 3: Was wir gern machen

Was machen diese **Leute** gern? Match each caption with the corresponding drawing.

1. _____ Dieser Herr **liest** gern.
2. _____ Diese Frau **isst** gern.
3. _____ Dieser **Mensch schläft** gern.
4. _____ Diese Frau **fährt** gern **Motorrad.**
5. _____ Dieser **Junge sieht** gern Videos.
6. _____ Dieser Mensch **läuft** gern.

Sprach-Info

In some German verbs, the stem vowel changes from **e** to **i**, **e** to **ie**, or **a** to **ä** in certain verb forms. Do you recognize these verbs?

Refer to *Verbs with Stem-Vowel Changes*, p. 76.

Neue Wörter

die Leute (*pl.*)   people
liest (lesen)   reads
isst (essen)   eats
der Mensch   person
schläft (schlafen)   sleeps
fährt (fahren)   rides
der Junge   boy
sieht (sehen)   sees, watches
läuft (laufen)   runs
schreiben   write

a. Ernst Immermüd

b. Herr Wurm

c. Frau Renner

d. Frau Schlemmer

e. Uschi Schnell

f. Gerhard Glotze

Was machen Sie gern?

	Ja	Nein
Hören Sie gern Musik?	☐	☐
Essen Sie gern Sushi?	☐	☐
Fahren Sie gern **Auto?**	☐	☐
Kochen Sie gern?	☐	☐
Schreiben Sie gern E-Mails?	☐	☐
Schwimmen Sie gern?	☐	☐
Laufen Sie gern?	☐	☐
Sprechen Sie gern Deutsch?	☐	☐
Trinken Sie gern Cappuccino?	☐	☐
Schicken Sie gern SMS?	☐	☐

Aktivität 8   Hin und her: Machen sie das gern?

Find out what the following people like to do or don't like to do by asking your partner.

BEISPIEL: **S1:**   Was macht Denise gern?

S2:   Sie reist gern. Was macht Thomas nicht gern?

S1:   Er fährt nicht gern Auto.

	Gern	Nicht gern
Thomas	arbeiten	Auto fahren
Denise		
Niko	Eis essen	Karten spielen
Anja		
Sie		
Ihr Partner / Ihre Partnerin		

Konzert in der Waldbühne in Berlin

Aktivität 9 Zwei Berliner°

Read the following questions and then scan the profiles of the two people from Berlin to find the answers to the questions.

1. Was trinkt Jasmin gern? Und Mehmet?
2. Was essen die beiden gern?
3. Wer hört gern klassische Musik? Wer hört gern die Wise Guys?
4. Was liest Mehmet gern?
5. Wer kocht gern?
6. Wer fährt gern ein Smart Cabrio?

Name: *Jasmin*
Alter: *23*
Lieblingsgetränk: *Rotwein*
Lieblingsessen: *Nudelgerichte*
Lieblingsmusik: *Klassische Musik, Jazz*
Lieblingsauto: *Smart Cabrio*
Lieblingsaktivität: *Unter den Linden mit Freunden im Café sitzen*
Hobbys: *im Internet surfen, lesen, kochen, Sport*

Name: *Mehmet*
Alter: *30*
Lieblingsgetränk: *Tee*
Lieblingsessen: *Hackbraten*
Lieblingsmusik: *die Wise Guys*
Lieblingsauto: *BMW*
Lieblingsaktivität: *ins Konzert in der Waldbühne gehen*
Hobbys: *Zeitung lesen, ins Kino gehen, wandern*

Im Café unter den Linden

Aktivität 10 Wer macht was gern?

Schritt 1: Find out who likes to do the following things by asking different classmates the questions below. If they answer *yes*, have them sign their name in the blank to the right (or keep track by jotting down the people's names on a separate sheet).

BEISPIEL: **S1:** Siehst du gern Filme?

S2: Ja, ich sehe gern Filme.

1. Wanderst du gern? _San Fransico - Danney_
2. Hörst du gern laute Musik? _hiphop - susann_
3. Liest du gern? _die Newspaper - Mike_
4. Surfst du gern im Internet? _Nein - elton_
5. Isst du gern Brokkoli? _Nein_
6. Fährst du gern Motorrad? _____

Schritt 2: Now ask three people in your class: **"Was machst du gern und was machst du nicht gern?"** Jot down their responses and report them to the class.

BEISPIEL: Jeff reist gern, aber er tanzt nicht gern.
Sharon spielt gern Karten, aber sie kocht nicht gern.
Dave hört gern Musik, aber er arbeitet nicht gern.

Sprach-Info

In order to turn down an invitation, you could offer the following excuses.

S1:	Wir gehen ins Konzert. Kommst du mit?	*We're going to the concert. Will you come along?*
S2:	Nein, ich habe keine Zeit.	*No, I don't have the time.*
	or	
S2:	Nein, ich habe keine Lust.	*No, I don't feel like it.*
	or	
S2:	Nein, ich habe kein Geld.	*No, I don't have any money.*

Aktivität 11 Interaktion

You receive invitations from several people. Do you want to accept or reject the invitations?

BEISPIEL: **S1:** Wir gehen heute tanzen. Kommst du mit?

S2: Schön. Ich komme mit. Ich tanze sehr gern.

oder: Ich habe keine Lust.

Einladung	**Reaktion**
Ich gehe / Wir gehen heute …	Ja, schön.
in ein Rockkonzert.	Gut.
ins Kino (*to a movie*).	Tut mir leid (*I'm sorry*).
ins Theater.	Ich habe …
schwimmen.	keine Zeit.
Tennis/Fußball spielen.	keine Lust.
	kein Geld.

Grammatik im Kontext

The Verb **haben**

The irregular verb **haben** (*to have*), like many other verbs, needs a direct object to form a complete sentence.

Wir **haben** eine Vorlesung um zwei Uhr.   *We have a lecture at two o'clock.*

Anja **hat** Zeit.   *Anja has time.*

haben			
ich	habe	wir	haben
du	**hast**	ihr	habt
er sie es	**hat**	sie	haben
Sie haben			

Analyse

Lesen Sie den Dialog.

Ein Gespräch zwischen zwei Studenten. Es ist 12 Uhr mittags.

Jürgen: Grüß dich, Petra. Hast du Hunger?

Petra: Warum fragst du?

Jürgen: Ich geh' jetzt essen. Ich hab' Hunger. Kommst du mit?

Petra: Na, gut. Da kommt übrigens Hans. Der hat bestimmt auch Hunger.

Hans: Habt ihr zwei vielleicht Hunger?

Petra: Ja, und wie! Aber ich hab' nicht viel Zeit. Um zwei haben wir nämlich eine Vorlesung.

▶ Which forms of the verb **haben** can you find in the dialogue?

▶ The **ich**-form of **haben** appears without the ending **-e.** What could be the reason for this?

Mittagszeit in der Mensa

Übung 1   Habt ihr Hunger?

Complete the sentences with **haben.**

Stephan, Klaus und Sabine sind Studenten in Bonn. Es ist gerade Mittagszeit.

Stephan _____[1] Hunger. Er sagt zu Sabine und Klaus: „Ich _____[2] großen Hunger. _____[3] ihr auch Hunger?" Sabine und Klaus _____[4] um zwei Uhr eine Vorlesung. Sie _____[5] also nicht viel Zeit. Klaus _____[6] kein Geld. Er sagt zu Stephan: „Du, ich _____[7] kein Geld. _____[8] du etwas Geld?" Stephan zu Klaus: „Du _____[9] Glück! Ich _____[10] heute gerade etwas Geld. Du _____[11] ja nie Geld." Klaus: „Da _____[12] du recht! Wie immer."

The Nominative and Accusative Cases°

Kasus: der Nominativ und der Akkusativ

In English, the subject and the direct object in a sentence are distinguished by their placement. The subject usually precedes the verb, whereas the direct object usually follows the verb.

In German, however, the subject and the object are not distinguished by their placement in the sentence. Instead, subjects and objects are indicated by grammatical cases. In this chapter you will learn about the nominative case (**der Nominativ**) for the subject of the sentence (as well as the predicate noun) and the accusative case (**der Akkusativ**) for the direct object.

German typically signals the case and the grammatical gender of a noun through different forms of the definite and indefinite articles that precede a noun.

The Indefinite Article°: Nominative and Accusative

Der unbestimmte Artikel

You are already familiar with the nominative case. Those are the forms you used in **Kapitel 1.** Here are the nominative and accusative forms of the indefinite article (*a/an*).

Nominative:	Das ist **ein** Stuhl.	*That is a chair.*
Accusative:	Ich brauche **einen** Stuhl.	*I need a chair.*
Nominative:	Das ist **eine** Zeitung.	*That is a newspaper.*
Accusative:	Wo finde ich hier **eine** Zeitung?	*Where do I find a newspaper here?*
Nominative:	Das ist **ein** Zimmer.	*That is a room.*
Accusative:	Ich brauche **ein** Zimmer.	*I need a room.*

Singular			
	Masculine	*Feminine*	*Neuter*
Nominative	ein Stuhl	eine Zeitung	ein Zimmer
Accusative	**einen** Stuhl	eine Zeitung	ein Zimmer

NOTE:

- Only the masculine indefinite article has a distinct accusative form: **einen.**
- There is no plural indefinite article, just as in English.

Übung 2 Neu in Göttingen

You will now hear a conversation between Stefan and Birgit. As you listen, check off what Stefan already has and what he still needs for his new apartment. Not all items are mentioned; leave those blank.

	Das hat Stefan	Das braucht Stefan
1. einen DVD-Spieler	☐	☐
2. eine Zimmerpflanze	☑	☒
3. eine Uhr	☐	☐
4. einen Couchtisch	☒	☐
5. einen Computer	☐	☐
6. einen Schreibtisch	☒	☐
7. ein Bücherregal	☒	☐
8. eine Kaffeemaschine	☒	☐
9. einen Schlafsack (*sleeping bag*)	☒	☒
10. ein Bett	☒	☐
11. einen Sessel	☐	☐

Übung 3 Was sehen Sie?

Das ist eine typische Studentenbude.

Da ist _____.

Das Zimmer hat _____.

Übung 4 Was ich habe und was ich brauche

Schritt 1: List three items that you already have and at least one item that you need. Tell your partner about these things.

BEISPIEL: Ich habe _____.

Ich brauche _____.

Schritt 2: Report to the class what your partner has and needs.

BEISPIEL: John hat einen Computer, einen Schreibtisch und ein Bett. Er braucht einen Sessel.

The Definite Article°: Nominative and Accusative

Der bestimmte Artikel

Here are the nominative and the accusative case forms of the definite article (*the*).

Nominative:	**Der** Stuhl kostet 70 Euro.	*The chair costs 70 euros.*
Accusative:	Ich kaufe **den** Stuhl.	*I am going to buy the chair.*
Nominative:	Wo ist **die** Zeitung?	*Where is the newspaper?*
Accusative:	Ich brauche **die** Zeitung.	*I need the newspaper.*
Nominative:	Was kostet **das** Zimmer?	*What does the room cost?*
Accusative:	Ich miete **das** Zimmer.	*I am going to rent the room.*

	Singular			Plural
	Masculine	*Feminine*	*Neuter*	*All Genders*
Nominative	der Stuhl	die Zeitung	das Zimmer	die Stühle
Accusative	**den** Stuhl	die Zeitung	das Zimmer	die Stühle

NOTE:

◗ Only the masculine definite article has a distinct accusative form: **den.**

◗ The plural has only one article for all three genders: **die.**

Sprach-Info

A few common masculine nouns have a special accusative singular form. For example:

NOMINATIVE	ACCUSATIVE
der Mensch	den Mensch**en**
der Student	den Student**en**
der Herr	den Herr**n**

Weak masculine nouns, as they are called, are indicated in the vocabulary lists of this book by the notation (**-en** *masc.*) or (**-n** *masc.*).

Übung 5 Die Studentenbude°

What do you think of what you see in this room?

BEISPIEL: Ich finde das Zimmer sehr klein.

Ich finde …

das Zimmer	nicht	praktisch/unpraktisch
das Bücherregal	zu (*too*)	komisch
der Computer	sehr	klein/groß
der Schreibtisch		modern/unmodern
der Drucker (*printer*)		schön
der Student		bequem/unbequem
die Schreibtischlampe		sympathisch
die Möbel		
das Bett		
die Zimmerpflanze		
der Kleiderschrank		
das Poster		
der Teppich		
der Nachttisch		

Eine Studentenbude

Übung 6 Was kaufen Sie?

Sie haben 500 Euro. Was kaufen Sie?

BEISPIEL: Ich kaufe ＿＿＿ für 130 Euro und … .

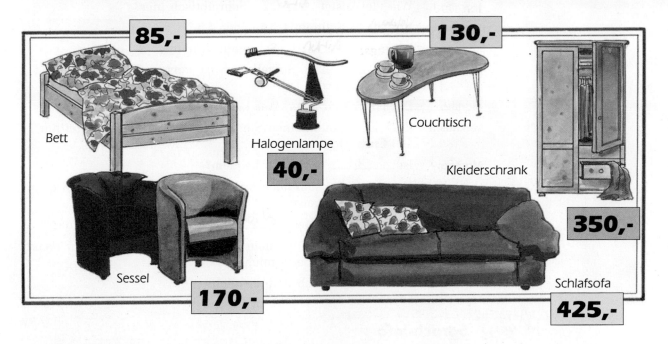

85,- Bett
Halogenlampe
40,-
130,- Couchtisch
Kleiderschrank
350,-
Sessel
170,-
Schlafsofa
425,-

The **der**-Words **dieser** and **welcher**

The word **dieser** (*this*) and the interrogative **welcher** (*which*) have the same endings as the definite article. For this reason they are frequently referred to as **der**-words.

Diese Wohnung ist zentral gelegen.	*This apartment is centrally located.*
Dieser Schreibtisch kostet 400 Euro.	*This desk costs 400 euros.*
Welchen Schreibtisch kaufst du?	*Which desk are you going to buy?*
Dieses Sofa ist nicht sehr bequem.	*This sofa is not very comfortable.*

All **der**-words follow the same pattern as the definite articles.

	Masculine	Feminine	Neuter	Plural
Nominative	die**ser**	die**se**	die**ses**	die**se**
	wel**cher**	wel**che**	wel**ches**	wel**che**
Accusative	die**sen**	die**se**	die**ses**	die**se**
	wel**chen**	wel**che**	wel**ches**	wel**che**

NOTE:

○ Just as with the definite article, only the accusative masculine has an ending different from the nominative.

Übung 7 Im Geschäft

Complete the sentences with the appropriate form of **dieser** or **welcher**.

Martina ist Studentin. Sie hat natürlich nicht viel Geld. Sie geht einkaufen.

Martina: Wie viel kostet _dieser_ Schreibtisch hier?

Verkäufer: _Welchen_ Schreibtisch meinen Sie?

Martina: Ich meine _diesen_ Schreibtisch hier.

Verkäufer: Ja also, _dieser_ Schreibtisch ist sehr preiswert. Der kostet nur 1 000 Euro.

Martina: Das ist viel zu teuer. Was kostet denn _dieses_ Sofa hier?

Verkäufer: _Welches_ Sofa meinen Sie? _Dieses_ Sofa hier kostet nur 500 Euro.

Martina: Ist _dieses_ Sofa auch bequem?

Verkäufer: Na, setzen Sie sich doch mal! _Dieses_ Sofa ist superbequem und wirklich preiswert.

Martina: Na, und was kostet _diese_ Lampe hier, die kleine da?

Verkäufer: Entschuldigung bitte, mein Boss sucht mich gerade. (*Er denkt*) _Diese_ Frau nervt mich.

Martina: _dieser_ Mensch irritiert mich!

Sprach-Info

In conversational German, the definite article is often used instead of a personal pronoun, particularly when emphasizing something. It is often placed at the beginning of the sentence.

Was kostet dieser Computer? —**Der** ist sehr preiswert, nur 600 Euro. —Gut, **den** kaufe ich.

Wie findest du die Wohnung von Klaus? —**Die** finde ich sehr gemütlich.

Übung 8 Fragen und Antworten

Complete each sentence by inserting a form of **dieser** in the question and the definite article as pronoun in the answer.

BEISPIEL: Was macht ___diese___ Frau sehr gern? —___Die___ macht sehr gern Kreuzworträtsel.

1. Was macht _diese_ Mensch schon wieder? —_Das_ schläft schon wieder.

2. Was kostet _diese_ Zeitung hier? —_die_ kostet nur zwei Euro.

3. Liest du _diese_ Zeitung oft? —_die_ lese ich immer.

4. Wie findest du _diesen_ Computer? —_Diesen_ finde ich ausgezeichnet.

5. Was kostet _diesen_ Bücherregal? —_der_ ist sehr preiswert, nur 250 Euro.

6. Wie findest du _diesen_ Zimmer? —_das_ ist sehr klein.

7. Kommt _diese_ Studentin aus den USA? —Ja, _der_ kommt aus Ohio.

8. Wohnt _die_ Student im Studentenwohnheim? —Nein, _der_ wohnt privat.

9. Papa, du hast doch zwei Autos. Brauchst du _diesen_ Mercedes (*m.*) heute? —Ja, _die_ brauche ich immer.

Negation°: **nicht** and **kein**

Verneinung

In **Kapitel 1** you learned to negate a simple statement by adding the word **nicht** (*not*) before a predicate adjective.

> Die Lampe ist **nicht** billig.   *The lamp is not cheap.*

You can also use **nicht** to negate an entire statement, or just an adverb.

> Karin kauft die Lampe **nicht**.   *Karin is not buying the lamp.*
>
> Ralf tanzt **nicht** besonders gut.   *Ralf doesn't dance particularly well.*

One other important way to express negation is by using the negative article **kein** (*no, not a, not any*), which parallels the forms of **ein**.

> —Ist das **eine** Zeitung?   *Is that a newspaper?*
> —Das ist **keine** Zeitung!   *That isn't a newspaper!*
>
> —Hast du **einen** Computer?   *Do you have a computer?*
> —Nein, ich habe **keinen** Computer.   *No, I don't have a computer.*
>
> —Hast du Geld?   *Do you have any money?*
> —Nein, ich habe **kein** Geld.   *No, I do not have any money.*
>
> —Sind das Studenten?   *Are those students?*
> —Nein, das sind **keine** Studenten.   *No, those are not students.*

NOTE:

▶ Use **kein** to negate a noun that is preceded by an indefinite article or no article at all.

▶ Unlike **ein,** the negative article **kein** has plural forms.

	Singular			Plural
	Masculine	*Feminine*	*Neuter*	*All Genders*
Nominative	kein Sessel	keine Lampe	kein Sofa	keine Stühle
Accusative	keinen Sessel	keine Lampe	kein Sofa	keine Stühle

Übung 9   Immer diese Ausreden!°   *Excuses, excuses!*

Everyone has a different excuse for turning down an invitation. Listen and check off the excuse given by each person.

1. Reinhard …
- ☐ hat keine Zeit.
- ☐ hat keine Lust.   *Reinm*
- ☒ hat kein Geld.   *Euro.*

2. Erika …
- ☐ hat keinen Freund.
- ☐ hat keine Zeit.   *disco*
- ☒ hat keine Lust.

3. Frau Becker …
- ☒ trinkt keinen Kaffee.   *Neraus*
- ☐ hat keine Lust.
- ☐ hat keine Zeit.

4. Jens und Ulla …
- ☒ haben kein Examen. —
- ☒ haben keine Zeit.
- ☐ haben keinen Hunger.

5. Peter …
- ☒ hat keine Lust.
- ☐ hat kein Geld.   *Fußbol fan*
- ☐ hat kein Auto.

**Zwei Störche
und ein Frosch**

[1]Die Masche zieht immer! *That line never fails.*

Übung 10   Ein Frühstück°

Was ist hier komisch (*funny*)? In Grimm's fairy tale "The Frog Prince," a prince turned into a frog is transformed back into a prince by a beautiful princess. The cartoon on the left draws on this story for its comical effect. Circle the correct option in each statement.

1. Die zwei Störche (*storks*) suchen ein/kein Frühstück.
2. Der Frosch hat ein/kein Problem.
3. Störche essen gern / nicht gern Frösche zum Frühstück.
4. Der Frosch ist ein/kein Prinz.
5. Der Frosch ist sehr / nicht sehr intelligent.
6. Die Störche essen heute ein/kein Frühstück.
7. Ich finde den Cartoon komisch / nicht komisch.

Übung 11   Susanne sucht ein Zimmer.

Fill each blank with **nicht** or the appropriate form of **kein**.

BEISPIEL: Susanne sucht ein Zimmer in Freiburg; sie braucht __keine__ Wohnung.

1. In der Schwarzwaldstraße ist ein Zimmer frei in einer Studenten-WG. Die Wohnung ist sehr schön, aber das Zimmer ist _____ möbliert.
2. In der Lessingstraße ist auch ein Zimmer frei. Es hat ein Bett, aber _____ Schreibtisch.
3. Sie findet das Zimmer _____ schön. Es ist viel zu klein und dunkel.
4. Das Zimmer ist auch _____ zentral gelegen.
5. Susanne hat _____ Auto. Sie fährt _____ gern Auto in der Stadt.
6. Im Studentenwohnheim ist momentan leider _____ Zimmer frei.
7. Zimmer suchen ist stressig. Es macht _____ Spaß (*m.*).
8. Susanne hat viel Arbeit im Studium. Sie hat also _____ viel Zeit für die Zimmersuche.
9. Stefan, Susannes Freund, wohnt bei seiner Familie in Freiburg. Da zahlt er _____ Miete.
10. Susannes Familie wohnt _____ in Freiburg; sie wohnt in Hamburg.

Übung 12   Wer hat das nicht?

Find out what your fellow students do not have.

BEISPIEL: **S1:** Wer hat kein Handy? →

   S2: Sieben Studenten haben kein Handy.

Wer hat kein- …?

Computer	Fahrrad	Stuhl
Stereoanlage	Zimmerpflanze	Wecker
Schreibtisch	Radio	Videorekorder
Lampe	Auto	Handy
Telefon	Motorrad	Poster im Zimmer
Sessel	Kommode	DVD-Spieler
Fernseher	Teppich	Geld
Sofa	Regal	

Verbs with Stem-Vowel Changes°

Verben mit Wechsel des Stammvokals

A number of common verbs have vowel changes in some of the present tense forms.

	fahren	schlafen	laufen	essen	sehen	lesen
ich	fahre	schlafe	laufe	esse	sehe	lese
du	**fährst**	**schläfst**	**läufst**	**isst**	**siehst**	**liest**
er sie } es	**fährt**	**schläft**	**läuft**	**isst**	**sieht**	**liest**
wir	fahren	schlafen	laufen	essen	sehen	lesen
ihr	fahrt	schlaft	lauft	esst	seht	lest
sie/Sie	fahren	schlafen	laufen	essen	sehen	lesen

NOTE:

▶ The vowel changes are in the second-person singular (**du**) and the third-person singular (**er, sie, es**).

Verbs with vowel changes in the present tense will be indicated in the vocabulary sections of this book as follows: **schlafen (schläft).**

Übung 13 Kontraste

Mr. and Mrs. Wunderlich don't have a lot in common. Create a profile of each of them using the phrases provided.

BEISPIEL: Frau Wunderlich fährt gern Motorrad.
Herr Wunderlich fährt gern Fahrrad.

fährt sehr gern Motorrad/Fahrrad
sieht gern Horrorfilme/Komödien
isst sehr gern Pizza/Sushi
liest die Zeitung / nur die Comics
läuft jeden Tag 10 Kilometer / macht keinen Sport

Übung 14 Was machen wir?

1. Ich _____ gern italienisch; meine Freundin _____ gern chinesisch. (essen)
2. Klaus und Petra _____ heute in der Mensa. (essen)
3. Petra fragt Klaus: „Was _____ du denn heute? (essen)
4. Hans braucht ein neues Handy. Er _____ viele Handys im Kaufhaus. (sehen)
5. Felix hat ein neues Motorrad. Morgen _____ er mit seinem Motorrad nach Hamburg. (fahren)
6. _____ du auch gern Motorrad? (fahren)
7. Herr Renner _____ jeden Tag dreimal um den Stadtpark. Dort _____ immer viele Jogger. (laufen)
8. Was _____ du jeden Tag? Ich _____ nur meine E-Mail! (lesen)
9. Manchmal _____ ich morgens bis 10 Uhr. Wie lange _____ du denn gewöhnlich? (schlafen)

Grammatik im Kontext   **71**

Übung 15 Was machen Sie gern, manchmal, nie, oft?

Tell a partner several things you do or don't like to do and how often:
(sehr) gern, manchmal (*sometimes*), **nie** (*never*), **(sehr) oft.** Report back to
the class.

BEISPIEL: **S1:** Ich esse sehr gern, ich tanze manchmal, ich laufe nie.

S2: John isst sehr gern, tanzt manchmal und läuft nie.

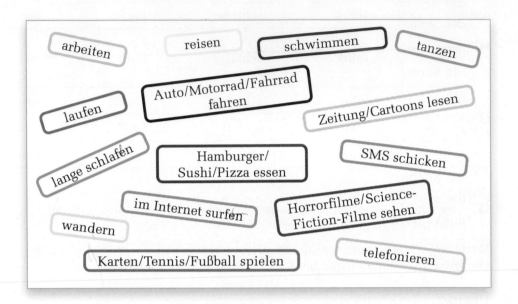

Substantive im Plural

The Plural of Nouns°

German forms the plural of nouns in several different ways. The following
chart shows the most common plural patterns and the notation of those
patterns in the vocabulary lists of this book.

Singular	Plural	Type of Change	Notation
das Zimmer	die Zimmer	*no change*	-
die Mutter	die Mütter	*stem vowel is umlauted*	¨
der Tag	die Tage	*ending* **-e** *is added*	**-e**
der Stuhl	die Stühle	*ending* **-e** *is added and stem vowel is umlauted*	**¨e**
das Buch	die Bücher	*ending* **-er** *is added and stem vowel is umlauted*	**¨er**
die Lampe	die Lampen	*ending* **-n** *is added*	**-n**
die Frau	die Frauen	*ending* **-en** *is added*	**-en**
die Studentin	die Studentinnen	*ending* **-nen** *is added*	**-nen**
das Radio	die Radios	*ending* **-s** *is added*	**-s**

NOTE:

- ▶ The definite article in the plural is **die** for all nouns, regardless of gender.
- ▶ Nouns ending in **or** or **ol** do not, with a few exceptions, change this ending in the plural.

Singular	Plural
der Amerikan**er**	die Amerikan**er**
das Zimm**er**	die Zimm**er**
der Sess**el**	die Sess**el**

However, the stem vowel may change, as follows:

die M**u**tter	die M**ü**tter
der V**a**ter	die V**ä**ter

- ▶ Most feminine nouns (over 90%) form the plural by adding **-n** or **-en** to the singular.

Singular	Plural
die Küche	die Küche**n**
die Arbeit	die Arbeit**en**
die Wohnung	die Wohnung**en**

- ▶ Feminine nouns ending in **-in** form the plural by adding **-nen** to the singular.

Singular	Plural
die Amerikaner**in**	die Amerikaner**innen**
die Mitbewohner**in**	die Mitbewohner**innen**

- ▶ Many masculine nouns form the plural by adding **-e.**

Singular	Plural
der Tisch	die Tisch**e**
der Teppich	die Teppich**e**

- ▶ Weak masculine nouns form the plural by adding **-en.**

Singular	Plural
der Mensch	die Mensch**en**
der Student	die Student**en**

- ▶ Nouns ending in vowels other than **-e** usually form the plural by adding **-s.**

Singular	Plural
das Handy	die Handy**s**
das Kino	die Kino**s**
das Sofa	die Sofa**s**

Although most nouns follow a predictable pattern in forming the plural, many do not. Make it a habit to learn the plural formation with each new noun you learn.

In order to use gender-inclusive language to refer to people, Germans frequently write forms such as **Student/in, Amerikaner/in,** or even **StudentIn, AmerikanerIn,** and for the plural of such nouns, **StudentInnen, AmerikanerInnen.**

Read at Home

Übung 16 Wie viele?

List items in your classroom and students in your class.

BEISPIEL: Das Klassenzimmer hat 27 Stühle.

Das Klassenzimmer hat …   Fenster (-)

Tür (-en)

Stuhl (¨e)

Tisch (-e)

Student (-en)

Studentin (-nen)

Computer (-)

Papierkorb (¨e)

Buch (¨er)

??

Übung 17 Zimmer zu vermieten

Supply the plural forms.

1. Mathias und Susanne suchen zwei _____ oder _____ für eine WG im Zentrum von Leipzig. (Mitbewohnerin, Mitbewohner)
2. Die schöne, große Wohnung hat vier _____. (Zimmer)
3. Sie hat auch eine Küche, zwei _____ und einen Balkon. (Bad).
4. Preiswerte _____ in zentraler Lage sind rar. (Wohnung)
5. Die _____ sind sehr hoch. (Miete)
6. Sie sind viel zu hoch für viele _____ und _____ wie Mathias und Susanne. (Studentin, Student)
7. Mathias und Susanne suchen zwei _____ oder _____. (Nichtraucherin, Nichtraucher)
8. Ein Zimmer in der Wohnung ist sehr groß und hat zwei _____ zum Garten. (Fenster)
9. Da hört man die _____ auf der Straße nicht so. (Auto)

Übung 18 Im Studentenwohnheim

Choose suitable nouns from the box at right to complete Kerstin's e-mail to Lea, making sure to put them in the plural.

Kerstin hat jetzt ein Zimmer im Studentenwohnheim in Berlin. Das Wohnheim ist ganz neu und modern. Hier ist Kerstins E-Mail an eine Freundin.

> Hallo, Lea! Na wie geht's? Ich hab' jetzt endlich ein Zimmer im Wohnheim. Gottseidank! Das Wohnheim hat 100 _____.ª Es gibt einen Computerraum, einen Fitnessraum, einen Musikraum und zwei _____.ᵇ Und wir haben auch fünf Gästezimmer für _____.ᶜ Ich liebe die vielen _____ᵈ in der Stadt. Man sieht dort immer viele _____ᵉ und _____.ᶠ Sie trinken Kaffee und diskutieren über alles und nichts. Ich habe übrigens eine _____ᵍ auf meinem Zimmer. Sie kommt aus Stuttgart und ist sehr sympathisch. Das Zimmer hat zwei _____,ʰ zwei _____ⁱ und zwei _____,ʲ aber nur *einen* Schreibtisch und *einen* Stuhl! Und wir haben nur ein Regal für die _____.ᵏ Ich schicke dir drei _____ˡ mit dieser E-Mail. Du siehst, es geht mir ausgezeichnet. Tschüss, Kerstin

das Bett
das Café
das Buch
der Student
das Foto
die Lampe
der Bierkeller (*pub*)
das Zimmer
der Kleiderschrank
die Studentin
der Besucher
die Mitbewohnerin

Sprache im Kontext

Videoclips

A Listen to what the following people say about where they live, and complete the information.

1. Sabine hat eine _____, Sie hat vier _____, eine _____ und ein _____. Die Wohnung hat ungefähr _____ Quadratmeter. Wiebke und ihr Mann _____ gern.

2. Nicoletta wohnt in Berlin-Kreuzberg in einer _____. Es ist eine _____. Man kann eine Wohnung über die Mitwohnzentrale, über die _____, über _____ oder am Schwarzen Brett finden.

3. Claudia hat eine helle _____ im vierten Stock. Das Wohnzimmer hat eine _Couch_, einen _Computer_ Schreibtisch mit einem _____, verschiedene _____, einen _____ und Regale mit CDs. Die Wohnung war nicht _möbliert_.

4. Harald _wohnt_ in Berlin-Kreuzberg in einer alten Fabrik. Die Wohnung hat eine große Küche, zwei _Schlafzimmer_ und ein _Kinderzimmer_. Harald _kocht_ gern vegetarisch und auch Fisch.

B Watch the interviews with Sabine and Claudia. Listen as they say what they still need for their apartments. Who needs what?

C Now describe your house, apartment, or room.

Lesen

Wie und wo wohnen junge Leute in Deutschland? In this section you will look at texts in which young people in Germany tell how they live.

Zum Thema

Wie wohnen Sie?

A Take a few moments to complete the questionnaire; then interview a partner to see how he/she answered the questions.

Wo wohne ich?

1. Ich wohne _____.
   a. in einem Studentenwohnheim
   b. in einer Wohnung
   c. bei meinen Eltern
   d. in meinem eigenen (*own*) Haus
   e. privat in einem Zimmer
   f. ??

2. Ich teile (*share*) mein Zimmer / meine Wohnung / mein Haus mit _____.
   a. einer anderen Person
   b. zwei, drei, vier, ... Personen
   c. niemand anderem. Ich wohne allein.

3. Ich habe _____.
   a. eine Katze (*cat*)
   b. einen Hund (*dog*)
   c. einen Goldfisch
   d. andere Haustiere (eine Kobra, einen Hamster, ...)
   e. keine Haustiere

4. Ich wohne gern/nicht gern _____.
   a. in einer Großstadt
   b. in einer Kleinstadt
   c. auf dem Land

5. Als Student hat man hier _____ Probleme, eine Wohnung zu finden.
   a. keine
   b. manchmal
   c. große

6. Die Mieten sind hier _____.
   a. niedrig
   b. hoch

B Report to the class what you found out about your partner.

Auf den ersten Blick

In the following passages students in Bonn, the former capital of the Federal Republic of Germany, and Rostock, a city in northeastern Germany, tell about their living arrangements. Skim through the texts, and for each one organize the vocabulary you recognize into the following categories.

Person	Housing	Objects Found in Room
BEISPIEL: Katja	Studentenwohnheim	Betten, Schreibtisch, Esstisch, Regale ...

So wohne ich

Name: Katja Meierhans
Wohnort: Rostock
Hauptfächer: Mathematik, Chemie

Während des Studiums wohne ich im Studenten-
5 wohnheim mit noch einer[1] Studentin auf einem
Zimmer; Gemeinschaftswaschräume[2] und WCs[3]
für den ganzen Flur[4] (22 Zimmer); im Raum sind
Betten, Schreibtisch, Esstisch, viele Regale, viele
Schränke. Ich bin zufrieden[5]. Zu Hause (300 km
10 von Rostock) wohne ich bei meinen Eltern. Wir
haben mein Zimmer zusammen ausgebaut[6],
deshalb[7] ist es natürlich mehr nach meinen
Wünschen. Ich fahre gern nach Hause, aber in
Rostock bin ich unabhängiger[8].

15 **Name:** Christina Stiegen
Wohnort: Niederkassel (Rheidt)
Hauptfächer: Politologie, Italienisch

Ich wohne in einer Wohnung etwas außerhalb
von[9] Bonn. Die Wohnung hat 52m², zwei Zimmer,
20 Küche, Diele[10], Bad. Ich teile mir[11] die Wohnung
mit meinem Freund, der auch in Bonn studiert. Es
handelt sich um[12] eine Dachwohnung[13].

Name: Jennifer Wolcott
Wohnort: Mönchengladbach
25 **Hauptfächer:** Englisch, Politische
Wissenschaften

Ich wohne in einem Zimmer (12m²) in einem
Studentenwohnheim. In dem Zimmer sind ein
Schreibtisch mit einer Schublade[14], ein Bett, ein
30 Regal, ein Kleiderschrank und ein Waschbecken[15]
mit Spiegel[16]. Ich habe einen Teppich[17] hingelegt,
Pflanzen auf die große Fensterbank[18] gestellt, noch
ein Regal (für meine vielen Bücher und meine
Stereoanlage). Außerdem habe ich Bilder, Poster
35 und Erinnerungen[19] an die weißen Wände gehängt.
Ich teile Bad/Toiletten und eine große Küche mit
zwanzig Studenten.

Name: Peter Kesternich
Wohnort: Euskirchen
40 **Hauptfächer:** Englisch, Geschichte

Ich wohne in einem Zimmer bei meinen Eltern.
Ich fahre jeden Morgen mit dem Zug[20] zur Uni
(ca. 50 Min.). Das ist für mich praktischer (und
billiger), als in Bonn ein Zimmer zu suchen.

---

[1]noch … one other [2]common washrooms [3]toilets [4]floor [5]content, satisfied [6]renovated [7]for that reason [8]more independent
[9]etwas … just outside of [10]front hall [11]teile … share [12]Es … It is [13]attic apartment [14]drawer [15]sink [16]mirror [17]carpet
[18]windowsill [19]mementos, souvenirs [20]train

Zum Text

A Look at the chart below and then scan the texts for specific information in order to complete it. If there is no information given for a
particular category, leave that space blank.

Name	Wohnort	Wie er/sie wohnt	Was im Zimmer ist	Weitere Informationen

1. Using the information you have written in the chart, construct
   sentences about the students. Have the rest of the class guess
   which person you are describing.

2. Now, using the information in the chart again, describe one of the
   people by creating true and false statements. The rest of the class
   has to say whether your statements are true or false.

B Read the texts more thoroughly and look at the following drawings. Which description most closely matches which drawing?

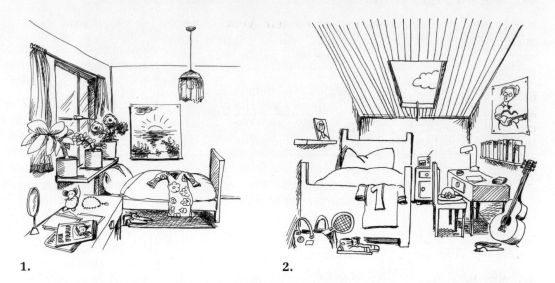

1.

2.

3.

4.

Zu guter Letzt

Wir suchen einen Mitbewohner / eine Mitbewohnerin.

In this chapter you have learned how to talk about student living situations and furnishings. In this project you will join others to interview a prospective roommate, choose a roommate, explain your choice, and report to the class.

Schritt 1: Work in groups of three or four. Imagine that you all live in a large apartment, house, or WG as roommates and that one of you is moving out. You are seeking a replacement for him/her. Create a flyer, in German, in which you describe what you have to offer. Feel free to consult and utilize the housing ads and flyers found in **Kapitel 2** as you create your own. You might start as follows:

> Wir, drei Studentinnen, suchen eine Mitbewohnerin für unsere Wohnung. ...

Distribute your housing flyer to classmates and find at least two people who want to interview for the room.

Schritt 2: Interview each applicant. Use German to ask the questions. You will want to ask the applicant several questions, such as whether he/she . . .

- is a student
- is also working
- is a (non)smoker
- has a pet (**einen Hund, eine Katze, einen Hamster**)
- owns a car, motorcycle, bicycle
- telephones frequently
- plays loud music (**laute Musik**)
- has a lot of visitors (**viel Besuch haben**)
- has a computer and will need a high-speed connection (**Computeranschluss**)
- considers herself/himself chaotic and eccentric or quiet and serious

The applicant might have questions, as well, such as . . .

- how large the room is
- whether the room is furnished
- how much the rent is
- whether there is a telephone, a garage, a yard
- how many people live in the apartment

Schritt 3: After you have interviewed prospective roommates, compare notes about the different people you interviewed, and decide whom to invite to become your roommate.

Schritt 4: Report back to the class on whom you have chosen and why.

BEISPIEL: Wir vermieten (*rent*) das Zimmer an Jeanine. Sie ist sehr nett und sympathisch. Sie studiert Informatik. Sie ist Nichtraucherin und spielt keine laute Musik. ...

Wortschatz

Im Kaufhaus — At the Department Store

das **Bett**, -en	bed
der **CD-Spieler**, -	CD player
der **Computer**, -	computer
der **Computeranschluss**, ¨e	computer connection
der **DVD-Spieler**, -	DVD player
der **Fernseher**, -	TV set
das **Foto**, -s	photograph
das **Handy**, -s	cell phone
der **Kleiderschrank**, ¨e	clothes closet
die **Kommode**, -n	dresser
die **Lampe**, -n	lamp
die **Möbel** (*pl.*)	furniture
der **Papierkorb**, ¨e	wastepaper basket
das **Poster**, -	poster
das **Radio**, -s	radio
das **Regal**, -e	shelf
das **Bücherregal**, -e	bookcase, bookshelf
der **Sessel**, -	armchair
das **Sofa**, -s	sofa
die **Stereoanlage**, -n	stereo
der **Stuhl**, ¨e	chair
das **Telefon**, -e	telephone
der **Teppich**, -e	rug, carpet
der **Tisch**, -e	table
der **Couchtisch**, -e	coffee table
der **Nachttisch**, -e	nightstand
der **Schreibtisch**, -e	desk
die **Uhr**, -en	clock
der **Videorekorder**, -	video recorder, VCR
der **Wecker**, -	alarm clock

Das Haus — The House

das **Bad**, ¨er	bathroom
der **Balkon**, -e	balcony
das **Fenster**, -	window
die **Garage**, -n	garage
der **Garten**, ¨	garden; yard
das **Haus**, ¨er	house
die **Küche**, -n	kitchen
die **Terrasse**, -n	terrace, patio
die **Tür**, -en	door
die **Wand**, ¨e	wall
das **Zimmer**, -	room
das **Arbeitszimmer**, -	workroom, study
das **Badezimmer**, -	bathroom
das **Esszimmer**, -	dining room
das **Schlafzimmer**, -	bedroom
das **Wohnzimmer**, -	living room

Sonstige Substantive — Other Nouns

das **Auto**, -s	car
der **Euro**, -s	euro
das **Geld**	money
der **Junge** (-n *masc.*), -n	boy
das **Kaufhaus**, ¨er	department store
der **Kunde** (-n *masc.*), -n / die **Kundin**, -nen	customer
die **Leute** (*pl.*)	people
der **Mensch** (-en *masc.*), -en	person, human being
die **Miete**, -n	rent
der **Mitbewohner**, - / die **Mitbewohnerin**, -nen	roommate, housemate
das **Motorrad**, ¨er	motorcycle
der **Nichtraucher**, - / die **Nichtraucherin**, -nen	nonsmoker
das **Problem**, -e	problem
das **Studentenwohnheim**, -e	dormitory
der **Tag**, -e	day
der **Verkäufer**, - / die **Verkäuferin**, -nen	salesperson
das **Video**, -s	video(tape)
die **Wohngemeinschaft**, -en (**WG**)	shared housing
die **Wohnung**, -en	apartment
die **Zeit**, -en	time
die **Zimmerpflanze**, -n	houseplant

Verben — Verbs

brauchen	to need
essen (isst)	to eat
fahren (fährt)	to drive, ride
fragen	to ask
haben (hat)	to have
Durst haben	to be thirsty
gern haben	to like (*a person or thing*)
Hunger haben	to be hungry
Lust haben	to feel like (*doing something*)
recht haben	to be correct
Zeit haben	to have time
kaufen	to buy
kosten	to cost
laufen (läuft)	to run, jog
lesen (liest)	to read
schlafen (schläft)	to sleep

schreiben	to write	niedrig	low
schwimmen	to swim	noch	still; yet
sehen (sieht)	to see	nur	only
sprechen (spricht)	to speak	preiswert	a bargain, inexpensive(ly)
suchen	to look for	recht	quite, rather
trinken	to drink	recht preiswert	quite inexpensive, reasonable

Adjektive und Adverbien — **Adjectives and Adverbs**

alle	all *everybody*	schon	already
bequem	comfortable, comfortably	schön	nice(ly), beautiful(ly)
		selten	rare(ly)
billig	inexpensive(ly), cheap(ly)	so	so, *in this way, that way*
		teuer	expensive(ly)
da	there *here*	viel/viele	much/many
dringend	desperate(ly)	wieder	again
dunkel	dark		
frei	free(ly)	**Sonstiges**	**Other**
genau	exact(ly)	dieser	this
gerade	just, exactly	etwas	something; somewhat, a little (*adverb*)
groß	big, large		
hässlich	ugly	kein	no, none, not any
hell	bright(ly), light	nichts	nothing
hoch	high(ly)	warum	why
klein	small	Was ist denn los?	What's the matter?
möbliert	furnished	weit (weg) von …	far (away) from …
unmöbliert	unfurnished	welcher	which
		zentral gelegen	centrally located

Das kann ich nun!

1. Sagen Sie:
   a. Wo und wie wohnen Sie?
   b. Wie hoch ist die Miete?
   c. Haben Sie Computeranschluss und ein Handy?

2. Nennen Sie vier Zimmer in einer Wohnung.

3. Nennen Sie fünf Möbelstücke in Ihrem Zimmer. Was haben Sie nicht? (Zwei Möbelstücke) Ich habe …

4. Was machen Sie gern? Nennen Sie drei Aktivitäten.

5. Nennen Sie die Artikel und Pluralformen von …
   a. Zimmer   e. Stuhl
   b. Buch   f. Mitbewohnerin
   c. Handy   g. Mensch
   d. Küche

6. Wie sagt man das auf Deutsch?
   a. A salesperson offers you a desk at a price that she considers reasonable, but you find it too expensive. Express your opinion.
   b. You are telling someone who has invited you for coffee that you have no time.
   c. You are telling someone that Frau Renner likes to ride a motorcycle.

3

Ein Essen im Garten

Familie und Freunde

In diesem Kapitel

- ▶ **Themen:** Family members, days of the week, months, holidays and celebrations, ordinal numbers

- ▶ **Grammatik:** Possessive adjectives; personal pronouns in accusative case; prepositions with accusative; **werden, wissen,** and **kennen**

- ▶ **Lesen:** „Wie feierst du deinen großen Tag?"

- ▶ **Landeskunde:** German holidays and celebrations, Otto von Bismarck, a family tree

- ▶ **Zu guter Letzt:** Eine Person vorstellen

VIDEOCLIPS

Familien und Feste

Families are important in every culture. We often define ourselves in terms of our family background. Even with the fast pace of modern life, family members take time to come together for important celebrations such as weddings, birthdays, and holidays.

A Below you see a picture of Thomas Neumann's family from Stuttgart with all of his relatives labeled. Your knowledge of cognate words and contextual guessing will help you understand what this vocabulary means. Look at the picture and identify the words for mother, father, sister, brother, grandfather, grandmother, father- and mother-in-law, sister-in-law, and niece.

At what kind of family celebration was the picture taken?

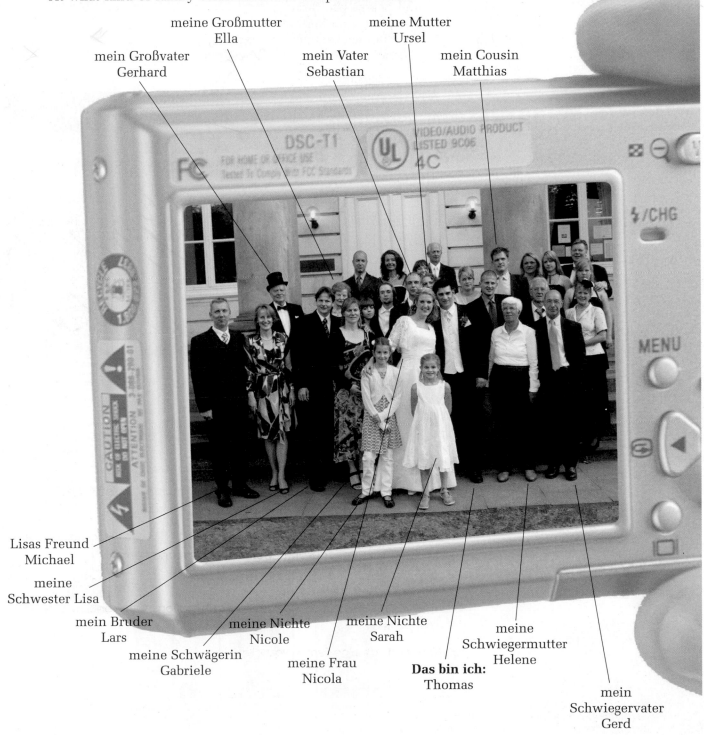

meine Großmutter
Ella

mein Großvater
Gerhard

mein Vater
Sebastian

meine Mutter
Ursel

mein Cousin
Matthias

Lisas Freund
Michael

meine
Schwester Lisa

mein Bruder
Lars

meine Schwägerin
Gabriele

meine Nichte
Nicole

meine Frau
Nicola

meine Nichte
Sarah

Das bin ich:
Thomas

meine
Schwiegermutter
Helene

mein
Schwiegervater
Gerd

B Now listen as Thomas' sister, Lisa, describes her family. As you listen, indicate whether the following statements are correct **(das stimmt)** or incorrect **(das stimmt nicht)**.

	Das stimmt	Das stimmt nicht
1. Das Foto zeigt Familie Neumann bei einer Geburtstagsfeier.	☐	☒
2. Familie Neumann wohnt in Leipzig.	☐	☒
3. Lisa Neumann hat zwei Brüder.	☐	☐
4. Ihr Bruder Thomas und Thomas' Frau, Nicola, sind Lehrer von Beruf.	☐	☐
5. Lisa plant eine Reise nach Kanada.	☐	☒
6. Lisas Bruder Lars hat zwei Kinder.	☒	☐
7. Thomas' Großvater Gerhard trägt einen Zylinder.	☐	☒

Wörter im Kontext

A family tree

Thema 1: Ein Familienstammbaum°
Bernd Thalhofers Familie

Look at Bernd Thalhofer's family tree to see how each person pictured is related to him. Then complete the activity about your own relatives that follows.

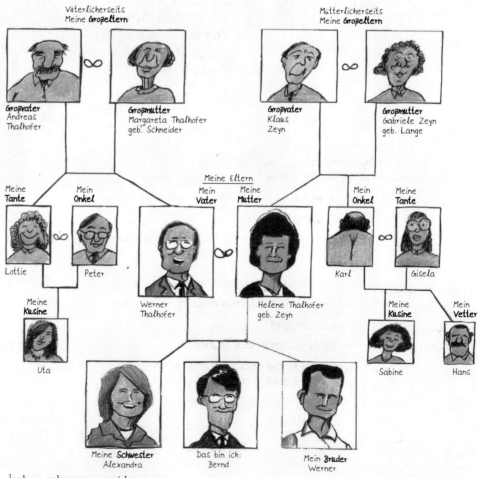

Väterlicherseits
Meine **Großeltern**

Mütterlicherseits
Meine **Großeltern**

Großvater
Andreas Thalhofer

Großmutter
Margareta Thalhofer geb.¹ Schneider

Großvater
Klaus Zeyn

Großmutter
Gabriele Zeyn geb. Lange

Meine Eltern

Meine **Tante**

Mein **Onkel**

Mein **Vater**

Meine **Mutter**

Mein **Onkel**

Meine **Tante**

Lottie

Peter

Werner Thalhofer

Helene Thalhofer geb. Zeyn

Karl

Gisela

Meine **Kusine**

Meine **Kusine**

Mein **Vetter**

Uta

Sabine

Hans

Meine **Schwester**
Alexandra

Das bin ich:
Bernd

Mein **Bruder**
Werner

¹geb. = geborene *maiden name*

Wer ist wer? How is each relative related to you?

1. der Bruder
2. der **Enkel**
3. die **Enkelin**
4. die **Geschwister** (*pl.*)
5. die **Großeltern** (*pl.*)
6. die **Großmutter** (**Oma**)
7. der **Großvater** (**Opa**)
8. die Kusine
9. der **Neffe**
10. die **Nichte**
11. der Onkel
12. der **Schwager**
13. die **Schwägerin**
14. die Schwester
15. die Tante
16. der Vetter

a. Mein _Neffe_: der **Sohn** meines (*of my*) Bruders oder meiner (*of my*) Schwester
b. Meine _____: die **Tochter** meiner Eltern
c. Meine _Nichte_: die Tochter meines Bruders oder meiner Schwester
d. Meine _Tante_: die Schwester meines Vaters oder meiner Mutter
e. Mein _____: der Sohn meines Sohnes oder meiner Tochter
f. Mein _____: der **Mann** meiner Schwester
g. Meine _____: die Söhne und Töchter meiner Eltern
h. Meine _____: die Mutter meines Vaters oder meiner Mutter
i. Mein _____: der Bruder meines Vaters oder meiner Mutter
j. Mein _____: der Sohn meiner Eltern
k. Mein _____: der Sohn meines Onkels und meiner Tante
l. Meine _Enkel_: die Tochter meines Sohnes oder meiner Tochter
m. Meine _Schwägerin_: die **Frau** meines Bruders
n. Meine _____: die Eltern meiner Eltern
o. Meine _Cousine_: die Tochter meines Onkels und meiner Tante
p. Mein _Großvater_: der Vater meines Vaters oder meiner Mutter

Neue Wörter

der **Enkel**	grandson
die **Enkelin**	granddaughter
die **Geschwister** (*pl.*)	siblings
die **Oma**	grandma
der **Opa**	grandpa
der **Neffe**	nephew
die **Nichte**	niece
der **Schwager**	brother-in-law
die **Schwägerin**	sister-in-law
der **Sohn**	son
die **Tochter**	daughter
der **Mann**	husband
die **Frau**	wife

Vetter - cousin (male)
Cousine - cousin (female)

Refer to *Possessive Adjectives*, p. 93.

Sprach-Info

As in English, to indicate that somebody is related to another person, add an **-s** to the person's name—though without an apostrophe.

Das ist Bernd **Thalhofers** Familie.

Bernds Eltern heißen Werner und Helene.

Another way to indicate relationships is with the preposition **von** (*of*).

Das ist die Familie **von** Bernd Thalhofer.

Die Eltern **von** Bernd heißen Werner und Helene.

The **von** construction is preferred if a name ends in an **-s** or a **-z.**

Die Frau **von** Markus heißt Julia.

Die Eltern **von** Frau Lentz kommen aus München.

Due to the influence of English, the apostrophe is being used more and more to express the possessive, though it is not officially acknowledged.

Aktivität 1 Wer ist das?

Unscramble the letters to find out which family member each item represents. The vocabulary at the top of the previous page will help you.

1. feeNf
2. eTtna
3. esKnui
4. treeVt
5. chNeti

6. klnOe
7. sewrStche
8. drerBu
9. tmßGorture
10. rVaet

Sprach-Info

To indicate that someone is related through a blended family or only through one parent, compounds can be formed using **Stief-** (*step*) and **Halb-** (*half*). The German equivalent to English *great* is the prefix **Ur-.**

Maria ist meine **Stiefschwester.**	*Maria is my stepsister.*
Mein **Halbbruder** heißt Jens.	*My half-brother is named Jens.*
Wilhelmine ist meine **Urgroßmutter.**	*Wilhelmine is my great-grandmother.*

Aktivität 2 Ein Interview

Schritt 1: Ask a person in your class about his/her family.

1. Wie heißen deine Eltern?
2. Wie viele Geschwister hast du?
3. Wie heißen deine Geschwister?
4. Wo wohnt deine Familie?
5. Wie alt sind deine Geschwister?
6. ??

Schritt 2: Report back to the class about your partner's family.

BEISPIEL: Jennys Familie wohnt in Toronto. Jenny hat fünf Brüder und drei Schwestern. Ihre Brüder heißen Mark, Stephen, …

Landeskunde-Info

Otto Eduard Leopold von Bismarck was born April 1, 1815 in Prussia of an aristocratic family. He became prime minister of Prussia in 1862 and remained so until 1890, during which time he oversaw the unification of Germany. He served as the first chancellor of the German Empire when it was formed in 1871. That role garnered him the title "The Iron Chancellor." Despite his conservative politics, Bismarck did develop a number of liberal social programs, most notably his insurance programs including health and old-age insurance. These were done to appease workers and in response to the rise of socialism in Germany.

▶ What are some other policies that Bismarck instituted to benefit workers of the German empire?

▶ What were some of the reasons he thought it necessary to institute a health and pension system for the German workers?

Aktivität 3 Ein berühmter Stammbaum

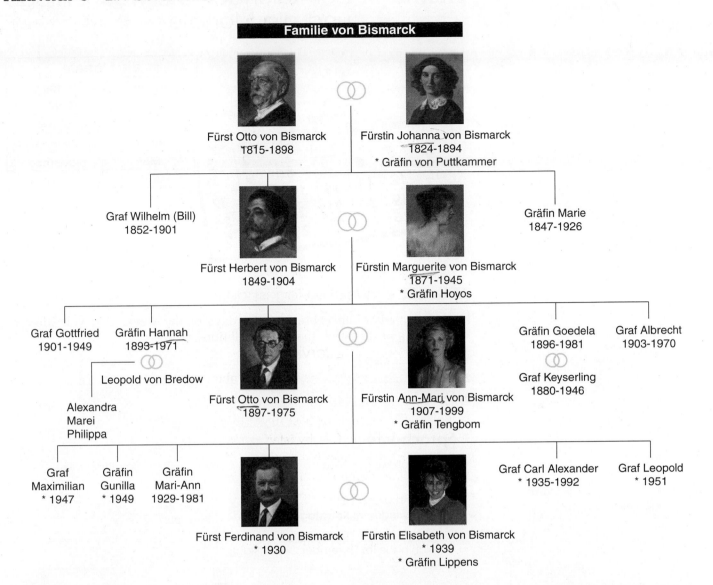

Familie von Bismarck

Fürst Otto von Bismarck
1815-1898

Fürstin Johanna von Bismarck
1824-1894
* Gräfin von Puttkammer

Graf Wilhelm (Bill)
1852-1901

Gräfin Marie
1847-1926

Fürst Herbert von Bismarck
1849-1904

Fürstin Marguerite von Bismarck
1871-1945
* Gräfin Hoyos

Graf Gottfried
1901-1949

Gräfin Hannah
1893-1971

Gräfin Goedela
1896-1981

Graf Albrecht
1903-1970

Leopold von Bredow

Graf Keyserling
1880-1946

Alexandra
Marei
Philippa

Fürst Otto von Bismarck
1897-1975

Fürstin Ann-Mari von Bismarck
1907-1999
* Gräfin Tengbom

Graf
Maximilian
* 1947

Gräfin
Gunilla
* 1949

Gräfin
Mari-Ann
1929-1981

Graf Carl Alexander
* 1935-1992

Graf Leopold
* 1951

Fürst Ferdinand von Bismarck
* 1930

Fürstin Elisabeth von Bismarck
* 1939
* Gräfin Lippens

The family of Otto von Bismarck was very prominent in nineteenth- and twentieth-century Germany. Fill in the missing information.

1. Wie heißt der ältere (*older*) Sohn von Otto von Bismarck und Fürstin Johanna? _____

2. Wie heißen die zwei Enkelinnen von Otto und Johanna? _____

3. Fürst Ferdinand von Bismarck ist der _____ von Fürstin Ann-Mari und Fürst Otto.

4. Gräfin Hannah ist die _____ von Otto und Johanna.

5. Fürstin Marguerite ist die _____ von Fürst Otto (*1897).

6. Graf Albrecht ist der _____ von Otto und Johanna.

Thema 2: Der Kalender: Die Wochentage und die Monate

Oktober

Montag	Dienstag	Mittwoch	Donnerstag	Freitag	Samstag	Sonntag
4	5	6	7	1	2	3
11	12	13	14	8	9	10
18	19	20	21	15	16	17
25	26	27	28	22	23	24
			29		30	31

die Monate	
Januar	Juli
Februar	August
März	September
April	Oktober
Mai	November
Juni	Dezember

Aktivität 4 Welcher Tag ist das?

Newspaper ads often abbreviate the days of the week. Can you identify which days of the week these abbreviations represent?

1. Mo _____
2. Fr _____
3. Do _____
4. So _____
5. Mi _____
6. Sa _____
7. Di _____

Refer to *The Verbs* **werden** and **wissen,** p. 102.

Sprach-Info

Use the following phrases to say the day or month when something takes place.

—Wann wirst du 21?
—Ich werde **am Samstag** 21.

—Wann hast du Geburtstag?
—Ich habe **im Dezember** Geburtstag.

Aktivität 5 Wie alt bist du?

Interview several classmates to learn their ages and birthdates.

BEISPIEL: S1: Wie alt bist du?

S2: Ich bin 23.

S1: Wann wirst du 24?

S2: Ich werde im August 24. Und du?

invitation

Aktivität 6 Eine Einladung° zum Geburtstag

Listen and take notes as Tom and Heike talk about an upcoming birthday party. Read the questions first before listening to the conversation.

1. Wer hat Geburtstag?
2. Wann ist der Geburtstag?
3. Wo ist die Party?
4. Wer kommt sonst noch (*else*)?
5. Kommt die Person am Telefon, oder nicht?

Aktivität 7 Hin und her: Verwandtschaften° relationships

Ask a partner questions about Bernd's family. How is each person related to Bernd?

BEISPIEL: **S1:** Wie ist Gisela mit Bernd verwandt?

S2: Gisela ist Bernds Tante.

S1: Wie alt ist sie denn?

S2: Sie ist 53.

S1: Wann hat sie Geburtstag?

S2: Im Februar.

Person	Verwandtschaft	Alter	Geburtstag
Gisela	Tante	53	Feb.
Alexandra	Schwester	25	März
Christoph	schwager	36	Dezember
Andreas	Großvater	80	Juni
Sabine	Kusine	19	August

Thema 3: Feste und Feiertage°

Geburtstagswünsche

Celebrations and holidays

Germans express birthday wishes in many ways. Here are some typical birthday wishes taken from German newspapers.

♥ Heike wird heute „21" Herzlichen Glückwunsch

Lieber Vater und Opa!
Zu Deinem 85. Geburtstag gratulieren
Hansi – Waltraud – Angela – Torsten
Birgit – Peter – Jan und Marco

Hallo Belinda!
Viel Glück und alles Gute zum 18. wünschen Mutti und Papa und der ganze Clan.
W. W. B. U. S. U. J. D. M. S. W. P. S. W. und Chris

Ralf hat Geburtstag!
Alles Gute!

Liebe Oma *Marie Sudhoff*
zu Deinem **80. Geburtstag** wünschen Dir Deine Kinder, Enkel und Urenkel alles Liebe und Gute.

Neue Wörter

wird (werden) turns, becomes
Herzlichen Glückwunsch (zum Geburtstag) Happy birthday!
gratulieren congratulate
Alles Gute! All the best!
wünschen wish

Analyse

- Find at least two different expressions of good wishes in the ads.
- Who are the family members who are sending birthday greetings to Belinda? to Marie Sudhoff?
- Marie Sudhoff is being addressed as "**liebe Oma.**" To which family member does the term **Oma** refer? What is another word for **Oma**?
- One birthday greeting gives no name but says only "**lieber Vater und Opa.**" Is this ad directed to one or two people? What clue(s) helped you arrive at your answer? What is another word for **Opa**?

Neue Wörter

neu new
kennen know
wichtig important
die Hochzeit wedding
heiratet (heiraten) is getting married
plant (planen) is planning
das Familienfest family gathering
wissen know
feiert (feiern) celebrates
es gibt there is
das Geschenk (Geschenke, *pl.***)** present
das Weihnachten Christmas
am Heiligen Abend on Christmas Eve
das Silvester New Year's Eve
um Mitternacht at midnight

Feiertage in der Familie Thalhofer

Valentinstag ist relativ **neu** für viele Deutsche. Bernd und Alexandra **kennen** diesen Tag aus den USA. Muttertag ist für Frau Thalhofer nicht so **wichtig,** aber ihre Familie gibt ihr **oft** Blumen.

Dieses Jahr gibt es noch eine **Hochzeit** in Bernds Familie. Seine Kusine Sabine **heiratet** nämlich im September. Die Familie **plant** ein großes **Familienfest** mit einem Abendessen in der Marxburg am Rhein. Bernds Großeltern feiern dieses Jahr ihre goldene Hochzeit, aber sie **wissen** noch nicht wo.

Die Marxburg am Rhein

Bernd hat im April Geburtstag. Dieses Jahr **feiert** er mit seiner Frau Bettina bei Freunden in Berlin. Natürlich feiern sie auch bei den Eltern in Köln, und **es gibt** auch eine kleine **Party** und natürlich auch **Geschenke.**

Weihnachten hat eine lange **Tradition. Am Heiligen Abend** gibt es Geschenke und ein Familienessen. Auch am ersten Weihnachtstag (25. Dezember) feiert die Familie zusammen. Am zweiten Weihnachtstag (26. Dezember) besucht die Familie die Großeltern, Tanten und Onkel.

Silvester sind Thalhofers oft bei Freunden. **Um Mitternacht** gibt es dann oft ein kleines Feuerwerk im Garten. Manchmal bleiben sie aber auch zu Hause.

Sprach-Info

To form most ordinal numbers (*first, second, third,* and so on) in German, add the suffix **-te** or **-ste** to the cardinal number. Note that the words for *first, third, seventh,* and *eighth* are exceptions to the rule.

eins	**erste**	neun	neun**te**
zwei	zwei**te**	zehn	zehn**te**
drei	**dritte**	elf	elf**te**
vier	vier**te**	zwölf	zwölf**te**
fünf	fünf**te**	dreizehn	dreizehn**te**
sechs	sechs**te**	. . .	. . .
sieben	**sieb(en)te**	zwanzig	zwanzig**ste**
acht	**achte**		

Ordinal numbers are normally used with the definite article.

Freitag ist **der erste** Oktober.

To talk about dates for special occasions, you can say:

Wann hast du Geburtstag? —**Am 18. (achtzehnten)** September.

Der erste Weihnachtstag ist **am 25. (fünfundzwanzigsten)** Dezember.

Note that ordinal numbers are written with a period: **der 4. Juli; am 4. Juli.**

Der erste

Hier klicken!

You'll find more about holidays and festivals in German-speaking countries in **Deutsch: Na klar!** on the World Wide Web at **www.mhhe.com/dnk6.**

Landeskunde-Info

Beim Volksfest

Legal holidays in German-speaking countries are largely religious holidays. The most important ones are Christmas (**Weihnachten**), New Year (**Neujahr**), and Easter (**Ostern**) and are celebrated for two days each. An important nonreligious holiday in Germany is the Day of German Unity (**Tag der deutschen Einheit**) on October 3.

There are a number of regional holidays as well. Mardi Gras (**Karneval** in the Rhineland and **Fasching** in southern Germany) is celebrated before Lent, in early spring. People get one day off work to participate in the merriment in and out of doors. Germans in northern and eastern regions do not celebrate Mardi Gras. Special festivals, so-called **Volksfeste,** are held in most communities, large and small, throughout Germany. Some of the better known ones are the yearly **Oktoberfest** in Munich and the **Kieler Woche** in the city of Kiel. The **Kieler Woche** is dedicated to sailing races on the Baltic Sea and draws sailing enthusiasts from around the world. Many local festivals have their origin in the Middle Ages, such as for instance the very popular **Schützenfeste** and **Kirmes. Schützenfeste** go back to target shooting practice during the Middle Ages when protecting a village or town was of great importance, whereas a **Kirmes,** now a general **Volksfest,** originated in a church-related celebration **(Kirchmess).**

Germans go all out for family celebrations such as weddings and silver and golden wedding anniversaries.

▶ Which holidays are national holidays in your country?

▶ Describe a regional or local festival to your classmates.

Aktivität 8 Feste und Feiertage

Match up the German holidays and celebrations with their English equivalents.

1. _____ Weihnachten
2. _____ Karneval
3. _____ Geburtstag
4. _____ Ostern
5. _____ Silvester
6. _____ Hochzeit
7. _____ der Heilige Abend
8. _____ Tag der deutschen Einheit

a. Mardi Gras
b. Christmas Eve
c. Easter
d. Labor Day
e. birthday
f. wedding
g. Memorial Day
h. German Unity Day
i. Christmas
j. New Year's Eve

Aktivität 9 Geburtstagsgrüße

Choose several of the following words and phrases to create birthday greetings for someone.

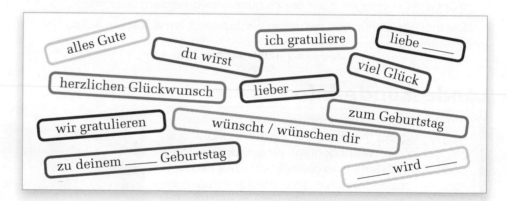

alles Gute

du wirst

ich gratuliere

liebe _____

herzlichen Glückwunsch

lieber _____

viel Glück

wir gratulieren

wünscht / wünschen dir

zum Geburtstag

zu deinem _____ Geburtstag

_____ wird _____

Aktivität 10 Eine Einladung zu einer Party

Invite someone to a party, using the expressions provided.

BEISPIEL: **S1:** Ich mache am Sonntag eine Party. Kommst du?

    S2: Am Sonntag? Vielen Dank. Ich komme gern.

   oder: Vielen Dank. Leider kann ich nicht kommen.

Other Excuses

Es tut mir leid. / Ich bin leider nicht zu Hause. / Ich fahre nämlich nach _____. / Mein Vater / Meine Mutter usw. (*and so on*) hat nämlich auch Geburtstag.

Neue Wörter

Es tut mir leid. I'm sorry.
leider unfortunately
nämlich namely, that is to say

Sprach-Info

When stating your reason for an action, use the adverb **nämlich.** Note that there is no exact equivalent of **nämlich** in English.

Ich kann nicht kommen. Ich fahre **nämlich** nach Hamburg.
I cannot come. The reason is, I am going to Hamburg.

Grammatik im Kontext

Possessive Adjectives°

Possessivartikel

Possessive adjectives (e.g., *my, your, his, our*) indicate ownership or belonging.

Sandra, 8 Jahre: *Meine Mutter Martina, mein Bruder Kelvin, meine Schwester Andrea, mein Vater Uli und ich beim Fahrrad fahren*

Dies ist Sandras Familie. Wer ist wer?

Wie heißt **deine** Schwester?	*What's your sister's name?*
Meine Schwester heißt Andrea.	*My sister's name is Andrea.*
Ihr Vater heißt Uli.	*Her father's name is Uli.*
Ihre Mutter heißt Martina.	*Her mother's name is Martina.*

Each possessive adjective corresponds to a personal pronoun.

Singular		Plural	
Personal Pronoun	**Possessive Adjective**	**Personal Pronoun**	**Possessive Adjective**
ich	**mein** *my*	wir	**unser** *our*
du	**dein** *your (informal)*	ihr	**euer** *your (informal)*
Sie	**Ihr** *your (formal)*	Sie	**Ihr** *your (formal)*
er	**sein** *his; its*		
sie	**ihr** *her; its*	sie	**ihr** *their*
es	**sein** *its*		

Unsere Freunde die Tiere

Possessives—short for possessive adjectives—take the same endings as the indefinite article **ein**. They are sometimes called **ein**-words because their endings are the same as those of **ein**. Unlike **ein**, however, they also have plural forms. They agree in gender, case, and number with the nouns they modify.

The nominative and accusative forms of **mein** and **unser** illustrate the pattern for all possessives.

	Singular			Plural
	Masculine	*Neuter*	*Feminine*	*All Genders*
Nominative	mein Freund unser Freund	mein Buch unser Buch	mein**e** Mutter unser**e** Mutter	mein**e** Freunde unser**e** Freunde
Accusative	mein**en** Freund unser**en** Freund	mein Buch unser Buch	mein**e** Mutter unser**e** Mutter	mein**e** Freunde unser**e** Freunde

NOTE:

▶ The masculine singular possessive adjective is the only one for which the accusative form differs from the nominative: **mein** → **meinen, unser** → **unseren.**

▶ The formal possessive adjective **Ihr** (*your*) is capitalized, just like the formal personal pronoun **Sie** (*you*).

▶ The possessive adjective **euer** (*your*) drops the **e** of the stem when an ending is added: e̶u̶ere → **eure**, e̶u̶eren → **euren.**

Analyse

▶ Scan the Valentine's Day greetings taken from a German newspaper and identify all possessive adjectives.

▶ In each case, determine whether the possessives refer to a male or female individual or to several people. What is the gender of each name or noun?

Herzliche Grüße zum Valentinstag

Liebe Beate,
ich liebe Dich
Dein Rainer
GF100037

Für meine Lieben
Helmut und Sandra
einen lieben Gruß und ein dickes
Küsschen[1]
Eure Doris Ma GF100081

Hallo Maus!
Nun ist es doch schon das 4. Jahr!
In Liebe Deine Katze
GE90558

Guten Morgen,
mein Tiger
Die Welt[2] ist wieder schön durch
Dich.
Dein Stern von Rio GD81183

Lieber Andre!
Alles Liebe zum Valentinstag.
Dein Häschen
GF100036

Liebe Christina
Zum Valentinstag herzliche Grüße
und alles Liebe und Gute wünscht
Dir Dein Vater
GC114748

---
[1] ein ... *a big kiss* [2] *world*

Übung 1   Herzlichen Glückwunsch! 🎧

You will hear eight congratulatory messages taken from a radio program. Write out who receives the greetings (**Empfänger/in**) and who sends them (**Absender/in**). Include the possessive adjectives you hear, if any. Follow the example.

Empfänger/in	Absender/in
1. *unsere Mutter*	*deine Kinder*
2. _____	_____
3. _____	_____
4. _____	_____
5. _____	_____
6. _____	_____
7. _____	_____
8. _____	_____

Übung 2   Unser Familienporträt

Dirk und Ute machen eine Website über ihre Familie.

Schritt 1: Complete each sentence with the correct form of **unser.**

1. Hier seht ihr _____ Haus in Bonn.
2. Und das ist _____ Familie.
3. In der Mitte seht ihr _____ Vater.
4. Da rechts ist _____ Bruder. Er heißt Dylan und ist 23 Jahre alt.
5. Und hier ist _____ Mutter. Sie heißt Lena und ist 47.
6. Die zwei Mädchen links sind _____ Kusinen.
7. Und hier vorne seht ihr _____ Hund. Er heißt Rakete.

Schritt 2: Now restate the sentences from **Schritt 1** using the correct form of **mein.**

BEISPIEL: Hier seht ihr mein Haus in Bonn.

Übung 3   Kombinationen: Was passt zusammen?

Combine elements from both columns to form sentences in which the personal pronoun in the first column matches the possessive adjective in the second. In some instances more than one match is possible.

BEISPIEL: Ich liebe mein Handy.

1. Ich liebe	ihre Kreditkarte.
2. Er feiert heute	Ihr Auto auf dem Parkplatz.
3. Sie suchen	mein Handy.
4. Du suchst	unsere Eltern.
5. Heute besuchen wir	ihre Kinder im Supermarkt.
6. Sie sucht	eure Freunde.
7. Morgen seht ihr	seinen Geburtstag.
8. Sie sehen	dein Fahrrad.

everyday life

Übung 4 Kleine Gespräche im Alltag°

Complete the minidialogues with appropriate possessive adjectives.

1. Claudia: Hier ist _____ neue Telefonnummer.

    Stefan: Gut, und _____ neue Adresse?

    Claudia: _____ neue Adresse ist Rosenbachweg 2.

2. Saskia: Und dies hier ist _____ Freund.

    Svea: Wie heißt er denn?

    Saskia: _____ Name ist Max.

    Svea: Max? Na, so was! So heißt nämlich _____ Hund.

3. Herr Weidner: Und was sind Sie von Beruf, Frau Rudolf?

    Frau Rudolf: Ich bin Automechanikerin.

    Herr Weidner: Und was ist _Ihr_ Mann von Beruf?

    Frau Rudolf: _Mein_ Mann ist Hausmann.

    Herr Weidner: Hausmann?

4. Frau Sanders: Ach, wie niedlich! Ist das _ihre_ Tochter?

    Frau Karsten: Ja, das ist _meine_ Tochter.

    Frau Sanders: Und ist das _ihr_ Hund?

    Frau Karsten: Ja, das ist _unser_ Hund. Das ist der Caesar.

5. Inge: Kennst du _mein_ Freund Klaus?

    Ernst: Ich kenne Klaus nicht, aber ich kenne _seine_ Schwester.

    Inge: Morgen besuchen wir _seine_ Eltern in Stuttgart.

6. Polizist: Ist das _ihr_ Auto?

    Frau Kunze: Ja, leider ist das _mein_ Auto.

    Polizist: Hier ist Parkverbot.

Übung 5 Persönliche Angaben

Schritt 1: Complete a personal profile of yourself. Add one or two items of your own choice.

_____ Name ist _____.

_____ Handynummer ist _____.

_____ Familie wohnt in _____.

_____ Mutter heißt _____.

Mein Vater heißt _____.

Mein Geschwister heißen _____.

Mein Geburtstag ist im _____. (z.B. Juli)

Mein Lieblingsband (*f.*) heißt _____.

Mein Hobby ist _____.

Mein Lieblingsbuch ist _____.

Schritt 2: Exchange personal profiles with someone in your class and report about him/her to the class.

BEISPIEL: Das ist Sam Lee. Seine Handynummer ist 555–8762. ...

Personal Pronouns in the Accusative Case°

You have already learned the personal pronouns for the nominative case. Here are the corresponding accusative forms.

Singular		Plural	
Nominative	**Accusative**	**Nominative**	**Accusative**
ich	**mich** *me*	wir	**uns** *us*
du	**dich** *you (informal)*	ihr	**euch** *you (informal)*
Sie	**Sie** *you (formal)*	Sie	**Sie** *you (formal)*
er	**ihn** *him; it*		
sie	**sie** *her; it*	sie	**sie** *them*
es	**es** *it*		

NOTE:

▶ The third-person singular pronouns **ihn, sie,** and **es** must agree in gender with the noun to which they refer.

▶ In the accusative case, **ihn** can mean *him* or *it,* and **sie** can mean *her* or *it* depending on the gender of the noun to which they refer.

—Kennst du **meinen Freund?**	*Do you know my friend?*
—Ja, ich kenne **ihn.**	*Yes, I know him.*
—Brauchst du **den Computer?**	*Do you need the computer?*
—Na klar brauche ich **ihn.**	*I absolutely do need it.*
—Hast du **meine Adresse?**	*Do you have my address?*
—Ich glaube, ich habe **sie.**	*I think I have it.*

Analyse

▶ Identify all personal pronouns in the ads and announcements and determine whether they are in the nominative or in the accusative case. Then provide the English meaning of each phrase.

Gourmets lieben ihn.

Mein Schatz,[1]
Ich liebe Dich.
Deine Jutta

GA140650

[1]*Mein ... My dear*

Wir sind da, wo Sie uns brauchen.

Ruth Brandt,
Unsere Omi ist das Liebste, was[1] wir haben, das wollen wir heute einmal[2] sagen:
WIR LIEBEN DICH

Deine Kinder
Deine Enkelkinder

[1]*das ... the dearest thing that*   [2]*just*

Übung 6 Wen kennst du?

Supply the missing direct-object personal pronouns corresponding to the nominative pronouns provided.

BEISPIEL: Ich kenne __euch__ (ihr).

1. Ich kenne _____ (du).
2. Kennst du _____ (ich) denn nicht?
3. Du kennst ja meine Familie. Oder kennst du _____ (sie) nicht?
4. Wir kennen _____ (ihr) aber schon lange.
5. Hier kommt Herr Wunderlich. Kennst du _____ (er)?
6. Herr Wunderlich kennt _____ (wir).
7. Ich kenne die Stadt nicht so gut. Meine Freundin kennt _____ (sie) aber sehr gut.

Love

Übung 7 Liebst° du das?

Take turns creating questions and answering them. Use a pronoun in your answer.

BEISPIEL: **S1:** Liebst du das komische rote Auto?

   S2: Ja, ich liebe es.

   oder: Nein, ich liebe es nicht.

Liebst du ...

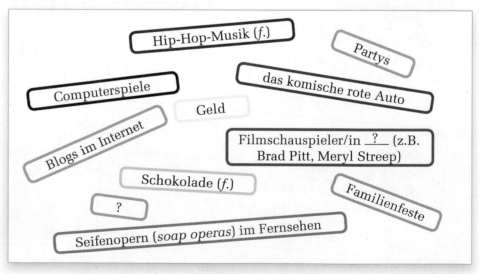

Übung 8   Im Café Kadenz

Several students are conversing at different tables at the Café Kadenz. Complete the blanks with appropriate personal pronouns in the nominative or the accusative case.

1. **A:** Wie findest _du_ den Professor Klinger?
   B: Also, ich finde _ihn_ unmöglich. _Er_ kommt nie pünktlich. Wir warten (*wait*) und warten, dann kommt _er_ endlich und liest seine Vorlesung, keine Diskussion, keine Fragen, nichts. _Er_ ist echt langweilig.
   A: Ich verstehe _dich_ nicht, Karin. Warum gehst du dann hin?
2. **C:** Machst du jetzt das Linguistik-Seminar?
   D: Ja, ich brauche _es_ für mein Hauptfach (*major*).
3. **E:** Und wie findest du deine Mitbewohner im Wohnheim?
   F: Ich finde _sie_ ganz prima. Da sind zwei Italienerinnen aus Venedig. _Sie_ sind wirklich nett. Ich verstehe _sie_ allerdings nicht immer.
4. **G:** Im Lumière läuft der Film „Die fetten Jahre sind vorbei". Kennst du _ihn_?
   H: Nein, aber die Filmkritiker finden _ihn_ ausgezeichnet.
5. **I:** Da kommt endlich unser Kaffee. Wie trinkst du _ihn_?
   J: Gewöhnlich trinke ich _ihn_ schwarz.
6. **K:** Meine Eltern besuchen _mich_ nächste Woche. Das ist immer stressig.
   L: Ja, ich verstehe _dich_ gut.

Übung 9   Wie findest du das?

With a partner, create five questions regarding student life. Then interview several people in your class.

BEISPIEL: **S1:** Wie findest du die Vorlesungen von Professor Ziegler?
   S2: Ich finde sie ausgezeichnet. Und du?
   S1: Ich finde sie zu lang.

das Essen (in der Mensa)	ausgezeichnet
der Kaffee (in der Mensa)	faul
das Leben (im Studentenwohnheim)	sympathisch/unsympathisch
die Uni-Zeitung	langweilig
die Studenten an der Uni	schlecht
die Mitbewohner (im Studentenwohnheim)	gut
	freundlich/unfreundlich
die Stadt _____	interessant
der Film _____	schön
das Buch _____	??
Freund/Freundin	
dein Zimmer	
??	

Prepositions with the Accusative Case°

You have already seen and used a number of German prepositions.

Ich studiere Architektur **in** Berlin.

Ich brauche eine Lampe **für** meinen Schreibtisch.

The use of prepositions, in English as well as in German, is highly idiomatic. An important difference, however, is that German prepositions require certain cases; that is, some prepositions are followed by nouns or pronouns in the accusative case, others by nouns or pronouns in other cases. In this chapter, we focus on prepositions that always require the accusative case.

Wir tun etwas **gegen** den Hunger.	*We are doing something against hunger.*
Es ist **gegen** fünf Uhr.	*It's around five o'clock.*
Herr Krause fährt **durch** die Stadt.	*Mr. Krause drives through town.*
Er braucht ein Geschenk **für** seine Tochter.	*He needs a gift for his daughter.*
Er geht **ohne** seine Frau einkaufen.	*He goes shopping without his wife.*
Die Geburtstagsfeier beginnt **um** sechs.	*The birthday party begins at six.*
Er sucht einen Parkplatz und fährt dreimal **um** den Marktplatz (**herum**).	*He looks for a parking space and drives around the marketplace three times.*

Accusative Prepositions	
durch	through, across
für	for
gegen	against; around (*with time*)
ohne	without
um	at (*with time*)
um (… herum)	around (*a place*)

Deutsche Welthungerhilfe

NOTE:

▶ When the preposition **um** is used to indicate movement around something, the word **herum** is often added after the place.

um die Stadt (**herum**)

▶ Three accusative prepositions often contract with the article **das**.

durch das → **durchs** Zimmer
für das → **fürs** Auto
um das → **ums** Haus

Übung 10 Kleine Geschenke

Uwe is having difficulty choosing birthday gifts for friends and relatives. Express your gift recommendations based on the facts provided about everyone. Include a suitable adjective in your answer, such as **perfekt, praktisch, originell, nett, gut,** or **schön.**

BEISPIEL: Seine Oma geht gern ins Café. →
Ich finde den Hut gut für seine Oma.

1. Seine Eltern reisen und fotografieren viel.
2. Sein Großvater wandert gern.
3. Sein Bruder Dirk schläft immer zu lange.
4. Seine Schwester Maria fährt nach Spanien.
5. Seine Freundin Sara liebt exzentrischen Schmuck (*jewelry*). *der Ring*
6. Seine Kusine Julia ist ein Fitnessfan. *Fitness-DVD*
7. Seine Mutter liest gern Detektivromane. *das Buch*
8. Sein Freund Marco ist etwas exzentrisch. *die Zehensocken*

[handwritten:] praktisch
Ich finde zwei Wanderstöcke für seinen Großvater.
Ich finde der wecker practica für seinen Bruder
Ich finde die Sonnenbrill perfect für seine Schwester
Ich finde die fitness-DVD

der Wecker   das Buch   die Zehensocken

der Ring   der Hut   die Fitness-DVD

zwei
Wanderstöcke   die Sonnenbrille   das Fotoalbum

Übung 11 Dieter braucht ein Geschenk

Choose the correct preposition.

1. Dieter braucht dringend ein Geburtstagsgeschenk _für_ seine Freundin Sonja. (um/für)
2. Leider hat Sonja schon alles, aber _ohne_ Geschenk geht es nicht. (ohne/durch)
3. Dieter gibt _um_ sieben Uhr abends eine kleine Party _für_ sie. (für/um)
4. Sonja hat Partys gern, aber sie ist _gegen_ große Partys. (gegen/ohne)
5. Dieter fährt also in die Stadt. Er fährt dreimal _um_ den Marktplatz herum. (um/durch) Er sucht einen Parkplatz. Er findet nichts.
6. Er fährt und fährt _durch_ die Straßen. (um/durch)
7. Er sucht und sucht _ohne_ Erfolg (success). (für/ohne) Was nun?
8. Er parkt schließlich illegal. Was tut er nicht alles _für_ Sonja. (ohne/für)
9. Was macht Sonja Spaß? Kochen! Also ein Kochbuch _für_ Vegetarier. (durch/für) Sonja ist nämlich Vegetarierin.
10. Im Buchladen geht Dieter _um_ den Tisch mit (with) Kochbüchern herum. (für/um)
11. Er sieht ein Buch: „Kochen _für_ Vegetarier _ohne_ Zeit". (ohne/für)
12. Das ist perfekt _für_ sie. (gegen/für)

The Verbs *werden* and *wissen*

Two common verbs that show irregularities in the present tense are **werden** (*to become*) and **wissen** (*to know*).

werden			
ich	werde	wir	werden
du	**wirst**	ihr	werdet
er sie es	**wird**	sie	werden
Sie werden			

wissen			
ich	**weiß**	wir	wissen
du	**weißt**	ihr	wisst
er sie es	**weiß**	sie	wissen
Sie wissen			

Übung 12 Kennen Sie eigentlich meine Familie?

Complete the sentences using the appropriate form of **werden**.

1. Ich _____ im September 16 Jahre alt.
2. Meine zwei Kusinen _____ am Samstag 13.
3. Mein kleiner Bruder Bernd _____ im November 11.
4. Meine kleine Schwester Sara _____ dieses Jahr 5 Jahre alt.
5. Mein Vater hat im Dezember Geburtstag. Er _____ 38 Jahre alt.
6. Mein Großvater fragt immer: „Wann _____ du 15?" Er vergisst (*forgets*), dass ich schon 15 bin!

Heidewitzka, Herr Kapitän!
Der beste Opa der Welt wird 70!

Es gratulieren:
David
Inge
Ulf
Uwe
Sandra
Schira
Afra

Helmut
2.7. 2011

Übung 13   Eine Umfrage: Wer wird wann wie alt?

Do a class poll:

1. Wer _____ dieses Jahr _____ Jahre alt?
2. Wie viele Leute _____ dieses Jahr 10?
3. Wann _____ du 50? 100? (Ich werde in 30 Jahren 50.)
4. Wann _____ dein Freund oder deine Freundin 19, 21, 25?

ZEITUNGSLESER WISSEN MEHR!

Wer kennt Goethe?

Johann Wolfgang von Goethe, 1749–1832

Sprach-Info

The verbs **wissen** and **kennen** both mean *to know*. **Wissen** means *to know facts*, while **kennen** means *to know or be acquainted/familiar with a person or thing*.

Ich **weiß** deine Telefonnummer nicht.	*I don't know your phone number.*
Ich **kenne** Herrn Meyer nicht persönlich, aber ich **weiß,** wer er ist.	*I don't know Mr. Meyer personally, but I know who he is.*
Weißt du, wo ich wohne?	*Do you know where I live?*

Note the comma before the indirect question.

Übung 14   Die neue Mitbewohnerin

Wendy, an exchange student from San Diego, is new in Göttingen and lives in a dorm. Listen to Wendy's questions and check off the appropriate negative responses.

	Weiß ich nicht.°	Kenne ich nicht.°		Weiß ich nicht.	Kenne ich nicht.
1.	☑	☐	5.	☑	☐
2.	☐	☑	6.	☑	☐
3.	☑	☐	7.	☑	☐
4.	☑	☐	8.	☑	☐

I don't know. (casual)

Übung 15   Wissen oder kennen?

Complete the minidialogues with the correct form of **wissen** or **kennen**.

1. **A:** _____ du Goethe?
   B: Nein, aber ich _____, wer er ist.
   A: _____ du seinen Roman, „Die Leiden (*sufferings*) des jungen Werther"?
   B: Nein, den _____ ich nicht. Aber mein Professor _____ ihn bestimmt.
2. **C:** _____ du, welcher Film heute im Odeon läuft?
   D: Das _____ ich nicht. Aber Toni _____ das bestimmt. Der _____ alles.

3. E: Wo wohnt ihr eigentlich jetzt?

   F: In der Schillerstraße. _____ du die?

   E: Nein. Ich _____ aber, wo die Goethestraße ist.

4. G: _____ ihr schon, wo ihr nächstes Semester studiert?

   H: Nein, wir _____ nur, dass wir nicht hier bleiben.

5. I: Ich _____, wo eine Wohnung frei wird.

   J: Wo denn?

   I: In der Weenderstraße.

   J: Die _____ ich nicht.

6. K: Ihr _____ doch den Peter Sudhoff?

   L: Tut mir leid, den _____ wir nicht.

inquisitive

Übung 16 Ein neugieriger° Mensch

Find out what your partner knows or does not know. Take turns asking each other questions starting either with **Kennst du ... ?** or **Weißt du ... ?** Choose elements from the list below and some of your own.

BEISPIEL: **S1:** Kennst du den Film „Julie und Julia" mit Meryl Streep?

        S2: Ja, den kenne ich. Weißt du, ... ?

        meine Familie?

        wo meine Familie wohnt?

        die Band _____ (z.B. „Wir sind Helden")?

        wie die Studentenzeitung hier heißt?

        den Film „Good bye, Lenin"?

        Angela Merkel?

        wer Angela Merkel ist?

Sprache im Kontext

Videoclips

In these videoclips, the people interviewed are talking about their families and various celebrations. As you watch, listen to what they say and think about how you would respond to the interviewer's questions.

A Watch the interviews with Doris and with Kurt Borowsky. Mark the following statements **richtig (R)** or **falsch (F)**.

1. Doris

_____ Doris ist verheiratet.

_____ Sie hat zwei Kinder.

_____ Die Kinder heißen Tina und Matthias.

_____ Die Familie feiert Weihnachten, Valentinstag und Ostern.

_____ Das Lieblingsfest von Doris ist Weihnachten.

_____ Doris hat heute Geburtstag.

2. Herr Borowsky

_____ Herr Borowsky wohnt in Berlin.

_____ Er hat eine kleine Familie.

_____ Er hat drei Enkelkinder.

_____ Er hat einen Bruder und zwei Schwestern.

_____ Er ist 67 Jahre alt.

_____ Er hat am 10. Februar Geburtstag.

B Now listen again to the questions asked by Michael, the interviewer. Write down four questions he asks and use them to interview two other students in the class. Then report your findings about one of the students to the class.

Lesen

Zum Thema

Eine Umfrage (*survey*). Fill out the questionnaire and compare answers.

A Welche Feiertage sind in Ihrer Familie wichtig?

	Wichtig	Unwichtig
1. Geburtstage	☐	☐
2. Hochzeitstage	☐	☐
3. religiöse Feiertage	☐	☐
4. nationale Feiertage	☐	☐
5. Muttertag	☐	☐
6. Vatertag	☐	☐

B Wie feiern Sie Ihren Geburtstag?

	Ja	Nein
1. Wir haben ein großes Familienfest.	☐	☐
2. Wir gehen ins Restaurant.	☐	☐
3. Familie und Freunde kaufen Geschenke für mich.	☐	☐
4. Ich mache an diesem Tag nichts Besonderes.	☐	☐
5. ??	☐	☐

Auf den ersten Blick

A Skim over the short texts below. Who are the respondents? What are their ages? What is the general topic?

B Now scan the texts more closely, looking for words of the following types.

- ❯ words relating to family
- ❯ words related to places where a celebration is held
- ❯ compound nouns: locate five compound nouns in the texts, and determine their components and their English equivalents

C The two most frequently used words in the texts are the verb **feiern** and the noun **Geburtstag.** How do they relate to the expression **"deinen großen Tag"** in the title? What is implied?

Landeskunde-Info

Ein runder Geburtstag ist immer ein besonders wichtiger Geburtstag. Das sind alle Geburtstage mit einer Null, zum Beispiel 20, 40 oder 50. Man feiert ihn oft groß mit Familie und Freunden in einem Lokal (*pub*). Oft gibt es ein Programm mit Reden (*speeches*), Musik und Gedichten.

Wie feierst du deinen großen Tag?

Anna, 18: Meine Zwillingsschwester[1] und ich feiern jedes Jahr zusammen[2]. Meistens machen wir eine große Party bei uns zu Hause. Unseren 18. Geburtstag haben wir bei unserer Oma im Partykeller gefeiert. Dort ist mehr Platz.

5 **Stefan, 15:** Ich gehe gerne auf Geburtstagspartys, aber ich gebe selber nicht gerne welche[3]. Deswegen feiere ich immer nur mit meinen Eltern und dem Rest der Verwandtschaft.

Patrick, 19: Seit ich 18 bin, feiere ich meinen Geburtstag nur mit meiner Freundin zusammen. Wir sind jetzt schon 10 seit zweieinhalb Jahren ein Paar.

Lennard, 19: Ich fahre für ein paar Tage nach Paris. Dort feiere ich dann zusammen mit meiner Brieffreundin.

Uta, 42: Ich habe am 26. März Geburtstag. Zu meinem Geburtstag lade ich meistens abends einige Freunde zu uns nach Hause ein. Ich mache 15 dann ein Buffet. Manche Freunde bringen auch etwas zu essen mit.

Bettina, 40: Ich feiere dieses Jahr einen runden[4] Geburtstag, meinen vierzigsten, und lade natürlich 40 Gäste ein, Freunde und Verwandte. Wir feiern in einem Restaurant in der Innenstadt. Es gibt ein kleines Programm mit Gedichten[5] und Musik. Und es gibt auch ein Super-Essen.

20 **Saskia, 30:** Der Geburtstag sieht gewöhnlich so bei uns aus: Das Geburtstagskind bekommt den Frühstückstisch schön gedeckt mit Kerzen[6] und Blumen aus dem Garten. Gleich morgens kommen auch die Geschenke von der Familie auf den Tisch. Am Abend kommen immer all unsere Freunde vorbei. Zu essen gibt es ein kleines kaltes Buffet, mit 25 etwas frischem Salat, Brot[7] und Käse. Wir tanzen auch schon mal zu später Stunde.

Teilweise aus: *JUMA* 2/2004, www.juma.de, Umfrage: Kristina Dörnenburg

---

[1]*Zwilling-* twin [2]*together* [3]*here: any* [4]*(birthday) ending in 0* [5]*poems* [6]*candles* [7]*bread*

Zum Text

A Now read the statements closely and complete the table. Try to guess meaning from the context as much as possible. Note which additional words you have to look up, if any, to find the information.

Name	Alter	Wie die Person feiert (groß, klein, allein, mit Freunden, mit Familie usw.)	wo die Person feiert

B What, if anything, did you find surprising about the way these people celebrate their birthdays? What differences, if any, are there between the way people celebrate their birthdays in your area and the way the Germans celebrate theirs?

C **Wie feiern Sie Ihren Geburtstag?** Now describe briefly how you typically spend your birthday, using the texts you have just read as a model.

Zu guter Letzt

Eine Person vorstellen°

introduce

Now that you have worked with the topic of family and friends, bring a picture of your family or several friends or a magazine picture depicting your "fictional family" to class.

Schritt 1: Jot down phrases or sentences in German that you might want to use in describing the people in your picture. Make sure that you include the following:

- names
- how the people are related to you if you are describing family members
- things they like to do
- when they celebrate their birthdays, and so forth.

Schritt 2: Now work in groups of three. Using the items you have jotted down, describe three of the people in the picture. Your description might go something like this:

> Das ist meine Tante. Sie heißt Barbara. Sie hat am 14. April Geburtstag. Sie ist sehr aktiv. Sie kocht gern und läuft gern.

Schritt 3: Each person in the group should ask the other two members two questions about others in the picture you did not describe. Sample questions might be:

- Wer ist das?
- Wie heißt er/sie?
- Ist das deine Schwester? dein Bruder?

Schritt 4: Ein Bericht. Finally, expand the information about your family or friends in a written report that might include information such as the following:

- wie groß die Familie ist
- wo sie wohnt
- wann sie Geburtstag haben
- wie sie Geburtstag feiern
- was Sie und andere Familienmitglieder (*family members*) oder Freunde gern machen (kochen, tanzen, Zeitung lesen, …)
- Lieblings… (-sport, -komponist, -musiker)
- Probleme (kein Geld, zu viel Geld, keine Hobbys, …)

Wortschatz

Der Stammbaum	**Family Tree**
der **Bruder, ¨**	brother
die **Eltern** (*pl.*)	parents
der **Enkel, -**	grandson
die **Enkelin, -nen**	granddaughter
die **Familie, -n**	family
die **Frau, -en**	wife
die **Geschwister** (*pl.*)	siblings
die **Großeltern** (*pl.*)	grandparents
die **Großmutter, ¨**	grandmother
der **Großvater, ¨**	grandfather
die **Kusine, -n**	(female) cousin
der **Mann, ¨er**	husband
die **Mutter, ¨**	mother
der **Neffe** (-n *masc.*), **-n**	nephew
die **Nichte, -n**	niece
die **Oma, -s**	grandma
der **Onkel, -**	uncle
der **Opa, -s**	grandpa
der **Schwager, ¨**	brother-in-law
die **Schwägerin, -nen**	sister-in-law
die **Schwester, -n**	sister
der **Sohn, ¨e**	son
die **Tante, -n**	aunt
die **Tochter, ¨**	daughter
der **Vater, ¨**	father
der **Vetter, -n**	(male) cousin

Die Wochentage	**Days of the Week**
der **Montag**	Monday
am **Montag**	on Monday
der **Dienstag**	Tuesday
der **Mittwoch**	Wednesday
der **Donnerstag**	Thursday
der **Freitag**	Friday
der **Samstag** / der **Sonnabend**	Saturday
der **Sonntag**	Sunday

Die Monate	**Months**
der **Januar***	January
im **Januar**	in January
der **Februar**	February
der **März**	March
der **April**	April
der **Mai**	May
der **Juni**	June
der **Juli**	July
der **August**	August
der **September**	September
der **Oktober**	October

___
****Jänner** is used in Austria.

der **November**	November
der **Dezember**	December

Feste und Feiertage	**Holidays**
das **Familienfest, -e**	family gathering
(der) **Fasching**	Mardi Gras (*southern Germany, Austria*)
das **Geschenk, -e**	gift, present
der **Heilige Abend**	Christmas Eve
die **Hochzeit, -en**	wedding
der **Kalender, -**	calendar
(der) **Karneval**	Mardi Gras (*Rhineland*)
der **Muttertag**	Mother's Day
das **Neujahr**	New Year's Day
(das) **Ostern**	Easter
die **Party, -s**	party
(das) **Silvester**	New Year's Eve
die **Tradition, -en**	tradition
der **Valentinstag**	Valentine's Day
das **Weihnachten**	Christmas
der **Weihnachtsbaum, ¨e**	Christmas tree

Verben	**Verbs**
feiern	to celebrate
geben (gibt)	to give
gratulieren	to congratulate
heiraten	to marry
kennen	to know (*be acquainted with a person or thing*)
planen	to plan
werden (wird)	to become, be
wissen (weiß)	to know (*something as a fact*)
wünschen	to wish

Adjektive und Adverbien	**Adjectives and Adverbs**
leider	unfortunately
morgen	tomorrow
nämlich	namely, that is to say
neu	new
verwandt mit	related to
wichtig	important

Ordinalzahlen	**Ordinal Numbers**
erste	first
der **erste Mai**	May first
am **ersten Mai**	on May first
zweite	second
dritte	third
vierte	fourth
fünfte	fifth

sechste	sixth	**Akkusativpronomen**	**Accusative Pronouns**
sieb(en)te	seventh	mich	me
achte	eighth	dich	you (*informal sg.*)
neunte	ninth	ihn	him; it
zehnte	tenth	sie	her; it; them
elfte	eleventh	es	it
zwölfte	twelfth	uns	us
dreizehnte	thirteenth	euch	you (*informal pl.*)
zwanzigste	twentieth	Sie	you (*formal*)

Possessivartikel	**Possessive Adjectives**	**Sonstiges**	**Other**
mein	my	**Alles Gute!**	All the best!
dein	your (*informal sg.*)	**es gibt**	there is, there are
sein	his; its	**Es tut mir leid.**	I'm sorry.
ihr	her; its; their	**Herzlichen Glück-**	Happy birthday!
unser	our	**wunsch zum**	
euer	your (*informal pl.*)	**Geburtstag!**	
Ihr	your (*formal*)	der **Hund, -e**	dog
		um Mitternacht	at midnight
Akkusativpräpositionen	**Accusative Prepositions**	**Wann hast du**	When is your birthday?
durch	through	**Geburtstag?**	
für	for	**Welches Datum ist**	What is today's/
gegen	against; around (+ *time*)	**heute/morgen?**	tomorrow's date?
ohne	without		
um	at (+ *time*)		
um (... herum)	around (*spatial*)		

Das kann ich nun!

1. Wer sind die folgenden Familienmitglieder?
   a. Mein Bruder und meine Schwester sind meine _____.
   b. Meine Mutter und mein Vater sind meine _____.
   c. Familie Renner hat drei _____: einen Sohn und zwei _____.

2. Drei wichtige Feiertage sind: _____, _____, und _____.

3. Zum Geburtstag wünscht man „_____ _____ zum Geburtstag!"

4. Wann haben Sie Geburtstag? Mein Geburtstag ist _____. Dann _____ ich _____ Jahre alt.

5. Wie sagt man das auf Deutsch?
   a. Is that your car, Mrs. Singer?
   b. Do you know our parents?
   c. His brother knows that.
   d. My sister knows him.

6. Welche Präpositionen mit dem Akkusativ fehlen hier?
   a. Ich kaufe ein Geschenk _____ meinen Freund.
   b. Meine Freunde gehen heute _____ mich auf die Party bei Klaus.
   c. Meine Oma geht oft _____ den Park.

7. Nennen Sie die Wochentage mit den Buchstaben D und M am Anfang.
   a. D _____ und D _____
   b. M _____ und M _____

Persönlichkeiten: Drei Kurzbiografien

Wolfgang Amadeus Mozart (1756–1791)

Wolfgang Amadeus Mozart,
ca. 1783

Leopold Mozart und seine Kinder
Wolfgang und „Nannerl", 1763

Geburtsort: Salzburg
Geburtsdatum: 27. Januar 1756
Sternzeichen: Wassermann[1]
Vater: Leopold
Mutter: Maria Anna

Geschwister: Marianne, genannt „Nannerl"
Verheiratet[2] mit: Constanze geb. Weber
Kinder: Karl und Wolfgang
Wohnort: Wien
Beruf: Kapellmeister und Komponist
Hauptwerke: Opern (z.B. „Don Giovanni", „Die Zauberflöte"); 41 Symphonien; Kirchenmusik (z.B. „Krönungsmesse"[3], „Requiem"); Konzerte und Kammermusik (z.B. „Eine kleine Nachtmusik")
Hobbys: Musik, Tanzen, Geselligkeit[4], Reisen
Lieblingskomponist: Joseph Haydn

[1]*Aquarius* [2]*married* [3]*Coronation Mass* [4]*conviviality*

Paula Modersohn-Becker (1876–1909)

Paula Modersohn-Becker,
Selbstbildnis

Geburtsort: Dresden
Geburtsdatum: 8. Februar 1876
Sternzeichen: Wassermann
Vater: Woldemar
Mutter: Mathilde
Geschwister: sechs; vier jüngere, zwei ältere
Verheiratet mit: Otto Modersohn
Kinder: Mathilde
Wohnort: zuletzt in Worpswede[1]
Beruf: Malerin

Hauptwerke: Landschaftsmalerei[2], Porträts, Stillleben
Hobbys: Musik, Tanzen, Kochen, Lesen, Zeichnen
Lieblingsdichter: Rainer Maria Rilke

Paula Modersohn-Becker: Worpsweder
Landschaft, um 1900

[1]*Worpswede ist ein Künstlerdorf in der Nähe von Bremen.* [2]*landscape painting*

Albert Einstein (1879–1955)

Geburtsort: Ulm
Geburtsdatum: 14. März 1879
Sternzeichen: Fisch
Vater: Hermann
Mutter: Pauline
Geschwister: Maria („Maja")
Verheiratet mit: zuerst Mileva, dann Elsa
Kinder: Hans und Eduard
Wohnort: zuletzt in Princeton, New Jersey
Beruf: Physiker (Nobelpreis, 1921)
Hauptwerk: Relativitätstheorie
Hobbys: Musik, Geige[1] spielen, Segeln[2]
Lieblingskomponist: Mozart
Lieblingsphilosoph: Immanuel Kant

[1]*violin* [2]*sailing*

Albert Einstein als Kind, mit seiner Schwester Maja

Aktivität 1 Darf ich vorstellen?

Suppose you had to introduce Mozart, Einstein, or Modersohn-Becker to someone at a party. Make three statements about each that characterize who they are.

BEISPIEL: Darf ich vorstellen, das ist Herr/Frau …

Er/Sie ist …

Er/Sie schreibt/malt/wohnt in …

Aktivität 2 Rollenspiel

Imagine that you could interview the people you just read about. With a partner, select one of the three, then create the interview. You could begin as follows:

BEISPIEL: **S1:** Wo sind Sie geboren, Frau Modersohn-Becker?

S2: In Dresden.

S1: Sind Sie verheiratet? …

Albert Einstein beim Segeln

Aktivität 3 Ein Steckbrief°

Choose a well-known historical person and gather information to write a **Steckbrief** about her or him. Present the information in class without revealing who the person is. Let the members of the class guess her or his identity.

wanted poster

Kapitel 4

Mein Tag

In diesem Kapitel

- ▶ **Themen:** Telling time, times of the day, daily plans, movies, music, theater

- ▶ **Grammatik:** Separable-prefix verbs; modal verbs; **möchte;** the imperative; the particles **bitte, doch, mal**

- ▶ **Lesen:** „In der S-Bahn komme ich endlich zum Lesen"

- ▶ **Landeskunde:** German theater, music, and film

- ▶ **Zu guter Letzt:** Ein Podcast über Sehenswertes an der Uni

Studenten nach der Vorlesung

Ein Tag im Leben von Jan, Jasmin und Beatrice

A In diesem  (Brief) sehen Sie fünf  (Bilder).
Die Bilder stehen für fünf Wörter oder Ausdrücke.
Die Ausdrücke sind alphabetisch geordnet.

Fahrrad

Haus(e)

Herz

Sonntag

Tasse Kaffee

Lesen Sie den Brief nun mit den Wörtern.

Sprach-Info

Just as in other cultures, SMS texting has become a way of life in German-speaking countries. Young people text more often than they talk on their **Handys.** There are even local, regional, and national contests to determine who the fastest SMS texter is. SMS texting in German makes liberal use of abbreviations. Here are a few examples.

bda–bis dann

8ung–Achtung

akla–Alles klar?

bvid–bin verliebt in Dich

DaD–denke an Dich

GiE–Ganz im Ernst

LMIR–lass mich in Ruhe

luauki–Lust auf Kino?

nfd–Nur für dich

thx–thanks/danke

t+–think positive / denke positiv

wasa–warte auf schnelle Antwort

B Schauen Sie den SMS Text an! Was bedeuten diese Abkürzungen (*abbreviations*)?

1. Nachm.
   a. Nachmittag
   b. Nach dem Essen
2. LG
   a. Lisa und Gerd
   b. Liebe Grüße

Was gibt es zum Essen und Trinken bei Emmi?

C Sie hören jetzt eine telefonische Einladung. Hören Sie zu und markieren Sie die richtige Information.

1. Die Einladung ist für _____.
   a. Sonntag
   b. Samstag
   c. Freitag
2. Erika und Thomas wollen _____.
   a. Dirk zu Kaffee und Kuchen einladen
   b. mit Dirk auf eine Party gehen
   c. mit Dirk ins Café gehen
3. Dirk soll _____ kommen.
   a. um 3 Uhr
   b. um 5 Uhr
   c. um 4 Uhr

Siehe *Modal Auxiliary Verbs*, S. 128.

Thema 1: Die Uhrzeit

Wie spät ist es?
Wie viel Uhr ist es?

Es ist eins.
Es ist **ein Uhr.**
Es ist dreizehn Uhr.

Es ist zehn (Minuten) **nach** eins.
Es ist ein Uhr zehn.
Es ist dreizehn Uhr zehn.

Es ist **Viertel nach** eins.
Es ist ein Uhr fünfzehn.
Es ist dreizehn Uhr fünfzehn.

Es ist **halb** zwei.
Es ist ein Uhr dreißig.
Es ist dreizehn Uhr dreißig.

Es ist zwanzig (Minuten) **vor** zwei.
Es ist ein Uhr vierzig.
Es ist dreizehn Uhr vierzig.

Es ist **Viertel vor** zwei.
Es ist ein Uhr fünfundvierzig.
Es ist dreizehn Uhr fünfundvierzig.

Es ist zehn (Minuten) vor zwei.
Es ist ein Uhr fünfzig.
Es ist dreizehn Uhr fünfzig.

Eine **Minute** hat sechzig **Sekunden,** eine **Stunde** sechzig Minuten und ein Tag vierundzwanzig Stunden.

Sprach-Info

In official timetables—for instance, in radio, television, movie, and theater guides—time is expressed according to the twenty-four-hour system.

1.00–12.00 Uhr	*1:00 A.M. to 12:00 noon*
13.00–24.00 Uhr	*1:00 P.M. to 12:00 midnight*

Midnight may also be referred to as **0 (null) Uhr.**

When writing time in numbers, German speakers usually separate hours and minutes with a period, instead of a colon as in English.

Aktivität 1 Zeitansagen°

Time announcements

Markieren Sie die Uhrzeiten, die Sie hören.

1. **a.** 7.38 **b.** 17.35 **c.** 17.30
2. **a.** 3.06 **b.** 2.06 **c.** 20.16
3. **a.** 14.00 **b.** 14.15 **c.** 14.05
4. **a.** 12.25 **b.** 10.24 **c.** 11.25
5. **a.** 19.45 **b.** 9.45 **c.** 19.40
6. **a.** 13.00 **b.** 3.40 **c.** 13.40
7. **a.** 0.15 **b.** 0.05 **c.** 0.45
8. **a.** 20.05 **b.** 20.50 **c.** 21.50

Analyse

Sehen Sie sich die Zeichnung an und beantworten Sie die Fragen.

- ▶ Wie spät ist es in New York?
- ▶ Wie spät ist es in Tokio?
- ▶ Wie spät ist es in Bombay?
- ▶ Die vierte Uhr zeigt (*shows*) die „gute alte Zeit". Warum hat der Mann wohl (*probably*) diese Uhr gern?

    a. Er hat Kuckucksuhren gern.

    b. Heute ist alles so hektisch.

    c. Die Kuckucksuhr geht langsamer als die anderen Uhren.

    d. ??

Aktivität 2 Wie viel Uhr ist es? Wie spät ist es?

BEISPIEL: Wie viel Uhr ist es? (Wie spät ist es?) →
Es ist Viertel nach sieben.

1.

2.

3.

4.

5.

6.

7.

Sprach-Info

To find out at what time something takes place, ask:

Um wie viel Uhr _____?

To say at what time something takes place, use the following expressions:

um ein Uhr (1.00 Uhr)

um ein Uhr zehn (1.10 Uhr)

um ein Uhr fünfzehn (1.15 Uhr)

um ein Uhr dreißig (1.30 Uhr)

um ein Uhr vierzig (1.40 Uhr)

um ein Uhr fünfundvierzig (1.45 Uhr)

Neue Wörter

das Wochenende weekend
steht ... auf (aufstehen)
  gets up
frühstückt (frühstücken) eats
  breakfast
ruft ... an (anrufen) calls up
trifft (treffen) meets

Aktivität 3 Was macht Hans-Jürgen am Wochenende?

Sehen Sie sich die Bilder an und ergänzen Sie Hans-Jürgens Pläne für das **Wochenende.**

7.05

7.20

7.45–8.30

1. Um _____ schläft Hans-Jürgen noch. Dann klingelt der Wecker.
2. Um _____ **steht** er endlich **auf.**
3. Von _____ bis _____ geht er joggen.

9.30

11.20

12.15

Siehe *Separable-Prefix Verbs,* S. 124.

4. Um _____ **frühstückt** er und liest die Zeitung.
5. Um _____ **ruft** er einen Freund **an.**
6. Um _____ **trifft** er eine Freundin im Café.

15.00

19.15

13.40

7. Um _____ **geht** er **einkaufen.**
8. Um _____ spielt Hans-Jürgen Fußball auf dem Sportplatz.
9. Um _____ ist er mit Freunden im Kino.

Aktivität 4   Mein Zeitbudget

Wie viel Zeit verbringen (*spend*) Sie **gewöhnlich** mit diesen Dingen?

Schritt 1: Tragen Sie in die Tabelle ein, wie viel Zeit Sie **pro Woche** mit jeder Tätigkeit verbringen.

Tätigkeit	Montag bis Freitag	Wochenende
Vorlesungen Labor Lesen Schreiben		
Nebenarbeit		
Essen: 　Frühstück 　Mittagessen 　Abendessen		
Einkaufen Sport Schlafen		
Zeit für mich: 　Fernsehen 　Zeitung/Bücher lesen 　Freunde besuchen 　Musik hören 　SMS schicken		

Schritt 2: Stellen Sie wenigstens 5 Fragen an einen Partner / eine Partnerin. Fragen Sie:

- ► Wie viel Zeit verbringst du in Vorlesungen? im Labor? mit Lesen? …
- ► Wie viel Zeit hast du für dich?

Schritt 3: Berichten Sie der Klasse, wie Ihr Partner / Ihre Partnerin seine/ihre Zeit verbringt.

BEISPIEL: Laura verbringt fünfzehn Stunden pro Woche mit Vorlesungen und zehn Stunden pro Woche mit Nebenarbeit. Sie hat nicht viel Zeit für Fernsehen aber hört oft Musik.

Neue Wörter

hat ... vor (vorhaben) is planning
einladen invite
der Vortrag lecture
die Vorlesung (university) lecture
abholen pick up
ausgehen go out
aufräumen straighten up
die Bibliothek library
kommt ... vorbei (vorbeikommen) comes by
spazieren gehen go for a walk
fernsehen watch TV

Thema 2: Pläne machen

Hans-Jürgens Wochenplan

Hans-Jürgen **hat** viel **vor** und plant seine Zeit immer sehr genau. Dies ist sein Wochenplan für die nächsten vier Tage.

15. DONNERSTAG

08.00 Karin im **Fitnesscenter** treffen
12.00 mit Thomas essen
15.30 Erika auf eine Tasse Kaffee **einladen**
19.30 zum **Vortrag** gehen

16. FREITAG

07.00 schwimmen gehen
10.15 in die Biologie-**Vorlesung** gehen
15.00 Konzerttickets **abholen**
20.00 mit Astrid und Max **ausgehen**

17. SAMSTAG

09.00 Wohnung **aufräumen**
14.00 Kurt in der **Bibliothek** treffen
21.00 Astrid **kommt vorbei**

18. SONNTAG

11.00 spät frühstücken
16.00 mit Astrid **spazieren gehen**
21.45 **fernsehen**: »Sabine Christiansen«[1]

[1]*a talk show host dealing mostly with political topics*

Tageszeiten

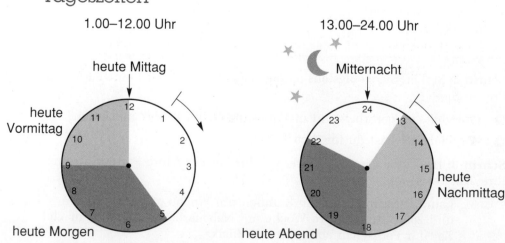

1.00–12.00 Uhr

heute Mittag
heute Vormittag
heute Morgen

13.00–24.00 Uhr

Mitternacht
heute Nachmittag
heute Abend

A Was **möchte** Hans-Jürgen machen – und wann? Sehen Sie sich Hans-Jürgens Wochenplan an und ergänzen Sie seine Pläne.

am Donnerstag, 15. Oktober

☐ **Heute Morgen** möchte Hans-Jürgen ins Fitnesscenter gehen.
☐ Heute **Mittag** möchte er ___essen mit Tomas___.
☐ Heute **Nachmittag** möchte er _____.
☐ Heute **Abend** möchte er zu einem ___Vortrag gehen___
   gehen.

am Freitag, 16. Oktober

☐ **Morgen früh** möchte Hans-Jürgen schwimmen gehen.
☐ Morgen **Vormittag muss** er _____.
☐ Morgen Nachmittag **soll** er _____.
☐ Morgen Abend möchte er _____.

am Samstag, 17. Oktober

☐ Samstagmorgen muss Hans-Jürgen die Wohnung aufräumen.
☐ Samstagnachmittag möchte er _____.
☐ Samstagabend _____ Astrid
   _____.

☐ Samstags ist er oft bis spät in der **Nacht** bei Freunden.

am Sonntag, 18. Oktober

☐ Sonntagvormittag möchte er _____.
☐ Sonntagnachmittag möchte er _____.
☐ Sonntagabend möchte er _____.

B Und Sie? Was möchten oder müssen Sie machen – und wann?

Neue Wörter

möchte   would like to
der Morgen   morning; tomorrow
der Mittag   noon
der Nachmittag   afternoon
der Abend   evening
früh   early
der Vormittag   morning, before noon
muss (müssen)   must
soll (sollen)   is supposed to
die Nacht   night

 Siehe *Modal Auxiliary Verbs,* S. 128.

Aktivität 5 Hin und her: Zwei Stundenpläne

Schritt 1: Milan und Frank sind 18 Jahre alt und gehen aufs Gymnasium (*secondary school*). Vergleichen Sie ihre Stundenpläne. Welche Fächer haben sie gemeinsam (*together*)?

BEISPIEL: **S1:** Welchen Kurs hat Milan montags um acht?

S2: Montags um acht hat Milan Physik. Welchen Kurs hat Frank um acht?

S1: Montags um acht hat Frank Französisch.

Schritt 2: Milan und Frank möchten Tennis spielen. Wann ist die beste Zeit? Wann haben sie beide frei?

Zeit	Montag	Dienstag	Mittwoch	Donnerstag	Freitag
8.00–8.45	Französisch	Mathe	Deutsch	Englisch	Mathe
8.50–9.35	Chemie	Musik	Deutsch	Englisch	Chemie
Pause					
9.50–10.35	Mathe	Sport	Bio-Chemie	Religion	Französisch
10.40–11.25	Englisch	Sport	Bio-Chemie	Französisch	iVFö
11.45–12.30	Deutsch	iVFö	Erdkunde	Erdkunde	Religion
12.35–13.20	Bio-Chemie	Französisch	Musik	Musik	Deutsch
13.20–14.30	Mittagspause	frei			frei
14.35–15.20	Physik	Handball	Englisch		Bio-Chemie
15.25–16.10	Physik		Chemie	frei	frei

Franks Stundenplan

Aktivität 6 Bist du heute Abend zu Hause?

Sie wollen einen Freund / eine Freundin besuchen. Sagen Sie, wann Sie vorbeikommen und wie lange Sie bleiben möchten. Benutzen Sie folgendes Sprechschema.

S1	S2
1. Bis du _____ zu Hause?	**2a.** Ja, ich bin zu Hause. **b.** Nein, ich bin leider nicht zu Hause.
3a. Kann ich dann _____ vorbeikommen? **b.** Schade. Wann kann ich denn mal vorbeikommen?	**4a.** Ja, gern. Ich sehe dich also _____. **b.** Kannst du _____ kommen?
5a. Schön. **b.** Ja, gern.	**6.** Wie lange kannst du denn bleiben?
7. _____ Stunde(n).	

Aktivität 7　Wie sieht Ihr Stundenplan aus?°

How does your schedule look?

Schritt 1: Schreiben Sie Ihren Stundenplan. Wann sind Ihre Kurse? Wann arbeiten Sie? Dann vergleichen Sie Ihren Stundenplan mit dem von zwei anderen Studenten/Studentinnen in Ihrem Kurs.

BEISPIEL: **S1:**　Was hast du donnerstags um 10?

　　　　　S2:　Donnerstags um 10 habe ich _____. Und du?

Schritt 2: Wer hat Kurse mit Ihnen zusammen? Berichten (*Report*) Sie der Klasse.

Thema 3: Kino, Musik und Theater

Jan:　Ich **gehe** heute Abend **ins Theater.** Willst du mit?

Ulla:　Nein, danke. Ich bin kein Theaterfan. Ich **möchte lieber ins Kino.**

Jan:　So! Was für **Filme** magst du denn?

Ulla:　**Am liebsten** Horrorfilme und Psychothriller. Die finde ich so **spannend.**

Jan:　Also, im Olympia läuft ein guter **Krimi.** Der soll sehr spannend sein.

Ulla:　Wann **fängt** das Kino denn **an?**

Jan:　Um 7.30 Uhr.

Ulla:　Gut. Ich **komme mit.**

Neue Wörter

möchte lieber　would rather
am liebsten　most preferably
spannend　suspenseful; exciting
der Krimi (Krimis, *pl.***)** detective story
fängt ... an (anfangen) begins
die Komödie (Komödien, *pl.***)** comedy
die Tragödie (Tragödien, *pl.***)** tragedy
das Theaterstück (Theaterstücke, *pl.***)**　play
die Oper (Opern, *pl.***)**　opera

▶　Was für Filme sehen Sie gern?

☑ Horrorfilme　　　　　☐ **Krimis**
☐ **Komödien**　　　　　☐ Science-fiction-Filme
☐ Psychothriller　　　　☐ Abenteuerfilme
☐ Liebesfilme　　　　　☐ Wildwestfilme

Was sehen Sie gern auf der Bühne (*on stage*)?

☐ **Tragödien**　　　　　☐ **Theaterstücke**
☐ Lustspiele (*comedies*)　☐ **Opern**
☐ Musicals　　　　　　☐ Tanz und **Ballett**

Was für Musik hören Sie gern?

☐ klassische Musik　　　☐ Jazz
☐ Heavy Metal　　　　　☐ Soul
☐ Rockmusik　　　　　　☐ Western-Musik
☐ Techno　　　　　　　☐ Rap
☐ alternative Musik　　　☐ Hip-Hop

Sprach-Info

To say where you are going, use the following expressions.

Ich gehe
{
ins Kino.
ins Theater.
ins Konzert.
in die Oper.
in die Disco.
}

Landeskunde-Info

Das kulturelle Leben in Deutschland hat eine lange Tradition, und das Interesse an Theater, Musik, Ballett und Film ist groß.

In den Groß- und Kleinstädten gibt es über 400 öffentliche und private Theater, und 130 professionelle Orchester bieten ein reiches Programm an klassischer und moderner Musik. Rund 35 Millionen Zuschauer besuchen jährlich mehr als 100 000 Theateraufführungen und 7 000 Konzerte. Auch in kleinen Städten gibt es Opernhäuser und Ballette. Die vielen Festspiele, wie zum Beispiel die Bayreuther Festspiele oder das Bachfest in Leipzig, sind international bekannt.

Der deutsche Staat subventioniert die meisten kulturellen Programme. Deshalb sind die Karten für Theater, Musik, Oper und Ballett nicht zu teuer. Viele Deutsche haben Abonnements (*subscriptions*) für Theater, Oper, Konzerte oder Ballett.

Auch der deutsche Film ist in den letzten Jahren populärer geworden. „Das Leben der anderen" (*The Lives of Others*) hat 2007 einen Oskar als bester ausländischer (*foreign*) Film gewonnen.

Schauspielhaus Düsseldorf

Eine moderne Ballettaufführung in Berlin

▶ Wie oft gehen Sie ins Theater?

▶ Was ist Ihr Lieblingstheaterstück (*favorite play*)?

invitations

Aktivität 8 Zwei Einladungen°

Sie hören zwei Dialoge. Wer spricht? Wohin möchten die Sprecher gehen? Warum ist es nicht möglich (*possible*)? Markieren Sie die richtige Information.

Dialog 1

1. Die Sprecher sind …
   a. ein Professor und ein Student.
   b. zwei Studentinnen.
   c. eine Studentin und ein Freund.

2. Der eine Sprecher möchte …
   a. zu Hause arbeiten.
   b. ins Kino.
   c. ins Konzert.

3. Die Sprecherin muss leider …
   a. arbeiten.
   b. in eine Vorlesung.
   c. einen Brief schreiben.

Dialog 2

1. Die Sprecher sind …
   a. zwei Studenten.
   b. zwei Professoren.
   c. ein Student und eine Freundin.

2. Die eine Sprecherin möchte …
   a. ins Kino.
   b. in eine Vorlesung.
   c. Karten spielen.

3. Der andere Sprecher …
   a. hat eine Vorlesung.
   b. hat Labor.
   c. muss in die Bibliothek.

Aktivität 9 Was machst du so° am Wochenende?

generally

Interviewen Sie Studenten/Studentinnen in der Klasse und finden Sie folgende Personen. Wer „ja" antwortet, muss unterschreiben.

BEISPIEL: **S1:** Gehst du tanzen, spazieren, laufen oder wandern?

S2: Ja, ich gehe tanzen.

S1: Unterschreib bitte hier.

Hier klicken!

Weiteres zum Thema Konzert und Theater finden Sie bei **Deutsch: Na klar!** im World-Wide-Web unter **www.mhhe.com/dnk6**.

Am Wochenende

1. _Lanron_ Wer geht tanzen, spazieren, laufen oder wandern?
2. _brandon_ Wer steht früh auf?
3. _____ Wer steht spät auf?
4. _Eldem_ Wer räumt das Zimmer, die Wohnung, den Schreibtisch auf?
5. _____ Wer geht ins Kino, ins Theater, in die Oper, ins Konzert, zu einer Technoparty? *gehts du tanze*
6. _____ Wer lädt Freunde ein?
7. _Sam Ja_ Wer sieht fern? *fern sieht*
8. _Ja_ Wer surft im Internet? *surft du im Internet*
Tonias

Aktivität 10 Was hast du vor?

Schauen Sie sich die Programme für Kino, Theater und Musik an. Sagen Sie, wohin Sie gehen wollen.

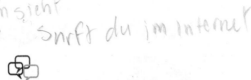

S1	S2
1. Was hast du am Samstag vor?	2. Ich gehe ins Kino / ins Theater / in die Oper / ? Willst du mit?
3. Was gibt es denn?	4. Einen Film / ein Musical / eine Oper / ? von (+ *name*).
5a. So? Wann fängt er/es/sie denn an? b. Ach, ich bleibe lieber zu Hause.	6a. _____: b. Schade.

Verben mit trennbaren Präfixen

Separable-Prefix Verbs°

You are already familiar with sentences such as the following:

Susanne und Peter **kommen** per Fahrrad **vorbei.**	*Susanne and Peter **are coming by** on their bikes.*
Ich gehe heute tanzen. **Kommst** du **mit?**	*I am going dancing today. Will you **come along?***

German, like English, has many two-part verbs that consist of a verb and a short complement that affects the meaning of the main verb. Examples of such two-part verbs in English are *to come by, to come along, to call up, to get up.*

Wüstenrot-Rendite[1]-Programm mit 470 Euro pro anno.
Jede Million fängt klein an.[2]

Ich rufe an.... *(Telefonieren ist einfach)*[3]

---

[1]*yield on investment* [2]fängt ... an: *begins* [3]*simple*

Kommen ... vorbei, kommst ... mit, fängt ... an, and **rufe ... an** are examples of such two-part verbs in German. They are also called separable-prefix verbs. In the infinitive, the separable part of these verbs forms the verb's prefix. The prefixes are always stressed.

> **án**rufen, **án**fangen, **vorbéi**kommen, **mít**kommen

In a statement or a question, the prefix is separated from the conjugated verb and placed at the end of the sentence.

—**Kommst** du heute Abend **vorbei?**	*Are you coming by tonight?*
—Ja, aber ich **rufe** vorher **an.**	*Yes, but I'll call first.*

Here are examples of some separable-prefix verbs introduced in this chapter.

Verb	Beispiel
abholen (holt ... ab) to pick up	Ich **hole** dich um 6 Uhr **ab.**
anfangen (fängt ... an) to begin	Wann **fängt** die Vorlesung **an?**
anrufen (ruft ... an) to call up	Ich **rufe** dich morgen **an.**
aufräumen (räumt ... auf) to straighten up	Er **räumt** sein Zimmer **auf.**
aufstehen (steht ... auf) to get up	Er **steht** um 9 Uhr **auf.**
aufwachen (wacht ... auf) to wake up	Wann **wachst** du gewöhnlich **auf?**
ausgehen (geht ... aus) to go out	Er **geht** oft allein **aus.**

einkaufen (kauft ... ein) to shop	Herr Lerche **kauft** immer morgens **ein**.
einladen (lädt ... ein) to invite	Ich **lade** dich zum Essen **ein**.
einschlafen (schläft ... ein) to fall asleep	Ich **schlafe** gewöhnlich nicht vor Mitternacht **ein**.
fernsehen (sieht ... fern) to watch TV	Sie **sieht** bis Mitternacht **fern**.
mitbringen (bringt ... mit) to bring along	Ich **bringe** eine Pizza **mit**.
mitkommen (kommt ... mit) to come along	**Kommst** du **mit**?
vorbeikommen (kommt ... vorbei) to come by	Wir **kommen** Sonntag **vorbei**.
vorhaben (hat ... vor) to plan to do	Was **hast** du heute **vor**?
zurückkommen (kommt ... zurück) to come back	Wann **kommst** du **zurück**?

¹ad ²geben ... auf *place*

NOTE:

▶ A separable-prefix verb shows all the same stem-vowel changes or other irregularities in the present tense as the base verb.

Hans **schläft** immer lange.	Er **schläft** um 23 Uhr **ein**.
Er **sieht** einen Film.	Er **sieht** heute Abend **fern**.

▶ Separable-prefix verbs are listed in the vocabulary of this book as follows:

an•rufen   ein•schlafen (schläft ein)   vor•haben (hat vor)

The Sentence Bracket°

Die Satzklammer

Separable-prefix verbs show a sentence structure that is characteristic for German: the conjugated verb and its complement form a bracket around the core of the sentence. The conjugated verb is the second element of the sentence, and the separable prefix is the last element.

		—— **Satzklammer** ——	
Ich	**rufe**	dich heute Abend	**an.**
Wann	**kommst**	du heute	**vorbei?**
Peter	**geht**	leider nicht	**mit.**

Another example of the sentence bracket (**Satzklammer**) can be seen in sentences with compound verbs such as **einkaufen gehen** (*to go shopping*), **tanzen gehen** (*to go dancing*), and **spazieren gehen** (*to go for a walk*).

		—— **Satzklammer** ——	
Ich	**gehe**	morgens	**einkaufen.**
Klaus und Erika	**gehen**	Sonntag mit Freunden	**tanzen.**
Daniel	**geht**	mit dem Hund	**spazieren.**

In the sentences above, the verb **gehen** and the infinitives **einkaufen, tanzen,** and **spazieren** form a bracket around the sentence core. You will encounter the concept of the sentence bracket in many other contexts involving verbs.

Übung 1 Daniels Tagesablauf

Daniel ist Künstler (*artist*), aber die Kunst (*art*) allein bringt nicht genug Geld ein. Sie hören jetzt eine Beschreibung von Daniels Tagesablauf. Markieren Sie alle passenden Antworten auf jede Frage.

1. Wann wacht Daniel gewöhnlich auf?
   a. sehr früh
   b. sehr spät
   c. um 5 Uhr

2. Wohnt Daniel allein?
   a. ja, allein
   b. nein, zusammen mit seinem Bruder
   c. nein, mit seiner Freundin

3. Was tut Daniel für die Familie Schröder?
   a. Er geht einkaufen.
   b. Er geht mit dem Hund spazieren.
   c. Er macht Reparaturen.

4. Wann fängt Daniels Arbeit im Hotel an?
   a. um 6 Uhr
   b. um 7 Uhr
   c. um 5 Uhr

5. Wann kommt Daniel nach Hause zurück?
   a. um 12 Uhr nachts
   b. um 6 Uhr abends
   c. so gegen 3 Uhr nachmittags

6. Was macht Daniel dann zuerst?
   a. Er geht schlafen.
   b. Er geht einkaufen.
   c. Er räumt das Zimmer auf.

7. Wann fängt Daniels Leben für die Kunst an?
   a. spät nachmittags
   b. am Wochenende
   c. so gegen Mitternacht

8. Was für Projekte hat Daniel der Künstler oft vor?
   a. Er komponiert (*composes*) Musik.
   b. Er macht Skulpturen aus Metall.
   c. Er fotografiert.

9. Wie verbringt Daniel manchmal seinen Abend?
   a. Er sieht fern.
   b. Er lädt Freunde ein.
   c. Er ruft Freunde an.

10. Wann schläft Daniel gewöhnlich ein?
    a. um 12 Uhr nachts
    b. nicht vor 1 Uhr nachts
    c. so gegen halb eins

Übung 2 Was Daniel macht

Erzählen Sie jetzt mithilfe der Fragen und Antworten in **Übung 1**, was Daniel jeden Tag macht.

BEISPIEL: Daniel wacht gewöhnlich sehr früh auf.

A date

Übung 3 Eine Verabredung°

Die folgenden Sätze sind eine Konversation zwischen Hans und Petra. Ergänzen Sie zuerst die Verben mit den fehlenden (*missing*) Präfixen. Arrangieren Sie dann die Sätze als Dialog, und üben Sie den Dialog mit einem Partner / einer Partnerin.

_____ Um acht. Ich komme um halb acht _____ und hole dich _____.

_____ Ja, ich gehe ins Kino. Im Olympia läuft ein neuer Film mit Keanu Reeves. Kommst du _____?

_____ Schön. Hinterher (*afterwards*) lade ich dich zu einem Bier _____.

_____ Gerne. Wann fängt der Film denn _____?

_1_ Hast du für heute Abend schon etwas _____?

Übung 4 Was ich so mache

Was machen Sie auch **immer, manchmal, selten, nie, oft, gewöhnlich?**

BEISPIEL: Daniel steht gewöhnlich sehr früh auf. →
Ich stehe nie früh auf.

1. Daniel steht gewöhnlich sehr früh auf.
2. Daniel geht nie am Wochenende einkaufen.
3. Lilo geht oft mit ihrem Hund spazieren.
4. Hans räumt selten sein Zimmer auf.
5. Lilo schläft gewöhnlich beim Fernsehen ein.
6. Daniel lädt manchmal abends Freunde ein.
7. Daniel schläft selten vor 1 Uhr nachts ein.
8. Lilo ruft ihre Eltern oft an.
9. Daniel geht selten mit Freunden aus.

Übung 5 Wie sieht dein Tag aus?

Schritt 1: Arbeiten Sie zu zweit (*in pairs*) und stellen Sie einander folgende Fragen. Formulieren Sie Ihre Antworten mithilfe der Ausdrücke auf der nächsten Seite. Schreiben Sie die Antworten auf.

- ▶ Was machst du gewöhnlich jeden Tag?
- ▶ Was machst du oft?
- ▶ Was machst du manchmal?
- ▶ Was machst du nie?

BEISPIEL: Ich stehe gewöhnlich vor sechs Uhr auf. Ich räume nie mein
Zimmer auf. ...

Schritt 2: Geben Sie jetzt einen kurzen Bericht von etwa vier Sätzen.

BEISPIEL: Keith steht gewöhnlich vor sechs Uhr auf. Er räumt nie sein
Zimmer auf. Er geht manchmal einkaufen. Jeden Tag geht er mit
Freunden aus.

Modal Auxiliary Verbs°

Modal auxiliary verbs (for example, *must, can, may*) express an attitude toward an action.

¹*novels*

Morgen **möchten** wir Tennis **spielen**.	*Tomorrow we **would like to play** tennis.*
Am Wochenende **wollen** wir Freunde **besuchen**.	*On the weekend we **want to visit** friends.*
Ich **kann** morgen **vorbeikommen**.	*I **can come by** tomorrow.*

NOTE:

▶ The modal auxiliary verb is the conjugated verb and is in the second position in a statement.

▶ Its complement—the verb that expresses the action—is in the infinitive form and stands at the end of the sentence.

▶ In German, sentences with modal auxiliaries and a dependent infinitive demonstrate the pattern of the sentence bracket (**Satzklammer**) that you learned earlier in this chapter.

─────── Satzklammer ───────

Morgen	**möchten**	wir Tennis	**spielen**.
Peter	**muss**	morgen leider	**arbeiten**.
Ich	**kann**	dich heute	**besuchen**.
Heute Abend	**wollen**	wir ins Kino	**gehen**.

German has the following modal verbs.

dürfen	to be allowed to, may	**Dürfen** wir hier rauchen? *May we smoke here?*
können	to be able to, can	Ich **kann** dich gut verstehen. *I can understand you well.*
mögen	to like, care for	**Mögen** Sie Bücher? *Do you like books?*
müssen	to have to, must	Er **muss** heute arbeiten. *He has to work today.*
sollen	to be supposed to, shall	Wann **sollen** wir vorbeikommen? *When are we supposed to come by?*
wollen	to want to, plan to do	**Willst** du mitgehen? *Do you want to go along?*

Hier dürfen Sie nicht parken!

The Present Tense of Modals

Modals are irregular verbs. With the exception of **sollen,** they have stem-vowel changes in the singular. Note also that the first- and third-person singular forms are identical and have no personal ending.

	dürfen	können	mögen	müssen	sollen	wollen
ich	**darf**	**kann**	**mag**	**muss**	**soll**	**will**
du	darfst	kannst	magst	musst	sollst	willst
er sie} es	**darf**	**kann**	**mag**	**muss**	**soll**	**will**
wir	dürfen	können	mögen	müssen	sollen	wollen
ihr	dürft	könnt	mögt	müsst	sollt	wollt
sie	dürfen	können	mögen	müssen	sollen	wollen
Sie	dürfen	können	mögen	müssen	sollen	wollen

Möchte (*would like*) is one of the most frequently used modal verbs. It is the subjunctive of **mögen.** Note that the first- and third-person singular forms are identical.

> Wir **möchten** morgen Tennis **spielen.** *We would like to play tennis tomorrow.*

möchte			
ich	**möchte**	wir	möchten
du	möchtest	ihr	möchtet
er sie} es	**möchte**	sie	möchten
Sie möchten			

NOTE:

- The modal **mögen** is generally used without a dependent infinitive.

  Er **mag** seine Arbeit im Hotel.   *He likes his work in the hotel.*

- The infinitive in a sentence with a modal verb may be omitted when its meaning is understood.

  Ich **muss** jetzt in die Vorlesung (**gehen**).   *I have to go to the lecture now.*

  Ich **möchte** jetzt nach Hause (**gehen**).   *I would like to go home now.*

  Er **will** das nicht (**machen**).   *He doesn't want to do that.*

Scan the headlines and visual.

▶ Identify all modal auxiliary verbs in the headlines and visual. Give the English equivalents of the sentences.

▶ What verbs express the action in those sentences?

▶ Mark the two parts of each sentence bracket.

▶ Why does the statement about Greenpeace not have an infinitive?

JEDER KANN AUS-GLEITEN UND FALLEN MAN DARF NUR NICHT LIEGENBLEIBEN [1]

AUS INDIEN

Ich möchte mehr Informationen über Greenpeace!

So schön (spannend, aufregend) kann Fernsehen sein

Die Studenten wollen streiken

[1]Jeder ... *Anyone can slip and fall; the trick is not to stay down.*

Übung 6   Wer möchte das?

Ergänzen Sie die Sätze mit der passenden Form von **möchte**.

1. Wir _____ heute Abend ins Kino gehen.
2. _____ ihr mitkommen?
3. Martina _____ lieber joggen gehen.
4. Ich _____ heute Abend zu Hause bleiben und meine Hausaufgaben machen.
5. _____ du auch zu Hause bleiben und arbeiten?
6. Andreas _____ sein Projekt für seinen Computerkurs fertig machen (*complete*).
7. Meine Freunde _____ alle heute Abend ins Kino gehen.

Übung 7   Was kann man da machen?

BEISPIEL: in der Bibliothek →

> S1:   Was kann man in der Bibliothek machen?
>
> S2:   Da kann man Bücher lesen!

1. im Restaurant	a. Filme sehen
2. im Kino	b. einkaufen
3. im Internetcafé	c. tanzen
4. in der Disco	d. Freunde treffen
5. im Kaufhaus	e. Bücher lesen
6. im Park	f. etwas essen und trinken
7. in der Bibliothek	g. spazieren gehen
	h. Computerspiele machen
	i. Freunde treffen

Sprach-Info

The indefinite pronoun **man** (*one, people, you, they*) is commonly used to talk about a general activity.

> **Man** darf hier nicht parken.
>
> *You (One) may not park here. (Parking is not allowed here.)*

Man is used with the third-person singular verb form.

Übung 8 Was darf man hier machen oder nicht?

BEISPIEL: Man darf hier nicht parken.

1.

2.

3.

4.

5.

6.

campen
schnell fahren
schwimmen
parken

spielen
rauchen (*smoke*)
von 8 bis 14 Uhr parken

Übung 9 Im Deutschen Haus

Chris und Jeff wohnen im Deutschen Haus an einer amerikanischen Universität. Sie sollen so oft wie möglich deutsch miteinander sprechen. Hören Sie zu, und kreuzen Sie die richtige Information an.

	Das stimmt	Das stimmt nicht
1. Chris muss für einen Test arbeiten.	☐	☐
2. Er redet laut (*aloud*) und stört (*disturbs*) seinen Mitbewohner Jeff.	☐	☐
3. Jeff wird jetzt böse (*annoyed*).	☐	☐
4. Chris kann nur laut lernen.	☐	☐
5. Chris geht in die Bibliothek.	☐	☐

Übung 10 Was sind die Tatsachen°?

Was wissen Sie über die beiden Bewohner des Deutschen Hauses? Bilden Sie Sätze.

Chris	soll	ins Badezimmer gehen
Jeff	muss	deutsche Grammatik lernen
	kann	ein A im Test bekommen
	will	nur laut Deutsch lernen
	möchte	Jeff nicht stören
	darf	auch arbeiten
		jetzt auch schlafen
		nicht arbeiten
		lesen

Hier darf man parken, aber wie?

facts

Übung 11   Was möchtest du lieber° machen?

Fragen Sie einen Partner / eine Partnerin: „Was möchtest du lieber machen?"

BEISPIEL: schwimmen gehen oder Tennis spielen? →

> **S1:** Was möchtest du lieber machen: schwimmen gehen oder Tennis spielen?
>
> **S2:** Ich möchte lieber Tennis spielen.

1. Zeitung lesen oder im Internet surfen?
2. fernsehen oder einkaufen gehen?
3. ins Café oder ins Kino gehen?
4. deine Familie anrufen oder eine E-Mail schicken?
5. ein Picknick machen oder spazieren gehen?
6. eine Party zu Hause machen oder ausgehen?
7. Freunde treffen oder allein sein?

Übung 12   Pläne für eine Party

Brigitte, Lisa und Anja haben endlich ein Dach (*roof*) über dem Kopf: eine Wohnung auf einem alten Bauernhof (*farm*). Jetzt planen sie eine Party. Setzen Sie passende Modalverben in die Lücken ein.

Brigitte: Also wen _____¹ (*want to*) wir denn einladen?

Lisa: Die Frage ist: Wie viele Leute _____² (*can*) wir denn einladen?

Anja: Im Wohnzimmer _____³ (*can*) bestimmt zwanzig Leute sitzen.

Lisa: Und tanzen _____⁴ (*can*) wir im Garten.

Anja: Und wer _____⁵ (*is supposed to*) für so viele Leute kochen?

Lisa: Ich _____⁶ (*want*) lieber nur ein paar Leute einladen.

Anja: Wir sagen, jeder _____⁷ (*is supposed to*) etwas zum Essen mitbringen.

Brigitte: Ich _____⁸ (*would like to*) Kartoffelsalat machen.

Lisa: Gute Idee. Das ist einfach, und das _____⁹ (*like*) alle.

Anja: Tut mir leid, aber ich _____¹⁰ (*like*) Kartoffelsalat nicht.

Brigitte: Ich _____¹¹ (*can*) auch Pizza oder Lasagne machen.

Lisa: Wir _____¹² (*may*) aber nicht nur Bier servieren, wir _____¹³ (*have to*) auch Mineralwasser oder Cola servieren.

Übung 13   Ein Picknick im Grünen

Einige Mitbewohner im internationalen Studentenwohnheim planen ein Picknick. Wer bringt was mit?

BEISPIEL: Andreas will ein Frisbee mitbringen. Er soll auch Mineralwasser mitbringen.

Jürgen aus München	wollen	Brot und Käse (*cheese*)	kaufen
Stephanie aus den USA	müssen	Mineralwasser	mitbringen
Paola und Maria aus Italien	möchte	Bier	machen
Nagako aus Tokio	sollen	ein Frisbee	
Michel aus Frankreich	können	eine Pizza	
ich		Kartoffelsalat	
		eine Kamera	
		einen Fußball	

Übung 14 Kommst du mit?

Arbeiten Sie zu zweit. Laden Sie Ihren Partner / Ihre Partnerin ein, etwas zu unternehmen (*do*).

BEISPIEL: **S1:** Ich will heute Tennis spielen. Möchtest du mitkommen?

 S2: Nein, leider kann ich nicht. Ich muss nämlich arbeiten.

oder: Ich möchte schon. Leider muss ich …

S1	S2
heute Abend ins Rockkonzert gehen	arbeiten
ins Kino gehen	meine Eltern besuchen
nach (+ *place*) fahren	zu Hause bleiben. (Mein Wagen ist kaputt.)
ins Café gehen	mein Zimmer aufräumen
Tennis spielen	Deutsch lernen (Ich habe eine Prüfung [*test*].)
Mini-Golf spielen	an einem Referat (*paper*) arbeiten
zu einer Party gehen	??
tanzen gehen	
??	

The Imperative°

The imperative is the verb form used to make requests and recommendations and to give instructions, advice, or commands. You are already familiar with imperative forms used in common classroom requests.

Der Imperativ

Bitte nehmen Sie Platz

Wiederholen Sie bitte.	*Repeat, please.*
Hören Sie zu!	*Listen!*
Sagen Sie das auf Deutsch.	*Say that in German.*
Nehmen Sie Platz!	*Be seated!*

These are examples of formal imperatives, used for anyone you would address as **Sie.** There are two additional imperative forms, used for informally addressing one or several people whom you would address individually as **du.** Imperatives in written German often end in an exclamation point, especially to emphasize a request or a command.

Overview of Imperative Forms			
Infinitive	*Formal*	*Informal Singular*	*Informal Plural*
kommen	**Kommen Sie** bald.	**Komm** bald.	**Kommt** bald.
fahren	**Fahren Sie** langsam!	**Fahr** langsam!	**Fahrt** langsam!
anrufen	**Rufen Sie** mich **an.**	**Ruf** mich **an.**	**Ruft** mich **an.**
sprechen	**Sprechen Sie** langsam!	**Sprich** langsam!	**Sprecht** langsam!
arbeiten	**Arbeiten Sie** jetzt!	**Arbeite** jetzt!	**Arbeitet** jetzt!
sein	**Seien Sie** bitte freundlich.	**Sei** bitte freundlich.	**Seid** bitte freundlich.

Formal Imperative

The formal imperative is formed by inverting the subject **(Sie)** and the verb in the present tense.

NOTE:

▶ The formal imperative has the same word order as a yes/no question; only punctuation or intonation identifies it as an imperative.

▶ The imperative of the verb **sein** is irregular.

Seien Sie bitte freundlich!   *Please be friendly.*

Particles and **bitte** with the Imperative

Requests or commands are often softened by adding the word **bitte** and particles such as **doch** and **mal. Bitte** can stand at the beginning, in the middle, or at the end of the sentence. The particles **doch** and **mal** follow the imperative form. They have no English equivalent.

Bitte nehmen Sie Platz.	*Please have a seat.*
Kommen Sie **doch** heute vorbei.	*Why don't you come by today?*
Rufen Sie mich **mal** an.	*Give me a call (some time). (Why don't you give me a call some time?)*

Im Café ist auch oben Platz.

office hour

Übung 15   In der Sprechstunde°

Mary Lerner geht zum Professor in die Sprechstunde. Kreuzen Sie an, ob es um eine Frage oder eine Aufforderung (*request or command*) geht.

	Frage	Aufforderung		Frage	Aufforderung
1.	☐	☐	6.	☐	☐
2.	☐	☐	7.	☐	☐
3.	☐	☐	8.	☐	☐
4.	☐	☐	9.	☐	☐
5.	☐	☐	10.	☐	☐

Informal Imperative

The singular informal imperative is used to request something of anyone you address with **du.** It is formed for most verbs simply by dropping the **-st** ending from the present-tense **du-**form of the verb and omitting the pronoun.

kommen: du **kommst** → **Komm!**

anrufen: du **rufst an** → **Ruf an!**

arbeiten: du **arbeitest** → **Arbeite!**

sprechen: du **sprichst** → **Sprich!**

But: sein: du **bist** → **Sei!**

Verbs that show a vowel change from **a** to **ä** (or **au** to **äu**) in the present tense have no umlaut in the imperative.

du **fährst** → **Fahr!**

du **läufst** → **Lauf!**

The plural informal imperative is used to request something from several persons whom you individually address with **du.**

Kommt doch mal zu uns.	*Why don't you come see us. (lit., Come to us.)*
Fahrt jetzt nach Hause.	*Drive home now.*
Gebt mir bitte etwas zu essen.	*Please give me something to eat.*
Seid doch ruhig!	*Be quiet!*

This imperative form is identical to the **ihr-**form of the present tense, but without the pronoun **ihr.**

[1]*enjoy*

Übung 16 Macht das, bitte!

Ergänzen Sie die Tabelle.

Formal	Informal Sing.	Informal Pl.
1. Kommen Sie, bitte!	Komm, bitte!	_____, bitte!
2. _____ leise, bitte!	Sprich leise, bitte!	_____ leise, bitte!
3. Laden Sie uns bitte ein.	_____ uns bitte _____.	_____ uns bitte _____.
4. _____ doch ruhig!	Sei doch ruhig!	_____ doch ruhig!
5. Fahren Sie langsam!	_____ langsam!	Fahrt langsam!
6. Rufen Sie mich mal an.	_____ mich mal _____.	Ruft mich mal an.
7. _____ das Buch mal.	_____ das Buch mal.	Lest das Buch mal.
8. Machen Sie schnell!	Mach schnell!	_____ schnell!

Übung 17 Wir duzen einander unter Studenten.°

Alle Studenten duzen einander. Setzen Sie die Imperativsätze in die **du**-Form.

BEISPIEL: Bitte, kommen Sie herein. → Bitte, komm herein.

1. Bitte, sprechen Sie etwas langsamer.
2. Arbeiten Sie nicht so viel!
3. Fahren Sie doch am Wochenende mit mir nach Heidelberg.
4. Bleiben Sie doch noch ein bisschen.
5. Besuchen Sie mich mal.
6. Bitte, rufen Sie mich morgen um 10 Uhr an!
7. Gehen Sie doch mal ins Kino.
8. Kommen Sie doch morgen vorbei.
9. Lesen Sie mal dieses Buch.
10. Sehen Sie mal, hier ist ein Foto von meiner Familie.
11. Seien Sie bitte ruhig!

Übung 18 Pläne unter Freunden

Sie möchten Ihren Freunden sagen, was sie alles tun sollen. Machen Sie aus den Fragen Imperativsätze. Benutzen Sie dabei auch **doch, mal** oder **bitte.**

BEISPIEL: Kommt ihr heute Abend vorbei? →
          Kommt bitte heute Abend mal vorbei!

1. Ladet ihr mich ein?
2. Ruft ihr mich morgen an?
3. Holt ihr mich ab?
4. Sprecht ihr immer deutsch?
5. Räumt ihr euer Zimmer auf?
6. Besucht ihr mich am Wochenende?
7. Kommt ihr morgen vorbei?
8. Seid ihr morgen pünktlich?

Übung 19 Situationen im Alltag

Ergänzen Sie die passende Form des Imperativs von **sein.**

1. Ich muss Sie warnen: Autofahren in Deutschland ist ein Abenteuer. _____ bitte vorsichtig!
2. Sie gehen mit zwei Freunden ins Konzert. Diese Freunde sind nie pünktlich und das irritiert Sie. Sie sagen zu ihnen: „_____ aber bitte pünktlich!"
3. Ihr Mitbewohner im Studentenwohnheim ist sehr unordentlich. Sie erwarten Ihre Eltern zu Besuch und bitten ihn: „_____ so nett und räum deine Sachen auf!"
4. Drei Mitbewohner im Studentenwohnheim spielen um drei Uhr morgens immer noch laute Musik. Sie klopfen irritiert gegen die Wand und rufen: „Zum Donnerwetter, _____ endlich ruhig!"
5. Frau Kümmel zu Frau Honig: „_____ bitte so nett und kommen Sie morgen vorbei!"

Sprache im Kontext

Videoclips

A Wie sind die Tagesroutinen von Jan und Beatrice? Was machen sie morgens und abends? Schauen Sie sich die Interviews mit Jan und Beatrice an und ergänzen Sie die Tabelle.

	Jan	Beatrice
Morgens	*7 Uhr – aufstehen*	
Abends		*0–1 Uhr – ins Bett gehen*

B Schauen Sie sich das Interview mit Jasmin an und ergänzen Sie die Informationen.

1. Jasmin _____ um 8 Uhr.
2. Um _____ oder _____ Uhr kommt sie von der Arbeit nach Hause.
3. Sie geht ungefähr um 22 Uhr ins _____.
4. Am Wochenende _____ sie lange, macht Sport oder geht _____.
5. Sie geht gern _____ _____.

C Und Sie? Machen Sie eine Tabelle für Ihre eigene (*own*) Tagesroutine. Erzählen Sie dann einem Partner / einer Partnerin, wie Ihr typischer Tag aussieht.

Lesen

Zum Thema

A Was trifft zu?

1. Wo wohnen Sie? Ich wohne …

☐ in einer Stadt.
☐ auf dem Land.
☐ in einem kleinen Dorf (*village*).
☐ in einem Vorort von _____.

2. Wie wohnen Sie? Ich wohne …

☐ in einem Studentenwohnheim.
☐ allein / mit anderen in einer Wohnung.
☐ bei meinen Eltern.
☐ ???

3. Wie kommen Sie zur Uni?

☐ Ich fahre mit dem Auto zur Uni.
☐ Ich benutze die öffentlichen Verkehrsmittel (den Bus, die U-Bahn [*subway*] usw.).
☐ Ich wohne auf dem Campus und gehe entweder zu Fuß (*on foot*) oder fahre mit dem Fahrrad.
☐ Ich wohne in der Nähe von der Uni und gehe entweder zu Fuß zur Uni oder fahre mit dem Fahrrad.

4. Für die Fahrt (*trip*) brauche ich …

☐ eine halbe Stunde oder weniger (*less*).
☐ eine Stunde oder weniger.
☐ mehr als eine Stunde.

B Ergänzen Sie die folgenden Aussagen.

1. Ich muss (nicht) früh aufstehen, denn…

2. Die meisten Studenten und Studentinnen an meiner Uni pendeln (*commute*) (nicht). Sie …

Auf den ersten Blick

A Look at the text without reading it. What type of text is "In der S-Bahn komme ich endlich zum Lesen"? What is your evidence?

☐ a blog about the life of students
☐ short personal reports in a newspaper
☐ letters to the editor

B Scan the title and subtitle, the photographs and captions and the boldfaced text. What type of information can you gather about the content of the reading? While you should avoid reading the text word for word, it is important to understand the article's subtitle: "Studierende aus dem Münchner Umland berichten über Vor- und Nachteile ihres Alltags als Pendler." Before you look up any words, see if you can guess the meaning of **Studierende** and **Münchner Umland**. **Erzählen** and **berichten** are synonyms. Accompanying each picture is a first-person **(ich)** narration. Can you guess then what **erzählen** and **berichten** mean? You know what **Tag** means. Can you guess the meaning of **Alltag?**

C **Guessing from Context.** As you read a text, you may be tempted to look up most of the words you do not know. Before reaching for a dictionary in book form or online, however, try to guess the meaning of words. Draw from your knowledge of cognates and the context.

◗ Guess the meaning of the compound nouns **Umland, Nachtleben,** and **Vororte** from the components and context.

◗ Look for related words and see if you can guess the meaning. If you know the meaning of the noun **Pendler** (*commuter*), you can probably guess the meaning of the verb **pendeln.**

◗ In this text there are a couple of examples of verbs used as nouns, for example **pendeln** = *to commute,* **das Pendeln** = (here) *commuting.* Can you find another example?

◗ Note the opposites **Vor- und Nachteile** in the subtitle. The hyphen after **Vor** indicates that it shares the stem **Teile** with the following word. Which do you think means "advantages" and which "disadvantages"?

- The comparative in German often parallels that in English with the **-er,** for example "pretty, prettier" and **schön, schöner.** Can you find another comparative in the text and guess its meaning?

- The expression **seit einem Jahr** appears several times in the text. From the context, can you guess what it means?

- Can you guess at the meaning of **entweder ... oder** in the sentence: **In die Uni komme ich entweder mit der BOB oder mit der S-Bahn?**

D **Using a dictionary.** When you find you really must use a dictionary, consider the following.

- Some forms found in texts differ from those listed in the dictionaries. For example, nouns and pronouns are listed in the nominative singular; verbs are listed under their infinitive forms; the comparatives of adjectives will not be listed. For example, you won't find **schöner** (*more beautiful*), but you will find **schön.**

- Many compound words are not listed in dictionaries. To discover their meaning, look up the components and determine the meaning of the compound from the definitions of its components.

- Some words have multiple meanings. Read through all possible meanings in the dictionary entry and choose the correct meaning of the word based on its use in the text.

For practice in using the dictionary, do the following exercise:

- How many meanings do you find for the words **pendeln** and **ziehen?** Which meanings of the words are used in the text?

- Under which entry would you find the verbs **stört, nervt,** and **vermisst?** Can you guess the meanings without looking them up?

- Underline all the words in the text that you do not understand. Choose five and look them up. In what form do they appear in the dictionary? How many meanings are given? Which meaning best fits the context?

„In der S-Bahn komme ich endlich zum Lesen"

Studenten erzählen: Studierende aus dem Münchner Umland berichten über Vor- und Nachteile ihres Alltags als Pendler

Kathrin Schwinghammer, 20:

5 „Ich komme aus Baierbrunn, dort wohne ich bei meinen Eltern. Seit zwei Semestern studiere ich Chemie an der LMU[1]. Ich fahre immer mit dem Auto, eine Kommilitonin[2] und ich bilden eine Fahrgemeinschaft. Mit
10 öffentlichen Verkehrsmitteln würden wir noch länger brauchen[3]."

Kathrin Schwinghammer fährt mit dem Auto zur Universität.

---

[1] = Ludwig-Maximilians-Universität   [2] *fellow student*   [3] *würden ... we would need even longer*

Dominik Bader, 22:

„Ich studiere Physikalische Technik an der
FH[4] und wohne in Seefeld bei Herrsching.
15 In meinem Elternhaus habe ich fast eine
eigene Wohnung; da sehe ich keinen Grund,
auszuziehen. Wenn ich in die Stadt ziehen
würde, müsste ich neben dem Studium
arbeiten[5]. Selbst verdientes Geld möchte ich
20 aber nicht in die Miete stecken[6], sondern
lieber in eine Reise. Ich will bald nach
Südafrika reisen. Am Pendeln stört mich vor
allem, dass ich immer so früh aufstehen
muss. Mich freut es aber, wenn ich in der
25 S-Bahn Leute treffe, die ich schon lange
nicht mehr gesehen habe."

Dominik Bader stört am Pendeln
das frühe Aufstehen.

Marianne Rösler, 21:

„Ich wohne seit einem Jahr nicht mehr zu
Hause. Aus dem kleinen Dorf, in dem meine
30 Eltern wohnen, bin ich nach Holzkirchen
gezogen[7], das ist nicht weit entfernt. Dort
wohne ich mit meinem Freund zusammen.
Näher an der Stadt möchte ich nicht
leben. Ich studiere an der LMU Geschichte
35 und Volkswirtschaftslehre und komme ins
zweite Semester. In die Uni komme ich
entweder mit der BOB[8] oder der S-Bahn.
Das dauert jedes Mal eine gute halbe
Stunde. Ein klarer Nachteil, wenn man
40 hier draußen wohnt, ist das fehlende[9]
Nachtleben. Aber damit kann ich leben –
ich bin kein Freund von Großstädten."

Marianne Rösler vermisst auf dem
Land nur das Nachtleben.

Robert Drozkowski, 21:

„In den nächsten Jahren möchte ich auf
45 jeden Fall in die Innenstadt ziehen.
Momentan bin ich aber noch zufrieden bei
meinen Eltern in Unterhaching. Dies ist eine
nette Gemeinde, in der ich mich wohl
fühle[10]. Es ist sicher schöner als viele andere
50 Vororte, andererseits hält mich hier auch
nichts Besonderes[11] – wenn ich die
Möglichkeit habe, mit Freunden in eine WG
in der Stadt zu ziehen, werde ich das sofort
machen. Ich studiere seit einem Jahr
55 Politikwissenschaften. Dafür fahre ich täglich
knapp zwei Stunden S-Bahn. Das Pendeln
zwischen Unterhaching und der Uni nervt
zwar, hat aber auch einen Vorteil: Während
der Fahrt komme ich endlich zum Lesen."

Robert Drozkowski möchte bald
nach München ziehen.

Aus: *Süddeutsche Zeitung online* 13.10.2006, www.sueddeutsche.de

---

[4] = Hochschule für angewandte Wissenschaften – FH München [5]Wenn ... *If I were to move to the city, I would have to work and study at the same time.* [6]in ... *put into the rent* [7]bin ... *I moved to Holzkirchen* [8] = Bayrische Oberland Bahn *Bavarian Regional Rail* [9]*lacking* [10]Dies ist ... *This is a nice community in which I feel comfortable.*
[11]andererseits ... *on the other hand, there is nothing in particular keeping me here*

Zum Text

A Überfliegen Sie (*Scan*) den Text und ergänzen (*complete*) Sie die Tabelle! Lesen Sie *nicht* Wort für Wort!

Name	Kathrin Schwinghammer	Dominik Bader	Marianne Rösler	Robert Drozkowski
wohnt in	*Baierbrunn*			
wohnt	*bei den Eltern*			
studiert	*Chemie*			
wo	*an der LMU*			
Wie kommt er/sie zur Uni?	*fährt mit dem Auto*			

B Schauen Sie sich die Liste unten an. Ist das ein Vorteil des Pendelns oder ein Nachteil?

	Vorteil	Nachteil
1. Man verbringt viel Zeit damit.	☐	☐
2. Man muss früh aufstehen.	☐	☐
3. Man kann im Grünen wohnen.	☐	☐
4. Man kann bei den Eltern billig wohnen.	☐	☐
5. Man kann in der S-Bahn lesen.	☐	☐

C Schauen Sie sich die Fotos und ihre Unterschriften (*captions*) noch mal an. Drücken (*Express*) die Unterschriften etwas Neutrales, einen Vor- oder Nachteil des Pendelns oder einen Wunsch (*wish*) aus?

	Neutral	Ein Wunsch	Vorteil des Pendelns	Nachteil des Pendelns
1. „Kathrin Schwinghammer fährt mit dem Auto zur Universität."	☐	☐	☐	☐
2. „Dominik Bader stört am Pendeln das frühe Aufstehen."	☐	☐	☐	☐
3. „Marianne Rösler vermisst auf dem Land nur das Nachtleben."	☐	☐	☐	☐
4. „Robert Drozkowski möchte bald nach München ziehen."	☐	☐	☐	☐

D Lesen Sie den Text noch einmal. Können Sie die Liste aus Aktivität C ergänzen? Suchen Sie im Text! Welche Sätze sind neutral, ein Wunsch, oder ein Vor- oder Nachteil des Pendelns oder draußen Wohnens?

1. neutral: „*Ich komme aus Baierbrunn*", ...

2. ein Wunsch:

3. Vorteil des Pendelns:

4. Nachteil des Pendelns:

Zu guter Letzt

sites worth seeing

Ein Podcast über Sehenswertes° an der Uni

During your German learning experience using **Deutsch: Na klar!** you will practice your German in presentational mode through a series of four podcasts. The first podcast deals with life at the university you are attending. Take the following steps to create your podcasts.

Schritt 1: Work with two other students in the class and make a list of three interesting places to see or things to do at your university.

Schritt 2: In your group, jot down words and phrases (in German) to describe these places or activities.

Schritt 3: Use the words and phrases to write a three-sentence description of each point of interest. This will serve as a script for the podcast.

Schritt 4: Using a digital video camera or other means of digital recording, visit the places you have chosen to present and film each member of the group describing one place, using the scripts you have written. You can be creative and go beyond the scripts, using as much German as you can. Make it a creative tour in German. (If you do not have ready access to a digital camera, check with your language lab or technology office.)

Schritt 5: Edit the podcast, adding titles, and/or vocabulary words you may want to highlight, and present it to the class. The podcast should not be longer than three minutes.

Schritt 6: Ask the class which site on campus that you presented was the most interesting to them, and why.

Wortschatz

Tage und Tageszeiten	Days and Times of Day
der **Morgen**	morning
der **Vormittag**	morning, before noon
der **Mittag**	noon
der **Nachmittag**	afternoon
der **Abend**	evening
die **Nacht**	night
heute **Morgen**	this morning
heute **Nachmittag**	this afternoon
morgen früh	tomorrow morning
morgen **Abend**	tomorrow evening
morgens	in the morning, mornings
vormittags	before noon
mittags	at noon
nachmittags	in the afternoon, afternoons
abends	in the evening, evenings
nachts	at night, nights
montags	Mondays, on Monday(s)
dienstags	Tuesdays, on Tuesday(s)
mittwochs	Wednesdays, on Wednesday(s)
donnerstags	Thursdays, on Thursday(s)
freitags	Fridays, on Friday(s)

samstags; sonnabends	Saturdays, on Saturday(s)
sonntags	Sundays, on Sunday(s)

Unterhaltung	Entertainment
das **Ballett, -e**	ballet
die **Disco, -s**	disco; dance club
in die **Disco gehen**	to go clubbing
das **Fernsehen**	watching television
der **Film, -e**	film
das **Kino, -s**	cinema, (movie) theater
ins **Kino gehen**	to go to the movies
die **Komödie, -n**	comedy
das **Konzert, -e**	concert
ins **Konzert gehen**	to go to a concert
der **Krimi, -s**	crime, detective, mystery film or book
die **Oper, -n**	opera
in die **Oper gehen**	to go to the opera
das **Theater, -**	(stage) theater
ins **Theater gehen**	to go to the theater
das **Theaterstück, -e**	play, (stage) drama
die **Tragödie, -n**	tragedy

Verben mit trennbaren Präfixen	Verbs with Separable Prefixes
ab•holen	to pick up (from a place)
an•fangen (fängt an)	to begin
an•rufen	to call (up)
auf•räumen	to clean up, straighten up
auf•stehen	to get up; to stand up
auf•wachen	to wake up
aus•gehen	to go out
ein•kaufen (gehen)	to (go) shop(ping)
ein•laden (lädt ein)	to invite
ein•schlafen (schläft ein)	to fall asleep
fern•sehen (sieht fern)	to watch television
mit•kommen	to come along
vorbei•kommen	to come by
vor•haben (hat vor)	to plan (to do)
zu•hören	to listen
zurück•kommen	to return, come back

Modalverben	Modal Verbs
dürfen (darf)	to be permitted to; may
können (kann)	to be able to; can
mögen (mag)	to care for; to like
möchte	would like to
müssen (muss)	to have to; must
sollen	to be supposed to; ought, should
wollen (will)	to want to; to plan to

Uhrzeiten	Time
die Minute, -n	minute
die Sekunde, -n	second
die Stunde, -n	hour
Um wie viel Uhr?	At what time?
Wie spät ist es? / Wie viel Uhr ist es?	What time is it?
Es ist eins. / Es ist ein Uhr.	It's one o'clock.
halb: halb zwei	half: half past one, one-thirty

nach: fünf nach zwei	after: five after two
um: um zwei	at: at two
Viertel: Es ist Viertel nach/vor zwei.	quarter: It's a quarter after/to two.
vor: fünf vor zwei	to, of: five to/of two

Sonstiges	Other
frühstücken	to eat breakfast
spazieren gehen	to go for a walk
Ich gehe spazieren.	I'm going for a walk.
treffen (trifft)	to meet
die Bibliothek, -en	library
das Fitnesscenter, -	gym
der Plan, ¨e	plan
die Tasse, -n	cup
eine Tasse Kaffee	a cup of coffee
die Vorlesung, -en	(university) lecture
der Vortrag, ¨e	lecture
die Woche, -n	week
pro Woche	per week
das Wochenende, -n	weekend
am liebsten: möchte am liebsten	would like to (do) most
doch	(intensifying particle often used with imperatives)
früh	early
gemütlich	cozy, cozily
gewöhnlich	usual(ly)
lieber: möchte lieber	would rather
mal	(softening particle often used with imperatives)
man	one, people, you, they
Hier darf man nicht parken.	You may not park here.
spannend	suspenseful, exciting
spät	late

Das kann ich nun!

1. Wie viel Uhr ist es? Sagen Sie die Zeit auf Deutsch: 6.00; 9.30; 12.45; 14.07; 17.15.

2. Was machen Sie gewöhnlich zwischen 6 Uhr morgens und 18 Uhr abends? Nennen Sie drei Dinge (things).

3. Was möchten Sie am Wochenende machen? Nennen Sie drei Dinge.

4. Bilden Sie Sätze.
   a. ich / morgens / um 7 Uhr / aufstehen
   b. die Vorlesung / um 11 Uhr / aufhören
   c. wir / einladen / 20 Leute / zur Party
   d. was / du / vorhaben / am Wochenende / ?

5. Wie sagt man das auf Deutsch?
   a. Please drop by at 6:00 p.m. (familiar singular)
   b. I can't go to the movies. I have to work.
   c. Please call me on Saturday morning. (formal)
   d. Would you like to go to the movies tonight? (familiar plural)
   e. Parking is not allowed here. (familiar singular)

Auf dem Markt

Kapitel 5

Einkaufen

In diesem Kapitel

- ▶ **Themen:** Talking about clothing, colors, types of foods, names of stores and shops
- ▶ **Grammatik:** The dative case; verbs that require the dative; dative prepositions; **wo, wohin,** and **woher**
- ▶ **Lesen:** „Die Obstverkäuferin" (Leonhard Thoma)
- ▶ **Landeskunde:** Clothing sizes, shopping, prices, weights and measures
- ▶ **Zu guter Letzt:** Eine Umfrage in der Klasse

VIDEOCLIPS

Einkaufen: was und wo?

144

A Sie sehen im Bild ein Kaufhaus. Wo findet man alles?

BEISPIELE: Computer findet man im vierten Stock.
Bücher findet man im Erdgeschoss.

4	Computer TV/DVD/CD Center Foto/Optik Elektrogeräte Telefon/Handy Shop Kundenrestaurant Toiletten
3	Bettwäsche Gardinen Teppiche Orientteppiche Geschenkartikel Glas/Porzellan Haushaltswaren Reisebüro
2	Jeans-Wear Mode-Boutiquen Kinderkonfektion Babywäsche Schuhe Sport/Fahrräder Camping Friseursalon
1	Damenkonfektion Damenwäsche Herrenkonfektion Herrenartikel Accessoires Handschuhe Bademoden Uhren/Schmuck
E¹	Lederwaren Lotto/Tabak Zeitschriften Parfümerie Kosmetik/Drogerie Schreibwaren Bücher Süßigkeiten
U²	Lebensmittel Toiletten

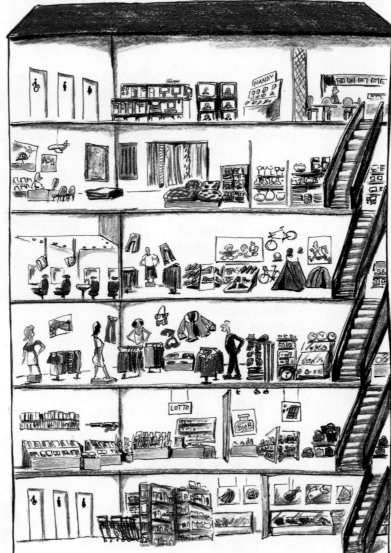

1. Schreibwaren
2. Schuhe
3. Pullover
4. Sportartikel
5. Telefonapparate
6. Teppiche
7. Handys
8. Brokkoli
9. DVD-Spieler
10. Parfüm
11. Fernseher
12. Kaffeetassen
13. Butter
14. Shampoo

- im Erdgeschoss
- im vierten Stock
- im Untergeschoss
- im dritten Stock
- im ersten Stock
- im zweiten Stock

¹E = Erdgeschoss (*ground floor*)
²U = Untergeschoss (*basement*)

B Sie hören nun vier Ansagen (*announcements*) im Kaufhaus. Markieren Sie, was die Sprecher beschreiben.

1. Kosmetik   Kameras   Fahrräder
2. Schmuck   Betten   Schuhe
3. Bücher   Kaffeemaschinen   Lederjacken
4. Jeans   Lampen   Fernseher

Wörter im Kontext

Thema 1: Kleidungsstücke

A **Klamotten, Klamotten!** Was sehen Sie im Schrank? Kreuzen Sie an!

Ich sehe ...

- ☐ einen **Hut**
- ☐ ein **Hemd**
- ☐ ein **Kleid**
- ☐ ein Polohemd
- ☐ ein **Sakko**
- ☐ ein Sweatshirt
- ☐ eine **Badehose**
- ☐ einen **Anzug**
- ☐ **Socken**
- ☐ ein **T-Shirt**
- ☐ einen **Badeanzug**
- ☐ einen Wintermantel
- ☐ einen **Rock**
- ☐ einen **Rucksack**
- ☐ einen **Schal**
- ☐ **Hausschuhe**
- ☐ **Jeans**
- ☐ einen **Koffer**
- ☐ einen **Pullover**

B Wer **trägt** was?

BEISPIEL: Die Frau trägt einen Schal, einen Mantel, eine Bluse, ...

C Was haben Sie alles zu Hause in Ihrem Kleiderschrank?

BEISPIEL: Ich habe ein Sakko, 15 T-Shirts, Hemden, 5 Hosen, Socken und Schuhe in meinem Kleiderschrank.

Analyse

Die Koffer-Checkliste notiert Kleidungsstücke für den Urlaub (*vacation*).

▶ Welche Kleidungsstücke sind für den Winter? Welche sind für den Sommer?

BEISPIEL: Sandalen sind für den Sommer.

▶ Welche Sachen auf dieser Liste tragen Sie besonders gern?

▶ Suchen Sie aus der Liste vier zusammengesetzte Wörter (*compounds*).

Bilden Sie nun Ihre eigenen Wörter.

BEISPIEL: Bade- + Hose = Badehose

Bade-		Anzug
Cord-		Mantel
Baumwoll-	+	Hose
Trainings-		Hemd
Leder-		Jacke
Regen-		Schuhe

Koffer-Checkliste
Für den Urlaub

☐ T-Shirts   ☐ Sweatshirts
☐ Shorts   ☐ Baumwollhosen
☐ Cordhosen   ☐ Trainings- und
                      Jogginganzüge
☐ Regenmantel   ☐ Sportschuhe
☐ Sandalen   ☐ Unterwäsche
☐ Badeanzug   ☐ Jacke
☐ Badehose   ☐ Handschuhe
☐ Blusen   ☐ Stiefel
☐ Röcke   ☐ Pullover
☐ Kleider   ☐ Mütze
☐ Hemden

Aktivität 1   Eine Reise nach Südspanien

Sie hören ein Gespräch zwischen Bettina und Markus. Sie planen für die Semesterferien eine Reise an die Küste von Südspanien mit einer Gruppe von Freunden. Was nimmt man da mit? Sind die Aussagen richtig oder falsch?

	Richtig	Falsch
1. Bettina und Markus nehmen einen Koffer und einen Rucksack mit.	☐	☐
2. Markus nimmt Shorts, ein paar T-Shirts und Jeans mit.	☐	☐
3. Bettina braucht unbedingt einen neuen Badeanzug.	☐	☐
4. Markus empfiehlt ihr, sie soll einen Bikini in Spanien kaufen.	☐	☐
5. Markus hat einen besonderen Gürtel für sein Geld.	☐	☐
6. Bettina steckt ihr Geld in die Schuhe.	☐	☐

Aktivität 2   Was tragen Sie gewöhnlich?

Sagen Sie, was Sie in den folgenden Situationen tragen.

BEISPIEL: Ich trage gewöhnlich Jeans und ein T-Shirt zur Uni. Zur Arbeit trage ich ein Sporthemd, eine Hose und ein Sakko.

zur Arbeit	einen Anzug
zur Uni	einen Badeanzug
im Winter	ein Kleid
im Urlaub auf Hawaii	ein Abendkleid
zu Hause	einen Wintermantel
auf einer Fete	Jeans
zu einer Hochzeit	ein T-Shirt
??	??

Aktivität 3   Ich brauche neue Bekleidung°.

Was brauchen Sie, und wo gibt es das? Was kostet das?

BEISPIEL: **S1:**   Ich brauch dringend ein Polohemd. Wo gibt es hier Polohemden?

S2:   Polohemden gibt es bei Strauss.

S1:   Weißt du, wie viel ein Polohemd da kostet?

S2:   Es gibt Polohemden für 19,95 Euro.

Schals	Schuhe	Polohemden
Blazer	Blusen	

Aktivität 4   Koffer packen!°

Let's pack our bags!

Spielen Sie in Gruppen von vier bis fünf Personen. So spielt man es:

BEISPIEL: **S1:**   Ich packe fünf Bikinis in meinen Koffer.

S2:   Ich packe fünf Bikinis und Sportschuhe in meinen Koffer.

S3:   Ich packe fünf Bikinis, Sportschuhe und Ledersandalen in meinen Koffer.

Wer etwas vergisst (*forgets*) oder falsch sagt, scheidet aus (*is eliminated*).

Thema 2: Beim Einkaufen im Kaufhaus

Julia braucht ein Geburtstagsgeschenk für ihren Vater. Ein **schickes** Hemd kann er immer gebrauchen.

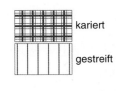

Verkäufer: Bitte sehr?

Julia: Ich möchte meinem Vater ein Sporthemd zum Geburstag schenken. Ich **hoffe,** Sie können mir da **helfen.**

Verkäufer: Welche **Größe** trägt Ihr Vater denn?

Julia: Ich bin **ziemlich sicher,** Größe 42.

Verkäufer: Und welche **Farbe** soll es sein?

Julia: Grün oder blau. Das sind seine Lieblingsfarben.

Verkäufer: **Wie gefällt Ihnen** dieses Hemd in Marineblau? Sehr schick und praktisch.

Julia: Die Farbe gefällt mir nicht so gut. Praktisch ist dunkelblau ja. Haben Sie das vielleicht in Hellblau?

Verkäufer: Hier habe ich ein Hemd in Hellblau **kariert**—sehr sportlich.

Julia: Ist das aus Baumwolle oder Synthetik?

Verkäufer: Wir haben nur Hemden aus Naturfasern (*natural fibers*)! Dies hier ist Baumwolle aus Ägypten.

Julia: Na gut. Das nehme ich dann. Und falls es ihm nicht **passt,** kann er es **umtauschen?**

Verkäufer: **Selbstverständlich,** mit Kassenbon (*receipt*). **Das macht** dann 75 Euro. Sie **zahlen** vorne an der **Kasse.**

Julia: Danke schön.

Verkäufer: Bitte sehr.

Neue Wörter

schickes (schick) stylish
hoffe (hoffen) hope
helfen help
die Größe size
ziemlich fairly
sicher sure
die Farbe color
Wie gefällt Ihnen ...? How do you like . . . ?
passt (passen) fits
umtauschen exchange
selbstverständlich of course
das macht that comes to
zahlen pay
die Kasse cashier, checkout
schenkt (schenken) is giving
empfiehlt (empfehlen) recommends
zeigt (zeigen) shows

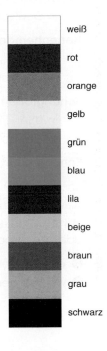

▶ Was passiert im Kaufhaus? Stimmt das oder stimmt das nicht?

	Das stimmt	Das stimmt nicht
1. Julia möchte ihrem Vater ein Sporthemd kaufen.	☐	☐
2. Sie **schenkt** ihm das zum Geburtstag.	☐	☐
3. Er trägt Größe 42.	☐	☐
4. Der Verkäufer **empfiehlt** Julia ein Hemd in Hellblau.	☐	☐
5. Das Hemd in Marineblau gefällt Julia sehr gut.	☐	☐
6. Der Verkäufer **zeigt** Julia ein Hemd aus Baumwolle.	☐	☐
7. Julias Vater kann das Hemd mit Kassenbon umtauschen.	☐	☐

Aktivität 5 Im Kaufhaus

Ergänzen Sie die fehlenden Informationen aus dem Dialog im Thema 2.

1. Die Kundin braucht _____.

2. Der Verkäufer möchte _____ und _____ wissen.

3. Die Kundin braucht _____ 42.

4. Größe 42 _____ dem Vater.

5. Das Hemd in Marineblau _____ ihr nicht.

6. Das Hemd ist aus _____.

7. Die Kundin _____ 75 Euro für das Hemd.

Landeskunde-Info

Size designations in Europe vary greatly from those in North America. Shown below are approximate correlations between U.S. and German sizes.

Kleine Preise auch für große Größen! Tolle Angebote,[1] wie z.B. sportliche Pullover in modischen Dessins

ab **€50,-**

[1]Tolle … *great deals*

Für Damen: Kleider, Mäntel, Jacken, Blusen

in USA	6	8	10	12	14	16
in Deutschland	34	36	38	40	42	44

Für Herren: Mäntel, Anzüge, Sakkos

in USA	36	38	40	42	44
in Deutschland	46	48	50	52	54

Herrenhemden

in USA	14	14½	15	15½	16	16½
in Deutschland	36	37	38	39	40	42

Schuhgrößen für Damen

in USA	5½	6½	7½	8½	9½	10½	11½	12½
in Deutschland	36	37	38/39	39/40	41	42	43/44	44/45

Schuhgrößen für Herren

in USA	6½	7½	8½	9½	10½	11½	12½	13½
in Deutschland	39/40	41	42	43/44	44/45	46	47	48/49

In many stores you will also find the sizes S, M, L, and XL (small, medium, large, and extra-large) for clothing. In addition, shoes are sometimes labeled with American sizes.

▶ Welche deutsche Schuhgröße haben Sie?

▶ Welche deutsche Hemden- oder Blusengröße haben Sie?

Aktivität 6 Gespräche im Geschäft

Was brauchen die Leute? In welcher Größe und in welcher Farbe? Ergänzen Sie die Tabelle.

	Was?	In welcher Größe?	In welcher Farbe?
Dialog 1			
Dialog 2			
Dialog 3			
Dialog 4			

Aktivität 7 Wer trägt was?

Finden Sie folgende Personen und bilden Sie Fragen. Wer **ja** sagt muss rechts unterschreiben (*sign*).

BEISPIEL: Wer trägt gern Rot?
Frage: Trägst du gern Rot?

Frage	Unterschrift
1. Wessen (*Whose*) Lieblingsfarbe ist Lila?	_____
2. Wem steht Blau sehr gut?	_____
3. Wem steht Grün nicht gut?	_____
4. Wer trägt gern bunte (*colorful*) Sachen?	_____
5. Wer trägt gern gestreifte oder karierte Sachen?	_____
6. Wer trägt Größe 39 in Hemden oder Blusen?	_____
7. Wer braucht die Schuhgröße 42?	_____

Aktivität 8 Wer ist das?

Beschreiben Sie, was und welche Farben jemand in Ihrem Deutschkurs trägt. Sagen Sie den Namen der Person nicht. Die anderen im Kurs müssen erraten (*guess*), wer das ist.

BEISPIEL: Diese Person trägt eine Bluse. Die Bluse ist rotweiß gestreift. Sie trägt auch Jeans; die sind blau. Und ihre Schuhe sind, hm, lila. Wer ist das? —Das ist Winona.

Aktivität 9 Ein Gespräch

Schritt 1: Arbeiten Sie zu zweit. Benutzen Sie die Wörter und Ausdrücke im Kasten und schreiben Sie zusammen ein Gespräch zwischen einem Verkäufer / einer Verkäuferin und einem Kunden / einer Kundin. Was für Kleidung möchten Sie kaufen? Wie beginnt das Gespräch?

Schritt 2: Spielen Sie jetzt das Gespräch zu zweit.

Sprach-Info

To talk about how clothing fits, how it looks, and whether you like it, you can use the following expressions.

Gefällt Ihnen dieses Hemd?

Do you like this shirt?

Ja, es **gefällt mir.**

Yes, I like it.

Größe 42 **passt ihr** bestimmt.

Size 42 will fit her for sure.

Das Hemd **steht dir** gut.

The shirt looks good on you.

Sprach-Info

The dative case is used with adjectives, sometimes in conjunction with the adverb **zu** (*too*).

300 Euro für dieses Kleid? Das ist **mir zu teuer.**

300 euros for this dress? *That's too expensive (for me).*

 Siehe *Verbs with a Dative Object Only*, S. 162.

Thema 3: Lebensmittel

Sonnenblumenbrot
je 750-g Laib

1.80
1 kg = 2,40

Schwälbchen
Haltbare Vollmilch
3,8% Fett,
1 l Packung
0,76

0.66
3,8%

Allgäuer Bio-Käse
Gouda, Tilsiter oder Butterkäse,
Schnittkäse/halbfester Schnittkäse
aus Deutschland, 45% Fett i.Tr.
0,95

100 g nur
Bio **0.67**

Orig, Lechtaler Salami
im Heißrauch gegart
100g

-.89

Bodensee-Äpfel
Kl.I, Sorten:Elstar, Jonagold,
Braeburn oder Idared
3-kg-Karton
(1 kg = 0,74)

2.22

Herz Allgäuer Bergkäse
45% Fett i. Tr.
100g

-.99

Franz. Speisekartoffel
Kl. 1, vorw. festkochend
Sorte Agatha
2,5 kg-Netz
1 kg = 0,80

1.99

AlnaturA Tee
verschiedene
Sorten,
100 g = 4,97 €

20 Aufgußbeutel
1.49

AlnaturA Bio-Säfte
verschiedene Sorten,
1 l = 2,25 €, 0,75 l Packung

1.69

A Welche Wörter kennen Sie schon? Kreuzen Sie an und geben Sie die englische Bedeutung. Wenn Sie die Wörter nicht kennen, fragen Sie andere Studenten/Studentinnen im Kurs.

- ☐ der Apfel
- ☐ der Aufschnitt
- ☐ die Banane
- ☐ das Bier
- ☐ der Blumenkohl
- ☐ der Brokkoli
- ☐ das Brot
- ☐ das Brötchen
- ☐ die Butter
- ☐ das Ei
- ☐ das Eis
- ☐ die Erdbeere
- ☐ frisch
- ☐ gefroren

- ☐ die Gurke
- ☐ das Hähnchen
- ☐ der Joghurt
- ☐ die Karotte
- ☐ die Kartoffel
- ☐ der Käse
- ☐ der Keks
- ☐ der Kuchen
- ☐ die Milch
- ☐ das Müsli
- ☐ der Pfeffer
- ☐ die Rasiercreme
- ☐ das Rindfleisch
- ☐ der Saft

- ☐ das Salz
- ☐ der Schinken
- ☐ das Schnitzel
- ☐ das Schweinefleisch
- ☐ der Tee
- ☐ das Toilettenpapier
- ☐ die Tomate
- ☐ die Traube
- ☐ der Truthahn
- ☐ das Wasser
- ☐ die Wurst
- ☐ die Zahnpasta
- ☐ zart
- ☐ der Zucker

B Nennen Sie drei **Lebensmittel** oder Produkte für jede Kategorie:

Obst	Gemüse	Fleisch	Getränke
_____	_____	_____	_____
_____	_____	_____	_____
_____	_____	_____	_____

C Mini-Umfrage: Interviewen Sie drei Studentinnen/Studenten. Was essen sie **jeden** Tag zum **Frühstück**? Zum **Mittagessen**? Zum **Abendessen**?

Landeskunde-Info

Deutsche kaufen in großen, modernen **Supermärkten** ein, aber es gibt immer noch viele Spezialgeschäfte, besonders in kleinen Städten, wie die **Metzgerei**, die **Bäckerei**, die **Konditorei**, den **Getränkeladen** und den **Obst- und Gemüsestand** auf dem Markt. **Medikamente** auf Rezept kann man in Deutschland nicht in einer **Drogerie** kaufen, sondern nur in einer **Apotheke**. Im **Bioladen** gibt es Produkte, die nicht mit chemischen Mitteln behandelt (*treated*) sind.

○ Kaufen Sie manchmal in Spezialgeschäften ein? Wenn ja, wo und was? Kaufen Sie auch im Bioladen ein? Welche Produkute?

○ Kaufen Sie lieber im Supermarkt oder in kleinen Geschäften ein?

Sprach-Info

The metric system is used in German-speaking countries. The following abbreviations are commonly used:

1 kg = 1 Kilogramm = 1000 Gramm = 2 Pfund

500 g = 500 Gramm = 1 Pfund

1000 ml = 1000 Milliliter

0,75 l = 0,75 Liter

1 l = 1 Liter

Kl. I = Klasse I (*top quality*)

Stck. = Stück (*piece*)

Aktivität 10 Kleine Läden

Was kauft man wo? Sagen Sie, wo man diese Dinge kaufen kann.

BEISPIEL: Brötchen kauft man in der Bäckerei.

am Obst- und Gemüsestand · in der Metzgerei · in der Bäckerei · im Bioladen · in der Konditorei · in der Drogerie

1. Brötchen
2. Trauben
3. Rindfleisch
4. Zahnpasta
5. Schinken
6. Blumenkohl
7. Vollkornbrot
8. Bio-Milch
9. Apfelstrudel

Aktivität 11 Wo? Was? Wie viel?

Sie hören drei Dialoge: in einer Bäckerei, auf dem Markt und in einer Metzgerei. Kreuzen Sie das richtige Geschäft an. Ergänzen Sie die Tabelle.

	Markt	Bäckerei	Metzgerei	Was?	Preis?
Dialog 1					
Dialog 2					
Dialog 3					

Aktivität 12 Preiswert einkaufen!

Stellen Sie sich vor, Sie haben nur 10 Euro für Essen und Trinken übrig und müssen damit ein ganzes Wochenende auskommen. Wählen Sie Waren aus den Anzeigen (*ads*) aus. Vergleichen Sie (*compare*) Ihre Listen im Kurs.

BEISPIEL: Wir kaufen ein Kastenweißbrot für €1,59; Schinkenaufschnitt für €1,79; Schokopudding für €0,79; Pizza für €1,99 und Fischstäbchen für €1,11.

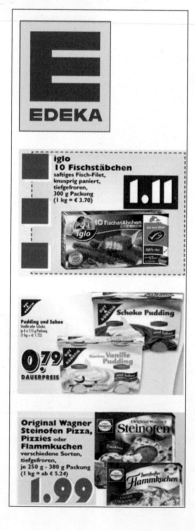

Aktivität 13 Einkaufstag für Jutta

Jutta muss einkaufen. Sie gibt nämlich eine Party. Schreiben Sie einen Text zu jedem Bild. Benutzen Sie Elemente aus beiden Spalten (*columns*) unten.

So beginnt die Geschichte.

Jutta gibt am Wochenende eine Party. Deshalb geht sie heute einkaufen ...

Zuerst geht sie ...	Obst und Gemüse – alles ganz frisch.
Zuletzt geht sie ...	Brot, Brötchen und Käsekuchen.
Dort kauft sie ...	und geht nach Hause.
Da gibt es ...	zur Bäckerei.
Dann geht sie ...	zum Lebensmittelgeschäft.
Jutta braucht auch ...	zur Metzgerei.
Deshalb geht sie auch ...	Würstchen zum Grillen.
Jetzt hat sie alles ...	Kaffee, Zucker, Milch und Käse.
In der Bäckerei kauft sie ...	auf den Markt.
Auf dem Markt kauft sie ...	Blumenkohl und Kartoffeln.
	Äpfel, Bananen und Trauben – alles ganz frisch.

Sprach-Info

The following words will help you organize your writing and help you put statements in order of occurrence.

zuerst first

deshalb therefore

dann then

zuletzt finally

Using these connectors will enable you to narrate effectively in German. Remember that if you begin your sentence with one of these connectors, your verb will immediately follow it.

Zuerst geht Jutta in die Bäckerei.

1.

2.

3.

4.

5.

Aktivität 14 Ein Menü für eine Party

Schritt 1: Planen Sie mit anderen Studenten eine Party am Wochenende. Was wollen Sie anbieten (*serve*)? Wählen Sie Getränke oder Speisen aus jeder Gruppe aus und bestimmen (*determine*) Sie die Zeit.

Zeit	heute Abend, am Wochenende, am Samstag, ???
zum Essen	Würstchen, Steaks, Hamburger, Kartoffelsalat, Kartoffelchips, Pommes frites, Salat, Gemüse, ???
zum Nachtisch	Eis, Pudding, frische Erdbeeren, Käsekuchen, ???
zum Trinken	Mineralwasser (Sprudel), Bier, Wein, ???

Schritt 2: Sprechen Sie über Ihre Pläne mit zwei oder drei anderen Studentinnen/Studenten im Kurs. Folgen Sie dem Modell.

S1	S2
1. Wollen wir _____ _____ grillen?	2. Gut. Machen wir _____ mit _____.
3. Und was servieren wir zum Nachtisch?	4. Warum nicht _____ oder _____? Was sollen wir dazu trinken?
5. _____ und _____ natürlich!	6a. Na, gut. b. Also, _____ schmeckt doch nicht dazu. Ich schlage vor (*suggest*), wir trinken _____.

In der Metzgerei kauft man Fleisch und Wurst.

Grammatik im Kontext

The Dative Case°

Der Dativ

As you have learned, the nominative case is the case of the subject; the accusative case is used for direct objects and with a number of prepositions. These cases are signaled by special endings of articles and possessive adjectives, as well as by different forms for personal pronouns.

Nominative		Accusative
Wer	braucht	einen Rucksack?
Der Student	braucht	einen Rucksack.
Der Rucksack	ist	für ihn.

Like the nominative and accusative cases, the dative has special forms for pronouns and endings for articles and possessive adjectives. You have already learned one common expression that uses dative pronouns.

Wie geht es **dir?**	*How are you?* (informal) (lit.: *How is it going for you?*)
Wie geht es **Ihnen?**	*How are you?* (formal)

The dative case serves several distinct functions. It is used primarily:

▶ for indirect objects (indicating the person to/for whom something is done); it answers the question **wem** (whom? to/for whom?).

Wem gehört der Koffer?	*To whom does the suitcase belong?*
Er zeigt **ihm** den Koffer.	*He shows the suitcase to him.*

▶ with certain verbs and expressions, such as **gehören** and **Spaß machen.**

Der Rucksack **gehört ihm.**	*The backpack belongs to him.*
Wandern **macht** mir **Spaß.**	*I like to hike.* (lit.: *Hiking is fun for me.*)

▶ with specific prepositions, such as **mit** and **zu.**

Der Kunde geht **mit dem** Rucksack **zur** Kasse.	*The customer goes to the cash register with the backpack.*

Personal Pronouns in the Dative

Gehört der Rucksack Thomas?	*Does the backpack belong to Thomas?*
Ja, der gehört **ihm.**	*Yes, it belongs to him.*
Wie gefällt **dir** der Rucksack?	*How do you like the backpack?*
Der Rucksack gefällt **mir** gut.	*I like the backpack.*
Einkaufen macht **uns** Spaß.	*We like to go shopping.*

The chart on the following page shows the personal pronouns in the dative case.

Singular		Plural	
Nominative	Dative	Nominative	Dative
ich	**mir** *to/for me*	wir	**uns** *to/for us*
du	**dir** *to/for you (informal)*	ihr	**euch** *to/for you (informal)*
Sie	**Ihnen** *to/for you (formal)*	Sie	**Ihnen** *to/for you (formal)*
er	**ihm** *to/for him; to/for it*		
Sie	**ihr** *to/for her; to/for it*	sie	**ihnen** *to/for them*
es	**ihm** *to/for it*		

Analyse

Scan the following ads.

◗ Find the dative object pronouns. What are the verbs that require the dative to be used?

◗ What is the nominative form of each of the dative pronouns?

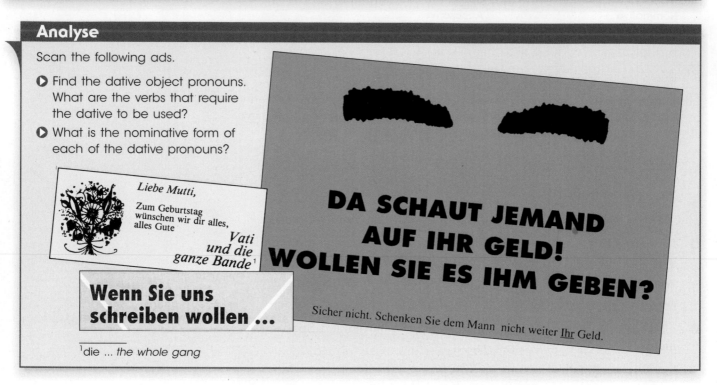

Liebe Mutti,

Zum Geburtstag wünschen wir dir alles, alles Gute

Vati und die ganze Bande[1]

Wenn Sie uns schreiben wollen ...

DA SCHAUT JEMAND AUF IHR GELD! WOLLEN SIE ES IHM GEBEN?

Sicher nicht. Schenken Sie dem Mann nicht weiter <u>Ihr</u> Geld.

[1]die ... *the whole gang*

Übung 1   Wem macht das Spaß?

Wie sagt man das anders? Setzen Sie Personalpronomen im Dativ in die Lücken.

BEISPIEL: Ich gehe gern einkaufen. Einkaufen gehen macht _mir_ Spaß.

1. Ich fotografiere gern. Fotografieren macht ＿＿ Spaß.
2. Mein Bruder Alex isst gern. Essen macht ＿＿ Spaß.
3. Mein Freund und ich, wir tanzen gern. Tanzen macht ＿＿ Spaß.
4. Die Studenten gehen gern in die Disco. In die Disco gehen macht ＿＿ Spaß.
5. Ich surfe gern im Internet. Im Internet surfen macht ＿＿ Spaß.
6. Meine Schwester kocht gern. Kochen macht ＿＿ Spaß.
7. Esst ihr gern Apfelstrudel frisch vom Bäcker? Apfelstrudel essen macht ＿＿ bestimmt Spaß.
8. Wir gehen gern einkaufen. Einkaufen gehen macht ＿＿ Spaß.
9. Was machst du gern? Karten spielen macht ＿＿ Spaß?
10. Was macht ihr gern? SMS schicken macht ＿＿ Spaß?

Übung 2   Das macht mir Spaß.

Schritt 1: Was macht dir Spaß? Was macht dir keinen Spaß? Arbeiten Sie zu zweit.

BEISPIEL: S1: Was macht dir Spaß?

S2: Fotografieren macht mir Spaß.

S1: Und was macht dir keinen Spaß?

S2: Einkaufen gehen macht mir keinen Spaß.

Schritt 2: Berichten Sie nun im Plenum über Ihre Partnerin / Ihren Partner.

BEISPIEL: Fotografieren macht Bob Spaß. Einkaufen gehen macht ihm keinen Spaß.

Übung 3   Hallo, wie geht's?

Ergänzen Sie die fehlenden Personalpronomen im Dativ.

1. **A:** Hallo, Sophia, wie geht es _____?

   B: Danke, es geht _____ gut.

   A: Und wie geht's deinem Freund?

   B: Ach, es geht _____ nicht besonders gut. Er hat zu viel Stress.

2. **C:** Hallo, Petra und Christoph. Na, wie geht es _____ denn?

   D: Danke, es geht _____ gut.

   C: Und was machen die Kinder?

   D: Ach, es geht _____ immer gut.

3. **E:** Guten Tag, Herr Professor Distelmeier.

   F: Guten Tag, Herr Liederlich. Wie geht es _____?

   E: Es geht _____ schlecht. Ich habe zu viel Arbeit.

4. **G:** Tag, Frau Merkel, wie geht es _____?

   H: Danke, es geht _____ gut. Und _____?

   G: Danke, auch gut. Und wie geht es Ihrer Mutter?

   H: Ach, es geht _____ nicht besonders. Sie schläft so schlecht.

Articles and Possessive Adjectives in the Dative

Der Verkäufer zeigt **dem** Kunden eine Digitalkamera.

The salesperson shows the customer a digital camera.

Er schenkt **seiner** Mutter eine Digitalkamera zum Geburtstag.

He is giving his mother a digital camera for her birthday.

Die Kamera gefällt **seinen** Eltern.

His parents like the camera.

The following chart shows the dative endings for definite and indefinite articles, possessive adjectives, and **der**-words. Note that the masculine and neuter endings are identical.

Masculine	Neuter	Feminine	Plural
dem (k)ein**em** mein**em** dies**em** } Mann	**dem** (k)ein**em** mein**em** dies**em** } Kind	**der** (k)ein**er** mein**er** dies**er** } Frau	**den** kein**en** mein**en** dies**en** } Männern Frauen Kindern
dem Kunden			**den** Kunden

NOTE:

● Nouns in the dative singular do not normally take an ending, except for the special masculine nouns that take an **-n** or **-en** in the accusative as well **(Kapitel 2).**

Nominative	Accusative	Dative
der Kunde	den Kunde**n**	dem Kunde**n**
der Student	den Student**en**	dem Student**en**

● In the dative plural, all nouns add **-n** to the ending, unless the plural already ends in **-n.** Plural nouns ending in **-s** do not add **-n.**

	Plural	Dative Plural
	die Männer	den Männer**n**
	die Frauen	den Frauen
but:	die Autos	den Autos
	die Handys	den Handys

The Dative Case for Indirect Objects

As in English, many German verbs take both a direct object and an indirect object. The direct object, in the accusative, will usually be a thing; the indirect object, in the dative, will normally be a person.

Michael kauft **seiner Freundin** eine Digitalkamera.

Der Verkäufer zeigt **ihm** mehrere Kameras.

Michael schenkt sie **ihr** zum Geburtstag.

NOTE:

● The dative object precedes the accusative object when the accusative object is a noun.

● The dative object follows the accusative object when the direct object (accusative) is a personal pronoun.

Following are some of the verbs that can take two objects in German:

empfehlen (empfiehlt)	to recommend	**schicken**	to send
geben (gibt)	to give	**zeigen**	to show
schenken	to give as a gift		

Übung 4 Situationen im Alltag

Sie hören vier Dialoge. Kreuzen Sie für jeden Dialog den Satz an, der zu dem Thema passt.

1. Hans braucht unbedingt etwas Geld.
   - ☐ Sein Freund kann ihm leider nichts geben.
   - ☐ Sein Freund gibt ihm 5 Euro.
2. Zwei Studentinnen brauchen Hilfe.
   - ☐ Ein Freund gibt ihnen etwas Geld.
   - ☐ Ein Herr zeigt ihnen den Weg zum Café.
3. Helmut hat Geburtstag.
   - ☐ Marianne schickt ihm eine Geburtstagskarte.
   - ☐ Marianne schenkt ihm eine CD.
4. Eine Studentin erzählt einem Studenten über ihren Tagesablauf.
   - ☐ Sie empfiehlt ihm Yoga.
   - ☐ Sie hat keine Zeit für Yoga.

Geben Sie Ihrem Haar einen modischen Kick... HENNA PLUS

Übung 5 Wortsalat!

Bilden Sie Sätze.

BEISPIEL: meinem Freund / macht / keinen Spaß / Telefonieren →
Telefonieren macht meinem Freund keinen Spaß.

1. einen Wecker / die Mutter / zum Geburtstag / ihrem Sohn / schenkt
2. ihren Freunden / schickt / diese Studentin / viele SMS / am Tag
3. den Studenten / zeigt / der Professor / eine Landkarte von Deutschland
4. dem Kunden / die Verkäuferin / einen preiswerten Computer / empfiehlt
5. du / das Handy / zum Geburtstag / gibst / deiner Schwester / ?
6. kauft / einen Ring / der Kunde / seiner Freundin
7. seiner Freundin / schenkt / zum Valentinstag / er / diesen Ring

Übung 6 So ein Stress!

Horst hat eine große Familie und viele Freunde. Wem schenkt Horst was?

BEISPIEL: Sein Onkel hört gern klassische Musik.
a. Er schenkt seinem Onkel eine CD.
b. Er schenkt ihm eine CD.

1. Seine Oma reist oft nach Hawaii.
2. Sein Bruder ist sportlich sehr aktiv.
3. Sein Vetter Kevin findet Fische interessant.
4. Seine Schwester Meike telefoniert pausenlos.
5. Seine Freundin Lisa wandert gern.
6. Seine Tante Marie liebt exzentrische Mode.
7. Sein Vater hat schon alles.
8. Seine Mutter trinkt morgens, mittags und abends Kaffee.
9. Seine Eltern planen eine Reise nach Spanien.

ein Aquarium mit zwei Goldfischen	das Handy	die Krawatte	die Sonnenbrille	der Kaffeebecher

der Reiseführer	die Inline-Skates	der Rucksack	der Hut

Verbs with a Dative Object Only

A number of common German verbs always take an object in the dative case. Note that these dative objects usually refer to people.

danken	Ich **danke dir** für die Karte.	*I thank you for the card.*
gefallen	Wie **gefällt Ihnen** dieses Hemd?	*How do you like this shirt?**
gehören	Der Mercedes **gehört meinem** Bruder.	*The Mercedes belongs to my brother.*
glauben	Ich **glaube dir.**	*I believe you.*
helfen	Der Verkäufer **hilft dem** Kunden.	*The salesperson is helping the customer.*
passen	Größe 48 **passt mir** bestimmt.	*Size 48 will surely fit me.*
schmecken	Das Brot **schmeckt mir.**	*That bread tastes good (to me).*
stehen	Das Kleid **steht dir** gut.	*The dress looks good on you.*

Verbs that take only a dative object are indicated in the vocabulary lists of this book as follows: (+ *dat.*)

A number of frequently used idiomatic expressions also require dative objects.

Wie geht es **dir?**	*How are you?*
Das tut **mir** leid.	*I'm sorry.*
Das ist **mir** egal.	*I don't care.*
Das macht **mir** Spaß.	*I like/enjoy that.*
Das ist **mir zu** teuer.	*That's too expensive (for me).*

honest

Übung 7   Sei ehrlich°!

Schritt 1: Wem gehört das?

BEISPIEL: s1:   Wem gehört der große Hut?

s2:   Der gehört dem Fotomodell Vanessa.

die karierte Hose
der große Hut
das komische Hemd
die langen Stiefel

Vanessa (das Fotomodell)   Michael (ihr Freund)   Mark (ihr Bruder)   Sabine (ihre Schwester)

---

*Lit.: *How does this shirt please you?*

Schritt 2: Wie gefällt dir das? Führen Sie ein Gespräch.

BEISPIEL: **S1:** Wie steht Vanessa der große Hut?

S2: Der Hut gefällt mir. Er steht ihr gut!

der große Hut	gefallen/gefällt		gut
das komische Hemd	passen/passt	ihm	nicht gut
die karierte Hose	sind/ist	ihr	zu eng
die langen Stiefel	stehen/steht	mir	zu groß
			zu kurz
			zu lang

Übung 8 Ein schwieriger° Kunde

difficult

Ergänzen Sie den Dialog mit passenden Verben aus dem Kasten und Pronomen im Dativ.

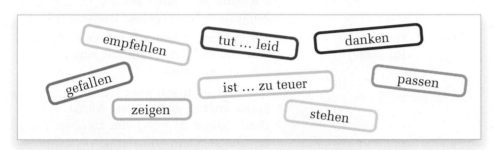

empfehlen   tut ... leid   danken   gefallen   ist ... zu teuer   passen   zeigen   stehen

Kunde: Ich brauche ein Geschenk für meine Freundin. Können Sie ____¹ vielleicht etwas ____²? (*recommend to me*)

Verkäufer: Eine Bluse vielleicht?

Kunde: ____³ Sie ____⁴ bitte eine Bluse in Größe 50. (*Show me*)

Verkäufer: Größe 50? Das ist aber sehr groß!

Kunde: Ich glaube, Größe 50 ____⁵ ____⁶ bestimmt. (*fits her*)

Verkäufer: Hier habe ich eine elegante Seidenbluse. In Schwarz.

Kunde: Nein, Schwarz ____⁷ ____⁸ nicht. (*look good on her*)

Verkäufer: Wie ____⁹ ____¹⁰ diese Bluse in Lila? (*do you like*)

Kunde: Schrecklich. Diese Farbe ____¹¹ ____¹² überhaupt nicht. (*I like*)

Verkäufer: Hier habe ich ein Modell aus Paris für 825 Euro. Ich garantiere, diese Bluse ____¹³ ____¹⁴ bestimmt. (*she will like*)

Kunde: Sie machen wohl Spaß. Das ____¹⁵ ____¹⁶ ____¹⁷. (*is too expensive for me*)

Verkäufer: Kann ich ____¹⁸ etwas anderes ____¹⁹? (*show you*)

Kunde: Können Sie ____²⁰ vielleicht ein T-Shirt ____²¹? (*show me*)

Verkäufer: Ja, natürlich. Hier habe ich ein ganz …

Kunde: Oh, je. Es ist schon halb sechs. Es tut ____²² ____²³. (*I'm sorry.*) Ich muss sofort gehen. Ich ____²⁴ ____²⁵ für Ihre Hilfe. (*thank you*) Auf Wiedersehen.

Prepositions with the Dative Case

Prepositions that require the dative case of nouns and pronouns include:

aus	from, out of	Richard kommt gerade **aus** dem Haus.
		Alexandra kommt **aus** Jena.
	(made) of	Das Hemd ist **aus** Polyester.
bei	near	Die Bäckerei ist **beim** Marktplatz.
	at (the place of)	Schicke Blusen gibt es **bei** Gisie.
	for, at (a company)	Manfred arbeitet **bei** VW.
	with	Sybille wohnt **bei** ihrer Großmutter.
mit	with	Herr Schweiger geht **mit** seiner Frau einkaufen.
		Mit einem Klick im Internet!
	by (means of)	Wir fahren **mit** dem Bus.
nach	to	Der Bus fährt **nach** Frankfurt.
		Ich fahre jetzt **nach** Hause.
	after	**Nach** dem Essen gehen wir einkaufen.
seit	since	**Seit** gestern haben wir schönes Wetter.
	for (time)	**Seit** einem Monat kauft sie nur noch Bio-Brot.
von	from	Das Brot ist frisch **vom** Bäcker.
		Frank kommt gerade **vom** Markt.
	by (origin)	Dieses Buch ist **von** Peter Handke.
zu	to	Wir gehen heute **zum** Supermarkt.
		Dirk muss schon um fünf Uhr **zur** Arbeit.
	at	Er ist jetzt wieder **zu** Hause.
	for	**Zum** Frühstück gibt es Müsli.

NOTE:

▶ **Nach Hause** and **zu Hause** are set expressions. **Nach Hause** is used to say that someone is *going* home, while **zu Hause** means someone is *at* home.

▶ The following contractions are common:

bei dem → **beim**	Jürgen kauft sein Brot nur **beim** Bäcker.
von dem → **vom**	Er kommt gerade **vom** Markt.
zu dem → **zum**	Er muss jetzt noch **zum** Bäcker.
zu der → **zur**	Dann geht er **zur** Bank.

Sprach-Info

The preposition **seit** is used with the present tense in German and refers to an action that started in the past and continues into the present. Note that in English, the present perfect tense is used in these contexts.

Seit wann lernst du Deutsch?	*How long have you been studying German?*
Seit drei Semestern.	*For three semesters (and still ongoing).*

German speakers frequently add the adveb **schon** for emphasis.

Ich plane schon seit einem Monat eine Grillparty.	*I have been planning a barbecue for a month.*

Übung 9 Ein typischer Tag

Sie hören eine Beschreibung von Maxis Tagesablauf. Was stimmt? Was stimmt nicht? Geben Sie die richtige Information an.

	Das stimmt	Das stimmt nicht
1. Maxi wohnt seit einem Monat in Göttingen.	☐	☐
2. Maxi wohnt allein in einer Wohnung.	☐	☐
3. Sie kann zu Fuß zur Universität gehen.	☐	☐
4. Maxi kommt gerade aus der Bibliothek.	☐	☐
5. Dann geht sie in die Mensa.	☐	☐
6. Maxi und Inge gehen zum Supermarkt.	☐	☐
7. Beim Bäcker kaufen sie ein Brot.	☐	☐
8. Maxi muss noch zur Bank.	☐	☐

Übung 10 Auskunft° geben

Information

Ergänzen Sie die fehlenden Präpositionen.

1. Sag mal, wo gibt es hier denn schicke Blusen? —_____ der Boutique Gisie.
2. Die Bluse steht dir gut. Ist sie _____ Polyester?
3. Ist diese Bluse neu? —Ja, sie ist ein Geschenk _____ meiner Mutter.
4. Das Brot schmeckt ausgezeichnet. Woher hast du es? —Es ist _____ der Bäckerei am Markt.
5. Gehst du zu Fuß zum Supermarkt? —Nein, ich fahre _____ dem Fahrrad.
6. Bitte, komm _____ dem Einkaufen sofort _____ Hause.
7. Ich plane schon _____ einem Monat eine Grillparty.
8. Wollen wir die Party _____ dir oder _____ mir _____ Hause machen?
9. Woher kommen diese Orangen? _____ Spanien.

Übung 11 Michaels Tag

Setzen Sie die fehlenden Präpositionen, Artikel und Endungen ein.

1. Michael wohnt _____ sein__ Bruder zusammen in einer alten Villa in Berlin.
2. Er geht schon _____ 6 Uhr _____ _____ Haus.
3. Er fährt _____ sein__ Motorrad _____ Arbeit.
4. Er arbeitet _____ Hotel Zentral.
5. Er arbeitet da schon _____ ein__ Jahr. Die Arbeit gefällt ihm sehr.
6. Er arbeitet _____ Leute__ _____ vielen Länder__ zusammen, z. B. _____ Spanien, Afghanistan und Amerika.
7. Abends _____ _____ Arbeit trifft er oft ein paar Freunde.
8. Dann geht er _____ sein__ Freunde__ in eine Kneipe.
9. Michael kocht gern. _____ Frühstück gibt es oft so etwas wie Rührei _____ Zwiebeln und Zucchini.
10. Das ist ein Rezept _____ Mexiko.
11. Er hat das Rezept _____ sein__ Freundin Marlene.

Übung 12 Ein Interview

Machen Sie mit den Fragen ein Interview und berichten Sie dann im Kurs.
(Benutzen Sie etwa 5 Fragen.)

1. Wann gehst du morgens aus dem Haus?
2. Wie kommst du zur Uni/Arbeit?
3. Arbeitest du? Wo? Gefällt dir die Arbeit?
4. Seit wann …?
5. Was machst du abends? Gehst du mit Freunden aus? Sitzt du vor dem Fernseher / am Computer?
6. Was macht dir besonders Spaß?
7. Was isst du gern zum Frühstück? zum Abendessen? Was magst du überhaupt nicht gern?
8. ???

Interrogative Pronouns° wo, wohin, and woher

Interrogativpronomen

The interrogative pronouns **wo** and **wohin** both mean *where*. **Wo** is used to ask where someone or something is located, **wohin** to ask about the direction in which someone or something is moving. **Woher** is used to ask where someone or something comes from.

Wo bist du denn jetzt?	Zu Hause.
Wo wohnst du?	In Berlin.
Wo kauft Maxi ihr Brot?	Beim Bäcker.
Wohin gehst du? (**Wo** gehst du **hin**?)	Zur Bank.
Wohin fährst du? (**Wo** fährst du **hin**?)	Nach Deutschland.
Woher kommen die Orangen? (**Wo** kommen die Orangen **her**?)	Aus Spanien.
Woher hast du die gute Wurst? (**Wo** hast du die gute Wurst **her**?)	Vom Metzger.

Note that the words **wohin** and **woher** are frequently split (**wo … hin, wo … her**), especially in conversation.

Brot vom Bäcker – täglich frisch

Übung 13 Wo, wohin, woher?

Bilden Sie die Fragen zu den Antworten.

BEISPIEL: Ich muss heute noch <u>zur Bank</u>. →
Wohin musst du heute noch? [*oder*]
Wo musst du heute noch hin?

1. Brötchen gibt es <u>beim Bäcker</u>.
2. Mark muss heute noch <u>zur Metzgerei</u>.
3. Sein Freund kommt gerade <u>vom Bioladen</u>.
4. Wir gehen später <u>zum Supermarkt</u>.
5. Antje ist heute <u>zu Hause</u>.
6. Die Leute kommen gerade <u>aus dem Kino</u>.
7. Sie gehen jetzt alle <u>nach Hause</u>.
8. Die Studentinnen trinken einen Kaffee <u>im Café Kadenz</u>.

Sprache im Kontext

Videoclips

A Schauen Sie sich das Interview mit Sara an. Lesen Sie die Fragen und streichen Sie (cross out) die Antwort durch, die nicht stimmt.

BEISPIEL: Was trägt Sara jetzt? [Jacke, H̶u̶t̶, Bluse]

1. Welche Blusengröße hat Sara? [38, 83]
2. Welche Schuhgröße hat sie? [51, 41]
3. Was nimmt Sara mit in Urlaub? [Jeans, Bikini, kurze Hosen]
4. Was trägt sie zu Hause? [Pyjama, Shorts, Kleider]
5. Sara kauft Lebensmittel. Was für Gemüse kauft sie? [Gurke, Karotten, grüne Bohnen]
6. Was für Obst kauft sie? [Äpfel, Erdbeeren, Orangen]
7. Sara muss auch Kosmetik kaufen. Was muss sie kaufen? [Zahnpasta, Shampoo, Toilettenpapier]

B Schauen Sie sich das Interview mit Harald an und beantworten Sie die Fragen.

1. Was für eine Hemdengröße hat Harald?
2. Was für eine Schuhgröße hat er?
3. Was trägt er im Sommerurlaub?
4. Was trägt er zur Arbeit?
5. Was für Lebensmittel kauft er?

C Schauen Sie sich das Interview mit Jasmin an. Was für Getränke kauft sie? Jasmin nennt auch ein Rezept für Auberginen. Wie bereitet (*prepare*) sie sie vor?

Lesen

Zum Thema

A Wo gehen Sie manchmal einkaufen? Was kann man da kaufen?

1. Auf dem Flohmarkt kann man _____ kaufen.
2. Auf dem Markt kann man _____ kaufen.
3. Im Supermarkt kann man _____ kaufen.
4. In kleinen Geschäften kann man _____ kaufen.
5. In einem Einkaufszentrum kann man _____ kaufen.
6. Im Internet kann man _____ kaufen.

B Wie ist der Kontakt zu den Menschen dort?

persönlich, unpersönlich, freundlich, unfreundlich, höflich, unhöflich, sehr menschlich

BEISPIEL: In einem Supermarkt ist der Kontakt gewöhnlich ___*unpersönlich*___.

1. auf dem Flohmarkt
2. auf dem Markt
3. in kleinen Geschäften
4. in einem Einkaufszentrum
5. im Internet

Obst- und Gemüsestand auf dem Markt

Auf den ersten Blick

Lesen Sie die ersten Abschnitte von „Die Obstverkäuferin" bis zu Zeile 15 „Niemand hat Zeit". Was assoziiert der Erzähler (*narrator*) mit „einkaufen"? Welche mit „shoppen"? Kreuzen Sie an.

	Einkaufen	Shoppen
1. Hosen, Schuhe, Sonnenbrillen	☐	☐
2. Brot, Käse, Obst und Wein	☐	☐
3. Supermarkt	☐	☐
4. Markt	☐	☐
5. nicht praktisch	☐	☐
6. nicht billig	☐	☐
7. Es macht Spaß.	☐	☐
8. Sprechen verboten!	☐	☐
9. Man plaudert.	☐	☐
10. Man kennt die Leute.	☐	☐
11. Niemand hat Zeit.	☐	☐

Die Obstverkäuferin

von Leonhard Thoma

Ich gehe gerne einkaufen. Nein, nicht shoppen. Ich meine nicht Hosen, Schuhe und Sonnenbrillen. Ich spreche von Brot und Käse, Obst und Wein.

Das kaufe ich sehr gerne. Aber nicht im Supermarkt. Ich gehe zu den
5 kleinen Geschäften in meiner Straße und vor allem°: auf den Markt.

Ich weiß: Das ist nicht praktisch, nicht billig und dauert lange. Na und? Es macht Spaß. Ich kenne die Leute in den Läden, wir grüßen uns freundlich, wir plaudern° über Wetter, Familie, Fußball.

vor ... *above all*

chat

Smalltalk, kann sein, aber menschlich und zivilisiert. Wir sind
10 Nachbarn° und im Laden bleiben wir Nachbarn. In anderen Geschäften   *neighbors*
ist es nicht ganz so: Da wird man Kunde und es gibt Verkäufer. Aber
auch dort redet man, höflich° von Mensch zu Mensch.   *politely*

Im Supermarkt aber gibt es keine Menschen, nur Konsumenten und
Kassierer. Sprechen verboten!
15 Niemand° hat Zeit. ...   *nobody*

Wie gesagt, da gehe ich lieber auf den Markt. Ein Paradies aus
Farben und Formen. Frische Luft°, frisches Leben! Menschen, laut,   *air*
lebendig, lustig.

Einkaufen, Leute treffen und plaudern. ... Die Straßenmusiker spielen
20 munter ihre Melodien. Alles offen, bunt, natürlich. Ein Volksfest. ...

Ich kenne die Verkäuferinnen. Leila und Fatima aus Marokko, Tata
aus Ekuador. Ihre Arbeit muss stressig sein, den ganzen Tag stehen, und
manche Kunden sind leider nicht sehr angenehm°. Aber die drei sind   *pleasant*
immer fröhlich° und haben etwas zu lachen°. Und sie haben Humor.   *cheerful / laugh*
25 Oft grüßen sie mit: „Hola joven!“ oder „Hola, guapo!“

Jung, schön ... nette Komplimente, denkt man zuerst. Aber dann
kapiert° man: Sie sagen das immer, auch zu dem alten zahnlosen   *understands*
Großväterchen hinter mir. Aber gut so. Vielleicht kein Kompliment, aber
ein schönes Ritual.
30 Sie sind wirklich lieb° und geben mir nur die frischesten Sachen.   *nice*
Nichts Altes, nichts Kaputtes.

Sie sind richtige Komplizinnen, vor allem Tata: Ich will ein Kilo
Mandarinen kaufen, aber sie sagt: „Achtung. Besser nicht. Die sind nicht
gut heute.“
35 Sie spricht leise, der Chef° ist auch da, der hört das nicht gerne.   *boss*
„Danke für den Tipp“, flüstere ich zurück, „was soll ich dann
nehmen?“
„Die Pfirsiche oder die Bananen, die sind heute besonders gut.“
Ich glaube, sie gibt diese Tipps nicht allen. Vor allem nicht den
40 Touristen.

Wir reden immer ein bisschen. Sie möchte ihr Deutsch verbessern°.   *improve*
Das ist meistens unser Thema. Jedes Gespräch° eine kleine Lektion.   *conversation*

Heute sprechen wir aber nicht über Deutsch. Und heute ist sie auch
nicht fröhlich. Sie ist sehr, sehr traurig. Ein Brief aus Ekuador. Ihr Mann
45 und ihre Tochter können nicht nach Europa kommen und hier mit ihr
leben. Keine Papiere, definitiv. Die Bürokratie. Sie muss aber hier
bleiben, sie brauchen das Geld.
„Keine Chance, ich habe meine Familie schon fast zwei Jahre nicht
mehr gesehen°“, sagt sie und zeigt mir ein Foto.   *habe gesehen = have seen*
50 „Aber kannst du sie nicht wenigstens besuchen?“, frage ich.

Nein, antwortet sie traurig. Die Papiere ..., es ist zu kompliziert. Und
dann verliert° sie vielleicht auch die Arbeit. Und vor allem ist der Flug°   *loses / flight*
so teuer. Ein Monatslohn für sie.
„Ekuador“, flüstert sie, „das ist so furchtbar weit weg.“
55 Eine andere Welt° und keine Brücke°.   *world / bridge*
Der Chef steht immer noch da, und die Leute warten.
„Ich muss weitermachen“, sagt sie schnell und versucht° wieder zu   *tries*
lächeln°.   *smile*
Ich gehe nach Hause. Sie tut mir leid, eine so traurige Geschichte. So
60 fern von zu Hause und kein Weg.
In der Küche packe ich meine Einkäufe aus und lege das Obst auf
den Tisch. Das Etikett° auf den Bananen: ‚Frisch aus Ekuador‘.   *label*

Zum Text

A Lesen Sie nun den ganzen Text einmal durch. Was erfährt (*finds out*) man über die Obstverkäuferinnen? Kreuzen Sie an.

	Tata	Leila	Fatima
1. … kommt aus Marokko.	☐	☐	☐
2. … kommt aus Ekuador.	☐	☐	☐
3. … ist immer fröhlich.	☐	☐	☐
4. … muss den ganzen Tag stehen.	☐	☐	☐
5. … hat Humor.	☐	☐	☐
6. … ist nett zu den Kunden.	☐	☐	☐
7. … möchte ihr Deutsch verbessern.	☐	☐	☐
8. … hat einen Mann und eine Tochter.	☐	☐	☐

B Der Erzähler erwähnt drei Obstverkäuferinnen, aber der Titel der Geschichte heißt „Die Obstverkäuferin". Welche der drei Obstverkäuferinnen meint er? Was erfahren wir über ihre Probleme? Kreuzen Sie an.

	Das stimmt	Das stimmt nicht	Keine Information
1. Sie spricht kein Deutsch.	☐	☐	☐
2. Sie ist fröhlich, weil sie einen Brief aus Ekuador bekommen hat.	☐	☐	☐
3. Sie lebt illegal in Europa.	☐	☐	☐
4. Sie lebt in Europa, weil sie dort Arbeit hat.	☐	☐	☐
5. Ihr Mann und ihre Tochter leben in Ekuador.	☐	☐	☐
6. Ihr Mann und ihre Tochter bekommen keine Papiere für eine Einreise nach Europa.	☐	☐	☐
7. Tata kann sie nicht besuchen, weil sie dann eventuell (*perhaps*) ihre Arbeit verliert.	☐	☐	☐

C Nachdem der Erzähler mit Tata gesprochen hat, denkt er: „Eine andere Welt und keine Brücke." Was ist diese andere Welt? Warum gibt es keine Brücke zu der anderen Welt?

D Die Geschichte endet mit dem Satz: „Das Etikett auf den Bananen: ‚Frisch aus Ekuador'." Welche Bedeutung hat dieser Satz für die Erzählung?

E Die achte Klasse eines Gymnasiums in Erfurt macht eine Umfrage darüber, wo Familien in anderen Ländern ihr Obst und Gemüse bekommen. Hier sind die Fragen der Schüler.

1. Gibt es bei euch einen Markt, wo man frisches Obst und Gemüse kaufen kann?
2. Woher kommt das Obst und Gemüse, das man bei euch kaufen kann?
3. Was für Obst und Gemüse wächst in eurer Gegend?
4. Gibt es in den Städten in eurer Gegend auch Gemüsegärten?
5. Haben eure Familien alle einen Garten mit Obst und Gemüse?

Schritt 1: Arbeiten Sie zu dritt. Beantworten Sie zuerst alle Fragen der Schüler gemeinsam.

Schritt 2: Schreiben Sie dann einen Bericht an die Schüler des Gymnasiums. So könnten Sie mit dem Bericht anfangen:

> „Liebe Schüler der achten Klasse,
>
> hier sind unsere Antworten auf eure Umfrage …“

Beenden Sie Ihren Bericht mit ein oder zwei Fragen an die Schüler. So könnten Sie den Bericht beenden:

> „Wir hoffen, ihr findet unseren Bericht nützlich. Und wir freuen uns, eine Antwort auf unsere Fragen zu bekommen.
>
> Mit freundlichen Grüßen, …“

Hier klicken!

Weiteres zum Thema Einkaufen finden Sie bei **Deutsch: Na klar!** im World-Wide-Web unter www.mhhe.com/dnk6.

Zu guter Letzt

Eine Umfrage in der Klasse

Wie geben Studenten/Studentinnen in Ihrer Klasse ihr Geld aus?

Schritt 1: Füllen Sie zuerst den Fragebogen (*questionnaire*) unten selbst aus.

Schritt 2: Interviewen Sie jetzt drei Studenten/Studentinnen und notieren Sie dabei Namen, Alter und Hauptfach (*major*). Benutzen Sie den Fragebogen und notieren Sie die Antworten.

Fragebogen

> 1. Gehen Sie gern einkaufen? Warum (nicht)?
> 2. Wofür geben Sie das meiste Geld aus?
>
> ☐ Miete   ☐ Studiengebühren
> ☐ Auto   ☐ Essen im Restaurant
> ☐ Kleidung   ☐ Lebensmittel
> ☐ Unterhaltung   ☐ etwas anderes
>
> 3. Was kaufen Sie und wie oft kaufen Sie es?
>
> **Was?**   **Wie oft?**
> ☐ Kaffee/Bier   jeden Tag
> ☐ Bücher   einmal
> ☐ Kleidung   zweimal ⎫ ⎧ in der Woche
> ☐ CDs, DVDs   dreimal ⎬ ⎨ im Monat
> ☐ Lebensmittel   alle fünf Jahre ⎩ im Jahr
> ☐ ein Auto   ???
> ☐ Möbel

Schritt 3: Für welche anderen Dinge, die nicht auf dieser Liste stehen, geben Studenten/Studentinnen ihr Geld aus? Notieren Sie sie.

Schritt 4: Was haben Sie herausgefunden? Fassen Sie die Informationen über eine Person, die Sie interviewt haben, schriftlich (*in writing*) zusammen und geben Sie der Person dieses Profil.

Wortschatz

Lebensmittel	**Groceries, Food**
der **Apfel**, ⸚	apple
der **Aufschnitt**	cold cuts
die **Banane**, -n	banana
das **Bier**, -e	beer
der **Blumenkohl**	cauliflower
der **Brokkoli**	broccoli
das **Brot**, -e	(loaf of) bread
das **Brötchen**, -	roll
die **Butter**	butter
das **Ei**, -er	egg
das **Eis**	ice cream; ice
die **Erdbeere**, -n	strawberry
das **Fleisch**	meat
das **Gemüse**	vegetables
das **Getränk**, -e	drink
die **Gurke**, -n	cucumber
das **Hähnchen**	chicken
der **Joghurt**	yogurt
die **Karotte**, -n	carrot
die **Kartoffel**, -n	potato
der **Käse**	cheese
der **Keks**, -e	cookie
der **Kuchen**, -	cake
die **Milch**	milk
das **Müsli**, -	granola; cereal
das **Obst**	fruit
der **Pfeffer**	pepper
das **Rindfleisch**	beef
der **Saft**, ⸚e	juice
das **Salz**	salt
der **Schinken**, -	ham
das **Schnitzel**, -	cutlet
das **Schweinefleisch**	pork
der **Tee**	tea
die **Tomate**, -n	tomato
die **Traube**, -n	grape
der **Truthahn**, ⸚e	turkey
das **Wasser**	water
die **Wurst**, ⸚e	sausage
der **Zucker**	sugar

Geschäfte	**Stores, Shops**
die **Apotheke**, -n	pharmacy
die **Bäckerei**, -en	bakery
die **Drogerie**, -n	toiletries and sundries store
die **Konditorei**, -en	pastry shop
der **Laden**, ⸚	store
der **Bioladen**, ⸚	natural-foods store
der **Getränkeladen**, ⸚	beverage store
der **Markt**, ⸚e	(open-air) market, marketplace
die **Metzgerei**, -en	butcher shop

der **Obst- und Gemüsestand**, ⸚e	fruit and vegetable stand
der **Supermarkt**, ⸚e	supermarket

Kleidungsstücke	**Articles of Clothing**
der **Anzug**, ⸚e	suit
der **Badeanzug**, ⸚e	bathing suit
die **Bluse**, -n	blouse
der **Gürtel**, -	belt
das **Hemd**, -en	shirt
die **Hose**, -n	pants, trousers
die **Badehose**, -n	swim trunks
der **Hut**, ⸚e	hat
die **Jacke**, -n	jacket
die **Jeans** (*pl.*)	jeans
die **Klamotte**, -n	duds, rags (*slang for clothing*)
das **Kleid**, -er	dress
die **Krawatte**, -n	necktie
der **Mantel**, ⸚	coat
die **Mütze**, -n	cap
der **Pullover**, -	pullover sweater
der **Rock**, ⸚e	skirt
das **Sakko**, -s	sport coat
der **Schal**, -s	scarf
der **Schlips**, -e	necktie
der **Schuh**, -e	shoe
der **Hausschuh**, -e	slipper
der **Tennisschuh**, -e	tennis shoe
die **Socke**, -n	sock
der **Stiefel**, -	boot
das **T-Shirt**, -s	T-shirt

Sonstige Substantive	**Other Nouns**
das **Abendessen**	evening meal
die **Brille**, -n	(pair of) eyeglasses
die **Farbe**, -n	color
das **Frühstück**	breakfast
die **Größe**, -n	size
die **Kasse**, -n	cash register; check-out, cashier
der **Koffer**, -	suitcase
das **Medikament**, -e	medicine
das **Mittagessen**	midday meal; lunch
die **Rasiercreme**, -s	shaving cream
der **Rucksack**, ⸚e	backpack
die **Tasche**, -n	handbag, purse
das **Toilettenpapier**	toilet paper
die **Zahnpasta**	toothpaste

Farben	**Colors**
beige	beige
blau	blue
braun	brown

gelb	yellow	kariert	plaid
grau	gray	schick	stylish(ly)
grün	green	sicher	sure(ly)
lila	purple	zart	tender(ly)
orange	orange	ziemlich	somewhat, rather, fairly
rot	red		
schwarz	black		
weiß	white		

Verben / Verbs

an • probieren	to try on
danken (+ dat.)	to thank
empfehlen (empfiehlt)	to recommend
gefallen (gefällt) (+ dat.)	to be pleasing to
Wie gefällt Ihnen …?	How do you like …?
gehören (+ dat.)	to belong to (a person)
glauben	to believe
helfen (hilft) (+ dat.)	to help
hoffen	to hope
mit • nehmen (nimmt mit)	to take along
nehmen (nimmt)	to take
passen (+ dat.)	to fit
schenken	to give (as a gift)
schmecken (+ dat.)	to taste (good)
stehen (+ dat.)	to look good (on a person)
Die Farbe steht mir.	The color looks good on me.
tragen (trägt)	to wear; to carry
um • tauschen	to exchange
zahlen	to pay
zeigen	to show

Sonstige Adjektive und Adverbien / Other Adjectives and Adverbs

frisch	fresh(ly)
gefroren	frozen
gestreift	striped

Dativpronomen / Dative Pronouns

mir	(to/for) me
dir	(to/for) you (informal sg.)
ihm	(to/for) him/it
ihr	(to/for) her/it
uns	(to/for) us
euch	(to/for) you (informal pl.)
ihnen	(to/for) them
Ihnen	(to/for) you (formal)

Dativpräpositionen / Dative Prepositions

aus	from; out of, (made) of
bei	at; near; with
mit	with; by means of
nach	after; to
seit	since; for (+ time)
von	of; from; by
zu	to; at; for

Sonstiges / Other

das macht	that comes to
egal: Das ist mir egal.	I don't care.
jeder	each, every
nach Hause	(to) home
selbstverständlich	of course, naturally
wem?	(to/for) whom?
wohin?	(to) where?
zu Hause	at home

Das kann ich nun!

1. Welche Kleidungsstücke tragen Sie jeden Tag?

2. Nennen Sie fünf Farben! Beginnen Sie mit Ihrer Lieblingsfarbe!

3. Sie reisen nach Hawaii. Was nehmen Sie im Koffer mit?

4. Was essen Sie jeden Tag? Was ist Ihr Lieblingsessen? Was trinken Sie jeden Tag?

5. Welche Frage passt?
   a. _____? —Die Jacke gefällt mir gut.
   b. _____? —Ja, bitte, zeigen Sie mir Tennisschuhe, Größe 42.
   c. _____? —Dieser Pullover ist zu klein.
   d. _____? —Ich schenke es (das T-Shirt) meinem Bruder.

6. Wo kauft man das?
   a. ein Sporthemd
   b. Obst und Gemüse
   c. Würstchen zum Grillen
   d. Brot und Brötchen
   e. Kaffee, Milch und Käse

7. Ergänzen Sie: **wo, woher,** oder **wohin!**
   a. _____ fährst du zum Einkaufen?
   b. _____ kommen diese Orangen?
   c. _____ kauft man frisches Obst und Gemüse am besten?

8. Mit wem machen Sie das gern?
   a. einkaufen gehen
   b. auf Partys gehen
   c. essen gehen

Kapitel 6

Wir gehen aus

In diesem Kapitel

- ▶ **Themen:** Talking about places to eat and drink, ordering in a restaurant

- ▶ **Grammatik:** Two-way prepositions; describing location and placement; expressing time with prepositions; the simple past tense of **sein, haben,** and modal verbs

- ▶ **Lesen:** „Die Soße" (Ekkehard Müller)

- ▶ **Landeskunde:** Regional food specialties, menus, sharing tables in restaurants, paying the bill, eating establishments

- ▶ **Zu guter Letzt:** Ihr Lieblings-restaurant bewerten

Ein Abend mit Freunden

VIDEOCLIPS

Bedienung, bitte

Pizzeria
AS
Internationale Spezialitäten
Italienisch - Chinesisch - Mexikanisch
Wir liefern Ihre Bestellung frei Haus[1] ab 8,00 Euro
0228
62 42 89
79 80 64
Internationale Spezialitäten
Italienisch - Chinesisch - Mexikanisch
TAGES-ANGEBOTE
unser Angebot außer Feiertag
Montag: Pizzatag
(außer Pizza-Pfannen)
5,00 Euro
(außer Pfannenpizzen und Calzoneria)
Dienstag: Gyrostag
5,00 Euro
Mittwoch: Nudeltag
(außer chin. Nudeln)
5,00 Euro
Donnerstag: Risotto- & Salattag
(außer chinesisch)
5,00 Euro
Geburtstag und Partyservice
Öffnungszeiten:
Mo - Fr von 17.00 - 23.00 Uhr
Sa und Feiertage von 17.00 - 23.00 Uhr
So von 14.00 - 23.00 Uhr
Bei einer Bestellung ab 23,- Euro erhalten Sie eine Flasche italienischen Wein oder 1 Liter alkoholfreies Getränk !!
Bestellservice
ab 8,- Euro Mindestbestellung
Von Weichs-Str. 18
53121 Bonn-Endenich

[1]frei ... *free delivery*

A „Pizzeria AS" ist ein Restaurant in Bonn.

- Was bedeutet der Name „AS"?
- Pizzeria AS ist nicht nur ein Pizzarestaurant. Was für internationales Essen bekommt man da?
- An welchen Tagen hat das Restaurant Tagesangebote?
- Welches Tagesangebot interessiert Sie besonders?
- Wie viel Geld muss man mindestens ausgeben, wenn man etwas frei Haus bestellt?
- Was bekommt man, wenn man mehr als 23 Euro für Essen ausgibt?

B Doris hat die Uni gewechselt und studiert jetzt in Berlin. Sie ist beim Info-Büro des Astas an der FU. Hören Sie jetzt ihr Gespräch mit der Asta-Referentin (*adviser*) und ordnen Sie die Charakterisierungen dem richtigen Restaurant zu.

Restaurant	Charakterisierung
1. e, f Brazil	**a.** gemütlich
2. h, a Kartoffelkeller	**b.** in der Oranienburger Straße
3. e, g Kellerrestaurant	**c.** macht viel Spaß
4. b, d Ristorante Italiano	**d.** nicht so teuer
in Berlin	**e.** österreichische Küche
	f. rappelvoll (*coll., crowded*)
	g. Rezepte von Helene Weigel
	h. vegetarisch

Thema 1: Lokale

Neue Wörter

vom Fass draft
täglich daily
geöffnet open
die Küche cuisine; kitchen
geschlossen closed
zum Mitnehmen food to go, take-out
der Ruhetag day that a business is closed

a.

www.cafeschulze.de

Coffee

Home
Caffe
Tagesrenner
Location
Kontakt
Aktuell
Gästebuch

frühstück
der morgenrenner
2 brötchen, 1 ei, konfitüre, honig, nutella, butter, 2,90
1 scheibe wurst, 1 scheibe käse, ohne getränk 4,60

eggs and ...
rührei mit schnittlauch 5,20
rührei mit schinken 4,20
2 spiegeleier
...alle gerichte mit brötchen und butter

Gasthaus ... in den »Ochsen« zum Wohlfühlen!

Original schwäbische Spezialitäten
Zünftige Hausmacher-Vesper
Pils- und Hefeweizen-Biere vom Faß
Gepflegte keimische Weine
Gartenwirtschaft
Nebenzimmer ca. 40 Personen
- Montag Ruhetag -

»Zum Ochsen«

Karl-Heinz Oetinger

Bottwartalstraße 2
71672 Marbach

www.ochsen-marbach.de
info@ochsen-marbach.de
Telefon: 07144-54 30
          07144-1 44 03
Fax:

b.

Kaiser von China
China Restaurant

• In der Kaiserpassage 18 / Eingang Wesselstraße
  53113 Bonn · Telefon (02 28) 65 88 30
• Restaurant Hong Kong
  Brassertufer 1 · 53111 Bonn · Tel. (02 28) 65 17 06
• Restaurant Hongdi / Siegburg
  mit schönem Biergarten am Mühlenbach · Auf der Kälke 1-3,
  beim Kreishaus · 53721 Siegburg · Tel. (0 22 41) 5 69 94

HONGDi

c.

Schmeckt's noch im ...

Balthasar Ristorante

Nach Führungswechseln in allen wichtigen Positionen wollte PRINZ wissen, wie sich das neue Team anstellt.

Küche ○○○○○
Atmosphäre ○○○○

Nett für laue Sommernächte: Die Terrasse bietet 75 Gästen Platz

d.

Maharani
Indien Pizza Service
Restaurant

Maharani Indisches Restaurant
Prager Str. 39
04317 Leipzig-Reudnitz
Telefon: 0341-9904742

e.

ÜBER 100 GERICHTE
ZUM GENIESSEN & MITNEHMEN!
SPEZIAL-MENÜS FÜR NUR 5,- €

Side
CAFÉ · BISTRO · RESTAURANT
INTERNET & GAMES

VORBESTELLUNG UNTER:
☎ 08621/ 20 15

DURCHGEHEND WARME KÜCHE

Hauptstr. 60, Altenmarkt a. d. Alz
Montag - Sonntag · 11.30 - 23.30

Inhaber: Evren Esat

f.

Wo gibt es das?

Schauen Sie sich die Anzeigen im **Thema 1** an. In welches Lokal können Leute gehen, die

▶ gern Pizza essen?

▶ gern auf der Terrasse sitzen?

▶ gern Bier vom Fass trinken?

▶ etwas zum Mitnehmen möchten?

▶ Vegetarier sind?

▶ gern schwäbische Spezialitäten essen?

▶ gern frühstücken?

▶ nicht viel Geld haben?

▶ gern Schnitzel essen?

Und Sie? In welches Lokal möchten Sie gehen? Warum?

Landeskunde-Info

German has many different words for places where one can eat or drink something.

das **Café**	café serving mainly desserts—**Kaffee und Kuchen**—but also offering a limited menu
der **Gasthof /** das **Gasthaus**	small inn with pub or restaurant
die **Gaststätte**	full-service restaurant
der **Imbiss**	fast-food stand; snack counter
die **Kneipe**	small, simple pub or bar; typical place where students gather (**Studentenkneipe**)
das **Lokal** das **Restaurant**	general word for an establishment that serves food and drinks
das **Wirtshaus**	pub serving mainly alcoholic beverages and some food

▶ Essen Sie lieber in einer Kneipe oder in einer Gaststätte?

▶ Wo essen Sie, wenn Sie wenig Zeit haben?

Ein Café in Duisdorf/Bonn

Ein Gasthof in Bad Suderode

Ein Imbiss in Berlin

Eine Kneipe in Berlin

Sprach-Info

To suggest to a friend that you do something together, you can use the expression **Lass uns (doch) ... :**

Lass uns doch ins Restaurant gehen!   *Let's go to a restaurant!*

Lass uns türkisch essen!   *Let's eat Turkish food!*

Aktivität 1   Lass uns essen!

Sie haben Hunger. Der Magen knurrt schon. In kleinen Gruppen, bespre-chen Sie, wie Sie essen möchten. Wozu entscheiden Sie sich?

S1:   Lass uns essen. Sag mir, wie?

S2:   Lass uns vegetarisch essen.

S3:   Nein, lass uns ... essen.

Knurr! Knuurr!

Lass uns essen. Sag mir, wie:

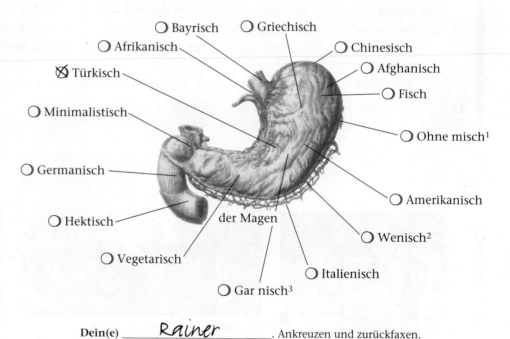

- ○ Bayrisch
- ○ Afrikanisch
- ⊗ Türkisch
- ○ Minimalistisch
- ○ Germanisch
- ○ Hektisch
- ○ Vegetarisch
- ○ Griechisch
- ○ Chinesisch
- ○ Afghanisch
- ○ Fisch
- ○ Ohne misch[1]
- ○ Amerikanisch
- ○ Wenisch[2]
- ○ Italienisch
- ○ Gar nisch[3]

der Magen

Dein(e) _____Rainer_____. Ankreuzen und zurückfaxen.

[1]mich   [2]wenig   [3]nichts

Aktivität 2   Umfrage

Beantworten Sie die Fragen.

1. Gehen Sie oft aus essen? Wie oft? Einmal die Woche, einmal im Monat?
2. Essen Sie gern griechisch, chinesisch, italienisch ... ?
3. Wie heißt Ihr Lieblingsrestaurant? Welche Spezialitäten gibt es dort?

4. Wann hat Ihr Lieblingsrestaurant Ruhetag? Oder ist es an allen Tagen der Woche geöffnet?

5. Was trinken Sie normalerweise, wenn Sie ausgehen?

6. Gibt es Cafés in Ihrer Stadt? Was kann man dort essen und trinken?

Aktivität 3 Ich habe Hunger. Ich habe Durst.

Wo gibt es was zu essen und zu trinken in Ihrer Stadt?

Vorschläge (*recommendations*) für Essen und Trinken:

Pizza
Bier (vom Fass)
griechische Küche
indische Spezialitäten (z.B. Lamm)

internationale Küche (z.B. chinesische oder italienische Spezialitäten)
ein Eis
eine Tasse Kaffee

S1	S2
1. Ich habe Hunger. Ich habe Durst.	**2.** Magst du _____? Isst du gern _____? Möchtest du _____?
3. Ja. Wo kann man das bekommen?	**4.** Im _____.
5. Wann ist es geöffnet? Ist es heute geöffnet?	**6a.** Ich weiß es nicht genau. **b.** Täglich von _____ bis _____.

Studenten beim Abendessen

Thema 2: Die Speisekarte, bitte!

Bad Oeynhausen
Herforder Str. 52
Tel. (05731) 3565
Fax (05731) 3536
Minden
Königswall 1-3
Tel. (0571) 21368
Fax (0571) 850581

die Knolle [1]©
das urige[2] Kartoffelhaus

Kleine Vorspeisen

Frittierte, frische Champignons.................... 3,10 €
mit Kräuterquark und kleinem Salatbuquette

Kartoffelspieß... 3,10 €
Kartoffeln, Speck, Zwiebeln, Paprika
mit Knoblauchcreme und Kräuterquark

Riesen Salatteller

Kleiner gemischter Salat............................. 3,20 €
Großer gemischter Salatteller...................... 6,60 €
mit Schinkenstreifen, Ei und Kräutercroutons

Salat "Korsika"... 7,50 €
mit Schinken, Ei, Schafskäse, Zwiebeln und Oliven

Hausgemachte Reibekuchen[3]

mit geräuchertem Lachs.............................. 8,40 €
und Senf-Dill-Sauce

mit Apfelmus.. 4,60 €

Vegetarisches, gesund und lecker...

Gemüse-Pilz-Pfanne................................... 7,20 €
mit Schupfnudeln[4] und Kräutern

Gebratene[5] Schupfnudeln.......................... 7,30 €
mit Zwiebeln, Lauch und Kräuterquark

Kartoffel-Käse-Rösti................................... 7,20 €
mit Tomaten, Basilikum und Mozzarella

Vom Grill und aus der Pfanne

Kartoffelhauspfanne "Die Knolle"................. 13,10 €
mit 2 Schweinemedaillons, Schweinerückensteak,
Speckbohnen, frischen Champignons,
Sauce Bérnaise und Bratkartoffeln

"Schwaben Pfanne"..................................... 13,50 €
3 Schweinemedaillons mit Champignons à la
Creme, Sauce Hollandaise, Schupfnudeln
und Brokkoli, überbacken mit Käse

hausgemachtes Gulasch.............................. 12,40 €
vom Rind und vom Schwein, frische Paprika,
frische Champignons, Zwiebeln, Apfelrotkohl und
Kartoffelklöße

Grillteller "Die Knolle".................................. 14,60 €
mit Rinderfilet, Schweinerückensteak,
Putenmedaillon, Grillspeck, Nackensteak, frischen
Champignons und Zwiebeln, dazu Kräuterbutter,
würzige Sauce und Pommes

Geflügel[6]

"Geflügelpfanne" Knolle.............................. 13,40 €
3 Putenmedaillons, frische Champignons, feines
Gemüse mit Sauce Bérnaise und Bratkartoffeln

kleinere Portion... 10,10 €

Geflügel-Grillteller..................................... 13,60 €
2 Putenmedaillons, 1 Hähnchenbrustfilet,
Pfeffersauce, Bratkartoffeln und gemischter Salat

kleinere Portion... 10,20 €

Lieblingsgerichte vom "Alten Fritz" überbacken mit Käse

"Schöne Gärtnerin"..................................... 8,70 €
Kartoffelauflauf mit Brokkoli, Blumenkohl,
Schinken und Käsesauce

Kartoffelauflauf "Hühnerdieb"...................... 9,40 €
mit Hähnchenfleisch, Champignons, Brokkoli,
Mais und Käsesauce

Kartoffelauflauf "Indisch"............................ 9,40 €
mit Geflügelstreifen, Currysauce, Mais, Tomaten,
und Porree

Kartoffel-Beziehungskisten

frische Bratkartoffeln aus der Pfanne mit ...

drei gebratenen Landeiern........................... 5,10 €
und Gewürzgurke

Nürnberger Pfanne..................................... 7,50 €
6 Nürnberger, Sauerkraut und Bratkartoffeln

Matjesfilet mit Hausfrauensauce.................. 9,70 €

Seemannspfännchen................................... 7,50 €
Champignons, Shrimps, Schnittlauch und
Spiegelei

Nachtisch

Sylter Rote Grütze...................................... 2,40 €
mit Vanillesauce

Warmer Apfelstrudel................................... 2,90 €
auf Vanillesauce

Schokoeisbecher.. 2,90 €
mit Eierlikör und Schlagcreme

Getränke

Pilsener............................... 0,2 l .... 1,90 €
Apfelsaft, Orangensaft............ 0,2 l .... 1,90 €
Sprudel, Cola, Fanta............... 0,2 l .... 2,20 €

[1]*tuber, spud*   [2]*cozy*   [3]*potato pancakes*   [4]*small potato dumplings*   [5]*fried*   [6]*fowl*

Spaß mit der Speisekarte. Schauen Sie sich die Speisekarte auf der vorigen Seite an und beantworten Sie die folgenden Fragen.

- Das Restaurant „Knolle" ist ein Kartoffelrestaurant. Was kann man bestellen, wenn man Kartoffeln *nicht* mag?
- Finden Sie **Kartoffelauflauf „Indisch"** auf der Speisekarte. Was ist an (*about*) diesem Auflauf indisch?
- Bei welchen anderen Speisen finden Sie geografische Namen?

A Suchen Sie die Wörter unten auf der Speisekarte im **Thema 2.** Können Sie vom Kontext erraten (*guess*), wie die Wörter auf Englisch heißen?

1. _____ das **Apfelmus**	**a.** pan
2. _____ die **Bohne**	**b.** French fries
3. _____ das **Gericht**	**c.** fried egg
4. _____ der **Grill**	**d.** sauerkraut
5. _____ der **Mais**	**e.** bean
6. _____ die **Olive**	**f.** bacon
7. _____ die **Paprika**	**g.** onion
8. _____ die **Pfanne**	**h.** olive
9. _____ die **Pommes (frites)** (*pl.*)	**i.** corn
10. _____ der **Salat**	**j.** plate
11. _____ das **Sauerkraut**	**k.** grill, barbecue
12. _____ der **Speck**	**l.** bell pepper
13. _____ das **Spiegelei**	**m.** applesauce
14. _____ der **Teller**	**n.** dish (*a prepared item of food*)
15. _____ die **Zwiebel**	**o.** salad

B Eine Mahlzeit (*meal*) besteht oft aus mehreren Gängen (*courses*): **Vorspeise, Hauptgericht, Beilage** und **Nachspeise (Nachtisch).** Dazu gibt es Getränke. Welche Speise gehört nicht in jede Kategorie? Streichen Sie aus, was nicht dazu gehört.

1. Vorspeise: **Suppe, Schweinebraten**
2. Hauptgericht: **Auflauf, Leberkäs, Senf, Weißwurst**
3. Beilage: **Nudeln, Bratkartoffeln, Schnitzel, Reis**
4. Nachtisch: **Apfelstrudel, Brezeln, Eisbecher**
5. Getränke: **Sprudel, Wein, Sahne, Pilsener**

Aktivität 4   So viele Speisen!

Welche Speise oder welches Wort ist das?

1. B e l a t f r a n k f o r t
2. S t a l a
3. S c k e p
4. S t u r e u k a r a
5. N e l d u
6. V e p r e s o s i
7. Z e b w e i l
8. H h h e n ä c n
9. P e n a n f
10. H i g e t u t p a c h r
11. A l u f u f a
12. S e e i g e p l i

Neue Wörter

die Vorspeise appetizer
das Hauptgericht main dish
die Beilage side dish
die Nachspeise dessert
der Nachtisch dessert
die Suppe soup
der Schweinebraten pork roast
der Auflauf casserole
der Leberkäs Bavarian-style meatloaf
der Senf mustard
die Weißwurst white sausage
die Bratkartoffeln (*pl.*) fried potatoes
die Brezel pretzel
der Eisbecher dish of ice cream
der Sprudel carbonated mineral water
die Sahne cream
das Pilsener Pilsner beer

Landeskunde-Info

Every area has its own regional specialties, while some dishes are available almost anywhere. Bavarian favorites include **Schweinshaxen** (pig's feet), **Spanferkel** (suckling pig), **Leberkäs** (a type of meatloaf), and **Weißwurst** (a type of veal sausage). North German dishes include **Matjeshering** (salted young herring) and **Hamburger Labskaus,** a sailor's casserole made of cured meat, pickled herring, and various other ingredients topped with a fried egg. In the Southwest and parts of Switzerland one commonly finds **Spätzle** or **Spätzli,** egg noodles generally served with butter and cheese. The Westphalians are known for their **Pumpernickel** bread, the Thuringians for their **Thüringer Bratwurst,** and the Viennese for the **Wiener Schnitzel,** a breaded, pan-fried veal cutlet.

Meat is frequently pork (**Schweinefleisch**). Beef (**Rindfleisch**) is also found on menus but is generally more expensive. Many restaurants have lighter fare such as chicken breast (**Hähnchen**) and turkey (**Truthahn** or **Pute**).

Favorite dessert items include **Rote Grütze,** a compote made from crushed strawberries, currants, and cherries, and—in Bavaria—**Kaiserschmarren,** a sweet crepelike omelet.

Be prepared to get a bottle of **Sprudel** (*mineral water*) if you request water in a restaurant, and don't expect to get a lot of ice with it. It is not customary to serve a guest tap water, whether in a restaurant or a private home.

Matjeshering auf Gemüse

Rote Grütze

▶ Welche Speisen oben essen Sie gern? nicht gern?

▶ Gibt es regionale Spezialitäten, wo Sie wohnen?

are ordering

Aktivität 5 Was bestellen° Norbert und Dagmar?

Hören Sie zu und ergänzen Sie die Tabelle.

Weißwurst mit Sauerkraut

	Norbert	Dagmar
Vorspeise		*Champignons*
Hauptgericht		
Beilage	*Reis*	
Getränk		

Aktivität 6   Was sollen wir bestellen?

Schritt 1: Schauen Sie sich die Speisekarte auf Seite 180 an und besprechen Sie zu zweit oder zu dritt, was Sie bestellen möchten. Pro Person
können Sie nur 20 Euro ausgeben.

BEISPIEL: Ich nehme Kartoffelspieß als Vorspeise. Als Hauptgericht nehme
ich Matjesfilet mit Hausfrauensauce. Und als Nachspeise nehme
ich rote Grütze.

Schritt 2: Notieren Sie Ihre Bestellung:

BEISPIEL: Vorspeise: €   3,10
Hauptgericht: €   9,70
Nachspeise: €   2,40
Summe: € 15,20

Vorspeise:
Hauptgericht:
Nachspeise:
Summe:

Hier klicken!

Weiteres zum Thema
Restaurant und
Gerichte finden Sie bei
Deutsch: Na klar! im World-
Wide-Web unter **www.mhhe.
com/dnk6.**

Aktivität 7   Im Restaurant

Bilden Sie kleine Gruppen. Eine Person spielt den Ober oder die Kellnerin
und nimmt die Bestellungen der Gäste an.

S1	S2
Ober/Kellnerin	**Gast**
1. Bitte schön. Was darf's sein?	**2.** Ich möchte gern _____.
3. Und zu trinken?	**4.** Bringen Sie mir bitte _____.
5. Sonst noch was? (*Anything else?*)	**6a.** Ja, _____. **b.** Nein, das ist alles.

Landeskunde-Info

When you are in a restaurant and want to get the server's attention, it is
polite to say **bitte schön.** Young people often call out **hallo,** but this is
very informal. In more formal restaurants, you may hear people call **Herr
Ober** if the server is male. Use the generic term **Bedienung** (**bitte**) to call
for a server.

In all but the most exclusive restaurants in German-speaking countries,
it is acceptable for people to ask to share a table if it is very crowded.
Simply ask: **Ist hier noch frei?** The answer might be: **Ja, hier ist noch frei.**
Or: **Nein, hier ist besetzt.**

‣ Wie ruft man die Bedienung in Ihrem Land? Was sagt man?

‣ Kann man in Ihrem Land im Restaurant mit Leuten, die man nicht
kennt, am Tisch sitzen?

Thema 3: Im Restaurant

Welches Bild passt zu welchem Mini-Dialog?

a.

b.

c.

d.

e.

f.

Neue Wörter

der Ober waiter

die Speisekarte menu

bestellen order

Was bekommen Sie? What will you have?

war (sein) was

hatte (haben) had

vielen Dank many thanks

Entschuldigen Sie. Excuse me.

Ist hier noch frei? Is this seat available?

Hier ist besetzt. This seat is taken.

da drüben over there

der Platz room, space

das Messer knife

der Löffel spoon

die Serviette napkin

die Gabel fork

voll full

hoffentlich I/we/let's hope

warten wait

mussten (müssen) had to

1. _____ — Herr **Ober,** die **Speisekarte,** bitte!

2. _____ — Wir möchten **bestellen.**
   — Ja, bitte, **was bekommen Sie?**
   — Ich nehme das Hähnchen.

3. _____ — Also, das **war** viermal Schnitzel und viermal Rotwein …
   — Nein, ich **hatte** den Grillteller.
   — Ach, ja. Das macht zusammen 68,40 Euro.
   — 70,– Euro.
   — **Vielen Dank.**

4. _____ — **Entschuldigen Sie,** bitte! **Ist hier noch frei?**
   — Nein, **hier ist besetzt,** aber **da drüben** ist **Platz.**

5. _____ — Herr Ober, ich habe **Messer, Löffel** und **Serviette,** aber keine **Gabel.**
   — Und ich habe keine Serviette.

6. _____ — Hier ist es aber ziemlich **voll. Hoffentlich** müssen wir nicht lange auf einen Platz **warten.**
   — Ja, wir **mussten** lange nach einem Parkplatz suchen.

Aktivität 8   Im Brauhaus Matz

Zwei Freunde, Jens und Stefanie, sind im Brauhaus Matz. Hören Sie zu, und ergänzen Sie den Text mit Informationen aus dem Dialog.

Stefanie und Jens suchen _eine Platz_ [1] in einem Restaurant. Es ist ziemlich _voll_ [2] Jens sieht zwei Leute an einem _Tisch_ [3] Da ist noch _Platz_ [4] für zwei Leute. Er geht an den Tisch und fragt: „Ist _hier nun Pried_ [5]?" Die Antwort am ersten Tisch ist: „_Nein_ [6]" Die Antwort am zweiten Tisch ist: „_Ja_ [7]"

J. Yacmis

Aktivität 9 Ist hier noch frei?

Bilden Sie mehrere Gruppen. Einige Personen suchen Platz.

S1	S2
1. Entschuldigen Sie. Ist hier noch frei?	**2a.** Ja, hier ist noch _____. **b.** Nein, hier ist leider _____. Aber da drüben ist noch _____.
3a. Danke schön. **b.** (*geht zu einem anderen Tisch*)	

Ist hier noch frei?

Aktivität 10 Wir möchten zahlen, bitte. 🎧

Was haben diese Leute bestellt? Wie viel kostet es? Kreuzen Sie an, was Sie hören.

	Getränke	Essen	Betrag
Dialog 1	☐ 2 Bier ☐ 3 Cola ☒ 3 Bier	☐ Knackwürste* ☒ Weißwürste ☒ Bockwürste† ☒ Sauerkraut ☐ Brot	☐ €10,00 ☐ €15,00 ☒ €18,50
Dialog 2	☐ 2 Tassen Tee ☒ 2 Tassen Kaffee ☐ 1 Tasse Kaffee	☐ 2 Stück Käsekuchen ☒ 1 Stück Käsekuchen ☒ 1 Stück Obsttorte	☐ €6,25 ☐ €4,25 ☒ €9,55
Dialog 3	☐ 2 Bier ☒ 5 Bier ☐ 3 Bier	☒ Leberknödelsuppe‡ ☒ Schweinskotelett ☒ Brezeln ☐ Weißwürste ☒ Sauerkraut	☐ €35,40 ☒ €39,40 ☐ €43,40

Landeskunde-Info

When adding up your restaurant bill **(Rechnung)**, your server will often ask whether you want to pay separately **(getrennt)** or together **(zusammen)**. When paying, you do not have to add a tip, as it is always included in your bill. The menu sometimes indicates this by stating:

Bedienungsgeld und Mehrwertsteuer enthalten.	*Tip (service fee) and value-added tax (federal sales tax) included.*

It is customary to round up the figures on your bill to the next euro, but this practice is entirely up to the individual.

> ● Wie viel Trinkgeld geben Sie im Restaurant?
> ● Ist Trinkgeld schon inklusive mit der Rechnung in Ihrem Land?

```
Kuffler                          ◎

SPATENHAUS
an der Oper

                              Rechnung
Seite 01
26.11.09          R-Nr.: 290
Ust.-ID Nr. DE221047804
                              Tisch 121/-

1x Tafelspitz/Sülze           12,50(1)
1x Hell 0,3                     3,10(1)


Netto(1)                Eur:    13,11
+ 19,0%                 MwSt:    2,49
Summe:
           Eur    15,60
```

_____

*a type of German frankfurter

†a type of German sausage similar to a hot dog in flavor and consistency

‡liver dumpling soup

Grammatik im Kontext

Two-Way Prepositions°

So far you have learned two kinds of prepositions: prepositions that are always used with the accusative case and others that are always used with the dative case.

In addition, a number of prepositions take either the dative or the accusative, depending on whether they describe a location or a direction. The most common two-way prepositions are these:

an	at, near, on
auf	on, on top of, at
hinter	behind, in back of
in	in
neben	next to
über	above, over
unter	under, beneath, below; among
vor	in front of; before
zwischen	between

Auf dem Bauernhof kann man gut frisches Obst und Gemüse kaufen.

NOTE:

▶ When answering the question **wo,** these prepositions take the dative case.

wo?	Stationary Location (Dative)
Wo kauft man Brot?	In **der** Bäckerei.
Wo zahlt der Kunde?	An **der** Kasse.
Wo kauft man frisches Gemüse?	Auf **dem** Bauernhof.
Wo soll ich warten?	Vor **dem** Geschäft.

▶ When answering the question **wohin,** they take the accusative case.

wohin?	Direction (Accusative)
Wohin geht Frau Glättli?	In **die** Bäckerei.
Wohin geht der Kunde?	An **die** Kasse.
Wo gehst du hin?	Auf **den** Markt.
Wo geht Herr Sauer hin?	In **das** Geschäft.

▶ The following contractions are common:

an dem → **am**	Das Kaufhaus steht **am** Markt.
an das → **ans**	Geh doch **ans** Fenster!
in dem → **im**	Frau Kraus isst **im** Restaurant.
in das → **ins**	Nikola geht gleich **ins** Geschäft.

Suchen Sie in den folgenden Anzeigen alle Präpositionen mit Dativ- oder Akkusativobjekten. Ordnen Sie sie ein.

wo? (Dativ)   **wohin?** (Akkusativ)

BEISPIEL: <u>im alten Forsthaus</u>   _____

Restaurant
Schubert-Stüberln

Küchenchef
Franz Zimmer

hinter dem Burgtheater, vis-à-vis der Universität,
beim Dreimäderlhaus

Schreyvogelgasse 4, 1010 Wien
Telefon für Tischreservierung 63 71 87

Mach' Dir ein paar schöne Stunden... geh' ins Kino

Parken! Problemlos!

3.000 kostenlose Parkplätze
direkt vor der Tür.

Fahren Sie
in unser großes Park-
haus an der Pelkoven-
straße.

PP

OLYMPIA
Einkaufszentrum

Hanauer Straße · Telefon 14160 02

Kulinarische Notizen

Ein Brevier für Genießer.

Biergartenromantik im alten Forsthaus

Übung 1   Wo kauft Mark ein?

Mark muss heute einkaufen. Hier ist sein Einkaufszettel. Wo gibt es das?

BEISPIEL: Käsekuchen →
Käsekuchen gibt es in der Konditorei.

die Bäckerei
die Buchhandlung
die Konditorei
der Markt
die Metzgerei
das Schuhgeschäft
der Supermarkt

> Einkaufszettel
> 250 g Aufschnitt
> Käsekuchen
> 150 g Emmentaler Käse
> 6 Brötchen
> 12 Würstchen zum Grillen
> 1 Pfund Kaffee
> Schwarzbrot
> 2 Flaschen Sprudel
> 4 Tomaten
> <u>nicht vergessen:</u>
> Wörterbuch
> Tennisschuhe

Übung 2 Am Feierabend°

Was machst du gern/oft/manchmal/nie am Feierabend?

BEISPIEL: **S1:** Gehst du gern ins Café?

S2: Ja, ich gehe gern ins Café.

oder Nein, ich gehe nicht gern ins Café.

der Biergarten	das Kino	der Sportklub
das Café	die Kneipe	die Stadt
die Disco	das Lokal	der Supermarkt
das Fitnesszentrum	das Restaurant	das Theater

Übung 3 Ein Einkaufszentrum

Wie kommt man dahin und was kann man dort machen? Schauen Sie sich die Werbung (unten) an und beantworten Sie die Fragen.

BEISPIEL: Wie kommt man zum Einkaufszentrum Spahn? →
Man kommt mit dem Bus dahin.

Nützliche Wörter

die Boutique
der Bus
die Buslinie
die Cafeteria
der Parkplatz
die Spielecke
das Studio

¹*children's play corner*

1. Mit welcher Buslinie kann man dahin fahren?
2. Wo gibt es etwas zu essen?
3. Wo kann man Lampen kaufen?
4. Wohin kann man seine Kinder bringen?
5. Wo gibt es Geschenke zu kaufen?
6. Wo kann man parken?

Wo und wann kann man parken?

Übung 4 Wo kann man hier parken?

Arbeiten Sie zu zweit. Sie sind mit einem Freund / einer Freundin mit dem Auto unterwegs und haben allerlei in der Stadt vor. Wo kann man da parken?

BEISPIEL: Sie müssen ins Kaufhaus Mertens. Sie brauchen unbedingt neue Jeans.

> **S1:** Ich muss ins Kaufhaus Mertens. Ich brauche unbedingt neue Jeans.
>
> **S2:** Hinter dem Kaufhaus ist ein Parkplatz. Lass uns da parken.

1. Sie möchten Karten für eine HipHop-Oper kaufen. Karten gibt es an der Theaterkasse im Stadttheater.
2. Sie wollen unbedingt ins Kaufhaus Mertens. Da gibt es ein Sonderangebot für Jeans.
3. Auf dem Marktplatz gibt es heute einen Flohmarkt. Das finden Sie immer interessant.
4. Sie wollen auch noch zur Uni. Sie müssen ein Buch zur Bibliothek zurückbringen.
5. Nachmittags brauchen Sie unbedingt einen Kaffee oder einen Tee. Das Altstadt-Café ist Ihr Lieblingscafé.
6. Sie müssen auch noch schnell zum Supermarkt.
7. Im Museum gibt es eine neue Ausstellung von afrikanischer Kunst. Haben Sie noch Zeit fürs Museum?

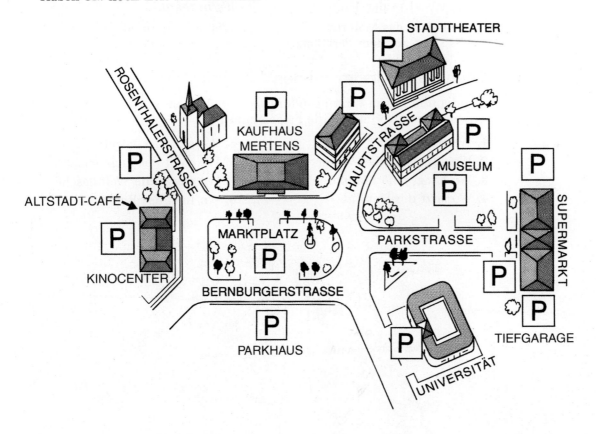

Describing Location

The verbs **hängen**, **liegen**, **sitzen**, **stecken**, and **stehen** indicate where someone or something is located.

hängen	to be (hanging)
liegen	to be (lying)
sitzen	to be (sitting)
stecken	to be (placed, often where it can't be seen)
stehen	to be (standing)

When a two-way preposition is used with one of these verbs indicating location, the object of the preposition is in the dative case. Remember, the interrogative pronoun **wo** asks where someone or something is located.

Wo hängt das Bild?	*Where is the picture hanging?*
Es hängt **im** Wohnzimmer.	*It's hanging in the living room.*
Wo liegt die Rechnung?	*Where is the bill?*
Sie liegt **auf dem** Tisch.	*It's on the table.*
Wo sitzen die Studenten?	*Where are the students sitting?*
Sie sitzen **auf einer** Bank im Park.	*They're sitting on a bench in the park.*
Wo steckt der Schlüssel nur?	*Where is the key? (I can't find it.)*
Er steckt **in der** Tür.	*It's in the door.*
Wo steht das Motorrad?	*Where is the motorcycle?*
Es steht **auf dem** Parkplatz.	*It's in the parking lot.*

Übung 5   Idylle im Grünen

Claudia und Jürgen verbringen (*are spending*) einen Samstagnachmittag im Grünen. Beantworten Sie die Fragen zum Bild.

1. Wo liegt Jürgen?
2. Wo sitzt Claudia?
3. Wo hängt eine Spinne?
4. Wo sitzt der Hund?

5. Wo sitzt der Vogel?
6. Wo steht der Picknickkorb?
7. Wo steckt die Weinflasche?
8. Wo liegt das Buch?

Übung 6　In einem Gartenlokal°

pub with a beer garden

Ergänzen Sie das passende Verb: **hängen, liegen, sitzen, stecken** oder **stehen**.

Andreas und Thomas ____¹ in einem Gartenlokal. Es ____² sehr schön im Grünen nicht weit von Bonn. Vor dem Lokal *stehen*³ viele Autos. Im Biergarten *hängen*⁴ Papierlaternen in den Bäumen. Auf dem Tisch vor Andreas und Thomas *stehen*⁵ zwei Gläser Bier. Unter dem Tisch direkt neben ihnen *sitzt*⁶ ein Hund. Um den Tisch *sitzen*⁷ vier Leute. Der Ober *steht*⁸ jetzt neben Andreas. Die Rechnung *liegt*⁹ schon auf dem Tisch. Andreas *steckt*¹⁰ die Rechnung in die Tasche. Er zahlt an der Kasse.

Describing Placement

The verbs **legen, setzen,** and **stellen,** as well as **hängen** and **stecken,** can indicate where someone or something is being put or placed.

hängen	to hang, to put/place
legen	to lay, to put/place
setzen	to set, to put/place
stecken	to put/place (where it can't be seen)
stellen	to stand, to put/place

When a two-way preposition is used with one of these verbs indicating placement, the object of the preposition is in the accusative case. The interrogative **wohin** asks where someone or something is being put or placed.

Wohin hängt der Mann das Bild?	*Where is the man hanging the picture?*
Er hängt es **an die** Wand.	*He's hanging it on the wall.*
Wohin legt der Kellner die Rechnung?	*Where is the waiter putting the bill?*
Er legt sie **auf den** Tisch.	*He's laying it on the table.*
Wohin setzt die Frau das Kind?	*Where is the woman putting the child?*
Sie setzt es **auf den** Stuhl.	*She's putting him/her on the chair.*
Wo steckt die Kellnerin das Geld **hin?**	*Where is the waitress putting the money?*
Sie steckt es **in die** Tasche.	*She's putting it in the (her) purse.*
Wohin stellt die Kellnerin den Teller?	*Where is the waitress putting the plate?*
Sie stellt ihn **auf den** Tisch.	*She's placing it on the table.*

Die Kellnerin stellt den Teller auf den Tisch.

Sprach-Info

The verb **setzen** is frequently used with a personal pronoun that reflects the subject of the sentence. Used in this reflexive way, the verb means to *sit down*.

Ich setze **mich** an den Tisch.	*I sit down at the table.*
Wir setzen **uns.**	*We sit down.*

In the third-person singular and plural this reflexive pronoun is always **sich.**

Die Studenten setzen **sich** auf die Bank.	*The students sit down on the bench.*

Übung 7 Im Lokal

Andreas trifft ein paar Freunde im „Nudelhaus". Ergänzen Sie die Sätze mit **hängen, legen, setzen, stecken** oder **stellen.**

1. Andreas und drei Studienfreunde _____ sich an einen Tisch beim Fenster.
2. Andreas _____ seinen Rucksack unter den Stuhl.
3. Michael _____ seinen Rucksack an seinen Stuhl.
4. Endlich kommt der Kellner und _____ die Speisekarte auf den Tisch.
5. Die vier bestellen zuerst etwas zu trinken. Der Kellner _____ vier Colas auf den Tisch.
6. Da kommt noch ein Freund, Phillip, an den Tisch zu ihnen. Andreas _____ noch einen Stuhl an den Tisch.
7. Phillip _____ sich neben Andreas.
8. Er _____ seine Bücher auf den Tisch.
9. Sein Handy _____ er in seinen Rucksack.

Sprach-Info

The verb **stehen** is used idiomatically to say that something has been stated (in print).

—Hier gibt es auch vegetarische Kost.   *They have vegetarian food here.*

—Wo **steht** das?   *Where does it say that?*

Übung 8 Ein Abend im Kartoffelkeller!

Ergänzen Sie die Sätze mit einem passenden Verb: **liegen, sitzen, stehen, legen, setzen** oder **stellen.**

1. Im Zentrum von Berlin _liegt_ das Restaurant „Kartoffelkeller".
2. Im Restaurant ist es heute sehr voll. An allen Tischen _____ schon Leute und einige suchen noch Platz.
3. Ein paar Leute _____ draußen vor dem Lokal und warten, dass jemand geht.
4. Man _____ hier auch sehr gemütlich. Und die Preise sind nicht so hoch. Deshalb ist es unter Studenten populär.
5. Endlich kommt eine Kellnerin und _liegt_ die Speisekarte auf den Tisch.
6. Auf der Speisekarte _steht_: „Spezialität unseres Hauses ist Kartoffelsuppe mit Brot."
7. Die Kellnerin _steht_ neben dem Tisch und wartet auf die Bestellung.
8. Am Nebentisch _sitzen_ einige Studenten und diskutieren laut.
9. Ein Student _setzt_ sich an die Theke (*counter*) und bestellt ein Bier.
10. Der Kellner _stellt_ das Bier vor ihn auf die Theke.

Übung 9 Die verlorene Theaterkarte

Michael kann seine Theaterkarte nicht finden. Wo steckt sie wohl? Eine
Person denkt sich aus, wo die Karte ist. Die anderen müssen raten (*guess*),
wo die Karte ist.

BEISPIEL: **S1:** Steckt die Theaterkarte in seiner Hosentasche?

    S2: Nein.

    S1: Liegt die Theaterkarte auf dem Schreibtisch?

    S2: Nein. (usw.)

das Weinglas
die Papiere (pl.)
die Büchertasche
die Sporttasche

Wo ist nur meine Theaterkarte?

Expressing Time with Prepositions

The following two-way prepositions always take the dative case when
expressing time:

vor drei Tagen	*three days ago*
vor dem Theater	*before the play*
in einer Stunde	*in one hour*
zwischen 5 und 7 Uhr	*between 5 and 7 o'clock*

You have learned several other prepositions expressing time—not two-way
prepositions—that also take the dative case.

nach dem Theater	*after the play*
seit einem Jahr	*for a year*
von 5 bis 7 Uhr	*from 5 to 7 o'clock*

The prepositions **um** and **gegen** always take the accusative case.

bis (um) 5 Uhr	*until 5 o'clock*
(so) gegen 7 Uhr	*around 7 o'clock*

Note: In German, expressions of time always precede expressions of place.

	Time	Place
Wir kommen	**so gegen zehn Uhr**	nach Hause.
Ich gehe	**heute**	ins Kino.

Übung 10 Was machst du gewöhnlich  um diese Zeit?

Arbeiten Sie zu zweit.

BEISPIEL: **S1:** Was machst du nach dem Deutschkurs?

S2: Da gehe ich in die Bibliothek.

von _____ bis _____	arbeiten
zwischen _____ und _____	schlafen
so gegen _____	essen
um _____	ausgehen
vor _____	einkaufen gehen
nach _____	fernsehen
??	??

Expressing Events in the Past

Like English, German has several tenses to express events in the past. The most common are the simple past tense (**das Imperfekt**) and the present perfect tense (**das Perfekt**).

▶ The simple past tense is used primarily in writing. However, in the case of **haben, sein,** and the modals, the simple past is common in conversation. In this chapter you will learn the simple past tense of these verbs; the simple past tense of all other verbs will be introduced in **Kapitel 10.**

▶ The present perfect tense (introduced in **Kapitel 7**) is preferred in conversation.

The Simple Past Tense of **sein** and **haben**

	sein	haben
ich	war	hatte
du	warst	hattest
er, sie, es	war	hatte
wir	waren	hatten
ihr	wart	hattet
sie/Sie	waren	hatten

Read the cartoon.

- ◗ What forms of the verbs **haben** and **sein** are used?
- ◗ The answer to the friend's question contains no verb or object because they are understood. What would the complete sentence be?
- ◗ How would the friend pose her questions if the speakers were adults addressing each other formally?

> Du warst in Paris? Hattest du denn keine Schwierigkeiten¹ mit deinem Französisch?

> Ich nicht, aber die Franzosen!

¹difficulties

Übung 11 Ausreden und Erklärungen°

Excuses and explanations

Ergänzen Sie **haben** oder **sein** im Imperfekt.

1. **A:** Warum _____ Sie gestern und vorgestern nicht im Deutschkurs, Herr Miller?

   B: Es tut mir leid, Herr Professor, aber meine Großmutter _____ krank (*sick*). Sie _____ Migräne.

2. **C:** _____ du gestern Abend noch in der Bibliothek?

   D: Nein, die _____ geschlossen. Außerdem _____ ich keine Lust zu arbeiten. Ich _____ aber im Kino!

3. **E:** Warum _____ Michael und Peter nicht auf der Party bei Ulla?

   F: Sie _____ keine Zeit.

4. **G:** Ihr _____ doch gestern im Café Käuzchen, nicht?

   H: Nein, wir _____ im Café Kadenz. Im Käuzchen _____ es zu voll.

   G: Wie _____ es denn?

   H: Die Musik _____ gut, aber der Kaffee _____ schlecht.

Übung 12 Wo warst du denn?

Fragen Sie Ihren Partner / Ihre Partnerin!

BEISPIEL: **S1:** Wo warst du denn Freitagabend?

S2: Da war ich im Theater.

S1: Wie war's denn?

S2: Sehr langweilig.

Wann	Wo	Wie
Freitagabend	auf dem Sportplatz	interessant
heute Morgen	auf einer Party	langweilig
gestern Abend	bei Freunden	nicht besonders gut
Samstagmorgen	im Kino	schön
??	im Restaurant	??
	im Theater	
	zu Hause	
	??	

The Simple Past Tense of Modals

Peter **wollte** gestern in die Disco. Ich **wollte** auch mit, ich **musste** aber zu Hause bleiben.

Peter wanted to go clubbing yesterday. I wanted to go along, too, but I had to stay home.

Wir **konnten** keinen Parkplatz auf der Straße finden.

We couldn't find a parking space on the street.

Sie **mussten** ins Parkhaus fahren.

They had to go into the parking garage.

	dürfen	können	mögen	müssen	sollen	wollen
ich	durfte	konnte	mochte	musste	sollte	wollte
du	durftest	konntest	mochtest	musstest	solltest	wolltest
er, sie, es	durfte	konnte	mochte	musste	sollte	wollte
wir	durften	konnten	mochten	mussten	sollten	wollten
ihr	durftet	konntet	mochtet	musstet	solltet	wolltet
sie/Sie	durften	konnten	mochten	mussten	sollten	wollten

NOTE:

▶ As with **haben** and **sein,** the first- and third-person singular forms and first- and third-person plural forms of the simple past tense of each modal are identical.

▶ Modals have no umlaut in the simple past tense.

¹In case

Übung 13 Ich wollte ... aber ich musste ...

Was wolltest du am Wochenende machen? Was musstest du machen?

A Ergänzen Sie **wollen** im Imperfekt.

1. Ich _____ zuerst mal lange schlafen.
2. Mein Freund _____ mit mir ins Café Käuzchen.
3. Bei gutem Wetter _____ wir Freunde im Park treffen.
4. Unsere Freunde _____ uns abholen.
5. _____ du am Wochenende nicht lange schlafen und dann ausgehen?

B Ergänzen Sie **müssen** im Imperfekt.

1. Ja, aber ich _____ früh aufstehen; ich _____ nämlich arbeiten.
2. Meine Freundin _____ auch arbeiten.
3. Am Nachmittag _____ wir einkaufen gehen.
4. Meine Freunde _____ ohne mich ausgehen.

Übung 14 Kleine Probleme

Ergänzen Sie die fehlenden Modalverben im Imperfekt.

Gestern Abend waren wir im Theater. Wir _____[1] (wollen) in der Nähe vom Theater parken. Da _____[2] (dürfen) man aber nicht parken. Wir _____[3] (können) keinen Parkplatz auf der Straße finden. Deshalb _____[4] (müssen) wir ins Parkhaus fahren. Katrin _____[5] (sollen) vor dem Theater auf uns warten. Sie _____[6] (müssen) lange warten. Nach dem Theater _____[7] (wollen) wir noch ins Café Kadenz. Da _____[8] (können) wir keinen Platz bekommen. Wir _____[9] (müssen) also nach Hause fahren.

Übung 15 Bei mir zu Hause

Wie war das bei Ihnen zu Hause? Erzählen Sie drei Dinge aus Ihrer Kindheit.

BEISPIEL: Als (*As a*) Kind musste ich abends schon früh ins Bett.

müssen	(immer) früh aufstehen
dürfen	abends (nie) lange aufbleiben
wollen	nach der Schule (nie) fernsehen
können	meiner Mutter / meinem Vater helfen
	(kein) Gemüse/Fleisch essen
	immer nur (Fußball/?) spielen
	immer nur am Computer spielen
	nur ab und zu ins Kino gehen
	??

Übung 16 Hin und her: Warum nicht?

Fragen Sie Ihren Partner / Ihre Partnerin, warum die folgenden Leute nicht da waren.

BEISPIEL: **S1:** Warum war Andreas gestern Vormittag nicht in der Vorlesung?

S2: Er hatte keine Lust.

Person	Wann	Wo	Warum
Andreas	gestern Vormittag	in der Vorlesung	keine Lust haben
Anke	Montag	zu Hause	
Frank			keine Zeit haben
Yeliz	heute Morgen	in der Vorlesung	
Mario			kein Geld haben
Ihr Partner / Ihre Partnerin			

Sprache im Kontext

Videoclips

A Schauen Sie sich das Interview mit dem Besitzer des Restaurants an und ergänzen Sie die Sätze.

1. Das Restaurant heißt ___.
   a. Geigenhafen
   b. Gugelhof
   c. Gartenlaube
2. Es gibt Spezialitäten vom ___, von Baden und von der Schweiz.
   a. Elsass
   b. Rheinland
   c. Mittelmeer
3. Eine Spezialität des Restaurants ist ___.
   a. Lamm provenzal
   b. Tarte flambée
   c. Steak tartare

B Schauen Sie sich die Szene im Restaurant an, wo die Gäste Essen bestellen. Wer bestellt was?

1. ___ Michael   a. Putenspieß
2. ___ Claudia   b. Kartoffelauflauf
3. ___ Ali   c. Schweineschnitzel
4. ___ Sara   d. Tomatensuppe

C Die Gäste sprechen über ihre Essgewohnheiten. Hören Sie zu und beantworten Sie folgende Fragen.

1. Wo isst Ali gern?
2. Was isst Claudia gern?
3. Was ist Saras Lieblingsessen?
4. Wer isst gern Falafel?
5. Was für Fast Food isst Claudia gern?

D Und Sie? Was essen und trinken Sie gern, wenn Sie ins Restaurant gehen?

Lesen

Zum Thema

Beantworten Sie die folgenden Fragen, bevor Sie den Text lesen.

1. Kochen Sie gern? Wenn nicht, kennen Sie jemand, der gerne kocht? Wer?
2. Was ist Ihr Lieblingsgericht? Ist es kompliziert oder einfach? Können Sie es kochen? Wenn ja, kochen Sie es nach Rezept oder nach Gefühl (*feeling*)?

Auf den ersten Blick

A Lesen Sie den Titel und die ersten vier Zielen des Textes und beantworten Sie die folgenden Fragen.

1. Mit wem spricht der Mann?
   - **a.** mit seiner Frau
   - **b.** mit jemandem am Telefon
   - **c.** mit sich selbst
2. Was macht der Mann?
   - **a.** Er isst.
   - **b.** Er kocht.
   - **c.** Er singt.

B Überfliegen Sie (*scan*) jetzt den Text. Welche Zutaten (*ingredients*) braucht der Koch in dieser Geschichte? Kreuzen Sie an!

☐ Salz   ☐ Essig   ☐ Paprika

☐ Zwiebeln   ☐ Tomaten   ☐ Knoblauch

☐ Wurst   ☐ Pfeffer   ☐ Karotten

☐ Wein   ☐ Kartoffeln   ☐ Oliven

Die Soße

von *Ekkehard Müller*

Selbstgespräch eines Mannes beim Kochen:

Hoffentlich ist die Soße richtig. Hoffentlich schmeckt sie gut.

Nein. Da fehlt° noch etwas.   *is missing*

Ich muss sie noch mehr salzen.

5 Oh weh! Das war zu viel.

Was mache ich jetzt?

Ich muss sie mit Wasser verdünnen°. Oh weh. Das war auch zu viel.   *dilute*

Jetzt schmeckt sie nach gar nichts.

Macht nichts. Das Wasser wird wieder verkochen.

10 Und das Salz???

Jetzt muss ich noch Zwiebeln schneiden.

Ich hätte° sie schon vorher …   *should have*

Au, das brennt in den Augen.

So. Die Zwiebeln sind auch schon drin. Wie schmeckt sie jetzt?

15 Besser. Viel besser.

Aber es fehlt noch etwas.

Ich muss noch Wein dazugeben.

Hm. Der schmeckt aber gut.

Und noch ein Glas.

20 Ausgezeichnet!

Oh weh! Jetzt habe ich keinen Wein mehr für die Soße.

Was mache ich?

Ich nehme Essig.

Brrrrrrrrr, zu sauer!

25 Wie rette° ich die Soße?   *save*

Ich weiß es. Mit Tomatenketchup. Das schadet nie°.   *schadet … never hurts*

Hier schon.

Jetzt muss noch Pfeffer rein. Endlich scharf!

garlic Und Paprika. Und Knoblauch°.

30 Schade, dass Knoblauch wie der Teufel stinkt.

Und jetzt, jetzt kommen noch Oliven in die Soße.

Ich mag Oliven.

remind Oliven erinnern° mich an Italien.

Und Italien erinnert mich an Sonne.

35 Und an das Meer.

Und an Fischer.

Ah, die Sonne!

Ah, das Meer!

Ah, die Fischer!

fragrance 40 Und der Duft° der Bäume im Frühling!

Herrlich!

Was raucht denn hier?

Ich gehe ins Gasthaus. Die Soße ist angebrannt.

Zum Text

A Lesen Sie den ganzen Text einmal durch und beantworten Sie dann
die folgenden Fragen.

1. Mit der Soße gibt es immer wieder ein neues Problem, aber der
Koch weiß immer wieder eine Lösung (*solution*). Wie löst er die
folgenden Probleme?

BEISPIEL: Die Soße schmeckt nach nichts. → Er salzt sie.

    a. Die Soße hat zu viel Salz.

    b. Er hat keinen Wein mehr.

    c. Die Soße ist zu sauer.

    d. Die Soße ist nicht scharf genug (*enough*).

    e. Die Soße ist angebrannt.

2. Was meinen Sie? Ist die Geschichte lustig, traurig, langweilig,
tragisch? Suchen Sie Stellen (*passages*) im Text, die das zeigen.

B Ist Ihnen schon mal etwas Ähnliches (*something similar*)
passiert? Was haben Sie gekocht? Erzählen Sie. Schreiben Sie
einen kurzen Bericht (*report*).

Zu guter Letzt

Ihr Lieblingsrestaurant bewerten

Haben Sie ein Lieblingsrestaurant? Gemeinsam mit anderen Studenten/
Studentinnen werden Sie jetzt ein Bewertungsformular (*evaluation form*)
für ein Restaurant entwickeln (*develop*), ausfüllen und darüber berichten.

Schritt 1: Machen Sie eine Liste mit Fragen über Ihr Lieblingsrestaurant,
zum Beispiel:

> Warum essen Sie dort?
>
> Wie ist die Atmosphäre?
>
> Essen Sie oft dort? Wie oft?
>
> Mit wem?
>
> Was essen Sie?
>
> Wie ist die Bedienung?
>
> Wie sind die Preise?
>
> Weitere Fragen?

Schritt 2: Arbeiten Sie in Gruppen zu dritt. Stellen Sie das Bewertungsformular zusammen. Benutzen Sie Fragen aus **Schritt 1.** Erstellen Sie mindestens 10 Fragen für Ihr Formular. Geben Sie dazu auch mögliche
Antworten an, z.B.

1. Wie oft essen Sie dort?
   ____-mal pro Woche
   ____-mal pro Monat
   ____-mal im Jahr
2. Wie ist die Atmosphäre?
   ☐ ruhig
   ☐ laut und lustig
   ☐ angenehm
3. …

Beantworten Sie die Fragen noch nicht!

Schritt 3: Machen Sie Fotokopien des Formulars und tauschen Sie sie mit
einer anderen Gruppe aus. Jeder bekommt also ein Formular zum Ausfüllen. Füllen Sie das Formular mit Bezug auf (*with reference to*) Ihr eigenes Lieblingsrestaurant aus.

Schritt 4: Berichten Sie der Klasse über Ihr Lieblingsrestaurant. Beschreiben Sie verschiedene Aspekte des Restaurants. Die Klasse entscheidet
(*decides*) Folgendes. Ist das Restaurant:

1. ausgezeichnet,
2. sehr gut,
3. gut,
4. mittelmäßig oder
5. unterdurchschnittlich?

Wortschatz

Lokale
der **Biergarten, ⸚**
das **Café, -s**
die **Gaststätte, -n**
der **Imbiss, -e**
die **Kneipe, -n**
das **Lokal, -e**
das **Restaurant, -s**
das **Wirtshaus, ⸚er**

**Eating and Drinking
Establishments**
beer garden
café
full-service restaurant
fast-food stand
pub, bar
restaurant, pub, bar
restaurant
pub

Im Restaurant
das **Apfelmus**
der **Apfelstrudel**
der **Auflauf**
die **Bedienung**
die **Beilage, -n**
die **Bohne, -n**
die **Bratkartoffeln** (*pl.*)
die **Brezel, -n**
der **Eisbecher, -**
die **Gabel, -n**
das **Gericht, -e**
der **Grill**
das **Hauptgericht, -e**
der **Kellner, -** / die
  Kellnerin, -nen
die **Küche**
der **Leberkäs**
der **Löffel, -**
der **Mais**
das **Messer, -**
die **Nachspeise, -n**
der **Nachtisch, -e**
die **Nudel, -n**
der **Ober, -**
die **Olive, -n**
die **Paprika**
die **Pfanne, -n**
das **Pilsener, -**
der **Platz, ⸚e**
die **Pommes frites** (*pl.*)
die **Rechnung, -en**
der **Reis**
der **Ruhetag, -e**
die **Sahne**
der **Salat, -e**
das **Sauerkraut**
der **Schweinebraten, -**
der **Senf**
die **Serviette, -n**
der **Speck**
die **Speise, -n**

In the Restaurant
applesauce
apple strudel
casserole
service
side dish
bean
fried potatoes
pretzel
dish of ice cream
fork
dish (*of prepared food*)
grill, barbecue
main dish
waiter / waitress, server

food, cuisine; kitchen
Bavarian-style meatloaf
spoon
corn
knife
dessert
dessert
noodle
waiter
olive
bell pepper
pan
Pilsner beer
place, seat
French fries
bill
rice
day that a business is closed
cream; whipped cream
salad; lettuce
sauerkraut
pork roast
mustard
napkin
bacon
dish (of prepared food)

die **Speisekarte, -n**
das **Spiegelei, -er**
der **Sprudel**
die **Suppe, -n**
der **Teller, -**
die **Vorspeise, -n**
der **Wein, -e**
die **Weißwurst, ⸚e**
die **Zwiebel, -n**

menu
fried egg (sunny-side up)
mineral water
soup
plate
appetizer
wine
white sausage
onion

Verben
bekommen
  Was bekommen Sie?
bestellen
entschuldigen
  Entschuldigen Sie!
hängen
lassen
  Lass uns (doch) …
legen
liegen
setzen

sitzen
stecken

stehen
stellen

warten

Verbs
to get
  What will you have?
to order
to excuse
  Excuse me!
to hang; to be hanging
to let
  Let's …
to lay, put (*in a lying position*)
to lie; to be located
to set; to put (*in a sitting
  position*)
to sit
to place, put (*inside*);
  to be (*inside*)
to stand; to be located
to stand up; place, put
  (*in an upright position*)
to wait

**Adjektive und
Adverbien**
alkoholfrei
besetzt
  Hier ist besetzt.
da drüben
geöffnet
geschlossen
getrennt
hoffentlich
täglich
vegetarisch
voll

**Adjectives and
Adverbs**
nonalcoholic
occupied, taken
  This place is taken.
over there
open
closed
separate(ly)
I hope
daily
vegetarian
full; crowded

Wechselpräpositionen
an
auf
hinter
in
neben
über
unter

Two-Way Prepositions
at, on, to, near
on, on top of, at
behind, in back of
in; to (*a place*)
next to, beside
over, above
under, below, beneath; among

vor	before, in front of	**von: von zwei bis drei Uhr**	from: from two to three o'clock
zwischen	between	**vor** (+ *dat.*)**: vor zwei Tagen**	ago: two days ago
Präpositionen (Temporal)	**Prepositions (Temporal)**	**zwischen: zwischen zwei und drei Uhr**	between: between two and three o'clock
bis (um): bis (um) fünf Uhr	until: until five o'clock	**Sonstiges**	**Other**
(so) gegen: (so) gegen fünf Uhr	around/about: around five o'clock	**Ist hier noch frei?**	Is this seat available?
in (+ *dat.*)**: in zwei Tagen**	in: in two days	**Vielen Dank!**	Many thanks!
nach: nach Dienstag	after: after Tuesday	**vom Fass**	on tap; draft
seit: seit zwei Jahren	since, for: for two years	**zum Mitnehmen**	(food) to go; take-out

Das kann ich nun!

1. Nennen Sie drei andere Lokalitäten, wo man essen und trinken kann.
   a. das Restaurant
   b. _____
   c. _____
   d. _____

2. Was ist Ihr Lieblingsessen? Ihr Lieblingsgetränk? Ihre Lieblingsnachspeise?

3. „**Wo**" oder „**wohin**"?
   a. _____ wollen wir gehen?
   b. _____ ist noch ein Platz frei?

4. Setzen Sie passende Präpositionen und Artikel ein.
   a. _____ _____ Konzert gehen Uwe und Ute _____ Restaurant.
   b. Ihr Auto steht _____ _____ Restaurant.
   c. Uwe setzt sich _____ _____ Tisch.
   d. Am Nebentisch liegt ein Hund _____ _____ Tisch.

5. Wie sagen Sie das?
   a. Ask if this seat is taken.
   b. Ask a server to bring you the menu.
   c. Order some mineral water and a dish of ice cream.
   d. Let the server know that you would like to pay.

6. Ergänzen Sie **sein** oder **haben** im Imperfekt. Wo _____ du gestern? —Ich _____ in der Uni. Wir _____ eine Gastvorlesung von einem Professor aus USA.

7. Setzen Sie ein passendes Modalverb im Imperfekt ein.
   a. Ich _____ nach der Vorlesung sofort in die Mensa.
   b. Wir _____ leider nicht mitkommen.
   c. Wir _____ nämlich zwei Stunden in der Vorlesung bleiben.

Begegnung mit der Kunst
der Gegenwart

Was ist Kunst? Das Wort „Kunst" kommt von „können". Ein Künstler oder eine Künstlerin ist ein „Könner"; jemand, der etwas „kann", z.B. malen, zeichnen, formen, komponieren, schreiben. Was erwarten Sie als Kunstbetrachter[1] von einem Kunstwerk? Soll es z.B. „schön" sein, provozieren, zum Nachdenken anregen[2] oder die Realität darstellen[3]?

Die Beispiele moderner und zeitgenössischer[4] deutscher Kunst auf diesen Seiten zeigen Kunst im Kontext von alltäglichen Dingen und ungewöhnlichen Medien. Viele Leute bewundern[5] diese Werke, andere nennen sie Werke von „Dilettanten und hochgemuten[6] Nichtskönnern". Was meinen Sie? (Zitat: aus S. 7, Faust / de Vries. „Hunger nach Bildern")

Tisch mit Aggregat, 1958/87. Joseph Beuys

„Flaschenpost", 1990.
Rolf Glasmeier

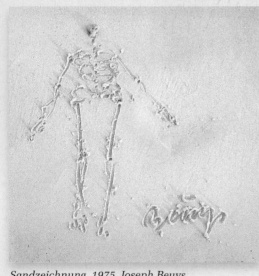

Sandzeichnung, 1975. Joseph Beuys

Aktivität 1   Kunstbewertung

A Was halten Sie von diesen Kunstgebilden? Wie würden Sie sie charakterisieren?

BEISPIEL: Ich finde die „Flaschenpost" sehr witzig.

☐ aggressiv	☐ dilettantisch
☐ hässlich	☐ komisch
☐ humorvoll	☐ originell
☐ komplex	☐ faszinierend
☐ radikal	☐ spektakulär
☐ schön	☐ kindisch
☐ verrückt	☐ fantasievoll
☐ kitschig	☐ kreativ
☐ witzig	☐ tief[7]
☐ provozierend	☐ ??

[1]*viewer of art* [2]*incite* [3]*represent* [4]*contemporary*
[5]*admire* [6]*arrogant* [7]*profound*

B Besprechen Sie die folgenden Fragen im Plenum.

1. Welches dieser Kunstwerke gefällt Ihnen besonders gut? Wenn Ihnen keins davon gefällt, warum nicht?

2. Erinnert Sie das eine oder andere dieser Kunstwerke an etwas, was Sie schon einmal, vielleicht in einem Museum, gesehen haben? Sind Ihnen die Namen der Künstler bekannt? Wenn ja, welche Namen?

3. Wer ist Ihr Lieblingskünstler / Ihre Lieblingskünstlerin?

4. Was für Kunstwerke oder Reproduktionen von Kunstwerken haben Sie in Ihrem Zimmer oder in Ihrer Wohnung?

5. Wenn Sie eins dieser Kunstwerke erwerben[1] könnten, welches würden Sie wählen, und warum?

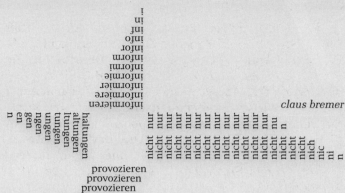

claus bremer

Konkrete Poesie

Hier sind zwei Beispiele konkreter Poesie. Charakteristisch für sie ist der visuelle Aspekt. Das Visuelle kann z.B. ein Piktogramm sein oder eine Figur, die mit Buchstaben und Wörtern gefüllt ist. Was halten Sie von Claus Bremers und Reinhard Döhls konkreter Poesie?

reinhard döhl

Aktivität 2 Sie sind dran.[2]

A Schreiben Sie jetzt Ihr eigenes konkretes Gedicht.

B Schreiben Sie ein Gedicht im Fünfzeilenformat:

Erste Zeile:	ein Substantiv
Zweite Zeile:	zwei Adjektive
Dritte Zeile:	drei Verben im Infinitiv
Vierte Zeile:	ein Satz, eine Frage oder ein Ausdruck
Fünfte Zeile:	Wiederholung der ersten Zeile, oder ein anderes Substantiv

---

[1]*acquire* [2]*Sie ... It's your turn.*

„Der Leser", 1981. Georg Jiri Dokoupil

Spaß am Wochenende

Kapitel 7

Freizeit und Sport

In diesem Kapitel

▷ **Themen:** Talking about sports and leisure pastimes, places to visit, seasons, and weather

▷ **Grammatik:** Coordinating conjunctions, the present perfect tense, the comparative

▷ **Lesen:** „Vergnügungen" (Bertolt Brecht)

▷ **Landeskunde:** Sports, hobbies, clubs, temperature conversion

▷ **Zu guter Letzt:** Ein Podcast über Ihre Universitätsstadt

VIDEOCLIPS

Pläne für die Freizeit

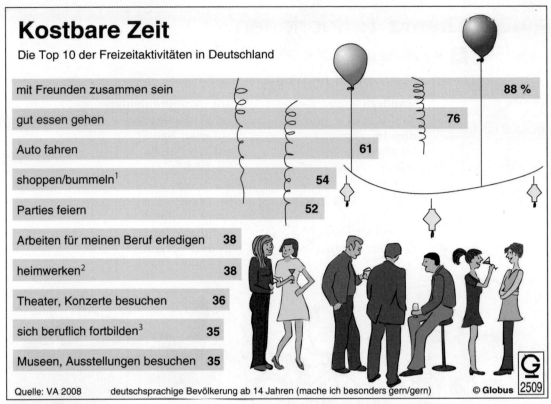

Kostbare Zeit

Die Top 10 der Freizeitaktivitäten in Deutschland

mit Freunden zusammen sein	88 %
gut essen gehen	76
Auto fahren	61
shoppen/bummeln[1]	54
Parties feiern	52
Arbeiten für meinen Beruf erledigen	38
heimwerken[2]	38
Theater, Konzerte besuchen	36
sich beruflich fortbilden[3]	35
Museen, Ausstellungen besuchen	35

Quelle: VA 2008   deutschsprachige Bevölkerung ab 14 Jahren (mache ich besonders gern/gern)   © Globus 2509

[1]bummeln *window shopping*   [2]*working on do-it-yourself home projects*   [3]sich ... *improving one's job skills*

A Schauen Sie sich die Grafik an und beantworten Sie die Fragen.

1. Was ist die beliebteste Freizeitaktivität der Deutschen?
2. Welche Freizeitaktivitäten haben mit Beruf zu tun?
3. Welche Freizeitaktivitäten haben 35% der Deutschen gern?
4. Was ist die beliebteste Freizeitaktivität in Ihrem Land?
5. Welche Freizeitaktivität haben Sie nicht so gern?

B Sie hören nun drei kurze Dialoge. Wie verbringen Ulrike, Wolfgang und Antje ihre Freizeit?

    1. Ulrike
        a. Tanzen
        b. sich mit Freunden treffen
        c. Kochen
        d. Lesen

    2. Wolfgang
        a. Fußball spielen
        b. Fernsehen
        c. Musik hören
        d. Rad fahren

    3. Antje
        a. ins Kino gehen
        b. Sport treiben
        c. Musik spielen
        d. im Internet surfen

Types of sports

Thema 1: Sportarten°

A Wo macht man das? Kombinieren Sie!

BEISPIEL: Man wandert im Wald oder am Fluss.

wandern	auf dem **Tennisplatz**
Rad fahren	im Fitnesscenter
angeln	auf dem **See**
tauchen	auf der **Straße**
reiten	im **Wald**
segeln	am **Fluss**
Bodybuilding machen	im **Meer**
schwimmen	im **Schwimmbad**
Tennis spielen	auf der **Wiese**
Aerobic machen	in den **Bergen**

1. Lisa macht jeden zweiten Tag Aerobic.

2. Uwe und Erich machen dreimal die Woche Bodybuilding.

3. Kerstin fährt Rad.

4. Heinz angelt oft im Sommer.

5. Manfred segelt gern.

6. Renate taucht gern.

7. Eva reitet jeden Tag.

B Die Karte „Naherholung" zeigt, welche Sportmöglichkeiten es in und um Göttingen gibt. Schauen Sie sich die Bildsymbole auf der Karte an. Welche Sportarten kann man hier treiben? Wo kann man das machen?

BEISPIELE: Man kann auf dem Kiessee segeln.
Man kann im Jahnstadion Fußball spielen.

im **Verein** kegeln   wandern   Golf spielen

Fußball spielen   angeln   reiten

tauchen, schwimmen   segeln   **joggen**

Tennis spielen   **Schlittschuh laufen**

Neue Wörter

der Verein club
das Freibad outdoor swimming pool
der Sportplatz athletic field
die Sporthalle sports arena
das Hallenbad indoor swimming pool
das Stadion stadium
das Eisstadion ice-skating rink

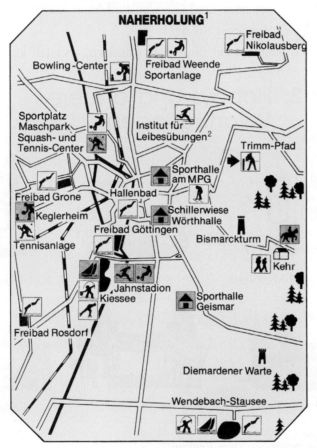

[1]local recreation   [2]physical education

Aktivität 1   Was braucht man für diese Sportarten?

Bilden Sie Sätze mit Elementen aus beiden Spalten (*columns*).

BEISPIEL: Zum Wandern braucht man Wanderschuhe.

zum Angeln	ein Fahrrad
zum Reiten	ein Segelboot
zum Wandern	einen Ball
zum Tauchen	eine Angelrute (*fishing pole*)
zum Fußball spielen	ein Pferd (*horse*)
zum Rad fahren	Wanderschuhe
zum Segeln	Schwimmflossen (*fins*)

Aktivität 2 Ein Gespräch über Sport

Bilden Sie kleine Gruppen und diskutieren Sie. Welche Sportarten treiben Sie gern? Wie oft?

BEISPIEL: S1: Ich jogge gern, und ich wandere auch gern.

S2: Wie oft machst du das?

S1: Ich gehe einmal im Monat wandern, aber ich jogge jeden Tag.

Thema 2: Hobbys und andere Vergnügungen°

pleasures

Siehe *Connecting Ideas: Coordinating Conjunctions,* S. 216.

Sie gehen oft ins Museum.

Sie bloggt.

Sie malt.

Er arbeitet am Wagen.

Sie spielen Schach.

Er faulenzt.

Neue Wörter

Freizeit verbringen spend free time
Sport treiben play sports
Schach spielen play chess
faulenzen do nothing, be lazy
die Briefmarke (Briefmarken, *pl.***)** postage stamp
sammeln collect
die Spielkarte (Spielkarten, *pl.***)** playing card
zeichnen draw
malen paint (pictures)
der Brief (Briefe, *pl.***)** letter
beliebt popular

○ Wie **verbringen** Sie Ihre **Freizeit?**

Schritt 1: Kreuzen Sie an, wie Sie Ihre Freizeit verbringen.

☐ **Sport treiben**
☐ Musik hören
☐ mit Freunden ausgehen
☐ Motorrad fahren
☐ ins Museum gehen
☐ **Karten** spielen
☐ Computerspiele spielen
☐ **Schach spielen**
☐ fernsehen
☐ **faulenzen**
☐ spazieren gehen

☐ **Briefmarken sammeln**
☐ **Spielkarten** sammeln
☐ **bloggen**
☐ **zeichnen**
☐ fotografieren
☐ Klavier spielen
☐ **malen**
☐ am **Wagen** arbeiten
☐ im Garten arbeiten
☐ **Briefe** schreiben
☐ ??

Schritt 2: Vergleichen Sie Ihre Liste mit der Liste von anderen Personen im Kurs. Können Sie drei gemeinsame Dinge finden? Was ist besonders **beliebt?**

Aktivität 3 In der Freizeit

Sie hören drei junge Leute über ihre Freizeit sprechen. Kreuzen Sie an, was sie machen.

1. Nina …
a. hört Musik. ☐
b. geht mit Freunden aus. ☐
c. spielt Computerspiele. ☐
d. fotografiert. ☐
e. zeichnet. ☐
f. malt. ☐

2. Thomas …
a. hat keine Freizeit. ☐
b. träumt (*dreams*) vom Motorrad fahren. ☐
c. fährt Ski im Traum. ☐
d. arbeitet am Wagen. ☐
e. bloggt. ☐

3. Annette …
a. geht Windsurfen. ☐
b. geht zum Flohmarkt. ☐
c. spielt Karten. ☐
d. sammelt Spielkarten. ☐
e. sammelt Briefmarken. ☐
f. surft im Internet. ☐

Aktivität 4 Wie hast du deine Freizeit verbracht?°

How did you spend your free time?

Fragen Sie einen Partner / eine Partnerin: Wie hast du in den letzten acht Tagen deine Freizeit verbracht? Nennen Sie mindestens drei Dinge.

BEISPIEL: Ich habe Musik gehört. Ich bin mit Freunden ausgegangen. Ich habe jeden Tag ferngesehen.

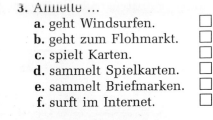

Siehe *Expressing Events in the Past*, S. 217.

mit Freunden	bin … ausgegangen
mit einem Freund	bin … in die Disco / ins Kino gegangen
mit einer Freundin	habe … Musik gehört/gespielt
allein	habe … ferngesehen/gebloggt

Aktivität 5 Möchtest du mitkommen?

Machen Sie eine Verabredung (*date*).

S1	S2
1. Ich gehe heute Bowling. Möchtest du mitkommen? ins Kino/Theater/Stadtbad/… in ein Rockkonzert / …	**2a.** Ja, gern, um wie viel Uhr denn? **b.** Ich kann nicht.
3a. Um ____ Uhr. Nach dem Abendessen um ____. Nach der Vorlesung um ____. **b.** Warum denn nicht?	**4a.** Wo wollen wir uns treffen (*meet*)? **b.** Ich muss arbeiten. Ich habe kein Geld / keine Zeit / …
5a. Vor dem Kino. / Vor der Bibliothek. / Im Studentenheim. / Bei mir zu Hause. / … **b.** Schade.	**6.** Gut. Ich treffe dich dann um ____.

Aktivität 6 Pläne für einen Ausflug°

excursion

Verena und Antje machen Pläne fürs Wochenende. Sie wohnen beide in Düsseldorf. Hören Sie sich den Dialog an, und markieren Sie dann die richtigen Antworten.

	Das stimmt	Das stimmt nicht	Keine Information
1. Verena und Antje planen einen Ausflug.	☐	☐	☐
2. Sie wollen im Neandertal wandern.	☐	☐	☐
3. Es dauert nur eine Stunde bis zum Neandertal.	☐	☐	☐
4. Der Weg führt durch den Wald.	☐	☐	☐
5. Auf dem Wege dahin wollen sie ein Picknick machen.	☐	☐	☐
6. Antje will ihren Freund Stefan einladen.	☐	☐	☐

Thema 3: Jahreszeiten und Wetter

Die Jahreszeiten

Die **Jahreszeiten:** der **Frühling**, der **Sommer**, der **Herbst**, der **Winter**. Welches Bild passt zu welcher Jahreszeit?

1. Der Berliner Wannsee im _____.

2. Oberammergau in Bayern im _____.

3. Der Grundlsee in Österreich im _____.

4. Das Städtchen Creuzburg im _____.

Das Wetter

Die Sonne	**Die Wolken**	**Der Regen**	**Das Gewitter**	**Der Schnee**
Die Sonne scheint.	**Es ist bewölkt.**	**Es regnet.**	**Es gibt ein Gewitter.**	**Es gibt Schnee.**
Es ist sonnig.	**Es ist kühl.**	**Es ist regnerisch.**	**Es blitzt und donnert.**	**Es schneit.**
Es ist angenehm/ heiter/warm/heiß.		**Es gibt einen Schauer.**	**Es ist schwül.**	**Es ist kalt.**

A Welche Jahreszeit ist das: Winter, Sommer, Frühling oder Herbst?

BEISPIEL: Die Blätter fallen von den Bäumen. →
Das ist Herbst.

1. Die Blätter (*leaves*) sind nicht mehr **so** grün **wie** im Sommer und **fallen** von den Bäumen. Es kann auch regnerisch werden.

2. Leute schwimmen im Freibad. An manchen Tagen ist der **Himmel wolkenlos.**

3. Es regnet viel und die Blumen blühen. Man braucht oft einen **Regenschirm.** Die Tage werden **länger als** im Winter.

4. Die Tage sind kurz. Für viele Menschen **dauert** diese Jahreszeit zu lang.

5. Es wird **kühler** als im Sommer und die Tage werden etwas **kürzer.**

6. Es ist sehr heiß und manchmal sogar schwül und unangenehm.

7. **Drinnen** ist es schön warm, **draußen** aber wirklich kalt. Die Sonne scheint selten. Ein starker **Wind** bläst und der Himmel ist oft bewölkt.

B Welcher **Wetterbericht** passt zu welchem Bild?

1. _____ Im Norden beginnt es zu regnen, und morgen regnet es den ganzen Tag. Am Abend: **Regen,** eventuell auch **Hagel.**

2. _____ Im Moment ist es bewölkt. Die **Temperatur** heute Nachmittag ist nur 7 **Grad,** aber heute Abend wird es kalt und **windig.**

3. _____ In der Karibik ist es sonnig, heiter und warm. Wir haben den ganzen Tag angenehme Temperaturen. Morgen wird es wieder heiß.

4. _____ Im Süden gibt es **starke** Gewitter. Was **passiert?** Es blitzt und donnert.

5. _____ In den Bergen schneit es im Moment. Die Skifahrer sind begeistert über den Schnee.

6. _____ Im Rheinland gibt es heute Morgen **Nebel,** nachher einzelne Wolken. Auch morgen neblig und kühl.

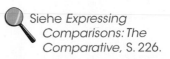
Siehe *Expressing Comparisons: The Comparative*, S. 226.

Neue Wörter

angenehm pleasant
heiter bright
heiß hot
das Gewitter (Gewitter, *pl.*) thunderstorm
es blitzt there's lightning
es donnert it's thundering
schwül humid
es schneit it's snowing
so ... wie as ... as
der Himmel sky
wolkenlos cloudless
der Regenschirm umbrella
länger (lang) longer
als than
dauert (dauern) lasts
kühler (kühl) cooler
kürzer (kurz) shorter
drinnen inside
draußen outside
der Wetterbericht weather report
der Hagel hail
der Grad (Grad, *pl.*) degree
starke (stark) strong
passiert (passieren) happens
der Nebel fog

a.

b.

c.

d.

e.

f.

Aktivität 7 Ein Wetterbericht für Deutschland

Schauen Sie sich den Wetterbericht und die Wettersymbole an. Was stimmt?

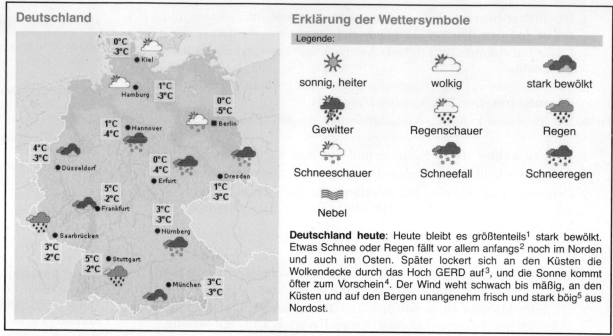

Deutschland

Erklärung der Wettersymbole

Legende:

sonnig, heiter — wolkig — stark bewölkt

Gewitter — Regenschauer — Regen

Schneeschauer — Schneefall — Schneeregen

Nebel

Deutschland heute: Heute bleibt es größtenteils[1] stark bewölkt. Etwas Schnee oder Regen fällt vor allem anfangs[2] noch im Norden und auch im Osten. Später lockert sich an den Küsten die Wolkendecke durch das Hoch GERD auf[3], und die Sonne kommt öfter zum Vorschein[4]. Der Wind weht schwach bis mäßig, an den Küsten und auf den Bergen unangenehm frisch und stark böig[5] aus Nordost.

[1]*largely* [2]*early* [3]*lockert sich auf breaks up* [4]*sight* [5]*gusty*

1. Dieser Wetterbericht ist wahrscheinlich für einen Tag im ...
   - **a.** Frühling.
   - **b.** Sommer.
   - **c.** Herbst.
   - **d.** Winter.

2. Wo ist es sonnig und heiter?
   - **a.** im Norden
   - **b.** im Osten
   - **c.** im Westen
   - **d.** nirgendwo

3. Wo gibt es Regen?
   - **a.** München
   - **b.** Hamburg
   - **c.** Stuttgart
   - **d.** Saarbrücken

4. Es ist stark bewölkt in ...
   - **a.** Düsseldorf.
   - **b.** München.
   - **c.** Berlin.
   - **d.** Hannover.

5. In Stuttgart gibt es ...
   - **a.** ein Gewitter.
   - **b.** Regen.
   - **c.** Nebel.
   - **d.** Schnee.

6. Die Tagestemperatur ist höher in Frankfurt als in
   - **a.** Stuttgart.
   - **b.** München.
   - **c.** Dresden.
   - **d.** Hannover.

7. Es ist wolkig, aber mit ein wenig Sonne in ...
   - **a.** Dresden.
   - **b.** Hamburg.
   - **c.** Erfurt.
   - **d.** Kiel.

8. Es schneit in ...
   - **a.** München.
   - **b.** Nürnberg.
   - **c.** Hannover.
   - **d.** Dresden.

9. Es gibt Nebel ...
   - **a.** im Norden.
   - **b.** im Süden.
   - **c.** im Westen.
   - **d.** nirgendwo.

Aktivität 8   Wetterberichte im Radio

Sie hören fünf kurze Wetterberichte für fünf Städte in Europa. Kreuzen Sie
die richtigen Informationen an und notieren Sie die Temperaturen in Grad
Celsius.

	Zürich	Wien	Berlin	Paris	London
sonnig	☐	☐	☐	☐	☐
warm	☐	☐	☐	☐	☐
bewölkt bis heiter	☐	☐	☐	☐	☐
(stark) bewölkt	☐	☐	☐	☐	☐
Nebel	☐	☐	☐	☐	☐
Schauer	☐	☐	☐	☐	☐
Regen	☐	☐	☐	☐	☐
Wind	☐	☐	☐	☐	☐
Gewitter	☐	☐	☐	☐	☐
Grad Celsius	___	___	___	___	___

Landeskunde-Info

The Fahrenheit temperature scale is
used in the United States, but the Celsius
scale is used elsewhere. Swedish astro-
nomer Anders Celsius (1701–1744) first
used a scale similar to the present-day
Celsius scale. The German physicist
Daniel Fahrenheit (1686–1736) defined
the Fahrenheit unit and also invented
the mercury thermometer.

To convert Celsius to Fahrenheit: divide
by 5, multiply by 9, and then add 32. To
convert Fahrenheit into Celsius: Subtract
32, divide by 9, and then multiply by 5.

- ▶ Check the current temperatures in
  Berlin, Vienna, and Zurich. Convert
  them into Celsius or Fahrenheit.
- ▶ What is the temperature in Celsius
  where you live?

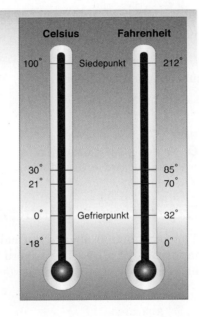

Aktivität 9   So ist das Wetter in …

Woher kommen Sie? Wie ist das Wetter dort?

BEISPIEL: Ich komme aus San Franzisko. Dort ist das Wetter im Sommer
oft kühl und neblig. Im Frühling ist es meistens sonnig. Und im
Winter regnet es.

Aktivität 10   Ihr Wetterbericht

Schauen Sie den Wetterbericht für die nächsten drei Tage in Ihrer Gegend
an. Dann berichten Sie Ihren Mitstudenten darüber. Beginnen Sie so:

BEISPIEL: Donnerstag wird es schwül und heiß. Temperaturen: 30–35 Grad
Celsius. Das Wetter für Freitag: morgens Nebel, dann sonnig,
30 Grad. Und am Samstag …

koordinierende Konjunktionen

Connecting Ideas: Coordinating Conjunctions°

Coordinating conjunctions connect words, phrases, or sentences. You already know **und** and **oder.**

> Herr **und** Frau Baumann sitzen vor dem Fernseher.

> War der Film langweilig **oder** amüsant?

Other coordinating conjunctions are:

aber	but, however
sondern	but, rather, on the contrary
denn	because, for

Erst muss ich heute arbeiten,	**und**	dann gehe ich Tennis spielen.
Ich möchte gern Tennis spielen,	**aber**	ich muss leider arbeiten.
Willst du mit zum Sportplatz,	**oder**	willst du zu Hause bleiben?
Ich möchte zum Sportplatz,	**denn**	da gibt es ein Fußballspiel.
Ich bleibe nicht zu Hause,	**sondern**	ich gehe zum Sportplatz.

NOTE:

▶ When used to connect sentences, coordinating conjunctions do not affect word order. Each sentence can be stated independently of the other.

Expressing a Contrast: **aber** vs. **sondern**

The conjunction **aber** is normally used for English *but* to express the juxtaposition of ideas. The adverb **zwar** is often added to the first contrasted element to accentuate the juxtaposition.

Das Spiel war kurz **aber** spannend.	*The game was short but exciting.*
Ich spiele **zwar** gern Tennis, **aber** nicht bei dem Wetter.	*I do like playing tennis, but not in this weather.*
Ich kann nicht schwimmen, **aber** ich möchte es lernen.	*I don't know how to swim, but I would like to learn.*

If a negative such as **nicht** or **kein** is part of the first contrasted element *and* two mutually exclusive ideas are juxtaposed, **sondern** must be used.

Es ist **nicht** warm, **sondern** kalt draußen.	*It isn't warm but rather cold outside.*
Das ist **kein** Regen, **sondern** Hagel!	*That's not rain but hail!*

Warm and **kalt,** as well as **Regen** and **Hagel,** in the above sentences, are mutually exclusive. Therefore **sondern** must be used.

Wer läuft mit?

Übung 1 Wie ist das Wetter?

Aber oder **sondern?** Ergänzen Sie die Sätze.

1. Gestern war es zwar kalt, _____ sonnig.
2. Bei uns gibt es im Winter keinen Schnee, _____ nur viel Regen.
3. Im Frühling wird es hier nie heiß, _____ im Sommer wird es manchmal sehr heiß.
4. Die Sonne scheint zwar, _____ ich glaube, es gibt heute ein Gewitter.
5. Es gibt heute keinen Regen, _____ Schnee.
6. Heute ist das Wetter angenehm, _____ morgen wird es heiß.
7. Es regnet zwar nicht, _____ ich nehme doch lieber einen Regenschirm mit.

Übung 2 Freizeitpläne

Ergänzen Sie: **und, aber, oder, denn, sondern.**

Jörg _____¹ seine Freundin Karin planen einen Ausflug _____² ein Picknick. Die Frage ist: wohin _____³ wann? Heute geht es leider nicht, _____⁴ es regnet, _____⁵ morgen haben beide keine Zeit. Also müssen sie bis zum Wochenende warten. Sie wollen diesmal nicht mit dem Auto ins Grüne fahren, _____⁶ mit ihren Fahrrädern. Das dauert zwar länger, _____⁷ es macht bestimmt mehr Spaß. Sie wollen an einen See, _____⁸ da können sie schwimmen gehen. Danach wollen sie ein Picknick im Wald _____⁹ am See machen. Karin ist nicht für die öffentlichen (*public*) Picknickplätze, _____¹⁰ da sind meistens zu viele Leute, Kinder _____¹¹ Hunde, Onkel _____¹² Tanten. Jörg lädt seinen Freund Andreas ein, _____¹³ der kann leider nicht mit. Es tut ihm leid, _____¹⁴ er muss arbeiten.

Expressing Events in the Past: The Present Perfect Tense°

das Perfekt

In German, the present perfect tense is generally used to talk about past events, although a number of common verbs (**sein, haben,** and the modals) typically use the simple past tense (**Imperfekt**) in conversation. There is essentially no difference in meaning between the two tenses.

Wo **warst** du gestern?	*Where were you yesterday?*
Gestern **habe** ich Fußball **gespielt.**	*I played soccer yesterday.*
Wer **hat** denn **gewonnen?**	*Who won?*
Wir **haben** fünf zu null **verloren.** Dann **sind** wir in die Kneipe **gegangen.**	*We lost five to zero. Then we went to the pub.*

NOTE:

▶ The present perfect tense in German, as well as English, is a compound tense. It consists of two parts: the present tense of the auxiliary verb **haben** or **sein** and a past participle (**Partizip Perfekt**). (You will learn about the auxiliaries on page 221.)

▶ The auxiliary verb (**haben** or **sein**) and the past participle form a sentence bracket (**Satzklammer**).

	┌─── **Satzklammer** ───┐	
Unsere Mannschaft	**hat**	fünf zu null	**verloren.**
Dann	**sind**	wir in die Kneipe	**gegangen.**

Uwe und Klaus reden über ihr Lieblingsthema: Fußball.

Uwe: Hast du schon gehört? Bayern München hat gestern gegen Dynamo Dresden verloren. Null zu zwei!

Klaus: Unglaublich! Hast du das in der Zeitung gelesen?

Uwe: Ich habe es im Fernsehen gesehen.

Klaus: Wie lange hat das Spiel gedauert?

Uwe: Etwas über zwei Stunden. Dynamo Dresden hat sehr gut gespielt. Letzte Woche haben sie auch gegen Bremen gewonnen; eins zu null.

Klaus: Ja, aber gegen den FC [Fußballclub] Nürnberg haben sie drei zu null verloren.

Fußball: in Deutschland sehr beliebt

❍ Identify the auxiliary verbs and past participles in the dialogue.

❍ What endings do the participles have?

❍ With what syllable do nearly all of the participles begin?

❍ What are the infinitives of these verbs?

German, like English, distinguishes between two types of verbs: so-called weak verbs (**schwache Verben**) and strong verbs (**starke Verben**). They form their past participles differently.

Weak Verbs

Ich habe **gehört,** Dynamo Dresden hat sehr gut **gespielt.**

I heard that Dynamo Dresden played very well.

Wer hat das **gesagt?**

Who said that?

Wir haben lange **gewartet.**

We waited for a long time.

NOTE:

❍ Weak verbs form the past participle by combining the verb stem with the prefix **ge-** and the ending **-(e)t.**

❍ The ending **-et** is used when the verb stem ends in **-t, -d,** or a consonant cluster such as in **regnen** or **öffnen.**

Infinitive	Prefix	Stem	Ending	Past Participle
hören	**ge-**	hör	**-t**	gehört
sagen	**ge-**	sag	**-t**	gesagt
warten	**ge-**	wart	**-et**	gewartet
regnen	**ge-**	regn	**-et**	geregnet

❍ Weak verbs ending in **-ieren** form the past participle without adding a prefix, but they do add a final **-t.**

Infinitive	Past Participle
diskutieren	diskutiert
fotografieren	fotografiert

Nürnberger Bratwurstglöcklein am Dom

Reserviert

für 5 Personen

Ab[1] 20.00 Uhr

[1]*starting at*

Übung 3 In meiner Kindheit

Drei Leute erzählen über ihre Hobbys als Kinder. Was hat ihnen Spaß gemacht? Was stimmt, und was wissen wir nicht?

	Das stimmt	Keine Information
1. Herr Harter hat gern …		
Trompete gespielt.	☐	☐
Briefmarken gesammelt.	☐	☐
viel Fernsehen geschaut.	☐	☐
2. Frau Beitz hat gern …		
mit ihrem Hund gespielt.	☐	☐
gemalt.	☐	☐
Comic-Hefte gesammelt.	☐	☐
3. Herr Huppert hat gern …		
Bücher von Karl May gesammelt.	☐	☐
mit Freunden Indianer gespielt.	☐	☐
im Schulorchester gespielt.	☐	☐
Fußball gespielt.	☐	☐

Landeskunde-Info

Generationen von jungen Deutschen lesen seit dem 19. Jahrhundert und auch heute noch die dramatischen Abenteuer-Romane von Karl May. Die populärsten Geschichten spielen im „romantischen Wilden Westen" Amerikas mit den Helden Winnetou und Old Shatterhand. Statt „cowboys and Indians" spielen deutsche Jungen „Indianer", wobei diese immer die Helden sind. So populär sind diese Geschichten, dass jährlich Karl-May-Spiele stattfinden, so z.B. in Bad Segeberg nördlich von Hamburg. Vor allem Familien mit Kindern besuchen diese Spiele, wo ihre Lieblingshelden auf der Bühne unter freiem Himmel den Sieg des Guten wahrmachen.

▶ Haben Sie als Kind Helden gehabt, die Sie gespielt haben?

▶ Gibt es in Ihrem Land ähnlich populäre Spiele für Familien?

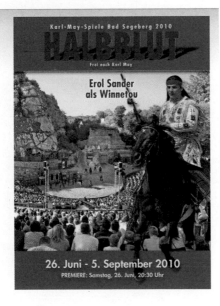

Übung 4 Im Nudelhaus

Was haben Inge und Claudia am Abend gemacht? Setzen Sie das Partizip Perfekt ein.

Inge und Claudia haben ein gemütliches Restaurant in der Stadt _____[1] (suchen). Draußen hat es _____[2] (blitzen) und _____[3] (donnern), ein Gewitter! Im Nudelhaus war es sehr voll. Der Kellner hat sie _____[4] (fragen): Haben Sie einen Tisch _____[5] (reservieren)? Sie haben ziemlich lange auf einen Platz _____[6] (warten). Der Kellner hat die Speisekarte auf den Tisch _____[7] (legen). Am Nebentisch haben einige Leute Karten _____[8] (spielen). Sie haben laut _____[9] (lachen [*to laugh*]). Das Essen hat sehr gut _____[10] (schmecken). Es hat nur 15 Euro _____[11] (kosten). Auf dem Weg nach Hause hat es immer noch _____[12] (regnen).

Übung 5 Ein Interview: Was und wie oft?

Was haben Sie schon einmal (*ever*) gemacht? Was noch nie (*never yet*)?

Schritt 1: Kreuzen Sie Ihre Antworten zuerst unten an.

Schritt 2: Arbeiten Sie dann zu zweit und stellen Sie einander abwechselnd Fragen.

BEISPIEL: **S1:** Hast du schon einmal Tango getanzt?

    S2: Ja, das habe ich schon einmal gemacht. Hast du schon einmal Trompete gespielt?

    S1: Nein, noch nie.

    oder   Ja, ich habe schon oft ...

	Schon einmal	Schon oft	Noch nie
1. den ganzen Tag faulenzen	☐	☐	☐
2. etwas sammeln (z.B. Briefmarken, ?)	☐	☐	☐
3. im Internet surfen/bloggen	☐	☐	☐
4. etwas spielen (z.B. Schach, Trompete, ?)	☐	☐	☐
5. eine Radtour machen	☐	☐	☐
6. mit Freunden über Politik diskutieren	☐	☐	☐
7. eine SMS schicken	☐	☐	☐

Strong Verbs

Heute habe ich Zeitung **gelesen.**	*Today I read the newspaper.*
Hast du schon Kaffee **getrunken?**	*Have you already drunk coffee?*
Dann sind wir zur Arbeit **gegangen.**	*Then we went to work.*

NOTE:

● Strong verbs form the past participle by placing the prefix **ge-** before the stem of the verb and adding the ending **-en.**

● Many show vowel and consonant changes in the past participle.

Infinitive	Prefix	Stem	Ending	Past Participle
gehen	**ge-**	gang	**-en**	gegangen
nehmen	**ge-**	nomm	**-en**	genommen
sitzen	**ge-**	sess	**-en**	gesessen
trinken	**ge-**	trunk	**-en**	getrunken

Following are several other familiar strong verbs and their past participles. A more complete list of strong and irregular verbs is in Appendix C.

Infinitive	Past Participle	Infinitive	Past Participle
essen	gegessen	schlafen	geschlafen
finden	gefunden	schreiben	geschrieben
geben	gegeben	sehen	gesehen
helfen	geholfen	sprechen	gesprochen
lesen	gelesen	stehen	gestanden

Übung 6 Kleine Probleme

Ergänzen Sie die fehlenden Partizipien.

BEISPIEL: Heute trinke ich Tee, aber gestern habe ich nur Wasser _getrunken_.

1. Heute geht es mir wieder gut, aber gestern ist es mir schlecht _____.
2. Isst du gern Sushi? —Das habe ich noch nie _____.
3. Mit wem sprichst du da? —Ich habe gerade mit meiner Mutter _____.
4. Ich hoffe, ich finde mein Handy wieder. Bis jetzt habe ich es immer noch nicht _____.
5. Ich sehe dich bald. Wir haben uns lange nicht _____.
6. Ich helfe dir gern. Du hast mir auch immer _____.
7. Wir stehen an der Bushaltestelle and warten. Gestern haben wir zwei Stunden im Regen _____ und auf den Bus _____.

Übung 7 Wie war's im Restaurant Nudelhaus?

Setzen Sie passende Partizipien der Verben im Kasten ein.

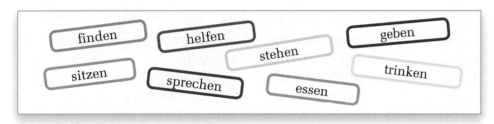

finden   helfen   geben   stehen   sitzen   sprechen   essen   trinken

```
      NUDELHAUS
     ROTE STR. 13
   37073 GÖTTINGEN
    TEL: 0551/42263

  #0001        06-01-11

  RECHNUNG-#      35

  GAST/TISCH#      3

  2 HEFEWEIZEN      €4,00
  1 GRUENE SCHINKEN €5,50
  1 VOLLKORNNUDELN  €5,25

  BAR-TL      €14,75

  ES BEDIENTE SIE
            KELLNER 1
```

1. Viele Leute haben vor dem Restaurant _____ und auf einen Platz gewartet.
2. Wir konnten zuerst keinen Platz finden. Dann haben wir endlich einen Platz _____.
3. Ich habe grüne Schinkennudeln _____, und wir haben Hefeweizen-Bier _____.
4. Am Tisch neben uns haben Touristen aus Brasilien _____.
5. Sie haben Portugiesisch _____.
6. Sie konnten nur wenig Deutsch. Wir haben ihnen mit der Speisekarte _____.
7. Sie haben mir ihre Visitenkarte (*business card*) mit E-Mail-Adresse _____. Ich soll sie in Brasilien besuchen!

The Use of **haben** or **sein** as Auxiliary

Most verbs use **haben** as the auxiliary verb in the present perfect tense.

Unsere Mannschaft **hat** das Fußballspiel **gewonnen.**	*Our team won the soccer game.*
Die Fans **haben** auf den Straßen **getanzt.**	*The fans danced in the streets.*

Sein is used with verbs that indicate movement from one place to another (e.g., **gehen** and **fahren**).

Wohin **ist** Rudi **gegangen?**	*Where did Rudi go?*
Er **ist** zum Fußballplatz **gegangen.**	*He went to the soccer field.*
Nach dem Spiel **ist** er nach Hause **gefahren.**	*After the game he went home.*

Other verbs that show motion from one place to another include **kommen (ist gekommen)**, **laufen (ist gelaufen)**, **fliegen (ist geflogen)** and **reiten (ist geritten)**.

Other important verbs using **sein** in the present perfect tense are **sein**, **bleiben**, **passieren**, and **werden**.

Wo **ist** Rudi gestern **gewesen?**	*Where was Rudi yesterday?*
Wir **sind** zu Hause **geblieben.**	*We stayed home.*
Unsere Mannschaft hat verloren? Wie **ist** das **passiert?**	*Our team lost? How did that happen?*
Nach dem Regen **ist** das Wetter wieder schön **geworden.**	*After the rain, the weather turned nice again.*

NOTE:

◐ Verbs conjugated with **sein** in the present perfect tense will be listed in the vocabulary sections as follows: **kommen, ist gekommen.**

Übung 8   Was hast du in deiner Freizeit gemacht?

Ergänzen Sie die Sätze mit der passenden Form von **sein** oder **haben**.

1. Ich _____ nichts gemacht. Es _____ die ganze Woche geregnet.
2. Ich _____ mit Freunden ins Kino gegangen.
3. Wir _____ einen alten Film mit Charlie Chaplin im Rialto gesehen.
4. Wir _____ zu Hause geblieben und _____ Karten gespielt.
5. Meine Eltern _____ zu Besuch gekommen. Ich hatte nämlich Geburtstag.
6. Ich _____ 21 geworden. Meine Freunde _____ mir eine große Party gemacht.
7. Mein Freund und ich _____ zum Wochenende nach London geflogen.
8. Wir _____ in die Berge gefahren und _____ eine Wandertour gemacht.

Übung 9   Hin und her: Wochenende und Freizeit

Wer hat was gemacht? Arbeiten Sie zu zweit.

BEISPIEL: **S1:** Was hat Dagmar gemacht?

S2: Sie ist zum Kegelklub gegangen.

Beim Töpfern in der Freizeit

wer	was
Dagmar	
Thomas	Fußball spielen
Jürgen	
Stefanie	einen Detektivroman lesen
Susanne	
Felix und Sabine	eine Radtour machen
die Kinder	

Landeskunde-Info

In ihrer Freizeit treiben viele Deutsche gern Sport; besonders beliebt sind Fußball, Rad fahren, Schwimmen und Wandern. Andere bleiben lieber zu Hause und machen Gartenarbeit, basteln (*do crafts*), sammeln Briefmarken, lesen oder sehen fern. Viele haben ein Hobby, das sie in einem Verein ausüben. In vielen Städten oder auch in kleinen Ortschaften gibt es Gesangs- und Heimatvereine, sowie Vereine für Schützen (*marksmen*), Amateurfunker (*ham radio operators*) und Kegler. In Deutschland sowohl wie in Österreich oder der Schweiz steht auch Skilaufen ganz oben auf der Liste.

▶ Gehören Sie einem Verein an?

▶ Welche Freizeitbeschäftigung macht Ihnen Spaß?

▶ Welche Sportart ist bei Ihrer Familie beliebt?

Wandern mit der ganzen Familie

Mixed Verbs

A few common verbs include features of both weak and strong verbs in the past participle. They are called mixed verbs. Like weak verbs, their participles end in **-t;** like most strong verbs, their verb stem undergoes a change.

Infinitive	Past Participle
bringen	gebracht
denken	gedacht
kennen	gekannt
wissen	gewusst

Past Participles of Verbs with Prefixes

Many German verbs consist of a base verb, such as **rufen** or **stellen,** and a prefix, such as **an-** or **be-,** to form verbs such as **anrufen** (*to call*) and **bestellen** (*to order*). The verb **anrufen,** as you learned in **Kapitel 4,** belongs to the group of verbs that have separable prefixes.

Ich **rufe** meinen Bruder **an.**	*I am calling my brother.*

When used in the present perfect tense, separable-prefix verbs form the past participle by inserting the **ge-** prefix between the separable prefix and the verb base. These verbs may be strong, weak, or mixed.

Ich habe meinen Bruder **angerufen.**	*I called my brother.*
Ich bin heute spät **aufgewacht.**	*I woke up late this morning.*
Wo hast du ihn **kennengelernt?**	*Where did you meet him?*

Other examples of separable-prefix verbs and their past participles include:

Infinitive	Past Participle
aufstehen	(ist) aufgestanden
ausgeben	ausgegeben
ausgehen	(ist) ausgegangen
einkaufen	eingekauft
einladen	eingeladen
zurückkommen	(ist) zurückgekommen

Other verbs, such as **bestellen** and **verbringen,** begin with prefixes that are not separable from the base, such as **be-, emp-, ent-, er-, ge-,** and **ver-.**

Hoffentlich **gewinnen** wir das Spiel.	*I hope we win the game.*
Er **verbringt** den ganzen Tag auf dem Fußballplatz.	*He spends the entire day on the soccer field.*
Der Gast **bestellt** eine Pizza.	*The guest orders a pizza.*

A verb with an inseparable prefix forms the past participle without an additional **ge-** prefix. These verbs may be either strong, weak, or mixed.

Wir haben das Spiel **gewonnen.**	*We won the game.*
Er hat den ganzen Tag auf dem Fußballplatz **verbracht.**	*He spent the entire day on the soccer field.*
Der Gast hat eine Pizza **bestellt.**	*The guest ordered a pizza.*

Other examples of inseparable-prefix verbs and their past participles include:

Infinitive	Past Participle
bezahlen	bezahlt
erzählen	erzählt
gefallen	gefallen
gewinnen	gewonnen
verlieren	verloren

Übung 10   Wie war das gestern?

Schritt 1: Ergänzen Sie zuerst die fehlenden Verbformen.

Infinitiv	Hilfsverb	Partizip Perfekt
1. aufstehen	*ist*	aufgestanden
2. bestellen	_____	_____
3. einladen	hat	_____
4. _____	ist	eingeschlafen
5. gefallen	_____	gefallen
6. _____	_____	mitgekommen
7. _____	hat	verloren

Schritt 2: Bilden Sie nun Sätze nach dem Beispiel.

BEISPIEL: Heute kaufe ich nicht ein.
Aber gestern *habe ich eingekauft*.

1. Ich stehe gewöhnlich früh auf.
   Aber gestern _____.
2. Unser Fußballverein gewinnt nie.
   Aber gestern _____.
3. Eigentlich gefällt mir Kegeln im Verein nicht.
   Aber gestern _____.
4. Dirk kommt nie zum Fußballspiel mit.
   Aber gestern _____.
5. Ich verliere nie beim Tennisspiel.
   Aber gestern _____.

Übung 11 Kleine Situationen

Ergänzen Sie das Partizip Perfekt.

1. Aus der Zeitung: Großer, graugetigerter Kater, rotes Halsband mit Glöckchen _____ (verlieren). Wer hat ihn _____ oder _____ (sehen, finden)? Er hört auf den Namen Charly.

2. In den letzten Tagen ist es recht kalt _____ (werden).

3. Wir haben gestern Abend noch lange über unsere Probleme _____ (diskutieren). Ich bin erst um drei Uhr nachts _____ (einschlafen). Und dann bin ich um sechs Uhr _____ (aufstehen).

4. Wir haben für acht Uhr einen Tisch im Nudelhaus _____ (reservieren). Wir haben alle eine Pizza _____ (bestellen).

5. **A:** Wo hast du deinen Freund _____ (kennenlernen)?

   B: Jemand hat ihn zu einer Party _____ (einladen). Gleich am nächsten Tag hat er mich _____ (anrufen).

6. **C:** Wie hat es euch im Nudelhaus _____ (gefallen)?

   D: Sehr gut. Warum bist du nicht _____ (mitkommen)?

   C: Ich habe nicht _____ (wissen), wo ihr wart.

Verloren/Gefunden

Großer, graugetigerter Kater, rotes Halsband mit Glöckchen. Wer hat ihn gesehen oder gefunden? Hört auf den Namen Charly. Finderlohn.

Übung 12 Wie war dein Wochenende?

Schritt 1: Sprechen Sie zu zweit über Ihr Wochenende. Nennen Sie drei Aktivitäten. Folgen Sie dem Beispiel.

BEISPIEL: **S1:** Was hast du letztes Wochenende gemacht?

S2: Zuerst habe ich meine Freundin angerufen.

S1: Und dann?

Hier sind einige mögliche Aktivitäten:

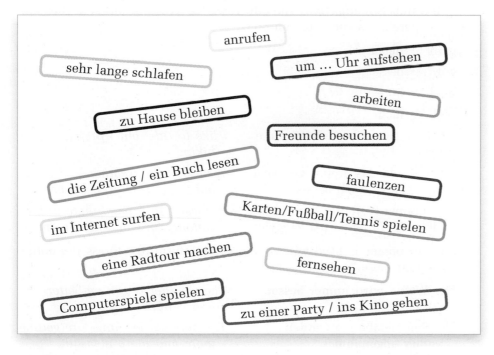

Schritt 2: Berichten Sie dann im Kurs.

Expressing Comparisons: The Comparative°

der Komparativ

Adjectives and adverbs have three forms: the basic form **(die Grundform),** the comparative **(der Komparativ),** and the superlative **(der Superlativ).** In this chapter you will learn about the comparative.

Der Winter kommt. Es wird **kühler.**	*Winter is coming. It is getting cooler.*
Es regnet **öfter.**	*It rains more often.*
Die Tage werden **kürzer.**	*The days are getting shorter.*

In German, the comparative is formed by adding **-er** to the basic form of the adjective or adverb. (Remember that in German, adverbs are identical to adjectives.) Unlike English, German has only one way to form the comparative, whereas English has two:

cool → cool**er**

often → **more** often

NOTE:

▶ Most adjectives of one syllable with the vowel **a, o,** or **u** have an umlaut in the comparative.

groß	→ größer		oft	→ öfter
kurz	→ kürzer		warm	→ wärmer

▶ Some adjectives that end in **-er** or **-el** drop an **e** when adding the **-er.**

teu**er** → teurer

dunk**el** → dunkler

A small number of adjectives and adverbs have irregular forms in the comparative. Here are some common ones.

gern → lieber

gut → besser

hoch → höher

viel → mehr

Ich reite **gern,** aber ich wandere **lieber.**	*I like to ride, but I prefer hiking.*
Gestern war das Wetter **gut,** aber heute ist es noch **besser.**	*Yesterday the weather was good, but today it is even better.*
Im Sommer regnet es hier nicht **viel;** im Winter regnet es **mehr.**	*It doesn't rain much here in the summer; in winter it rains more.*

The adverb **immer** is used with a comparative form to express the notion of "more and more."

Das Wetter wird **immer besser.**	*The weather is getting better and better.*
Die Sommerabende werden **immer angenehmer.**	*The summer evenings are getting more and more pleasant.*

The conjunction **als** (*than*) links the two parts of a comparison.

Das Wetter ist besser im Süden **als** im Norden.	*The weather is better in the South than in the North.*

▶ Scan the excerpts from German weather reports and identify adjectives and adverbs in the comparative. What are the basic forms of those adjectives and adverbs?

Freundlicher, bis 23 Grad

Es wird wieder sommerlicher. Der Himmel ist wechselnd bewölkt mit sonnigen Abschnitten. Die Temperatur steigt auf 2?

WETTER

23/10 Der Himmel ist heute meist nur leicht bewölkt, und nach Angaben der Meteorologen soll es auch trocken bleiben. Mittwoch und Donnerstag wird es noch wärmer.

Heute in Norddeutschland

Im Norden Deutschlands gibt es heute einen Mix aus Sonne und Wolken. An der Nordsee ist der Himmel wolkiger.

Übung 13 Wie war das Wetter?

Ergänzen Sie die Sätze mit dem Adjektiv im Komparativ.

BEISPIEL: In Berlin war es warm, aber in Hamburg war es noch _____*wärmer*_____.

1. Im Westen war es bewölkt, aber im Norden war es noch _____.
2. Heute ist es kalt und windig, aber gestern war es noch _____ und _____.
3. Am Meer war es sonnig, aber in den Bergen war es noch _____.
4. Am Nachmittag war es angenehm, aber am Abend war es noch _____.
5. Zu Weihnachten hat es viel geschneit, aber an Neujahr hat es noch _____ geschneit.
6. Das Wetter in Österreich hat mir gut gefallen, aber in Italien hat mir das Wetter noch _____ gefallen.
7. Auf dem Land gibt es oft Gewitter im Sommer, aber in den Bergen gibt es noch _____ Gewitter.

> ### Sprach-Info
>
> The particle **noch** (*even*) intensifies a comparative.
>
> Morgen wird es **noch** wärmer.
> *Tomorrow it's getting even warmer.*

Übung 14 Vergleiche

Bilden Sie Sätze nach dem Muster.

BEISPIEL: in Berlin = 35 Grad Celsius / in Frankfurt = 25 Grad C (heiß) →
    In Berlin ist es heißer als in Frankfurt.

1. in Österreich = 20 Grad C / in der Schweiz = 25 Grad C (warm)
2. in den Bergen = −2 Grad C / in der Stadt = 10 Grad C (kalt)
3. die Tage im Winter / die Tage im Sommer (kurz)
4. die Tage im Sommer / die Tage im Winter (angenehm)
5. das Wetter im Frühling / das Wetter im Herbst (regnerisch)
6. das Wetter heute / das Wetter gestern (gut)
7. die Temperatur gestern / die Temperatur heute (hoch)
8. in London / in Kairo (es regnet viel)

Expressing Equality

Use **so ... wie** (*as . . . as*) to express equality. Use **nicht so ... wie** to express inequality.

Das Wetter im Norden ist **so** schlecht **wie** im Süden.	*The weather in the North is as bad as in the South.*
Im Süden regnet es **nicht so** viel **wie** im Norden.	*It doesn't rain as much in the South as in the North.*

The adverb **genauso** (*just/exactly as*) can replace **so** to emphasize the point being made.

Österreich ist **genauso** schön **wie** die Schweiz.	*Austria is just as beautiful as Switzerland.*

Übung 15   Vergleiche: Was ist Ihre Meinung?

Bilden Sie Sätze nach dem Beispiel.

BEISPIELE: Wandern gefällt mir / gut / Schwimmen →
   Wandern gefällt mir besser als Schwimmen.
oder   Schwimmen gefällt mir nicht so gut wie Wandern.
oder   Wandern gefällt mir so/genauso gut wie Schwimmen.

1. Aerobic gefällt mir	gut	Bodybuilding
2. Ein Volkswagen kostet	viel	ein BMW
3. Ein BMW fährt	schnell	ein Volkswagen
4. Ich finde Kegeln	interessant	Golf spielen
5. Ich höre klassische Musik	gern	Popmusik
6. Am Wochenende schlafe ich	lang	in der Woche
7. Wanderschuhe sind	bequem	Sandalen

Übung 16   Was meinst du?

Arbeiten Sie zu zweit und wechseln Sie einander ab (*take turns*). Folgen Sie dem Beispiel.

BEISPIEL: Ich gehe lieber _____ als _____. (ins Kino, in die Disco, ins Theater, ...)

   S1:   Ich gehe lieber ins Kino als ins Theater. Und du?

   S2:   Ich gehe genauso gern ins Theater wie ins Kino.

   oder   Ich gehe nicht so gern ins Kino wie ins Theater.

   oder   Ich gehe auch lieber ins Kino als ins Theater.

1. Ich mag _____ lieber als _____. (Musik hören, Bloggen, Fernsehen, ...)

2. Ich finde _____ schöner als _____. (klassische Musik, Rapmusik, Heavymetal, ...)

3. Ich trage _____ lieber als _____. (Sandalen, Stiefel, Turnschuhe, ...)

4. _____ gefällt mir besser als _____. (Rad fahren, Schlittschuh laufen, Inlineskaten, ...)

5. Ich finde _____ interessanter als _____. (Wien, Berlin, Zürich, ...)

6. _____ schlafe ich länger als _____. (an Wochentagen, am Wochenende, montags, ...)

7. _____ gefällt mir besser als _____. (Camping, Wandern, Segeln, ...)

Segeln macht mehr Spaß als Wandern.

Sprache im Kontext

Videoclips

A Jan, Dennis und Beatrice sprechen über ihre Freizeit. Was machen sie nicht in der Freizeit? Streichen Sie die Aktivitäten durch, die sie nicht machen.

1. Jan ...
verbringt seine Freizeit
   im Freien
geht ins Kino
trifft Freunde
sieht fern
macht Sport

2. Dennis ...
geht ins Kino
geht ins Museum
treibt Sport
trifft Freunde

3. Beatrice ...
geht ins Kino
trifft gern Freunde
macht Sport
hört Musik

B Herr Borowsky verbringt seine Freizeit ein bisschen anders. Wie verbringt er seine Freizeit?

C Welche Sportarten treiben Jan und Dennis?

D Wo haben diese Leute den Urlaub verbracht? Kombinieren Sie.

1. _____ Jan
2. _____ Beatrice
3. _____ Herr Borowsky
4. _____ Dennis

a. in Ägypten
b. in Wien
c. in Guatemala
d. auf den Kanarischen Inseln und in Bayern

E Und Sie? Was machen Sie in der Freizeit? Wo haben Sie letztes Jahr Ihren Urlaub verbracht?

Lesen

Zum Thema

A Wie viel Freizeit hat man in verschiedenen Ländern? Schauen Sie sich die Tabelle „Arbeitsfrei" auf der nächsten Seite an. Beantworten Sie die folgenden Fragen mithilfe der Tabelle.

1. Wie viele Urlaubstage haben die Deutschen im Jahr?
2. Welches Land hat mehr Urlaubstage — die Schweiz oder Österreich?
3. Wer hat mehr Freizeit — die Belgier oder die Niederländer?
4. Wie viele Urlaubstage haben die US-Amerikaner?

B Was machen die Deutschen in ihrer Freizeit? Schauen Sie sich die Grafik auf Seite 207 an. Vergleichen Sie Ihre Freizeitbeschäftigungen mit denen der Deutschen.

   ◗ Was machen Sie gern in Ihrer Freizeit?
   ◗ Stehen Ihre Freizeitaktivitäten auf der Liste?

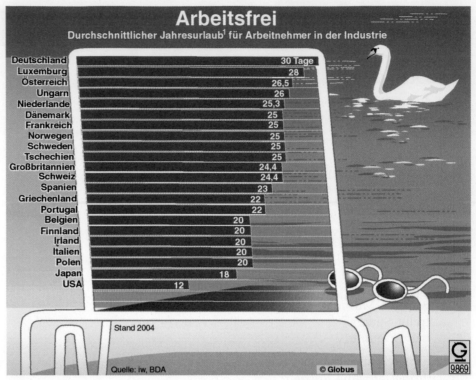

Arbeitsfrei
Durchschnittlicher Jahresurlaub[1] für Arbeitnehmer in der Industrie

Deutschland	30 Tage
Luxemburg	28
Österreich	26,5
Ungarn	26
Niederlande	25,3
Dänemark	25
Frankreich	25
Norwegen	25
Schweden	25
Tschechien	25
Großbritannien	24,4
Schweiz	24,4
Spanien	23
Griechenland	22
Portugal	22
Belgien	20
Finnland	20
Irland	20
Italien	20
Polen	20
Japan	18
USA	12

Stand 2004

Quelle: iw, BDA   © Globus

[1]Durchschnittlicher ... *average annual vacation*

C Machen Sie eine Liste der sechs beliebtesten Freizeitaktivitäten in Ihrer Klasse. Vergleichen Sie Ihre Klasse mit den Deutschen.

1. Was ist die beliebteste Freizeitbeschäftigung in Ihrer Klasse?
2. Was steht an zweiter Stelle (*place*) für die Klasse?
3. Steht diese Aktivität auf der Liste der Deutschen?
4. Welche Unterschiede (*differences*) und Ähnlichkeiten (*similarities*) gibt es?

Auf den ersten Blick

A Assoziationen: Woran denken Sie, wenn Sie _____ hören?

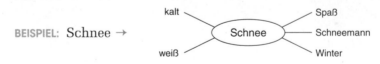

BEISPIEL: Schnee → kalt / Spaß / Schnee / weiß / Schneemann / Winter

1. Reisen
2. Schwimmen
3. freundlich sein
4. bequeme Schuhe
5. Hund
6. Buch
7. neue Musik
8. Singen

B Lesen Sie den Titel und überfliegen (*scan*) Sie den Text.

1. Was für ein Text ist das?
   a. ein Artikel aus einer Zeitung
   b. ein Gedicht (*poem*)
   c. ein Brief
2. Wie heißt der Autor?
3. Kennen Sie andere Werke (*works*) von ihm? Wenn ja, welche?

Vergnügungen

von Bertolt Brecht

Der erste Blick[1] aus dem Fenster am Morgen
Das wiedergefundene alte Buch
Begeisterte Gesichter[2]
Schnee, der Wechsel der Jahreszeiten
5 Die Zeitung
Der Hund
Die Dialektik
Duschen, Schwimmen
Alte Musik
10 Bequeme Schuhe
Begreifen[3]
Neue Musik
Schreiben, Pflanzen
Reisen
15 Singen
Freundlich sein.

Bertolt Brecht 1898–1956

Focus on words?

---

[1]*glance* [2]*Begeisterte … enthusiastic faces* [3]*understanding*

Zum Text

A Die Wörter **Duschen, Pflanzen, Reisen** können die Pluralformen sein von: **Dusche** (*shower*), **Pflanze** (*plant*), **Reise** (*trip*); oder sie können auch Verbalformen sein: **Duschen** = *taking a shower;* **Pflanzen** = *planting;* **Reisen** = *traveling.* Wie versteht Brecht diese Wörter wahrscheinlich? Als Dinge (Objekte) oder als Aktivitäten? Warum ist das wichtig?

B Sind Brechts Vergnügungen ungewöhnlich oder ganz normal? Welche finden Sie ungewöhnlich? Warum?

C Schreiben Sie ein Gedicht mit dem Titel „Vergnügungen". Arbeiten Sie dann zu zweit und tauschen Sie Ihre Gedichte aus. Lesen Sie das Gedicht Ihres Partners / Ihrer Partnerin vor.

Zu guter Letzt

Ein Podcast über Ihre Universitätsstadt

Machen Sie einen Podcast über Ihre Stadt für deutschsprachige Touristen.

Schritt 1: In Gruppen zu viert, schauen Sie sich Thema 1 und 2 an und notieren Sie mindestens fünf Freizeitaktivitäten, die man in Ihrer Universitätsstadt machen kann, z.B. wandern, segeln, Rad fahren.

Schritt 2: Mit einer Digitalkamera gehen Sie an die Orte, wo man diese Aktivitäten macht, und filmen Sie die Freizeitaktivitäten. Sie sollen nicht mehr als drei Minuten pro Aktivität filmen.

Schritt 3: Mit der Gruppe schauen Sie sich die Aktivitäten auf dem Film an und wählen Sie für jede Aktivität drei Szenen. Benutzen Sie nur diese Aktivitäten für Ihr Projekt.

Schritt 4: Schreiben Sie zu jeder Aktivität einen kurzen Text.

BEISPIEL: „Nicht weit von der Uni gibt es einen Wald mit einem See. Dort wandern und segeln viele Leute.“

Schritt 5: Schneiden Sie Film und Text zusammen. Der Film soll nicht länger als vier Minuten sein.

Schritt 6: Zeigen Sie den Film Ihrer Klasse. Nach dem Film sollen die anderen Studenten sagen, was für andere Freizeitaktivitäten man an diesen Orten machen kann.

BEISPIEL: „Nicht weit von der Uni gibt es einen Wald. Er heißt Huesten Woods. Dort wandern und segeln viele Leute. Viele Studenten fahren dort auch Rad.“

Wortschatz

Sport und Vergnügen	**Sports and Leisure**	der **Fluss**, ̈-e	river
angeln	to fish	das **Freibad**, ̈-er	outdoor swimming pool
bloggen	to blog	das **Hallenbad**, ̈-er	indoor swimming pool
Bodybuilding machen	to do bodybuilding, weight training	das **Meer**, -e	sea, ocean
		das **Schwimmbad**, ̈-er	swimming pool
der **Brief**, -e	letter	der **See**, -n	lake
die **Briefmarke**, -n	postage stamp	die **Sporthalle**, -n	sports arena
faulenzen	to be lazy, lie around	der **Sportplatz**, ̈-e	athletic field
die **Freizeit**	free time	das **Stadion**, *pl.* **Stadien**	stadium
der **Fußball**, ̈-e	soccer; soccer ball		
Fußball spielen	to play soccer	der **Tennisplatz**, ̈-e	tennis court
joggen	to jog	der **Wald**, ̈-er	forest
die **Karte**, -n	card	die **Wiese**, -n	meadow
malen	to paint		
Rad fahren (fährt Rad), ist Rad gefahren	to bicycle, ride a bike	**Die Jahreszeiten**	**Seasons**
		das **Frühjahr**	spring
reiten, ist geritten	to ride (horseback)	der **Frühling**	spring
sammeln	to collect	der **Herbst**	autumn, fall
Schach spielen	to play chess	der **Sommer**	summer
Schlittschuh laufen (läuft), ist gelaufen	to ice-skate	der **Winter**	winter
segeln	to sail		
die **Spielkarte**, -n	playing card	**Das Wetter**	**Weather**
der **Sport**, *pl.* **Sportarten**	sports, sport	das **Gewitter**, -	thunderstorm
		der **Grad**	degree(s)
Sport treiben, getrieben	to play sports	**35 Grad**	35 degrees
		der **Hagel**	hail
tauchen	to dive	der **Himmel**	sky
Tennis spielen	to play tennis	der **Nebel**	fog
(Zeit) verbringen, verbracht	to spend (time)	der **Regen**	rain
		der **Regenschauer**, -	rain shower
der **Verein**, -e	club, association	der **Regenschirm**, -e	umbrella
der **Wagen**, -	car	der **Schnee**	snow
zeichnen	to draw	die **Sonne**	sun
		Die Sonne scheint.	The sun is shining.
Orte	**Locations**	der **Sonnenschein**	sunshine
der **Berg**, -e	mountain	die **Temperatur**, -en	temperature
das **Eisstadion**, *pl.* **Eisstadien**	ice-skating rink	der **Wetterbericht**, -e	weather report

der **Wind, -e**	wind	**fallen (fällt), ist**	to fall
die **Wolke, -n**	cloud	**gefallen**	
		fliegen, ist geflogen	to fly
blitzen	to flash	**passieren, ist passiert**	to happen
Es blitzt.	There's lightning.	**reservieren**	to reserve
donnern	to thunder	**verlieren, verloren**	to lose
Es donnert.	It's thundering.		
regnen	to rain	**Sonstiges**	**Other**
Es regnet.	It's raining.	**als**	than
schneien	to snow	**beliebt**	popular
Es schneit.	It's snowing.	**denn**	because, for
		draußen	outside
angenehm	pleasant	**dreimal**	three times
bewölkt	overcast, cloudy	**drinnen**	inside
heiß	hot	**einmal**	once
heiter	fair, bright	**einmal die Woche**	once a week
kalt; kälter	cold; colder	**einmal im Monat**	once a month
kühl	cool	**einmal im Jahr**	once a year
kurz; kürzer	short; shorter	**früher**	earlier, once, used to
lang; länger	long; longer		(*do, be, etc.*)
neblig	foggy	**genauso**	just/exactly as
regnerisch	rainy	**gestern**	yesterday
schwül	muggy, humid	**jeden Tag**	every day
sonnig	sunny	**oder**	or
stark; stärker	strong; stronger	**so ... wie**	as ... as
warm; wärmer	warm; warmer	**sondern**	but, rather
windig	windy	**zweimal**	twice
wolkenlos	cloudless		

Andere Verben	**Other Verbs**
bringen, gebracht	to bring
dauern	to last; to take

Das kann ich nun!

1. Nennen Sie drei Sportarten. Wie oft treiben Sie Sport?

2. Was braucht man?
   a. Zum Wandern braucht man _____.
   b. Zum Fußball spielen braucht man _____.
   c. Zum Radfahren braucht man _____.

3. Nennen Sie drei Freizeitaktivitäten. Was machen Sie gern in Ihrer Freizeit?

4. Wie gut können Sie das? Verwenden Sie **besser als** oder **(nicht) so gut wie** in Ihren Antworten.
   a. Schach spielen vs. Karten spielen
   b. Fahrrad fahren vs. Schlittschuh laufen
   c. singen vs. tanzen

5. Setzen Sie eine passende Konjunktion ein.
   a. Ist es kalt _____ warm draußen?
   b. Ich bin nicht zum Sportplatz gegangen, _____ ich bin zu Hause geblieben.
   c. Mein Freund segelt gern, _____ ich reite lieber.

6. Wie heißen die vier Jahreszeiten? Beschreiben Sie sie.

7. Setzen Sie die richtige Form von **haben** oder **sein** ein.
   a. Wann _____ das passiert?
   b. Wo _____ der Mann gestanden?
   c. Wann _____ seine Frau gekommen?
   d. Wann _____ sie ihn nach Hause gebracht?
   e. Wir _____ die ganze Zeit bei ihm geblieben.

8. Wie sagt man das im Perfekt?
   a. Wir gehen aus.
   b. Er spielt Fußball.
   c. Ich weiß das leider nicht.
   d. Er bestellt eine Pizza im Restaurant.
   e. Das Wetter wird besser.

Kapitel **8**

Wie man fit und gesund bleibt

Zu zweit macht Joggen mehr Spaß.

In diesem Kapitel

- ▶ **Themen:** Talking about health and fitness, the human body, common illnesses and health complaints, morning activities

- ▶ **Grammatik:** Subordinating conjunctions, indirect questions, reflexive pronouns and verbs

- ▶ **Lesen:** „Sage mir, was du isst ..." (Monika Hillemacher)

- ▶ **Landeskunde:** Health spas in Germany, visits to the doctor, **Apotheken** and **Drogerien,** German breakfast

- ▶ **Zu guter Letzt:** Ein idealer Fitnessplan

A Schauen Sie sich die Anzeige für Baden-Baden an, einen Kurort (*spa*) in Deutschland. Was kann man in Baden-Baden unternehmen (*do*)? Machen Sie eine Liste mit diesen Kategorien.

BEISPIEL:	**Sport**	**Unterhaltung**	**Gesundheit**
	schwimmen	ins Theater gehen	in die Sauna gehen

B Was machen diese Leute in Baden-Baden? Kreuzen Sie an.

	Herr/Frau Lohmann	Herr Kranzler	Frau Dietmold
Golf	☐	☐	☐
Karten spielen	☐	☐	☐
Massage	☐	☐	☐
Mini-Golf	☐	☐	☐
Sauna	☐	☐	☐
Schwimmen	☐	☐	☐
Spazierengehen	☐	☐	☐
Tanzen	☐	☐	☐
Theater	☐	☐	☐
Thermalbad	☐	☐	☐
Tischtennis	☐	☐	☐
Trinkkur	☐	☐	☐
Wandern	☐	☐	☐

Hier klicken!

Weiteres zum Thema
Kurorte finden Sie bei
Deutsch: Na klar! im
World-Wide-Web unter
www.mhhe.com/dnk6.

Landeskunde-Info

There are many health spas **(Heilbäder und Kurorte)** throughout Germany, and Germans can choose to spend several weeks at a spa after an illness or when they feel stressed from their jobs. The national health-care system **(Krankenkasse)** subsidizes such a stay to a degree if rest and recuperation **(Kur und Erholung)** are prescribed by a physician, and if the **Kur** will either minimize or delay development of a potential condition or treat a chronic one. The necessity of such treatment is evaluated on a case-by-case basis. Faced with increasing health-care costs, fewer demands for **Kur und Erholung** at health spas, and the recent trends toward **Wellness,** these resorts are having to reinvent themselves. To be sure, the traditional **Kur** is still available, but at more cost to the patient. These **Kurorte** now offer additional activities such as exercise and **Wellness** programs, family excursions, and, at some, even gambling. Some resorts now offer conference facilities so that participants can combine meetings with some type of recreation. At some health spas people go on a **Trinkkur:** at prescribed intervals they drink a glass of the healthful mineral waters for which some spas are famous.

- What kind of health care system is available in your country?
- Are there equivalents to **Wellness** programs available in your country?

Wörter im Kontext

Neue Wörter

die Gesundheit health
tue (tun) do
versuche (versuchen) try
die Arbeit work
meistens mostly
zu Fuß on foot
der Kräutertee herbal tea
ab und zu now and then
deshalb for that reason
rauche (rauchen) smoke
d.h. = das heißt that is
wenig little
regelmäßig regularly
besonders especially
die Luft air
mich fit halten (sich fit halten) keep fit
mich beeilen (sich beeilen) hurry up
mindestens at least
mache Urlaub (Urlaub machen) go on vacation
anstrengend strenuous
die Krankenschwester nurse
achte auf (achten auf) pay attention to
die Biolebensmittel *(pl.)* organic foods
entweder ... oder either . . . or
mich entspannen (sich entspannen) relax

Thema 1: Fit und gesund

Was machen diese Leute, um **fit** zu bleiben?

TINA: Für meine **Gesundheit tue** ich viel. Ich esse vegetarisch, **versuche** so gut es geht, den **Stress** in meinem Leben zu reduzieren. Zur **Arbeit** gehe ich **meistens zu Fuß.** Ich trinke viel **Kräutertee** und nur selten **Alkohol,** und **ab und zu** ein Glas Wein zum Essen.

WALTER: **Fitness** ist mir sehr wichtig. **Deshalb rauche** ich nie und esse **gesund, d.h. (das heißt) wenig** Fleisch und viel Gemüse. Ich treibe **regelmäßig** Sport, **besonders** an der frischen **Luft.** Ich möchte **mich fit halten.** So, und jetzt muss ich **mich beeilen.** Ich muss ins Fitnesscenter.

ANITA: **Mindestens** zweimal im Jahr **mache** ich **Urlaub,** denn meine Arbeit ist sehr **anstrengend.** Ich bin nämlich **Krankenschwester.** Ich **achte auf** meine Gesundheit und esse nur **Biolebensmittel, entweder** direkt vom Bauernhof **oder** vom Bioladen. Ich mache jede Woche Yoga. Da kann ich **mich** richtig **entspannen.**

A Was machen Tina, Walter und Anita für ihre Gesundheit? Kombinieren Sie!

1. Stress _____	**a.** trinken
2. regelmäßig _____	**b.** machen
3. mit Yoga _____	**c.** Alkohol trinken
4. Kräutertee _____	**d.** achten
5. gesund _____	**e.** rauchen
6. auf die Gesundheit _____	**f.** sich entspannen
7. ab und zu _____	**g.** reduzieren
8. oft Urlaub _____	**h.** essen
9. nie _____	**i.** Sport treiben
10. Biolebensmittel _____	**j.** essen

B Tina, Walter und Anita leben gesund. Wählen Sie die richtige Antwort.

1. Wie kommt Tina zur Arbeit?

   a. zu Fuß   **b.** mit dem Rad   **c.** mit dem Auto

2. Wie oft trinkt Tina ein Glas Wein?

   a. nie   **b.** ab und zu   **c.** einmal in der Woche

3. Wie viel Fleisch isst Walter?

   a. viel   **b.** wenig   **c.** keins

4. Wie oft treibt Walter Sport?

   a. einmal im Monat   **b.** regelmäßig   **c.** nie

5. Was für Lebenmittel isst Anita?

   a. Biolebensmittel   **b.** Lebensmittel vom Supermarkt

6. Wie oft macht Anita Urlaub?

   a. mindestens zweimal im Jahr   **b.** einmal im Jahr   **c.** nicht mehr als alle zwei Jahre

7. Wie entspannt sich Anita?

   a. Sie joggt.   **b.** Sie läuft Schlittschuh.   **c.** Sie macht Yoga.

a.

b.

c.

Aktivität 1   Meine Fitnessroutine

Schritt 1: Was machen Sie, um fit und gesund zu bleiben? Kreuzen Sie an!

1. ☐ joggen	**8.** ☐ nicht rauchen
2. ☐ ins Fitnesscenter gehen	**9.** ☐ mich entspannen
3. ☐ vegetarisch essen	**10.** ☐ viel an die frische Luft gehen
4. ☐ meditieren	**11.** ☐ viel zu Fuß gehen
5. ☐ Urlaub machen	**12.** ☐ Yoga machen
6. ☐ wenig Alkohol trinken	**13.** ☐ viel Wasser trinken
7. ☐ Stress reduzieren	**14.** ☐ ??

Schritt 2: Sagen Sie nun, wie oft Sie das tun.

BEISPIEL: Ich trinke jeden Tag viel Wasser.

nie	jeden Tag
selten	mindestens/meistens einmal/zweimal die Woche
ab und zu	einmal/zweimal/dreimal im Jahr
manchmal	??
regelmäßig	

Siehe *Reflexive Pronouns and Verbs*, S. 248.

Schritt 3: Sagen Sie nun, warum Sie das tun oder nicht tun.

BEISPIELE: Ich jogge nicht. Das ist mir zu langweilig.
Ich esse vegetarisch. Das ist gut für die Gesundheit.

macht mir (keinen) Spaß
ist gut/schlecht für die Gesundheit
macht krank
kostet zu viel Geld
habe keine Zeit/Lust dazu (*for that*)
ist zu anstrengend
ist (un)gesund
reduziert Stress
ist mir zu langweilig
??

fitness adviser **Aktivität 2** Beim Fitnessberater°

Spielen Sie ein Gespräch zwischen einem Fitnessberater und einer Klientin. Was darf man tun? Was soll man nicht tun?

BEISPIEL: **S1:** Darf ich Wein trinken?

S2: Ja, aber nicht zu viel. Trinken Sie lieber viel Wasser.

S1: Und wie viele Stunden soll ich pro Nacht schlafen?

S2: Mindestens sieben Stunden.

Fleisch essen	Kräutertee trinken
Vitamintabletten einnehmen	Kaffee trinken
Urlaub machen	??
Sport treiben	

body # Thema 2: Der menschliche Körper°

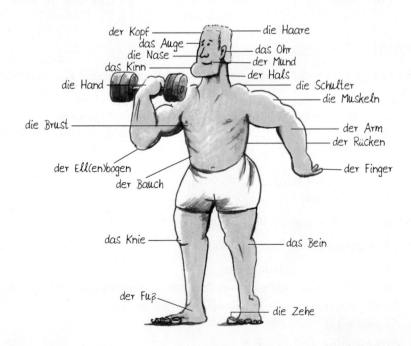

Ein Telefongespräch

Christoph: Schmidt.

Uta: Hallo, Christoph? Hier ist Uta.

Christoph: Ja, grüß dich, Uta.

Uta: Nanu! Was ist denn los? Du **klingst** ja so **deprimiert**.

Christoph: Ich liege im Bett. Ich **fühle mich hundsmiserabel**.

Uta: **Was fehlt dir** denn?

Christoph: Ich habe eine **Erkältung**, vielleicht **sogar** die **Grippe**. Der Hals **tut mir weh**, ich kann **kaum schlucken, mir ist schlecht**. Ich habe **Fieber**, **Halsschmerzen, Husten** und **Schnupfen**. Ich habe auch **Kopfschmerzen** und bin so **müde** und **schlapp**. Und morgen muss ich eine Arbeit bei Professor Höhn **abgeben**.

Uta: **So ein Pech.** Warst du schon beim **Arzt**?

Christoph: Nein.

Uta: Wie lange bist du denn schon **krank**?

Christoph: Seit **fast** zwei Wochen schon.

Uta: Du bist **verrückt**! Geh doch **gleich** zum Arzt. Er kann dir sicher was* **verschreiben**.

Christoph: Aber ich kriege (*get*) wohl keinen **Termin**.

Uta: **Das macht nichts.** Geh einfach in die **Sprechstunde**.

Christoph: Na gut. Ich danke dir für den **Rat**.

Uta: **Nichts zu danken** ... Ich wünsche dir **gute Besserung**!

> Ich fühle mich hundsmiserabel.

Neue Wörter

klingst (klingen) sound
deprimiert depressed
fühle mich (sich fühlen) feel
hundsmiserabel really lousy
Was fehlt dir? What's wrong with you?
die Erkältung cold
sogar even
die Grippe flu
tut weh (wehtun) hurts
kaum scarcely
schlucken swallow
mir ist schlecht I feel bad, I feel sick to my stomach
das Fieber fever
die Halsschmerzen (*pl.*) sore throat
der Husten cough
der Schnupfen head cold
die Kopfschmerzen (*pl.*) headache
müde tired
schlapp worn out
abgeben drop off, give to
so ein Pech what bad luck
der Arzt doctor
krank sick
fast almost
verrückt crazy
gleich right away
verschreiben prescribe
der Termin appointment
Das macht nichts. That doesn't matter.
die Sprechstunde office hours
der Rat advice
nichts zu danken don't mention it
gute Besserung get well soon

A Stimmt das oder stimmt das nicht?

	Das stimmt	Das stimmt nicht
1. Uta spricht mit Christoph am Telefon.	☐	☐
2. Christoph fühlt sich heute viel besser.	☐	☐
3. Er war gestern beim Arzt.	☐	☐
4. Uta ist deprimiert.	☐	☐
5. Uta gibt Christoph Rat.	☐	☐
6. Sie bringt Christoph zum Arzt.	☐	☐

B Was ist los mit Christoph? Ergänzen Sie!

1. Christoph klingt _____.
2. Er fühlt sich _____.
3. Er hat eine _____.
4. Der Hals _____ ihm _____.
5. Er hat auch _____, _____, _____ und _____.
6. Christoph ist seit zwei Wochen _____.

---

*__Was,__ as used here, is a shortened form of **etwas.** It occurs often in colloquial German.

Aktivität 3 Christophs Geschichte

Erzählen Sie Christophs Geschichte. Benutzen Sie die Bilder.

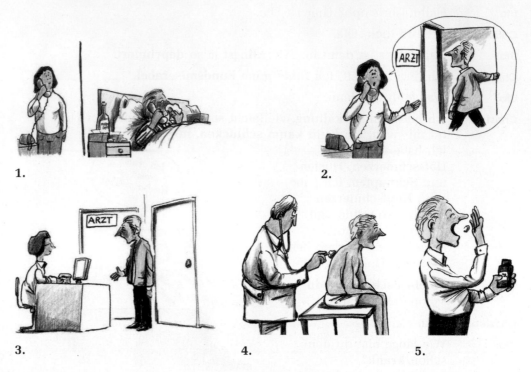

1.

2.

3.

4.

5.

Aktivität 4 Im Aerobic-Kurs

Sie hören eine Aerobic-Lehrerin beim Training im Aerobic-Kurs. Nummerieren Sie alle Körperteile in der Reihenfolge von 1–10, so wie Sie sie hören. Einige Wörter auf der Liste kommen nicht im Hörtext vor.

_____ Arme	_____ Füße	_____ Knie	_____ Muskeln
_____ Bauch	_____ Hals	_____ Kopf	_____ Rücken
_____ Beine	_____ Hände	_____ Ohren	_____ Schultern
_____ Finger			

Landeskunde-Info

Die Deutschen, so heißt es, sind die Arztbesuchseuropameister[1]. Niemand in Europa geht so oft und so gern zum Arzt wie die Deutschen. Achtzehnmal pro Jahr gehen sie zum Arzt. Montag ist der beliebteste Tag für Arztbesuche. Am Montag gehen im Durchschnitt 8 Prozent der Bevölkerung zum Arzt, während es an anderen Tagen 4 Prozent sind. Und die häufigsten Beschwerden? Schauen Sie sich die Grafik an.

◗ Wie oft gehen Sie jedes Jahr zum Arzt?

◗ Was sind die häufigsten Diagnosen in Ihrem Land?

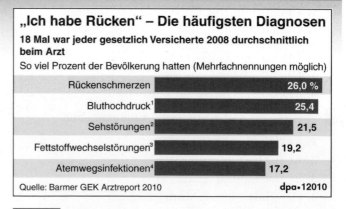

„Ich habe Rücken" – Die häufigsten Diagnosen

18 Mal war jeder gesetzlich Versicherte 2008 durchschnittlich beim Arzt

So viel Prozent der Bevölkerung hatten (Mehrfachnennungen möglich)

Rückenschmerzen	26,0 %
Bluthochdruck[1]	25,4
Sehstörungen[2]	21,5
Fettstoffwechselstörungen[3]	19,2
Atemwegsinfektionen[4]	17,2

Quelle: Barmer GEK Arztreport 2010   dpa•12010

_____
[1]Meister = *champions*

[1]*high blood pressure* [2]*vision problems* [3]*metabolic problems*
[4]*respiratory infections*

Aktivität 5 Beschwerden°

Was fehlt diesen Leuten? Was sollten sie dagegen tun? Markieren Sie Ihre Antworten.

Dialog 1

| Leni hat: | Rückenschmerzen | eine Erkältung | Kopfschmerzen |
| Doris empfiehlt: | Geh zum Arzt. | Leg dich ins Bett. | Nimm Aspirin. |

Dialog 2

| Doris hat: | Kopfschmerzen | Bauchschmerzen | Fieber |
| Leni empfiehlt: | Geh zum Arzt. | Trink Kamillentee. | Leg dich ins Bett. |

Dialog 3

| Patient hat: | keine Energie | Halsschmerzen | kann nicht schlafen |
| Arzt empfiehlt: | mehr Schlaf | Kur im Schwarzwald | Tabletten gegen Stress |

Sprach-Info

Use the following phrase to talk about how you feel:

> Ich **fühle mich** nicht wohl.   *I don't feel well.*

The person with the symptoms refers to himself or herself with a pronoun in the dative case.

> **Mir ist schlecht.**   *I feel sick to my stomach.*
>
> **Mir ist warm/kalt.**   *I feel warm/cold.*

The verb **fehlen** with the dative case is frequently used to ask "What is the matter?"

> **Was fehlt dir/ihm denn?**   *What's the matter with you/him?*

Use the verb **wehtun** with the dative case to say that something hurts.

> Die Füße **tun mir/ihm/ihr weh.**   *My/His/Her feet hurt.*

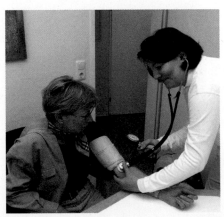

¹lozenges

Aktivität 6 Was fehlt dir denn?

Arbeiten Sie zu zweit und fragen Sie einander: „Was fehlt dir denn?"
Antworten Sie mit einem guten Rat.

BEISPIEL: **S1:** Ich fühle mich so schlapp.

  S2: Geh nach Hause und leg dich ins Bett.

Beschwerden	**Ratschläge**
Ich fühle mich so schlapp.	Nimm ein paar Aspirin.
Der Hals tut mir weh.	Geh …
Ich habe …	in die Sauna.
Kopfschmerzen.	nach Hause.
Rückenschmerzen.	zum Arzt.
Husten.	Leg dich ins Bett.
Schnupfen.	Nimm mal Vitamin C.
eine Erkältung.	Trink heißen Tee mit Rum.
Fieber.	??
Ich kann nicht schlafen.	
Mir ist schlecht.	

Was fehlt Ihnen?

Thema 3: Morgenroutine

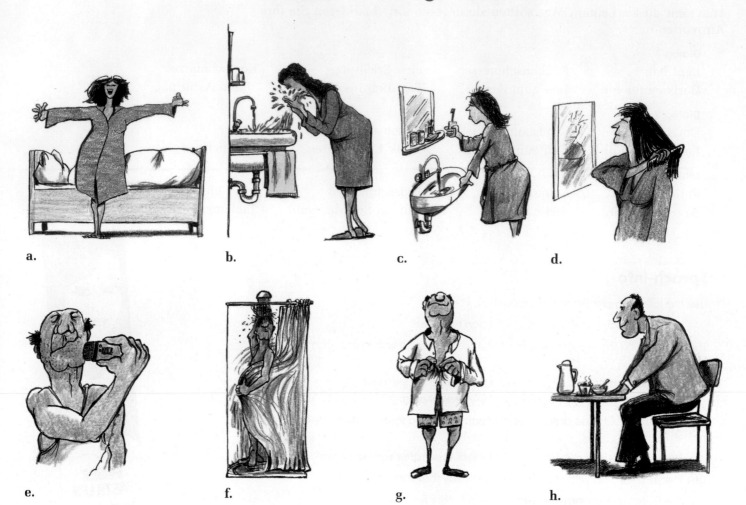

a.

b.

c.

d.

e.

f.

g.

h.

A Was bedeuten die Wörter und Ausdrücke? Kombinieren Sie!

1. sich duschen   *to shave*
2. sich setzen   *to stretch*
3. sich kämmen   *to brush one's teeth*
4. sich strecken   *to shower*
5. sich das Gesicht waschen   *to sit down*
6. sich rasieren   *to comb one's hair*
7. sich anziehen   *to wash one's face*
8. sich die Zähne putzen   *to get dressed*

B Was machen Herr und Frau Lustig morgens? Was passt zu welchem Bild?

1. _____ Er **rasiert sich.**
2. _____ Sie **streckt sich.**
3. _____ Sie **kämmt sich.**
4. _____ Sie **putzt sich die Zähne.**
5. _____ Er **duscht sich.**
6. _____ Er **setzt sich** an den Tisch.
7. _____ Sie **wäscht sich** das **Gesicht.**
8. _____ Er **zieht sich an.**

Aktivität 7 Meine Routine am Morgen

Was machen Sie jeden Morgen? Hier sind einige Dinge, die man morgens oft macht. In welcher Reihenfolge machen Sie alles jeden Morgen? Nummerieren Sie die Aktivitäten von 1 bis 8.

_____ Ich ziehe mich an.

_____ Ich dusche mich.

_____ Ich wasche mir das Gesicht.

_____ Ich kämme mich.

_____ Ich strecke mich.

_____ Ich rasiere mich.

_____ Ich setze mich an den Frühstückstisch.

_____ Ich putze mir die Zähne.

Aktivität 8 Hin und her: Meine Routine – deine Routine

Jeder hat eine andere Routine. Was machen diese Leute und in welcher Reihenfolge? Machen Sie es auch so?

BEISPIEL: **S1:** Was macht Alexander morgens?

S2: Zuerst rasiert er sich und putzt sich die Zähne. Dann kämmt er sich. Danach setzt er sich an den Tisch und frühstückt.

Wer	Was er/sie morgens macht
Alexander	zuerst / sich rasieren / sich die Zähne putzen dann / sich kämmen danach / sich an den Tisch setzen / frühstücken
Elke	
Tilo	zuerst / sich duschen / sich rasieren dann / sich an den Tisch setzen / frühstücken danach / sich die Zähne putzen
Kamal	
Sie	zuerst / ?? dann / ?? danach / ??
Ihr Partner / *Ihre Partnerin*	zuerst / ?? dann / ?? danach / ??

Grammatik im Kontext

Connecting Sentences

unterordnende Konjunktionen

Subordinating Conjunctions°

Subordinating conjunctions are used to connect a main clause and a dependent clause. Four frequently used subordinating conjunctions are **dass** (*that*), **ob** (*whether, if*), **weil** (*because*), and **wenn** (*whenever, if*).

Ich hoffe, **dass** du bald gesund wirst.	*I hope that you'll get well soon.*
Weißt du, **ob** Mark krank ist?	*Do you know whether Mark is ill?*
Mark bleibt zu Hause, **weil** er eine Erkältung hat.	*Mark is staying at home because he has a cold.*
Ich gehe ins Fitnessstudio, **wenn** ich Zeit habe.	*I go to the fitness center whenever I have time.*

NOTE:

▶ A comma always separates the main clause from the dependent clause.

▶ In dependent clauses the conjugated verb is placed at the end.

▶ In the case of a separable-prefix verb, the prefix is joined with the rest of the verb.

Main Clause	Dependent Clause
Er bleibt zu Hause,	weil er eine Erkältung **hat.**
Ich weiß nicht,	ob er schon zum Arzt gegangen **ist.**
Er hat gesagt,	dass er zu Hause bleiben **muss.**
Ich bin sicher,	dass er **mitkommt.**

If the dependent clause precedes the main clause, the main clause begins with the conjugated verb, followed by the subject.

Dependent Clause	Main Clause
Weil Mark krank war,	**musste** er zu Hause bleiben.
Wenn wir Zeit haben,	**gehen** wir am Wochenende ins Fitnesscenter.
Ob Hans Zeit hat,	**weiß** ich nicht.

Indirect Questions

An indirect question is made up of an introductory clause and a question. Interrogative pronouns function like subordinating conjunctions in indirect questions. The conjugated verb is placed at the end.

Direct Question	Indirect Question
Warum kauft Herr Stierli so viel Vitamin B?	Ich weiß nicht, **warum** Herr Stierli so viel Vitamin B **kauft.**
Was hat er vor?	Ich möchte wissen, **was** er **vorhat.**

A yes/no indirect question is introduced by the conjunction **ob.**

> Geht er zu einer Party?   Ich möchte wissen, **ob** er zu einer Party **geht.**

Übung 1   Es geht ihm hundsmiserabel.

Suchen Sie passende Nebensätze für die Sätze in der linken Spalte. Mehrere Antworten sind manchmal möglich.

1. Tobias liegt im Bett, _____
2. Inge möchte wissen, _____
3. Inge hofft, _____
4. Er sagt ihr, _____
5. Sie fragt ihn, _____
6. Sie besucht ihn, _____

    a. dass er schon seit vier Tagen krank ist.
    b. wie es ihm geht.
    c. weil er die Grippe hat.
    d. wenn er wieder gesund ist.
    e. dass er endlich zum Arzt geht.
    f. ob er schon beim Arzt war.

Übung 2   Ein großer Erfolg°

success

Schauen Sie sich den Cartoon „Herr Stierli" an. Beantworten Sie die Fragen, indem Sie die Konjunktion **weil** benutzen (*use*).

von René Fehr

1. Warum ist Herr Stierli zur Apotheke gegangen? (Er wollte Vitamin B kaufen.)
2. Warum hat er fünf Packungen Vitamin B gekauft? (Er braucht mehr Energie.)
3. Warum war Herr Stierli sehr stolz (*proud*)? (Er war sehr populär bei den Gästen auf der Party.)
4. Warum hat er so großen Erfolg? (Er hat viel Vitamin B eingenommen.)

Übung 3   Was meinen Sie?°

What's your opinion?

BEISPIEL: **S1:**   Obst ist die beste Nahrung (*food*).

        S2:   Ich bezweifle, dass Obst die beste Nahrung ist.

Redemittel

Ich bezweifle, dass …
Ich glaube auch, dass … / Ich bin sicher, dass …

1. Vitamin C ist gut gegen Erkältungen.
2. Klassische Musik ist gut gegen Stress.
3. Rauchen ist ungesund.
4. Yoga reduziert Stress.
5. Gesund ist, was gut schmeckt.
6. Bier macht dick.
7. Vegetarisches Essen ist ideal.
8. Zucker macht aggressiv.
9. Knoblauch (*garlic*) hilft gegen Vampire.

Essen macht Spaß

Jeder Deutsche trinkt im Leben 3060 Liter Bier

Lachen macht gesund!

MOZART GEGEN STRESS

health-conscious

Übung 4 Wie gesundheitsbewusst° sind Sie?

Fragen Sie einen Partner / eine Partnerin, was er/sie für Fitness und die Gesundheit tut und warum.

BEISPIEL: S1: Gehst du regelmäßig ins Fitnesscenter?

S2: Nein.

S1: Warum nicht?

S2: Weil ich das langweilig finde.

S1: Fragen	S2: Antworten
vegetarisch essen	finde das langweilig
Vitamintabletten einnehmen	kostet zu viel
oft zu Fuß gehen	mag ich (nicht)
Kräutertee / Kaffee / viel Wasser trinken	reduziert Stress
rauchen	macht mir (viel/keinen) Spaß
Yoga machen	habe keine Zeit dazu
regelmäßig ins Fitnesscenter gehen	ist sehr gesund/ungesund
Biolebensmittel kaufen	gefährdet die Gesundheit
Kalorien zählen	

Landeskunde-Info

In deutschsprachigen Ländern kauft man Medikamente, sogar Aspirin, in der **Apotheke**. Aber auch Vitamine und pflanzliche Heilmittel (homöopathische Mittel) bekommt man dort. Zahnpasta, Seife und Kosmetikartikel kauft man in der **Drogerie** oder auch im Supermarkt.

▶ Sind homöopathische Mittel weit verbreitet in Ihrem Land?

▶ Wo kaufen Sie Medikamente?

Medikamente gibt es in der Apotheke.

Schwabentor Apotheke

Übung 5 Das mache ich, wenn ...

Sagen Sie, wann Sie das machen.

BEISPIEL: Ich gehe zum Arzt, wenn ich krank bin.

Ich gehe zum Arzt, ...
    zum Zahnarzt, ...
    in die Sauna, ...
    in die Drogerie, ...
    in die Apotheke, ...
Ich bleibe im Bett, ...
Ich nehme viel Vitamin C
    ein, ...
Ich esse Hühnersuppe, ...
Ich trinke Kräutertee, ...

Ich brauche Zahnpasta.
Ich habe zu viel gegessen.
Ich brauche Aspirin.
Ich fühle mich hundsmiserabel.
Ich habe die Grippe.
Ich fühle mich schlapp.
Ich habe eine Erkältung.
Ich bin krank.
Ich habe Zahnschmerzen.
??

Übung 6 Was tun Sie gewöhnlich?

Sagen Sie, was Sie in diesen Situationen machen.

BEISPIEL: Wenn ich eine Erkältung habe, trinke ich viel Kräutertee.

Wenn ich eine Erkältung habe,
Wenn ich nicht einschlafen kann,
Wenn ich gestresst bin,
Wenn ich mich hundsmiserabel
    fühle,

im Bett bleiben
Kräutertee trinken
im Internet surfen
Rotwein mit Rum trinken
viel Vitamin C einnehmen
Hühnersuppe essen
ein Buch lesen
meditieren
Musik hören
??

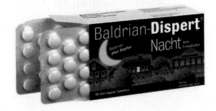

Übung 7 Ich muss es mir überlegen°.

think it over

Kirsten möchte Drachenfliegen (*hang gliding*) lernen. Ihr
Freund Stefan ist sehr skeptisch. Was will er genau wissen?

BEISPIEL: Wo kann man das lernen? →
    Er will wissen, wo man das lernen kann.

Er will wissen, ...

1. Wie gefährlich (*dangerous*) ist das eigentlich?
2. Warum muss es ausgerechnet Drachenfliegen sein?
3. Was braucht man an Ausrüstung (*equipment*)?
4. Muss man nicht zuerst einen Führerschein (*driver's
   license*) machen?
5. Was kostet ein Kurs?
6. Willst du nicht lieber wandern gehen?

Reflexive Pronouns and Verbs°

When the subject and pronoun object of a sentence refer to the same person, the object is called a reflexive pronoun.

Ich wasche **mich.**	*I wash myself.*
Die Studenten informieren **sich** über die Kosten.	*The students are informing themselves about the costs.*

Reflexive pronouns are identical to personal pronouns except for the third-person forms and the formal **Sie**-forms, all of which are **sich.**

Wander-Vögel

informieren sich
jeden Samstag im
REISE-JOURNAL
der Rheinischen Post

Reflexive Pronouns			
	Acc.	**Dat.**	
(ich)	mich	mir	*myself*
(du)	dich	dir	*yourself*
(Sie)	sich	sich	*yourself (formal)*
(er/sie)	sich	sich	*himself/herself*
(wir)	uns	uns	*ourselves*
(ihr)	euch	euch	*yourselves*
(Sie)	sich	sich	*yourselves (formal)*
(sie)	sich	sich	*themselves*

Verbs with Accusative Reflexive Pronouns

German uses reflexive pronouns much more extensively than does English. Some verbs are always used with an accusative reflexive pronoun. The English equivalent of many such verbs has no reflexive pronoun at all.

Er hat **sich erkältet.**	*He caught a cold.*
Wir müssen **uns beeilen.**	*We have to hurry.*
Bitte, **setzen** Sie **sich.**	*Please sit down.*

The infinitives of these verbs are **sich erkälten, sich beeilen,** and **sich setzen.**

NOTE:

❯ The reflexive pronoun comes after the conjugated verb.

❯ It follows pronoun subjects in questions and the formal imperative.

Infinitive: **sich setzen** (*to sit down*)		
ich setze **mich**		wir setzen **uns**
du setzt **dich**		ihr setzt **euch**
er sie } setzt **sich** es		sie setzen **sich**
Sie setzen **sich**		

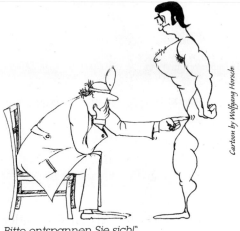

Cartoon by Wolfgang Horsch

„Bitte entspannen Sie sich!"

Verbs that *always* use an accusative reflexive pronoun include:

sich ausruhen	to rest
sich beeilen	to hurry
sich entspannen	to relax
sich erholen	to recuperate
sich erkälten	to catch cold

Verbs that *typically* use an accusative reflexive pronoun include:

sich (hin)legen	to lie down
sich (hin)setzen	to sit down
sich informieren (über)	to inform oneself (about)
sich (wohl) fühlen	to feel (well)

Analyse

Schauen Sie sich den Cartoon an.

▶ Lesen Sie, was Wurzel denkt, und identifizieren Sie die Sätze mit reflexiven Verben.

▶ Wie fühlt sich Wurzel heute?

▶ Fühlt er sich gewöhnlich so gut? Wie oft hat er sich schon so gefühlt?

▶ Warum fühlt er sich am Ende ganz deprimiert?

¹unusual ²sign

¹*each time*

Übung 8 Beim Arzt

Sie hören eine Besprechung zwischen Herrn Schneider und seinem Arzt. Markieren Sie die richtigen Antworten auf die Fragen.

1. Warum hat Herr Schneider einen Termin beim Arzt?
    a. Er hat einen chronischen Schluckauf (*hiccups*).
    b. Er hat sich beim Fitnesstraining verletzt.
    c. Er fühlt sich so schlapp.

2. Was ist die Ursache (*cause*) seines Problems?
    a. Seine Arbeit bringt viel Stress mit sich.
    b. Er sitzt den ganzen Tag am Schreibtisch.
    c. Seine Arbeit ist so langweilig.

3. Was empfiehlt ihm der Arzt?
    a. Er soll sich eine andere Arbeit suchen.
    b. Er soll sich im Schwarzwald vom Stress erholen.
    c. Er soll Sport treiben.

4. Wie reagiert Herr Schneider auf diese Vorschläge?
    a. Er ist sehr enthusiastisch.
    b. Er hat keine Zeit für eine Kur im Schwarzwald.
    c. Er interessiert sich nicht für Sport.

5. Was verschreibt ihm der Arzt?
    a. einen täglichen Spaziergang
    b. regelmäßig meditieren
    c. Vitamintabletten

6. Warum meint der Arzt, dass Herr Schneider mit seinen Nerven am Ende ist?
    a. Er hat einen Schluckauf und weiß es nicht.
    b. Er entspannt sich oft.
    c. Er redet zu viel und zu schnell.

Was macht er da? Er erkältet sich bestimmt.

Verbs with Reflexive Pronouns in the Accusative or Dative

A number of German verbs may be used with a reflexive pronoun in either the accusative or the dative case. They include:

sich anziehen	*to get dressed*
sich kämmen	*to comb one's hair*
sich verletzen	*to injure oneself*
sich waschen	*to wash oneself*

Reflexive Pronoun in Accusative	**Reflexive Pronoun in Dative**
Ich ziehe **mich** an.	Ich ziehe **mir** die Jacke an.
I get dressed.	*I put my jacket on.*
Ich wasche **mich**.	Ich wasche **mir** die Hände.
I wash myself.	*I wash my hands.*
Du hast **dich** verletzt.	Du hast **dir** den Fuß verletzt.
You've injured yourself.	*You've injured your foot.*
Ich kämme **mich**.	Ich kämme **mir** die Haare.
I'm combing my hair.	*I'm combing my hair.*
—	Ich putze **mir** die Zähne.
	I brush my teeth

NOTE:

▶ The reflexive pronoun is in the dative case if the sentence also has a direct object in the accusative.

▶ The expression **sich die Zähne putzen** is used only with the dative reflexive pronoun.

Übung 9 Morgenroutine

Morgens geht es bei der Familie Kunze immer recht hektisch zu. Ergänzen Sie die fehlenden Reflexivpronomen.

Herr Kunze duscht _____¹ zuerst. Dann rasiert er _____.² Seine Frau ruft: „Bitte, beeil _____,³ ich muss _____⁴ auch noch duschen."

Cornelia, die siebzehnjährige Tochter, erklärt: „Ich glaube, ich habe _____⁵ erkältet. Ich fühle _____⁶ so schlapp. Ich lege _____⁷ wieder hin." Frau Kunze zu Cornelia: „Zieh _____⁸ bitte sofort an! Du fühlst _____⁹ so schlapp, weil du so spät ins Bett gegangen bist." Cornelia: „Ja, ja, ich ziehe _____¹⁰ ja schon an."

Frau Kunze zu Thomas, dem siebenjährigen Sohn: „Es ist schon halb acht, und du musst _____¹¹ noch kämmen. Hast du _____¹² überhaupt schon gewaschen? Und hast du _____¹³ auch die Zähne geputzt?"

Sabine, die zwölfjährige Tochter, duscht _____¹⁴ schon seit fünfzehn Minuten.

Herr und Frau Kunze setzen _____¹⁵ endlich an den Frühstückstisch. Herr Kunze zu seiner Frau: „Wir müssen _____¹⁶ beeilen. Wo sind denn die Kinder?" Er ruft ungeduldig: „Könnt ihr _____¹⁷ nicht ein bisschen beeilen? Es ist schon acht Uhr."

So ist es jeden Morgen: Alle müssen _____¹⁸ beeilen.

Übung 10 Ratschläge°

Was kann man Ihnen in diesen Situationen raten?

BEISPIEL: **S1:**   Ich fühle mich hundsmiserabel.

S2:   Leg dich ins Bett.

oder   Du musst dich ins Bett legen.

Trimm Dich am Feierabend

1. Es ist sehr kalt draußen.
2. Sie haben sich erkältet.
3. Sie fühlen sich hundsmiserabel.
4. Sie haben den ganzen Tag mit Arbeit verbracht.
5. Sie müssen in einer Minute an der Bushaltestelle sein.
6. Sie haben sich den Fuß verletzt.

sich beeilen
sich ins Bett legen
sich entspannen
sich (ins Café) setzen
sich warm anziehen
sich ausruhen
??

Übung 11 Wie oft machen Sie das?

Fragen Sie jemand, wie oft er/sie die folgenden Dinge macht.

BEISPIEL: sich die Zähne putzen →

S1:   Putzt du dir jeden Tag die Zähne?

S2:   Natürlich putze ich mir jeden Tag die Zähne.

sich die Zähne putzen	nie
sich die Haare kämmen	ab und zu
sich rasieren	oft
sich die Haare waschen	jeden Tag/Morgen/Abend
sich duschen	einmal/zweimal die Woche

Expressing Reciprocity

A reflexive pronoun is used to express reciprocity.

Martina und Jörg **lieben sich.**	*Martina and Jörg love each other.*
Sie **treffen sich** im Café.	*They meet (each other) in the café.*
Sie **haben sich** vor zwei Wochen **kennengelernt.**	*They met each other two weeks ago.*
Sie **rufen sich** oft **an.**	*They call each other frequently.*

Übung 12 Der neue Freund

Martina erzählt ihrer Freundin Katrin über ihren neuen Freund Jörg. Benutzen Sie die Verben unten in einem kleinen Bericht.

Hier ist der Anfang:
Wir haben uns vor zwei Wochen kennengelernt.

1. sich kennenlernen (wo)
2. sich anrufen (wie oft)
3. sich treffen (wo, wie oft)
4. sich sehr gut verstehen
5. sich lieben

Sprache im Kontext

Videoclips

A Im Interview erklären diese Leute, warum sie ihre Lebensmittel im Bioladen kaufen. Verbinden (*Connect*) Sie die Person mit dem Grund (*reason*).

1. Frau Simon
2. Maria
3. Peter

Der Käse aus dem Bioladen schmeckt besser als Käse aus einem Supermarkt.

Bauern gebrauchen keine Chemikalien für die Bioprodukte.

Biosäfte sind gesünder als die herkömmlichen Säfte.

B Und Sie? Kaufen Sie auch im Bioladen ein? Warum? (Warum nicht?)

C Welche Symptome haben diese Leute, wenn sie krank sind? Markieren Sie Oliver und/oder Maria.

Oliver	Maria	
☐	☐	hat oft eine Erkältung
☐	☐	hat Halsschmerzen
☐	☐	hat Fieber und Husten
☐	☐	hat Schnupfen
☐	☐	hat manchmal die Grippe

D Welche Symptome haben Sie, wenn Sie krank sind?

E Und was machen diese Leute, wenn sie krank sind?

1. Oliver badet heiß, schwitzt (*sweats*), _____ sich ins Bett, _____ viel und trinkt _____.
2. Maria legt sich auf die _____, trinkt Tee mit Honig und versucht, abzuschalten (*switch off*).

F Was machen Sie, wenn Sie krank sind?

Landeskunde-Info

Auf dem deutschen Frühstückstisch findet man traditionell Brot und Brötchen mit Butter, Marmelade, Honig und Käse, eventuell auch Aufschnitt und ein gekochtes Ei. Cerealien wie Müsli gehören auch zum Frühstück. Zum Trinken gibt es Kaffee oder Tee und Fruchtsaft.

▶ Was essen und trinken Sie gewöhnlich zum Frühstück? Kreuzen Sie an.

Trinken		Essen	
Kaffee	☐	Müsli	☐
Tee	☐	Cornflakes, Cerealien	☐
Milch	☐	Brot, Brötchen oder Toast	☐
Saft	☐	Pfannkuchen	☐
Wasser	☐	Eier	☐
Cola	☐	Speck, Schinken	☐
_____	☐	Obst	☐
		_____	☐

Lesen

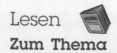

Zum Thema

A Wie gesund essen Sie? Was betrifft Sie? Kreuzen Sie an.

Essen Sie gesund?

Wie oft essen bzw. trinken Sie ...	täglich	mehrmals pro Woche	selten	nie
Getreideprodukte (Vollkornbrot, Weißbrot, Cerealien, Reis, Pasta usw.)	☐	☐	☐	☐
frisches Obst und Gemüse, Fruchtsaft ohne Zucker	☐	☐	☐	☐
Milchprodukte (Vollmilch, Magermilch, Quark, Joghurt, Käse usw.)	☐	☐	☐	☐
Wurst, Schinken, Speck, Aufschnitt	☐	☐	☐	☐
Fleisch (Rindfleisch, Schweinefleisch usw.)	☐	☐	☐	☐
Geflügel	☐	☐	☐	☐
Fisch, Meeresfrüchte	☐	☐	☐	☐
Butter	☐	☐	☐	☐
Süßigkeiten	☐	☐	☐	☐
Cola, Limonade	☐	☐	☐	☐
Bier, Wein, Alkohol	☐	☐	☐	☐
Kaffee, Tee	☐	☐	☐	☐

B Vergleichen Sie Ihre Essgewohnheiten untereinander in kleinen Gruppen. Was haben Sie erfahren? Berichten Sie dann im Kurs darüber.

BEISPIEL: Stephanie isst viel Obst und Gemüse, aber Robert isst gesünder als sie. Er isst nie Fast Food und wenig Fleisch.

Auf den ersten Blick

A Schauen Sie sich den Titel und den Untertitel an. Was ist das Thema?

☐ Was man zum Frühstück essen soll.

☐ Frühstück essen ist nicht wichtig.

☐ Das Frühstück sagt etwas über unseren Charakter.

B Lesen Sie den ersten Absatz und kreuzen Sie an.

1. Was steht im Text?

☐ 60% aller Studenten essen morgens kein Frühstück.

☐ 60% aller Studenten essen morgens Frühstück.

☐ Nur 40% aller Studenten essen morgens Frühstück.

2. Warum sollte man besser jeden Morgen gut frühstücken? Mit einem Frühstück im Bauch ...

☐ kann man sich besser konzentrieren.

☐ kann man den Stress an der Uni besser ertragen.

☐ bleibt man gesund.

Sage mir, was du isst …
Was das Frühstück über den Charakter verrät°

reveals

von Monika Hillemacher

Haben Sie schon wieder mal keine Zeit gehabt? Typisch! Nur etwa 60 Prozent der Studenten essen morgens Frühstück. Dabei kann man Uni-Stress viel besser mit einem Frühstück im Bauch verkraften°.

cope with

Essen und trinken am Morgen kann jeder. Ernährungsexperte Gerhard
5 Jahreis: „Jeder Mensch hat seinen ganz individuellen Rhythmus. Wichtig ist nicht, wann jemand frühstückt, sondern nur, dass und was er frühstückt."

Auf den Fitness-Speiseplan gehören Milch und Milchprodukte wie Trinkmilch, Joghurt und Käse, Müsli, frisches Obst, Vollkornbrot oder -brötchen und ausreichend Getränke wie Kaffee, Tee, Saft oder
10 Wasser. Käse, Quark° und Joghurt sind wahre Kraftpakete°. Und wer oft Vollmilch, Cerealien mit Milch oder Joghurtvarianten auf dem Tisch hat, bleibt schlanker. Frische Produkte sind besser als Multivitaminsaft oder Mineralstofftabletten.

fresh yogurt-like cheese / power packs

Am Wochenende lassen Studenten das Frühstück besonders gerne
15 unter den Tisch fallen. Es gibt dann manchmal einen Brunch mit Freunden und Familie.

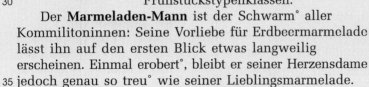

„Sage mir, was du frühstückst und ich sage dir, wer du bist", behauptet Professor Gebert von der Universität Münster: „Der Charakter bestimmt
20 das Frühstück mit." Der Psychologe und Soziologe fragt Studenten regelmäßig nach ihren Frühstücksgewohnheiten. Allerdings schaut er in erster Linie Männern auf den Teller, weil sie –
25 anders als ihre Kommilitoninnen° – „Gewohnheitsmenschen° und somit berechenbarer° sind." Das Resultat sind Professor Geberts (nicht ganz ernst gemeinte)
30 Frühstückstypenklassen.

fellow (female) students
creatures of habit
more predictable

Der Marmeladen-Mann

Der **Marmeladen-Mann** ist der Schwarm° aller Kommilitoninnen: Seine Vorliebe für Erdbeermarmelade lässt ihn auf den ersten Blick etwas langweilig erscheinen. Einmal erobert°, bleibt er seiner Herzensdame
35 jedoch genau so treu° wie seiner Lieblingsmarmelade.

heartthrob

conquered
loyal

Der Müsli-Raspler

Der **Müsli-Raspler**° startet mit frisch gepresstem O-Saft, biologisch – logisch. Macht sich viele Gedanken über das Essen, die Umwelt°, das Leben im
40 Allgemeinen, grübelt° viel über dies und das.

grater

environment
ponders

Der **Beifahrersitz-Frühstücker**° isst und
45 trinkt im Auto, in der
Der Beifahrersitz-Frühstücker

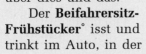

Bahn, im Bus, auf dem Rad, im Laufschritt. Diese Spezies macht vieles schnell nebeneinander°, fühlt sich spontan.

multitasking breakfaster

at the same time

Der **Guck-zurück-Typ**° verschlingt° wahllos
50 alles, was er im Kühlschrank findet. Professor

take-my-chances type / wolfs down

Der Guck-zurück-Typ

reflection
society
scatterbrains

Gebert nennt ihn ein Spiegelbild° der modernen „Spontan-
und Spaß-Gesellschaft°." Nicht einmal für den Kauf von
Brot und Butter haben „solche Chaoten° einen Plan."
    Der **Espresso-Mann** stürzt seinen morgendlichen
55 Kaffee hinunter. Symbol für ein „Leben auf der
Überholspur°. Er will alles erleben°. Schnell. Sofort.
Langweilig ist es nie, dazu ist sein Leben viel zu kurz."

fast lane / experience

Quelle: Monika Hillemacher; adaptiert aus: „Sage mir, was du
isst ...", UNICUM, April 2005. Illustrationen: © Sabine Kühn,
www.sabinekuehn.de.

Der Espresso-Mann

Zum Text

A **Über Speisen und Ernährung.** Lesen Sie die ersten drei Abschnitte
und beantworten Sie die folgenden Fragen.

1. Was stimmt? Ernährungsexperten sagen, es ist wichtig, ...
   ☐ *wann* man frühstückt.   ☐ *wo* man frühstückt.
   ☐ *dass* und *was* man frühstückt.

2. Was steht *nicht* auf dem deutschen Fitness-Speiseplan für das
   Frühstück?
   ☐ Milch und Milchprodukte   ☐ Vollkornbrot
   ☐ Speck und Eier   ☐ Weißbrot
   ☐ frisches Obst   ☐ Bier
   ☐ Kartoffeln und Fleisch   ☐ Vitamintabletten

3. „Am Wochenende lassen Studenten das Frühstück besonders gerne
   unter den Tisch fallen." Was bedeutet das?
   ☐ Die Studenten essen kein Frühstück.
   ☐ Sie essen das Frühstück auf dem Tisch.
   ☐ Das Frühstück fällt unter den Tisch.

4. Was machen Studenten oft am Wochenende?
   ☐ Sie essen Frühstück mit Freunden oder mit der Familie.
   ☐ Sie gehen mit Freunden oder mit der Familie zum Brunch.
   ☐ Sie essen nur ein Mittagessen.

B Lesen Sie nun den Rest des Textes. Was passt zu den Frühstückstypen?
Kombinieren Sie!

1. Der Marmeladen-Mann ...   isst und trinkt im Auto.
2. Der Müsli-Raspler ...   trinkt den Kaffee sehr schnell.
3. Der Beifahrersitz-Frühstücker ...   macht sich Gedanken über
                                        die Umwelt.
4. Der Guck-zurück-Typ ...   isst gern Erdbeermarmelade.
5. Der Espresso-Mann ...   hat keinen Plan für sein Leben.

C Meinungen und Interpretationen zum Text

1. Es heißt im Text, es ist nicht wichtig, *wann* man frühstückt,
   sondern nur, *dass* und *was* man frühstückt. Was ist Ihre Meinung?
2. Vergleichen Sie, was Sie gewöhnlich zum Frühstück essen, mit
   dem was auf dem Fitness-Speiseplan steht.

BEISPIEL: Ich esse Joghurt, aber trinke keinen Kaffee.

3. Professor Gebert von der Universität Münster behauptet:, „Der Charakter bestimmt das Frühstück mit." Was bedeutet das? Stimmen Sie ihm zu? (Ja oder nein, und warum?)

D Frühstückstypen in der Klasse

1. Welcher Frühstückstyp sind Sie? Schreiben Sie zwei oder drei Sätze über Ihre Frühstücksgewohnheiten und berichten Sie im Plenum.

BEISPIEL: **S1:** Ich bin eine Marmeladen-Frau! Ich esse jeden Tag Frühstück! Ich esse aber nur Orangenmarmelade.

S2: Freitags bin ich ein Espresso-Mann und Montags ein Beifahrersitz-Frühstücker. Dienstags, mittwochs und donnerstags schlafe ich lange und esse kein Frühstück.

2. Machen Sie nun eine Liste aller Frühstückstypen in Ihrer Klasse. Welcher Typ ist besonders populär? Haben Sie noch andere Typen in der Klasse, die im Text nicht vorgekommen (*appeared*) sind?

Zu guter Letzt
Ein idealer Fitnessplan

Machen Sie einen idealen Fitnessplan für sich.

Schritt 1: Schreiben Sie eine Liste mit Fitnessaktivitäten, die Sie während der letzten Woche gemacht haben. Analysieren Sie die Liste:

- Sind Sie viel zu Fuß gegangen?
- Haben Sie Sport getrieben?
- Haben Sie sich zu wenig entspannt?
- Was sehen Sie als positiv, was als negativ?

Schreiben Sie nun eine Liste mit allem, was Sie während der letzten Woche gegessen haben. Analysieren Sie die Liste:

- Haben Sie gesund gegessen?
- Haben Sie zu viel Fast Food gegessen?

Schritt 2: Möchten Sie mehr für Ihre Gesundheit tun? Was ist der ideale Fitnessplan für Sie? Machen Sie nun mithilfe der Informationen, die Sie in **Schritt 1** gesammelt haben, einen idealen Fitnessplan für sich.

BEISPIEL:

Mein idealer Fitnessplan

Sport treiben	Essen und trinken	Sonstiges
dreimal die Woche joggen	mehr Gemüse essen	weniger Fernsehen
_____	_____	_____
_____	_____	_____
_____	_____	_____

Schritt 3: Tauschen Sie Ihre Listen und Fitnessplan mit einem Partner / einer Partnerin aus. Lesen Sie die Fitnesspläne und machen Sie dann einander einige Vorschläge (*suggestions*). Sie können sie entweder annehmen (*accept*) oder ablehnen (*reject*).

BEISPIEL: Enstpanne dich öfter und geh zu Fuß zur Uni.

Schritt 4: Revidieren (*revise*) Sie nun Ihren Fitnessplan und machen Sie eventuell Korrekturen oder Änderungen (*changes*).

Hier klicken!

Weiteres zum Thema Gesundheit finden Sie bei **Deutsch: Na klar!** im World-Wide-Web unter **www.mhhe.com/dnk6.**

Wortschatz

Körperteile	Parts of the Body
der **Arm**, -e	arm
das **Auge**, -n	eye
der **Bauch**, ̈e	stomach, belly
das **Bein**, -e	leg
die **Brust**, ̈e	chest; breast
der **Ell(en)bogen**, -	elbow
der **Finger**, -	finger
der **Fuß**, ̈e	foot
das **Gesicht**, -er	face
das **Haar**, -e	hair
der **Hals**, ̈e	throat, neck
die **Hand**, ̈e	hand
das **Kinn**, -e	chin
das **Knie**, -	knee
der **Kopf**, ̈e	head
der **Mund**, ̈er	mouth
der **Muskel**, -n	muscle
die **Nase**, -n	nose
das **Ohr**, -en	ear
der **Rücken**, -	back
die **Schulter**, -n	shoulder
die **Zehe**, -n	toe

Gesundheit und Fitness	Health and Fitness
der **Alkohol**	alcohol
die **Arbeit**, -en	work; assignment; paper
der **Arzt**, ̈e / die **Ärztin**, -nen	physician, doctor
die **Biolebensmittel** (*pl.*)	organic foods
die **Erkältung**, -en	cold
das **Fieber**	fever
die **Fitness**	fitness
die **Gesundheit**	health
die **Grippe**	flu
der **Husten**	coughing, cough
der **Krankenpfleger**, / die **Kranken-schwester**, -n	nurse
der **Kräutertee**	herbal tea
die **Luft**, ̈e	air
der **Rat**	advice
die **Schmerzen** (*pl.*)	pains
die **Halsschmerzen**	sore throat
die **Kopfschmerzen**	headache
der **Schnupfen**	nasal congestion; head cold
die **Sprechstunde**, -n	office hours
der **Stress**	stress
der **Termin**, -e	appointment

Verben	Verbs
ab·geben (gibt ab), abgegeben	to drop off, give to
achten auf (+ *acc.*)	to pay attention to
sich **an·ziehen**, angezogen	to get dressed
sich **aus·ziehen**, ausgezogen	to get undressed
sich **beeilen**	to hurry up
sich **duschen**	to shower
sich **entspannen**	to relax
sich **erholen**	to get well, recover
sich **erkälten**	to catch a cold
sich **fit halten** (hält), gehalten	to keep fit, in shape
sich (**hin·**)**legen**	to lie down
sich (**hin·**)**setzen**	to sit down
sich **informieren** (über)	to inform oneself (about)
sich **kämmen**	to comb (one's hair)
sich **rasieren**	to shave
rauchen	to smoke
schlucken	to swallow
sich **strecken**	to stretch
tun, getan	to do
sich **verletzen**	to injure oneself
verschreiben, verschrieben	to prescribe
versuchen	to try, attempt
sich **waschen** (wäscht), gewaschen	to wash oneself
weh·tun, wehgetan (+ *dat.*)	to hurt
Das tut mir weh.	That hurts.
sich (**wohl**) **fühlen**	to feel (well)
sich die **Zähne putzen**	to brush one's teeth

Adjektive und Adverbien	Adjectives and Adverbs
ab und zu	now and then, occasionally
anstrengend	tiring, strenuous
besonders	especially
deprimiert	depressed
deshalb	therefore
entweder ... oder	either . . . or
fast	almost
fit	fit, in shape
gesund	healthy, healthful, well
gleich	immediately
hundsmiserabel (*coll.*)	sick as a dog
kaum	hardly, scarcely
krank	sick, ill

manchmal	sometimes	**Sonstiges**	**Other**
meistens	mostly	**d.h. (= das heißt)**	that is, i.e.
mindestens	at least	**Das macht nichts.**	That doesn't matter.
müde	tired	**Gute Besserung!**	Get well soon!
regelmäßig	regular(ly)	**klingen**	to sound
schlapp	weak, worn out	Du klingst	You sound so
sogar	even	so deprimiert.	depressed.
verrückt	crazy	**Mir ist schlecht.**	I'm sick to my stomach.
wenig	little, few	**Nichts zu danken.**	No thanks necessary;
			Don't mention it.
Unterordnende	**Subordinating**	**So ein Pech!**	What a shame!
Konjunktionen	**Conjunctions**		(What bad luck!)
dass	that	**Urlaub machen**	to go on vacation
ob	whether	**Was fehlt Ihnen/dir?**	What's the matter?
weil	because	**zu Fuß gehen**	to go on foot, to walk
wenn	if, when		

Das kann ich nun!

1. Nennen Sie sechs Körperteile mit Artikel und Plural.

2. Beschreiben Sie Ihre Morgenroutine. Bilden Sie mindestens drei Sätze mit reflexiven Verben.

3. Sie telefonieren mit einem Freund. Er klingt krank, kann kaum sprechen und hustet. Was fragen Sie ihn? Was empfehlen Sie ihm? Was wünschen Sie ihm?

4. Was machen Sie, wenn Sie eine Erkältung haben?

   Wenn ich eine Erkältung habe, …

5. Sie gehen zum Arzt, weil Sie sich hundsmiserabel fühlen. Der Arzt fragt: „Was fehlt Ihnen denn?" Was sagen Sie?

6. Was tun Sie für Fitness und Gesundheit? (Nennen Sie drei Dinge.) Wenn Sie nichts tun, sagen Sie bitte, warum Sie nichts tun.

7. Sie haben sich erkältet, aber Sie müssen unbedingt zur Arbeit. Sie reden mit einem Freund / einer Freundin über diese Situation. Was sagen Sie zu ihm/ihr?
   a. Ich weiß nicht, ob …
   b. Ich kann heute nicht zu Hause bleiben, weil …
   c. Ich glaube nicht, dass …

9

In der Stadt

Auf dem Münsterplatz mit Beethovendenkmal in Bonn

In diesem Kapitel

- ▶ **Themen:** Talking about hotel and lodging, places in the city, asking for and giving directions
- ▶ **Grammatik:** The genitive case, attributive adjectives
- ▶ **Lesen:** „Die Gitarre des Herrn Hatunoglu" (Heinrich Hannover)
- ▶ **Landeskunde:** Services of tourist information offices, Wittenberg history
- ▶ **Zu guter Letzt:** Eine Webseite für Touristen

VIDEOCLIPS

Hier gefällt es mir!

A Dresden liegt im Bundesland Sachsen südlich von Berlin an der Elbe. Es gibt viele Sehenswürdigkeiten (*tourist attractions*) in und um die Stadt. Für Jugendliche gibt es in Dresden besonders viel zu erleben.

Dresden.

Junges Dresden: Freizeit, Unterhaltung, Szene

Dresden hat viele Facetten[1]: weltberühmte Museen und Sehenswürdigkeiten, eine romantische Elblandschaft[2], sächsische[3] Gemütlichkeit und eine bunte Szenekultur. Ein Abend in Dresden muss nicht immer Oper, Konzert oder Theater bedeuten. Wer außerdem Lust auf einen Kneipenbummel[4] hat, kommt in der Dresdner Neustadt voll auf seine Kosten[5]. In der Hauptstraße, der Rähnitzgasse und der Königstraße gibt es Restaurants unterschiedlichster Couleur. Internationale und sächsische Küche findet man auch rings um den Albertplatz. Von hier aus geht's die Alaunstraße entlang, wo sich urige[6] Szenekneipen und internationale Spezialitätenrestaurants abwechseln. Günstige Übernachtungsmöglichkeiten finden Sie in Dresdens Jugendherbergen[7] und Hostels.

Ein Tag in Dresden

Zwinger
Dresdens schönstes barockes Bauwerk[8] befindet sich im Zentrum der Altstadt. Nach starken Beschädigungen[9] im Zweiten Weltkrieg und raschem Wiederaufbau beherbergt der Zwinger heute kostbare Sammlungen.

Semperoper
Dresdens Operntradition reicht bis in die Renaissance zurück. Feinsinnige[10] Architektur und besondere Akustik machen die Dresdner „Semperoper" zu einem der Höhepunkte der Theaterarchitektur des 19. Jahrhunderts.

[1]*dimensions* [2]*Elbe river landscape* [3]*Saxon* [4]*pub crawl* [5]*kommt voll auf seine Kosten finds everything he/she needs* [6]*rustic* [7]*youth hostels* [8]*structure* [9]*damage* [10]*tasteful*

Suchen Sie die fehlenden Informationen im Text oben.

1. Die _____ in Dresden sind weltberühmt.
2. Wenn man Kultur erleben möchte, kann man abends in die _____, ins _____ oder ins _____ gehen. Wenn man das nicht will, kann man auch in der Dresdner Neustadt einen _____ machen.
3. Wenn man essen will, findet man _____ und _____ Küche rings um den Albertplatz in Dresden.
4. In Dresden kann man in _____ und in _____ übernachten.
5. Das Opernhaus in Dresden heißt _____.

Suchen Sie mehr Informationen über Dresden. Was würden Sie gern dort machen?

B Sie machen eine Stadtführung (*guided tour*) durch Dresden. Der Fremdenführer (*tour guide*) erzählt einige Tatsachen über die Stadt. Hören Sie zu und kreuzen Sie an, was stimmt und was nicht stimmt.

	Das stimmt	Das stimmt nicht
1. Heute leben etwa 500 000 Einwohner in Dresden.	☐	☐
2. Die erste deutsche Lokomotive kommt aus Dresden.	☐	☐
3. Bierdeckel, Kaffeefilter und Shampoo hat man in Dresden erfunden.	☐	☐
4. In Dresden hat Richard Wagner die erste deutsche Oper geschrieben.	☐	☐
5. Die Stadt bietet viel Kultur an: Musik, Museen und Theater.	☐	☐
6. Dresden ist die europäische Hauptstadt des Films.	☐	☐

Hier klicken!
Weiteres zum Thema Dresden finden Sie bei **Deutsch: Na klar!** im World-Wide-Web unter www.mhhe.com/dnk6.

accommodations

Thema 1: Unterkunft° online buchen

Neue Wörter

die Bettwäsche linens
der Parkplatz parking space
der Internetzugang Internet access
der Föhn hair dryer
der Kühlschrank refrigerator
der Stock floor

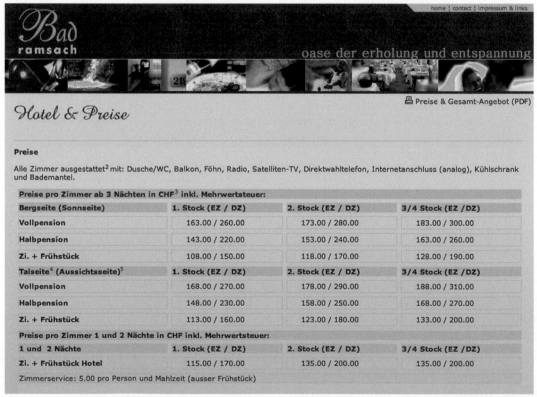

AO HOSTEL BERLIN Fhain — Bei uns schlafen Sie zum Frühstückspreis!

Alle Preise pro Person und Nacht inkl. MwSt.

Möchten Sie die aktuellen Preise für ein bestimmtes Datum wissen? Sehen Sie im Bereich <u>BUCHEN</u> nach.

Einzelzimmer*	ab	30.00 €
Zweibettzimmer*	ab	17.00 €
Kleines Mehrbettzimmer (4-6 Betten) mit Dusche und WC	ab	13.00 €
Kleines Mehrbettzimmer (4-6 Betten)	ab	10,50 €
Großes Mehrbettzimmer (8-10 Betten) mit Dusche und WC	ab	10,50 €
Großes Mehrbettzimmer (8-10 Betten)	ab	10.00 €

* inklusive Frühstück und Bettwäsche

Ergänzungen

Bettwäsche	3,00 € / einmalig
Handtuch	1,00 € / einmalig
Frühstücksbuffet	5,00 € / Tag
Fahrradverleih[3]	10,00 € / Tag
Parkplatz	3,00 € / Tag (max. 6,00 €)
Internetzugang	1,00 € / 20 Minuten

home | contact | impressum & links

Bad ramsach — oase der erholung und entspannung

🖶 Preise & Gesamt-Angebot (PDF)

Hotel & Preise

Preise

Alle Zimmer ausgestattet[2] mit: Dusche/WC, Balkon, Föhn, Radio, Satelliten-TV, Direktwahltelefon, Internetanschluss (analog), Kühlschrank und Bademantel.

Preise pro Zimmer ab 3 Nächten in CHF[3] inkl. Mehrwertsteuer:

Bergseite (Sonnseite)	1. Stock (EZ / DZ)	2. Stock (EZ / DZ)	3/4 Stock (EZ /DZ)
Vollpension	163.00 / 260.00	173.00 / 280.00	183.00 / 300.00
Halbpension	143.00 / 220.00	153.00 / 240.00	163.00 / 260.00
Zi. + Frühstück	108.00 / 150.00	118.00 / 170.00	128.00 / 190.00
Talseite[4] (Aussichtsseite)[5]	**1. Stock (EZ / DZ)**	**2. Stock (EZ / DZ)**	**3/4 Stock (EZ /DZ)**
Vollpension	168.00 / 270.00	178.00 / 290.00	188.00 / 310.00
Halbpension	148.00 / 230.00	158.00 / 250.00	168.00 / 270.00
Zi. + Frühstück	113.00 / 160.00	123.00 / 180.00	133.00 / 200.00

Preise pro Zimmer 1 und 2 Nächte in CHF inkl. Mehrwertsteuer:

1 und 2 Nächte	1. Stock (EZ / DZ)	2. Stock (EZ / DZ)	3/4 Stock (EZ /DZ)
Zi. + Frühstück Hotel	115.00 / 170.00	135.00 / 200.00	135.00 / 200.00

Zimmerservice: 5.00 pro Person und Mahlzeit (ausser Frühstück)

[1]*current*   [2]*furnished*   [3]*(abbreviation for Swiss francs)*   [4]*valley side*   [5]*view side*

Sprach-Info

Bei Hotelwerbungen findet man oft folgende Bezeichnungen:

Vollpension	*all meals included*
Halbpension	*one meal besides breakfast included*
Pauschalangebot	*package offer*

Die folgenden Abkürzungen sind auch typisch:

EZ	= **das Einzelzimmer**	*single room*
DZ	= **das Doppelzimmer**	*double room*
DU	= **die Dusche**	*shower*
WC	= **die Toilette** (Engl. *water closet*)	*toilet*
inkl.	= **inklusive**	*included, including*

A Was ist Ihnen wichtig, wenn Sie in einem **Hotel**, einer **Pension** oder einer **Jugendherberge übernachten** wollen? Die **Unterkunft** sollte …

- ☐ **in der Nähe** des **Bahnhofs** liegen.
- ☐ in der **Innenstadt** (im **Zentrum**) liegen.
- ☐ ein Restaurant im Haus haben.
- ☐ Kabelfernsehen oder Radio haben.
- ☐ in ruhiger **Lage** sein.
- ☐ Bad/Dusche/WC im Zimmer haben.
- ☐ Frühstück **im Preis enthalten.**
- ☐ einen **Parkplatz** in der Nähe haben.
- ☐ Hunde **erlauben.**
- ☐ Telefon im Zimmer haben.
- ☐ im Bad einen **Föhn** haben.
- ☐ preiswert sein.
- ☐ **günstig liegen** (z.B. im Zentrum).
- ☐ einen **Kühlschrank** im Zimmer haben.
- ☐ **Internetzugang** haben.
- ☐ in einer **Fußgängerzone** liegen.
- ☐ **Bettwäsche** haben.

B **Daniel in Berlin.** Daniel war drei Tage in Berlin. Er wollte nicht viel Geld für _____ [1] (*lodging*) ausgeben, aber sie sollte _____ _____ [2] (*be conveniently located*), am besten in der _____ [3] (*inner city*). Er hat dort auch eine preiswerte Unterkunft in einer _____ [4] (*youth hostel*) gefunden: ein _____ [5] (*single room*) mit WC und _____ [6] (*shower*). _____ [7] (*breakfast*) und _____ [8] (*linens*) waren im Preis enthalten. Das Zimmer hatte kein Telefon und auch keinen _____ [9] (*Internet access*). Dafür musste man extra bezahlen.

C **Frau Heilmann macht Kurzurlaub.** Frau Heilmann wollte sich ein paar Tage entspannen und hat in Bad Ramsach in der Schweiz Kurzurlaub gemacht. Das Hotel war in ruhiger _____ [10] (*location*). Sie hatte ein _____ [11] (*single room*) mit Vollpension auf der Talseite des Hotels im zweiten _____ [12]. Das Zimmer war etwas teuer – es hat 178 CHF pro Nacht gekostet, aber es war sehr schön ausgestattet mit Telefon, WC, _____ [13] (*shower*) und einem _____ [14] (*refrigerator*) und es hatte auch einen Balkon mit Blick auf das schöne Tal.

Aktivität 1 Zwei telefonische Zimmerbestellungen

Was stimmt? Markieren Sie die richtigen Antworten.

Erstes Telefongespräch

1. Der Gast braucht ein …
   - **a.** Einzelzimmer.
   - **b.** Doppelzimmer.
2. Er braucht das Zimmer für …
   - **a.** eine Nacht.
   - **b.** mehrere (*several*) Nächte.
3. Das Hotel hat ein Zimmer frei …
   - **a.** ohne Bad.
   - **b.** mit Bad.
4. Frühstück ist im Preis …
   - **a.** nicht enthalten.
   - **b.** enthalten.
5. Der Gast …
   - **a.** muss ein anderes Hotel finden.
   - **b.** nimmt das Zimmer.

Zweites Telefongespräch

1. Das Jugendgästehaus hat …
   - **a.** nur Doppelzimmer.
   - **b.** nur Mehrbettzimmer.
2. Das Haus ist …
   - **a.** ganz neu.
   - **b.** sehr alt.
3. Die Übernachtung kostet …
   - **a.** mehr als 20 Euro.
   - **b.** weniger als 20 Euro.
4. Jedes Zimmer hat …
   - **a.** WC and Dusche.
   - **b.** fünf Betten.
5. Das Gästehaus liegt …
   - **a.** auf dem Lande.
   - **b.** in der Nähe der Innenstadt.

Landeskunde-Info

„Tourist i" (*for information*) ist für viele Besucher in deutschen Städten der erste Stopp. Meist liegt er am Hauptbahnhof oder an einem anderen zentralen Ort. Hier können Touristen viel Wissenswertes über die neue Stadt erfahren. Sie können zum Beispiel Empfehlungen für Restaurants bekommen, eine Stadtrundfahrt buchen und Prospekte (*brochures*) von der Stadt erhalten. Hier gibt es auch eine Zimmervermittlung. Da kann der Besucher ein Zimmer in einem Hotel oder einer Pension finden.

- ▶ Wo bekommen Sie Information über eine Stadt, die Sie besuchen wollen?
- ▶ Buchen Sie Hotelzimmer online oder rufen Sie das Hotel an?

Aktivität 2 Unterkunft in Berlin

Sie reisen mit Freunden und suchen eine Unterkunft in Berlin. Schauen Sie sich die Webseite „AO Hostel" im **Thema 1** genau an und überlegen Sie sich, in was für einem Zimmer Sie übernachten wollen. Gebrauchen Sie die folgenden Ausdrücke.

BEISPIEL: Ich schlage vor, wir übernachten in einem Mehrbettzimmer. Das ist nicht so teuer.

Ich schlage vor, …
Mir gefällt … besser.
Ich brauche … im Zimmer.
… ist mir zu teuer.

Thema 2: Im Hotel

Teil A: *Herr Thompson* **kommt** *im Hotel „Mecklenheide"* **an.** *Zuerst muss er* **sich anmelden.**

Rezeption:	Guten Abend.
Gast:	Guten Abend. Ich habe ein Zimmer für zwei Nächte bestellt.
Rezeption:	**Auf welchen Namen,** bitte?
Gast:	Thompson.
Rezeption:	Ah, ja. Herr Thompson. Ein Einzelzimmer mit Bad. **Würden Sie** bitte das **Anmeldeformular ausfüllen?**
Gast:	Möchten Sie auch meinen **Reisepass** sehen?
Rezeption:	Nein, das ist nicht nötig. Ihr Zimmer liegt im ersten Stock, Zimmer 21. Hier ist **der Schlüssel.** Der **Aufzug** ist hier **rechts.**
Gast:	Danke.
Rezeption:	Wir bringen Ihr **Gepäck** aufs Zimmer. Haben Sie nur den einen Koffer?
Gast:	Ja ... **Übrigens,** wann gibt es morgens Frühstück?
Rezeption:	Zwischen 7 und 10 Uhr im **Frühstücksraum** hier gleich **links** im **Erdgeschoss.**
Gast:	Danke sehr.
Rezeption:	Bitte sehr. Ich wünsche Ihnen einen **angenehmen Aufenthalt.**

der dritte Stock
der zweite Stock
der erste Stock
das Erdgeschoss

Neue Wörter

kommt ... an (ankommen) arrives
zuerst first
sich anmelden register, check in
die Rezeption reception desk
würden Sie ... ausfüllen would you fill out ...
das Anmeldeformular registration form
der Reisepass passport
der Schlüssel key
der Aufzug elevator
rechts to the right
das Gepäck luggage
übrigens by the way
links to the left
angenehm pleasant
der Aufenthalt stay

Teil B: *Herr Thompson ruft die Rezeption an und* **beschwert sich,** *weil der Fernseher nicht* **funktioniert.**

Rezeption:	Rezeption.
Thompson:	Guten Abend. Der Fernseher in meinem Zimmer ist **kaputt.** Es gibt kein Bild, keinen Ton, nichts.
Rezeption:	**Das tut mir leid,** Herr Thompson. Ich schicke **sofort** jemand auf Ihr Zimmer. Wenn er den **Apparat** nicht gleich **reparieren** kann, bringen wir Ihnen einen anderen.
Thompson:	Vielen Dank. **Auf Wiederhören.**
Rezeption:	Auf Wiederhören.

Neue Wörter

beschwert sich (sich beschweren) complains
kaputt broken
Das tut mir leid. I'm sorry.
sofort immediately
der Apparat TV set
reparieren repair
auf Wiederhören good-bye (*on the phone*)

▶ Bilden Sie Sätze!

1. _b_ Ich habe ein Einzelzimmer ...
2. ___ Würden Sie bitte das Anmeldeformular ...
3. ___ Ihr Zimmer liegt ...
4. ___ Wir bringen Ihr Gepäck ...
5. ___ Ich wünsche Ihnen einen ...
6. ___ Der Fernseher im Zimmer ...

a. ist kaputt.
b. bestellt.
c. angenehmen Aufenthalt.
d. ausfüllen?
e. aufs Zimmer.
f. im ersten Stock.

Aktivität 3 Im Hotel Mecklenheide

Was passiert? Ergänzen Sie!

1. Herr Thompson bekommt ein _____ mit Bad im ersten _____.
2. Er muss das Anmeldeformular _____.
3. Seinen _____ muss er aber nicht vorzeigen.
4. Er bekommt den _____ zum Zimmer und nimmt den _____ in den ersten Stock.
5. Jemand vom Hotelpersonal bringt sein _____ aufs Zimmer.
6. Er kann zwischen 7 und 10 Uhr im Frühstücksraum im _____ frühstücken.
7. Herr Thompson _____ sich, weil der Fernseher in seinem Zimmer _____ist.
8. Jemand vom Hotelpersonal soll den Fernseher _____.

Hier klicken!

Weiteres zum Thema Hotel und Unterkunft finden Sie bei **Deutsch: Na klar!** im World-Wide-Web unter **www.mhhe.com/dnk6.**

Aktivität 4 Die Geschichte von Herrn Thompson

Sehen Sie sich die Bilder von Herrn Thompson im Hotel an. Schreiben Sie für jedes Bild einen Satz und erzählen Sie die Geschichte von Herrn Thompson.

1.

2.

3.

4.

5.

6.

Thema 3: Ringsum° die Stadt
Lutherstadt Wittenberg

All around

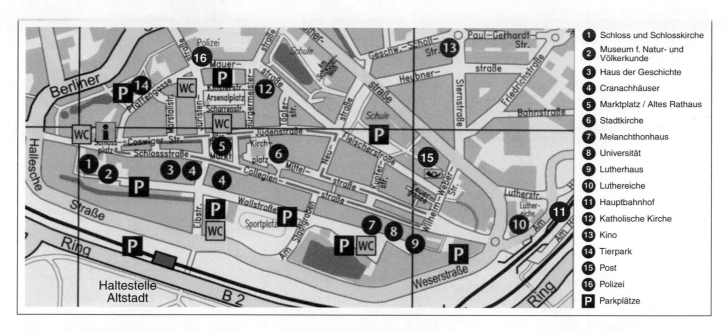

1. Schloss und Schlosskirche
2. Museum f. Natur- und Völkerkunde
3. Haus der Geschichte
4. Cranachhäuser
5. Marktplatz / Altes Rathaus
6. Stadtkirche
7. Melanchthonhaus
8. Universität
9. Lutherhaus
10. Luthereiche
11. Hauptbahnhof
12. Katholische Kirche
13. Kino
14. Tierpark
15. Post
16. Polizei
P. Parkplätze

A Verbinden Sie das deutsche Wort mit dem Englischen.

1. ___ die **Kirche**	**a.** bank
2. ___ das **Museum**	**b.** city hall
3. ___ die **Post**	**c.** museum
4. ___ die **Bank**	**d.** castle
5. ___ die **Polizei**	**e.** police
6. ___ das **Kino**	**f.** post office
7. ___ das **Schloss**	**g.** stop/station (*bus, train, etc.*)
8. ___ die **Haltestelle**	**h.** movie theater
9. ___ der **Tierpark**	**i.** main train station
10. ___ das **Rathaus**	**j.** church
11. ___ der **Hauptbahnhof**	**k.** zoo

Das Lutherhaus in der Collegienstraße

Neue Wörter

nach dem Weg fragen to ask for directions

Entschuldigung excuse me

gehen Sie ... entlang (entlanggehen) go along

biegen Sie ... ein (einbiegen) turn

immer geradeaus straight ahead

bis zur as far as, up to

gegenüber vom across from the

weit far

ungefähr about, approximately

Nach dem Weg fragen

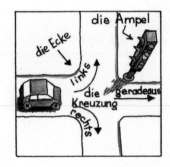

*Ein **Tourist** steht in Wittenberg vor der Stadtkirche und fragt nach dem Weg.*

Tourist: **Entschuldigung,** wie komme ich am besten zum Lutherhaus?

Passant: **Gehen Sie** hier die Mittelstraße **entlang.** Dann **biegen Sie** rechts in die Wilhelm-Weber Straße **ein.** Gehen Sie **immer geradeaus bis zur** Collegienstraße. Da finden Sie das Lutherhaus. Es liegt **gegenüber vom** Restaurant „Am Lutherhaus".

Tourist: Ist es **weit** von hier?

Passant: Nein. **Ungefähr** 15 Minuten zu Fuß.

B Sie stehen am alten Markt am Rathaus und kennen Wittenberg jetzt sehr gut. Einige Touristen fragen Sie nach dem Weg.

Tourist 1: Wie komme ich am besten zum Haus der Geschichte?

Sie: _____ _____ (*go along*) die Elbstraße _____. Dann _____ _____ (*turn*) rechts _____. Das Haus der Geschichte ist auf der linken Seite.

Tourist 2: Sind das Schloss und die Schlosskirche _____ (*far*) von hier?

Sie: Nein, _____ (*about*) zehn Minuten zu Fuß. Gehen Sie die Schlossstraße _____ _____ (*straight ahead*). Dann sehen Sie das Schloss und die Schlosskirche.

Aktivität 5 Drei Touristen

Drei Leute fragen nach dem Weg. Wohin wollen sie? Wie kommen sie dahin?

	Dialog 1	Dialog 2	Dialog 3
Wohin man gehen will			
Wie man dahin kommt			

Aktivität 6 Hin und her: In einer fremden° Stadt

unfamiliar

Sie sind in einer fremden Stadt. Fragen Sie nach dem Weg. Benutzen Sie die Tabelle.

BEISPIEL: **S1:** Ist das Landesmuseum weit von hier?

      S2: Es ist sechs Kilometer von hier, bei der Universität.

      S1: Wie komme ich am besten dahin?

      S2: Nehmen Sie die Buslinie 7, am Rathaus.

Wohin?	Wie weit?	Wo?	Wie?
Landesmuseum	6 km	bei der Universität	Buslinie 7, am Rathaus
Bahnhof	15 Minuten	im Zentrum	mit dem Taxi
Post			
Schloss	15 km	außerhalb der Stadt	mit dem Auto
Opernhaus			

Aktivität 7 In Wittenberg

Schauen Sie sich den Stadtplan von Wittenberg im **Thema 3** an und fragen Sie jemand im Kurs, wie Sie am besten an einen bestimmten Ort kommen.

BEISPIEL: Sie stehen am Haus der Geschichte (Nummer 3 im Stadtplan). →

      S1: Entschuldigung, wie komme ich am besten zum Markt?

      S2: Geh geradeaus bis zur Elbstraße. Bieg dann links ein. Der Markt ist auf der rechten Seite gleich an der Ecke.

Sie stehen ...

am Haus der Geschichte
vor der katholischen Kirche
am Schloss
am Tierpark
vor der Stadtkirche
vor dem Kino
am Hauptbahnhof
vor dem alten Rathaus
am Markt

Sie wollen ...

ins Kino
zum Schloss
zum alten Rathaus
zum Markt
zur Stadtkirche
zum Hauptbahnhof
in den Tierpark

Redemittel

Entschuldigung, wie komme ich
  am besten zum/zur _____?
Wie weit ist es bis zum/zur _____?
immer geradeaus
bis zur Kreuzung/Ampel
Geh die _____-straße entlang.
Bieg links/rechts in die _____
  -straße ein.
gleich an der Ecke / um die Ecke
auf der rechten/linken Seite
Es ist zehn Minuten zu Fuß.

 Siehe *Attributive Adjectives*, S. 275.

Landeskunde-Info

Wittenberg: Ein Blick in die Geschichte

1180	erste urkundliche Erwähnung (*mention*) von Wittenberg
1502	Gründung der Wittenberger Universität
1508	Martin Luther kommt nach Wittenberg. Er wird Theologieprofessor.
1517	Luther veröffentlicht (*publishes*) seine 95 Thesen an der Tür der Schlosskirche. Die Reformation beginnt.
1537	Lucas Cranach, ein berühmter Maler der Reformation, wird Bürgermeister der Stadt.
1618–1648	der dreißigjährige Krieg: Wittenberg erleidet (*suffers*) Schäden.
1817	Schließung der Wittenberger Universität
1883	Eröffnung des Reformationsmuseums „Lutherhaus"
1994	Die Universität wird wieder belebt (*revived*).
1996	Das Lutherhaus, das Melanchthonhaus und die Stadt- und Schlosskirche werden Teil des Weltkulturerbes (*world cultural heritage*) der UNESCO.

Martin-Luther-Denkmal am Markt

▶ Was sind zwei wichtige Daten in der Geschichte Ihrer Stadt oder Ihrer Universität? Was ist da passiert?

▶ Schreiben Sie eine kurze Geschichte von Ihrer Stadt in tabellarischer Form (sowie oben) und berichten Sie der Klasse über die Geschichte.

Quelle: www.wittenberg.de (adaptiert)

Aktivität 8   Wie kommt man dahin?

Fragen Sie nach dem Weg in Ihrer Stadt oder auf Ihrem Campus. Wählen Sie passende Fragen und Antworten aus jeder Spalte (*column*).

BEISPIEL: **S1:** Entschuldigung, wo ist hier die Post?

S2: Da nehmen Sie am besten den Bus.

S1: Wo ist die Haltestelle?

S2: Gleich da drüben an der Kreuzung.

Fragen	Antworten
Wie kommt man hier zum Supermarkt / zur Bibliothek / zur Sporthalle?	immer geradeaus
	bis zur Ampel
	nächste Kreuzung rechts/links
Wie weit ist es bis ins Zentrum?	Da nehmen Sie am besten _____ (den Bus, z.B. Linie 8).
Entschuldigung, wo ist hier die Post (Bank, Mensa)?	gleich da drüben / gleich an der Ecke
Wo ist die Haltestelle?	fünf Minuten zu Fuß
??	??

¹*GPS*

The Genitive Case°

The genitive case typically indicates ownership, a relationship, or the characteristics of another noun.

Der Wagen **meines Vaters** steht auf dem Parkplatz.	*My father's car is in the parking lot.*
Die Lage **des Hotels** ist günstig.	*The location of the hotel is convenient.*
Das Hotel liegt im Zentrum **der Stadt.**	*The hotel is located in the center of town.*

Singular			Plural
Masculine	*Neuter*	*Feminine*	*All Genders*
des eines unseres dieses } Vaters / Gastes *but:* Studenten	des eines unseres dieses } Hotels	der einer unserer dieser } Stadt	der unserer dieser } Gäste

NOTE:

▶ Most masculine and neuter nouns add **-s** in the singular genitive case.

in der Nähe des Bahnhof**s**	*in the vicinity of the train station*
die Lage dieses Hotel**s**	*the location of this hotel*

▶ Masculine and neuter nouns of one syllable often add **-es.**

die Unterschrift des Gast**es**	*the guest's signature*
in der Nähe des Schloss**es**	*in the vicinity of the castle*

▶ Masculine nouns that add **-n** or **-en** in the dative and the accusative also add **-n** or **-en** in the genitive case.

das Gepäck des Student**en**	*the student's luggage*

▶ A noun in the genitive follows the noun it modifies.

In spoken German, the genitive case is often replaced by the preposition **von** and the dative case.

in der Nähe **vom Bahnhof**	*in the vicinity of the railroad station*

To ask for the owner of something, use the interrogative pronoun **wessen** (*whose*).

Wessen Koffer ist das?	*Whose suitcase is that?*
Wessen Unterschrift ist das?	*Whose signature is that?*

Proper Names in the Genitive

Martinas Koffer   *Martina's suitcase*

Herrn Kramers Reisepass   *Mr. Kramer's passport*

Hessen: das Herz **Deutschlands**   *Hesse: the heart of Germany*

NOTE:

◗ A proper name in the genitive normally precedes the noun it modifies.

◗ Proper names in the genitive add **-s** regardless of the person's gender, but without an apostrophe in contrast to English.

◗ The name of a country or a region in the genitive case may precede or follow the noun it modifies.

Analyse

◗ Identify the genitive expressions in the illustrations.

◗ What nouns are modified by the genitive attributes?

◗ Give appropriate English translations of these phrases.

VERANSTALTUNGEN

Samstag. 06. August 2011	August
20.00 Uhr **Die Nacht der Vampire**	
Bergtheater Thale	**01**

KAUFHAUS DES WESTENS
Wo finde ich was?

In der Nikolaikirche

Café deR BegegNung

Wappen der Stadt Köln

Vienna

Übung 1   Was für eine Stadt ist Wien°?

Sie sind gerade in Wien. Beschreiben Sie die Stadt.

BEISPIEL: Wien ist eine Stadt der Tradition.

Wien ist eine Stadt ...

die Kaffeehäuser	die Architektur	das Theater
die Museen	die Kirchen	die Musik
die Schlösser	der Walzer (*waltz*)	

Übung 2   Wo liegt Ihr Hotel?

Beschreiben Sie die Lage Ihres Hotels in Wien.

BEISPIEL: Unser Hotel liegt in der Nähe eines Cafés.

Unser Hotel liegt in der Nähe ...

die Donau (*Danube*)	der Dom (*cathedral*)	ein Park
die Universität	das Rathaus	ein Schloss
der Bahnhof	das Opernhaus	eine Bank
die Ringstraße	das Zentrum	die Post

Übung 3 Spiel mit Wörtern

In der deutschen Sprache gibt es viele zusammengesetzte (*compound*) Wörter. Oft kann man sie auseinander (*apart*) nehmen und mit einem Genitivobjekt ausdrücken.

Schritt 1: Nehmen Sie zuerst die zusammengesetzten Wörter in Spalte A auseinander.

BEISPIEL: die Hotellage →
 die Lage des Hotels

Schritt 2: Bilden Sie dann Sätze mit den Satzteilen in Spalte B.

BEISPIEL: Die Lage des Hotels ist sehr günstig im Zentrum.

A	B
1. die Hotellage	**a.** ist nicht weit von hier entfernt.
2. der Übernachtungspreis	**b.** liegt auf dem Tisch im Hotelzimmer.
3. der Hotelmanager	**c.** ist am Wochenende geschlossen.
4. der Autoschlüssel	**d.** ist in der Tiefgarage im Hotel.
5. das Stadtzentrum	**e.** beträgt 130 Euro pro Person.
6. die Universitätsbibliothek	**f.** heißt Johannes Tiefenbach.
7. der Hotelparkplatz	**g.** ist sehr günstig im Zentrum.

Übung 4 Wem gehört das?

Wessen Sachen sind das? Arbeiten Sie zu zweit.

BEISPIEL: **S1:** Wessen Gepäck ist das?

 S2: Das ist das Gepäck des Gastes.

1. das Gepäck	meine Schwester
2. der Rucksack	der Student
3. der Reisepass	der Herr auf Zimmer 33
4. die Unterschrift (*signature*)	der Gast
5. die Koffer	die Touristen
6. der Schlüssel	unsere Freunde
7. die Kreditkarte	der Tourist
8. die Kamera	die Passantin

Prepositions with the Genitive

A number of prepositions are used with the genitive case. Here are several common ones:

außerhalb	*outside of*	außerhalb der Stadt
innerhalb	*inside of, within*	innerhalb einer Stunde
trotz	*in spite of*	trotz des Regens
während	*during*	während des Sommers
wegen	*because of*	wegen der hohen Kosten

In colloquial German, **trotz, während,** and **wegen** may also be used with the dative case.

Übung 5 Notizen von einer Reise nach Wien

Wählen Sie die passenden Präpositionen.

1. _____ unserer Reise nach Wien haben wir viel gesehen. (Trotz / Während)
2. _____ der hohen Hotelpreise haben wir in einer kleinen Pension übernachtet. (Wegen / Trotz)
3. Die Pension hat _____ der Stadt gelegen. (während / außerhalb)
4. _____ der vielen Touristen war es in Wien schön. (Trotz / Wegen)
5. _____ der vielen Besucher mussten wir lange vor der Spanischen Reitschule warten. (Innerhalb / Wegen)

inquiries

Übung 6 Erkundigungen°

Arbeiten Sie zu zweit. Sie sind bei der Information einer Stadt und fragen nach dem Weg.

BEISPIEL: **S1:** Bitte schön, wie komme ich zum Rathaus?

S2: Das Rathaus liegt gleich hier in der Nähe des Marktplatzes. Gehen Sie rechts die Hauptstraße entlang.

Wie komme ich ...	Er/sie/es liegt ...
das Rathaus	auf der anderen Seite
das Hotel Zentral	außerhalb
ein Parkplatz	direkt gegenüber von
der Naturpark	gleich hier
das Kunstmuseum	in der Nähe
die Post	in der Mitte
die Universität	neben
eine Bank	Gehen Sie die _____-straße entlang.

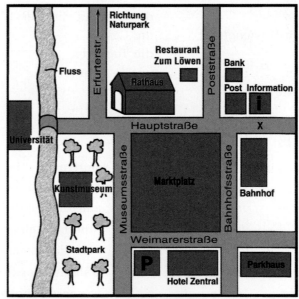

Stadtplan

Attributive Adjectives°

You are already familiar with predicate adjectives. Predicate adjectives do not take endings.

> Der Bahnhof ist **alt.**
>
> Das Hotel ist **preiswert.**
>
> Die Bedienung ist **freundlich.**

When adjectives precede the nouns they modify, they are called attributive. Attributive adjectives do take endings.

> Der **alte** Bahnhof liegt in der Nähe des Hotels.
>
> Das **preiswerte** Hotel liegt außerhalb der Stadt.
>
> Die **freundliche** Bedienung hat mir gefallen.

Adjectives after a Definite Article

Whenever an adjective follows a definite article or other **der**-word, such as **dieser** or **jeder**, it takes the ending **-e** or **-en** (depending on the case and gender).*

	Singular			Plural
	Masculine	*Neuter*	*Feminine*	*All Genders*
Nom.	der groß**e** Park	das schön**e** Wetter	die lang**e** Straße	die alt**en** Häuser
Acc.	den groß**en** Park	das schön**e** Wetter	die lang**e** Straße	die alt**en** Häuser
Dat.	dem groß**en** Park	dem schön**en** Wetter	der lang**en** Straße	den alt**en** Häusern
Gen.	des groß**en** Parks	des schön**en** Wetters	der lang**en** Straße	der alt**en** Häuser

Übung 7 Notizen von einem Besuch

Ergänzen Sie die Endungen.

1. Diese historisch_____ Stadt hat viele Sehenswürdigkeiten.
2. Das alt_____ Rathaus liegt direkt am Marktplatz.
3. Neben dem alt_____ Rathaus steht das neu_____ Opernhaus.
4. In der Nähe des alt_____ Rathauses liegt die berühmt_____ Kirche.
5. Morgen besuchen wir das alt_____ Rathaus.
6. Trotz des kalt_____ Wetters haben wir einen Spaziergang gemacht.
7. Der Groß_____ Garten ist der Name eines Parks in Dresden.
8. Heute besuchen wir den Groß_____ Garten.
9. Unser Hotel liegt am Groß_____ Garten.
10. Die viel_____ Touristen in Dresden kommen aus der ganzen Welt.

> ### Sprach-Info
>
> When two or more adjectives modify a noun, they have the same ending.
>
> Das **kleine historische** Hotel liegt in der Altstadt.

Obst aus dem Alten Land

---

*This type of adjective ending is traditionally referred to as a *weak* adjective ending.

Das familienfreundliche Museum.
Eintritt frei für Kinder bis 16 Jahre.

Übung 8 Wie war es in der Stadt?

Bilden Sie Sätze mit Adjektiven. Folgen Sie dem Beispiel.

BEISPIEL: Die Menschen waren alle sehr freundlich. →
Die freundlichen Menschen haben mir gefallen.

1. Die Häuser waren sehr alt.
2. Das Hotel war klein und gemütlich.
3. Das Frühstück im Hotel war ausgezeichnet.
4. Die Straßen waren sauber.
5. Das Bier war ausgezeichnet.
6. Der Marktplatz war klein.
7. Die Bedienung im Restaurant war leider unfreundlich.
8. Aber der Bürgermeister war sehr freundlich.
9. Das Museum war sehr familienfreundlich.

Ein Volksfest in Bayern

Übung 9 In der Stadt

Setzen Sie passende Adjektive aus der Liste in die Lücken.

klein   modern
groß   bequem
alt   historisch
neu

1. Das _____ Rathaus liegt neben der _____ Post.
2. Neben dem _____ Rathaus ist ein Park.
3. In dem _____ Park gibt es einen kleinen See.
4. Vor der _____ Kirche steht eine Statue.
5. In den _____ Hotels übernachten viele Touristen.
6. Auf dem _____ Marktplatz kann man täglich Obst und Gemüse kaufen.
7. In dieser _____ Stadt kann man gut leben.
8. Diese _____ Stadt hat mir sehr gefallen.

Ein warmer Sommertag am Elbufer in Dresden

Adjectives after an Indefinite Article

Adjectives preceded by indefinite articles, possessives, or other **ein**-words follow the same pattern as adjectives preceded by **der**-words, except in three instances: the masculine nominative and the neuter nominative and accusative.

Heute war **ein** schön**er** Tag.	*Today was a nice day.*
Das ist **mein** neu**es** Haus.	*This is my new house.*
Ich suche **ein** klein**es** Hotel.	*I'm looking for a small hotel.*
Wo ist **Ihr** neu**er** Wagen?	*Where is your new car?*

	Singular			Plural
	Masculine	*Neuter*	*Feminine*	*All Genders*
Nom.	ein groß**er** Park	ein schön**es** Haus	eine lang**e** Straße	keine neu**en** Geschäfte
Acc.	einen groß**en** Park	ein schön**es** Haus	eine lang**e** Straße	keine neu**en** Geschäfte
Dat.	einem groß**en** Park	einem schön**en** Haus	einer lang**en** Straße	keinen neu**en** Geschäften
Gen.	eines groß**en** Parks	eines schön**en** Hauses	einer lang**en** Straße	keiner neu**en** Geschäfte

Übung 10 Sehenswürdigkeiten in einer Stadt

Ergänzen Sie die Adjektive.

Hier ist …

1. ein deutsch＿＿ Restaurant.
2. eine bekannt＿＿ Universität.
3. ein alt＿＿ Rathaus.
4. eine modern＿＿ Fußgängerzone.
5. eine historisch＿＿ Altstadt.
6. ein groß＿＿ Flughafen.
7. ein berühmt＿＿ Kunstmuseum.
8. ein gemütlich＿＿ Biergarten.
9. ein groß＿＿, modern＿＿ Bahnhof.

hometown

Übung 11 Was gibt es in Ihrem Heimatort°?

Stellen Sie Fragen über den Heimatort eines Partners / einer Partnerin in Ihrer Klasse. Benutzen Sie die „Sehenswürdigkeiten" in **Übung 10** für Ihre Fragen. Berichten Sie dann im Plenum.

BEISPIEL: **S1:** Gibt es in deinem Heimatort ein deutsches Restaurant?

S2: Nein, es gibt kein deutsches Restaurant da.

oder Ja, es gibt ein deutsches Restaurant. Es heißt Suppenküche.

Adjectives without a Preceding Article

An attributive adjective that is not preceded by a **der-** or an **ein-**word takes an ending that signals the case, gender, and number of the noun that follows. With the exception of the genitive singular masculine and neuter, these endings are identical to those of the **der-**words.

da**s** Obst → Wo bekommt man hier frisch**es** Obst?

Where can you get fresh fruit?

di**e** Brötchen → Hier gibt es jeden Tag frisch**e** Brötchen.

You can get fresh rolls here every day.

bei de**m** Wetter → Bei schlecht**em** Wetter bleibe ich zu Hause.

In bad weather I stay home.

	Singular			Plural
	Masculine	*Neuter*	*Feminine*	*All Genders*
Nom.	schön**er** Park	gut**es** Wetter	zentral**e** Lage	alt**e** Häuser
Acc.	schön**en** Park	gut**es** Wetter	zentral**e** Lage	alt**e** Häuser
Dat.	schön**em** Park	gut**em** Wetter	zentral**er** Lage	alt**en** Häusern
Gen.	schön**en** Parks	gut**en** Wetter**s**	zentral**er** Lage	alt**er** Häuser

NOTE:

◐ An adjective in the genitive singular masculine or neuter always takes the **-en** ending.

Übung 12 Informationen

Ergänzen Sie die Sätze mithilfe von der Information in „Analyse" auf Seite 27%.

1. Das Kartoffelhaus nennt sich ein total _____ Wirtshaus.
2. Es bietet _____ Küche und _____ Mittagstisch.
3. Das Hotel Arcade bietet _____ Lage, _____ Komfort, _____ Zimmer und eine _____ Tiefgarage.
4. Im Hotel gibt es ein Restaurant mit _____ Küche.
5. Fischers Fritz fängt nur _____ Fische.

Circle all attributive adjectives in the illustrations.
Then determine:

▶ the gender, case, and number of the noun.

▶ why a particular adjective ending is used.

Fischers Fritz
fischt frische Fische

Kartoffelhaus № 1®

Das total unmögliche Wirtshaus

Quedlinburg
Breite Straße 37 – Ecke Klink
Tel. 0 39 46 / 70 83 34

Öffnungszeiten:
täglich von 11.00–24.00 Uhr
warme Küche 11.00–24.00 Uhr
täglich preiswerter Mittagstisch
Biergarten mit 60 Sitzplätzen

HOTEL

ARCADE

member of
PULLMAN INTERNATIONAL HOTELS

Das **A** und **O** für Bonn!
ARCADE   OPTIMAL

Sie suchen:

- das Hotel im Herzen der Stadt
- maximalen Komfort, moderne Einrichtung[1]
- die gehobene[2] Mittelklasse
- ein Tagungshotel

- **gastfreundlich**

Wir bieten:

- **zentrale Lage,** unmittelbar in der Nähe der Fußgängerzone
- 147 **gastfreundliche Zimmer** mit Dusche, WC, Telefon, Kabel-TV u. Radio
- **preiswerte Übernachtung** mit reichhaltigem[3] Frühstücksbuffet, **Restaurant** mit internationaler Küche
- 3 Konferenzräume für 10—150 Personen
- eigene **Tiefgarage**

- **preiswert** • **zentral**

Im Sommer
frische
Buttermilch
0,5 Liter 2,50 €

[1] *furnishings*   [2] *upper*   [3] *lavish*

Übung 13 Bei uns in der Stadt

Sie hören zwei kurze Hörtexte. Ergänzen Sie die fehlenden Adjektive, die Sie hören.

Text 1

A: Willkommen im _____ Theater unserer Stadt. Wir machen Theater für _____ Menschen zwischen 5 und 10 Jahren. Im _____ Haus präsentieren wir ein _____ Musical für die _____ Familie.

B: Unser Programm finden Sie auch auf unserer _____ Homepage. Besuchen Sie uns bald mit der _____ Familie, jung und alt.

Text 2

A: Entschuldigung, wo geht es hier zum Rathaus?

B: Meinen Sie das _____ oder das _____ Rathaus?

A: Oh, es gibt zwei? Ein _____ und ein _____? Ich meine das Rathaus mit dem _____ Glockenspiel.

B: Also, das ist das _____ Rathaus. Gehen Sie geradeaus, dann die _____ Straße links. Das Rathaus liegt auf der _____ Seite.

A: _____ Dank.

Das Rathaus in München am Marienplatz

Übung 14 Hin und her: Was gibt es hier?

Fragen Sie einen Partner / eine Partnerin nach den fehlenden Informationen.

BEISPIEL: **S1:** Was gibt es beim Gasthof zum Bären?

S2: Warme Küche.

S1: Was gibt es sonst noch?

S2: Bayerische Spezialitäten.

Wo?	Was?	Was sonst noch?
Gasthof zum Bären		
Gasthof Adlersberg	ein Biergarten / gemütlich	liegt in Lage / idyllisch
Gasthaus Schneiderwirt		
Hotel Luitpold	liegt in Lage / idyllisch	Zimmer / rustikal
Restaurant Ökogarten		

Adjectives Referring to Cities and Regions

Das Hotel liegt in der **Frankfurter** Innenstadt.

Wo trägt man **Tiroler** Hüte?

Wo isst man **Wiener** Schnitzel?

A city or regional name can be used attributively by adding **-er** to the name of the city or region. This is one of the rare instances where an adjective is capitalized in German. No further changes are made. One country name can also be used in this way: **die Schweiz.**

> Essen Sie gern **Schweizer** Käse?

Übung 15 Berichte

Sie sind gerade von einer Reise nach Hause gekommen. Nun müssen Sie berichten.

Was hast du da gesehen oder gemacht?

BEISPIEL: **S1:** Was hast du in Köln gemacht?

S2: Da habe ich den Kölner Dom besichtigt.

1. in Hamburg / den Hafen (*harbor*) besichtigt
2. in Bremen / die Stadtmusikanten gesehen
3. in Düsseldorf / die berühmte Altstadt besucht
4. in Dortmund / Bier getrunken
5. in Berlin / eine Weiße mit Schuss getrunken [ein Spezialgetränk aus Bier und Saft]
6. in München / Weißwurst gegessen
7. in der Schweiz / Käse gekauft
8. in Wien / Walzer getanzt

Die Bremer Stadtmusikanten

Sprache im Kontext

Videoclips

A Hotel Jurine: Interview mit Nadine Schulz. Nadine arbeitet im Hotel. Sie gibt viele Informationen über das Hotel. Was sagt sie?

1. Der Name des Hotels ist _____ _____ des Inhabers.
2. Das Hotel hat 53 _____.
3. Ein Einzelzimmer kostet zwischen _____ und _____ Euro.
4. Ein _____ kostet zwischen 80 und 140 Euro.
5. Die Zimmer haben _____, WC, _____, Telefon und _____.

B Wie gefällt Doris und Beatrice das Hotel? Was sagen sie?

C Michael fragt Dennis nach dem Weg zum Alexanderplatz. Was sagt Dennis? Nummerieren Sie die Sätze in der richtigen Reihenfolge.

_____ und dann kannst du es nicht verfehlen

_____ du gehst am besten immer geradeaus

_____ und dann gehst du immer geradeaus circa fünf Minuten

_____ vorne an der Ampel gehst du nach links

_____ Nächste gleich wieder rechts

Lesen

Zum Thema

A Machen Sie eine Liste von den Vorteilen (*advantages*) und Nachteilen (*disadvantages*) des Stadtlebens.

B **Was würden Sie machen?**

1. Sie müssen für eine Prüfung lernen, und Ihr Mitbewohner / Ihre Mitbewohnerin spielt sehr laute Musik.
2. Sie studieren Musik (Trompete) und müssen jeden Tag üben. Ihre Nachbarn im Haus beschweren sich immer, wenn Sie spielen.

Auf den ersten Blick

A In dem folgenden Text stehen die Verben im Imperfekt (*simple past*). Suchen Sie den Infinitiv in der zweiten Spalte.

1. _____ spielte	**a.** schlagen (*to hit*)
2. _____ gab	**b.** sprechen
3. _____ stieß	**c.** grüßen
4. _____ losging	**d.** ausziehen (*to move out*)
5. _____ blies	**e.** einziehen (*to move in*)
6. _____ schlug	**f.** losgehen (*to start, begin*)
7. _____ traf	**g.** anfangen
8. _____ grüßte	**h.** stören (*to disturb*)
9. _____ einzog	**i.** stoßen (*to pound*)
10. _____ auszog	**j.** spielen
11. _____ sprach	**k.** blasen (*to blow*)
12. _____ anfing	**l.** treffen
13. _____ störte	**m.** geben

B Lesen Sie bis Zeile (*line*) 11. Wo findet die Geschichte statt (*takes place*)? Wie könnte die Geschichte weitergehen?

Die Gitarre des Herrn Hatunoglu

von Heinrich Hannover

Frau Amanda Klimpermunter spielte oft und gern Klavier. Aber sie
wohnte in einem großen Mietshaus. Und da gab es manchmal Ärger° mit   *trouble*
den Mietern der Nachbarwohnungen. Denn die Wände und Decken des
Hauses waren dünn°.   *thin*

5   In der Wohnung unter Frau Klimpermunter wohnte Herr Maibaum.
Wenn oben Klavier gespielt wurde, fühlte sich Herr Maibaum in seiner
Ruhe gestört° und schimpfte°. Dann stieß er ein paarmal mit einem   *disturbed / yelled, swore*
Besenstiel an die Decke. Aber Frau Klimpermunter spielte weiter. Und so
schaffte sich Herr Maibaum eines Tages eine Trompete an. Und immer,
10 wenn Frau Klimpermunters Klaviermusik losging, trompetete er kräftig°   *powerfully, vigorously*
dagegen.

    Das störte nun den Nachbarn des Herrn Maibaum, der sich schon
über das Klavier genug geärgert hatte. Und jetzt auch noch die Trompete,
das war zu viel. Ein paarmal klopfte° er mit einem Holzpantoffel gegen   *knocked*
15 die Wand. Aber Herr Maibaum trompetete weiter. Und so schaffte sich
der Nachbar, er hieß Fromme-Weise, eine Posaune an. Und immer, wenn
das Klavier und die Trompete im Haus ertönten, blies er laut wie ein
Elefant auf der Posaune.

    Aber das störte nun Frau Morgenschön, die Wand an Wand mit
20 Herrn Fromme-Weise wohnte. Ein paarmal schlug sie mit dem Kochlöffel
gegen die Wand, aber das kümmerte ihren Nachbarn nicht. Und so
kaufte sie sich eine Flöte und düdelte° dazwischen, wenn die anderen   *noodled*
Musikanten im Haus loslegten.

    Das störte Herrn Bollermann, der unter Frau Morgenschön wohnte.
25 Er kaufte sich ein Schlagzeug und haute, wenn die anderen herumtönten,
kräftig auf die Pauke. Das gab nun alle Tage einen Höllenlärm im Haus,
ein fürchterliches Durcheinander – tüdelüdelüt-bumsbums-trärä-trara-
bumspeng … Wenn man sich auf der Treppe traf, grüßte keiner den
anderen, man knallte° mit den Türen, es gab immer Krach° im Haus,   *slammed / noise*
30 auch wenn keiner Musik machte.

    Aber dann zog Herr Hatunoglu ins Haus ein, ein Ausländer, wie man
schon am Namen merkt. Er brachte eine Gitarre mit und freute sich,
daß im Haus musiziert wurde. „Da kann ich ja auch ein bißchen Gitarre
spielen", sagte er. Aber obwohl man die Gitarre bei dem Lärm, den
35 die anderen Hausbewohner mit ihren Instrumenten machten, gar nicht
hören konnte, waren sich plötzlich alle einig: „Die Gitarre ist zu laut."
Plötzlich sprachen sie wieder miteinander.

    „Finden Sie nicht auch, daß der Herr Hatunoglu mit seiner Gitarre
einen unerträglichen Lärm macht?"
40   „Ja, Sie haben recht, der Mann muß raus."

    Sie grüßten sich wieder auf der Treppe und hörten auf,° sich   *hörten … stopped*
gegenseitig zu nerven. Dem Herrn Hatunoglu aber machten sie das Leben
schwer°. Wenn er anfing, auf der Gitarre zu spielen, klopften sie von   *difficult*
oben und von unten und von allen Seiten mit Besenstielen, Kochlöffeln
45 und Holzpantoffeln an Wände und Decken und riefen: „Aufhören! Ruhe
im Haus!"

„Was haben die Leute bloß gegen meine Gitarre?" fragte Herr
Hatunoglu. Und eines Tages zog er aus.
    Kaum war Herr Hatunoglu ausgezogen, ging der Krach im Haus
50 wieder los. Sobald Frau Klimpermunter den ersten Ton auf dem Klavier
gespielt hat, packen die anderen Hausbewohner ihre Instrumente aus
und legen los: Tüdelüdelüt-bumsbums-trärä-trara-bumspeng … Sie
sprechen auch nicht mehr miteinander und grüßen sich nicht mehr auf
der Treppe. Und sie knallen wieder mit den Türen. Aber abends, wenn
55 sie völlig entnervt ins Bett gehen, flüstern sie vor sich hin: „Was war das
doch für eine schöne, ruhige Zeit, als noch der Herr Hatunoglu mit
seiner Gitarre im Haus wohnte."

Zum Text

A Wer wohnt wo? Setzen Sie die Namen der Bewohner in das erste
Bild ein. Sehen Sie sich nun auch die anderen Bilder an. Welches
Instrument gehört zu welcher Person? Welches „Schlagzeug" gehört
zu welcher Person?

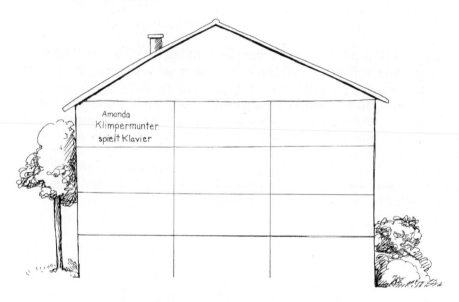

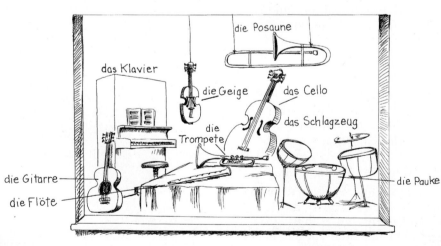

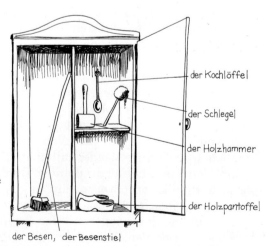

B Stimmt das? Stimmt das nicht? Oder steht das nicht im Text?

	Das stimmt	Das stimmt nicht	Das steht nicht im Text
1. Herr Hatunoglu ist unfreundlich.	☐	☐	☐
2. Nachdem Herr Hatunoglu einzieht, sprechen die Nachbarn wieder miteinander.	☐	☐	☐
3. Er spielt Gitarre und ist sehr froh, dass die anderen Bewohner so viel Musik machen.	☐	☐	☐
4. Die anderen Bewohner sagen, sie mögen Herrn Hatunoglu nicht, weil er so laut ist.	☐	☐	☐
5. Herr Hatunoglu lädt oft Freunde ein, und sie sind sehr laut.	☐	☐	☐
6. Sobald Herr Hatunoglu auszieht, werden die anderen Bewohner miteinander viel freundlicher.	☐	☐	☐

C Die folgenden Wörter stehen im Text. Welches Wort gehört nicht in die Gruppe? Sagen Sie warum.

BEISPIEL: Holzpantoffel   Klavier   Besen →
Klavier gehört nicht dazu. Frau Klimpermunter spielt Klavier.
Die Nachbarn schlagen mit dem Holzpantoffel und Besen gegen
die Wand, wenn sie Musik hören.

1. sich etwas anschaffen	düdeln	trompeten
2. Nachbarn kümmern	die Tür knallen	Krach machen
3. klopfen	schlagen	flüstern
4. anschaffen	aufhören	kaufen

D Interviewen Sie Herrn Hatunoglu und eine weitere Person im Haus.
Schreiben Sie mindestens drei Fragen für jede Person auf. Arbeiten
Sie in Gruppen zu viert. Zwei Studenten/Studentinnen übernehmen
die Rollen. Die anderen interviewen die beiden.

Zu guter Letzt

Eine Webseite für Touristen

Entwerfen Sie eine Webseite über Ihre Stadt für Touristen.

Schritt 1: Suchen Sie im Internet einen Stadtplan von Ihrer Heimatstadt
oder Universitätsstadt. Identifizieren Sie die wichtigsten Sehenswürdigkeiten, z.B. Denkmäler (*monuments*), Gebäude (*buildings*), Plätze und Parks.

Schritt 2: Schreiben Sie einen kurzen Text über fünf bis sieben Sehenswürdigkeiten in der Stadt. Suchen Sie auch passende Fotos dazu.

Schritt 3: Stellen Sie nun alles zusammen und machen Sie die Webseite.
Benutzen Sie die Stadt Wittenberg als Modell (www.wittenberg.de).

Schritt 4: Tauschen Sie Ihre Webseite mit einem Partner / einer Partnerin
aus. Jeder muss dann drei Fragen über die Webseite vorbereiten.

Schritt 5: Stellen Sie Ihrem Partner / Ihrer Partnerin die Fragen und notieren Sie die Antworten. Berichten Sie dann der Klasse, was Sie über die
Stadt gelernt haben.

Wortschatz

In der Stadt	**In the City**	der **Schlüssel,** -	key
die **Ampel, -n**	traffic light	der **Stock,**	floor, story
der **Bahnhof, ⸚e**	train station	*pl.* **Stockwerke**	
die **Bank, -en**	bank	die **Übernachtung, -en**	overnight stay
die **Fußgängerzone, -n**	pedestrian zone	die **Unterkunft, ⸚e**	accommodation
das **Hotel, -s**	hotel	das **WC, -s**	bathroom, toilet
die **Innenstadt, ⸚e**	downtown		
die **Jugendherberge, -n**	youth hostel	**Nach dem Weg fragen**	**Asking Directions**
die **Kirche, -n**	church	**bis: bis zum/zur**	to, as far as
die **Kreuzung, -en**	intersection	**gegenüber von**	across from
die **Lage, -n**	location	(+ *dative*)	
das **Museum,** *pl.* **Museen**	museum	**geradeaus**	straight ahead
der **Passant (-en** *masc.*),	passerby	**immer geradeaus**	(keep on going) straight ahead
-en / die			
Passantin, -nen		**links**	left
die **Pension, -en**	bed and breakfast, small family-run hotel	**nach links**	to the left
		rechts	right
die **Polizei**	police, police station	**nach rechts**	to the right
die **Post,** *pl.* **Postämter**	post office	**weit**	far
das **Rathaus, ⸚er**	city hall		
das **Schloss, ⸚er**	castle, palace	die **Ecke, -n**	corner
der **Tierpark, -s**	zoo	**an der Ecke**	at the corner
der **Tourist (-en** *masc.*),	tourist	die **Haltestelle, -n**	bus stop
-en / die		die **Mitte**	middle, center
Touristin, -nen		**in der Mitte (der Stadt)**	in the center (of the city)
der **Weg, -e**	way, path; road		
das **Zentrum,** *pl.* **Zentren**	center (of town)	die **Nähe**	vicinity
		in der Nähe (des Bahnhofs)	near (the train station)
Im Hotel	**At the Hotel**		
das **Anmeldeformular, -e**	registration form	**Verben**	**Verbs**
der **Apparat, -e**	set, appliance (*such as TV, telephone, camera*)	**ab·reisen, ist abgereist**	to depart
der **Aufenthalt, -e**	stay; layover	**an·kommen, ist angekommen**	to arrive
der **Aufzug, ⸚e**	elevator		
die **Bettwäsche**	linens	**sich an·melden**	to check in, register
das **Doppelzimmer, -**	room with two beds, double room	**aus·füllen**	to fill out
		sich beschweren über	to complain about
die **Dusche, -n**	shower	(+ *acc.*)	
das **Einzelzimmer, -**	room with one bed, single room	**ein·biegen**	to turn, make a turn
		entlang·gehen, ist entlanggegangen	to walk along
das **Erdgeschoss, -e**	ground floor		
der **Föhn, -e**	hair dryer	**erlauben**	to allow, permit
der **Frühstücksraum, ⸚e**	breakfast room	**funktionieren**	to work, function
das **Gepäck**	luggage	**reparieren**	to repair
der **Internetzugang**	Internet access	**übernachten**	to stay overnight
die **Kreditkarte, -n**	credit card		
der **Kühlschrank, ⸚e**	refrigerator	**Adjektive und Adverbien**	**Adjectives and Adverbs**
der **Parkplatz, ⸚e**	parking space; parking lot	**günstig**	favorable, convenient(ly)
der **Preis, -e**	price; cost	**günstig liegen**	to be conveniently located
im Preis enthalten	included in the price		
der **Reisepass, ⸚e**	passport	**kaputt**	broken
die **Rezeption**	reception desk		

sofort	immediately	**Sonstige Ausdrücke**	**Other Expressions**
übrigens	by the way	**Auf welchen Namen?**	Under what name?
ungefähr	about, approximately	**Auf Wiederhören!**	Good-bye! (*on telephone*)
zuerst	first, at first	**Das tut mir leid.**	I'm sorry.
		Entschuldigung	excuse me
Genitivpräpositionen	**Genitive Prepositions**	**jemand nach dem Weg fragen**	to ask someone for directions
außerhalb	outside of	**Wie komme ich am besten dahin?**	What's the best way to get there?
innerhalb	inside of, within	**Würden Sie (bitte) … ?**	Would you (please) …?
trotz	in spite of		
während	during, while		
wegen	because of, on account of		

Das kann ich nun!

1. Sie sind beim Informationszentrum einer deutschen Stadt und suchen ein Zimmer. Nennen Sie 3–4 Dinge, die Ihnen wichtig sind.

2. Sie sind an der Rezeption eines Schweizer Hotels. Sie haben eine Reservierung. Was sagen Sie?

3. Sie sind in einer fremden Stadt und suchen das Rathaus. Fragen Sie jemand auf der Straße nach dem Weg.

4. Sie sind in einem Hotel in einer deutschen Stadt und berichten einem Freund per E-Mail etwas über das Hotel. Wie sagen Sie dies auf Deutsch?
   a. *My room is on the first floor.*
   b. *The hotel is located in the center of town near the railroad station.*
   c. *Behind the hotel is a big, beautiful park.*
   d. *In the park there is a small lake.*

5. Wie sagt man auf Deutsch:
   a. *street crossing*
   b. *traffic light*
   c. *straight ahead*

6. Sie schreiben eine Postkarte aus Wien. Ergänzen Sie die Adjektivendungen.
   Wien ist eine sehr schön___ Stadt mit viel___ interessanten Museen und historisch___ Kirchen. Neben meinem Hotel liegt ein alt___ Schloss. Hinter dem alt___ Schloss liegt ein wunderschön___ Park. Gestern habe ich im Restaurant ein Wien___ Schnitzel gegessen. Zum Glück haben wir gut___ Wetter.

7. Was fischt Fischers Fritz?

Die Entwicklung der Stadt

Im Laufe der Zeit hat sich das Bild der Stadt sehr verändert[1]. Viele Städte in Deutschland, wie auch anderswo in Europa, haben aber zum Teil ihren ursprünglichen[2] Charakter aus der mittelalterlichen Zeit erhalten[3]. Sie sind stolz auf ihre Vergangenheit, die oft bis ins Mittelalter und manchmal bis in die Römerzeit zurückreicht. Köln wurde zum Beispiel im Jahre 50 gegründet, Erfurt im 9. Jahrhundert. Die Geschichte Goslars reicht in das 10. Jahrhundert zurück. Gelegentlich sind sogar noch Überreste alter Bauten und Denkmäler[4] aus frühen Zeiten zu sehen.

Aktivität 1   Mittelalterliche Städte

Wie sahen Städte im Mittelalter aus? Was gehörte zum typischen Stadtbild? Kreuzen Sie an.

- ☐ Restaurants
- ☐ Gefängnis[5]
- ☐ Burg/Schloss
- ☐ Universität
- ☐ Kirche/Dom
- ☐ Bürgerhäuser[6]
- ☐ Wachttürme[7]
- ☐ Krankenhaus
- ☐ Markt
- ☐ Geschäfte
- ☐ Parks
- ☐ Bibliothek
- ☐ Schule
- ☐ Fabrik
- ☐ Stadtmauer[8]
- ☐ Rathaus
- ☐ Museum
- ☐ Stadttor[9]

[1]changed   [2]original   [3]preserved   [4]Bauten ... buildings and monuments   [5]prison   [6]patrician houses   [7]watchtowers   [8]city wall   [9]city gate

Aktivität 2   Nürnberg damals

Schauen Sie sich jetzt die Stadtansicht von Nürnberg aus dem Jahr 1533 auf der nächsten Seite an. Identifizieren Sie die Hauptmerkmale der Stadt.

1. _____ Burg
2. _____ Kirche
3. _____ Brücke
4. _____ Bürgerhäuser
5. _____ Stadtmauer
6. _____ Wachtturm

▶ Welche(s) Gebäude[10] bildete(n) den Kern[11] einer mittelalterlichen Stadt? Warum?

▶ Wer wohnte in der Stadt? Wer wohnte außerhalb der Stadt?

[10]building(s)   [11]center

Erfurt

Köln

Nürnberg heute

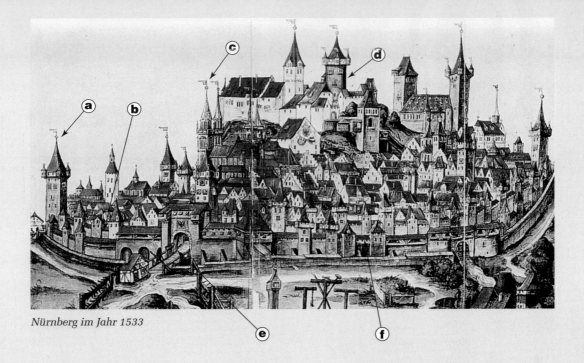

Nürnberg im Jahr 1533

Aktivität 3 Nürnberg heute

Vergleichen Sie die Zeichnung von Nürnberg im Jahr 1533 mit dem Stadtplan von Nürnberg heute. Obwohl die Stadt während des Zweiten Weltkriegs fast völlig zerstört[1] wurde, sind noch einige Bauten und Denkmäler aus dem Mittelalter und der Renaissance erhalten. Wie viele der folgenden Bauten und Denkmäler können Sie auf dem Stadtplan finden?

1. St. Sebaldus Kirche (14. Jahrhundert)
2. St. Lorenz Kirche (13.–14. Jahrhundert)
3. das Rathaus (14. Jahrhundert)
4. die Stadtmauer (14.–15. Jahrhundert)
5. der Schöne Brunnen (1389–1396)
6. die Burg (11.–12. Jahrhundert)

Aktivität 4 Auf den Spuren[2] der Stadtentwicklung

Wählen Sie eine Stadt in Ihrem Land aus. Es kann auch Ihre Heimatstadt sein. Beschreiben Sie folgendes:

▶ Wie sah die Stadt vor 100 Jahren aus?

▶ Was gehörte damals zum Stadtbild?

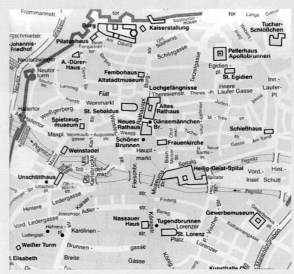

Stadtplan von Nürnberg heute

▶ Gab es einen Mittelpunkt der Stadt? Wenn ja, was gehörte dazu? Ein Markt, eine Kirche oder ein anderes Gebäude?

▶ Welche alten Bauten und Denkmäler sind noch in dieser Stadt erhalten? Welche sind verschwunden[3]? Warum?

---

[1]*destroyed*   [2]*Auf … On the trail*   [3]*disappeared*

Einsteigen, bitte!

Auf Reisen

In diesem Kapitel

▶ **Themen:** Talking about travel, vacations, modes of transportation, items to take on vacation

▶ **Grammatik:** The superlative, adjectival nouns, the simple past tense, the conjunction **als,** the past perfect tense

▶ **Lesen:** „The American Dream" (Bernd Maresch)

▶ **Landeskunde:** German vacations, German geography, dealing with a travel agency, buying a train ticket, **Sächsische Schweiz**

▶ **Zu guter Letzt:** Ein Reisebericht

VIDEOCLIPS

Wohin im Urlaub?

A Was planen Sie für Ihren nächsten Urlaub? Was interessiert Sie? Lesen Sie die folgenden Anzeigen.

⊙ Auf welcher Reise kann man eine Fremdsprache lernen?

⊙ Welche Reisen sind für sportliche Leute am geeignetsten (*most suited*)? Welche Sportarten kann man auf diesen Reisen machen?

⊙ Welche Reise verbindet (*connects*) Sport und Kultur? Welche verbindet Action mit Erholung in der Natur?

⊙ Was macht Ihnen persönlich in den Ferien Spaß: eine Fremdsprache lernen? Tennisspielen lernen? eine Kanutour machen? Mountainbiking?

Tennis, Biken, Wassersport, Marathon und vieles mehr
AKTIV URLAUB

SportScheck Reisen

Sun and Fun Sportreisen GmbH
Franz-Joseph-Str 43
D-80801 Munchen

Hammer Str. 418
48153 Münster
Telefon 0251/87188-0

RUCKSACK REISEN
Aktivurlaub, Gruppenreisen und Kanutouren

Wildwasser-Kajak

Eine faszinierende Sportart, die Action und Adrenalin mit intensiver Erholung in unverbrauchter[1] Natur verbindet. Erlernbar für jeden, der bereit ist, im Team zu agieren und Spaß zu haben. Die Reviere[2] in Frankreich, Slowenien und Österreich zählen zu den Klassikern des Wildwassersports.

[1]unspoiled   [2]preserves

SPANISCH in LATEINAMERIKA

z.B. Bolivien

2 Wo Einzelunterricht[3] 25 Std/Wo
Wochenend-Tourenprogramm
Unterkunft m. VP bei Gastfamilie
Kleinkinderbetreuung[4]

schon ab € 700,–

ALR Wolfgang Retz Postfach 390 153/D
Conrädstr. 16/4 Berlin 13509
Tel: (030) 805 49 30 Fax: (030) 805 15 52

[3]one-on-one instruction
[4]child care

TENNIS & KULTUR IN PRAG

€ 200,–

1 Wo inkl.: 5x2(4) Std. Tennistraining
+ HP + Kulturprogramm · Info + Buchung:
Tel. (089) 53 94 34 od. 53 64 35 · Fax 532 84 70
Tamar-Reisen · Häberlstraße 13 · München 80337

B Sie hören drei Gespräche über den Urlaub. Wo haben die Urlauber ihre Ferien verbracht? Was haben sie unternommen?

wo	**was**
1. a. an der Nordsee	**a.** segeln
b. an der Ostsee	**b.** Camping
2. a. Mexiko	**a.** Spanisch lernen
b. Bolivien	**b.** tauchen
3. a. in den Dolomiten	**a.** Bergsteigen
b. im Schwarzwald	**b.** wandern

Thema 1: Ich möchte verreisen

Wie reisen Sie am liebsten?

▶ Kreuzen Sie an!

☐ mit dem Wagen ☐ mit dem **Flugzeug** ☐ mit dem Fahrrad

☐ mit dem **Zug** / mit der **Bahn** ☐ mit dem **Taxi** ☐ mit dem Motorrad

☐ mit dem **Schiff** ☐ **per Autostop** ☐ mit dem **Bus**

BEISPIEL: Ich reise am liebsten mit dem Bus.

A Und warum? Was finden Sie …

am **interessant**esten?	am langweiligsten?	am praktischsten?
am **sicher**sten?	am **gefährlich**sten?	am **laut**esten?
am **schnell**sten?	am **langsam**sten?	am bequemsten?

BEISPIEL: Reisen mit dem Bus ist am interessantesten. Man sieht mehr.

B Fragen Sie jemand, wie er oder sie **verreisen** möchte.

BEISPIEL: **S1:** Also Sven, du möchtest verreisen? Wohin?

S2: Nach Marokko.

S1: Wie kommst du dahin?

S2: Mit dem Schiff.

S1: Und warum?

S2: Das ist am interessantesten.

Siehe *Expressing Comparisons: The Superlative*, S. 300.

Neue Wörter

sicher safe
schnell fast
gefährlich dangerous
langsam slow
laut loud
verreisen go on a trip
die Reise trip
vergessen forgotten
der Handschuh (Handschuhe, *pl.***)** glove
der Reiseführer travel guide
der Strand beach
das Sonnenschutzmittel suntan lotion, sunscreen
das Handgepäck carry-on luggage
das Bargeld cash
der Reisescheck (Reiseschecks, *pl.***)** travelers' check
der Personalausweis ID card
die Fahrkarte (Fahrkarten, *pl.***)** ticket
die Platzkarte (Platzkarten, *pl.***)** seat-reservation cards
der Fahrplan schedule
das Navi (Navigationssystem) GPS system

Ihre Checkliste vor der Reise – haben Sie nichts vergessen?

In den Koffer packen …

Bekleidung
☐ Unterwäsche
☐ Regenmantel
☐ **Handschuhe**
☐ Jogginganzug
☐ Schlafanzug
☐ Schal
☐ Sportbekleidung

Schuhwerk
☐ Hausschuhe
☐ Turnschuhe

Toilettensachen
☐ Hautcreme
☐ Zahnpasta
☐ Haarshampoo
☐ Zahnbürste

Für Ihre Aktivitäten im Urlaub
☐ Kamera, Filme
☐ **Reiseführer**
☐ Stadtpläne
☐ Landkarten

Für den Strand
☐ **Sonnenschutzmittel**
☐ Badehose/Badeanzug
☐ Sonnenbrille

Für die Berge
☐ Wanderstock
☐ Wanderschuhe
☐ Rucksack

Das sollte im Handgepäck nicht fehlen …
☐ Reiseapotheke
☐ Reiselektüre

Auch das muss mit - aber nicht im Koffer!
☐ **Bargeld**
☐ **Reisechecks,** Euroschecks
   Achtung! Scheckkarte!
☐ Reisepass, **Personalausweis**
☐ **Fahrkarten**
☐ **Platzkarten**
☐ **Fahrplan**
☐ Kofferschlüssel
☐ Wohnungsschlüssel
☐ Handy
☐ **Navi**

Aktivität 1   Alles für die Reise

Diese Wörter haben alle mit Reisen zu tun. Welches Wort in jeder Gruppe passt nicht?

1. Stadtplan, Landkarte, Reiseführer, Zahnbürste
2. Badeanzug, Sportbekleidung, Stadtplan, Regenmantel
3. Bargeld, Turnschuhe, Reiseschecks, Reisepass
4. Wanderschuhe, Wanderstock, Kofferschlüssel, Rucksack

Aktivität 2   Haben Sie etwas vergessen?

Schauen Sie sich die Reise-Checkliste aus **Thema 1** an und nennen Sie drei Dinge aus der Liste, die Sie unbedingt (*absolutely*) mitnehmen würden.

BEISPIEL: Ich möchte eine Mountainbike-Tour machen. Ich nehme Sonnenschutzmittel, eine Kamera, und mein Navi mit.

eine Wanderreise durch Europa	eine Safari nach Afrika
eine Reise nach Hawaii	eine Reise nach _____

Landeskunde-Info

Deutsche Arbeitnehmer bekommen im Jahr durchschnittlich (*on average*) sechs Wochen bezahlten Urlaub. Das erklärt, warum der Urlaub ein so wichtiges Thema ist. Wie kann man sechs Wochen freie Zeit sinnvoll planen? Die meisten, vor allem Familien, nehmen den größten Teil des Urlaubs im Sommer, wenn die Kinder Ferien (*school holidays*) haben. Viele Deutsche machen auch im Winter Urlaub: Sie fahren in den Bergen Ski oder suchen ein wärmeres Klima im Süden. Und viele wollen sich im Urlaub weiterbilden. Sie reisen in verschiedene Länder, um mehr über Land und Leute zu erfahren.

▶ Wie viel Urlaub bekommt man durchschnittlich in Ihrem Land?

▶ Wohin fahren Sie gerne im Urlaub?

Aktivität 3 Hin und her: Was nehmen sie mit?

Wohin fahren diese Leute im Urlaub? Was nehmen sie mit? Und warum? Ergänzen Sie die Informationen.

BEISPIEL: **S1:** Wohin fährt Angelika Meier in Urlaub?

S2: Sie fährt in die Türkei.

S1: Warum fährt sie in die Türkei?

S2: Weil …

S1: Was nimmt sie mit?

S2: Sie nimmt …

Personen	Wohin?	Warum?	Was nimmt er/sie mit?
Angelika Meier	in die Türkei	sich am Strand erholen	Buch, Sonnenbrille, Badesachen
Peter Bayer			
Roland Metz	nach Thüringen	wandern, Weimar besichtigen	Stadtpläne, Reiseführer, Wanderschuhe
Sabine Graf			

Advantages and disadvantages

Aktivität 4 Vorteile und Nachteile°

Alles hat seine Vorteile und Nachteile. Was meinen Sie?

BEISPIELE: Mit dem Fahrrad sieht man viel, aber es ist anstrengend.
Mit dem Auto geht es schneller, aber es ist _____ .

mit dem/der _____	geht es	nicht	bequem / anstrengend
Bahn (Zug)	ist es	sehr	billig / teuer
Bus	kostet es	zu	praktisch / unpraktisch
Fahrrad	sieht man		romantisch / langweilig
Flugzeug			schnell / langsam
Wagen (Auto)			sicher / gefährlich
per Autostop			viel / wenig
zu Fuß			
??			

Thema 2: Im Reisebüro

*Gespräch im **Reisebüro** zwischen einer Kundin (Claudia) und einem Angestellten, Herrn Meier.*

Claudia: Mein Freund und ich möchten dieses Jahr mal einen Aktivurlaub machen. Können Sie etwas **vorschlagen**?

Herr M.: Ja, gern. Wofür interessieren Sie sich denn? Sind Sie sportlich **aktiv**?

Claudia: Wir fahren oft Rad. Und wir wandern gern.

Herr M.: Wie wäre es (*How about*) dann mit einer Radreise durchs Elsass? Da kann man viel **erleben** und **unternehmen**. Oder ein Segelkurs an der Ostsee?

Claudia: Ach, ein Segelkurs ist nichts für mich. Ich kann nicht so gut schwimmen.

Herr M.: Und eine Wandertour? Hier habe ich ein **Reiseprospekt** mit **Wanderwegen** durch Deutschland. Es gibt so viele **Möglichkeiten**. Hier ist zum Beispiel ein **Angebot** für eine siebentägige Wandertour auf dem Malerweg im Nationalpark Sächsische Schweiz.

Claudia: Davon habe ich schon gehört. Es soll sehr schön dort sein.

Herr M.: Bestimmt. Man wandert durch eine wildromantische **Landschaft** mit Bergen und Wäldern. Viele Maler haben da gemalt. Daher (*For this reason*) der Name Malerweg.

Claudia: Klingt interessant. Und was kostet das?

Herr M.: Also, sieben Übernachtungen in kleinen Landhotels, mit Frühstück, Gepäcktransport und **Verpflegung** unterwegs **insgesamt** 395 Euro **pro Person**. Das kann ich jederzeit für Sie **buchen**.

Claudia: Das klingt gut. Mein Freund liebt die **Natur**, solange er nicht im **Zelt** übernachten muss. Wir werden es **uns überlegen**. Zwei Freunde von uns wollen eventuell auch mitkommen. **Zu viert** macht es noch mehr Spaß!

▶ Ergänzen Sie:

1. Im Reisebüro kann man eine Reise _____.
2. Das Reisebüro hat ein _____ für eine Wandertour.
3. Über die Reise kann man im _____ lesen.
4. Die Tour auf dem Malerweg im Nationalpark Sächsische Schweiz dauert _____.
5. Die Wandertour geht durch eine wildromantische _____.
6. Der Preis für die Wandertour ist _____.
7. Claudia will zwei Freunde einladen und die Reise _____ machen.

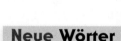

Neue Wörter

das Reisebüro travel agency
vorschlagen suggest
erleben experience
unternehmen do, undertake
der Reiseprospekt travel brochure
der Wanderweg hiking trail
die Möglichkeit possibility
das Angebot offer
die Landschaft landscape
die Verpflegung meals
insgesamt altogether
buchen book
das Zelt tent
uns überlegen (sich überlegen) think over
zu viert as a foursome

Eine Wandertour von vier Tagen ist eine **viertägige** Wandertour. Eine Reise von einer Woche ist eine **einwöchige** Reise. Ein Aufenthalt von fünf Monaten ist ein **fünfmonatiger** Aufenthalt. So macht man es:

ein-	-stündig	
zwei-	-tägig	
drei- +	-wöchig	} + Adjektivendung
...	-monatig	

Landeskunde-Info

Die Sächsische Schweiz ist eine wildromantische Landschaft bekannt für ihre Wälder und bizarren Felsengebilde (im Elbsandsteingebirge), entlang der Elbe, im nordöstlichen Teil Deutschlands. Der Malerweg, der durch diesen Naturpark führt, gehört zu den schönsten und beliebtesten Wanderwegen Deutschlands.

▶ Wo gibt es beliebte Wanderwege in Ihrer Gegend?

▶ Wo möchten Sie gern eine Wandertour machen?

Ein Blick auf die Elbe

Hier klicken!

Weiteres zum Thema Reisen finden Sie bei **Deutsch: Na klar!** im World-Wide-Web unter www. mhhe.com/dnk6.

Aktivität 5   Eine Wandertour — tolle Idee!

Claudia Siemens trifft sich mit ihren Freunden Philipp und Monika im Café und berichtet über die Wandertour. Ergänzen Sie die Sätze mit Informationen aus dem Gespräch im **Thema 2.**

Claudia: Sascha und ich wollen eine _____[1] in der Sächsischen Schweiz machen. Habt ihr Lust mitzukanmen?

Monika: Wie lange dauert diese Tour denn?

Claudia: _____.[2]

Monika: Und wo übernachtet man?

Claudia: _____.[3]

Philipp: Was soll das denn kosten?

Claudia: _____.[4]

Philipp: Wie steht es mit Gepäck und Essen?

Claudia: _____.[5]

Monika: Was meinst du, Philipp? Sollen wir das machen?

Philipp: Also, gut, das ist mal was anderes.

Aktivität 6 Pläne für einen interessanten Urlaub

Sie hören vier Gespräche im Reisebüro. Wie, wohin und warum wollen die
Leute in Urlaub fahren? Wie lange wollen sie dort bleiben?

Personen	Wie?	Wohin?	Warum?	Wie lange?
1. Nicola Dinsing				
2. Marianne Koch und Astrid Preuß				
3. Herbert und Sabine Lucht				
4. Sebastian Thiel				

Aktivität 7 Überredungskünste°

Art of persuasion

Versuchen Sie, einen Partner / eine Partnerin zu einem Plan für einen
gemeinsamen Urlaub zu überreden (*persuade*). Die Anzeigen (*ads*) in **Alles
klar?** bieten mögliche Reisen.

S1	S2
1. Ich möchte dieses Jahr nach/in ____. Willst du mit?	2. Was kann man denn da unternehmen?
3. Man kann da zum Beispiel ____.	4. Ist das alles? Was sonst noch?
5. Nein, man kann auch ____.	6. Wo übernachtet man denn?
7. ____.	8. Wie viel soll das kosten?
9. ____.	10. Wie kommt man dahin?
11. ____.	12a. Ich will es mir überlegen. b. Ich weiß nicht, das ist mir zu ____ (teuer, langweilig usw.). c. Klingt gut. Ich komme mit.

Wanderwege in den Alpen

Thema 3: Eine Fahrkarte, bitte!

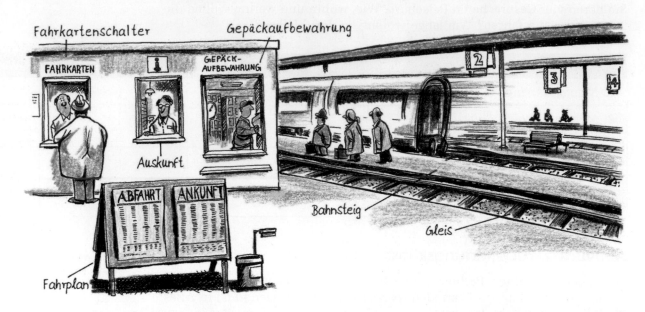

Wo ist das?

1. Am _____ kauft man Fahrkarten für den Zug.
2. Der Zug fährt von _____ 2 ab.
3. Man bekommt Informationen über Züge bei der _____.
4. Auf dem _____ kann man lesen, wann ein Zug ankommt oder abfährt.
5. Die Leute stehen auf dem _____ und warten auf den Zug.

Reiseverbindungen

Deutsche Bahn **DB**

VON Bad Harzburg   Gültig[1] am Montag, dem 09.08.
NACH Hamburg Hbf
ÜBER

BAHNHOF   UHR   ZUG   BEMERKUNGEN[2]

Bad Harzburg   ab 10:46 E   3622
 Hannover Hbf   an 12:25
                  ab 12:43 ICE 794   Zugrestaurant
Hamburg Hbf   an 13:56

[1]valid [2]notes

Am Fahrkartenschalter im Bahnhof

Michael: Eine Fahrkarte nach Hamburg, bitte.

Angestellter: **Hin und zurück?**

Michael: Nein, **einfach, zweiter Klasse,** bitte.

Angestellter: Das macht €42. Das ist übrigens der Sparpreis für Jugendliche. Haben Sie Ihren Ausweis dabei?

Michael: Ja, natürlich. Wann fährt denn der nächste Zug?

Angestellter: In dreißig Minuten. In Hannover müssen Sie dann **umsteigen.**

Michael:	Habe ich da gleich **Anschluss?**
Angestellter:	Sie haben achtzehn Minuten Aufenthalt. Dann können Sie mit dem ICE weiter nach Hamburg fahren. Für den ICE müssen Sie allerdings noch einen Platz reservieren. Möchten Sie im Großraumwagen sitzen, oder lieber in einem Abteil?
Michael:	Lieber in einem Abteil. Wann komme ich in Hamburg an?
Angestellter:	Um 13.56 Uhr.
Michael:	Danke schön.
Angestellter:	Bitte sehr.

Hier klicken!

Weiteres zum Thema Bahnfahren finden Sie bei **Deutsch: Na klar!** im World-Wide-Web unter **www.mhhe.com/dnk6.**

Aktivität 8 Michaels Pläne

Ergänzen Sie den Text mit Informationen aus dem Dialog.

Michael fährt mit dem _____[1] nach Hamburg. Er kauft seine Fahrkarte am Schalter im _____.[2] Er fährt zweiter _____.[3] Der nächste Zug nach Hannover fährt in _____[4] ab. Michael muss in Hannover _____.[5] Dort hat er gleich _____[6] an den ICE nach Hamburg. Für den ICE muss er einen _____[7] reservieren.

Aktivität 9 Am Fahrkartenschalter

Sie hören drei kurze Dialoge am Fahrkartenschalter. Setzen Sie die richtigen Informationen in die Tabelle ein.

Information	Dialog 1	Dialog 2	Dialog 3
Fahrkarte nach			
1. oder 2. Klasse			
einfach oder hin und zurück			
für wie viele Personen			
Platzkarten?			

Cartoons: Bernd Eisert

„Geben Sie doch endlich zu, dass Sie sich verfahren haben!!!"

Der Superlativ

Expressing Comparisons: The Superlative°

In **Kapitel 7** you learned how to express comparisons using the comparative.

Gestern war das Wetter **schön.** Heute ist es noch **schöner.**	*Yesterday the weather was nice. Today it is even nicer.*
Ich reise gern **bequem.** Mit dem Zug reist man **bequemer** als mit dem Wagen.	*I like traveling comfortably. By train, you travel more comfortably than by car.*

In this chapter you will learn about the superlative form of adjectives and adverbs. The superlative indicates the highest degree of a quality or quantity.

Mit dem Zug fährt man **am bequemsten.**	*Traveling by train is the most comfortable.*
Zu Fuß ist es **am schönsten.**	*Walking is the nicest.*
Mit dem Heißluftballon sieht man **am meisten.**	*By hot air balloon you see the most.*

Mit dem Heißluftballon sieht man am meisten.

Zu Fuß ist es am schönsten.

NOTE:

⊙ The superlative form of adverbs and predicate adjectives is **am _____-sten.**

⊙ German has only one form of the superlative, in contrast to English (*most* and *-(e)st*).

bequem	**am bequemsten**	*the most comfortable*
freundlich	**am freundlichsten**	*the most friendly/the friendliest*
schnell	**am schnellsten**	*the fastest*

⊙ Most adjectives of one syllable with the vowel **a, o,** or **u** in the stem add an umlaut in the superlative.

hoch	**am höchsten**	*highest*
lang	**am längsten**	*longest*

⊙ Adjectives ending in **-s, -ß, -z,** or **-t** add **-esten** to the basic form.

heiß	**am heißesten**	*hottest*
kurz	**am kürzesten**	*shortest*

⊙ Some common irregular forms are:

gern	**am liebsten**	*most preferred*
groß	**am größten**	*biggest, largest*
gut	**am besten**	*best*
viel	**am meisten**	*most*

Übung 1 Zur Wiederholung: kurz und bündig

Ergänzen Sie die Tabelle mit den fehlenden Formen.

Grundform	Komparativ	Superlativ
1. bequem	bequemer	am bequemsten
2. _____	jünger	_____
3. hoch	_____	_____
4. _____	mehr	_____
5. _____	lieber	_____
6. _____	besser	_____
7. laut	_____	_____
8. _____	_____	am kürzesten

Übung 2 Wo mag das sein?

Schritt 1: Ergänzen Sie zuerst die Fragen mit dem Superlativ des Adjektivs oder Adverbs in Klammern.

BEISPIEL: Wo regnet es ___*am meisten*___? (viel)

1. Wo sind die Berge _____? (hoch)
2. Wo schmeckt das Bier _____? (gut)
3. Wo sind die Bierkrüge (*beer mugs*) _____? (groß)
4. Wo verbringen die Deutschen einen warmen Sommerabend
   _____? (gern)
5. Wo feiert man _____? (viel)
6. Wo singt man _____? (laut)
7. Wo fahren die Autos _____? (schnell)
8. Wo übernachtet man _____? (günstig)

Schritt 2: Arbeiten Sie nun zu zweit und beantworten Sie abwechselnd (*taking turns*) die Fragen in **Schritt 1.** Im Kasten unten sind mögliche Antworten.

BEISPIEL: **S1:** Wo regnet es am meisten?

S2: Ich glaube, am meisten regnet es in Norddeutschland.

Übung 3 Hin und her: Wie war der Urlaub?

Herr Ignaz Huber aus München war drei Wochen im Urlaub in Norddeutschland. Er war zwei Tage in Hamburg, eine Woche in Cuxhaven und nicht ganz zwei Wochen auf der Insel Sylt. Stellen Sie Ihrem Partner / Ihrer Partnerin Fragen über Herrn Hubers Urlaub. Benutzen Sie den Superlativ.

BEISPIEL:
S1: Wo war es am wärmsten?

S2: Am wärmsten war es in Cuxhaven.

	In Hamburg	In Cuxhaven	Auf der Insel Sylt
1. *Wo war es (kalt/warm)?*			
2. *Wo waren die Hotels (günstig/teuer)?*	150 Euro	90 Euro mit Halbpension	200 Euro
3. *Wo hat es (viel) geregnet?*			
4. *Wo war das Hotelpersonal (freundlich)?*	freundlich	sehr freundlich	unfreundlich
5. *Wo war der Strand (schön)?*			
6. *Wo hat das Essen (gut) geschmeckt?*	ziemlich gut	nicht besonders	ausgezeichnet

Attributive Adjectives in the Comparative

When adjectives in the comparative are used attributively, i.e. before a noun, they take adjective endings.

Ich brauche einen größer**en** Koffer.	*I need a larger suitcase.*
Wir suchen ein günstiger**es** Hotel.	*We are looking for a more reasonably priced hotel.*
Günstiger**e** Hotels findet man in kleiner**en** Städten.	*You'll find more reasonably priced hotels in smaller towns.*
Wo finde ich ein besser**es** Restaurant?	*Where do I find a better restaurant?*

NOTE:

▷ Attributive adjectives in the comparative add appropriate adjective endings to the comparative forms:

größer-	Hier ist ein größer**er** Koffer.
besser-	Wo gibt es ein besser**es** Restaurant?
kleiner-	Das kleiner**e** Hotel war günstiger.

▷ **Mehr** and **weniger** (the comparatives of **viel** and **wenig**) do not take adjective endings.

Ich brauche **mehr** Geld für die Reise.	*I need more money for the trip.*
Ich habe jetzt **weniger** Zeit zum Reisen.	*I now have less time for traveling.*

Übung 4 Werners Reisevorbereitungen

Werner erzählt von seinen Reisevorbereitungen. Hören Sie zu und markieren Sie die passende Antwort.

1. Werner braucht …
   a. mehr Geld. **b.** mehr Zeit. **c.** mehr Arbeit.
2. Er braucht auch …
   a. einen kleineren Koffer. **b.** einen größeren Koffer.
   c. zwei kleinere Koffer.
3. Er nimmt _____ mit.
   a. die kleinere Kamera **b.** die neuere Kamera **c.** die größere Kamera
4. Dies ist Werners …
   a. längster Urlaub. **b.** teuerster Urlaub. **c.** kürzester Urlaub.

Übung 5 Probleme im Urlaub

Herr Ignaz Huber aus München fährt in Urlaub. Aber überall gibt es Probleme.

BEISPIEL: Das Hotel ist zu teuer. →
           Er wünscht sich ein preiswerteres Hotel.

Hier sind einige passende Adjektive für die Antworten.

   lang, neu, gut, höflich, groß, gemütlich, bequem, kühl, preiswert

1. Sein Mietwagen ist zu klein. Er wünscht sich einen _____ Mietwagen.
2. Das Hotelzimmer ist ungemütlich. Er wünscht sich ein _____ Hotelzimmer.
3. Das Bett ist zu kurz. Er wünscht sich ein _____ Bett.
4. Das Bad ist zu klein. Er wünscht sich ein _____ Bad.
5. Der Fernseher im Zimmer ist schon sehr alt. Er wünscht sich einen _____ Fernseher.
6. Die Bedienung ist unhöflich. Er wünscht sich eine _____ Bedienung.
7. Das Essen ist schlecht. Er wünscht sich _____ Essen.
8. Seine Wanderschuhe sind unbequem. Er wünscht sich _____ Wanderschuhe.
9. Das Wetter ist oft zu heiß. Er wünscht sich _____ Wetter.
10. Der Urlaub ist viel zu kurz. Er wünscht sich einen _____ Urlaub.

Attributive Adjectives in the Superlative

Arnstadt ist die **älteste** Stadt Thüringens.

Arnstadt is the oldest city in Thuringia.

In Thüringen gibt es die **schönsten** Rathäuser.

The most beautiful city halls are in Thuringia.

Das **beste** Bier gibt es in München.

You'll find the best beer in Munich.

Die **meisten** Deutschen leben in der Stadt.

Most Germans live in a city.

NOTE:

▶ Attributive adjectives in the superlative add **-(e)st** plus an appropriate adjective ending to the adjective.

▶ A definite article usually precedes the adjective in the superlative.

Landeskunde-Info

Wissenswertes über Deutschland

- ◗ Zwei Drittel allen Weins kommt aus Rheinland-Pfalz.
- ◗ Mecklenburg-Vorpommern hat 600 Seen.
- ◗ Nordrhein-Westfalen hat mehr Industrie als die anderen Bundesländer.
- ◗ Die meisten Touristen und Besucher landen auf dem Frankfurter Flughafen.
- ◗ Berlin hat über drei Millionen Einwohner.
- ◗ Meißen produziert das berühmteste Porzellan.
- ◗ Die größte Insel ist Rügen (926 km²).
- ◗ Der längste Fluss ist der Rhein (865 km), der zweitlängste ist die Elbe (700 km).
- ◗ Der höchste Berg ist die Zugspitze (2962 m), der zweithöchste ist der Watzmann (2713 m).
- ◗ Die Universität Heidelberg existiert seit 1386.

Burg Katz am Rhein

Facts **Übung 6** Tatsachen° über Deutschland

Die meisten Antworten finden Sie oben in der Landeskunde-Info.

BEISPIEL: Berlin ist die größte Stadt Deutschlands.

Bayern	ist	das nördlichste Bundesland
Bremen	hat	die meiste Industrie
Frankfurt	produziert	die höchsten Berge
Berlin		die älteste Universität
Heidelberg		das berühmteste Porzellan
Nordrhein-Westfalen		das kleinste Bundesland
Meißen		den größten Flughafen
Rheinland-Pfalz		die größte Stadt
Mecklenburg-Vorpommern		den meisten Wein
Schleswig-Holstein		die meisten Seen
??		??

Übung 7 Eine Reise nach Österreich

Sie planen eine Reise nach Österreich und brauchen Information. Was möchten Sie wissen?

1. Wie heißt die _____ (schön) Stadt Österreichs?
2. Wo findet man die _____ (preiswert) Hotels?
3. Wo liegen die _____ (interessant) Sehenswürdigkeiten?
4. Welches ist das _____ (alt) Schloss in Wien?
5. Wo gibt es die _____ (viel) Cafés?
6. In welchem Café gibt es den _____ (gut) Kaffee?
7. Wo gibt es die _____ (freundlich) Leute?
8. Wie heißt der _____ (groß) Vergnügungspark in Österreich?

Adjectival Nouns°

Adjectives can be used as nouns. As nouns, they are capitalized.

Deutsche und Amerikaner
bezahlen Rechnungen oft mit
Plastik.

*Germans and Americans
frequently pay their bills
with credit cards.*

Die meisten **Deutschen** zahlen
mit Scheckkarte oder in bar.

*Most Germans pay with a debit
card or cash.*

NOTE:

▶ An adjectival noun takes the same endings as an attributive adjective.

Ein **deutscher** Tourist hat mich
nach dem Weg gefragt.

*A German tourist asked me
for directions.*

Ein **Deutscher** hat mich nach
dem Weg gefragt.

*A German asked me for
directions.*

▶ The gender and number of an adjectival noun are determined by what it designates: people are masculine or feminine.

ein Deutsch**er** = a German
(*man*)

der Deutsch**e** = the German
(*man*)

eine Deutsch**e** = a German
(*woman*)

die Deutsch**e** = the German
(*woman*)

[zwei] Deutsch**e** = [two] Germans

die Deutsch**en** = the Germans

▶ The case of the adjectival noun depends on its function within the sentence.

Eine Deutsche hat den Zoo
gesucht.

*A German (woman) was
looking for the zoo.*

Ich habe **der Deutschen** den
Weg gezeigt.

*I showed the German (woman)
the way.*

▶ Abstract concepts are neuter. They are frequently preceded by words such as **etwas, nichts,** or **viel.**

Steht in der Zeitung **etwas
Neues?** Es gibt **nichts Neues.**

*Is there anything new in the
paper? There is nothing new.*

Er hat **viel Interessantes** von
seiner Reise erzählt.

*He told a lot of interesting
things about his trip.*

Übung 8 Die Urlauber sind alle aus Deutschland.

Ergänzen Sie die Sätze mit dem Wort **deutsch** als Nomen.

BEISPIEL: Die _Deutschen_ reisen gern.

1. Das Traumziel (*dream destination*) der _____ ist Spanien.
2. In Hotels auf Mallorca findet man fast nur _____.
3. Herr Keller ist aus Deutschland. Er ist _____.
4. Frau Keller ist auch _____.
5. Für die _____ sind Sonne und Meer sehr wichtig.
6. Die _____ liegen den ganzen Tag am Strand in der Sonne.
7. Abends gehen sie mit anderen _____ in die Discos.
8. Am Ende des Urlaubs fliegen die _____ von der Sonne gebräunt nach Deutschland zurück.

In the comic panels:

NA-WIE WARS IM URLAUB?

EIN BISSCHEN ZU HEISS- WAS?

DIESE BRÄUNE SOLL JA GARNICHT GESUND SEIN

SIE SIND DOCH NUR NEIDISCH

HORSCH

Übung 9 Was erwarten diese Leute vom Urlaub?

BEISPIEL: Ich möchte im Urlaub etwas ___Schönes___ (schön) erleben.

1. Herr Lüders aus Berlin will nichts _____ (anstrengend). Er braucht nur gutes Wetter, Sonne und Meer.

2. Das Reisebüro Fröhlich bietet eine Reise zum Mars zum Sparpreis von nur 50 000 Euro. Das ist wirklich etwas _____ (toll)! Ich buche das sofort.

3. Ingrid und ihr Freund Horst möchten mit dem Rad durch Portugal fahren. Da sieht man viel _____ (interessant).

4. Herr und Frau Lindemann wollen nichts _____ (neu) sehen. Wie jedes Jahr fahren sie in die Alpen.

5. Marion sucht etwas _____ (ungewöhnlich). Sie bucht einen Kochkurs in der Toskana.

Narrating Events in the Past: The Simple Past Tense°

das Imperfekt

You recall that in conversation about events in the past, the present perfect tense is preferred except for the verbs **haben, sein,** and modal verbs. These verbs are commonly used in the simple past tense in conversation as well as in written or formal language.

The simple past tense of other verbs is generally used in German to narrate past events in writing or in formal speech. By choosing this tense, the narrator or writer generally establishes a distance from the events.

Weak Verbs°

Schwache Verben

Weak verbs form the simple past tense by adding the marker **-(e)te** to the stem.

Wir **packten** unsere Sachen in einen Rucksack.	*We packed our things in a backpack.*
Wir **warteten** auf den Bus.	*We waited for the bus.*
Die Fahrt **dauerte** drei Stunden.	*The trip took three hours.*
Wir **übernachteten** in einer Jugendherberge.	*We stayed at a youth hostel.*

NOTE:

○ The first- and third-person singular are identical, as are the first- and third-person plural.

○ Verbs with stems ending in **-t** or **-d,** as well as some verbs with a consonant + **-n** in the stem (e.g., **regnen, öffnen**), add **-ete** to the stem.

reisen			
ich	reiste	wir	reisten
du	reistest	ihr	reistet
er sie es	reiste	sie	reisten
Sie reisten			

warten			
ich	wartete	wir	warteten
du	wartetest	ihr	wartetet
er sie es	wartete	sie	warteten
Sie warteten			

○ Weak verbs with separable and inseparable prefixes have the same past tense stem as the base verb.

In Wien **besuchten** sie die Spanische Reitschule.	*In Vienna they visited the Spanish Riding School.*
Die Familie **reiste** letzten Donnerstag **ab.**	*The family departed last Thursday.*

Übung 10   Kleine Erlebnisse° im Urlaub

experiences

Ergänzen Sie die Sätze mit passenden Modalverben im Imperfekt: **dürfen, können, müssen, wollen.**

BEISPIEL: Wir __*wollten*__ per Autostop nach Spanien fahren.

1. Niemand _____ uns mitnehmen.
2. Wir _____ zwei Stunden an der Autobahn warten.
3. Ein Fahrer _____ uns bis nach Freiburg mitnehmen.
4. Wir _____ in der Jugendherberge übernachten, aber dort war kein Platz mehr.
5. Deshalb _____ wir im Park übernachten.
6. Im Park _____ man aber nicht übernachten. Es war verboten.
7. Wir _____ aber noch eine Übernachtung auf einem Bauernhof bekommen.

Übung 11   Eine Reise nach Spanien

Rainer, zehn Jehre alt, hat in der Schule über seine Sommerferien geschrieben. Setzen Sie Rainers Sätze ins Imperfekt.

BEISPIEL: Wir haben eine Reise nach Spanien gemacht. →
          Wir machten eine Reise nach Spanien.

1. Schon drei Wochen vor der Reise habe ich meinen Koffer gepackt.
2. Bei unserer Abfahrt in Deutschland hat es viel Regen gegeben.
3. Wir haben auf einem Campingplatz übernachtet.
4. Am Urlaubsort hat es auch jeden Tag geregnet. So ein Pech!
5. Wir haben in einer kleinen Stadt gewohnt.
6. Wir haben alle Museen da besucht.
7. Die Reise hat nicht viel Spaß gemacht.
8. Das Schlimmste (*worst*): In Deutschland ist ein Traumsommer gewesen.

Eine kleine Pause auf Reisen

Strong Verbs°

Strong verbs change their stem vowel in the simple past tense. Many verbs that are strong in English are also strong in German. You will find a comprehensive list of strong verbs in the Appendix.

Im Stau auf der Autobahn

| | Familie Stieber **fuhr** im Urlaub nach Spanien. | *The Stieber family drove to Spain on their vacation.* |

Familie Stieber **fuhr** im Urlaub nach Spanien. — *The Stieber family drove to Spain on their vacation.*

Sie **standen** lange im Stau auf der Autobahn. — *They were in a traffic jam on the Autobahn for a long time.*

Der Urlaub **fing** nicht gut **an.** — *The vacation did not start out well.*

	fahren	stehen	anfangen	verlieren
ich	fuhr	stand	fing an	verlor
du	fuhr**st**	stand**est**	fing**st** an	verlor**st**
er sie es	fuhr	stand	fing an	verlor
wir	fuhr**en**	stand**en**	fing**en** an	verlor**en**
ihr	fuhr**t**	stand**et**	fing**t** an	verlor**t**
sie/Sie	fuhr**en**	stand**en**	fing**en** an	verlor**en**

NOTE:

▶ The first- and third-person singular are identical; they have no personal endings.

▶ A past tense stem ending in a **-d, -t,** -or **-s** adds **-est** to the **du-**form and **-et** to the **ihr-**form.

▶ Like weak verbs, strong verbs with separable and inseparable prefixes have the same past tense stem as the base verb.

Mixed Verbs°

Several verbs change their stem vowel *and* add **-te** to the changed stem in the simple past, combining aspects of both strong and weak verbs. These verbs include:

bringen → brachte	kennen → kannte	verbringen → verbrachte
denken → dachte	nennen → nannte	wissen → wusste

The simple past tense of **werden** (*to become*) is **wurde.**

The conjunction **als** has several important functions in German. You have learned to use it in the comparison of adjectives and adverbs.

Mit dem Zug fährt man bequemer **als** mit dem Bus.

Additionally, **als** can be used as a subordinating conjunction meaning *when*, referring to a one-time event in the past. Sentences with the conjunction **als** are often in the simple past tense, even in conversation.

Als meine Reise nach Russland begann, war es schon Winter.	*When my trip to Russia began, it was already winter.*
Als ich am Morgen aufwachte, fand ich mich mitten im Dorf.	*When I woke up in the morning, I found myself in the middle of the village.*

Analyse

Sonderbares° Erlebnis einer Reise

Der Baron von Münchhausen lebte im 18. Jahrhundert und hatte einige merkwürdige Abenteuer. Man nannte ihn auch den „Lügenbaron" (*"lying baron"*), weil man ihm seine Geschichten nicht glaubte. Lesen Sie die folgende Geschichte. Identifizieren Sie dann alle Verben im Imperfekt. Machen Sie eine Liste mit den Verben und geben Sie den Infinitiv an. Welche Verben sind stark? Welche sind schwach? Sie finden die starken Verben im Anhang (*Appendix*).

Münchhausens Reise nach Russland

Meine Reise nach Russland begann im Winter. Ich reiste zu Pferde°, weil das am bequemsten war. Leider trug ich nur leichte Kleidung, und ich fror° sehr. Da sah ich einen alten Mann im Schnee. Ich gab ihm meinen Reisemantel und ritt weiter. Ich konnte leider kein Dorf° finden. Ich war müde und stieg vom Pferd ab°. Dann band° ich das Pferd an einen Baumast° im Schnee und legte mich hin. Ich schlief tief und lange. Als ich am anderen Morgen aufwachte, fand ich mich mitten in einem Dorf auf dem Kirchhof°. Mein Pferd war nicht da, aber ich konnte es über mir hören. Ich schaute in die Höhe° und sah mein Pferd am Wetterhahn des Kirchturms° hängen. Ich verstand sofort, was passiert war. Das Dorf war in der Nacht zugeschneit° gewesen. In der Sonne war der Schnee geschmolzen°. Der Baumast, an den ich mein Pferd gebunden hatte°, war in Wirklichkeit die Spitze des Kirchturms gewesen. Nun nahm ich meine Pistole und schoss° nach dem Halfter°. Mein Pferd landete ohne Schaden° neben mir. Dann reiste ich weiter.

Bizarre

zu ... *on horseback*
froze

village / stieg ... *got off the horse*
tied / *branch of a tree*

churchyard (cemetery)

in ... *up*
am ... *on the weather vane on top of the church tower* / *snowed under*
melted
gebunden ... *had tied*

shot / *halter*
damage

diary

Übung 12   Aus Münchhausens Tagebuch°

Ergänzen Sie die Verben im Imperfekt.

Ich _____¹ (beginnen) meine Reise nach Russland im Winter. Ich _____² (reisen) zu Pferde, weil das am bequemsten _____.³ (sein) Leider _____⁴ (frieren) ich sehr, weil ich nur leichte Kleidung _____.⁵ (tragen) Plötzlich _____⁶ (sehen) ich einen alten Mann im Schnee. Ich _____⁷ (geben) ihm meinen Mantel und _____⁸ (reiten) weiter. Bald _____⁹ (sein) ich müde und _____¹⁰ vom Pferd _____.¹¹ (ab•steigen) Ich _____¹² (binden) das Pferd an einen Baumast im Schnee. Dann _____¹³ ich mich _____¹⁴ (hin•legen) und _____ _____.¹⁵ (ein•schlafen) Als ich am anderen Morgen _____¹⁶ (auf•wachen), _____¹⁷ (finden) ich mich mitten in einem Dorf. Ich _____¹⁸ (wissen) zuerst nicht, wo mein Pferd war. Ich _____¹⁹ (kennen) keinen Menschen in diesem Dorf.

Übung 13   Münchhausens Reise

Sie hören die Geschichte von Münchhausens Reise nach Russland mit sechs Veränderungen (*changes*). Können Sie sie identifizieren?

Übung 14   Wann war das?

Sie müssen einen Fragebogen (*questionnaire*) für eine Umfrage ausfüllen. Können Sie sich erinnern?

BEISPIEL: Wann haben Sie den Führerschein gemacht? →
           Ich war 17, als ich den Führerschein machte.

1. Wann sind Sie zuerst in den Kindergarten gekommen?
2. Wann haben Sie das erste Geld verdient?
3. Wann haben Sie sich zum ersten Mal verliebt (*fell in love*)?
4. Wann haben Sie den Führerschein gemacht?
5. Wann haben Sie Ihre beste Freundin oder Ihren besten Freund kennengelernt?
6. Wann haben Sie Ihre erste Reise ins Ausland gemacht? Wohin?
7. Wann haben Sie schwimmen gelernt? (oder einen anderen Sport)

The Past Perfect Tense°

The past perfect tense describes an event that precedes another event in the past.

Bevor wir in Urlaub fuhren, **hatten** wir alle Rechnungen **bezahlt.**	*Before we went on vacation we **had paid** all the bills.*
Nachdem wir auf Mallorca **angekommen waren,** gingen wir sofort an den Strand.	*After we **had arrived** in Mallorca, we immediately went to the beach.*

The conjunctions **bevor** and **nachdem** are commonly used to connect sentences with the simple past and past perfect tenses.

To form the past perfect, combine the simple past of **haben** (*hatte*) or **sein** (*war*) and the past participle of the main verb. Verbs using **sein** in the present perfect tense also use **sein** in the past perfect.

Present Perfect	**Past Perfect**
Ich **bin** gegangen.	Ich **war** gegangen. (*I had gone.*)
Wir **haben** bezahlt.	Wir **hatten** bezahlt. (*We had paid.*)

Übung 15 Die Fahrt hatte kaum begonnen.

Ergänzen Sie die Sätze durch Verben im Plusquamperfekt.

1. Ich _____ schon früh aus dem Haus _____ (gehen), denn mein Flugzeug nach Frankfurt flog um 8 Uhr ab.
2. Ich _____ am Tag zuvor ein Taxi _____ (bestellen).
3. Am Flughafen fiel mir ein (*I remembered*), dass ich die Schlüssel in der Haustür _____ _____ (vergessen).
4. Kein Wunder, denn letzte Nacht _____ ich kaum _____ (schlafen).
5. Sobald ich am Flughafen _____ _____ (ankommen), rief ich eine Nachbarin (*neighbor*) an.
6. Der Flug nach Frankfurt war verspätet (*late*). Nachdem wir drei Stunden _____ _____ (warten), konnten wir endlich abfliegen.

Sprache im Kontext

Videoclips

A Thomas Möllmann arbeitet im Reisebüro. Schauen Sie sich das Interview mit ihm an und ergänzen Sie die folgenden Informationen.

1. Ein Reiseziel, das im Moment „in" ist, ist _____.
2. Andere beliebte Reiseziele der Kunden sind _____ und die _____ _____.
3. Wie kommen die meisten Kunden an den Urlaubsort?
4. Herr Möllmann hat dieses Jahr eine _____ an die _____ gemacht. Er ist mit der _____ gefahren.
5. Herr Möllmann hat vor, in ungefähr sechs Wochen nach _____ zu reisen.
6. Herr Möllmann arbeitet seit ungefähr _____ Jahren im Reisebüro.

B Was sind beliebte Reiseziele in Ihrem Land?

C Alex spricht über seine Urlaubspläne und seinen Urlaub letztes Jahr. Hören Sie sich das Interview an und machen Sie sich Notizen in der Tabelle. Benutzen Sie dann Ihre Notizen, um 3–4 Sätze über seinen Urlaub zu schreiben.

Am schönsten ist's im eigenen Land

Wo die Deutschen 2005 ihren Urlaub verbrachten

Deutschland	32,0 %
Spanien	10,6
Italien	7,7
Österreich	6,1
Türkei	5,1
Osteuropa	5,0
Frankreich, Monaco	4,7
Griechenland	3,6
Kroatien, Slowenien	3,4
Skandinavien	3,4
Tunesien, Marokko, Ägypten	2,7
USA, Kanada	2,3
Asien	2,1
Karibik	1,5

Datenbasis: 4000 befragte Personen ab 14 Jahren im Januar 2006.
Quelle: BAT Freizeit-Forschungsinstitut

Urlaub dieses Jahr:	
Wohin? Wie lange?	
Wie kommt er dahin?	
Wo hat er gebucht?	
Urlaub letztes Jahr:	
Wo? Wie lange? Mit wem?	
Was hat er mitgenommen?	
Was hat er erlebt?	

D Fragen Sie drei Personen in der Klasse, wohin sie dieses Jahr in Urlaub fahren und wo sie letztes Jahr waren. Berichten Sie der Klasse darüber.

Lesen

Zum Thema

A **Ihr letzter Urlaub.** Beantworten Sie die folgenden Fragen und vergleichen Sie Ihre Antworten untereinander.

1. Wann haben Sie zum letzten Mal Urlaub gemacht?
2. Wohin sind Sie gefahren?
3. Sind Sie allein oder mit Freunden gefahren?
4. Was haben Sie dort gemacht?
5. Wie war das Wetter dort?
6. Wie lange waren Sie dort?
7. Was hat Ihnen dort (nicht) gefallen?

B **Ein Aktivurlaub.** Die Werbung „Sportreisen" unten zeigt viele Möglichkeiten für einen Aktivurlaub. Schauen Sie sich die Tabelle mit einem Partner / einer Partnerin an.

❍ Welche Sportart interessiert Sie besonders in diesem Angebot?

❍ Wo finden diese Aktivitäten statt *(take place)*?

❍ Was macht man alles da?

❍ Für welche Sportart muss man besonders fit sein?

❍ Welche Reise möchten Sie buchen? Warum?

SPORTREISEN ...

Sportart	Ort	Leistungen	Reisetermin	Preis	Grad*
Rafting	Colorado/ USA	zwei Übernachtungen im Hotel, Transfer, Raftingtour, Bootsführer, alle Mahlzeiten während der Tour, Camping-ausrüstung, Anreise in Eigenregie[1]	1., 8., 15. und 22.9.	ab 800 € für 7 Tage	●●
Katamaran-segeln	Levkada/ Griechenland	Flug, Übernachtungen im Appartement, kostenlose Benutzung der Katamarane und Segelflotte,[2] Teilnahme am Unterricht[3]	1., 8., 15., 22. und 29.9.	ab 715 € pro Woche	●●●
Tauchen	Villi Varu/ Malediven	Flug ab Düsseldorf, sechs Übernachtungen mit Vollpension, Sechs-Tage-Tauchpaket à 1 Tauchgang[4] täglich und 2 Haus-riff-Tauchgänge (inkl. Boot, Flasche, Blei und Bleigurt)[5]	3., 10., 17. und 24.9.	115 € pro Woche	●
Aktiv-Camp	Berchtes-gaden/ Deutschland	Schnupperkurs[6] im Klettergarten,[7] River-Rafting auf der Saalach, Mountainbike-Tour, Bergwanderung, Paragliding-Schnupper-kurs, sechs Übernachtungen mit Frühstück, Ausrüstung,[8] Führung[9]	6.–12.9.	300 €	●
Surfen	Bonaire/ Karibik	Flug ab Amsterdam, Übernachtung im Appartement mit Selbstversorgung[10] oder im Hotel mit Frühstück, Surfboard-Miete 115 Euro pro Woche	6., 13., 20. und 27.9.	ab 1100 € pro Woche	●●
Reiten	Costa Blanca/ Spanien	Flug, acht Tage mit sieben Übernachtungen im Appartement mit Selbstversorgung, Reitprogramm, Reitführung, Unterlagen, Qualifikation: sicher in den Grundgangarten,[11] gute Kondition	9.–16.9.	ab 1050 €	●●

* Zeigt den Grad der körperlichen[12] Fitneß, die der Teilnehmer[13] mitbringen muß: ●●● = sehr gut trainiert, ●● = körperlich fit, ● = auch für Anfänger[14]

[1]Anreise ... *passage excluded* [2]*sailing fleet* [3]Teilnahme ... *participation in instruction* [4]*dive* [5]Blei ... *weight and weight belt* [6]*sampler class* [7]*climbing garden* [8]*equipment* [9]*guide* [10]*no meals provided* [11]sicher ... *secure in all the basic paces* [12]*physical* [13]*participant* [14]*beginners*

Auf den ersten Blick

A Überfliegen Sie das Lesestück. Kreuzen Sie an. Der Text berichtet über:

☐ die Arbeitserfahrung eines deutschen Studenten in den USA

☐ eine Reise für Studenten in die USA

☐ eine Beschreibung von Städten und Regionen in den USA

B Präziser bitte! Suchen Sie diese Informationen im Text!

1. Wie lange war Bernd insgesamt in den USA?

2. Was hat er in den USA gemacht?

3. In welchen Bundesstaaten hat er gearbeitet?

von Bernd Maresch

Jobben in den USA

Just another summer of my life?! „ … aber es wird noch ein bisschen
dauern, es ist gerade rush-hour in New York City", säuselt° mir die
freundliche amerikanische Stimme ins Ohr. Vor ein paar Minuten sind
wir im JFK-Airport gelandet. Nun bin ich im Land der unbegrenzten
5 Möglichkeiten, die Vordiplomprüfungen sind vorbei, die Semesterferien
liegen vor mir, und warum sollte ich diese nicht jobbenderweise° in den
USA verbringen, um die Mythen dieses Landes kennenzulernen?

New York Times Square: Im Land der unbegrenzten Möglichkeiten

Was folgte, waren drei aufregende Monate, die ich als „American
Dream" bezeichne: In Manhattan arbeitete ich zusammen mit 20 jungen
10 Leuten aus zwölf Nationen im „New York Student Center". Mit einem
Drücken° im Magen starte ich zu meinem ersten Auftrag: Ich sollte eine
Gruppe von 35 Briten am JFK in Empfang nehmen° und sie über die
„dos & don'ts" dieser Stadt aufklären. Es war ein seltsames Gefühl, allein
in einer fremden Stadt vor einer Gruppe englischsprechender Menschen
15 zu stehen und ihnen in ihrer Muttersprache mit meinem deutsch-
akzentuierten Englisch das Programm zu erklären.

Bruce Willis im Central Park

New York zeigte sich von seiner weltstädtischen° Seite. Zu acht wohnten
wir in einem großzügigen° Appartement, das wir in der Nähe von SoHo
20 anmieteten. Die Seiten meines Tagebuchs der folgenden Wochen lesen
sich wie ein Star-Report aus der Yellow-Press: Wir trafen Bruce Willis
beim Rollerbladen im Central Park. Bon Jovi gab ein Spontan-Konzert am
Times Square vor dem Auftritt bei David Letterman.

Nach sechs Wochen wechselte ich den Schauplatz. Arbeiten mit
25 Rangern in einem von Utahs Nationalparks. Die pralle° Natur stand freilich
im krassen° Gegensatz zum New Yorker Großstadtleben. Unsere Crew lebte
selbstversorgend in „bunk houses" inmitten des Uinta National Forest.
Arbeitslohn erhielten wir in Form von Unterkunft und Verpflegung°.

Jeep, Motorboot und Pferde

30 Wir mussten hart zupacken°: Holzzäune errichten°, Pipelines für Tränken°
der Waldtiere in den Boden graben und Wanderwege anlegen. Dabei

---

Glossary (margin notes):

- murmurs — *säuselt*
- while working — *jobbenderweise*
- sinking feeling — *Drücken*
- in … to receive — *in Empfang nehmen*
- cosmopolitan — *weltstädtischen*
- spacious — *großzügigen*
- intense — *pralle*
- stark — *krassen*
- Unterkunft … room and board — *Verpflegung*
- knuckle down / Holzzäune … build wooden fences / watering — *zupacken / Holzzäune errichten / Tränken*

standen uns ein Jeep, ein Motorboot und Pferde zur Verfügung. Ein Demolition-Derby, ein echtes Rodeo, Indianerkultur in Form von alten Felsmalereien° und historische Ausgrabungen an einem alten
35 Schlachtfeld spiegelten die Höhepunkte im Leben einer amerikanischen Kleinstadt wider.

rock paintings

Der berühmte Arches Naturpark im Bundesstaat Utah

Nach vier Wochen in Utah führte mich der Weg nach California, wo ich den Rest meines Aufenthaltes verbrachte. Noch in Deutschland hatte ich Amerikaner kennengelernt, die ich nun besuchte. Und so flog ich
40 nach San Francisco. Die Gastfreundschaft ging so weit, dass ich das Auto benutzen konnte, was mir so manchen Ausflug auf den Highway No. 1 und nach Napa Valley möglich machte.

Als Clou° für mein Studium konnte ich in den Bibliotheken von Berkeley und Stanford University so manches Schnäppchen° für meine
45 anstehende Hausarbeit erstöbern°, wenngleich es mich nach einem Besuch an einer amerikanischen Uni gar nicht mehr zum Studium nach Hause zog.

(coll.) side benefit

find

uncover

„ … erreichen wir in Kürze Frankfurt am Main. Wir bitten Sie, die Gurte° anzulegen und hoffen, Sie hatten einen guten Flug und einen angenehmen Aufenthalt." Die Stimme der Stewardess weckt mich, und
50 erst nach Beginn des Semesters an einer deutschen Hochschule wurde mir so richtig bewusst°, dass mein „American Dream" wahr gewesen ist.

seat belts

wurde … I truly realized

—Quelle: Bernd Maresch; adaptiert aus: "The American Dream," *UNICUM,*
April 2006

Zum Text

A Lesen Sie nun den Text etwas genauer. Was stimmt und was stimmt nicht?

	Das stimmt	Das stimmt nicht
1. Bernd wollte seine Semesterferien in den USA verbringen, um die Mythen des Landes kennenzulernen.	☐	☐
2. Sein erster Auftrag war in New York, wo er eine Gruppe von 25 Deutschen im Empire State Gebäude empfangen sollte.	☐	☐

	Das stimmt	Das stimmt nicht
3. In Manhattan traf er Brad Pitt auf seinem Motorrad.	☐	☐
4. Nach New York arbeitete Bernd in einem Nationalpark in Utah.	☐	☐
5. Dort hat Bernd ein Demolition-Derby und ein echtes Rodeo erlebt.	☐	☐
6. Die dritte Station seines Aufenthaltes in den USA war Kalifornien.	☐	☐
7. Dort hat Bernd einen alten deutschen Freund besucht, den er von seiner Heimatstadt kannte.	☐	☐

B **Drei Schauplätze.** Was hat Bernd dort gesehen und erlebt? Machen Sie sich Notizen zu jedem Schauplatz und erzählen Sie, was Bernd dort gemacht hat.

New York	Utah	Kalifornien

C Bernd hat viele Höhepunkte seines Aufenthaltes in Amerika beschrieben aber nur wenige Details gegeben. Was möchten Sie zusätzlich noch gern wissen? Formulieren Sie drei Fragen für Bernd, wo Sie ihn nach mehr Details fragen.

D Bernd benutzt drei Arten von „Englisch" in seinem Reisebericht: (1) eingedeutschte (*Germanized*) Wörter, (2) Namen auf Englisch für Sehenswürdigkeiten in Amerika und (3) andere englische Wörter.

1. Suchen Sie diese Wörter und sortieren Sie sie in drei Kategorien.

(1) Eingedeutschte Wörter	(2) Namen auf Englisch	(3) Andere englische Wörter
jobben	*Napa Valley*	*American Dream*

2. Suchen Sie deutsche Wörter oder Äquivalente für die Wörter, die Sie in Kategorie 3 gefunden haben.
3. Warum benutzt Bernd wohl diese drei Kategorien von Wörtern?

E **Bernds Reisebericht kurz und bündig** (*in a nutshell*). Erzählen Sie Bernds Reisebericht mithilfe des folgenden Rasters (*template*) nach.

---

1. Bernds Aufenthalt begann _____.
2. Dort arbeitete er _____.
3. Für seinen ersten Auftrag musste er _____.
4. In New York erlebte er _____.
5. Nach seinem Aufenthalt in New York _____.
6. Dort musste er schwere Arbeit machen, z.B. _____.
7. Danach _____.
8. Dort _____.
9. Für Bernd war die Reise nach Amerika _____.

F **Diskutieren Sie.** Wie lernt man ein fremdes Land am besten kennen? Zum Beispiel: Würden Sie auch jobben wie Bernd, oder lieber als Tourist im Reisebus durch ein Land fahren? Welche anderen Möglichkeiten kennen Sie? Was sind die Vor- und Nachteile?

Zu guter Letzt

Ein Reisebericht

Haben Sie je eine interessante Reise gemacht? allein? mit Freunden oder mit Familie? Schreiben Sie einen Bericht darüber – so kreativ wie möglich. Wenn Sie wollen, können Sie einen fiktiven Reisebericht oder im Stil von Bernd Maresch schreiben.

Schritt 1: Beginnen Sie mit einem Zitat (*quote*), das den Ton und die Stimmung Ihres Berichts angibt, z.B. aus einem Roman, einer Geschichte oder einem Lied. Das Zitat kann auf Englisch oder auf Deutsch sein. Erklären Sie dann, warum Sie die Reise gemacht haben.

- Freunde oder Familie besuchen?
- etwas Exotisches erleben?
- ein neues Land oder eine neue Stadt kennenlernen?
- einen Ferienjob finden?
- ??

Schritt 2: Schreiben Sie über zwei oder drei spezifische, interessante Erlebnisse auf der Reise. Geben Sie möglichst viele Details. Haben Sie interessante Leute kennengelernt oder ungewöhnliche Dinge gesehen oder erlebt? (Benutzen Sie bitte drei Adjektive in der Komparativform und drei in der Superlativform. Gebrauchen Sie auch mindestens zehn Verben im Imperfekt.)

Schritt 3: Beenden Sie Ihren Reisebericht mit einer Überraschung (*surprise*) oder einer interessanten Bemerkung (*comment*) für den Hörer oder den Leser. Seien Sie hier so kreativ wie möglich.

Schritt 4: In kleinen Gruppen zu viert lesen Sie Ihre Reiseberichte Ihren Mitstudenten und Mitstudentinnen vor. Sie sollen Ihnen Fragen über den Reisebericht stellen und raten, ob Ihre Geschichte wahr ist oder nicht.

Wortschatz

Beginning with this chapter, the vocabulary section at the end of each chapter will list strong or irregular verbs with their principal parts as follows: **bringen, brachte, gebracht** or **fahren (fährt), fuhr, ist gefahren.**

Verkehrsmittel / **Means of Transportation**

die **Bahn, -en**	railway; train
der **Bus,** *pl.* **Busse**	bus
das **Flugzeug, -e**	airplane
das **Schiff, -e**	ship
das **Taxi, -s**	taxicab
der **Zug, ⸚e**	train

Im Reisebüro / **At the Travel Agency**

das **Angebot, -e**	(special) offer; selection
die **Fahrkarte, -n**	ticket
die **Reise, -n**	trip
das **Reisebüro, -s**	travel agency
der **Reiseprospekt, -e**	travel brochure

Unterwegs / **En Route**

die **Abfahrt, -en**	departure
die **Ankunft, ⸚e**	arrival
der **Anschluss, ⸚e**	connection
die **Auskunft, ⸚e**	information
der **Bahnsteig, -e**	(train) platform
der **Fahrkarten-schalter, -**	ticket window
der **Fahrplan, ⸚e**	schedule
die **Gepäckaufbe-wahrung**	baggage check
das **Gleis, -e**	track
die **Landschaft, -en**	landscape
die **Möglichkeit, -en**	possibility, opportunity
die **Natur**	nature
das **Navi, -s (das Navigationssystem)**	GPS
die **Platzkarte, -n**	seat reservation card
der **Reiseführer, -**	travel guide (book)
der **Strand, ⸚e**	beach
die **Verpflegung**	meals
der **Wanderweg, -e**	hiking trail

Zum Mitnehmen auf Reisen / **Things to Take Along on a Trip**

das **Bargeld**	cash
das **Handgepäck**	carry-on luggage
der **Handschuh, -e**	glove
die **Kamera, -s**	camera
der **Personalausweis, -e**	ID card
der **Reisescheck, -s**	traveler's check

das **Sonnenschutzmittel**	suntan lotion, sunscreen
das **Zelt, -e**	tent

Verben / **Verbs**

ab·fahren (fährt ab), fuhr ab, ist abgefahren	to depart, leave
buchen	to book (a trip)
ein·steigen, stieg ein, ist eingestiegen	to board, get into (*a vehicle*)
erleben	to experience
packen	to pack
sich überlegen, überlegt	to think over
um·steigen, stieg um, ist umgestiegen	to transfer, change (trains)
unternehmen (unter-nimmt), unternahm, unternommen	to undertake, to do
vergessen (vergisst), vergaß, vergessen	to forget
verreisen, ist verreist	to go on a trip
vor·schlagen (schlägt vor), schlug vor, vorgeschlagen	to suggest, propose

Adjektive und Adverbien / **Adjectives and Adverbs**

aktiv	active(ly)
gefährlich	dangerous(ly)
insgesamt	altogether, total
jung	young
langsam	slow(ly)
laut	loud(ly)
schnell	quick(ly), fast
sicher	safe(ly)

Sonstiges / **Other**

alles	everything
als (*subord. conj.*)	when
bevor (*subord. conj.*)	before
einfach	one-way (ticket); simple
erster/zweiter Klasse fahren	to travel first/second class
hin und zurück	round-trip
nachdem (*subord. conj.*)	after
per Autostop reisen	to hitchhike
pro Person	per person
sportlich aktiv	active in sports
zu zweit, zu dritt, zu viert, ...	as a twosome, threesome, foursome, ...

Das kann ich nun!

1. Sagen Sie, wie Sie am liebsten reisen.

2. Sagen Sie, was Sie am liebsten im Urlaub machen.

3. Sie sind mit Freunden unterwegs in Deutschland und gehen in ein Reisebüro. Sie suchen Information über Wandertouren in den Alpen. Sagen Sie etwas über:
   a. was Sie möchten
   b. wie lange, wie viele Leute (kleine/große Gruppe)
   c. die Kosten

4. Sie stehen am Fahrkartenschalter am Kölner Hauptbahnhof. Sie wollen eine Tagesreise von Köln nach Düsseldorf machen. Was sagen Sie?

5. Sie packen Ihren Koffer für eine Reise in die Schweiz im August. Sagen Sie, was Sie mitnehmen.

6. Sie kommen von der Reise zurück und berichten in Ihrem Deutschkurs auf Deutsch:
   a. *The food tasted best in smaller restaurants.*
   b. *Staying overnight in a youth hostel was the the best deal* (**günstig**).
   c. *The most beautiful and best-known mountain is called* **das Matterhorn.**

7. Sie berichten über eine Reise. Schreiben Sie mithilfe der folgenden Notizen einen Bericht im Imperfekt.

   Reise in Frankfurt beginnen / in einem kleinen Hotel günstig übernachten / am nächsten Morgen mit dem Zug von Frankfurt nach Berlin fahren / am späten Nachmittag in Berlin ankommen / sehr lange auf ein Taxi warten / in einem gemütlichen Restaurant im Hotel essen

Kapitel **11**

Der Start in die Zukunft

Bei der Arbeit im Labor

In diesem Kapitel

▶ **Themen:** Talking about career expectations, the world of work, professions, and job applications

▶ **Grammatik:** Future tense, relative clauses, **was für (ein)**, negating sentences with **nicht** and **kein**

▶ **Lesen:** „Abi 2009: Rein ins Leben"; „Sara, 22, 1. Lehrjahr als Fotografin"

▶ **Landeskunde:** Help-wanted ads, applying for a job, the German school system, civilian service

▶ **Zu guter Letzt:** Berufswünsche

VIDEOCLIPS

Mein Beruf – mein Leben

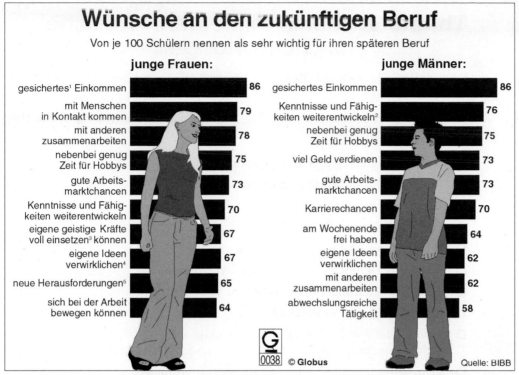

Wünsche an den zukünftigen Beruf

Von je 100 Schülern nennen als sehr wichtig für ihren späteren Beruf

junge Frauen:

gesichertes[1] Einkommen	86
mit Menschen in Kontakt kommen	79
mit anderen zusammenarbeiten	78
nebenbei genug Zeit für Hobbys	75
gute Arbeitsmarktchancen	73
Kenntnisse und Fähigkeiten weiterentwickeln	70
eigene geistige Kräfte voll einsetzen[3] können	67
eigene Ideen verwirklichen[4]	67
neue Herausforderungen[5]	65
sich bei der Arbeit bewegen können	64

junge Männer:

gesichertes Einkommen	86
Kenntnisse und Fähigkeiten weiterentwickeln[2]	76
nebenbei genug Zeit für Hobbys	75
viel Geld verdienen	73
gute Arbeitsmarktchancen	73
Karrierechancen	70
am Wochenende frei haben	64
eigene Ideen verwirklichen	62
mit anderen zusammenarbeiten	62
abwechslungsreiche Tätigkeit	58

G
0038 © Globus   Quelle: BIBB

[1]*secure*   [2]Kenntnisse ... *continuing to develop knowledge and skills*   [3]*fully apply one's intellectual strengths*   [4]*realizing*   [5]*challenges*

A Was wollen junge Deutsche vom Beruf? Die Informationen finden Sie im Schaubild.

○ Das Wichtigste für den Beruf junger Frauen und junger Männer ist _____.

○ _____ ist wichtiger für junge Frauen als für junge Männer.

○ _____ und _____ sind genauso wichtig im Beruf für junge Frauen.

○ Für junge Männer sind _____ und _____ genauso wichtig im Beruf.

○ Welche Berufswünsche haben junge Frauen, die junge Männer nicht haben und umgekehrt (*vice versa*)? Suchen Sie fünf Unterschiede.

B Sie hören Gabriele Sommer über ihre Berufspläne sprechen.

○ Wie ist sie auf ihre Berufswahl gekommen?

○ Wo studiert sie?

○ Was studiert sie?

○ Was hat sie in ihrem späteren Berufsleben vor?

Wörter im Kontext

wishes

expectations

Thema 1: Meine Interessen, Wünsche° und Erwartungen°

Wie **stellen** Sie **sich** Ihr **Berufsleben vor?** Was erwarten Sie vom Beruf? Kreuzen Sie an.

Neue Wörter

stellen sich vor (sich vorstellen) imagine

das Berufsleben professional life

selbstständig independent(ly)

der Arbeitsplatz position, workplace

mich … beschäftigen (sich beschäftigen) occupy myself

im Freien outdoors

die Gelegenheit opportunity

im Ausland abroad

das Gehalt salary

verdienen earn

abwechslungsreich varied

die Tätigkeit position; activity

erfolgreich successful

der Chef / die Chefin manager, boss

der Mitarbeiter (Mitarbeiter, pl.) / die Mitarbeiterin (Mitarbeiterinnen, pl.) co-worker, colleague

die Technik technology

die Ausbildung training

das Ansehen prestige

das Büro office

verantwortlich responsible

die Firma firm, company

herausfordert (herausfordern) challenges

Ich möchte gern:	Wichtig	Unwichtig
▶ **selbstständig** arbeiten	☐	☐
▶ einen sicheren **Arbeitsplatz** haben	☐	☐
▶ **mich** mit Finanzen **beschäftigen**	☐	☐
▶ **im Freien arbeiten**	☐	☐
▶ **Gelegenheit** zum Reisen haben	☐	☐
▶ **im Ausland** arbeiten	☐	☐
▶ ein gutes **Gehalt** haben (viel Geld **verdienen**)	☐	☐
▶ eine **abwechslungsreiche Tätigkeit** haben	☐	☐
▶ ohne viel Arbeit **erfolgreich** sein	☐	☐
▶ einen **Chef** / eine **Chefin** haben, der/die meine Arbeit anerkennt (*appreciates*)	☐	☐
▶ sympathische **Mitarbeiter/Mitarbeiterinnen** haben	☐	☐
▶ mit Menschen zu tun haben	☐	☐
▶ mit Computer **Technik**/Elektronik arbeiten	☐	☐
▶ eine kurze **Ausbildung**zeit haben	☐	☐
▶ Prestige/**Ansehen** haben	☐	☐
▶ im **Büro** arbeiten	☐	☐
▶ eine **verantwortliche** Position bei einer großen **Firma** haben	☐	☐
▶ einen Beruf haben, der mich **herausfordert**	☐	☐

Vergleichen Sie Ihre Antworten untereinander. Suchen Sie jemand im Kurs, mit dem Sie mehr als fünf Antworten gemeinsam haben.

Aktivität 1 Drei junge Leute

Sie hören drei junge Leute über ihre Interessen, Wünsche und Erwartungen sprechen. Was tun sie gern oder nicht gern? Was ist ihnen wichtig oder nicht wichtig?

Person	Was er/sie (nicht) gern tut	Was ihm/ihr (nicht) wichtig ist
Tina		
Markus		
Andrea		

Aktivität 2 Wenn ich groß bin …

Schauen Sie die Grafik an und beantworten Sie die Fragen.

Wenn ich groß bin, werde ich …

Mädchen	So viel Prozent der 8- bis 19-Jährigen nannten als Traumberuf		Jungen
(Bank)Kauffrau	9,4 %	9,7 %	Kfz-Mechatroniker
Tierärztin	7,1	8,5	(Bank)Kaufmann
Tierpflegerin	6,5	7,8	handwerklicher Beruf
Lehrerin	5,4	6,6	Polizist
Krankenpflegerin	5,3	6,3	Fußballprofi
andere soziale, therapeutische Berufe	5,0	6,1	Ingenieur
Friseurin	4,6	5,3	weiß noch nicht
weiß noch nicht	3,8	3,4	Forscher, Erfinder
Musikerin, Sängerin	3,4	3,3	Informatiker
Kindergärtnerin	3,3	3,1	Koch

Quelle: Eltern Family März 2008   Mehrfachnennungen möglich © Globus 2011

1. Welcher Beruf ist für Mädchen am populärsten? für Jungen?
2. Welcher Beruf hat mit Sport zu tun?
3. Welche Berufe haben mit Tieren zu tun?
4. In welchem Beruf arbeitet man mit Kindern?
5. Für welche Berufe braucht man musikalisches Talent?

Aktivität 3 Hin und her: Wer macht was, und warum?

Ergänzen Sie die Informationen.

BEISPIEL: **S1:** Was macht Corinna Eichhorn?

      S2: Sie ist Sozialarbeiterin.

      S1: Warum macht sie das?

      S2: Weil …

Name	Beruf	Warum?
Corinna Eichhorn	Sozialarbeiterin	Menschen helfen
Karsten Becker		
Erika Lentz	Filmschauspielerin	mit Menschen zu tun haben
Alex Böhmer		

Aktivität 4 Berufswünsche

Fragen Sie einen Partner / eine Partnerin: „Was erwartest du von deinem Beruf? Was ist dir nicht so wichtig?" Verwenden Sie einige der folgenden Redemittel.

BEISPIEL: **S1:** Mir ist ein sicherer Arbeitsplatz wichtig.

S2: Ein sicherer Arbeitsplatz ist mir nicht so wichtig, aber ich erwarte, dass ich Gelegenheit zum Reisen habe.

<table>
<tr><td>Redemittel</td><td>Erwartungen</td></tr>
<tr><td>Mir ist _____ (nicht) wichtig.</td><td>ein gutes Gehalt (haben)</td></tr>
<tr><td>Ich erwarte, dass _____.</td><td>viel Kontakt mit Menschen (haben)</td></tr>
<tr><td>Ich möchte gern _____.</td><td>Menschen helfen</td></tr>
<tr><td>An erster Stelle kommt _____.</td><td>Spaß an der Arbeit (haben)</td></tr>
<tr><td>_____ interessiert mich (nicht).</td><td>nette Mitarbeiter/Mitarbeiterinnen (haben)</td></tr>
</table>

Gelegenheit zum Reisen (haben)

selbstständig arbeiten

im Freien arbeiten

im Ausland arbeiten

Ansehen (haben)

einen sicheren Arbeitsplatz (haben)

kreativ arbeiten

flexible Arbeitszeit (haben)

??

Ein Schornsteinfeger arbeitet meistens im Freien.

Thema 2: Berufe

BERUFE

Gesundheitswesen
Arzt/Ärztin
Krankenpfleger/Krankenschwester
Psychologe/Psychologin
Sozialarbeiter/Sozialarbeiterin
Tierarzt/Tierärztin
Zahnarzt/Zahnärztin

Verwaltung
Rechtsanwalt/Rechtsanwältin
Diplomat/Diplomatin
Finanzbeamter/Finanzbeamtin
Personalchef/Personalchefin

Technischer Bereich
Elektroinstallateur/Elektroinstallateurin
Ingenieur/Ingenieurin
Mechaniker/Mechanikerin
Radio- oder Fernsehtechniker/
  Radio- oder Fernsehtechnikerin

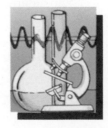

Naturwissenschaften
Biotechnologe/Biotechnologin
Chemiker/Chemikerin
Laborant/Laborantin
Meteorologe/Meteorologin
Physiker/Physikerin

Wirtschaft und Handel
Geschäftsmann/Geschäftsfrau
Informatiker/Informatikerin
Kaufmann/Kauffrau
Sekretär/Sekretärin

Verkehrswesen
Flugbegleiter/Flugbegleiterin
Flugingenieur/Flugingenieurin
Pilot/Pilotin
Reisebüroleiter/Reisebüroleiterin

Kommunikationswesen
Bibliothekar/Bibliothekarin
Dolmetscher/Dolmetscherin
Journalist/Journalistin
Nachrichtensprecher/Nachrichtensprecherin

Kreativer Bereich
Architekt/Architektin
Designer/Designerin
Fotograf/Fotografin
Künstler/Künstlerin
Musiker/Musikerin
Schauspieler/Schauspielerin
Zeichner/Zeichnerin

Welcher Beruf passt zu welcher Beschreibung?

BEISPIEL: Eine Architektin entwirft Häuser.

1. _____ spielt im Film oder auf der Bühne (*stage*).
2. _____ spielt in einem Orchester.
3. _____ **untersucht** Patienten.
4. _____ **entwirft** Gebäude, Häuser und Wohnungen.
5. _____ verkauft Produkte einer Firma.
6. _____ hat mit Computern zu tun.
7. _____ malt Bilder.
8. _____ arbeitet in einer Bibliothek.
9. _____ **übersetzt** Texte mündlich (*orally*).
10. _____ repariert Autos.

a. Arzt/Ärztin
b. Informatiker/Informatikerin
c. Schauspieler/Schauspielerin
d. Bibliothekar/Bibliothekarin
e. Automechaniker/Automechanikerin
f. Musiker/Musikerin
g. Architekt/Architektin
h. Kaufmann/Kauffrau
i. Dolmetscher/Dolmetscherin
j. Künstler/Künstlerin

Neue Wörter

der Zahnarzt / die Zahnärztin dentist
der Rechtsanwalt / die Rechtsanwältin lawyer, attorney
der Handel sales, trade
der Geschäftsmann / die Geschäftsfrau businessman/businesswoman
der Informatiker / die Informatikerin computer scientist
der Kaufmann / die Kauffrau salesman/saleswoman
der Bibliothekar / die Bibliothekarin librarian
der Dolmetscher / die Dolmetscherin interpreter
der Künstler / die Künstlerin artist
der Schauspieler / die Schauspielerin actor
der Zeichner / die Zeichnerin graphic artist
untersucht (untersuchen) examines
entwirft (entwerfen) designs
übersetzt (übersetzen) translates

Aktivität 5 Was meinen Sie?

Suchen Sie Ihre Antworten auf die folgenden Fragen in der Liste von Berufen im **Thema 2**.

1. Wer hat die gefährlichste Arbeit?
2. Welcher Beruf hat das meiste Prestige?
3. Wer hat mit Tieren zu tun?
4. Wer arbeitet meistens in einem Büro?
5. Wer verdient das meiste Geld?
6. Für welche Berufe muss man studieren?
7. Welche Arbeit bringt den meisten Stress mit sich?
8. Wer hat die längsten Arbeitsstunden?
9. Wer hat die langweiligste Arbeit?

Aktivität 6 Hin und her: Berühmte° Personen

famous

Diese berühmten Menschen, die alle einen Beruf ausübten, hatten auch andere Interessen. Ergänzen Sie die Informationen.

BEISPIEL: **S1:** Was war Martin Luther von Beruf?

S2: Er war Priester.

S1: Was für andere Interessen hatte er?

S2: Er interessierte sich für Literatur, Musik und die deutsche Sprache.

Siehe *The Interrogative Pronoun* **was für (ein)**, S. 337.

Name	Beruf	Interessen
Martin Luther		
Käthe Kollwitz	Künstlerin	Politik
Bertha von Suttner		
Rainer Werner Fassbinder	Filmregisseur	Literatur, Theater
Marlene Dietrich		
Willi Brandt	Politiker	Ski fahren, Lesen

Aktivität 7 Welcher Beruf ist der richtige?

Machen Sie eine Liste von den Kriterien, die Ihnen im Beruf wichtig sind. Benutzen Sie die Vokabeln vom **Thema 1**. Fragen Sie dann jemand im Kurs, was für einen Beruf er/sie Ihnen empfehlen würde.

BEISPIEL: **S1:** Ich möchte eine abwechslungsreiche Tätigkeit haben, vielleicht im Büro arbeiten und viel Kontakt mit Menschen haben. Was empfiehlst du mir?

S2: Ich empfehle dir, Kaufmann/Kauffrau zu werden.

Landeskunde-Info

Mit sechs Jahren beginnt für Kinder in Deutschland die Schule. Alle Kinder gehen zuerst vier Jahre lang gemeinsam auf **die Grundschule.** Danach trennen sich die Wege.

Ein Teil der Schüler und Schülerinnen geht dann auf **die Hauptschule,** die nach dem neunten oder zehnten Schuljahr mit dem Hauptschulabschluss endet. Danach suchen sich die meisten Schulabgänger eine Ausbildungsstelle für einen praktischen Beruf. Zweimal die Woche müssen die „Azubis" (Auszubildende oder Lehrlinge) auf **die Berufsschule** gehen. Dort lernen sie vor allem praktische Fächer für den künftigen Beruf.

Ein anderer Teil der Schüler und Schülerinnen geht von der Grundschule auf **die Realschule.** Sie endet nach dem zehnten Schuljahr mit dem **Abschluss** der **mittleren Reife.** Danach geht man auf eine **Fach-schule** oder auch auf eine **Berufsschule.**

Als dritte Möglichkeit gibt es **das Gymnasium,** das auf ein Universitätsstudium vorbereitet. Das Gymnasium umfasst acht Klassen. (Vor kurzem ist die Zeit auf dem Gymnasium von neun auf acht Jahre reduziert worden.) Am Ende des Gymnasiums machen Schüler **das Abitur.** Ohne Abitur (**Hochschulreife**) kann man nicht studieren.

▶ In welchem Alter beginnt für Kinder die Schule in Ihrem Land?

▶ Muss man in Ihrem Land einen bestimmten Schulabschluss haben, um studieren zu können?

▶ Was halten Sie von einem Schulsystem mit drei verschiedenen Schulen?

Der erste Schultag: Der Ernst des Lebens beginnt.

Das Schulsystem in Deutschland

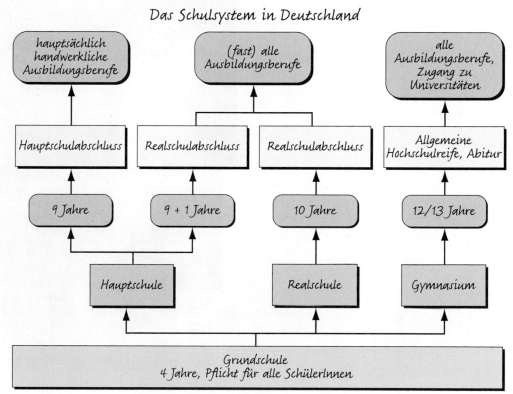

© David Nutting and Regine Reister. Used by permission.

Thema 3: Stellenangebote und Bewerbungen

Ein Stellenangebot

Sehen Sie sich das Stellenangebot an und beantworten Sie die Fragen.

Für alle, die Leistung zeigen wollen.
Julia Enders, Auszubildende, Allianz Gruppe

Kauffrau/-mann für Versicherungen und Finanzen. Haben Sie einen guten Schulabschluss, Mittlere Reife/Abitur? Sind Sie kontaktfreudig, kommunikativ, selbstbewusst? Dann werden Sie Profi in Kundenbetreuung, -beratung und Verkauf zu Versicherung und Finanzdienstleistung. Jetzt bewerben!
www.ausbildung.allianz.de

Hoffentlich Allianz.

Allianz ⑪

Allianz Deutschland AG, Personal Berufsausbildung, Anja Großmann
Postfach 1130, 85765 Unterföhring, Tel. 089.92529-25221, anj.grossmann@allianz.de

Allianz advertisement Photography: Christoph Franke, www.chfranke.de; Idea + Design: Christina Schels, www.bueroschels.de.

Hier klicken!

Weiteres zum Thema Stellenanzeigen finden Sie bei **Deutsch: Na klar!** im World-Wide-Web unter **www.mhhe.com/dnk6.**

- Wie heißt die Firma, die Mitarbeiter sucht?
- Für welchen Beruf sucht diese Firma Azubis (Auszubildende)?
- Welchen Schulabschluss muss man für diesen Beruf haben?
- Welche Qualifikationen und Eigenschaften sind der Firma wichtig?
- In welchem Bereich (*area*) der Firma soll der Bewerber / die Bewerberin arbeiten?

Eine Bewerbung

Wie **bewirbt** man **sich um** eine **Stelle?** Bringen Sie folgende Schritte in eine logische Reihenfolge.

_____ einen tabellarischen **Lebenslauf** schreiben

_____ ein **Bewerbungsformular** ausfüllen

__1__ Interessen, Wünsche und Erwartungen mit Familie und Freunden besprechen

_____ **Unterlagen** (Abiturzeugnis oder anderen Abschluss und **Zeugnisse** von früheren **Arbeitgebern**) sammeln

_____ **sich auf** das **Vorstellungsgespräch vorbereiten**

_____ die Stellenangebote in der Zeitung durchlesen

_____ Informationen über verschiedene Karrieren und Berufe sammeln

_____ zum **Arbeitsamt** an der Uni gehen und mit **Berufsberatern** sprechen

Neue Wörter

bewirbt sich (sich bewerben) um   applies for
die Stelle   position, job
der Lebenslauf   résumé
das Bewerbungsformular   application form
die Unterlagen (*pl.*)   documentation
das Zeugnis (Zeugnisse, *pl.***)**   recommendation; report card
der Arbeitgeber   employer
sich vorbereiten auf   to prepare for
das Vorstellungsgespräch   job interview
das Arbeitsamt   employment office
der Berufsberater   employment counselor

Aktivität 8   Ein Stellenangebot

Schauen Sie sich noch einmal das Angebot der Firma auf Seite 328 an und setzen Sie passende Wörter aus dem Kasten in die Lücken ein.

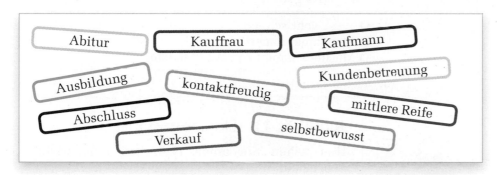

Abitur   Kauffrau   Kaufmann   Ausbildung   kontaktfreudig   Kundenbetreuung   Abschluss   mittlere Reife   Verkauf   selbstbewusst

1. Die Firma Allianz sucht junge Leute, die _____ oder _____ werden wollen.
2. Die Firma bietet eine _____ in _____ und _____.
3. Die Bewerber/Innen müssen einen guten _____ von der Schule haben.
4. Dies kann entweder _____ oder _____ sein.
5. Die Bewerber/Innen sollen _____, kommunikativ und _____ sein.

Aktivität 9   Ein Gespräch unter Freunden

Was stimmt? Was stimmt nicht? Korrigieren Sie die falschen Aussagen.

	Das stimmt	Das stimmt nicht
1. Petra sucht einen Ausbildungsplatz.	☐	☐
2. Petra ist noch nicht zum Arbeitsamt gegangen.	☐	☐
3. Petra hat ein interessantes Stellenangebot in der Zeitung gefunden.	☐	☐
4. Petra hat sich um eine Ausbildungsstelle beworben.	☐	☐
5. Petra hat die Firma sofort angerufen.	☐	☐
6. Petra ist sehr enthusiastisch, weil sie die Firma gut kennt.	☐	☐
7. Die Firma verlangt, dass Bewerber Biologie studiert haben.	☐	☐

Aktivität 10 Ein Gespräch über eine Stellensuche

Führen Sie mit einem Partner / einer Partnerin ein Gespräch über eine Stellensuche. Sie können die Anzeige in diesem Kapitel oder Anzeigen aus einer Zeitung oder dem Internet zur Information benutzen.

S1	S2
1. Was wirst du _____ machen? ◑ nach dem Studium ◑ in den Semesterferien ◑ ??	2. Ich werde eine Stelle _____ suchen. ◑ in einem Büro ◑ bei einer Firma ◑ in einer Fabrik ◑ ??
3. Wie findet man _____?	4. Man muss mindestens _____ (2/3/4/5/?) Dinge machen: _____. ◑ Informationen über verschiedene Berufe sammeln ◑ Stellenangebote in der Zeitung / im Internet durcharbeiten ◑ zur Arbeitsvermittlung an der Uni gehen ◑ Freunde/Familie/Bekannte fragen ◑ zum Arbeitsamt / zur Berufsberatung gehen ◑ ??
5. Was braucht man für eine Bewerbung?	6. Man muss gewöhnlich _____.
7. Wie lange dauert es, bis _____?	8. ◑ _____ geht schnell. ◑ Manchmal dauert es _____. ◑ Meistens dauert es _____ Monate.
9. Na, dann viel Glück!	10. Vielen Dank!

Lebenslauf

Name	Birgit Hermsen
Geburtsdatum	22. Dezember 1986
Geburtsort	Bonn
Eltern	Friedrich Hermsen Elsbeth Hermsen, geb. Marx

Ausbildungsgang

1990–1994	Grundschule: Elisabethschule, Bonn
1994–2001	Realschule, Bonn
1999–2000	Austauschschülerin in USA (Experiment in International Living) Redwood City, Kalifornien
2001	Realschulabschluss: Mittlere Reife
2001–2003	Ausbildung als Bürokauffrau, Bonn Reisebüro Wilmers
Seit 2003	Reisebürokauffrau, Bonn Reisebüro am Markt
Familienstand	ledig
Interessen	Reisen (USA, Nepal, Australien und Neuseeland) Sport (Tennis, Reiten) Lesen und Musik

Aktivität 11 Ein Lebenslauf

Hier sehen Sie einen typischen tabellarischen Lebenslauf.

Schritt 1: Beantworten Sie die Fragen:

◑ Welche Schulen hat Birgit in Bonn besucht?

◑ Welche Ausbildung hat sie gemacht?

◑ Was ist ihr jetziger Beruf?

◑ Welche anderen Interessen hat Birgit?

Schritt 2: Nun erzählen Sie Birgits Lebenslauf in vollständigen Sätzen. Benutzen Sie folgendes Format.

BEISPIEL: Birgit ist am 22. Dezember 1986 in Bonn geboren.
Von _____ bis _____ …
Seit …
Danach …

Grundschule besucht
Realschule besucht
Ausbildung als Bürokauffrau gemacht
als Reisebürokauffrau in Bonn gearbeitet

Future Tense°

Das Futur

You recall that in German the present tense can also refer to future action, particularly when an adverb of time is present.

Nächstes Jahr macht Sabine ein Praktikum in den USA.	*Next year Sabine is going to do an internship in the USA.*
Morgen schickt sie mehrere Bewerbungen ab.	*Tomorrow she will send off several applications.*

In German, the future tense is used most frequently to express future time when the context provides no other explicit reference to the future.

Eines Tages **werde** ich Erfolg **haben.**	*Someday I will be successful.*
Millionen **werden** meine Bücher **kaufen.**	*Millions will buy my books.*
Wir **werden** mal **sehen.**	*We shall see (if that's the case).*

kaufen			
ich	werde kaufen	wir	werden kaufen
du	wirst kaufen	ihr	werdet kaufen
er sie es	wird kaufen	sie	werden kaufen
Sie werden kaufen			

NOTE:

- The future tense is formed with the auxiliary verb **werden** and the infinitive of the main verb.

- The auxiliary **werden** and the infinitive at the end of the sentence form a sentence bracket (**Satzklammer**).

Eines Tages **werden** Millionen meine Bücher **kaufen.**

Was möchtest du werden?

Übung 1 Wunschträume

Was ist Ihr Wunschtraum? Was werden Sie eines Tages sein? Wo werden Sie wohnen?

BEISPIEL: Ich werde Millionär sein.
Ich werde in einem Schloss wohnen.

Was?	Wo?
Akrobat/Akrobatin beim Zirkus	auf dem Mars
Präsident/Präsidentin von …	in einem Schloss
Astronaut/Astronautin	in einer Grashütte auf Tahiti
Fußballspieler/Fußballspielerin	in einer netten kleinen Villa
Milliardär/Milliardärin	in einem Wohnwagen
berühmte/r Schauspieler/ Schauspielerin	im Weißen Haus
berühmte/r Sänger/Sängerin	in einer Kommune
??	in einer großen Villa
	??

Analyse

Lesen Sie den Cartoon „Poesie" (*Poetry*).

Poesie von Erich Rauschenbach

Eines Tages werde ich mit meinen Gedichten¹ Erfolg haben²!

Dann werden mich die Kritiker in den Himmel heben³, und Millionen werden meine Bücher kaufen!

Ich werde berühmt⁴ sein und sehr, sehr reich dazu.

Dann werde ich mir jeden, aber auch jeden Wunsch erfüllen!

Das Problem ist nur, was mach ich danach⁵?

Am besten ist es wohl, ich mache weiter⁶ wie bisher⁷, und schreibe nur für eine kleine, ausgewählte Leserschaft⁸.

▶ Identify the verbs in each sentence. Which verbs clearly refer to the present?

▶ How does the poet express his hopes for the future?

▶ For each sentence expressing the poet's hopes for the future, state the unspoken reality of his present life.

BEISPIEL: Er hat jetzt keinen Erfolg mit seinen Gedichten.

¹poems
²Erfolg … *be successful*
³in den … *praise me to the skies*
⁴famous
⁵afterward
⁶mache … *continue*
⁷wie … *as before*
⁸ausgewählte … *select readership*

Expressing Probability

The future tense is also used in German to express probability, often with the adverb **wohl** or **wahrscheinlich** (*probably*).

Consider the following hypothetical scenario concerning the unsuccessful poet of the cartoon "*Poesie.*"

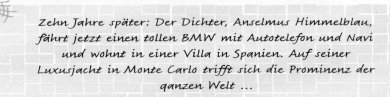

*Zehn Jahre später: Der Dichter, Anselmus Himmelblau,
fährt jetzt einen tollen BMW mit Autotelefon und Navi
und wohnt in einer Villa in Spanien. Auf seiner
Luxusjacht in Monte Carlo trifft sich die Prominenz der
ganzen Welt ...*

What is probably true about Anselmus?

Er **wird wohl** endlich Erfolg haben.	*He is probably finally successful.*
Millionen **werden** jetzt **wahrscheinlich** seine Bücher **kaufen.**	*Millions are probably buying his books now.*
Er **wird wohl** sehr reich **sein.**	*He is probably very rich.*

Übung 2 Wahrscheinlich

Reden Sie mit mindestens zwei Leuten. Jemand hat gerade eine Million Dollar in der Lotterie gewonnen. Was wird er/sie wahrscheinlich mit dem Geld machen?

BEISPIEL: **S1:** Meine Mutter hat eine Million Dollar gewonnen.

S2: Was wird sie mit dem Geld machen?

S1: Sie wird sich wahrscheinlich einen tollen Ferrari kaufen.

Wer?	Was?
Mutter	das Geld auf die Bank bringen
Vater	nach Florida ziehen
Eltern	(sich) ein Schloss in Frankreich kaufen
Freundin	vielen Leuten helfen
Freund	(sich) ein tolles Motorrad kaufen
ich	auf eine Insel in der Karibik ziehen
??	eine Weltreise machen
	??

Describing People or Things: Relative Clauses°

Relativsätze

A relative clause provides additional information about a person or an object named in the main clause.

XYZ Company is looking for bright and energetic trainees *who are interested in a career in communications technology.*

XYZ Company is looking for trainees *whose background includes a degree in computer science.*

XYZ Company is looking for trainees *for whom the sky is the limit.*

The Relative Pronoun°

In German, a relative clause is always introduced by a relative pronoun. The forms of the relative pronoun are identical to those of the definite article, except in the genitive singular and the genitive and dative plural.

	Singular			Plural
	Masculine	*Neuter*	*Feminine*	*All Genders*
Nominative	der	das	die	die
Accusative	den	das	die	die
Dative	dem	dem	der	**denen**
Genitive	**dessen**	**dessen**	**deren**	**deren**

Nominative Subject

Ich wünsche mir einen Job, **der** Spaß macht.

I want a job **that** is fun.

Accusative Object

Wie heißt der junge Mann, **den** du gestern kennengelernt hast?

What is the name of the young man (**whom**) you met yesterday?

Dative Object

Sind Sie einer von den Menschen, **denen** ein sicherer Arbeitsplatz wichtig ist?

Are you one of those people **to whom** a secure position is important?

Genitive Object

Wir sind eine Firma, **deren** Produkte weltbekannt sind.

We are a company **whose** products are known worldwide.

Prepositional Object

Informatikerin ist ein Beruf, **für den** ich mich interessiere.

Computer scientist is an occupation **in which** I am interested.

NOTE:

‣ Relative pronouns correspond in gender and number to their antecedent—that is, to the noun to which they refer.

‣ The case of the relative pronoun is determined by its function within the relative clause. It can be the subject, an object, or a prepositional object.

‣ The conjugated verb is placed at the end of the relative clause.

ein Beruf, für den ich mich interessiere.

‣ A relative clause in German is always set off from the rest of the sentence by a comma.

‣ The relative pronoun cannot be omitted as it sometimes can in English.

Der Personalchef, **den** ich kürzlich kennenlernte, ...

The personnel director I met recently . . . (The personnel director whom I met recently . . .)

Die Berufsberaterin, **mit der** ich sprach, ...

The career adviser I spoke with . . . (The career adviser with whom I spoke . . .)

KONSTRUKTEURE,
denen Ihr Radius zu eng ist...'

Malte Fischer
Beratung · Schlehenweg 2
und Management · D-5063 Overath
für Unternehmen · Tel. 02206/2231

Ich will einen Job, der zu mir passt.

Wir suchen einen qualifizierten

Mitarbeiter

der mindestens ein Jahr Erfahrung mit Airlines vorweisen kann.

Wir suchen noch Hausfrauen, Rentner, Studenten oder Berufstätige, die es frühmorgens in ihren Betten nicht mehr aushalten.

Lesen Sie, was Leute lesen, die Karriere machen wollen.

▶ Identify the main clause and the relative clause(s) in each of the four ads.

▶ About whom or what do the relative clauses provide information?

▶ Where is the conjugated verb placed in each relative clause?

Übung 3 Attribute

Ergänzen Sie die Relativpronomen. Wie heißen die Sätze auf Englisch?

A. Nominativ

1. Gabriele ist eine Frau, _____ selbstständig arbeiten möchte.
2. Nicholas ist ein Mann, _____ selbstständig arbeiten möchte.
3. Das sind junge Leute, _____ selbstständig arbeiten möchten.
4. Dies ist eine Firma, _____ junge Leute mit Verkaufstalent sucht.
5. ABC ist ein Unternehmen, _____ Azubis sucht.

B. Akkusativ

1. Wie heißt der Arzt, _____ du gestern kennengelernt hast?
2. Wie heißt die Ärztin, _____ du gestern kennengelernt hast?
3. Wie heißt der Schauspieler, _____ du gern kennenlernen möchtest?
4. Wie heißen die Musiker, _____ du gern hören möchtest?
5. Wie heißt das Buch, _____ du zum Geburtstag bekommen hast?

C. Dativ

1. Wir suchen eine Studentin, _____ Reisen Spaß macht.
2. Wir suchen einen Studenten, _____ Auto fahren Spaß macht.
3. Wir suchen Leute, _____ Technik Spaß macht.
4. Er ist ein Mensch, _____ Prestige sehr wichtig ist.
5. Plus ist eine Firma, _____ motivierte Manager wichtig sind.

D. Genitiv

1. Dies ist eine Firma, _____ Produkte überall bekannt sind.
2. Dies ist ein Unternehmen, _____ Produkte überall bekannt sind.
3. Das sind Schulen, _____ Schüler eine gute Ausbildung bekommen.

Übung 4　So bin ich.

Schritt 1: Kreuzen Sie drei Dinge an, die auf Sie zutreffen (*apply*).

Ich bin ein Mensch, … der Gruppenarbeit nicht mag. ☐
der gut zuhören kann. ☐
dem man vertrauen (*trust*) kann. ☐
dem Lernen Spaß macht. ☐
den alle Leute mögen. ☐
dem kreative Arbeit gefällt. ☐
der gut organisieren kann. ☐
der sich gut allein beschäftigen kann ☐

Schritt 2: Arbeiten Sie nun zu viert und machen Sie eine Liste mit den Qualitäten, die in Ihrer Gruppe vorkommen (*are found*).

BEISPIELE: Es gibt drei Leute, die Gruppenarbeit nicht mögen.
Es gibt einen Studenten, dem kreative Arbeit gefällt.
Es gibt eine Studentin, die gut organisieren kann.

Übung 5　Qualifikationen

Die folgenden Sätze sind aus Stellenangeboten in deutschen Zeitungen. Setzen Sie die passenden Relativpronomen ein.

1. Unsere Firma sucht Abiturienten, _____ Kreativität und Flexibilität besitzen.
2. Wenn Sie eine junge Dame sind, _____ sich für technische Berufe interessiert, schicken Sie uns Ihre Bewerbung.
3. Wir suchen einen Auszubildenden (Azubi), _____ das Bäckerhandwerk lernen möchte.
4. Elektroniker ist ein Beruf, für _____ sich viele junge Leute interessieren.
5. Wir sind eine Firma, mit _____ Sie über Ihre Zukunft reden sollten.
6. Ist Ihnen die Umwelt, in _____ Sie leben, wichtig? Dann werden Sie doch Umwelt-Techniker, ein Beruf für engagierte Menschen, _____ unsere Umwelt wichtig ist.
7. Wir suchen junge Leute, _____ ein gesundes Selbstbewusstsein (*self-confidence*) haben.
8. Wir suchen junge Leute, _____ einen sicheren Arbeitsplatz suchen und _____ bei der Post Karriere machen wollen.

Übung 6　Ein gefährlicher Beruf

Herr Grimmig, Briefträger von Beruf, hat – wie Sie sehen – mal wieder einen schlechten Tag. Schauen Sie sich zuerst die zwei Bilder an.

Schritt 1: Was sind hier die Tatsachen (*facts*)? Kombinieren Sie.

1. Der kleine Junge	**a.** hat die Polizei geholt.
2. Nikos Hund, Fritz,	**b.** heißt Niko.
3. Der Hund hat den Briefträger	**c.** hat alles gesehen.
4. Nikos Vater, Herr Sauer,	**d.** schreibt alles genau auf.
5. Frau Kluge, die Nachbarin,	**e.** ins Bein gebissen.
6. Der Briefträger, Herr Grimmig,	**f.** ist sehr böse über den Hund.
7. Der Polizist, Herr Gründlich,	**g.** hasst Briefträger.

Nützliche Wörter	
hassen	*to hate*
beißen, gebissen	*to bite*
böse	*angry*
holen	*to fetch, get*
auf•schreiben, aufgeschrieben	*to write down*

Schritt 2: Sagen Sie nun mithilfe der Tatsachen etwas über diese Situation.

BEISPIEL: Fritz ist der Hund. Er hasst Briefträger. →
Fritz ist der Hund, der Briefträger hasst.

1. Fritz ist der Hund, …
2. Niko ist …,
3. Herr Grimmig ist …,
4. Frau Kluge ist …,
5. Herr Sauer ist …,
6. Herr Gründlich ist …,

The Interrogative Pronoun° **was für (ein)**

Das Interrogativpronomen

Nominative

Was für ein Beruf ist das?	*What kind of a profession is that?*
Was für eine Firma ist das?	*What kind of a firm is that?*

Accusative

Was für einen Chef hast du?	*What kind of a boss do you have?*
Was für eine Chefin hast du?	*What kind of a boss do you have?*
Was für Arbeit machst du dort?	*What kind of work do you do there?*

In **was für einer** Firma arbeitest du?	*What kind of a firm do you work for?*
Mit **was für einem** Kollegen arbeitest du?	*What kind of a colleague do you work with?*
Mit **was für** Kollegen arbeitest du?	*What kind of colleagues do you work with?*

NOTE:

▶ The interrogative pronoun **was für (ein)** is always followed by a noun.

▶ The case of the noun that follows **was für (ein)** depends on its function in the sentence. In this context, **für** does not function as a preposition and, therefore, does not determine the case of the noun.

▶ The expression is always **was für** (without **ein**) when the noun is plural.

Übung 7 Ein unkonventioneller Klub

Hören Sie zu und markieren Sie die richtigen Antworten. Mehrere Antworten können stimmen. Die Sprecher sind Sven und Anja, zwei gute Freunde.

1. Anja …
   a. liest ein Buch.   **b.** sieht fern.   **c.** schreibt ein Buch.
2. *Das literarische Oktett* ist …
   a. ein Gedicht.   **b.** der Titel eines Buches.   **c.** der Name eines Klubs.
3. Die Autoren sind …
   a. Schüler.   **b.** Studenten.   **c.** Hausfrauen.
4. Im Buch stehen …
   a. Geschichten.   **b.** Gedichte.   **c.** Geschichten und Bilder.
5. Die Themen, über die die Autoren schreiben, beziehen sich auf …
   a. Politik.   **b.** Sex.   **c.** Liebe.   **d.** Studentenalltag.
6. Anja findet das Buch …
   a. langweilig.   **b.** originell.   **c.** dumm.   **d.** provozierend.

Übung 8 Ein Interview

Ergänzen Sie zuerst die Sätze mit der passenden Form von **was für (ein)**. Arbeiten Sie dann zu zweit und stellen Sie einander abwechselnd diese Fragen und beantworten Sie sie.

BEISPIEL: **S1:** *Was für* Filme siehst du am liebsten?

        S2: Am liebsten sehe ich Dokumentarfilme.

1. _____ Bücher liest du gern? (z.B. Biografien, Krimis, Science Fiction)
2. _____ Wagen fährst du?
3. _____ Musik hörst du gern?
4. _____ Kleidung trägst du am liebsten?
5. _____ Getränke trinkst du am liebsten?
6. _____ Job hast du? (z.B. interessant, langweilig, …)
7. _____ Beruf findest du wirklich interessant?
8. In _____ Stadt lebst du oder möchtest du leben? (z.B. Kleinstadt, Großstadt, in überhaupt keiner Stadt, …)

Negating Sentences

Summary: The Position of **nicht**

You recall that **nicht** (*not*) is used in negation when the negative article **kein** cannot be used. The position of **nicht** varies according to the structure of the sentence.

When **nicht** negates a specific sentence element, it precedes that sentence element.

> Ich komme **nicht heute,** sondern morgen.

> Wir haben **nicht viel Geld.**

When **nicht** negates an entire statement, it generally stands at the end of the sentence.

> Petra kommt morgen leider **nicht.**

> Sie gibt mir das Buch **nicht.**

However, **nicht** precedes:

● *predicate adjectives*	Petras Bewerbungsbrief ist **nicht lang.**
● *predicate nouns*	Das ist **nicht Petras Brief.**
● *verbal complements at the end of the sentence*	
a. *separable prefixes*	Sie schickt den Brief **nicht ab.**
b. *past participles*	Sie hat sich **nicht beworben.**
c. *infinitives*	Sie will sich **nicht bewerben.**
● *prepositional phrases*	Sie hat sich **nicht um die Stelle** beworben.

Übung 9 Schwierige° Zeiten

difficult

Beantworten Sie alle Fragen negativ mit **nicht.**

BEISPIEL: Hat Hans die Prüfung bestanden (*passed*)? →
        Nein, er hat die Prüfung nicht bestanden.

1. Hat er sich um die Stelle bei der Zeitung beworben?
2. Kennt er den Personalchef der Zeitung?
3. Hat er einen Lebenslauf geschrieben?
4. Hat er ein Bewerbungsformular ausgefüllt?
5. Hat er seine Bewerbung zur Post gebracht?
6. Hat er mit Berufsberatern gesprochen?
7. Hat der Personalchef ihn gestern angerufen?
8. Hat der Personalchef ihn zum Gespräch eingeladen?
9. Hat er sich auf das Vorstellungsgespräch vorbereitet?
10. War der Personalchef sehr beeindruckt?
11. Hat Hans die Stelle bekommen?
12. War er traurig?
13. Wird er sich noch einmal bewerben?

Negation: **noch nicht / noch kein(e);**
nicht mehr / kein(e) … mehr

To respond negatively to a question that includes the adverb **schon** (*already, yet*), use either **noch nicht** (*not yet*), **noch kein** (*no . . . yet*), or **noch nie** (*never yet*) in your answer.

Geht Ute **schon** zur Schule?   Nein, sie geht **noch nicht** zur Schule.

Hat Dieter **schon** eine Stelle?   Nein, er hat **noch keine** Stelle.

To respond negatively to a question that includes the adverb **noch** or **immer noch** (*still*), use either **nicht mehr** or **kein … mehr** (*no longer*) in your answer.

Ist Sabine **immer noch** arbeitslos?
—Nein, sie ist **nicht mehr** arbeitslos.

Hat Dieter **noch** Arbeit?
—Nein, er hat **keine** Arbeit **mehr.**

Übung 10   Leider, noch nicht

Arbeiten Sie zu zweit und stellen Sie einander Fragen.

BEISPIEL: **S1:**   Weißt du schon, was du nach dem Studium machen willst?

S2:   Nein, das weiß ich noch nicht.

1. Weißt du schon, wo du arbeiten möchtest?
2. Hast du schon eine Stelle für den Sommer?
3. Hast du heute schon die Zeitung gelesen?
4. Hast du dich schon um eine Stelle beworben?
5. Hast du den Personalchef der Firma schon angerufen?
6. Hast du schon ein Angebot von der Firma bekommen?

Übung 11   Nein, nicht mehr

Beantworten Sie die Fragen mit **ja** und dann mit **nein**. Arbeiten Sie zu dritt und wechseln Sie sich ab.

BEISPIEL: **S1:**   Studiert Barbara noch?

S2:   Ja, sie studiert immer noch.

S3:   Nein, ich glaube, sie studiert nicht mehr.

1. Wohnt Barbara noch in Heidelberg?
2. Arbeitet Andreas immer noch als Reiseführer?
3. Hat Anna noch Arbeit?
4. Hat Klaus noch ein Motorrad?
5. Macht Astrid die Arbeit als Journalistin noch Spaß?
6. Spricht sie immer noch so enthusiastisch über ihre Arbeit?
7. Ist Maximilian immer noch unzufrieden?

Videoclips

A Schauen Sie sich die Interviews mit Oliver, Jasmin und Alex an. Wie sind sie zu ihrem Beruf gekommen? Ergänzen Sie die Sätze.

1. Oliver ist selbstständig, er ist _____.
2. Er hat eine _____ in neuen Medien wie Fernsehen und Computeranimation gemacht.
3. An seinem Beruf gefällt ihm die _____.
4. Olivers Beruf ist aber sehr _____.
5. Jasmin ist _____ bei der Deutschen Bank.
6. Wie hat sie ihre Stelle bekommen? Sie hat die _____ in der Zeitung gelesen und hat sich _____.
7. Sie hat ihren _____ mit Passfoto an die Bank geschickt und hat ein _____ erhalten.
8. Alex ist _____ von Beruf.
9. Wie hat er seine Stelle bekommen? Von einer Freundin hat er erfahren, dass eine _____ frei war.
10. Er hat sich _____.
11. Alex arbeitet seit _____ Jahren in diesem Beruf.

B Was für Schulen haben Peter und Jasmin besucht? Kreuzen Sie an.

	Peter	Jasmin
Grundschule	☐	☐
Gesamtschule	☐	☐
Gymnasium	☐	☐
Realoberschule	☐	☐
Universität	☐	☐

C Was wollten Oliver, Jasmin und Alex als Kinder werden? Und Sie? Was wollten Sie als Kind werden?

D Was werden Peter, Jasmin und Alex in zwanzig Jahren tun?

E Und Sie? Was werden Sie in zwanzig Jahren tun?

Lesen

Zum Thema

Was sind Traumberufe für junge Leute?

Schritt 1: Arbeiten Sie zu dritt und machen Sie eine Liste mit drei Traumberufen.

Was ist ein Grund (*reason*), warum junge Leute sich für diese Berufe interessieren?

Schritt 2: Vergleichen sie diese Liste mit zwei anderen Gruppen in der Klasse. Haben Sie Traumberufe gemeinsam (*in common*)? Welche?

Schritt 3: Nennen sie die fünf populärsten Traumberufe in der Klasse.

Landeskunde-Info

In Deutschland ist ein Jahr Militärdienst Pflicht (*required*) für deutsche Männer. Im Allgemeinen geht der junge Deutsche mit 18 Jahren oder direkt nach der Ausbildung zum Militär. Viele sind Kriegsdienstverweigerer (*conscientious objectors*) und machen stattdessen Zivildienst. Das bedeutet, dass sie während dieser Zeit in einem Krankenhaus, Altenheim oder einem anderen sozialen oder auch ökologischen Bereich arbeiten. Oft helfen die sogenannten „Zivis" älteren Menschen zu Hause oder auch im Pflegeheim. So helfen sie z.B. morgens beim Anziehen, besorgen Mahlzeiten und helfen in der Wohnung.

▶ Ist Militärdienst Pflicht bei Ihnen?

▶ Was halten Sie von Zivildienst?

Unter Schulfreunden

Auf den ersten Blick 1

Überfliegen Sie die kurzen Texte über die Pläne von jungen Leuten, die ihr Abitur 2009 in Hamburg gemacht haben. Suchen Sie folgende Informationen in den Texten:

▶ Wer interessiert sich für Sprachen?

▶ Wer interessiert sich für technische Berufe?

▶ Wer interessiert sich für einen Beruf im kulturellen oder künstlerischen Bereich?

▶ Wer will studieren?

▶ Wer will eine Lehre machen?

▶ Wer weiß noch nicht, was er/sie machen möchte?

Lucas Hornung freut sich auf mehr Freiheit. Seinen Zivildienst möchte er im Ausland machen. Gerne in einem Land, in dem Französisch gesprochen wird. Spanisch und English kann er bereits. Während der Schulzeit hat er ein Jahr lang in Costa Rica gelebt. Seine Gasteltern
5 möchte er gerne mal nach Deutschland einladen, sobald er das Geld dazu hat.

Pascal Schoenmakers jobbt neben der Schule dreimal pro Woche bei einer Film- und Musikproduktion. Dort lernt er, Werbefilme zu schneiden und Bilder zu bearbeiten. Das gefällt ihm so gut, dass er
10 gerne Medientechnik studieren möchte, um später als Kameramann oder Cutter zu arbeiten. Nach dem Abi wird er eine kleine Auszeit vom Lernen nehmen.

Jonas Schmidt leidet zwar nicht an der Schule. Aber er freut sich darauf, weniger eingeschränkt° zu sein und endlich das zu tun, was °restricted
15 er sich selbst ausgesucht hat. Am liebsten möchte er Politologie studieren. Denn er hat eine Leidenschaft° für Nachrichten und °passion politische Reportagen. Er würde gerne selbst einmal über Politik berichten, vielleicht für das Fernsehen.

Katja Dos Santos Rocha hat gemischte Gefühle, wenn sie an die Zeit
20 nach der Schule denkt, denn sie weiß noch nicht, was sie dann machen möchte. Sicher ist, dass es etwas mit Sprachen sein soll, denn sie spricht Englisch, Portugiesisch, Spanisch und Französisch. Sicher ist aber auch, dass sie nicht studieren wird. Interessant fände sie eine Ausbildung zur Flugbegleiterin.

25 **Jovanka Backhus** singt, seit sie ein kleines Kind war. Inzwischen nimmt sie an der Jungen Akademie der Jugendmusikhochschule jede Woche Gesangs- und Klavierstunden. Ob sie Musik studieren möchte, weiß sie noch nicht. Sie könnte sich auch vorstellen, Innenarchitektin zu werden. Denn außer Musik mag sie in der Schule am liebsten Mathe
30 und Kunst.

Yoran Zeid würde am liebsten sein ganzes Leben lang studieren. Bevor er in den Niederlanden, der Heimat seiner Mutter, ein Medizinstudium beginnt, möchte er seine Sprachkenntnisse verbessern. Ein halbes Jahr lang will er durch arabische Länder reisen. Sein Traum wäre, Israel zu
35 besuchen, das sein Vater, ein Palästinenser, als Kind verlassen musste.

Courtesy of DIE ZEIT.

Zum Text 1

Beantworten Sie die folgenden Fragen.

1. Wer von diesen jungen Leuten hat die interessantesten Pläne?
2. Finden Sie die Pläne dieser jungen Leute typisch?
3. Sehen Sie hier etwas, was man in Ihrem Lande ungewöhnlich finden würde?

Auf den ersten Blick 2

Lesen Sie jetzt das folgende Interview mit Sara, die ihren Traumjob gefunden hat. Sie wird Fotografin.

Sara, 22 Jahre, 1. Lehrjahr als Fotografin

Wie sieht dein Tag als Fotografin aus?

frames

exception

Ich mache alles, was mit dem Laden zu tun hat, also Kunden bedienen, Rahmen° verkaufen, Bilder fertig machen und am Computer Bilder
5 ausdrucken. Dann kommt noch Laborarbeit dazu. Das ist aber eher die Ausnahme.° Und dann natürlich das Fotografieren. Da ich erst im ersten Lehrjahr bin, mache ich bis jetzt nur Pass- und Bewerbungsbilder. Das heißt, ich pudere die Kunden, setze sie ins richtige Licht und fotografiere sie. Dann setze ich mich an den Computer, drucke die
10 Bilder aus, schneide sie und gebe sie dem Kunden. Ich assistiere aber auch bei Shootings. Auswärts arbeiten wir auch, also zum Beispiel bei Hochzeiten und Reportagen fotografieren.

Deine Lieblingsaufgabe

Im Labor arbeite ich sehr gern, weil man da viele Freiheiten hat, die
15 Bilder noch zu verändern und zu bearbeiten. Und das Fotografieren an sich macht mir natürlich Spaß. Außerdem ist es auch interessant, mit so vielen unterschiedlichen Menschen umzugehen.

Welche... What do you have to put up with?

(lit.: What toads do you have to swallow?)

Welche Kröten musst du schlucken?°

Am Wochenende arbeiten, das heißt jeden Samstag, weil ich ja in einem
20 ganz normalen Fotogeschäft arbeite. Außerdem sind Hochzeiten und andere Außentermine oft am Wochenende. Das ist nicht immer so schön.

Ohne was geht es nicht?

Man sollte einen Blick fürs Bild haben, kreativ sein, eigene Ideen haben und diese umsetzen wollen. Wenn man Porträtfotografin werden möchte,
25 sollte man auch gut mit Menschen umgehen können. Denn wenn man Porträts macht, muss man sich auf die Menschen, die man fotografiert, einlassen können. Man muss aber auch mit dem Computer umgehen mögen, weil immer mehr Bilder digital bearbeitet werden.

Und nach der Ausbildung?

30 Ich würde gerne für ein Magazin arbeiten. Aber ganz genau festgelegt hab' ich mich noch nicht. Das schöne als Fotografin ist ja, dass es in jedem Bereich was gibt: Mode, Reisefotografie, Porträts, sogar im Krankenhaus oder bei der Polizei. Es gibt nichts, was nicht fotografiert wird. Das heißt, man kann überall arbeiten. Ich selbst würde gerne Fotografie und Reise
35 verbinden. Mein Traum wäre es, zum Beispiel für ein Magazin wie Geo zu fotografieren.

Zum Text 2

A Ergänzen Sie die Informationen über Saras Aufgaben.

Im Laden muss Sara Kunden _____ (*wait on*) und _____ (*frames*) verkaufen. Sie muss auch _____ (*pictures*) fertig machen und am Computer Bilder _____ (*print*). Weil Sara erst im ersten _____ (*apprenticeship year*) ist, darf sie nur _____- (*passport*) und Bewerbungsbilder machen.

B Welche der folgenden Arbeiten macht Sara gern? Welche nicht so gern?

	Gern	Nicht gern	Keine Information
1. Fotografieren	☐	☐	☐
2. im Labor arbeiten	☐	☐	☐
3. Kunden bedienen	☐	☐	☐
4. verschiedene Menschen kennenlernen	☐	☐	☐
5. am Wochenende arbeiten	☐	☐	☐

C Machen Sie eine Liste der Eigenschaften, die wichtig sind, um diesen Beruf auszuüben.

D **Zukunftspläne.** Sara beschreibt ihre Pläne für die Zukunft. Lesen Sie diesen Teil des Interviews noch einmal durch. Welche drei Fragen möchten Sie Sara über Ihre Zukunftspläne stellen?

Zu guter Letzt

Berufswünsche

Was sind Ihre Berufswünsche? Wie sehen Sie Ihren zukünftigen Beruf? Machen Sie eine Umfrage in der Klasse und analysieren Sie die Ergebnisse.

Schritt 1: Was würden (*would*) Sie über Ihre eigenen Berufswünsche sagen? Schreiben Sie drei Möglichkeiten für jede der vier Kategorien.

BEISPIEL: Das würde mir gefallen. →
- im Labor experimentieren
- alten Leuten helfen
- Baupläne entwerfen

1. Das würde mir gefallen.
2. Dort würde ich gern arbeiten.
3. Das würde ich gern machen.
4. Für eine gute Stelle würde ich ...

Schritt 2: Machen Sie aus jeder der vier Kategorien eine Frage.

BEISPIEL: Was würde dir an diesem Beruf gefallen?

Schritt 3: Interviewen Sie fünf Studenten/Studentinnen in der Klasse. Stellen Sie ihnen die vier Fragen und schreiben Sie die Antworten auf.

Schritt 4: Arbeiten Sie in Gruppen und stellen Sie eine Liste von allen Antworten auf die vier Fragen zusammen.

Schritt 5: Analysieren Sie die Antworten. Gibt es Ähnlichkeiten in den Antworten der Studenten/Studentinnen?

Wortschatz

Arbeitswelt	**World of Work**
das **Ansehen**	prestige
der **Arbeitsplatz, ⸚e**	workplace; position
die **Ausbildung**	(career) training
das **Ausland** (no pl.)	foreign countries
im Ausland	abroad
das **Berufsleben**	professional life
das **Büro, -s**	office
der **Chef, -s** / die **Chefin, -nen**	manager, boss, head
das **Einkommen**	income
die **Entwicklung, -en**	development
der **Erfolg, -e**	success
Erfolg haben	to be successful
die **Firma**, pl. **Firmen**	firm, company
das **Gehalt, ⸚er**	salary
die **Gelegenheit, -en**	opportunity
das **Leben** (no pl.)	life
die **Leistung, -en**	performance
der **Mitarbeiter, -** / die **Mitarbeiterin, -nen**	co-worker, colleague; employee
die **Tätigkeit, -en**	activity; position
die **Technik, -en**	technique; technology

Berufe	**Professions**
der **Bibliothekar, -e** / die **Bibliothekarin, -nen**	librarian
der **Dolmetscher, -** / die **Dolmetscherin, -nen**	interpreter
der **Geschäftsmann**, pl. **Geschäftsleute** / die **Geschäftsfrau, -en**	businessman/ businesswoman
der **Handel**	sales, trade
der **Informatiker, -** / die **Informatikerin, -nen**	computer scientist
der **Kaufmann**, pl. **Kaufleute** / die **Kauffrau, -en**	salesman/saleswoman
die **Kundenbetreuung**	customer service
der **Künstler, -** / die **Künstlerin, -nen**	artist
der **Mechaniker, -** / die **Mechanikerin, -nen**	mechanic
der **Psychologe** (-n masc.), -n/ die **Psychologin, -nen**	psychologist
der **Rechtsanwalt, ⸚e** / die **Rechtsanwältin, -nen**	lawyer, attorney
der **Schauspieler, -** / die **Schauspielerin, -nen**	actor
der **Zahnarzt, ⸚e** / die **Zahnärztin, -nen**	dentist
der **Zeichner, -** / die **Zeichnerin, -nen**	graphic artist

Stellensuche	**Job Search**
das **Abitur, -e**	*examination at the end of Gymnasium*
der **Abschluss, ⸚e**	completion; degree
der **Arbeitgeber, -** / die **Arbeitgeberin, -nen**	employer
das **Arbeitsamt, ⸚er**	employment office
der **Berufsberater, -** / die **Berufsberaterin, -nen**	employment counselor
die **Bewerbung, -en**	application
das **Bewerbungsformular, -e**	application form
die **Eigenschaft, -en**	characteristic
die **Grundschule, -n**	primary school
das **Gymnasium**, pl. **Gymnasien**	secondary school
der **Kontakt, -e**	contact
der **Lebenslauf**	résumé
die **Stelle, -n**	position, job
das **Stellenangebot, -e**	job offer; help-wanted ad
die **Unterlagen** (pl.)	documentation, papers
der **Verkauf**	sales
die **Versicherung, -en**	insurance
das **Vorstellungsgespräch, -e**	job interview
die **Website, -s**	website
das **Zeugnis, -se**	report card; transcript; recommendation (from a former employer)
die **Zukunft**	future

Verben	**Verbs**
sich **beschäftigen** (mit)	to occupy oneself (with)
besitzen, besaß, besessen	to own, possess
sich **bewerben** (um) (bewirbt), bewarb, beworben	to apply (for)
entwerfen (entwirft), entwarf, entworfen	to design
heraus•fordern	to challenge
her•stellen	to produce, manufacture
sich **interessieren** für (+ acc.)	to be interested in
nach•denken (über + acc.), dachte nach, nachgedacht	to think (about)
übersetzen, übersetzt	to translate
untersuchen, untersucht	to examine
verdienen	to earn; to deserve
sich **vor•bereiten** (auf + acc.)	to prepare (for)

sich (*dat.*) vor•stellen	to imagine	selbstständig	independent(ly)
sich (*acc.*) vor•stellen	to introduce	verantwortlich	responsible
		wahrscheinlich	probably
Adjektive und Adverbien	**Adjectives and Adverbs**	wohl	probably
abwechslungsreich	varied, diverse		
kontaktfreudig	outgoing	**Sonstiges**	**Other**
erfolgreich	successful(ly)	im Freien	outdoors
selbstbewusst	self-assured	was für (ein)	what kind of (a)

Das kann ich nun!

1. Beschreiben Sie in drei Sätzen, was Ihnen für Ihren zukünftigen Beruf wichtig ist.

2. Welche Berufe sind gemeint?
   a. Man arbeitet auf der Bühne.
   b. Man untersucht Patienten.
   c. Man repariert Autos.
   d. Man entwirft Gebäude und Häuser.
   e. Man verkauft Produkte einer Firma.

3. Wenn man sich um eine Stelle bewirbt, muss man oft einen tabellarischen _____ schreiben. Sehr wichtig für eine erfolgreiche Bewerbung sind die _____ von früheren Arbeitgebern.

4. In Deutschland gibt es mehrere Schultypen. Nennen Sie drei.

5. Wenn man in Deutschland studieren will, muss man am Ende des Gymnasiums _____ machen.

6. Wie sagt man das auf Deutsch? Benutzen Sie **werden**.
   a. *Someday I will be rich and famous.*
   b. *My brother is going to be a pilot.*
   c. *Niels is probably at home now.*

7. Ergänzen Sie die Sätze mit Relativpronomen.
   a. Ich bin ein Mensch, _____ weiß, was er will.
   b. Meine Mutter ist eine Frau, _____ man vertrauen kann.
   c. Niko ist der Junge, _____ Hund den Briefträger gebissen hat.

8. Wie heißen die Fragen? Wie heißen die Antworten?
   a. _____ ? —Das ist ein BMW Sportkabriolett.
   b. _____ ? —Ich habe sehr nette Kollegen.
   c. _____ ? —Er hat noch nicht von der Firma gehört.
   d. Hast du noch Arbeit? —Nein, _____ .
   e. Studierst du immer noch? —Nein, _____ .

12

Unser Heim im Grünen

Haus und Haushalt

In diesem Kapitel

- ▶ **Themen:** Talking about money matters, housing, the home, renting, and household appliances

- ▶ **Grammatik:** Verbs with fixed prepositions, **da-** and **wo-**compounds, subjunctive II, **würde**

- ▶ **Lesen:** „Die drei Geldtypen"

- ▶ **Landeskunde:** BAföG, paying for university study, store hours

- ▶ **Zu guter Letzt:** Ein Podcast über Geldtypen

VIDEOCLIPS

Beatrice, Dennis und Jan
sprechen über ihre Finanzen

Mehr als nur ein Notgroschen[1]

Sparverhalten im Frühjahr 2009

48,6 Prozent der Bundesbürger sparen (Herbst 2008: 44,5 %)

Wozu?

Altersvorsorge[2]	65,8 %
Konsum[3]	59,9
Erwerb[4] u. Renovierung von Wohneigentum	50,6
Kapitalanlage[5]	36,7
Kinder	5,7
Notgroschen	4,7

Wie?

6,9 %	festverzinsl. Wertpapiere, Bundesschatzbriefe
12,5	Aktien
20,9	Investmentfonds
20,9	Riester-Vertrag
21,1	Immobilien[6]
31,9	kurzfristige Geldanlage
37,9	Renten- u. Kapitallebens-versicherung
38,3	Girokonto[7]
38,3	Bausparvertrag[8]
55,7	Sparbuch

Quelle: Verband der Privaten Bausparkassen, TNS Infratest   Mehrfachnennungen   © Globus 2936

[1]*emergency fund for a rainy day* [2]*planning for retirement* [3]*consumer goods* [4]*acquisition*
[5]*investments* [6]*real estate* [7]*checking account* [8]*savings plan to purchase/build a home*

A Die Deutschen sparen aus verschiedenen Gründen. Die Grafik zeigt, wofür sie sparen.

Wozu sparen die Deutschen?

◐ Wie viele Deutsche sparen insgesamt? _____

◐ Die deutschen Sparer sparen am meisten für _____.

◐ Mehr als die Hälfte aller Sparer spart für _____ und
_____.

◐ Weniger als 6% spart für die _____.

◐ Am wenigsten sparen sie für einen _____.

Und wie sparen sie?

◐ Die meisten Sparer besitzen ein _____.

◐ Ungefähr 13% der Sparer investieren Geld in _____.

◐ Etwas mehr als 21% der Sparer kaufen _____.

◐ _____ haben einen Bausparvertrag.

B „Was bedeutet euch Geld?" Diese Frage haben wir Jens, Lucia und Elke gestellt. Hören Sie ihre Antworten. Schreiben Sie J (Jens), L (Lucia) oder E (Elke) neben die zutreffenden Aussagen.

1. ___ lange Urlaub machen und dann wieder arbeiten
2. ___ Armen (*poor people*) helfen
3. ___ Geld für medizinische Forschung spenden (*donate*)
4. ___ ein eigenes Geschäft aufmachen
5. ___ ein neues Auto oder eine neue Wohnung kaufen
6. ___ investieren
7. ___ weiter studieren – vielleicht im Ausland
8. ___ Geld für Welthungerorganisationen spenden

Wörter im Kontext

Neue Wörter

geben ... aus (ausgeben)
spend
durchschnittlich on
average
die Ausgabe (Ausgaben, *pl.***)**
expense

Siehe *Asking Questions:*
wo*-Compounds,* S. 362.

Thema 1: Finanzen der Studenten

A Wie **geben** Studenten in Deutschland ihr Geld **aus**? Schauen Sie sich
das Schaubild an.

> ❿ Wie viel Geld brauchen Studenten **durchschnittlich** pro Monat?

> ❿ Wofür geben sie das meiste Geld aus? das wenigste Geld?

> ❿ Woher bekommen Studenten das meiste Geld?

> ❿ Das Budget ist nur für Studenten, die nicht bei den Eltern wohnen.
> Wofür würden Studenten, die bei den Eltern wohnen, wahrschein-
> lich weniger Geld ausgeben?

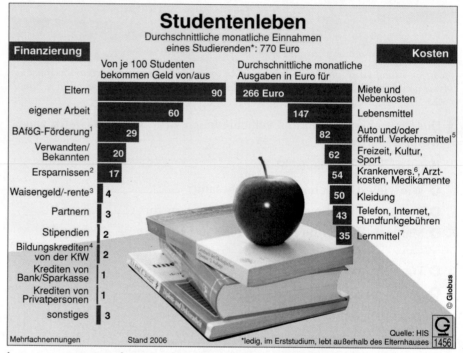

[1]*government stipend* [2]*savings* [3]*support for orphans* [4]*student loans* [5]*public
transportation* [6]*Krankenversicherung health insurance* [7]*school supplies*

B Schauen Sie näher! Wie leben deutsche Studenten? Antworten Sie
mit Informationen aus der Grafik.

> ❿ Wie viel Geld brauchen deutsche Studenten **monatlich** für
> Lebensmittel? für Kleidung? für die Gesundheit?

> ❿ Was gehört alles in die Rubrik „Freizeit"?

> ❿ Was gehört alles in die Rubrik „Lernmittel"?

C Ihr monatliches Budget:

> ❿ Wofür geben Sie monatlich Geld aus und durchschnittlich ungefähr
> wie viel?

> ❿ Wofür geben Sie das meiste Geld aus? das wenigste?

> ❿ Wofür geben Sie nur ab und zu oder gar kein Geld aus?

D Prozent Ihrer monatlichen Ausgaben:

_____ Miete

_____ **Nebenkosten** im **Haushalt** (**Strom, Heizung,** eigenes Telefon, Handy, Wasser)

_____ Auto (**Benzin, Reparaturen**)

_____ Fahrtkosten (öffentliche Verkehrsmittel, z.B. Bus, Flugzeug, Fahrten nach Hause)

_____ **Ernährung** (Essen, Trinken, Mensa, Restaurants)

_____ **Studiengebühren** (pro Semester, pro Quartal)

_____ Lernmittel (Bücher, **Hefte, Bleistifte, Kugelschreiber, Papier,** Sonstiges)

_____ Freizeit (Kino, Theater, Partys, Hobbys)

_____ **sparen** (**Sparkonto,** Sparschwein)

_____ **Versicherungen,** Arztkosten, Medikamente

_____ INSGESAMT (_total_)

◆ Haben Sie genügend (_enough_) **Einnahmen**? Haben Sie am Ende des Monats etwas Geld **übrig,** oder sind Sie **pleite**?

◆ Müssen Sie sich manchmal Geld von Freunden oder Ihrer Familie leihen? Unterstützen Ihre Eltern Sie finanziell?

◆ Sind Sie sparsam? Müssen Sie nebenbei **jobben?**

◆ Vergleichen Sie Ihre monatlichen Ausgaben mit denen eines Mitstudenten / einer Mitstudentin. Wer hat höhere monatliche Ausgaben?

Neue Wörter

Nebenkosten (_pl._)   utilities
der Strom   electricity
die Heizung   heat
das Benzin   gasoline
die Ernährung   food
Studiengebühren (_pl._)
   tuition
das Heft (**Hefte,** _pl._)
   notebook
der Bleistift (**Bleistifte,** _pl._)
   pencil
der Kugelschreiber
   (**Kugelschreiber,** _pl._)
   ballpoint pen
sparen   to save
das Sparkonto   savings
   account
Einnahmen (_pl._)   income
übrig   left over
pleite   broke
unterstützen   support
sparsam   thrifty
jobben   work (at a
   temporary job)
vergleichen   compare

Landeskunde-Info

Wie finanziert man das Studium in Deutschland?

◆ Eltern: Nach dem Gesetz (_law_) müssen Eltern für die Ausbildung ihrer Kinder zahlen, und zwar bis zum Abschluss einer Berufsausbildung, oder für Abiturient/innen bis zum Abschluss eines Studiums.

◆ Stipendien oder Darlehen (_loans_): Das **BAföG** (= _B_undes_a_usbil-dungs_fö_rderungs_g_esetz) ist ein deutsches Gesetz, das die staatliche Unterstützung von Schüler/innen und Student/innen regelt. BAföG besteht aus Darlehen und Zuschüssen (_grants_).

◆ Jobben: Studierende können während des Studiums nebenbei jobben.

Lange Zeit war das Studium an staatlichen Universitäten in Deutschland kostenlos, das heißt es gab keine allgemeinen Studiengebühren (_tuition_). Diese Zeiten sind vorbei. Seit 2005 gibt es in den meisten Bundesländern allgemeine Studiengebühren. Sie sind allerdings verschieden in den Bundesländern, z.B., zur Zeit zahlen Studenten in Baden-Württemberg 800 Euro pro Semester, in Berlin dagegen ist es weiterhin kostenlos.

◆ Wie finanziert man das Studium in Ihrem Land?
◆ Was für Gebühren muss man in Ihrem Land an der Uni zahlen?

Aktivität 1 Pleite oder nicht?

Schauen Sie sich Ihr monatliches Budget im **Thema 1** an. Vergleichen Sie jetzt Ihre Ausgaben mit den Ausgaben eines Partners / einer Partnerin und berichten Sie darüber. Gebrauchen Sie folgende Redemittel.

> Ich gebe das meiste Geld für _____ aus.
> Das wenigste Geld gebe ich für _____ aus.
> Ich gebe nur ab und zu oder gar kein Geld für _____ aus.
> Für _____ und _____ gebe ich mehr/weniger Geld aus als mein Partner / meine Partnerin.

Aktivität 2 Andreas Dilemma

Lesen Sie den Dialog und ergänzen Sie die Sätze unten.

Siehe *The Subjunctive*, S. 363.

Andrea: Sag mal, könntest du mir einen Gefallen (*favor*) tun?

Stefan: Was denn?

Andrea: Würdest du mir bis Ende der Woche 50 Euro leihen? Ich bin total pleite.

Stefan: Fünfzig Euro? Das ist viel Geld.

Andrea: Ich musste 100 Euro für Bücher ausgeben. Und jetzt habe ich keinen Cent mehr übrig. Ich warte auf Geld von meinen Eltern.

Stefan: Hm, ich würde es dir gern leihen. Aber 50 Euro habe ich selber nicht mehr. Ich kann dir höchstens 20 Euro leihen.

Andrea: Ich zahle es dir bis Ende des Monats bestimmt zurück.

Stefan: Eben hast du gesagt, bis Ende der Woche.

Andrea: Ja, ja. Das Geld von meinen Eltern kann jeden Tag kommen.

Stefan: Na gut. Hier ist ein Zwanziger.

Andrea: Vielen Dank.

Andrea hat kein _____[1] mehr; sie ist total _____.[2] Sie möchte sich von Stefan _____.[3] Sie hat nämlich ihr ganzes Geld für _____[4] ausgegeben. Deshalb hat sie jetzt nichts mehr für Essen und Trinken _____.[5] Stefan kann ihr aber _____[6] leihen. Andrea hofft, dass sie Stefan das Geld bis _____[7] zurückzahlen kann. Sie wartet auf _____.[8]

Aktivität 3 Drei Studentenbudgets

Vergleichen Sie die Ausgaben der drei Studenten in der Tabelle auf der nächsten Seite und beantworten Sie die Fragen.

1. Wie viel Geld geben Marion, Wolfgang und Claudia insgesamt monatlich aus?
2. Wofür geben sie das meiste Geld aus?
3. Wer bezahlt die höchste Miete? Wo ist die Miete billiger?
4. Wer hat die höchsten Ausgaben für Telefon, Internet und Rundfunk- und Fernsehgebühren?
5. Wer hat die höchsten Kosten für Bücher und Lernmittel?
6. Was ist – außer Miete – günstig, wenn man im Studentenwohnheim wohnt?
7. Wer unterstützt die drei Studenten finanziell?
8. Warum hat Marion keine Ausgaben für Verkehrsmittel?
9. Wer lebt am sparsamsten?

	Marion	Wolfgang	Claudia
Studienfach	Übersetzer (*translator*)/ Dolmetscher	Medizin	Romanistik/Politik
Unterhalt (support)	Eltern	BAföG	jobben
Miete	200 Euro (1 Zi, Studenten- wohnheim)	300 Euro (1 Zi, Küche, Bad außerhalb)	400 Euro (1 Zi, Küche, Bad)
Verkehrsmittel	keine (alles mit dem Fahrrad erreichbar)	60 Euro	50 Euro
Lebensmittel und Mensa	200 Euro	250 Euro	200 Euro
Bücher und Lernmittel	30 Euro	70 Euro	40 Euro
Telefon, Internet, Rundfunk- und Fernsehgebühren	35 Euro (kein Internet)	60 Euro (eigenes Telefon)	80 Euro
Freizeit	70 Euro	80 Euro	100 Euro
Fahrt nach Hause	20 Euro (Mitfahrgelegenheit) 40 Euro (mit der Bahn)	—	20 Euro
Sonstiges	40 Euro	35 Euro	40 Euro

Aktivität 4 Einnahmen und Ausgaben

Vier Studenten sprechen über ihre monatlichen Einnahmen und Ausgaben. Kreuzen Sie das Zutreffende (*the items that apply*) an. Notieren Sie unter „Ausgaben", wie viel die Studenten für ihre Miete ausgeben.

	Stefanie	Gert	Susanne	Martin

1. Einnahmen von:
  a. Job während des Semesters   ☐ ☐ ☐ ☐
  b. Job während der Semesterferien   ☐ ☐ ☐ ☐
  c. Eltern   ☐ ☐ ☐ ☐
  d. Stipendium/BAföG   ☐ ☐ ☐ ☐

2. Ausgaben für:
  a. Zimmer (privat)   ____ ____ ____ ____
  b. Studentenwohnheim   ____ ____ ____ ____
  c. eigene Wohnung   ____ ____ ____ ____
  d. Wohngemeinschaft   ____ ____ ____ ____

Thema 2: Unsere eigenen vier Wände°

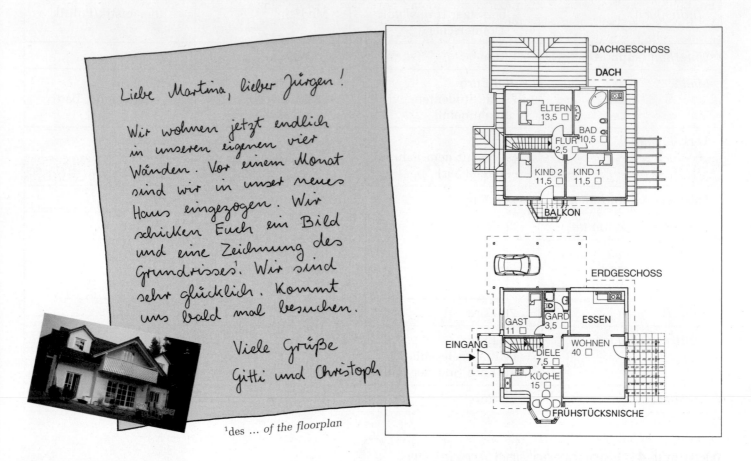

Liebe Martina, lieber Jürgen!

Wir wohnen jetzt endlich in unseren eigenen vier Wänden. Vor einem Monat sind wir in unser neues Haus eingezogen. Wir schicken Euch ein Bild und eine Zeichnung des Grundrisses¹. Wir sind sehr glücklich. Kommt uns bald mal besuchen.

Viele Grüße
Gitti und Christoph

¹des ... *of the floorplan*

Neue Wörter

eigen own
eingezogen (einziehen)
 moved in
die Zeichnung drawing
bald soon
das Dachgeschoss attic, top
 floor
der Eingang entrance
die Garderobe closet
die Diele entry, foyer
die Treppe staircase
unten below, downstairs
oben above; upstairs

Schauen Sie sich die **Zeichnung** von Gittis und Christophs neuem Haus an. Ergänzen Sie dann die folgenden Sätze durch ein passendes Wort aus der Liste:

Bad	Esszimmer	Schlafzimmer
Dachgeschoss	**Frühstücksnische**	Terrasse
Diele	**Gästezimmer**	**Treppe**
Erdgeschoss	Küche	Wohnzimmer

1. Das Haus hat zwei Stockwerke: ein _____ und ein _____.

2. Vom **Eingang** kommt man zuerst in die _____.

3. Links neben der Diele ist eine **Garderobe** und ein _____.

4. Von der Diele geht man rechts in die _____ und eine kleine _____.

5. **Unten** liegen noch zwei Zimmer: ein _____ und ein _____.

6. Das Wohnzimmer führt auf die _____ und in den Garten.

7. In der Diele führt eine _____ nach **oben** ins Dachgeschoss.

8. Im Dachgeschoss sind drei _____ und ein _____.

Aktivität 5   Die ideale Wohnung

Drei Leute (Frau Heine, Herr Zumwald und Thomas) berichten, was für eine Wohnung sie suchen, und was ihnen in der Wohnung wichtig oder unwichtig ist. Stellen Sie zuerst fest, wer welchen Wohnungstyp sucht. Dann notieren Sie in der Tabelle, was jedem wichtig (w) oder unwichtig (u) ist.

Wer sucht:

ein älteres Haus außerhalb der Stadt?   _____

eine Neubauwohnung in der Innenstadt?   _____

eine gemütliche Altbauwohnung in der Stadt?   _____

wichtig/unwichtig	Frau Heine	Herr Zumwald	Thomas
Lage			
Zentralheizung			
Balkon			
Garage			
Garten			
Teppichboden (carpeting)			
Waschmaschine			

Aktivität 6   Hin und her: Eine neue Wohnung

Diese Leute haben entweder eine neue Wohnung oder ein neues Haus gekauft. Wer hat was gekauft? Wie viele Stockwerke gibt es? Wie groß ist das Wohnzimmer? Wie viele WCs oder Badezimmer gibt es?

BEISPIEL: **S1:**   Was für eine Wohnung hat Bettina Neuendorf gekauft?

    S2:   Eine Eigentumswohnung.

    S1:   Wie viele Stockwerke hat die Wohnung?

    S2:   Eins.

    S1:   Und wie viele Schlafzimmer? ...

Person	Typ	Stockwerke	Schlafzimmer	Wohnzimmer	WC/Bad
Bettina Neuendorf	Eigentumswohnung	eins	eins, aber auch ein kleines Gästezimmer	mit Esszimmer kombiniert 30 Quadratmeter	eins
Uwe und Marion Baumgärtner					
Sven Kersten	Eigentumswohnung	zwei	zwei, eins als Gästezimmer benutzt	mit Esszimmer zusammen 35 Quadratmeter, Balkon vom Wohnzimmer	zwei, ein WC und ein Bad
Carola Schubärth					

Siehe *Prepositional Objects: da-Compounds*, S. 360.

Aktivität 7 Der Grundriss

Schritt 1: Sie sehen hier unten einen Grundriss. Identifizieren Sie, wo das Wohnzimmer, das Esszimmer, die Küche, das Schlafzimmer und andere Räume sind. Beschreiben Sie dann, wo die Zimmer liegen.

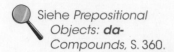

> Zuerst kommt man in ____. Rechts von ____ ist ____. Von der ____ führt eine Tür ins ____. Links neben der ____ ist ein ____ und daneben ein ____. Vom Wohnzimmer geht man auf ____.

Schritt 2: Zeichnen Sie nun den Grundriss Ihrer Wohnung oder einer Fantasiewohnung. Geben Sie jemandem die Zeichnung und beschreiben Sie ihm/ihr, wo die Zimmer liegen. Ihr Partner / Ihre Partnerin setzt die Zimmernamen in den Grundriss. Schauen Sie sich dann die Zeichnung an, um zu sehen, ob alles richtig identifiziert ist.

> Beginnen Sie so: Zuerst kommt man in ____.

Thema 3: Unser Zuhause
Mieten und Vermieten

Neue Wörter

mieten to rent (from someone)
vermieten to rent out (to someone)
die Umgebung vicinity

[1]auf ... *in the country* [2]Gö = Göttingen *university town in north central Germany* [3]*community* [4]*since* [5]*lead*

A Lesen Sie das Mietgesuch (*rental flyer*). Wer sucht was und wo?

1.

Land-WG sucht Mitbewohner(in)!

Wir, Bruno (26) und Britta (21), Hund und Katze, vermieten eine ganze obere Etage in einem älteren Bauernhaus 1 1/2 Zimmer, ca 38 qm[1]. Benutzbar[2] sind Küche, Bad, großer Garten. Die Miete beträgt monatlich €300,— plus €30,— Nebenkosten. 20 km von Göttingen. Ab 1. Juni.

2. Mieter gesucht für große, helle 3 Zimmer in Neubau, ab 1. August, ca. 70 qm. Balkon, eingerichtete Küche (Spülmaschine, Kühlschrank, Mikrowellenherd), Waschraum mit Waschmaschine, Zentralheizung, Teppichboden, Bad und WC, Garage. Zu Fuß ca. 15 Minuten von der Universität, 5 vom Bahnhof, 10 Minuten vom Zentrum.Tiere nicht erwünscht. Miete €400,— Nebenkosten €60,—.

[1]qm = Quadratmeter *square meters*   [2]*available for use*

B Lesen Sie nun die zwei Mietangebote (*rental ads*). Welches Angebot empfehlen Sie Brigitte und Matthias?

1. Ich finde Angebot Nummer _____ ideal für Brigitte und Matthias, denn es gibt dort _____.

2. Ich empfehle Brigitte und Matthias Angebot Nummer _____, denn _____. Es gibt jedoch ein Problem: _____

C Was passt zusammen?

1. _____ Mit diesem **Gerät** macht man den Teppichboden sauber.

2. _____ Dieses Gerät wäscht die Wäsche.

3. _____ Man kann damit das Essen schnell zubereiten.

4. _____ Damit trocknet man die Wäsche.

5. _____ Dieses Gerät spült das **schmutzige** Geschirr.

6. _____ Das ist ein Haus auf dem Land.

7. _____ Das ist ein modernes Haus.

8. _____ Ein anderes Wort für „Region".

a. das **Bauernhaus**
b. der **Mikrowellenherd**
c. der **Staubsauger**
d. der **Wäschetrockner**
e. der **Neubau**
f. die **Spülmaschine**
g. die **Waschmaschine**
h. die **Umgebung**

Aktivität 8   Ist die Wohnung noch frei?

Frau Krenz hat eine große, helle Dreizimmerwohnung zu vermieten. Die Anzeige stand in der Zeitung. Herr Brunner hat auf die Anzeige hin angerufen. Er weiß, wie groß die Wohnung ist und wie hoch die Miete ist. Was möchte er noch von der Vermieterin wissen? Kreuzen Sie alles Zutreffende an.

1. Herr Brunner möchte wissen,
☐ ob die Heizung in den Nebenkosten einbegriffen ist.
☐ ob die Küche einen Mikrowellenherd hat.
☐ wie er vom Haus in die Innenstadt kommt.
☐ wo die Wohnung liegt.
☐ ob es einen Aufzug gibt.
☐ wo man parken kann.
☐ ob Hund und Katze willkommen sind.

2. Frau Krenz möchte von Herrn Brunner wissen,
☐ wie viele Kinder er hat.
☐ ob er verheiratet ist.
☐ ob er Arbeit hat.
☐ wann er vorbeikommen kann.
☐ wann er einziehen möchte.

Wohnqualität

Was ist den Deutschen für die Wohnqualität wichtig?

▶ Am wichtigsten für die Deutschen sind die _____.

▶ Besonders wichtig für 15% der Bundesbürger sind _____ und _____.

▶ Für 18% der Deutschen muss die Wohnlage _____ sein.

▶ _____, das heißt Nähe zu Bus, U-Bahn oder Straßenbahn, ist für 14% der Deutschen wichtig.

▶ Welche drei Dinge sind Ihnen für die Wohnqualität wichtig?

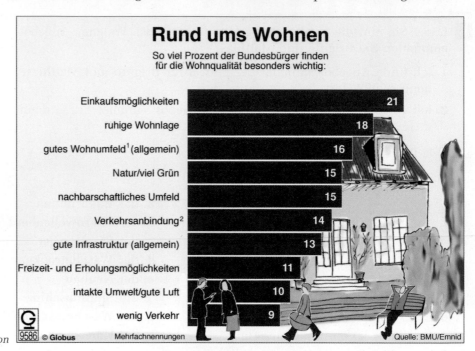

Rund ums Wohnen

So viel Prozent der Bundesbürger finden
für die Wohnqualität besonders wichtig:

Einkaufsmöglichkeiten	21
ruhige Wohnlage	18
gutes Wohnumfeld[1] (allgemein)	16
Natur/viel Grün	15
nachbarschaftliches Umfeld	15
Verkehrsanbindung[2]	14
gute Infrastruktur (allgemein)	13
Freizeit- und Erholungsmöglichkeiten	11
intakte Umwelt/gute Luft	10
wenig Verkehr	9

9586 © Globus   Mehrfachnennungen   Quelle: BMU/Emnid

[1]*nice surroundings*
[2]*access to public transportation*

Aktivität 9   Ein interessantes Angebot

Sie interessieren sich für ein Mietangebot, das Sie in der Zeitung gesehen haben und rufen deshalb den Vermieter / die Vermieterin an.

S1 Vermieter/Vermieterin	S2 Anrufer/Anruferin
1. State your last name.	2. Greet the person, state your last name, and ask whether the apartment is still available.
3. Say it is still available.	4. Ask how much the rent is.
5. State a price.	6. Ask whether this price includes all household bills.
7. State that everything is included (**inklusive**) except the heat.	8. Tell the landlord/landlady that you have a cat or dog.
9. Say that it's all right.	10. Find out where the apartment is located.
11. Give the address and location. Suggest to the caller a time when he/she can come to see it.	12. Say that the time is suitable.
13. Say good-bye.	14. Say good-bye.

Grammatik im Kontext

Verbs with Fixed Prepositions

Many German verbs require the use of fixed prepositions; these verb-preposition combinations are usually different from their English equivalents.

Ich interessiere mich **für** schnelle Autos.	*I'm interested **in** fast cars.*
Wir warten **auf** den Bus.	*We are waiting **for** the bus.*
Die Studenten ärgern sich **über** die hohen Studiengebühren.	*The students are annoyed **about** the high cost of tuition.*

The following are examples of verbs that take fixed prepositions:

Angst haben vor (+ *dat.*)	*to be afraid of*
sich ärgern über (+ *acc.*)	*to be annoyed about*
sich beschäftigen mit	*to occupy oneself with*
sich bewerben um	*to apply for*
denken an (+ *acc.*)	*to think of*
sich freuen auf (+ *acc.*)	*to look forward to*
sich freuen über (+ *acc.*)	*to be happy about*
sich interessieren für	*to be interested in*
verzichten auf (+ *acc.*)	*to do without*
sich vor•bereiten auf (+ *acc.*)	*to prepare for*
warten auf (+ *acc.*)	*to wait for*

Übung 1   So ist es im Leben

Was passt zusammen? Suchen Sie nach Kombinationen im Kasten oder erfinden Sie Ihre eigenen.

1. Ich warte schon lange auf …
2. Ich ärgere mich über …
3. Ich möchte mich um … bewerben.
4. Ich freue mich auf …
5. Ich interessiere mich für …
6. Ich kann nicht auf … verzichten.
7. Ich beschäftige mich gern mit …
8. Ich freue mich über …
9. Ich denke oft an …

Technologie
eine Tasse Kaffee
das Semesterende
Musik
Urlaub auf Hawaii
die hohen Preise für …
einen Anruf von Freunden
Hausarbeit
eine Arbeit im Ausland
mein Handy
ein Praktikum bei …
die Party am Wochenende
kleine Geschenke
Probleme mit dem Computer

Prepositional Objects: **da**-Compounds°

In German, a personal pronoun following a preposition generally refers to a person.

Jan wartet auf **die Chefin.**	*Jan is waiting for the boss.*
Er wartet schon lange **auf sie.**	*He has been waiting for her for a long time.*

When the object of a preposition refers to a thing or an idea, this is represented by a **da**-compound consisting of the adverb **da** and a preposition.

Wer ist **für eine Erhöhung der Studiengebühren?**	*Who is for a tuition increase?*
Nicht viele Leute sind **dafür.**	*Not many people are for it.*
Die Studenten sind **dagegen.**	*The students are against it.*

NOTE:

▶ **Da-** becomes **dar-** when the preposition begins with a vowel.

Kim wartet auf Geld von ihrem Vater. Sie wartet schon eine Woche **darauf.**	*Kim is waiting for money from her father. She has been waiting for it for a week.*

▶ **Da-/Dar-** can combine with most accusative, dative, and two-way prepositions.

The adverbs **dahin** ([*going*] *there*) and **daher** ([*coming*] *from there*) are commonly used with verbs of motion.

Fliegt Kim **nach Spanien?**	—Ja, sie fliegt morgen **dahin.**
Wann gehst du **zur Bank?**	—Ich komme gerade **daher.**

Dahin is often abbreviated to **hin.**

Jan muss noch zur Bank.	Er geht später **hin.**

Da may be placed at the beginning of a sentence and **hin** at the end.

Gehst du oft ins Museum?	—**Da** gehe ich nur selten **hin.**

Analyse

▶ Identify all **da**-compounds in the following text.
▶ What noun does each **da**-compound refer to?
▶ Restate all **da**-compounds as prepositional objects using the nouns to which they refer.

BEISPIEL: dafür → Sabines Zimmer → für ihr Zimmer

Sabines Zimmer im Studentenwohnheim
Sie zahlt nur 150 Euro im Monat dafür. Links an der Wand ist ein Waschbecken. Darüber hängt ein Spiegel. Daneben hängt ein Haken mit einem Handtuch. Rechts an der Wand steht ein Schreibtisch. Darauf liegen viele Bücher und Papiere. Hinten an der Wand steht ein Bett. Darunter stehen Sabines Schuhe und rechts daneben steht ein kleines Bücherregal. Dahinter ist ein Fenster. Davor steht ein Vogelkäfig. Sabines Kanarienvogel, Caruso, wohnt darin und singt pausenlos.

der Spiegel

der Vogelkäfig

das Waschbecken

Übung 2 Gemeinsames und Kontraste

Sabine und Jürgen haben einiges, aber nicht alles, gemein (*in common*).

BEISPIEL: Sie interessiert sich für klassische Musik. →
Er interessiert sich nicht _dafür_.

1. Jürgen gibt viel Geld für sein Auto aus. Sabine gibt nichts _____ aus.
2. Er spricht nicht gern über seine Finanzen. Sie spricht oft _____.
3. Er hat nur wenig Geld für die Freizeit übrig. Sie hat auch nur wenig _____ übrig.
4. Sie freut sich immer über kleine Geschenke. Er freut sich auch _____.
5. Sie kann gut auf Fernsehen verzichten. Er kann nicht _____ verzichten.
6. Sie denkt immer an alle Geburtstage. Er denkt nie _____.
7. Er geht immer pünktlich zur Vorlesung. Sie geht nie pünktlich _____.
8. Er ärgert sich über die laute Musik im Wohnheim. Sie ärgert sich überhaupt nicht _____.
9. Sie freut sich auf das Ende des Studiums. Er freut sich auch _____.

Übung 3 Beschreibungen und Situationen

Setzen Sie passende Pronominaladverbien in die Lücken ein.

1. In meinem Zimmer steht ein Sofa. _Davor_ steht ein kleiner Tisch. _____ liegen tausend Dinge.
2. —Wir wollen heute ins Kino. —Wann geht ihr _____?
3. Im Sommer ziehe ich in eine neue Wohnung um. Ich freue mich schon _____.
4. Letztes Jahr hat Robert in Göttingen studiert und viel Spaß gehabt. Er denkt noch oft _____.
5. Gestern kam endlich ein Scheck von Melanies Familie. Sie hat sich sehr _____ gefreut. Sie hat lange _____ gewartet.
6. Morgen hat Thomas eine Klausur (*test*). Er hat keine Angst _____. Er hat sich gut _____ vorbereitet. Aber er muss schon um acht Uhr an der Uni sein. Er ärgert sich _____, weil er sich nämlich so früh noch nicht gut konzentrieren kann.

Übung 4 Eine Umfrage im Deutschkurs

Stellen Sie einander Fragen in kleinen Gruppen oder im Plenum.

BEISPIEL: Wie viele Leute haben Angst vor Prüfungen? →
Sechs Leute haben Angst davor.

1. Wie viele Leute interessieren sich für Politik? für Sport? für Yoga?
2. Wer hat Angst vor Prüfungen?
3. Wer denkt (oft, nie, manchmal) an das Leben nach dem Studium?
4. Wie viele Leute sind für oder gegen eine nationale Krankenversicherung? Wer soll dafür zahlen: Arbeitgeber? Arbeitnehmer? der Staat?
5. Wer freut sich auf das Ende des Studiums? auf eine Reise im Sommer?
6. Wer ärgert sich über die hohen Preise für Bücher? die hohen Studiengebühren?

Asking Questions: **wo**-Compounds°

Pronominaladverbien mit **wo**

Questions with prepositions asking about persons use **wen** or **wem** depending on the case required.

Auf wen wartest du?	*Who are you waiting for?* *(For whom . . .)*
Mit wem fährst du in Urlaub?	*Who are you going on vacation with? (With whom . . .)*
Über wen redet ihr?	*Who are you talking about? (About whom . . .)*

When asking questions with prepositions involving things or ideas, German normally uses a **wo**-coumpound.

Wofür interessiert er sich?	*What is he interested in?*
Woran denkst du?	*What are you thinking of?*
Worauf warten Sie?	*What are you waiting for?*

NOTE:

▶ Wo- becomes **wor-** when the preposition begins with a vowel, as for example **woran, worauf, worüber.**

▶ It is possible to start a prepositional question with **für was, an was,** or **auf was** instead of using a **wo**-compound; however, **wo**-compounds are preferred in standard German.

Übung 5 Das möchte ich wissen!

Formulieren Sie zuerst Fragen. Arbeiten Sie dann zu zweit und beantworten Sie die Fragen abwechselnd (*taking turns*).

BEISPIEL: **S1:** Wofür gibst du viel Geld aus?

S2: Für mein Handy. Worauf freust du dich?

Wofür . . .	freust du dich?
Womit . . .	denkst du oft?
Woran . . .	gibst du viel Geld aus?
Worauf . . .	interessierst du dich?
Worüber . . .	hast du Angst?
Wovor . . .	ärgerst du dich?
	beschäftigst du dich am liebsten?
	kannst du nicht verzichten?

The Subjunctive°

Der Konjunktiv

So far you have learned to make statements, make requests, and ask questions using the indicative mood. The subjunctive mood is used to express polite requests and to convey wishful thinking, conjectures, and conditions that are contrary to fact. You are already familiar with one frequently used subjunctive form: **möchte** (*would like*), commonly used to express a polite request.

Expressing Requests Politely

Ich **möchte** gern bezahlen.	*I would like to pay.*
Ich **hätte** gern eine Tasse Kaffee.	*I would like a cup of coffee.*
Könntest du mir einen Gefallen tun?	*Could you do me a favor?*
Würdest du mir 50 Euro leihen?	*Would you lend me 50 Euros?*

The forms **möchte, hätte, könntest,** and **würdest** are subjunctive forms of the verbs **mögen, haben, können,** and **werden.** They are frequently used in polite requests.

The Present Subjunctive II°: **haben, werden, können, mögen**

Konjunktiv II Präsens

	haben	werden	können	mögen
ich	hätte	würde	könnte	möchte
du	hättest	würdest	könntest	möchtest
er sie es	hätte	würde	könnte	möchte
wir	hätten	würden	könnten	möchten
ihr	hättet	würdet	könntet	möchtet
sie	hätten	würden	könnten	möchten
Sie	hätten	würden	könnten	möchten

The Present Subjunctive II is based on the simple past forms.

NOTE:

▶ Irregular weak verbs and strong verbs with an **a, o,** or **u** in the simple past add an umlaut to the vowel.

Infinitive	Simple Past	Present Subjunctive
haben →	hatte →	**hätte**
werden →	wurde →	**würde**

▶ Modals with an umlaut in the infinitive retain this umlaut in the subjunctive.

können →	konnte →	**könnte**
mögen →	mochte →	**möchte**

▶ Modals with no umlaut remain unchanged

wollen →	wollte →	**wollte**

Übung 6 Im Café: Was hätten Sie gern?

BEISPIEL: Ich _hätte gern_ ein Stück Käsekuchen.

1. Was _____ Sie _____?
2. Wir _____ einen Platz am Fenster.
3. Ich _____ einen Espresso.
4. Kerstin _____ einen Eiskaffee.
5. Herr und Frau Haese _____ einen Platz draußen.
6. Wir _____ zwei Eisbecher mit Vanilleeis und Sahne.
7. _____ du _____ ein Stück Kuchen?

Übung 7 Wünsche im Restaurant

Formulieren Sie die Wünsche und Fragen sehr höflich.

BEISPIEL: Ich will ein Bier. →
        Ich hätte gern ein Bier.
   oder Ich möchte gern ein Bier.

1. Wir wollen die Speisekarte.
2. Ich will eine Tasse Kaffee.
3. Mein Freund will ein Bier.
4. Und was wollen Sie?
5. Willst du ein Stück Kuchen?
6. Wollen Sie sonst noch etwas?
7. Wir wollen die Rechnung.

Übung 8 Etwas höflicher, bitte!

Drücken Sie die folgenden Wünsche höflicher aus.

BEISPIEL: Leih mir bitte 50 Euro. →
        Könntest du mir bitte 50 Euro leihen?
   oder Würdest du mir bitte 50 Euro leihen?

1. Tu mir bitte einen Gefallen.
2. Tut mir bitte einen Gefallen.
3. Leih mir bitte 100 Euro.
4. Wechseln Sie mir 200 Euro.
5. Geben Sie mir etwas Kleingeld.
6. Hilf mir bitte!
7. Helft mir bitte!
8. Unterschreiben Sie bitte.

Könnten Sie mir vielleicht drei Euro
geben? Ich möchte ein Eis.

The Use of **würde** with an Infinitive

In spoken German, one of the most commonly used forms of the subjunctive is **würde** plus infinitive. Like English *would*, the **würde** form can be used with almost any infinitive to express polite requests or wishes, or to give advice.

Würdest du mir **helfen?**   *Would you help me?*

Ich **würde** gerne **mitkommen.**   *I would like to come along.*

NOTE:

▶ Verbs that are generally not used with **würde** include **sein, haben, wissen,** and the modals.

Übung 9   Wie würden Sie darauf reagieren?

BEISPIEL: Sie haben eine Reise nach Österreich gewonnen. →
   Ich würde mich darüber freuen.

1. Sie sollen mit Freunden Bungee-Jumping gehen.
2. Sie hören, eine Freundin hat eine Million Dollar gewonnen.
3. Sie haben ein Praktikum bei einer deutschen Firma bekommen.
4. Sie sind im Supermarkt und haben Geld und Kreditkarte zu Hause gelassen.
5. Sie haben Ihre Autoschlüssel verloren.
6. Ihre Freunde planen eine Reise in die Karibik.

Ich hätte Angst davor.
Ich würde mich darüber freuen.
Ich würde mich darüber ärgern.
Ich würde das nicht glauben.
Ich würde das (nicht) machen.
?

Expressing Wishes and Hypothetical Situations

Ich **wünschte,** ich **wäre** mit der Arbeit fertig.

I wish I were finished with work.

Dann **würde** ich ins Kino mitkommen.

Then I would come along to the movies.

Ich **käme** gerne mit.

I would like to come along.

Wenn Benzin doch nicht so teuer **wäre.**

If only gasoline weren't so expensive.

Wenn ich nur **wüsste,** wo meine Schlüssel sind.

If I only knew where my keys were.

Wenn sie doch nur wüsste ...

The Present Subjunctive II: Strong and Weak Verbs

	kommen	sein	wissen	wünschen
ich	käme	wäre	wüsste	wünschte
du	käm(e)st	wär(e)st	wüsstest	wünschtest
er sie es	käme	wäre	wüsste	wünschte
wir	kämen	wären	wüssten	wünschten
ihr	kämet	wär(e)t	wüsstet	wünschtet
sie	kämen	wären	wüssten	wünschten
Sie	kämen	wären	wüssten	wünschten

NOTE:

▶ Strong verbs with **a, o,** or **u** in the simple past tense add an umlaut in the Subjunctive II. All strong verbs also add the ending **-e** in the first and third person singular. The **-e-** in the second person is optional.

Infinitive	Simple Past	Present Subjunctive
kommen	→ kam	→ käme
sein	→ war	→ wäre
fahren	→ fuhr	→ führe
bleiben	→ blieb	→ bliebe
gehen	→ ging	→ ginge

▶ While the Subjunctive II forms of strong verbs are increasingly replaced with **würde** plus infinitive, they are still used with a few common verbs like **gehen, kommen, fahren,** and **bleiben.** You will encounter such Subjunctive II forms mostly in writing.

¹dig up   Uli Stein 2006,

- ▶ The Present Subjunctive II of weak verbs is identical to the simple past tense.

  wünschen → wünschte → wünschte

  However, normally **würde** plus infinitive is used with weak verbs.

- ▶ Irregular weak verbs, as already pointed out on p. 363, add an umlaut to **a, o,** or **u** in the Subjunctive II.

  wissen → wusste → wüsste

- ▶ For emphasis, the particles **doch** and **nur** are often added to wishes introduced with **wenn.**

Übung 10 Was sind die Tatsachen hier?

Folgen Sie dem Beispiel.

BEISPIEL: Wenn ich nur wüsste, wo meine Autoschlüssel sind. →
         Ich weiß aber nicht, wo sie sind.

1. Ich wünschte, ich hätte keine Kreditkarte. Dann hätte ich keine Schulden.
2. Ich wünschte, die Kosten für das Studium wären nicht so hoch.
3. Ich wünschte, ich könnte genug Geld für eine Weltreise sparen.
4. Klaus wünschte, er würde nicht so viel Geld für SMS ausgeben.
5. Wenn ich nur wüsste, wo wir eine preiswerte Wohnung in München finden können.
6. Wenn ich nur mehr Zeit für Sport hätte.
7. Mein Freund würde sich gern einen BMW kaufen.
8. Ich wünschte, das Semester wäre zu Ende.
9. Die Studenten wünschten, sie müssten nicht so schwer arbeiten.

Übung 11 Nichts ist perfekt. Was wünschten diese Leute?

BEISPIEL: Peter hat nie Zeit für mich.
         Ich wünschte, *er hätte mehr Zeit für mich.*

1. Ich habe wenig Zeit für meine Freunde.
   Ich wünschte, …
2. Herr Schmidt fährt viel zu schnell auf der Autobahn.
   Seine Frau wünschte, …
3. Christine kommt nie pünktlich zur Klasse.
   Ich wünschte, …
4. Es gibt kein interessantes Programm im Fernsehen.
   Wir wünschten, …
5. Max ist fast immer total pleite.
   Er wünschte, …
6. Unsere Gäste gehen gar nicht nach Hause. (Es ist schon nach Mitternacht.)
   Wir wünschten, …
7. Ich weiß nicht, wo mein Handy ist.
   Ich wünschte, …
8. Klaus muss sehr viel Geld für Reparaturen an seinem Wagen ausgeben.
   Er wünschte, …

Übung 12 Heikle Situationen

Was würden Sie an seiner oder ihrer Stelle tun?

BEISPIEL: Felix wartet und wartet auf seine Freundin. An seiner Stelle würde ich allein ins Kino gehen.

1. Lukas   **2.** Marie   **3.** Tina   **4.** Herr Hansen   **5.** Felix

Landeskunde-Info

In Deutschland gibt es das sogenannte Ladenschlussgesetz (*law regulating store hours*). Die einzelnen (*individual*) Bundesländer regeln die Öffnungszeiten. In den meisten Ländern dürfen die Geschäfte montags bis samstags rund um die Uhr öffnen, wenn sie wollen. In einigen Ländern müssen sie spätestens um 22.00 Uhr schließen. In kleineren Städten und auf dem Land jedoch schließen viele Geschäfte besonders am Samstag schon vor 18.00 Uhr und sie sind oft auch nachmittags zwischen 12.00–14.00 Uhr geschlossen.

Am Sonntag und an Feiertagen bleibt praktisch alles geschlossen. Es gibt aber einige Ausnahmen: Bäckereien, Konditoreien und Blumengeschäfte dürfen für einige Stunden verkaufen. Apotheken sowie Geschäfte an Bahnhöfen und Flughäfen dürfen auch sonntags geöffnet sein.

Die Bank ist geschlossen!

◐ Was sehen Sie als Vorteil von Ladenschlussgesetzen? Was als Nachteil?

◐ Vergleichen Sie Ladenschlussgesetze in Ihrem Land/Staat mit denen in Deutschland. Gibt es solche Gesetze bei Ihnen?

Talking about Contrary-to-Fact Conditions

Compare the following sentences:

Wenn ich Geld **brauche, gehe** ich zur Bank.	*When I need money, I go to the bank.*
Wenn ich Geld **hätte, würde** ich mir einen neuen Wagen **kaufen.**	*If I had money, I would buy a new car.*
Wenn die Geschäfte in Deutschland länger geöffnet **wären, könnte** man vielleicht auch sonntags **einkaufen.**	*If the stores in Germany were open longer, one might be able to go shopping on Sundays as well.*

The first example states a condition of fact. The second and third examples state conditions that are contrary to fact. In the second one, the implication is that the speaker does not have enough money to buy a new car. In such cases, the Subjunctive II is used.

Analyse

Die Schnecke in diesem Cartoon singt ein bekanntes deutsches Volkslied (*folk song*).

▶ Circle the verbs that express the snail's wishful thinking. Note that these verb forms differ from those you have learned: they have no **-e** ending. What could be the reason for this?

▶ State the three things the snail wishes to be, to have, or to do. (Note that the suffix **-lein,** when added to a noun, makes a diminutive of this noun.)

    der Vogel (*bird*) → das Vöglein

    der Flügel (*wing*) → das Flüglein

    Sie möchte ...

▶ Was sind die Tatsachen (*facts*) ihres Lebens?
Eine Schnecke ist kein Vöglein; sie hat ... und ...

▶ Interessiert sich die zweite Schnecke für die Sängerin? Was würden Sie als Beweise (*evidence*) dafür anführen?

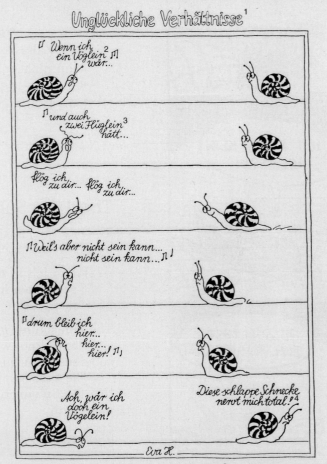

Unglückliche Verhältnisse[1]

[1]Er *Wenn ich ein Vöglein[2]* Er *wär...*

Er *und auch zwei Flüglein[3] hätt...*

Flög ich zu dir... Flög ich zu dir...

[1]*Weil's aber nicht sein kann... nicht sein kann...* [1]Er

[1]*drum bleib ich hier... hier... hier!* [1]Er

Ach, wär ich doch ein Vögelein!

Diese schlappe Schnecke nervt mich total![4]

— Eva H. —

[1]Unglückliche ... *Unhappy conditions* [2]*little bird* [3]*little wings* [4]Diese ... *This lame snail is getting on my nerves.*

Übung 13 Was würden Sie machen, wenn … ?

Sagen Sie, was Sie machen würden, wenn alles anders wäre.

BEISPIEL: Wenn ich Talent hätte, würde ich Opernsängerin werden.

Wenn ich Zeit hätte,	ein berühmter / eine berühmte ___??___
Geld	(z.B. Sänger/Sängerin) werden.
Talent	interessante Leute kennenlernen.
??	öfter ins Kino gehen.
	meine Familie öfter anrufen.
	einen tollen neuen Wagen kaufen.
	??

Übung 14 Rat geben

Stellen Sie sich vor, ein Freund / eine Freundin hat ein Problem. Was raten Sie?

BEISPIEL: **S1:** Ich kann nicht schlafen. Was soll ich nur machen?

S2: Wenn ich nicht schlafen könnte, würde ich etwas fernsehen.
oder Du solltest etwas fernsehen.

Problem	Rat
habe Zahnschmerzen	Arbeit suchen
kann nicht schlafen	Geld von jemand leihen
bin immer müde und schlapp	sofort zum Zahnarzt gehen
habe kein Geld	mehr Sport treiben
??	nicht so spät schlafen gehen
	aufstehen und Computerspiele spielen
	??

The Past Subjunctive II°   Der Konjunktiv II der Vergangenheit

The Past Subjunctive II is used to express wishes and conjectures concerning events in the past.

Wenn ich in der Lotterie **gewonnen hätte, wäre** ich überglücklich **gewesen.**	*If I had won the lottery, I would have been ecstatic.*

The conjecture (*If I had . . .*) speculates about an event in the past: The speaker did not win the lottery. Both English and German require the past subjunctive in this case.

The Past Subjunctive II forms are derived from the past perfect tense. Use the Subjunctive II form **hätte** or **wäre** plus the past participle of the main verb.

Infinitive	Past Perfect	Past Subjunctive II
kaufen	ich hatte gekauft	ich hätte gekauft
sein	ich war gewesen	ich wäre gewesen

Ich wünschte, ich **hätte** den neuen Porsche nicht **gekauft.**	*I wish I had not bought the new Porsche.*
Ein gebrauchter Wagen **wäre** billiger **gewesen.**	*A used car would have been cheaper.*

NOTE:

▶ Use **hätte** or **wäre** according to the same rules that determine the use of **haben** or **sein** in the perfect tense (see **Kapitel 7**).

Ich **habe** die Miete **bezahlt.**   Lars **hätte** die Miete nicht **bezahlt.**

Er **ist** in die Stadt **gefahren.**   Ich **wäre** nicht in die Stadt **gefahren.**

A clause stating a hypothetical situation usually begins with the conjunction **wenn.** As in English, the conjunction can be omitted, in which case the conjugated verb is placed at the beginning.

Wenn wir das nur gewusst hätten!   *If we had only known that!*

Hätten wir das nur gewusst!   *Had we only known that!*

Analyse

Schauen Sie sich den Cartoon an.

▶ Find the verb forms in the past subjunctive and give their infinitives.

▶ What is the woman speculating about?

▶ What stereotype does the cartoon allude to? Formulate a conclusion to the hypothesis **"Wenn ich als Blondine geboren wär(e) …"**

▶ What is the reality of her life?

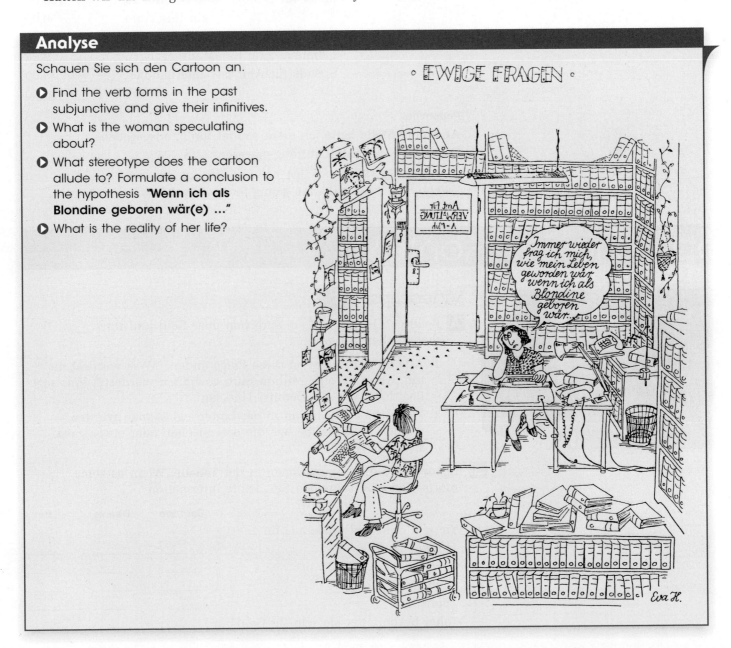

Übung 15 Andreas ist total pleite

Wie ist das passiert? Sie sehen hier Andreas' Ausgaben für eine Woche. Schauen Sie sich die Liste an. Wofür hat er Ihrer Meinung nach (*in your opinion*) zu viel Geld ausgegeben? Machen Sie ein paar Vorschläge (*suggestions*), was Sie anders gemacht hätten.

	Ausgaben
Geburtstagsgeschenk, Buch und Blumen für Freundin	€ 65,00
drei Sporthemden	120,00
neuer Drucker für seinen Computer	80,00
zweimal im Kino	22,00
zwei CDs auf dem Flohmarkt	6,50
zweimal mit Freunden in der Kneipe	25,00
Bücher für Biologie und Informatik	125,00
Benzin fürs Auto	90,00
Lebensmittel	48,00
dreimal zum Essen ausgegangen	59,00
Spende für Amnesty International	25,00
Handy	20,00

Redemittel

An seiner Stelle hätte ich nicht so viel für … ausgegeben.

Das wäre wirklich nicht nötig gewesen.

Braucht er wirklich … ? Ich hätte …

Zweimal … ? Einmal wäre genug (*enough*) gewesen.

Sprache im Kontext

Videoclips

A Beatrice, Dennis und Jan sprechen über Geld und ihre monatlichen Ausgaben.

1. Alle drei beantworten diese Frage anders: „Was würdest du tun, wenn du eine Million Euro gewinnen würdest?" Was sagt Beatrice? Was sagt Dennis? Und Jan?
2. Wenn Sie eine Million in der Lotterie gewinnen würden, würden Sie dasselbe wie die drei machen oder etwas ganz anderes? Was?

B Ergänzen Sie die Informationen in der Tabelle. Wenn es keine Information gibt, schreiben Sie „keine Information".

Wie viel Geld gibt er/sie aus für …	Beatrice	Dennis	Jan
Miete?	_____	_____	_____
Telefon?	_____	_____	_____
Lebensmittel?	_____	_____	_____
Sonstiges?	_____	_____	_____
Woher bekommt er/sie sein/ihr Geld?	_____	_____	_____

C Schauen Sie sich alle drei Interviews noch einmal an. Wen beschreiben diese Sätze? Schreiben Sie **B** für Beatrice, **D** für Dennis und **J** für Jan.

1. _____ kann nicht sehr gut mit Geld umgehen.
2. _____ will in der Zukunft Lehrer werden und kleine Kinder unterrichten.
3. _____ wohnt mit einer Freundin zusammen und teilt die Kosten.
4. _____ wohnt allein in einer Wohnung mit Kochnische.
5. _____ macht ein Magisterstudium in Kulturwissenschaften und studiert noch Politik dazu.
6. _____ lebt relativ sparsam.

Lesen

Zum Thema

Ein Interview. Interviewen Sie drei Studenten in der Klasse über das Thema Geld. Benutzen Sie die folgenden Fragen. Schreiben Sie die Antworten auf.

1. Hast du als Kind Taschengeld bekommen? Wie viel und wie oft?
2. Sollen Kinder Taschengeld bekommen? Warum / warum nicht?
3. Was war dein erster bezahlter Job? Was für Arbeit hast du gemacht? Wie hast du dein Geld ausgegeben?

Auf den ersten Blick

A Lesen Sie den Titel des Lesestücks auf Seite 374 und beantworten Sie die Frage im Untertitel. Spekulieren Sie!

1. Was könnten die drei Geldtypen sein?
   - ☐ drei verschiedene Währungen (*currencies*).
   - ☐ drei Beschreibungen von Menschen und wie sie ihr Geld ausgeben.

2. Ergänzen Sie die folgenden Sätze.
   - ▶ Wenn man klotzt, zeigt man, dass man viel _____ hat.
   - ▶ Wenn man knausert, gibt man _____ .
   - ▶ Wenn man gut haushalten kann, dann _____ .

B Dieser Text „Die drei Geldtypen" ist eine Meinungsumfrage. Sie müssen auf fünf Fragen oder Aussagen reagieren. Wählen Sie zwei davon und reagieren Sie persönlich.

BEISPIEL: Kaufen oder nicht? →
    Ich kaufe nicht viel. Ich gehe nicht gern einkaufen.

C Was für ein Geldtyp sind Sie? Kreuzen Sie an!

- ☐ Ich lebe auf Pump (*credit*).
- ☐ Ich spare Geld.
- ☐ Ich leihe meinen Freunden immer Geld.
- ☐ Ich kaufe keine CDs. Ich lade Musik vom Internet runter.
- ☐ Ich hebe den Kassenzettel immer auf, wenn ich etwas kaufe.
- ☐ Ich kaufe nur das, was ich wirklich brauche.
- ☐ Ich gehe mit Geld vernünftig um.
- ☐ Ich bin knauserig.

Die drei Geldtypen

to skimp / to show off / to budget

Knausern°, klotzen° oder haushalten° – oder wie gehst du mit dem lieben Geld um?

Kaufen oder nicht?

sich gönnen *grant or indulge (oneself)*

5 **A** Man lebt nur einmal. Deshalb sollte man sich ruhig auch mal was gönnen°.

B Sparen geht bei mir vor Ausgeben. Schließlich soll es später kein böses Erwachen geben und die meisten Dinge brauche ich eigentlich gar nicht.

10 **C** Wenn mir was wirklich wichtig ist, will ich es mir auch kaufen. Dafür würde ich dann auch bei anderen Dingen kürzer treten.

So bringst du Musik in dein Leben ...

own

A Mit CDs ist es wie mit Büchern. Es ist einfach schön, sie selber zu besitzen°.

15 **B** Musik höre ich für mein Leben gerne, aber jede CD muss ich mir deshalb noch lange nicht kaufen. Das meiste läuft ja sowieso im Radio oder ich kann es bei meiner Freundin anhören.

tausche aus *share, exchange*

C Mit meinen Freunden tausche ich oft CDs aus°. Meine absoluten Hits will ich aber schon selber haben.

20 ## Was machst du mit dem Kassenzettel?

why / receipt

A Bezahlt ist bezahlt, wozu° da noch die Quittung° aufheben?

fussy

B In Punkto Geld Ausgeben bin ich sehr penibel° und schreibe alles immer genau auf.

25 **C** Rechnungen hebe ich nur von größeren Dingen auf, auf die ich auch Garantie habe.

Hast du etwas zu verleihen?

A Ich leihe gerne anderen mal was aus. Und guten Freunden erst recht.

30 **B** Ich laufe anderen nicht gerne hinterher. Deswegen leihe ich anderen auch nicht gerne was aus – weder Geld noch Sachen.

C Ausleihen ist für mich kein Problem, wenn ich genau weiß, dass ich die Dinge dann auch wieder kriege.

Was machst du am Wochenende?

35 **A** Kino, Billard spielen oder Disco. Zusammen mit meinen Freunden fällt mir eigentlich immer was ein.

B Wir sind eine richtig gute Clique. Am Wochenende leihen wir uns oft Videos aus oder kochen was zusammen.

40 **C** Ich bin gerne unterwegs. Am Monatsende bin ich dann aber wegen leerer Kassen öfters mal mit Freunden zu Hause.

Ergebnis

Dreimal A und mehr. Du genießt das Leben und Langeweile ist für dich ein Fremdwort. Allerdings musst du aufpassen, dass du dabei nicht über deine Verhältnisse lebst und etwas mehr Ordnung und Überblick über 45 deine Finanzen könnte auch nicht schaden. Von Käufen oder Vergnügungen auf Pump solltest du eher die Finger lassen.

Dreimal B und mehr. Du bist zufrieden mit deinem Alltag, auch wenn die großen Überraschungen und spontanen Entscheidungen eher nicht dein Ding sind. Aber du findest dich ziemlich kompliziert und beneidest 50 Leute, die die Sachen cool angehen und einfach nur genießen° können. Ordnung ist dir wichtig und du denkst oft an morgen. Das sind gute Voraussetzungen°, um den Überblick über deine Finanzen zu halten. Dann kannst du sicher auch entspannter° an das Thema Geld rangehen.

Dreimal C und mehr. Du weißt was Spaß macht, doch von offenen 55 Rechnungen hältst du nichts. Das hört sich nach einer gesunden Mischung an. Deshalb sind Finanzen meist kein Thema für dich. Falls du doch mal über die Stränge geschlagen hast, trittst du bei anderen Ausgaben etwas kürzer, so dass alles wieder im Lot ist. Meistens zumindest!

enjoy

preconditions
in a more relaxed fashion

Zum Text

A Lesen Sie die Meinungsumfrage noch einmal durch und kreuzen Sie bei jedem Punkt A, B, oder C an.

1. Was ist das Resultat? Wo sind Sie gelandet? Schauen Sie die Ergebnisse an: Dreimal A und mehr? Dreimal B und mehr? Dreimal C und mehr?

2. Stimmt das mit Ihrer Antwort auf Aktivität C in **Auf den ersten Blick** überein?

3. Reden Sie zu dritt über Ihre Ergebnisse. Sind diese identisch? ganz verschieden?

B **Rat geben.** Was raten Sie jemandem, der in Kategorie A oder B fällt? Benutzen Sie die Vokabeln und Ausdrücke aus diesen Kategorien.

BEISPIEL: Ich würde dir raten: Kauf nichts auf Pump. Du musst Ordnung in deine Finanzen bringen. Lass die Finger von Käufen, die du nicht brauchst.

Sie: _____

_____

Zu guter Letzt

Ein Podcast über Geldtypen

Arbeiten Sie in Gruppen zu dritt und stellen Sie einen der drei Geldtypen in einem Podcast dar.

Schritt 1: Wählen Sie zuerst den Geldtyp aus:

▶ jemand, der knausert

▶ jemand, der klotzt

▶ jemand, der gut haushaltet

Schritt 2: Entwickeln Sie einen Sketch! Ihre Szene sollte zwei oder drei Charakteristiken des Geldtyps darstellen. Für Knausern könnten Sie, z.B., eine geizige (*stingy*) Person darstellen, die im Restaurant so wenig Geld wie möglich ausgeben will, bestellt nur ein Glas Wasser zu trinken und sehr wenig zu essen. Und wie ist das mit Trinkgeld? Die Kurzszene sollte wenigstens 15 Zeilen lang sein, und jede Person in Ihrem Team hat eine Rolle.

Schritt 3: Filmen Sie Ihren Sketch!

Schritt 4: Schreiben Sie eine kurze Einleitung zu Ihrem Sketch: Was ist der Zweck von diesem Podcast? Was finden Sie interessant daran?

Schritt 5: Präsentieren Sie Ihren Podcast der Klasse.

Wortschatz

Geldangelegenheiten	**Money Matters**
die **Ausgabe, -n**	expense
das **Benzin**	gasoline
der **Bleistift, -e**	pencil
die **Einnahmen** (*pl.*)	income
die **Ernährung**	food, nutrition
der **Haushalt, -e**	household
das **Heft, -e**	notebook
die **Heizung**	heat, heating system
der **Kugelschreiber, -**	ballpoint pen
der **Müll**	trash, garbage
die **Nebenkosten**	utilities; extra costs
das **Papier, -e**	paper
die **Reparatur, -en**	repair
das **Sparkonto,** *pl.* **Sparkonten**	savings account
der **Strom**	electricity
die **Studiengebühren** (*pl.*)	tuition, fees

Das Haus	**The House**
das **Bauernhaus, ̈er**	farmhouse
das **Dach, ̈er**	roof
das **Dachgeschoss, -e**	top floor, attic
die **Diele, -n**	front hall
der **Eingang, ̈e**	entrance
die **Etage, -n**	floor, story
der **Flur, -e**	hallway

die **Frühstücksnische, -n**	breakfast nook
die **Garderobe, -n**	wardrobe; closet
das **Gästezimmer, -**	guest room
das **Gerät, -e**	appliance, device
der **Mikrowellenherd, -e**	microwave oven
der **Neubau, -ten**	modern building
die **Spülmaschine, -n**	dishwasher
der **Staubsauger, -**	vacuum cleaner
der **Teppichboden, ̈**	wall-to-wall carpeting
die **Treppe, -n**	staircase
die **Umgebung, -en**	area, neighborhood, vicinity
die **Waschmaschine, -n**	washing machine
der **Wäschetrockner, -n**	clothes dryer

Verben	**Verbs**
sich ärgern über (+ *acc.*)	to be annoyed about
aus·geben (gibt aus), gab aus, ausgegeben	to spend (*money*)
bauen	to build
bitten um, bat, gebeten	to ask for, request
denken an (+ *acc.*), **dachte, gedacht**	to think about, of
ein·richten	to furnish, equip
ein·ziehen in (+ *acc.*), **zog ein, ist eingezogen**	to move in
sich freuen auf (+ *acc.*)	to look forward to
sich freuen über (+ *acc.*)	to be glad about
jobben	to work (*at a temporary job*)

mieten	to rent (*from someone*)	pleite	broke, out of money
sparen	to save	schmutzig	dirty
unterstützen, unterstützt	to support	sparsam	thrifty
vergleichen, verglich, verglichen	to compare	spätestens	at the latest
		übrig	left over
vermieten	to rent out (*to someone*)	unten	below; downstairs
verzichten auf (+ *acc.*)	to do without	nach unten	below; downstairs (*directional*)

Adjektive und Adverbien — **Adjectives and Adverbs**

ab	from, as of
ab 1. Juni (ab erstem Juni)	as of June 1st
bald	soon
deswegen	because of that
durchschnittlich	on average
eigen	own
ganz	complete(ly), total(ly), entire(ly)
monatlich	monthly
oben	above; upstairs
nach oben	above; upstairs (*directional*)

Sonstiges — **Other**

an deiner Stelle	if I were you, (if I were) in your place
die **Angst, ⸚e**	fear
Angst haben vor (+ *dat.*)	to be afraid of
der **Gruß, ⸚e**	greeting
viele Grüße	best wishes
die **Katze, -n**	cat
das **Tier, -e**	animal
die **Zeichnung, -en**	drawing

Das kann ich nun!

1. Machen Sie eine Liste mit den fünf größten Ausgaben, die Sie monatlich haben.

2. Beschreiben Sie das Haus, in dem Sie wohnen, das Haus Ihrer Eltern oder das Haus von Freunden. Wie viele Zimmer gibt es? Was für Zimmer? Wo liegen sie? Was für Geräte gibt es?

3. Beschreiben Sie Ihr Zimmer oder Ihr Klassenzimmer. Benutzen Sie dabei Wörter wie: **daneben, dazwischen, darauf, darunter,** usw.

4. Formulieren Sie passende Fragen zu folgenden Antworten. (Use a **wo**-compound.)
   a. _____? —Das Kind hat Angst vor Gewitter.
   b. _____? —Die Studenten beschäftigen sich mit Politik.
   c. _____? —Wir warten auf die Post.

5. Wie sagt man dies sehr höflich auf Deutsch?
   a. *You are at a restaurant and would like a table by the window. (two ways)*
   b. *You would like to see the menu.*
   c. *You would like to pay by credit card.*

6. Sie haben viele Wünsche. Wie drückt man sie auf Deutsch aus?
   a. *You wish you had more time and money.*
   b. *You wish you could stay home today.*
   c. *You are asking someone, very politely, to help you.*

7. Schreiben Sie die Sätze zu Ende.
   a. Wenn ich das Geld für eine Reise hätte, _____.
   b. Wenn ich gewusst hätte, dass es ein Gewitter gibt, _____.
   c. Du hast eine Erkältung? An deiner Stelle _____.

Viertes Zwischenspiel

Deutsche Einwanderung[1] nach Nordamerika

Laut US-Census aus dem Jahre 2000 gibt es ca. 43 Millionen Amerikaner deutscher Abstammung[2] in den USA. Die ersten Deutschen kamen schon 1608 nach Jamestown in Virginia. Die Menschen verließen ihre Heimat hauptsächlich aus religiösen, politischen oder wirtschaftlichen Gründen.

Im Jahre 1683 wanderten achtzehn Quäker und Mennoniten-Familien aus Krefeld mit Franz Daniel Pastorius (1651–1719) nach Pennsylvanien aus, wo sie die erste deutsche Siedlung[3], Germantown, gründeten. Die Beziehung zwischen Krefeld und Germantown wird bis heute aktiv gepflegt.

Amische in Lancaster County, Pennsylvanien

Germuntown in Pennsylvanien

1688 initiierte Pastorius mit Mitgliedern der Quäker-Gemeinde den ersten Protest gegen Sklaverei in Amerika. Sie verfassten eine Schrift gegen Sklaverei und verbreiteten sie unter den Mitgliedern ihrer religiösen Gemeinde.

Die Vorfahren der Amischen wurden in Europa wegen ihrer Religion verfolgt[4]. (Der Name „Amisch" kommt von dem Begründer der Sekte, dem Prediger Jakob Amman.) Noch heute leben viele Amische in den USA und Kanada. Die größten Siedlungen findet man in Ohio, Pennsylvanien und Indiana. Viele Amische sind dreisprachig: zu Hause sprechen sie ihren altdeutschen Dialekt und in der Kirche sprechen sie Hochdeutsch. Außerhalb der Gemeinschaft sprechen sie Englisch.

Im Jahre 1848 gab es in den deutschen Staaten eine demokratische Revolution. Deutschland existierte damals noch nicht als vereinigte Nation. Die Revolution scheiterte[5] allerdings und viele der Revolutionäre mussten flüchten[6]. Einer dieser Revolutionäre war Carl Schurz (1829–1906), der später im Bürgerkrieg und in der amerikanischen Regierung eine prominente Rolle spielte. Seine Frau Margarethe Schurz etablierte 1855 den ersten Kindergarten in Amerika in Watertown, Wisconsin, wo sie und ihr Mann sich eine Farm gekauft hatten.

Im 19. Jahrhundert gab es eine steigende Massenemigration Deutscher aus wirtschaftlichen Gründen. Sie suchten im Land der „unbegrenzten[7] Möglichkeiten" einen Neuanfang. So verließ Johann Jakob Astor 1784 seine Heimat in Walldorf bei Heidelberg. Mit 25 Dollar in der Tasche landete er in New York. Er brachte es zu einem Vermögen[8] im Immobilien-[9] und Pelzhandel[10].

Im Jahr 1847 wanderte Levi Strauss (1829–1902) von Bayern in die USA aus. 1853 kam er nach Kalifornien, wo er den Goldgräbern[11] stabile Hosen aus einem Material mit dem französischen Namen „serge de Nîmes" verkaufte. Danach wurde das Material „Denim" benannt. Wer hätte sich je vorstellen können, dass diese „Denims" als „Jeans" die Uniform von Generationen junger Menschen in der ganzen Welt sein würden?

In den 30er-Jahren des 20. Jahrhunderts flohen viele prominente deutsche und österreichische, jüdische sowie nicht-jüdische Intellektuelle vor politischer und rassistischer Verfolgung durch die Hitler-Diktatur nach Nordamerika, unter anderem Albert Einstein, Thomas Mann, Paul Tillich, Billy Wilder und Bertolt Brecht.

---

[1]*immigration* [2]*heritage* [3]*settlement* [4]*persecuted*

[5]*failed* [6]*flee* [7]*unlimited* [8]*fortune* [9]*real estate* [10]*fur trade*
[11]*gold-diggers*

Chronologie deutscher Einwanderung nach Amerika

1608   Deutsche Glasmacher kommen nach Jamestown in Virginia.

1683   Mennoniten und Quäker gründen Germantown, Pennsylvanien.

1732   Erste deutschsprachige Zeitung in Nordamerika, *Die Philadelphische Zeitung*, erscheint.

1741   Die Herrnhuter Brüdergemeinde (*Moravian Brethren*) siedelt im Bundesstaat Pennsylvanien an.

1743   Christoph Sauer druckt die erste deutsche Bibel in Amerika.

1750   Die erste große Welle deutscher Einwanderer kommt nach Neuschottland.

1777   Deutsche spielen eine große Rolle im amerikanischen Revolutionskrieg.

1845   Deutsche gründen Neu Braunfels in Texas.

1850–90   Massenmigration Deutscher nach Amerika

1894   Es gibt mehr als 800 deutschsprachige Zeitungen und Zeitschriften in Amerika.

1917   Erster Weltkrieg: antideutsche Hysterie bricht aus; die deutsche Sprache wird verboten.

1933   Hitler kommt an die Macht; jüdische und nichtjüdische Intellektuelle und Künstler verlassen Deutschland.

1950–   Über 120.000 Deutsche wandern nach Amerika aus.

Quelle: Adams, Willi Paul: *The German Americans: An Ethnic Experience* (1993).

Aktivität 2   Menschen und Momente

Es gibt viele wichtige Personen und Momente in der Geschichte der deutschen Einwanderung nach Nordamerika. Treiben Sie etwas Forschung und suchen Sie Informationen zu den folgenden Namen. Warum sind sie von Bedeutung?

1. Nikolaus de Meyer
2. Hessische Truppen
3. *Illinois Staatsanzeiger*
4. Mary McCauley
5. Barbara Heck
6. Joseph Hiester
7. J. A. Sutter
8. Frederick Pabst

Aktivität 3   Mini-Forschungsprojekte

1. Schreiben Sie eine Kurzbiografie eines Einwanderers / einer Einwanderin mit Bildern als Posterpräsentation.

2. Erforschen Sie die deutschen Wurzeln (*roots*) Ihrer Stadt oder Ihrer Region und schreiben Sie einen Bericht darüber.

3. Berichten Sie über eines der folgenden Themen:

   a. eine deutschsprachige Zeitung in Ihrem Land

   b. Nordamerikanische Firmen, die von Deutsch-Amerikanern gegründet wurden

4. Erstellen Sie eine Grafik über deutsche Einwanderung nach Nordamerika bzw. in Ihr Heimatland.

Aktivität 1   Historische Tatsachen

Verbinden Sie die passenden Satzteile miteinander.

1. Die ersten Deutschen ...
2. Dreizehn Krefelder Quäker und Mennoniten-Familien ...
3. Im 19. Jahrhundert ...
4. Margarethe Schurz ...
5. Carl Schurz musste sein Heimatland ...

a. ... gab es mehr als 800 deutschsprachige Zeitungen und Zeitschriften in Amerika.

b. ... gründete den ersten Kindergarten in Amerika.

c. ... kamen schon 1608 nach Jamestown.

d. ... aus politischen Gründen verlassen.

e. ... gründeten 1683 Germantown.

Barbara Heck

Medien und Technik

In diesem Kapitel

▶ **Themen:** Talking about television, newspapers, and other media; technology, computers

▶ **Grammatik:** Infinitive clauses with **zu,** verbs **brauchen** and **scheinen,** infinitive clauses with **um ... zu,** indirect discourse

▶ **Lesen:** „Gute Freunde im Netz" (Kerstin Kohlenberg)

▶ **Landeskunde:** Radio and television, inventions

▶ **Zu guter Letzt:** Podcast: Eine neue Erfindung

Gibt's was Neues in der Zeitung?

In der Zeitung steht ...

A Hier sehen Sie verschiedene deutschsprachige Zeitungen.

- ◐ Finden Sie drei Zeitungen, die deutsche Städtenamen tragen.
- ◐ Welche Zeitung ist für das Rheinland?
- ◐ Welche Zeitung erscheint wöchentlich (*weekly*)?
- ◐ Welche Zeitung erscheint hauptsächlich in Süddeutschland?
- ◐ Welche Zeitungen sind überregional, d.h. sie erscheinen in ganz Deutschland mit Nachrichten aus der ganzen Welt?

B Sie hören vier kurze Berichte aus dem Radio. Welche Schlagzeile passt zu welchem Bericht? Schreiben Sie die passende Zahl (1–4) vor die Schlagzeile.

_____ Kluges (*smart*) Köpfchen vorm Mittagessen

_____ Spender (*donor*) der Woche

_____ Unbekanntes Dorf im Iran entdeckt

_____ Autodieb (*car thief*) auf Surfbrett gefangen

Wörter im Kontext

Thema 1: Medien

Was gibt's im Fernsehen?

Thomas: Was gibt's denn heute Abend im Fernsehen?

Barbara: Nach den **Nachrichten** kommt im zweiten **Programm** um 20.15 Uhr ein Krimi, „Kommissar Süden und der Luftgitarrist".

Thomas: Ein Krimi, nein danke! Das ist nichts für mich. **Das ist mir zu blöd.** Was gibt's denn bei RTL?

Barbara: Eine Seifenoper, „Gute Zeiten, schlechte Zeiten" oder die Quiz-Show, „Wer wird Millionär?".

Thomas: Auch **nichts Gescheites.**

Barbara: Was für eine **Sendung** möchtest du denn sehen?

Thomas: Na, vielleicht Sport … oder einen **Dokumentarfilm.** Ich kann **mich** noch nicht **entschließen.**

Neue Wörter

die Nachrichten (*pl.*) news
das Programm program, channel
Das ist mir zu blöd. I think that's really stupid.
nichts Gescheites nothing decent
die Sendung TV program
mich … entschließen (sich entschließen) decide
der Bericht report
der Spielfilm movie, feature film
ansehen watch
Such dir was aus! (sich etwas aussuchen) Choose something!
Wie wäre es mit … ? How about…?
Na und? So what?
auf jeden Fall in any case
Wovon handelt sie? (handeln von) What's it about?

ZDF

17.15 hallo deutschland 95-933
Boulevardmagazin
17.45 Leute heute 264-556
Journal mit Pierre Geisensetter
18.00 SOKO 5113 16-204
TIPP Dtl. 2006/07. Schlitzohr. (Wh.)

KRIMISERIE

Schickl (Wilfried Klaus, l.) befragt Meister Ehinger (Martin Lüttge)

Leichenfund im Englischen Garten. Der Tote hat ein Loch im Kopf und ein aufgerissenes Ohrläppchen. Er war ein Zimmermannsgeselle auf der Walz. Nur gut, dass Hauptkommissar Horst Schickl den alten Freund Franz Ainfachnur als Verstärkung für den verletzten Theo angefordert hat. Denn in dessen Heimatstadt Meutenstetten kennt man sich mit traditionellem Brauchtum aus. **Mit** Hartmut Schreier, Bianca Hein, Christofer v. Beau, Michael Baral, Frank Ruttloff
19.00 heute 50-020
19.20 Wetter 7-915-001
19.25 WISO wiso.zdf.de 9-877-321
Wirtschaft & Soziales
Geplant u. a. Tipp: Mietnebenkosten – Was dürfen Vermieter berechnen? Moderation: Michael Opoczynski

20.15 Kommissar Süden und der Luftgitarrist Dtl. 2009 4-496-469
TIPP

TV-KRIMI

NEU Weiß Süden (Ulrich Noethen, l.) mehr? Kollege Martin Heuer (Martin Feifel) vermutet es

Martin Heuer, Freund und Kollege von Kommissar Tabor Süden, steht bei der WM-Ausscheidung im Luftgitarrespielen im Finale. Plötzlich ist sein härtester Konkurrent unauffindbar: Edward Loos, Architekt und Eigenbrötler, kann sich doch nicht in Luft aufgelöst haben. Nicht der einzige Fall für das Vermisstendezernat 11. Ein Mann behauptet steif und fest, seine durch den Tsunami im Jahr 2004 umgekommene Frau in der Münchner U-Bahn gesehen zu haben. – Ebenso ungewöhnlich wie düster.
Tabor Süden .... Ulrich Noethen
Sonja Feyerabend .... Jeanette Hain
Freya Epp .... Johanna Bantzer
und: Hubertus Hartmann, Olivia Pascal, Harry Täschner, Anka Lea Sarstedt, Philipp Moog. Regie: Dominik Graf **90 Min.**
INFO Zweiter Film der Reihe nach Friedrich Ani, der auch das Drehbuch schrieb.
21.45 heute-journal Mit S. Seibert 426-730
22.12 Wetter 202-157-662

RTL

19.05 Alles, was zählt   751-317
Familienserie, Dtl. 2009 (659)
Céline äußert ihren Unmut: Sie fürchtet, dass Maximilian durch die Zusammenarbeit mit Simone wieder in ein Netz von Lügen und Intrigen gerät. Nina erwischt Axel erneut mit ihrer Nebenbuhlerin. Annette nimmt überraschend Kontakt zu Ingo auf. Neue Chance, neues Glück?

19.40 Gute Zeiten,   2-046-556
schlechte Zeiten (4222)

SERIE

Kampfhähne: Leon (Daniel Fehlow, l.) und Tayfun (Tayfun Baydar)
Herzklopfen bei Emily: Lenny bittet um ein Treffen. Ist Caroline damit für ihn passé? Nach Gerners Attacke fragt sich Jasmin, ob Dominik wirklich eine verkorkste Frau wie sie verdient hat. Tayfun arbeitet bei Leon seine Spielschulden ab, doch von Versöhnung keine Spur.

20.15 Wer wird Millionär?   841-865
TIPP Deutschland 2009

QUIZSHOW

Wieder kommt es auf Schnelligkeit an: Der / die Schnellste macht bei Günther Jauch das Rennen
Erstmals diente das Quiz, beziehungsweise das indische Pendant zu „WWM?", als Vorlage für einen Film. Das in Indien fast nur mit indischen Darstellern gedrehte Bollywood-Märchen „Slumdog Millionaire?" (Kinostart war der 19. März) handelt vom bisher größten Tag im Leben des 18-jährigen Jamal Malik: Nur eine Frage trennt ihn vom Hauptpreis in der Quizshow „Who Wants to Be a Millionaire?". Doch kurz vor dem Finale wird der Kandidat beschuldigt, betrogen zu haben… Der britische Regisseur Danny Boyle wurde für sein Werk mit acht Oscars belohnt. – Nä. Show: Freitag

WEITERE SPIELFILME

11.30 NDR Rache ist süß 🅢🅦
KOMÖDIE Starreporter Jeff soll für seinen rachsüchtigen Boss einen dunklen Fleck auf der weißen Weste einer attraktiven Richterin finden… Nette Unterhaltung. SV 5-187-268
USA 1941 D Walter Pidgeon, Rosalind Russell, Edward Arnold R Norman Taurog 80 Min. →12.50 ➡

20.15 PRO 7 Borderline – Unter Mordverdacht
NEU: THRILLER Gefängnispsychologin Lila wird verdächtigt nach einem Sorgerechtsstreit um die beiden Kinder, ihren Ex-Mann und dessen Freundin ermordet zu haben. Sie glaubt, den wahren Täter aus ihrem Umfeld zu kennen… Spannend. SV 83-341
USA 2002 D Gina Gershon, Sean Patrick Flanery, Eddie Driscoll R Evelyn Purcell 105/87 Min. →22.00 ↗

21.45 BR Bella Martha
LIEBESKOMÖDIE Martha kann gut kochen, aber vom Genießen versteht sie nichts. Ein temperamentvoller Italiener und ein kleines Mädchen tauen das Herz der verschlossenen Köchin auf… Garniert mit feinem Humor. SV 7-202-744
Dtl./Ital. 2001 D Martina Gedeck, Sergio Castellitto B+R Sandra Nettelbeck 100 Min. →23.25 ↗

22.05 MDR Tatort: Das Phantom
TV-KRIMI Schenk erkennt, daß er vor Jahren einen Unschuldigen hinter Gitter gebracht hat. Bevor er den Fehler wieder gutmachen kann, bricht der junge Mann aus und tötet einen Polizisten… Melancholische Story. SV 3-728-812
Dtl. 2003 D Klaus J. Behrendt, Dietmar Bär, Roman Knizka R Kaspar Heidelbach 90 Min. →23.35 ↗

23.20 SWR Virus im Paradies (1)
TV-THRILLER Der Tod eines bretonischen Hühnerzüchters alarmiert Ärzte und Politiker. Die Hühner werden getötet, es beginnt die Jagd auf das Virus… 2. Teil: am Mi. SV 9-844-687
Frkr./Schw./Island/Belg. 2003 D Richard Bohringer R Oliver Langlois 90 Min. →0.50 ↗

0.45 DAS VIERTE Cocktail für eine Leiche 🅢🅦
THRILLER Um ihrem Professor zu beweisen, daß ein perfekter Mord möglich ist, töten zwei Studenten einen Kommilitonen und geben am Tatort eine Party… Von nur einem Kamerastandpunkt aus gedrehter Klassiker. SV 41-952-850
USA 1948 D James Stewart, Farley Granger, John Dall R Alfred Hitchcock FSK 12 90/76 Min. →2.15 ↗

SYMBOLE: ⬆ Großartig   ↗ Gelungen
↘ Annehmbar   ⬇ Schwach

Barbara: Um 20.15 Uhr gibt es ein Fußballspiel … und später um 22.40 Uhr kommt ein **Bericht** über die Arbeitslage in Deutschland. Aber keine Dokumentarfilme. Ich möchte mir mal einen guten **Spielfilm ansehen.**

Thomas: Du hast ja das Programm für heute Abend. **Such dir was aus!**

Barbara: **Wie wäre es mit** „Cocktail für eine Leiche" von Hitchcock?

Thomas: So ein alter Schinken (*old hat*).

Barbara: **Na und?** Das ist **auf jeden Fall** ein guter, alter Klassiker. Ach, nein, Moment, der kommt erst um 0.45 Uhr.

Thomas: Lass mal sehen … Um 22.05 Uhr läuft im MDR „Tatort: Das Phantom."

Barbara: Das ist mir auch zu spät.

Thomas: Wie wäre es mit einer Liebeskomödie, „Bella Martha" um 21.45 Uhr?

Barbara: Klingt gut. **Wovon handelt** sie denn?

Ergänzen Sie die folgenden Sätze. Die Informationen finden Sie im Gespräch zwischen Barbara und Thomas.

1. „Kommissar Süden und der Luftgitarrist" läuft im zweiten _____.
2. Thomas möchte vielleicht Sport oder einen _____ sehen.
3. Barbara möchte gern einen _____ sehen.
4. Thomas meint, Serien wie „Gute Zeiten, schlechte Zeiten" sind nichts _____.
5. Um 22.40 kommt im Zweiten Programm ein _____ über die Arbeitslage in Deutschland.
6. Barbara fragt Thomas, wovon der Film „Bella Martha" _____.

Was steht in der Zeitung?

Hier sind einige typische Rubriken (*sections*) aus der Zeitung, bzw. der
Zeitschrift.

A Welche Rubriken …

- ❍ lesen Sie immer? nie? manchmal?

- ❍ finden Sie am interessantesten?

B Finden Sie nun eine passende Schlagzeile für die Rubriken.

Rubriken

Lokalnachrichten	**Wirtschaft** und **Börse**	Reisen
Inland	Arbeit und Karriere	**Horoskop**
Ausland	Wissen und **Forschen**	Kultur
Politik	Menschen und Medien	
Aktuelles	Sport	

SCHLAGZEILEN

Outsourcing:
Die Arbeit wandert aus

Zehn Fragen zu Afghanistan

Niedersachsens Justizminister kritisiert Kanzlerin

USA gehen gegen
Cyberkriminalität vor

DELFINE[1] ERKENNEN
SICH AM NAMEN

Atomstreit mit Iran

MACHT IHR BERUF NOCH SPASS

Mallorca: Ab in den Urlaub!

15 Kinder bei Busunfall schwer verletzt

Bayreuther Festspiele
am 25. Juli eröffnet

WIRD DER RHEIN SAUBERER?

Kabinett verabschiedet Rekordschulden-Haushalt

Fußball-Weltmeisterschaft:
12 Städte, 32 Mannschaften, 64 Spiele

Räuber mit Karnevalsmaske überfällt Kiosk

BÖRSE REAGIERT MIT ABSTURZ

Klima in Kopenhagen wird immer schlechter

WAS SAGEN UNS DIE STERNE?

"Ich wollte keinen typischen Familienfilm"

Firmen sollen Twitter für Kundenservice nutzen

[1]*dolphins*

Aktivität 1   Das Fernsehprogramm

Suchen Sie im Fernsehprogramm eine Sendung, die zu jeder der folgenden
Kategorien passt.

BEISPIEL: Spielfilm →
   Um 20.15 Uhr kommt der Spielfilm „Der Mann auf der Brücke"
   im ersten Programm.

1. Nachrichten
2. Komödie (*f.*)
3. Talk-Show (*f.*)
4. Krimi (*m.*)
5. Reportage (*f.*)
6. Dokumentarfilm
7. Sportsendung
8. Spielfilm
9. Wetterbericht
10. Seifenoper

SPIELFILME DES TAGES

20.15 SUPER RTL

Edward mit den Scherenhänden

TRAGIKOMÖDIE Der Humunculus Edward (Johnny Depp) ist die letzte, unvollkommene Schöpfung eines verstorbenen Erfinders: Statt mit Händen ist er nur mit Scheren ausgestattet. Die

USA 1990 R: Tim Burton D: Johnny Depp, Winona Ryder, Dianne Wiest, Anthony Michael Hall, Robert Oliveri, Kathy Baker, Conchata Ferrell

Avon-Beraterin Peg findet den Jüngling und bringt ihn in ihre Reihenhausidylle, wo er bald eifrig Hecken und Frisuren stutzt. Die Liebe zur jungen Kim (Winona Ryder) wird ihm zum Verhängnis.

115 Min. → 22.10   49-187-510
Satirischer Märchentrip

ACTION   SPANNUNG   EROTIK   HUMOR
●   ●●   ●●

FSK: 6

20.15 DAS ERSTE

Der Mann auf der Brücke

DRAMA Der Kioskbesitzer Bernie (Peter Lerchbaumer, l.) will sich das Leben nehmen - und rettet dabei zufällig das des kleinen Lukas. Dessen Vater (Stephan Kampwirth), der Politiker Tornow, benutzt den Selbstmordkandidaten für seine Wahlkampagne.

90 Min. → 21.45   9-790-442
Sensibel und ungewöhnlich

ACTION   SPANNUNG   EROTIK   HUMOR

21.45 BAYERN

Good Woman – Ein Sommer in Amalfi

DRAMA 1930. Die New Yorkerin Erlynne (Helen Hunt, mit Mark Umbers) reist an die Amalfi-Küste. Sie hofft auf die Bekanntschaft spendabler Herren. Tatsächlich zückt für die reiche Mr. Windermere das Scheckbuch. Leider ist er verheiratet.

85 Min. → 23.10   8-853-423
Tolle Oscar-Wilde-Adaption

ACTION   SPANNUNG   EROTIK   HUMOR

SERIE

21.15 PRO 7

Harper's Island

MINISERIE Auf Harper's Island trifft sich eine Hochzeitsgesellschaft (u. a. Christopher Gorham, l.). Ein Serienkiller sorgt dafür, dass die Gästeliste immer kürzer wird. – Die Serie endet mit Folge 13 und der Auflösung, wer der Mörder ist.

60 Min. → 22.15   8-772-626
Folge: Einer nach dem anderen

INFO & WISSEN

22.15 RTL

stern TV

INFOMAGAZIN Heute beschäftigt sich Günther Jauch mit „Kindern am Rande der Gesellschaft". So fragt er, was aus den Kindern von Köthen wurde: 1994 berichtete das Magazin erstmals über einen kriminellen Neunjährigen und seine Brüder.

105 Min. → 0.00   504-591
Moderation: Günther Jauch

54

DAS ERSTE   ARD

5.00 Tagesschau	2-531-046
5.05 Plusminus	3-954-572
5.30 Morgenmagazin	59-967-336
9.00 heute	40-423
9.05 Rote Rosen	9-994-336
9.55 Wetter	3-864-591
10.03 Brisant	300-092-862
10.25 Der Dicke	4-166-125
11.15 In aller Freundschaft	3-157-249
12.00 heute mittag	58-404
12.15 ARD-Buffet	9-567-423
Ratgeber	
13.00 Mittagsmagazin	71-012
Magazin	
14.00 Tagesschau	34-268
14.10 Rote Rosen	2-023-244
Telenovela	
15.00 Tagesschau	87-336
15.10 Sturm der Liebe	8-650-046
Telenovela	
Mit Ivanka Brekalo	
16.00 Tagesschau	52-626
16.10 Elefant, Tiger & Co.	3-866-881
Doku-Soap	
Heiße Ware	
17.00 Tagesschau	13-713
17.15 Brisant	7-911-684
18.00 Verbotene Liebe	16-249
18.25 Marienhof	6-354-688
18.50 Eine für alle	65-133
Herzensangelegenheiten	
19.20 Das Quiz	320-171
19.45 Wissen vor 8	7-839-881
19.50 Das Wetter	4-984-591
19.55 Börse im Ersten	4-983-862
20.00 Tagesschau	66-607

DRAMA

20.15 Der Mann auf der Brücke
FILM   9-790-442
➡ D 2009
Mit Henry Stange, Stephan Kampwirth, Claudia Michelsen
Der lebensmüde Bernie (Peter Lerchbaumer) rettet versehentlich das Leben des kleinen Lukas. Der erobert das Herz des Pessimisten.
Erstausstrahlung   **Siehe Tipp**

21.45 hart aber fair   2-959-607
LIVE Frank Plasberg diskutiert mit Politikern und Prominenten über aktuelle Themen, die Deutschland beschäftigen.

23.00 Tagesthemen	8-423
23.30 Berlin – Prenzlauer Berg	54-220
Doku	
0.15 Nachtmagazin	966-737
0.35 Leaving Las Vegas – Liebe	

FILM bis in den Tod   1-184-263
⬆ Drama, USA 1995
Mit Nicolas Cage, Elisabeth Shue, Julian Sands

2.20 Tagesschau	16-051-843
2.25 Sturm der Liebe	6-847-089
3.15 Berlin – Prenzlauer Berg	4-715-621
Doku	
4.00 Bahnstrecken	7-050-114
4.10 Tagesschau	19-991-843
4.15 hart aber fair	7-544-060

ZDF   ZDF

5.00 hallo deutschland	9-508-442
5.30 Morgenmagazin	59-965-978
9.00 heute	48-065
9.05 Volle Kanne –	
Service täglich	2-567-775
Magazin	
10.30 Alisa – Folge deinem Herzen	1-873-794
Telenovela	
11.15 Die Rosenheim-Cops	3-148-591
Krimiserie	
12.00 heute mittag	56-046
12.15 drehscheibe Dt.	9-565-065
13.00 Mittagsmagazin	38-442
Magazin	
14.00 heute – in Dt.	33-539
14.15 Die Küchenschlacht	82-607
Kochshow	
Alfons Schuhbeck sucht den Spitzenkoch	
15.00 heute – Sport	86-607
15.15 Tierische Kumpel	7-159-607
Doku-Soap	
16.00 heute – in Europa	51-997
16.15 Alisa – Folge deinem Herzen	9-192-591
Telenovela	
17.00 heute – Wetter	11-355
17.15 hallo deutschland	77-539
17.45 Leute heute	379-022
Magazin	
18.00 SOKO Wismar	41-794
Krimiserie. Am helllichten Tag	
18.50 Lotto Ziehung	2-201-997
19.00 heute	32-626
19.20 Wetter	7-824-959
19.25 Küstenwache	8-381-171
Spionage auf der Ostsee	

MAGAZIN

20.15 Aktenzeichen XY: ... ungelöst   9-798-084
LIVE U.a. Nürtingen: Überfall auf einen Drogeriemarkt / Koblenz: Führt Auto zum Täter? Kripo jagt Bankräuber
Rudi Cerne bittet um Hinweise in einem Vermisstenfall.
Ein Familienvater aus Hagen ist seit zwei Jahren verschwunden.

21.45 heute-journal	291-046
22.15 Abenteuer Wissen	852-171
Wissensmagazin, D 2009	
Die fruchtbare Erde – Mit den Füßen getreten	
22.45 auslandsjournal	7-308-065
23.15 Markus Lanz	1-595-607
0.20 heute nacht	5-080-896
0.35 Neue braune Welle	2-190-060
Die Jugend im Visier der Rechtsextremen	
1.20 SOKO Wismar	2-101-176
Krimiserie	
2.05 heute	16-038-992
2.10 Abenteuer Wissen	6-813-447
Wissensmagazin, D 2009	
2.40 Markus Lanz	7-638-060
3.55 heute	91-716-379
4.00 auslandsjournal	4-959-195
4.30 @rt of animation	7-049-008
4.45 Leute heute	2-692-089

RTL   RTL

5.10 Posch ermittelt	3-979-881
5.35 Explosiv	3-960-133
6.00 Punkt 6	4-784-249
7.30 Alles was zählt	9-978
8.00 Unter uns	5-797
8.30 Gute Zeiten, schlechte Zeiten	4-268
9.00 Punkt 9	5-997
9.30 Mitten im Leben!	51-317
10.30 Mein Baby	4-404
11.00 Die Kinderärzte	5-133
11.30 Unsere erste gemeinsame Wohnung	8-220
12.00 Punkt 12	619-268
14.00 Oliver Geissen	34-626
Moderation: Oliver Geissen	
15.00 Mitten im Leben!	92-626
Doku-Soap	
16.00 Mitten im Leben!	96-442
Von mutigen ersten Schritten in eine bessere Zukunft über aufreibende Familienkonflikte bis hin zu berührenden Auseinandersetzungen mit harten Schicksalsschlägen.	
17.00 Ritas Welt	9-751
Sex in Gang vier	
17.30 Unter uns	4-828
Daily Soap	
18.00 Explosiv	1-997
18.30 Exclusiv	11-794
18.45 RTL aktuell	744-292
19.05 Alles was zählt	805-713
Daily Soap	
19.40 Gute Zeiten, schlechte Zeiten	3-614-713

COACHINGSHOW

20.15 Nachbarschaftsstreit – Kolb greift ein   690-133
Der Rechtsanwalt und Mediator Ernst Andreas Kolb setzt zerstrittene Nachbarn an einen Tisch. Er hat schon viele verfahrene Situationen erlebt und bei schon mehr als einem Nachbarschaftsstreit einen Ausweg gefunden. Heute: Familie Knopf vs. Kleingarten

21.15 Unser neues Zuhause	6-686-510
22.15 stern TV	504-591
LIVE Das Fernsehmagazin mit Günther Jauch **Siehe Tipp**	
0.00 Nachtjournal	5-195
Mod.: Christof Lang	
0.27 Wetter	202-243-973
0.35 Extra – Das RTL-Magazin	
Mod.: Birgit Schrowange	7-542-331
1.40 Nachbarschaftsstreit – Kolb greift ein	6-854-379
Coachingshow	
2.30 Oliver Geissen	6-909-843
Mod.: Oliver Geissen	
3.20 Nachtjournal	9-671-398
Mod.: Christof Lang	
3.50 Das Strafgericht	7-014-398
Gerichtsshow	
Vorsitz: Richter Ulrich Wetzel	
4.40 Unsere erste gemeinsame Wohnung	2-645-282

⬆ gelungen   ⮕ annehmbar   ⬇ schwach   ARD, ZDF: alle Showviewzahlen mit VPS

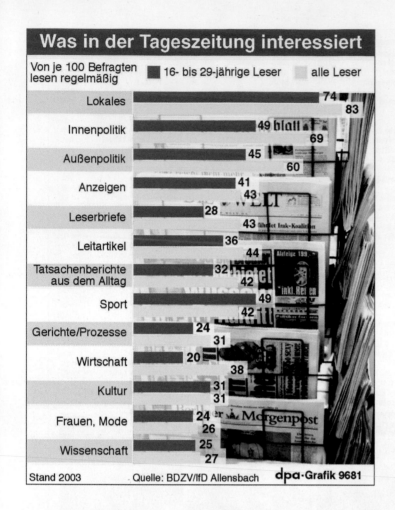

Was in der Tageszeitung interessiert

Von je 100 Befragten lesen regelmäßig — ■ 16- bis 29-jährige Leser   □ alle Leser

Kategorie	16- bis 29-jährige Leser	alle Leser
Lokales	74	83
Innenpolitik	49	69
Außenpolitik	45	60
Anzeigen	41	43
Leserbriefe	28	43
Leitartikel	36	44
Tatsachenberichte aus dem Alltag	32	42
Sport	49	42
Gerichte/Prozesse	24	31
Wirtschaft	20	38
Kultur	31	31
Frauen, Mode	24	26
Wissenschaft	25	27

Stand 2003   Quelle: BDZV/IfD Allensbach   **dpa·Grafik 9681**

Aktivität 2   Was in der Zeitung interessiert

Schritt 1: Zeitungssprache. Was bedeuten diese Wörter und Ausdrücke?

1. Lokales
2. Anzeigen
3. Leitartikel
4. Tatsachenberichte aus dem Alltag
5. Gerichte/Prozesse
6. Wirtschaft
7. Wissenschaft

a. *economy*
b. *court proceedings*
c. *ads*
d. *lead articles*
e. *local news*
f. *science*
g. *everyday news*

Schritt 2: Was lesen die Deutschen? Schauen Sie sich die Grafik an.

1. Die meisten Deutschen lesen hauptsächlich _____.

2. Sechzehn- bis neunundzwanzigjährige Leser interessieren sich mehr für _____ als alle Leser.

3. Genau ein Viertel der 16- bis 29-jährigen Leser liest über _____.

4. Sechzig Prozent aller Leser interessiert sich für _____.

5. _____ ist für alle Leser und auch für 16- bis 29-jährige Leser mit 31 Prozent gleich interessant.

Hier klicken!

Weiteres zum Thema Medien finden Sie bei **Deutsch: Na klar!** im World-Wide-Web unter **www.mhhe.com/dnk6.**

Aktivität 3   Hin und her: Wie informieren sie sich?

Wie informieren sich diese Personen? Was lesen sie zur Unterhaltung? Stellen Sie Fragen an Ihren Partner / Ihre Partnerin.

BEISPIEL: **S1:**   Was sieht Martin gern im Fernsehen? Was liest er oft?

S2:   Er _____.

Person	Fernsehshows	Zeitungen und Zeitschriften
Martin	Talk-Shows und Dokumentarfilme	*die Zeit*
Stephanie		
Patrick	Quizsendungen wie „Der Preis ist heiß", die Nachrichten	*die Frankfurter Allgemeine* und *Stern*
Kristin		
Mein Partner / Meine Partnerin		

Landeskunde-Info

Lange Zeit gab es in Deutschland nur drei Programme. Die ARD (Arbeitsgemeinschaft der Rundfunkanstalten Deutschlands) – auch „Erstes Programm" genannt – und das ZDF (Zweites Deutsches Fernsehen) senden auch heute noch das erste und zweite Programm. Das „Dritte Programm" besteht aus regionalen Sendern aus ganz Deutschland. In diesen drei Programmen werden die meisten Sendungen nicht durch Werbung unterbrochen. Alle Werbespots werden blockweise zu einem bestimmten Zeitpunkt gezeigt. Jeder Haushalt muss für Radio und Fernsehen eine Gebühr, die sogenannte Rundfunkgebühr, bezahlen. Man zahlt die Gebühr an die GEZ (Gebühreneinzugszentrale).

Ich zahl. Die Rundfunkgebühren

WDR N1/97121

www.gez.de

☐ Ich bin noch nicht bei der GEZ angemeldet
☐ Ich bin schon angemeldet unter der Nr. _____

Name   Geburtsdatum

Straße/Hausnummer

Postleitzahl   Ort

Ich melde an   ☐ Radio   ☐ Fernsehgerät   ab

Ich zahle   ☐ jährlich im Voraus   ☐ vierteljährlich im Voraus
                zum 1. Januar   zum 1. Januar, April, Juli, Oktober
             ☐ halbjährlich im Voraus   ☐ in der Mitte eines Dreimonats-
                zum 1. Januar, Juli   zeitraumes jeweils zum 15.

Ich zahle   ☐ per Überweisung/mit Zahlschein   ☐ Lastschrift (s.u.)

Kontonummer   Bankleitzahl

Bank/Sparkasse   Kontoinhaber

Datum   Unterschrift

Bitte informieren Sie die GEZ, wenn Sie umziehen oder einen Umzug planen. Formulare zur **Änderungsmeldung** liegen bei Banken und Sparkassen aus. Auch telefonisch, per Fax oder im Internet können Sie (unter Angabe Ihrer Teilnehmer-Nummer) Ihre Anschrift korrigieren lassen. **Bitte melden Sie sich hier ab und unter neuer Anschrift wieder an.** www.gez.de

GEZ Service-Hotline 0180 501 65 65 · Faxline 0180 582 10 10 (12 Cent/Min)

Übrigens: Für Radio und TV zahlen Sie nur 53 Cent am Tag

Antwort

GEZ

50656 Köln

Heutzutage gibt es in deutschsprachigen Ländern eine Vielfalt an Fernsehprogrammen. Kabelfernsehen und Satellitenprogramme, z.B. PRO 7, NBC Super-Channel und CNN, sind sehr beliebt und zeigen viele Sendungen im amerikanischen Stil. Kabelfernsehen muss man abonnieren. Für Sender wie Premiere (sogenannte Pay TV) muss man weitere Gebühren bezahlen.

▶ Gibt es bei Ihnen Programme ohne Werbung im Fernsehen?

▶ Für welche Programme muss man bei Ihnen bezahlen?

Aktivität 4   Das sehe ich gern!

Was mögen Sie im Fernsehen? Warum? Was finden Sie nicht besonders gut im Fernsehen? Geben Sie Beispiele.

BEISPIEL: Ich mag Serien, zum Beispiel „Tatort". Die finde ich spannend. Aber Quizsendungen finde ich schrecklich langweilig.

Krimis	gewöhnlich	aktuell
Nachrichten	immer	interessant
Dokumentarfilme	meistens	komisch
Quizsendungen	schrecklich	langweilig
Talk-Shows	sehr	schlecht
Seifenopern		spannend
Sport		unterhaltsam
Serien		
Musik		
Komödien		
Musicals		
Dramen		

SERIE
18.10 PRO 7
Die Simpsons

SPIELFILME DES TAGES
22.30 ZDF
The Good German – In den Ruinen von Berlin

INFO & WISSEN
22.15 ZDF
Abenteuer Wissen

SERIE
14.50 PRO 7
The Big Bang Theory

UNTERHALTUNG
18.00 VOX
mieten, kaufen, wohnen

SPORT
18.30 DAS ERSTE
Bundesliga

SHOW
20.15 VOX
Kocharena

23.00 NDR
Psycho

Aktivität 5 Eine Sendung auswählen

Besprechen Sie mit einem Partner / einer Partnerin, was Sie heute Abend sehen möchten. Wählen Sie eine Sendung aus dem Fernsehprogramm in **Aktivität 2** aus.

S1	S2
1. Was gibt es heute Abend im Fernsehen?	2. Um ＿＿ gibt es ＿＿.
3. Was ist denn das?	4a. Das ist eine Sendung über ＿＿. b. Keine Ahnung, klingt aber interessant.
5. Wer spielt mit?	6. Hier steht ＿＿.
7. Wie lange dauert das?	8a. ＿＿ Stunden/Minuten b. Von ＿＿ Uhr bis ＿＿ Uhr.
9. Was gibt es sonst noch?	10a. Magst du ＿＿? b. Wie wäre es mit ＿＿?
11a. Ja, das finde ich ＿＿. b. Nein, ich sehe lieber ＿＿. c. Ich lese heute Abend lieber.	12. Na gut.

Thema 2: Leben mit Technik

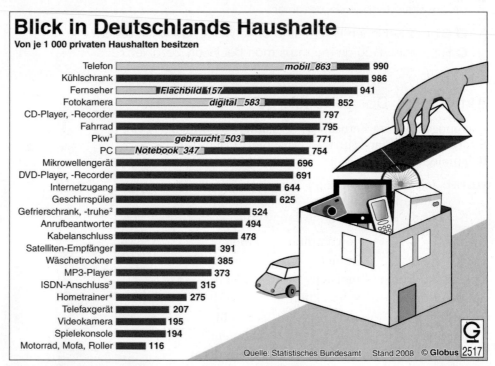

Blick in Deutschlands Haushalte
Von je 1 000 privaten Haushalten besitzen

Telefon	*mobil 863* 990
Kühlschrank	986
Fernseher	*Flachbild 157* 941
Fotokamera	*digital 583* 852
CD-Player, -Recorder	797
Fahrrad	795
Pkw[1]	*gebraucht 503* 771
PC	*Notebook 347* 754
Mikrowellengerät	696
DVD-Player, -Recorder	691
Internetzugang	644
Geschirrspüler	625
Gefrierschrank, -truhe[2]	524
Anrufbeantworter	494
Kabelanschluss	478
Satelliten-Empfänger	391
Wäschetrockner	385
MP3-Player	373
ISDN-Anschluss[3]	315
Hometrainer[4]	275
Telefaxgerät	207
Videokamera	195
Spielekonsole	194
Motorrad, Mofa, Roller	116

Quelle: Statistisches Bundesamt Stand 2008 © Globus 2517

[1]*automobile* [2]*freezer* [3]type of communications link; here: *high-speed Internet* [4]*home exercise equipment*

A Schauen Sie sich das Schaubild an und beantworten Sie die Fragen.

> ○ Wie viele Haushalte haben einen Fernseher? einen Pkw? eine **Digitalkamera?** einen PC? **Internet?** ein **Notebook?**

> ○ Haben Deutsche öfter **Kabelanschluss** oder einen **Satelliten-Empfänger?**

> ○ Welche Geräte im Schaubild hat man in den letzten dreißig Jahren **erfunden?** Was sind **Erfindungen** der letzten fünfzig Jahre?

> ○ Welche von diesen Geräten besitzen Sie?

B Wozu benutzt man die folgenden Geräte? Verbinden Sie die Satzteile. Für manche Geräte sind mehrere Anworten möglich!

BEISPIEL: Man benutzt eine Digitalkamera, um Fotos zu machen.

1. eine Digitalkamera
2. einen Computer
3. einen Kabelanschluss / einen Satelliten-Empfänger
4. ein **Faxgerät**
5. einen Laptop / ein Notebook
6. einen MP3-Player
7. einen **Anrufbeantworter**
8. einen **Drucker**
9. eine **Videokamera**
10. einen Hometrainer

a. um unterwegs am Computer zu arbeiten
b. um Musik digital zu **speichern** und abzuspielen
c. um mehr Programme im Fernsehen zu **empfangen**
d. um **Dokumente** über das Telefonnetz zu schicken
e. um telefonische Nachrichten zu **hinterlassen**
f. um Dokumente und Bilder zu **drucken**
g. um fit zu bleiben
h. um **E-Mails** zu schicken
i. um Videos **aufzunehmen**
j. um Fotos zu machen

Neue Wörter

der Kabelanschluss cable TV connection
der Satelliten-Empfänger satellite receiver
der Anrufbeantworter answering machine
erfunden (erfinden) invented
die Erfindung (Erfindungen, *pl.*) invention
der Drucker printer
speichern store, save
empfangen receive
hinterlassen leave (behind)
drucken print
aufzunehmen (aufnehmen) to record

 Siehe *Infinitive Clauses with* **um ... zu** S. 394.

Aktivität 6 Am Computer

Die Sprache der modernen Technologie kommt zum großen Teil aus dem Englischen. Die moderne Computertechnologie verwendet auch viele Symbole. Verbinden Sie die Symbole mit ihren üblichen (*conventional*) Bedeutungen.

1. _____ ✉
2. _____ 💾
3. _____ 🗑
4. _____ ☝
5. _____ 🔊
6. _____ ▶▶
7. _____ ✂
8. _____ 🖨

a. Audio/Video vorspulen (*fast forward*)
b. das Dokument drucken
c. das Dokument speichern
d. den Text ausschneiden (*cut*)
e. das Dokument löschen (*delete*)
f. eine E-Mail lesen
g. Hier kann man etwas hören.
h. Hier kann man klicken.

Aktivität 7 Da kann man …

Suchen Sie passende Verben zu den Substantiven. (Manchmal ist mehr als eine Antwort richtig.)

BEISPIEL: Am Computer kann man E-Mails bekommen.

Am Computer kann man …

1. E-Mails _____.
2. Softwareprogramme _____.
3. ein Thema oder ein Wort _____.
4. eine Zeitung im Internet _____.
5. über viele Themen _____.
6. Dokumente _____.

bloggen	lesen	herunterladen/downloaden
googeln	kaufen	twittern
speichern		schicken
bekommen	schreiben	

Aktivität 8 Die Geschichte einer Erfindung

Lesen Sie den Text über den Korkenzieher und beantworten Sie die Fragen auf der folgenden Seite.

Der Korkenzieher

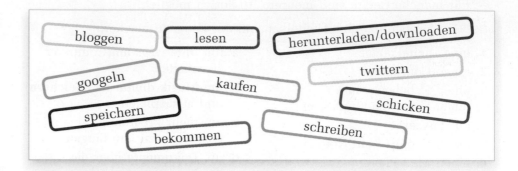

Man weiß nicht genau, wer den Korkenzieher erfunden hat. Ein Prototyp stammt aus England. Und wer ist auf die Idee gekommen, eine Flasche mit einer Art Korkenzieher zu öffnen? Soldaten wahrscheinlich. Im 17. Jahrhundert haben Soldaten verklemmte[1] Kugeln aus ihren Gewehren[2] gebohrt[3]. Das war das Prinzip für den ersten „Korkenzieher". Samuel Henshall, ein Pfarrer aus Oxford in England hat im Jahr 1795 das erste Patent für einen Korkenzieher angemeldet. Seinen einfachen Stangenkorkenzieher findet man auch heute noch.

Aber wer brauchte damals einen Korkenzieher? Soldaten vielleicht, aber vor allem reiche Aristokraten, denn nur sie konnten sich gute Weine aus Frankreich leisten. Im Laufe der Zeit wurde es Mode, die Weinflasche bei Tisch zu entkorken. Ein Korkenzieher musste leicht zu bedienen sein; aber er sollte auch ästhetisch schön sein. Die Geschichte des Korkenziehers zeigt, wie dieses Werkzeug praktisch angefangen aber im Laufe der Zeit sich zu einem eleganten Instrument entwickelt hat

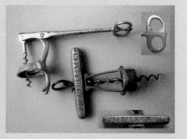

Korkenzieher aus alten Zeiten

[1]jammed [2]guns [3]drilled

1. Wer kam zuerst auf die Idee, Flaschen mit einer Art Korkenzieher zu öffnen?
2. Wie kamen sie auf diese Idee?
3. Wer hat das erste Patent für einen Korkenzieher angemeldet?
4. Warum hatten Aristokraten Korkenzieher nötig?
5. Warum sollten Korkenzieher auch ästhetisch schön sein?

Aktivität 9 Ein findiger Kopf

Wie erfinderisch sind Sie? Beschreiben Sie eine nützliche (*useful*) Erfindung.

BEISPIEL: Medizin →
  Ein Hustenbonbon, das wie Schokolade schmeckt.

Bereiche
1. Medizin
2. Technik
3. Verkehr
4. Haushalt
5. Tiere
6. Stadtplanung
7. Umwelt
8. Häuser

Aktivität 10 Hin und her: Erfindungen durch die Jahrhunderte

Sie möchten erfahren, wer was, und wann, erfunden hat. Arbeiten Sie zu zweit.

BEISPIELE: **S1:** Wer hat _____ erfunden?

   S2: _____.

   S1: Wann hat er/sie es erfunden?

   S2: (Im Jahre) _____.

oder **S1:** Was hat _____ erfunden?

   S2: Er/Sie hat _____ erfunden.

   S1: In welchem Jahr?

   S2: (Im Jahre) _____.

Erfinder	Erfindung	Jahr
	der Buchdruck mit beweglichen Lettern (*movable type*)	
	das Alkoholthermometer	
Karl von Drais	das Fahrrad (Draisine)	1817
Herta Heuwer		
Gottlieb Daimler	das Motorrad	1885
Rudolf Diesel	der Dieselmotor	1893
Wilhelm Conrad Röntgen		
Melitta Bentz	der Kaffeefilter	1908

Der Infinitivsatz

Infinitive Clauses with **zu**°

Infinitive clauses may be complements of verbs, nouns, or adjectives. When used this way, the infinitive is always preceded by **zu.**

Familie Baier **hat vor,** einen neuen Computer **zu kaufen.**	*The Baier family is planning to buy a new computer.*
Es macht mir **Spaß,** E-Mail aus der ganzen Welt **zu bekommen.**	*I enjoy receiving e-mail from all over the world.*
Es ist **leicht,** einen Brief per E-Mail **zu schicken.**	*It is easy to send a letter via e-mail.*

NOTE:

▶ The infinitive with **zu** is always the last element of the sentence.

▶ With separable-prefix verbs, **zu** is placed between the prefix and the main verb.

Ich habe versucht, dich gestern **anzurufen.**	*I tried to call you yesterday.*
Du hast versprochen **vorbeizukommen.**	*You promised to come by.*

▶ A comma generally sets off an infinitive clause that includes more than just the infinitive with **zu.** No comma is used otherwise.

Übung 1 Felix

Felix studiert Medien an der Hochschule für Technik in Dresden. Er ist ein Erstsemester und es gibt viel Neues für ihn. Bilden Sie Sätze.

BEISPIEL: Er hat sich entschlossen, einen neuen Laptop zu kaufen.

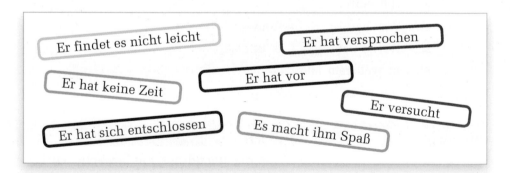

Er findet es nicht leicht · Er hat versprochen · Er hat keine Zeit · Er hat vor · Er versucht · Er hat sich entschlossen · Es macht ihm Spaß

1. ein Zimmer in einer WG finden
2. seine Familie regelmäßig anrufen
3. jeden Mittwoch zum Kickboxen gehen
4. jeden Abend ausgehen
5. etwas Geld mit Jobben verdienen
6. im Inter-Treff Klub Studenten kennenlernen
7. einen neuen Laptop kaufen
8. jeden Tag die Zeitung lesen

Übung 2 Meiner Meinung nach …

Drücken Sie Ihre Meinung aus.

BEISPIEL: Es macht mir Spaß, Seifenopern anzusehen.

Ich habe keine Zeit	stundenlang am Computer sitzen
Es macht mir (keinen) Spaß	im Internet surfen
Ich finde es langweilig	Computerspiele/Videospiele spielen
wichtig	Kriegsfilme/Sportsendungen im Fernsehen ansehen
schwierig	eine Fremdsprache lernen
interessant	über Politik diskutieren
spannend	per E-Mail korrespondieren
schwer	mein Horoskop in der Zeitung lesen
	jeden Tag die Zeitung lesen
	Nachrichten im Fernsehen ansehen
	Radio hören
	einen guten Job finden
	studieren und nebenbei jobben

Übung 3 Aus dem Kalender

Schauen Sie sich Cornelias Kalender an. Was hat sie vor? Was darf sie nicht vergessen?

BEISPIEL: Sie hat vor, Sonntag mit Klaus ins Kino zu gehen.
　　　　　Sie darf nicht vergessen, Montag …

Sonntag	19.30 mit Klaus ins Kino gehen
Montag	nicht vergessen: Videogerät zur Reparatur bringen Reise nach Spanien buchen
Dienstag	nicht vergessen: Radio und Fernsehen anmelden 14.30 Prof. Hauser: Seminararbeit besprechen
Mittwoch	Job für den Sommer suchen
Donnerstag	nicht vergessen: Mutter anrufen, Geburtstag!
Freitag	Seminararbeit fertig schreiben 20.00 Vera treffen: Café Kadenz
Samstag	14.00 mit Klaus Tennis spielen 20.30 „Casablanca" im Fernsehen ansehen

Übung 4 Gute Vorsätze° für die Zukunft

resolutions

Schritt 1: Sie haben vor, in Zukunft alles besser zu machen. Was haben Sie sich versprochen? Was haben Sie vor? Überlegen Sie sich zwei gute Vorsätze.

BEISPIELE: Ich habe vor, weniger Geld für CDs auszugeben.
　　　　　Ich habe mir versprochen, nicht so viel im Internet zu surfen.

Schritt 2: Vergleichen Sie Ihre Vorsätze mit den Vorsätzen eines Partners / einer Partnerin. Haben Sie gemeinsame Vorsätze? Wenn ja, welche? Was sind die häufigsten guten Vorsätze Ihrer Kursmitglieder?

Übung 5 Nichts scheint zu funktionieren

Was scheint hier los zu sein? Folgen Sie dem Beispiel.

BEISPIEL: Das Telefon klingelt nicht. Warum nicht? (Es ist kaputt.) →
Es scheint kaputt zu sein.

1. Der Computer funktioniert mal wieder nicht. (Er ist kaputt.)
2. Hast du meine Nachricht nicht bekommen? Ich habe eine Nachricht auf deinem Anrufbeantworter hinterlassen. (Er funktioniert nicht.)
3. Meine Kamera funktioniert nicht. (Sie braucht eine neue Batterie.)
4. Bei Firma Bär meldet sich niemand am Apparat. (Niemand ist im Büro.)
5. Drei von meinen Kollegen sind heute nicht zur Arbeit gekommen. (Sie sind alle krank.)

Übung 6 Nein, heute nicht

Arbeiten Sie zu zweit und stellen Sie einander Fragen. Was musst du heute noch machen?

BEISPIEL: S1: Musst du heute arbeiten?

S2: Nein, heute brauche ich nicht zu arbeiten. Musst du heute … ?

1. im Labor arbeiten
2. Hausaufgaben machen
3. in die Vorlesung gehen
4. den Computer benutzen
5. Rechnungen bezahlen
6. eine deutsche Zeitung im Internet lesen
7. einen neuen Anrufbeantworter kaufen
8. einen Bericht über Fernsehen in Deutschland schreiben

Infinitive Clauses with **um … zu**

German uses many different ways to explain the reasons for an action. You have already learned a number of them. Compare the following sentences.

Warum spart Stefan?

1. Stefan spart **für einen neuen Computer.** ← Prepositional phrase

2. Stefan will einen neuen Computer kaufen. **Deswegen** muss er jetzt sparen. ← Adverb: **deswegen** = *therefore*

3. Stefan spart. Er will **nämlich** einen Computer kaufen.   ← Adverb:
nämlich = *the reason being*

4. Stefan spart, **denn** er will einen Computer kaufen.   ← Coordinating conjunction:
denn = *because*

5. Stefan spart, **weil** er einen Computer kaufen möchte.   ← Subordinating conjunction:
weil = *because*

Yet another way to explain one's reasons for an action is with an infinitive clause with **um … zu.**

Stefan spart, **um** einen neuen Computer **zu kaufen.**   *Stefan is saving money in order to buy a new computer.*

Manche Leute leben, **um zu arbeiten.**   *Some people live in order to work.*

Ich arbeite schwer, **um** mich auf das Examen **vorzubereiten.**   *I am working hard to prepare for the exam.*

Sie müssen kein Fisch sein,   um Meerwasser[1] trinken zu können.

[1]*sea water*

Übung 7   Was sind die Gründe° dafür?   *reasons*

Geben Sie die Gründe an. Benutzen Sie dabei **um … zu, weil, nämlich, denn** oder **deswegen.**

BEISPIEL: Ich muss sparen. Ich möchte mir einen Plasmamonitor kaufen. →
       Ich muss sparen, um mir einen Plasmamonitor zu kaufen.
  oder Ich will mir einen Plasmamonitor kaufen. Deswegen muss ich sparen.

1. Barbara macht den Fernseher an. Sie will die Nachrichten sehen.

2. Thomas setzt sich in den Sessel. Er will die Tageszeitung lesen.

3. Barbara schaut sich das Filmprogramm an. Sie sucht sich einen Spielfilm aus.

4. Thomas programmiert den Fernseher. Er möchte die Fußballweltmeisterschaft aufnehmen.

5. Stephanie füllt ein Formular aus. Sie meldet ihr Radio und ihren Fernseher an.

6. Oliver überfliegt nur die Schlagzeilen in der Zeitung. Er will Zeit sparen.

7. Andreas hört sich die Tagesschau an. Er informiert sich über Politik.

Indirect Discourse°

When you report what another person has said, you can quote that person verbatim, using direct discourse. In writing, this is indicated by the use of quotation marks. Note that in German, opening quotation marks are placed just below the line.

Direct Discourse

Der Autofahrer behauptete: „Ich habe den Radfahrer nicht gesehen."

The automobile driver claimed, "I did not see the bicyclist."

Another way of reporting what someone said uses indirect discourse—a style commonly found in newspapers. In this case, German often uses subjunctive verb forms, especially the indirect discourse subjunctive, also called Subjunctive I.

Indirect Discourse

Der Autofahrer behauptete, er **habe** den Radfahrer nicht **gesehen.**

The driver claimed he had not seen the bicyclist.

In using the indirect discourse subjunctive, a speaker or writer signals that the information reported does not necessarily reflect the speaker's own knowledge or views. The indirect discourse subjunctive establishes distance between the reporter and the topic. This is useful when people want to be objective or neutral.

„Na, Schatz, steht was Interessantes in der Zeitung?"

Konjunktiv I: Präsens

Subjunctive I: Present Tense°

The present tense of the indirect discourse subjunctive, Subjunctive I, is derived from the stem of the infinitive. Only the verb **sein** has a complete set of forms that are commonly used in modern German. For all other verbs, Subjunctive I forms are mostly limited to the third-person singular.

NOTE:

◗ Except for **sein,** all verbs add **-e** to the infinitive stem to form the third-person singular.

haben	→	er/sie/es **habe**
können	→	er/sie/es **könne**
tun	→	er/sie/es **tue**
wissen	→	es/sie/es **wisse**

Subjunctive I	
Infinitive	**sein**
ich	sei
du	sei(e)st
er/sie/es	sei
wir	seien
ihr	sei(e)t
sie/Sie	seien

Übung 8 Was man über Fernsehen gesagt hat

Ergänzen Sie die Sätze mit dem Konjunktiv I von **sein.**

1. Herr Schwarz hat gesagt, ohne Fernsehen _____ sein Leben schöner.
2. Frau Schwarz meinte, für Kinder _____ Programme wie „Die Sendung mit der Maus" etwas Besonderes.
3. Man hat mir gesagt, ohne Fernsehen _____ ich nicht gut informiert. So ein Quatsch.
4. Die Frau von der Marktforschung fragte, warum wir nicht am Fernsehen interessiert _____.
5. Man hat mir berichtet, dass du jetzt ganz ohne Fernseher _____.
6. Frau Schmidt meinte, ohne ihre tägliche Telenovela _____ sie nicht glücklich.
7. Familie Schulte hat gesagt, die Sportprogramme _____ immer ausgezeichnet.

If indirect discourse requires the use of any other verb forms, then Subjunctive II is used. It is quite common to use exclusively Subjunctive II or **würde** + infinitive for all indirect discourse. The following examples demonstrate the possibilities.

Der Student sagte, er **sei (wäre)** krank und **habe (hätte)** keine Zeit.	*The student said he is sick and has no time.*
Es **tue (täte)** ihm leid, dass er nicht zur Vorlesung kommen **könne (könnte)**.	*He is sorry that he cannot come to the lecture.*
Er **gebe (gäbe)** seine Hausarbeit morgen **ab. (würde … abgeben)**	*He will turn in his homework tomorrow.*
Die Wähler meinten, sie **wüssten** nicht, wem man glauben **könne (könnte)**.	*The voters said they don't know whom to believe* (lit. *whom one can believe*).
Politiker behaupten, sie **würden** immer die Wahrheit **sagen.**	*Politicians claim they always tell the truth.*

Analyse

Lesen Sie die folgenden Texte und markieren Sie alle Verben in indirekter Rede. Was sind die Infinitive der Verben? Wie würden Sie diese Sätze auf English ausdrücken?

Im Fernsehen hat man berichtet, das Land sei in einer großen Krise. Niemand wisse, wie es enden soll. Niemand habe eine Lösung.[1]

Technikstress: Telefonieren, Fernsehen, Internet surfen; der moderne Mensch sei zwar immer bestens informiert, aber manchmal ziemlich gestresst von zu viel Technik.

Ein Kriminologe und Jugendforscher schreibt, der durchschnittliche männliche Schüler bringe es auf 5 Stunden Medienkonsum am Tage. Das sei ein krankes Leben. Je mehr Zeit Kinder am Fernseher und Computer verbrächten, desto[3] schlechter seien sie in der Schule. In einigen Computerspielen könne man eine Erklärung für die erhöhte Gewaltbereitschaft[4] finden.

Und wie war's heute in der Schule?

Prima. Frau Koch hat gesagt, wenn alle so wären wie ich, könnten sie die Schule dichtmachen[2]!

[1]*solution* [2]*to close down* [3]*je mehr … desto schlechter the more . . . the worse* [4]*erhöhte … increased violence*

Übung 9 Das stand in der Zeitung

Berichten Sie in indirekter Rede, was in der Zeitung stand.

BEISPIEL: Der Mensch denkt am schnellsten vor dem Mittagessen. →
In der Zeitung stand, der Mensch denke am schnellsten vor dem Mittagessen.

1. Man soll also schwierige Probleme zwischen 11 and 12 Uhr lösen.
2. Die Sinne (*senses*) funktionieren dagegen besser abends.
3. Das Abendessen schmeckt deshalb besser als das Frühstück.
4. Wir sind deshalb abends für Theater, Musik und auch für die Liebe am empfänglichsten (*most receptive*).
5. Für den Sport ist der Spätnachmittag ideal.
6. Man wird spätnachmittags nicht so schnell müde.

excuses

Übung 10   Immer diese Ausreden°

Sie hören drei Dialoge. Machen Sie sich zuerst Notizen. Erzählen Sie dann mithilfe Ihrer Notizen, was das Problem ist und was für Ausreden (*excuses*) die Personen in den Dialogen haben.

BEISPIEL: Peter hat gesagt, er könne nicht mit ins Kino …

Sprecher/in	Problem	Ausrede
1. Peter		
2. Jens		
3. Ursula		

Subjunctive I: Past Tense

To express the past tense in indirect discourse, use the Subjunctive I of the auxiliary verb **sein** or **haben** and the past participle of the main verb.

Die Autofahrerin behauptete, der Motorradfahrer **sei** bei Rot **gefahren.**

The driver claimed the motorcyclist ran a red light.

Sie **habe** ihn nicht rechtzeitig **gesehen.**

She did not see him in time.

NOTE:

▶ Whether to use **sein** or **haben** depends on the main verb. The choice is identical to which auxiliary the verb would use in the perfect tenses.

Er **ist** gefahren.   →   Er **sei** gefahren.

Sie **hat** gesehen.   →   Sie **habe** gesehen.

▶ With **haben,** only the third-person singular Subjunctive I, **habe,** is used; Subjunctive II is used for the remaining forms.

Der Motorradfahrer berichtete, seine Bremsen **hätten** nicht funktioniert.

The motorcyclist reported that his brakes weren't functioning.

▶ Subjunctive II is increasingly used for all forms in past-tense indirect discourse. There is no **würde** form in this case.

Übung 11 Ungewöhnliches° aus den Nachrichten

Unusual happenings

Schreiben Sie die folgenden Sätze in indirekter Rede der Vergangenheit um. Benutzen Sie dabei Konjunktiv I oder Konjunktiv II.

Heute habe ich im Radio gehört:

1. Im Südwesten Irans hat man ein unbekanntes Dorf entdeckt.
2. Ein Mann im Gorillakostüm hat in den Straßen von Dallas 50-Dollar-Scheine an Fußgänger verteilt (*distributed*).
3. Im Jahre 1875 haben die Leute noch 65 Stunden pro Woche gearbeitet. Heutzutage arbeiten die meisten nur noch 39 Stunden pro Woche im Durchschnitt.
4. Bei einer Verkehrskontrolle in Cocoa Beach ist ein Autodieb ins Meer gesprungen. Er ist immer weiter raus geschwommen. Ein Polizist in voller Uniform hat sich auf ein Surfbrett geschwungen und hat den Dieb nach zehn Minuten eingeholt.
5. Gestern ist auf einem Spielplatz in Russland ein UFO gelandet. Die Leute, die aus dem UFO gestiegen sind, sind sehr freundlich gewesen. Nach kurzer Zeit sind sie wieder abgeflogen.

Übung 12 Sensationelles aus der Presse

Lesen Sie zuerst die zwei kurzen Berichte aus einer Zeitung und unterstreichen Sie die Verben in indirekter Rede. Erzählen Sie dann den Bericht in direkter Rede. Hier ist der Anfang: „Gestern Abend ist bei einer Geburtstagsfeier in einem Restaurant ein Geburtstagskuchen explodiert. ...“

A In der Zeitung stand, gestern Abend sei bei einer Geburtstagsfeier in einem Restaurant ein Geburtstagskuchen explodiert. Der Kellner habe zu viel Cognac über den Kuchen gegossen. Die Gäste und der Kellner seien, Gott sei Dank, unverletzt gewesen.

B In einem Kölner Kiosk habe ein Mann seine Zigaretten mit einem 600-Euro-Schein bezahlt. Der Verkäufer habe geglaubt, es handele sich um einen neuen, noch nicht bekannten Schein. Er habe dem „Kunden" über 500 Euro Wechselgeld zurückgegeben. Erst ein Bekannter des Verkäufers habe die blaue Banknote als Fälschung erkannt und habe die Polizei gerufen. Der Mann mit den Zigaretten sei spurlos verschwunden°.

sei ... disappeared without a trace

Sprache im Kontext

Videoclips

Jasmin, Peter und Maria sprechen über ihre Lese- und Fernsehgewohnheiten.

A Schauen Sie sich die Interviews mit Jasmin und Maria an und füllen Sie die Tabelle aus. Wenn die Person keine Information zu dem Thema gibt, schreiben Sie „keine Information."

	Peter	Jasmin	Maria
Welche Zeitung liest du?			
Was liest du zuerst?			
Welchen Teil liest du ganz genau?			
Was überfliegst du?			
Was siehst du im Fernsehen?			
Welche Filme siehst du gern im Kino?			

B Schauen Sie sich das Interview mit Peter an und beantworten Sie die Fragen.

1. Welche Tageszeitungen liest er?

2. Peter vergleicht drei verschiedene Zeitungen, den *Tagesspiegel,* die *Welt* und die *Süddeutsche Zeitung.* Wie beschreibt er jede Zeitung?
   a. den *Tagesspiegel:* _____.
   b. die *Welt:* _____.
   c. die *Süddeutsche Zeitung:* _____.

3. Welche Zeitung liest er nie? Warum?

4. Was liest Peter ganz genau? Was überfliegt er?

C Ein Interview. Benutzen Sie die Tabelle in **Teil A,** um zwei andere Personen zu interviewen. Machen Sie Notizen zu jedem Interview und berichten Sie der Klasse darüber.

Lesen

Zum Thema

A Wie wichtig sind die folgenden Sachen in Ihrem Leben? Kreuzen Sie zuerst an, was sehr wichtig und was nicht so wichtig ist. Geben Sie an, wie viele Stunden pro Woche Sie damit verbringen. Ordnen Sie sie dann in eine Reihenfolge (1–6) ein: 1 = das wichtigste.

	sehr wichtig	nicht so wichtig	Stunden pro Woche	Reihenfolge
Fernsehen	☐	☐	_____	_____
Radio hören	☐	☐	_____	_____
Zeitung lesen	☐	☐	_____	_____
am Computer arbeiten	☐	☐	_____	_____
im Internet surfen	☐	☐	_____	_____
Bücher lesen	☐	☐	_____	_____
Videos, Filme sehen	☐	☐	_____	_____
Musik hören	☐	☐	_____	_____

B Was liegt an erster Stelle unter Ihren Klassenmitgliedern? Wie viel Zeit verbringen sie damit?

C Womit beschäftigen Sie sich, wenn Sie am Computer sitzen? Kreuzen Sie alles an, was Sie machen.

☐ bloggen
☐ chatten
☐ Filme/Fotos herunterladen
☐ forschen, Information für Kurse und Referate sammeln
☐ Fotos bearbeiten
☐ Hausaufgaben machen
☐ im Internet surfen
☐ Instant-Messaging betreiben
☐ mailen
☐ Musik hören und herunterladen
☐ Nachrichten lesen
☐ Sonstiges: _____

D Berichten Sie kurz über die drei wichtigsten Dinge, die Sie am Computer machen.

Auf den ersten Blick

A Schauen Sie sich den Titel des Lesetexts an und lesen Sie die zwei ersten Sätze. Was erwarten Sie von diesem Text?

☐ Informationen über die Freunde junger Deutscher
☐ einen Bericht über den negativen Einfluss von Computer und Fernsehen
☐ Informationen über die Rolle vom Computer im Leben junger Deutscher

B Überfliegen Sie den Artikel und suchen Sie im Text Wörter, die etwas mit Computer und Internet zu tun haben. Machen Sie eine Liste. Woher stammt das Vokabular zum größten Teil?

C Was passt zusammen?

BEISPIEL: Man schaltet den Computer an.

1. Man schaltet _____.
2. Man klickt _____.
3. Man checkt _____.
4. Man lädt _____.
5. Man googelt _____.
6. Man bearbeitet _____.
7. Man surft _____.

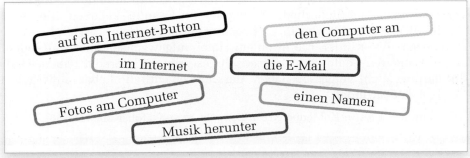

auf den Internet-Button   den Computer an

im Internet   die E-Mail

Fotos am Computer   einen Namen

Musik herunter

Gute Freunde im Netz

Das Leben am Laptop

von Kerstin Kohlenberg

Wer heute 17 ist, kennt ein Leben ohne Internet nicht. Für die meisten ist der Computer wichtiger als Fernsehen.

Seit einigen Wochen sind die Ferien vorbei. Mel
5 geht wieder zur Schule. Sie kommt aus der Schule nach Hause, schmeißt den Rucksack auf den Sessel in ihrem Zimmer, zieht die Turnschuhe aus und schaltet den Computer im Wohnzimmer an. Sie ist allein in der Wohnung. Heute gehört ihr der Familiencomputer
10 ganz allein.

Sie geht in die Küche, macht sich ein Stück Pizza warm und trägt es zurück zum Computer. Ihr tägliches Ritual beginnt. Mel klickt auf den Internet-Button, schaltet den MSN-Messenger an, ein Programm, das ihr sagt, dass Lisa
15 online ist und der Rest ihrer Freunde noch offline. Sie checkt ihre E-Mail bei Hotmail – nur ein Kettenbrief°, den sie weiterschickt – sie checkt ihre E-Mail bei Yahoo – ihre Mutter aus Paris. Dann betritt° sie ihr Leben: Skyblog.com. Das tägliche Ritual geht weiter. Mel surft, guckt sich die Top 40 Lieder an, und wenn ihr ein neues Lied gefällt, dann
20 lädt sie es herunter. Musik und ihre Freunde, das ist es, was Mel interessiert. Dass sie gestern Spinoza° gegoogelt hat, liegt daran, dass sie über ihn ein Referat° in der Schule halten muss.

Ihre Internet-Seite berichtet über Mel: Sie ist 17 Jahre alt, hat viele Freunde, und fährt oft nach Paris. Ihre Mutter lebt nämlich jetzt wieder
25 in Paris. Die Eltern sind geschieden. Mel lebt mit ihrem Vater und ihrem Bruder in Berlin. Mel hat vier Freundinnen und auch einen Freund und geht auf ein französisches Gymnasium in Berlin.

Mels Generation ist mit dem Computer aufgewachsen. Der war vor ein paar Jahren noch vor allem ein Spielzeug der Jungen. Doch
30 inzwischen ist er auch für Mädchen wie Mel ein wichtiger Teil des Lebens. Von den Jugendlichen in Deutschland zwischen 12 und 19 haben so gut wie alle, nämlich 96 Prozent, mindestens einen Computer zu Hause. 85 Prozent haben Internet-Zugang, ein Drittel surft vom eigenen Zimmer aus. Mehr als die Hälfte dieser Internet-Nutzer
35 ist über 10 Stunden pro Woche online. Eine Stuttgarter-Studie berichtet, dass für Mädchen der Computer noch hinter Fernsehen, Radio und Büchern rangiert. Für Jungen dagegen ist der Computer der wichtigste Zeitvertreib°.

Was an Mel und ihren Freunden auffällt°, ist ihre fehlende° Angst
40 vor Menschen. Die Sicherheit, mit der sie auf Fremde° zugehen, die Offenheit°, mit der sie von ihren Leben erzählen, wirken überraschend erwachsen. Wie Kinder, die in einem Hotel aufgewachsen sind und jeden Tag mit anderen Leuten am Speisetisch gesessen und geredet haben. Und die darüber nicht vergessen haben, dass das eigentliche Leben außerhalb
45 des Hotels stattfindet.

Adaptiert aus: Kerstin Kohlenberg, *Die Zeit,* Nr. 41, 6 Oktober 2005, S. 68

Marginal glosses:
- chain letter
- enters
- Baruch Spinoza *(philosopher)*
- report
- pastime
- is striking / lack of
- strangers
- candor

Zum Text

A Lesen Sie nun den Text genauer und suchen Sie Information über Mel. Was erfahren wir über die folgenden Themen?

Familie _____

Freunde _____

Schule _____

Interessen _____

B Die Rolle des Computers

1. Was erfahren wir über junge Deutsche und die Rolle des Computers in ihrem Leben?

2. Glauben Sie, dass es einen Unterschied zwischen jungen US-Amerikanern/Kanadiern und jungen Deutschen im Gebrauch des Computers gibt?

C Im letzten Abschnitt des Artikels sagt die Autorin des Artikels, was ihr bei diesen jungen Berlinern aufgefallen ist:

○ die fehlende Angst vor Menschen

○ die Sicherheit, mit der sie auf Fremde zugehen

○ die Offenheit, mit der sie von ihrem Leben erzählen

○ sie wirken überraschend erwachsen

1. Sehen Sie diese Qualitäten als etwas Positives oder haben sie auch eine negative Seite?

2. Können Sie sich damit identifizieren?

D Die Autorin schließt mit einem Vergleich (*comparison*). Mit wem vergleicht sie die junge Generation, die mit dem Computer aufgewachsen ist? Finden Sie diesen Vergleich passend (*fitting*)?

Zu guter Letzt

Podcast: Eine neue Erfindung

Sind Sie kreativ und erfinderisch? Benutzen Sie Ihr Talent, um eine neue Erfindung auf den Markt zu bringen. Machen Sie einen Podcast, wo Sie die Erfindung darstellen.

Schritt 1: In Gruppen zu dritt überlegen Sie sich eine Kategorie für die Erfindung, z.B. Kommunikation, Auto/Transport, Computertechnologie oder Haushalt. Was ist der Zweck (*purpose*) der Erfindung? Wie soll die Erfindung das Leben leichter oder interessanter machen?

Schritt 2: Jede Gruppe arbeitet nun die Einzelheiten (*details*) ihrer Erfindung aus. Wie sieht sie aus? Wie funktioniert sie? Welche Materialien braucht man für die Erfindung?

Schritt 3: Zeichnen Sie die Erfindung als Poster. Dann konstruieren Sie sie!

Schritt 4: Machen Sie einen Film über die Geschichte Ihrer Erfindung. Eine Person erzählt die Geschichte der Erfindung, eine Person zeigt die Erfindung und beschreibt den Zweck und eine Person nimmt alles mit Digitalkamera auf. Schneiden Sie den Film zusammen.

Schritt 5: Präsentieren Sie der Klasse den Film und beantworten Sie Fragen über Ihre Erfindung.

Wortschatz

Im Fernsehen — **On Television**

der **Bericht, -e** — report
der **Dokumentarfilm, -e** — documentary (film)
das **Programm, -e** — station, TV channel; program
die **Sendung, -en** — TV or radio program
der **Spielfilm, -e** — feature film, movie
die **Unterhaltung** — entertainment
  zur Unterhaltung — for entertainment

Die Presse — **The Press**

das **Abo(nnement), -s** — subscription
die **Börse, -n** — stock market
das **Horoskop, -e** — horoscope
das **Inland** — at home, domestic, national
  im Inland und Ausland — at home and abroad
die **Nachrichten** (*pl.*) — news
  die Lokalnachrichten — local news
die **Politik** — politics
die **Schlagzeile, -n** — headline
die **Wirtschaft** — economy
die **Zeitschrift, -en** — magazine; periodical

Technik — **Technology**

der **Anrufbeantworter, -** — answering machine
die **Digitalkamera, -s** — digital camera
das **Dokument, -e** — document
der **Drucker, -** — printer
die **E-Mail, -s** — e-mail
die **Erfindung, -en** — invention
das **Faxgerät, -e** — fax machine
das **Internet** — Internet
der **Kabelanschluss, ̈e** — cable TV connection
das **Notebook, -s** — notebook computer
der **Satelliten-Empfänger** — satellite receiver
die **Videokamera, -s** — video camera

Verben — **Verbs**

abonnieren — to subscribe
sich (*dat.*) **etwas an•schauen** — to watch, look at
sich (*dat.*) **etwas an•sehen (sieht an), sah an, angesehen** — to look at, watch
auf•nehmen (nimmt auf), nahm auf, aufgenommen — to record (e.g., on video)

sich etwas aus•suchen — to select, find, choose something
behaupten — to claim, assert
berichten — to report, narrate
drucken — to print
empfangen (empfängt), empfing, empfangen — to receive
sich entschließen, entschloss, entschlossen — to decide
erfinden, erfand, erfunden — to invent
forschen — to do research
handeln (von) — to deal with, be about
  Wovon handelt es? — What's it about?
hinterlassen (hinterlässt), hinterließ, hinterlassen — to leave (behind) (e.g., a message)
sich melden — to answer (phone)
  Niemand meldet sich. — No one is answering.
scheinen, schien, geschienen — to seem, appear
speichern — to save, store
überfliegen, überflog, überflogen — to skim (a text), read quickly
sich unterhalten (unterhält), unterhielt, unterhalten — to entertain oneself; to converse

Adjektive und Adverbien — **Adjectives and Adverbs**

aktuell — current, topical
  Aktuelles — current events
blöd (*colloquial*) — stupid
gescheit — intelligent, bright; sensible, decent
  nichts Gescheites — nothing decent
unterhaltsam — entertaining

Ausdrücke — **Expressions**

auf jeden Fall — in any case
Das ist mir zu blöd. — I think that's really stupid.
Na und? — So what?
Wie wäre es mit … ? — How about … ?

Das kann ich nun!

1. Sie reden mit Freunden über Fernsehen und Zeitung. Füllen Sie die Lücken mit einem passenden Ausdruck aus dem Kasten.

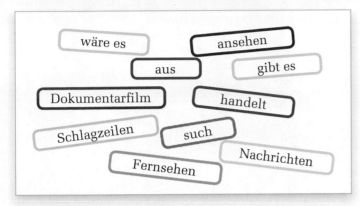

wäre es   ansehen   aus   gibt es   Dokumentarfilm   handelt   Schlagzeilen   such   Nachrichten   Fernsehen

   a. Na, was _____ denn heute Abend im _____?
   b. Um 20.00 Uhr kommen die _____.
   c. Wie _____ mit einem _____ über die Sahara?
   d. Ich möchte mir lieber einen guten Spielfilm _____.
   e. Na gut, _____ dir was _____.
   f. Wovon _____ der Film übrigens?
   g. Die _____ in der *Bild* Zeitung zeigen immer nur Sensationelles.

2. Was sehen Sie gerne im Fernsehen? Wofür interessieren Sie sich nicht?

3. Nennen Sie zwei deutschsprachige Zeitungen (aus Deutschland, Österreich oder der Schweiz). Was lesen Sie gewöhnlich in der Zeitung? Was nie?

4. Nennen Sie drei technologische Geräte und erklären Sie, wozu sie nützlich sind.

5. Schreiben Sie die folgenden Sätze zu Ende.
   a. Ich habe heute vor, _____. (*to go to the movies*)
   b. Kai hat versucht, _____. (*to call me yesterday*)
   c. Er hat während des Semesters gejobbt, _____. (*in order to pay his rent*)

6. Berichten Sie folgende Information in indirekter Rede.
   a. Der Junge sagte: „Ich habe das Comic-Heft nicht genommen."
   b. Er sagte: „Das Geld dafür ist in meiner Tasche."
   c. Inge behauptet: „Ich sehe nicht gern Seifenopern im Fernsehen."
   d. Der Reporter fragte: „Worum handelt es sich?"
   e. In der Zeitung steht: „Immer mehr Berliner wandern aus. Sie suchen bessere Arbeit und wärmeres Klima."
   f. Der Reporter berichtet: „Der Autofahrer ist bei Rot gefahren und hat den Radfahrer nicht gesehen."

Kapitel

14

Die öffentliche Meinung

Berliner gegen
Atomkraft

In diesem Kapitel

- ▶ **Themen:** Talking about global problems, public opinion, the environment, and using discussion strategies

- ▶ **Grammatik:** Passive voice, the present participle

- ▶ **Lesen:** „Was in der Zeitung steht" (Reinhard Mey)

- ▶ **Landeskunde:** The environment, speed limits in Europe, recycling

- ▶ **Zu guter Letzt:** Globale und lokale Probleme

VIDEOCLIPS

Globale Probleme

Jugendliche in Deutschland:
Die Sorgen in der Welt von morgen

Von je 100 Jugendlichen* halten für die größten Herausforderungen der Welt

Armut[1] in vielen Ländern	75
Klimawandel[2], Umweltzerstörung	73
Mangel[3] an Nahrung[4] und Trinkwasser	70
Rohstoffknappheit[5]	58
Ausbreitung[6] von Seuchen[7] und Krankheiten weltweit	53
Verbreitung von Massenvernichtungswaffen[8]	49
Krieg[9] und bewaffnete[10] Konflikte	48
Wirtschafts- und Finanzkrise	46
Internationaler Terrorismus	42
Wachstum[11] der Weltbevölkerung	36

© Globus

G 2999

Quelle: Bertelsmann Stiftung   Mehrfachnennungen   *von 14 bis 18 Jahren   Stand 2009

[1]*poverty*   [2]*climate change*   [3]*shortage*   [4]*food*   [5]*shortage of raw materials*
[6]*spread*   [7]*contagious diseases*   [8]*weapons of mass destruction*   [9]*war*
[10]*armed*   [11]*growth*

A Jugendliche in Deutschland interessieren sich für globale Probleme und halten diese zehn Probleme für die größten Herausforderungen (*challenges*) der Welt. Schauen Sie sich die Themen in der Grafik an. Lesen Sie dann die folgenden Aussagen. Auf welches Problem bezieht sich jede Aussage?

1. Mehr als 6 Millionen Kinder sterben jedes Jahr an vermeidbaren (*avoidable*) Ursachen.

2. Jeden Tag sterben 6 000 Menschen an HIV/Aids.

3. Alle 3,6 Sekunden verhungert (*starves to death*) ein Mensch irgendwo auf der Welt.

4. Viele Entwicklungsländer haben finanzielle Probleme und brauchen internationale Hilfe.

5. Mehr als eine Milliarde Menschen haben keinen Zugang zu sauberem Trinkwasser.

6. Anschläge von Terroristen töten täglich Menschen in vielen Ländern.

7. Mineralien und Holzreserven werden weltweit knapp.

8. Einige Länder besitzen oder entwickeln Massenvernichtungswaffen im Namen der Selbstverteidigung.

B Sie hören jetzt eine Beschreibung von vier verschiedenen Seminaren über Probleme in der Welt. Welche Themen behandeln diese Seminare? Schreiben Sie die entsprechende Nummer vor jedes Thema.

_____ Kriminalität/Gewalt   _____ Menschenrechte

_____ Umweltverschmutzung   _____ Medizin/Umwelt

Wörter im Kontext

Neue Wörter

die Welt world
sich Sorgen machen um worry about
die Arbeitslosigkeit unemployment
die Armut poverty
die Krankheit (Krankheiten, *pl.*) disease, illness
die Ausländerfeindlichkeit hatred of foreigners
die Drogensucht drug addiction
die Gewalttätigkeit violence
der Klimawandel climate change
die Regierung government
der Krieg war
die Obdachlosigkeit homelessness
die Verletzung violation
das Menschenrecht (Menschenrechte, *pl.*) human right
möglich possible
die Lösung (Lösungen, *pl.*) solution
lösen solve
der Fortschritt (Fortschritte, *pl.*) progress
teilnehmen (an) participate (in)
die Forschung research
die Gefahr (Gefahren, *pl.*) danger
einführen introduce
verbreiten spread
Obdachlose homeless persons
entwickeln develop
schaffen create
umschulen retrain
wählen elect
streng strictly
öffentlich public
das Verkehrsmittel (Verkehrsmittel *pl.*) means of transportation
fördern promote
vermindern lessen
verbieten forbid
der Lärm noise
sich engagieren get involved
schützen protect

Thema 1: Globale Probleme

A Was sind Ihrer Meinung nach die drei größten Probleme in der **Welt**, in Ihrem Staat und in Ihrer Heimatstadt? Wor**um machen** Sie **sich Sorgen**?

	Welt	Staat	Stadt
Arbeitslosigkeit	☐	☐	☐
Armut und **Hunger**	☐	☐	☐
Ausbreitung von **Krankheiten** und Seuchen	☐	☐	☐
Ausländerfeindlichkeit	☐	☐	☐
Drogensucht	☐	☐	☐
Gewalttätigkeit und **Terrorismus**	☐	☐	☐
Klimawandel und Umweltzerstörung	☐	☐	☐
Korruption in der **Regierung**	☐	☐	☐
Krieg	☐	☐	☐
Obdachlosigkeit	☐	☐	☐
Rassismus	☐	☐	☐
Rechtsextremismus	☐	☐	☐
Rohstoffknappheit	☐	☐	☐
Verletzung der **Menschenrechte**	☐	☐	☐
Wirtschaftskrisen	☐	☐	☐

B **Mögliche Lösungen.** Wie kann man diese Probleme **lösen**? Wie können **Fortschritte** gemacht werden? Suchen Sie aus der folgenden Liste passende Ausdrücke (*expressions*), um Ihre Meinung auszudrücken.

BEISPIEL: In meiner Heimatstadt ist Obdachlosigkeit ein großes Problem. Man sollte mehr Sozialbauwohnungen bauen.

- **an Demonstrationen** gegen _____ **teilnehmen**
- mehr Fußgängerzonen einrichten
- mehr Geld für **Forschung** ausgeben
- Kinder und Jugendliche besser über die **Gefahren** von Alkohol und **Drogen** informieren
- mehr Recyclingprogramme **einführen** und **verbreiten**
- mehr Sozialbauwohnungen für **Obdachlose** bauen
- Alternativenergie, Solar- und Windenergie **entwickeln**
- neue Arbeitsplätze **schaffen**
- Arbeitslose **umschulen**
- verantwortungsbewusste **Politiker** und **Politikerinnen wählen**
- Strom- (Elektrizität-) und Wasserverbrauch **streng** reduzieren
- **öffentliche Verkehrsmittel fördern**
- Giftstoffe (*toxics*) **vermindern** oder **verbieten**
- Stressfaktoren (z.B. **Lärm**) reduzieren
- **sich** politisch **engagieren**
- Umwelt **schützen**
- Luftverschmutzung kontrollieren

Die Kunst der Diskussion

Fünf Studenten sollen in Team-Arbeit einen Vortrag über ein globales oder lokales Problem für ihr Hauptseminar in Soziologie vorbereiten. Sie sitzen im Uni-Café und diskutieren.

Christian: Also, was **meint** ihr? Sollen wir ein globales Thema wie Terrorismus **behandeln**?

Cornelia: Aktuell ist es schon, aber ich würde lieber ein Problem behandeln, das uns hier in Deutschland täglich **betrifft**, z.B. Arbeitslosigkeit oder **Umweltverschmutzung**.

Erman: ... oder auch Ausländerfeindlichkeit.

Niels: **Im Grunde genommen** sind ja all diese Probleme global.

Alexandra: **Ich bin der Meinung**, Umweltschutz ist besonders wichtig, gerade jetzt, wo wir mehr alternative Energie produzieren müssen.

Niels: Ja, Solarenergie und Windenergie. Könnt ihr euch das vorstellen: hinter jedem Haus ein **Windrad** im Garten?

Cornelia: **So ein Unsinn!** Ich **halte** das **für übertrieben.**

Erman: Das ist deine Meinung, nicht unbedingt meine.

Cornelia: Also, ich **stimme** Alexandra **zu**, Umweltschutz und Klimawandel sind relevant und enorm wichtig. Es betrifft uns alle. Und **außerdem** gibt es viel darüber zu sagen.

Christian: **Stimmen** wir **ab**: Wer ist **dafür** und wer **dagegen**?

Alle: Dafür.

Christian: Nun gut. Ich mache auch mit. Wie sollen wir das Thema behandeln?

Erman: Jeder soll sich einen Aspekt des Themas aussuchen. Ich würde z.B. gern mehr über alternative Energie erfahren.

Cornelia: Und ich möchte mich mit **Bürgerinitiativen** zum Klimawandel beschäftigen.

Christian: Ich hab' mal von einer Bürgerinitiative gehört, die gegen Handys in Bussen und Bahn war, und jetzt gibt es Ruhezonen bei der Bahn. **Meiner Meinung nach** ist das auch Umweltschutz.

Alexandra: Also, ich schlage vor, wir machen jetzt gleich einen konkreten Plan, wer welchen Aspekt des Themas behandelt.

Niels: Tut mir leid, dass ich **unterbrechen** muss. Ich muss jetzt leider weg. Ich habe eine Vorlesung. Wann treffen wir uns wieder?

Alexandra: Ich schicke dir eine Mail mit allen Informationen.

Alle: Tschüss.

Neue Wörter

meint (meinen) think
behandeln deal with
betrifft (betreffen) affects
die Umweltverschmutzung environmental pollution
im Grunde genommen basically
ich bin der Meinung I am of the opinion
der Umweltschutz environmental protection
das Windrad wind power generator
So ein Unsinn! Nonsense!
ich halte ... für ... I think ... is/are ...
übertrieben exaggerated
ich stimme (dir/Alexandra) zu I agree (with you/Alexandra)
außerdem besides
stimmen ab (abstimmen) take a vote
(ich bin) dafür (I am) for that
(ich bin) dagegen (I am) against that
der Bürger citizen
meiner Meinung nach in my opinion
unterbrechen interrupt

Windräder erzeugen saubere Energie

Ergänzen Sie die folgenden Sätze mit Ausdrücken und Informationen aus dem Dialog oben.

1. Cornelia möchte ein Thema _____, das sie in Deutschland täglich _____.

2. Alexandra ist der _____, dass _____ besonders wichtig ist. Niels _____ ihr zu.

3. Christian erwähnt eine _____, die früher gegen Handys in Bussen und Bahn demonstriert hat.

4. Niels muss _____, denn er hat eine Vorlesung.

Aktivität 1   Hin und her: Probleme und Lösungen

Stellen Sie Ihrem Partner / Ihrer Partnerin Fragen zu den folgenden Problemen, um herauszufinden, welche möglichen Lösungen es gibt.

BEISPIEL: **S1:**   Was kann man gegen Krieg tun?

S2:   Man kann an Antikriegsdemonstrationen teilnehmen.

Probleme	Mögliche Lösungen
Krieg	an Antikriegsdemonstrationen teilnehmen
Inflation	
Drogensucht	Informationen über die Gefahren von Drogen verbreiten
Umweltverschmutzung	
Verletzung der Menschenrechte	Organisationen wie Amnesty International unterstützen
Obdachlosigkeit	
Arbeitslosigkeit	Arbeiter umschulen

Aktivität 2   Probleme in der Stadt

Vier Leute sprechen über Probleme in ihrer Stadt und wie man sie lösen könnte. Setzen Sie die passende Nummer (1–4) vor das Problem, über das der Sprecher / die Sprecherin redet, und markieren Sie auch die Lösung, die er/sie vorschlägt.

Sprecher	Problem	Lösung
_____	Atomkraft (*nuclear power*)	**a.** Solarenergie
		b. Windenergie
_____	Giftstoffe in Nahrungsmitteln	**a.** strenge Staatskontrolle
		b. weniger Gemüse essen
_____	Verkehr	**a.** Tempolimit
		b. Wagen am Stadtrand parken
_____	Lärm	**a.** weniger Flugzeuge
		b. Autos verbieten

Express your opinion!

Aktivität 3   Nehmen Sie Stellung!°

In Vierergruppen, äußern Sie sich zu einigen Problemen im **Thema 1.** Benutzen Sie dabei die Redemittel im **Thema 1.** Jemand nennt das Gesprächsthema; die anderen sagen ihre Meinung.

BEISPIEL: **S1:**   Verkehrsbelästigung (*traffic disturbances*)

S2:   Ich bin der Meinung, man sollte Autos in der Innenstadt verbieten.

S3:   Meiner Meinung nach sollte man mehr Fußgängerzonen haben.

S4:   Ich finde es schade, dass Leute immer ihren Wagen benutzen. Sie sollten öfter zu Fuß gehen.

Aktivität 4 Um welche Probleme geht es hier?

Buttons, Aufkleber (*stickers*) und Poster sind beliebte Formen, die Meinung zu äußern (*express*).

Schritt 1: Schauen Sie sich die Buttons und Poster an und stellen Sie fest, wofür oder wogegen sie sind. Schreiben Sie dann die passenden Zahlen in die Liste.

a. _____ gegen Energie-
      verschwendung

b. _____ gegen Armut

c. _____ gegen Autoabgase
      (*emissions*)

d. _____ gegen Welthunger

e. _____ für den Tierschutz

f. _____ gegen Rauchen

g. _____ gegen Obdachlosigkeit

h. _____ gegen Krieg

i. _____ für höhere Gehälter

j. _____ gegen Pestizide in
      Nahrungsmitteln

k. _____ gegen Atomenergie

l. _____ für sauberes
      Trinkwasser

Schritt 2: Wählen Sie ein Problem aus **Thema 1** und entwerfen Sie einen Button, einen Aufkleber oder ein Poster.

Nr. 3, 6, 9, 12: Die Plakate sind Motive des Wettbewerbs „Farbe bekennen. Gegen globale Armut" des deutschen Bundesministeriums für wirtschaftliche Zusammenarbeit und Entwicklung (BMZ) zum Aktionsprogramm 2015. Weitere Informationen erhalten Sie unter www.ap2015.de.

Neue Wörter

die Wegwerfflasche (Wegwerfflaschen, *pl.***)** nonrecyclable bottle

die Getränkedose (Getränkedosen, *pl.***)** beverage can

mit umweltfreundlicher Verpackung with environmentally friendly packaging

vorziehen (+ *dat.*) give preference to . . . (over . . .)

die Plastiktüte (Plastiktüten, *pl.***)** plastic bag

verwenden use

verbrauchen consume

das Arzneimittel (Arzneimittel, *pl.***)** medication

anschaffen buy, acquire

isolieren insulate

die Sammelstelle (Sammelstellen, *pl.***)** recycling center

der Abfall (Abfälle, *pl.***)** waste

Thema 2: Umwelt

Was kann man für die Umwelt tun?

A Die Zeitschrift „Natur" fragte ihre Leser, „Bei welchen dieser Punkte auf der Liste glauben Sie, dass Sie mehr für die Umwelt tun könnten?" Hier sind die Antworten. Welche drei Punkte sind für Sie am wichtigsten? Was tun Sie persönlich für die Umwelt?

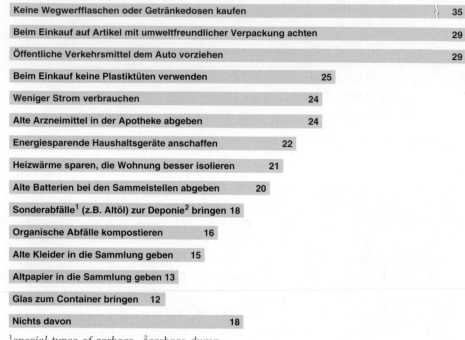

Keine Wegwerfflaschen oder Getränkedosen kaufen	35
Beim Einkauf auf Artikel mit umweltfreundlicher Verpackung achten	29
Öffentliche Verkehrsmittel dem Auto vorziehen	29
Beim Einkauf keine Plastiktüten verwenden	25
Weniger Strom verbrauchen	24
Alte Arzneimittel in der Apotheke abgeben	24
Energiesparende Haushaltsgeräte anschaffen	22
Heizwärme sparen, die Wohnung besser isolieren	21
Alte Batterien bei den Sammelstellen abgeben	20
Sonderabfälle[1] (z.B. Altöl) zur Deponie[2] bringen	18
Organische Abfälle kompostieren	16
Alte Kleider in die Sammlung geben	15
Altpapier in die Sammlung geben	13
Glas zum Container bringen	12
Nichts davon	18

[1]*special types of garbage* [2]*garbage dump*

B Wie kann man beim Energieverbrauch sparen? Welche von den Tipps im Schaubild befolgen Sie, um der Umwelt zu helfen?

BEISPIEL: Wenn ich aus dem Zimmer gehe, schalte ich das Licht aus.

1. kochen
2. Kühlschrank
3. warmes Wasser
4. Licht
5. heizen
6. Computer
7. ?

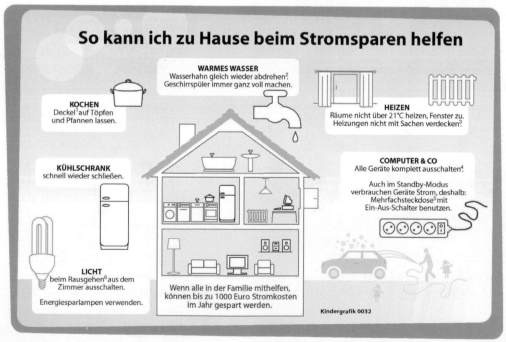

So kann ich zu Hause beim Stromsparen helfen

KOCHEN Deckel[1] auf Töpfen und Pfannen lassen.

KÜHLSCHRANK schnell wieder schließen.

LICHT beim Rausgehen[6] aus dem Zimmer ausschalten. Energiesparlampen verwenden.

WARMES WASSER Wasserhahn gleich wieder abdrehen[2]. Geschirrspüler immer ganz voll machen.

HEIZEN Räume nicht über 21°C heizen, Fenster zu. Heizungen nicht mit Sachen verdecken[3].

COMPUTER & CO Alle Geräte komplett ausschalten[4]. Auch im Standby-Modus verbrauchen Geräte Strom, deshalb: Mehrfachsteckdose[5] mit Ein-Aus-Schalter benutzen.

Wenn alle in der Familie mithelfen, können bis zu 1000 Euro Stromkosten im Jahr gespart werden.

Kindergrafik 0032

[1]*lids* [2]*turn off* [3]*cover* [4]*shut off* [5]*power strip* [6]*leaving, going out*

Landeskunde-Info

In allen Ländern Europas außer in der Bundesrepublik gibt es eine Höchstgeschwindigkeit auf der Autobahn. In Deutschland ist die Richtgeschwindigkeit (*suggested speed*) 130 km pro Stunde auf der Autobahn. Natürlich gibt es streckenweise (*for certain stretches*) Geschwindigkeitsbegrenzungen, zum Beispiel an Baustellen. Über der Autobahn sind manchmal Kameras angebracht, die einen Wagen, der zu schnell fährt, filmen. Man bekommt dann einen Strafzettel (*ticket*) mit dem Bild des Wagens und dem Nummernschild ins Haus geschickt. Niemand kann dann sagen: Das war jemand anders.

▷ Finden Sie es fair, dass es Kameras über der Autobahn gibt?

▷ Gibt es Tempolimits auf den Autobahnen bei Ihnen?

Aktivität 5 Langsamer, bitte!

Sie hören zuerst ein Gespräch zwischen Andreas, einem deutschen Autofahrer, und Jennifer, seinem Gast aus den USA. Hören Sie zuerst den Dialog, und lesen Sie die Sätze unten. Bringen Sie dann die Sätze in die richtige Reihenfolge.

_____ Bei uns ist die Höchstgeschwindigkeit (*speed limit*) 110 km pro Stunde.

_____ Wahrscheinlich eine Baustelle (*construction zone*) in der Nähe.

_____ Also doch ein Tempolimit. Gott sei Dank. Bei 100 km pro Stunde fühle ich mich direkt wie zu Hause.

_____ Keine Angst. Der Wagen schafft das spielend.

_____ Dann kann man gleich zu Fuß gehen.

_____ Schau mal. Dort ist ein Schild. Höchstgeschwindigkeit 100 km pro Stunde.

_1_ Fliegen wir eigentlich oder fahren wir?

Tempolimits auf Autobahnen

Erlaubte Höchstgeschwindigkeiten für Pkw in km/h

Land	km/h
Norwegen	90
Schweden	110
Großbritannien	112
Irland	
Belgien	
Finnland	120
Griechenland	
Niederlande	
Portugal	
Schweiz	
Serbien/Monten.	
Spanien	
Türkei	
Bulgarien	
Dänemark	
Frankreich	
Italien	
Kroatien	130
Luxemburg	
Österreich	
Polen	
Slowakei	
Slowenien	
Tschechien	
Ungarn	
Deutschland*	

*empfohlene Richtgeschwindigkeit

Quelle: ADAC

dpa— Grafik 5036   Stand 2007

Analyse

Berufe im Umweltbereich werden immer beliebter. Hier sind drei neue Berufe.

▷ Beate Lehmkuhl. Fachärztin für Umweltmedizin. Was hat sie studiert? Wo arbeitet sie jetzt?

▷ Ralph Hantschel. Geoökologe. Wo hat er studiert? Wo arbeitet er jetzt?

▷ Siegfried Müller. Entsorger (*waste management engineer*). Was hat er studiert? Wo arbeitet er jetzt?

Beate Lehmkuhl, 41, ist Fachärztin für Umweltmedizin in Hamburg. Sie studierte Humanmedizin in Freiburg. „Ich beschäftige mich hauptsächlich mit Schadstoffen und ihrer Wirkung auf den Menschen. Diese Schadstoffe sind in Boden, Wasser, Luft, Lebensmitteln und in Dingen, die wir jeden Tag benutzen."

Ralph Hantschel, 34, zählt zu den ersten Studienabgängern der Geoökologie: „Die Ausbildung in Bayreuth war intensiv und gut." Heute sucht er Wege zu einer umweltverträglichen Landwirtschaft und ist beim Forschungszentrum für Umwelt und Gesundheit (GSF) tätig.

Siegfried Müller vom Amt für Abfallwirtschaft der Stadt München: „Es macht Spaß. Aber die Verwaltungswege erscheinen mir mitunter zu lang." Der 32jährige studierte Physik. Er arbeitet in der Entsorgungsplanung.

Das Passiv

The Passive Voice°

So far you have learned to express sentences in German in the active voice. In the active voice, the subject of a sentence performs the action expressed by the verb. In the passive voice, the subject is acted on by an agent, the person or thing performing the action. This agent is not always named, because it is either understood, unimportant, or unknown. Compare the following sentences.

Active Voice

Viele Leute lesen täglich eine Zeitung.	*Many people read a newspaper daily.*
Welche Zeitung lesen die Deutschen am meisten?	*Which paper do Germans read the most?*

Passive Voice

In Deutschland werden viele Zeitungen verkauft.	*Many newspapers are sold in Germany.*
Welche Zeitung wird am meisten gelesen?	*Which newspaper is read the most?*

The active voice emphasizes the subject that carries out an activity; in the passive voice the emphasis shifts to the activity itself. For this reason, the passive voice tends to be more impersonal. It is commonly used in newspapers, scientific writing, and descriptions of procedures and activities.

Formation of the Passive Voice

The passive voice is formed with the auxiliary verb **werden** and the past participle of the main verb. (English uses *to be* and the past participle.) Although it can be used in all personal forms, the passive occurs most frequently in the third-person singular or plural. Following are the commonly used tenses of the passive.

Present

Die Zeitung **wird verkauft.**	*The newspaper is (being) sold.*

Simple Past

Die Zeitung **wurde verkauft.**	*The newspaper was (being) sold.*

Present Perfect

Die Zeitung **ist verkauft worden.**	*The newspaper has been sold.*

Past Perfect

Die Zeitung **war verkauft worden.**	*The newspaper had been sold.*

NOTE:

❯ In the perfect tenses of the passive, the past participle **geworden** is shortened to **worden.**

❯ The presence of **worden** in any sentence is a clear signal that the sentence is in the passive voice.

Hier werden Zeitungen verkauft.

You now know three ways in which the verb **werden** can function.

1. **werden** as independent verb (*to become*)
2. **werden** + infinitive (future tense)
3. **werden** + past participle (passive voice)

Read the headlines and captions and determine . . .

▶ how the verb **werden** is used in each case (independent verb, future tense, passive)

▶ the position of the past participle in
   a. a main clause in the passive voice
   b. a dependent clause in the passive voice

In jeder Minute werden 21 Hektar[1] Regenwald vernichtet[2]

Schon in wenigen Jahren wird es die „Grünen Lungen[3] der Erde" nicht mehr geben

---

GREENPEACE

Wie konnten Sie es zulassen[4], daß unsere Erde[5] in so kurzer Zeit vergiftet[6] wurde?

Du meinst, Fleisch essen und Umweltschutz vertragen sich?

Denk mal genau nach!

Wenn dir wirklich was an diesem Planeten liegt, werde Vegetarier!

Muß unser Dorf so häßlich werden?

---

[1]Hektar = *2.47 acres* [2]*destroyed* [3]*lungs* [4]*allow* [5]*earth* [6]*poisoned*

Expressing the Agent

As already noted, the agent causing the action in a passive voice sentence is often not stated. However, when it is stated, the agent is expressed with the preposition **von** (+ *dat.*).

> Wie viel Geld wird **vom Staat** für Umweltschutz ausgegeben?
>
> *How much money is spent for environmental protection **by the government**?*

When the action is caused by an impersonal force, the preposition **durch** (+ *acc.*) is used.

> Die Ozonschicht wird **durch Luftverschmutzung** zerstört.
>
> *The ozone layer is being destroyed **by air pollution**.*

Sentences in the passive voice that state the agent can also be expressed in the active voice. There is no difference in meaning, only in emphasis.

PREPOSITIONAL
OBJECT
SUBJECT (AGENT)
PASSIVE: Jedes Jahr wird **viel Geld vom Staat** für Umweltschutz ausgegeben.

SUBJECT (AGENT)　　　　　DIRECT OBJECT
ACTIVE: **Der Staat** gibt jedes Jahr **viel Geld** für Umweltschutz aus.

Note that the subject in the passive voice sentence becomes the direct object in the active voice sentence, and the subject in the active voice sentence becomes the prepositional object (**von**) in the passive voice sentence.

Übung 1　In der Schweiz

Ergänzen Sie die folgenden Sätze mit Verben im Passiv Präsenz.

1. In der Schweiz _____ vier Sprachen _____: Deutsch, Französisch, Italienisch und Rätoromanisch. (sprechen)
2. In 17 Kantonen _____ Deutsch _____. (sprechen)
3. Jährlich _____ rund drei Milliarden Franken für Umweltschutz _____. (ausgeben)
4. 237 Liter Wasser _____ per Person pro Tag _____. (verbrauchen)
5. Im Durchschnitt _____ mehr Kaffee von den Schweizern als von den Deutschen _____. (trinken)
6. Die Bahn _____ zweimal so oft von den Schweizern _____ wie von den Deutschen. (benutzen)

Übung 2　Wissen über Deutschland

Bilden Sie Sätze im Passiv Präsens.

1. in Deutschland / innovative Energietechnologien vom Staat / fördern
2. immer mehr Passivhäuser / bauen
3. ein Passivhaus / mit Erdwärme / heizen
4. Strom für ein Passivhaus / durch Solaranlagen / gewinnen
5. erneuerbare Energie / durch Wind, Wasser und Sonne / produzieren
6. durch Wind, Wasser und Sonne / keine klimaschädlichen Emissionen / erzeugen
7. der Verbrauch an Wasser in Haushalt und Industrie / langsam / reduzieren
8. viele Solarzellen und Windräder / aus Deutschland / in die ganze Welt / exportieren

Übung 3 Wer handelt hier?

Ergänzen Sie die folgenden Sätze im Passiv mit **von** oder **durch**.

Ein Passivhaus mit Solaranlage

1. In den 80er-Jahren ist das Ozonloch _____ Wissenschaftlern entdeckt worden.
2. Die Umwelt wird _____ Luftverschmutzung zerstört.
3. Die Aktion „Saubere Luft" wird _____ vielen Bürgern unterstützt.
4. Bei der Initiative „Gegen Atomkraft" sind einige Studenten _____ der Polizei verhaftet (*arrested*) worden.
5. Die Bürgerinitiative „Kein Handy in Bus und Bahn" ist _____ Zeitung und Fernsehen verbreitet worden.
6. Strom für ein Passivhaus wird _____ Solaranlagen gewonnen.

Übung 4 Achtung, Uhren umstellen!

Lesen Sie folgende Nachricht über die Sommerzeit (*daylight saving time*).

1. Identifizieren Sie alle Sätze im Passiv.
2. Was sind die Tatsachen?

   a. Die Uhren …
   b. Die Nacht …
   c. Die Sommerzeit …
   d. Das Ziel (*goal*) …

Achtung, Uhren umstellen: Die Sommerzeit beginnt

BM/dpa Hamburg, 26. März

Der Osterhase[1] bringt in diesem Jahr auch die Sommerzeit: In der Nacht zum Sonntag um 2 Uhr werden die Uhren auf 3 Uhr vorgestellt; die Nacht wird um eine Stunde verkürzt. Die Sommerzeit endet am 24. September–traditionsgemäß wieder eine Sonntag-Nacht.

   Die Sommerzeit war in der Bundesrepublik Deutschland – nach 30 Jahren Unterbrechung[2] – erstmals 1980 wieder eingeführt worden. Das eigentliche[3] Ziel, Energie einzusparen, wurde jedoch nicht erreicht. Dafür genießen[4] viele ihre Freizeit an den langen hellen Abenden.

In der Nacht zum Sonntag...

...Uhr 1 Stunde vorstellen

[1]*Easter Bunny* [2]*interruption* [3]*real* [4]*enjoy*

Nützliche Wörter	
die Uhr umstellen	*to change the clock*
die Uhr vorstellen	*to set the clock ahead*
verkürzen	*to shorten*
einführen	*to introduce*
erreichen	*to reach*

Expressing a General Activity

Sometimes a sentence in the passive voice expresses a general activity without stating a subject at all. In such cases, the "impersonal" **es** is generally understood to be the subject, and therefore the conjugated verb always appears in the third-person singular. This grammatical feature has no equivalent in English.

Hier wird gerudert.	*People are rowing here.*
Im Fernsehen wird viel über Terrorismus gesprochen.	*There's a lot of talk about terrorism on television.*
Hier wird Deutsch gesprochen.	*German (is) spoken here.*

Eins – und eins – und eins ...

Hier wird mächtig gerudert! **Jochen** sitzt zwischen **Peter** und **Stefan**, **Armin** sitzt zwischen **Martin** und **Thomas**. Vorn in einem Boot sitzt **Peter**, während **Martin** hinten sitzt. **Kalli** und **Stefan** rudern nicht in demselben Boot. Wer ist wer?

Lösung: 1. Stefan, 2. Jochen, 3. Peter, 4. Martin, 5. Armin, 6. Thomas, 7. Kalli

Übung 5 Was ist hier los?

Beschreiben Sie, was die Leute auf diesen Bildern machen. Gebrauchen Sie die Verben:

debattieren	essen	Musik machen	tanzen
demonstrieren	feiern	reden	trinken
diskutieren	lachen	singen	

BEISPIEL: Da wird gefeiert und ...

2.

1.

3.

Landeskunde-Info

In vielen Orten Deutschlands können alte Medikamente in die Apotheke zurückgebracht werden, damit sie nicht in den Abfall geworfen werden und als Giftstoffe die Umwelt gefährden. Andere potentiell gefährliche Substanzen wie alte Batterien und Farben werden von „Umweltbussen" abgeholt.

- ▶ Was sollte man auf keinen Fall mit alten Medikamenten machen?
- ▶ Was machen Sie mit alten Medikamenten?

Beispiele für Gefahrensymbole

Gifte	Leicht entzündlich	Ätzend	Gesundheitsschädlich

Übung 6 Hin und her: Zwei umweltbewusste Städte

In zwei Städten, Altstadt und Neustadt, wird für eine bessere Umwelt gesorgt.

BEISPIEL: **S1:** Was ist in Altstadt zuerst gemacht worden?

S2: Zuerst sind die Bürger über Umweltschutz informiert worden. Und in Neustadt?

S1: Zuerst sind …

	Altstadt	**Neustadt**
zuerst		Tipps für umweltbewusstes Leben an alle Bürger verteilen
dann		Bürger zum Energiesparen motivieren
danach		in öffentlichen Gebäuden Energiesparlampen anschaffen
schließlich		auf Pestizide in Parks verzichten
zuletzt		Fahrradfahren im täglichen Leben fördern

The Passive with Modal Verbs

Modal verbs used with a passive infinitive convey something that should, must, or can be done. Only the present tense, the simple past tense, and the present subjunctive of modals are commonly used in the passive.

Die Umwelt **muss geschützt werden.**
The environment must be protected.

Die Natur **darf** nicht **zerstört werden.**
Nature must not be destroyed.

Recyclingprogramme **sollten gefördert werden.**
Recycling programs ought to be promoted.

Alte Medikamente **können** in die Apotheke **zurückgebracht werden.**
Old medications can be returned to the pharmacy.

NOTE:

○ The passive infinitive consists of the past participle of the main verb and **werden:**

Active Infinitive	Passive Infinitive
schützen *to protect*	geschützt werden *to be protected*
zerstören *to destroy*	zerstört werden *to be destroyed*
vermeiden *to avoid*	vermieden werden *to be avoided*
fördern *to promote*	gefördert werden *to be promoted*
zurückbringen *to return*	zurückgebracht werden *to be returned*

Schützt Flüsse und Auen

Diese Lebensräume vieler wildlebender Tier- und Pflanzenarten dürfen nicht weiter zerstört werden!

Spendenkonto: 1703-203, Postgiroamt Hamburg, oder werden Sie Mitglied im Bund der aktiven Naturschützer.

Übung 7   Aus Liebe zur Umwelt

Was kann und muss gemacht werden? Folgen Sie dem Beispiel.

BEISPIEL: die Umwelt schonen / müssen →
Die Umwelt muss geschont werden.

1. alle Menschen über Umweltschutz informieren / müssen
2. mehr Energie sparen / sollen
3. Recyclingprogramme fördern / sollen
4. Altglas sammeln / können
5. Wälder und Flüsse schützen / müssen
6. Alternativenergie entwickeln / müssen
7. Luftverschmutzung vermindern / müssen
8. Klimawandel verhindern / können
9. Abfälle wie Plastiktüten und Einwegflaschen vermeiden / müssen
10. Altbatterien nicht in den Müll werfen / dürfen
11. Wegwerfprodukte (wie z.B. Einmal-Rasierer, Einmal-Fotoapparate) nicht kaufen / sollen
12. Verpackungen (wie die Mehrweg-Eierbox) wieder ins Geschäft bringen / können

Übung 8   Was ist das Problem?

Was soll, kann oder darf damit (nicht) gemacht werden?

BEISPIEL: Digitaluhren können nicht repariert werden.

1. Billiguhren (Digitaluhren)
2. Einmal-Fotoapparate
3. alte Batterien
4. Einwegflaschen
5. alte Medikamente
6. Giftstoffe

a. vom Umweltbus abholen
b. in fast alle Apotheken zurückbringen
c. nur für einen Film gebrauchen
d. nicht in den Müll werfen
e. nicht wieder füllen
f. nicht reparieren

Landeskunde-Info

Viele Menschen leben heutzutage viel umweltbewusster als früher. Sie sind daran interessiert, wie man die Umwelt schützen kann und wie man selbst mithelfen kann, umweltfreundlicher zu leben. Dieses Umweltbewusstsein zeigt sich auch in der modernen Sprache. So gebraucht man oft **alt** als Präfix, wenn man von Dingen spricht, die zur Deponie, zu Sammelstellen oder zur Wiederverwertung gebracht werden; z.B. **Altbatterien, Altöl, Altpapier, Altglas** und **Altkleidung.** Das Altglas wird nach Farben sortiert: **Braunglas, Grünglas** und **Weißglas.**

Abfall oder Müll (*garbage*) wie Plastiktüten, Einwegflaschen (*bottles that can't be returned*) und Batterien werden auch zu besonderen Sammelstellen gebracht. In Deutschland versucht man Abfall, der nicht wiederverwertet werden kann, total zu eliminieren. Jede Gemeinde (*community*) bestimmt, wie man die Müllabfuhr (*garbage collection*) organisiert und was man dafür bezahlt. Es gibt strenge Regeln, welcher Artikel in welche Abfalltonne gehört. In manchen Gemeinden wird Abfall in der Abfalltonne gewogen (*weighed*) und danach richtet sich die Bezahlung. Manchmal gibt es sogar spezielle Abfalltonnen nur für Kinderwindeln (*diapers*), die dann auch gewogen werden. Man bezahlt also nach Gewicht, auch wenn man Dinge selbst zu einem Recyclinghof bringt.

▶ Muss man bei Ihnen Abfall streng sortieren?
▶ Welche Dinge recyceln Sie?

Use of **man** as an Alternative to the Passive

Generally, the passive voice is used whenever the agent of an action is unknown. One alternative to the passive is to use the pronoun **man** in the active voice.

Passive Voice	Active-Voice Alternative
Die Gefahr ist nicht erkannt worden.	**Man hat** die Gefahr nicht **erkannt.**
The danger was not recognized.	*People (One) did not recognize the danger.*
Die Zerstörung der Altstadt muss verhindert werden.	**Man muss** die Zerstörung der Altstadt **verhindern.**
The destruction of the old city must be prevented.	*People (One) must prevent the destruction of the old city.*

Übung 9 Was kann man für die Umwelt tun?

Bilden Sie neue Sätze mit **man.**

BEISPIEL: Wegwerfprodukte sollen vermieden werden. →
Man soll Wegwerfprodukte vermeiden.

1. Die Umwelt darf nicht weiter zerstört werden.
2. Altpapier und Glas sollten zum Recycling gebracht werden.
3. In Göttingen ist Geld für den Umweltschutz gesammelt worden.
4. Mehr Recycling-Container sind aufgestellt worden.
5. Chemikalien im Haushalt sollen vermieden werden.
6. Batterien sollen nicht in den Hausmüll geworfen werden.
7. Der Wald muss besonders geschützt werden.

Hier klicken!

Weiteres zum Thema Umwelt finden Sie bei **Deutsch: Na klar!** im World-Wide-Web unter **www.mhhe.com/dnk6.**

Übung 10 Lebensqualität

Was kann man tun, um die Lebensqualität zu verbessern? Bilden Sie zwei Sätze je mit **man** und Passiv.

BEISPIEL: alte Zeitungen →
Man kann alte Zeitungen zum Recycling bringen.
Alte Zeitungen können zum Recycling gebracht werden.

alte Zeitungen	bauen
Plastiktüten	fördern
Windenergie	vermeiden
Kinderspielplätze	sammeln
Altpapier	schützen
öffentliche Verkehrsmittel	benutzen
Wälder	zum Recycling bringen
Verpackungen	
die Wohnung	kompostieren
organische Abfälle	besser isolieren
Altglas	wieder ins Geschäft bringen
mehr Fußgängerzonen	

The Present Participle°

The present participle (ending in *-ing* in English) is used in a more limited way in German than it is in English. In German it functions primarily as an adjective or an adverb. As an attributive adjective (preceding a noun), the participle takes appropriate adjective endings. The present participle of a German verb is formed by adding **-d** to the infinitive.

Infinitive	Present Participle
kommen	kommend (*coming*)
steigen	steigend (*climbing, increasing*)

Present Participle as Attributive Adjective

im **kommenden** Sommer	*in the coming (next) summer*
die **steigende** Arbeitslosigkeit	*increasing unemployment*

Present Participle as Adverb

Jennifer spricht **fließend** Deutsch.	*Jennifer speaks German fluently.*

Übung 11 In der Zeitung

Worüber liest man fast täglich? Ergänzen Sie die Sätze mit einem Partizip Präsens.

Man liest oft über …

1. ___wachsende___ Obdachlosigkeit. (wachsen)
2. die _____ Preise. (steigen)
3. _____ Studenten. (demonstrieren)
4. _____ Arbeitslosigkeit. (wachsen)
5. die _____ Luftverschmutzung. (steigen)
6. die _____ Arbeiter. (streiken)
7. die _____ Menschen. (hungern)

Sprache im Kontext

Videoclips

A Claudia, Harald und Wiebke sprechen über die Probleme in der Welt.

1. Was sind für sie die drei größten Probleme heute?
2. Und für Sie? Was sind für Sie die drei größten Probleme heute in der Welt?

B Harald spricht über ein ganz spezifisches Problem in Berlin. Erklären Sie das Problem.

C Wiebke spricht über Aids und was dagegen gemacht wird. Was sagt sie? Ergänzen Sie ihre Worte.

„Ich verfolge in der Zeitung ab und zu die Entwicklung von Aids. Ich sehe, dass es in Afrika sehr stark _____ hat, dass auch die _____ Versorgung für Aids noch nicht das _____, was es bringen könnte. Man arbeitet an Wirkstoffen und _____, aber die Versorgung zum Beispiel für _____ Leute in Afrika oder für Leute in den Ostblockländern ist nicht so gut. Und Medikamente sind auch nicht so verfügbar, wie man sich das _____.“

D Was tun Claudia und Wiebke für die Umwelt? Schauen Sie sich die Interviews an und schreiben Sie vor jede Aussage entweder **C** für Claudia oder **W** für Wiebke.

_____ sammelt Zeitungen

_____ benutzt öffentliche Verkehrsmittel oder Fahrrad

_____ bringt leere Flaschen zurück

_____ benutzt Stoffbeutel statt Plastikbeutel

_____ lässt das Wasser beim Zähneputzen nicht laufen

_____ badet und duscht weniger und wäscht sich mehr, denn es ist gesünder für die Haut

_____ gebraucht so wenig Strom wie möglich

E Und Sie? Was machen Sie für die Umwelt?

Lesen

Zum Thema

Die Skandalpresse. In den meisten Ländern gibt es Zeitschriften, die von den jüngsten Sensationen und Skandalen berichten. Auch im Fernsehen wird oft von sensationellen und skandalösen Ereignissen (*events*) berichtet, die aber oft erfunden sind.

Interviewen Sie zwei Kursmitglieder. Schreiben Sie die Antworten auf und berichten Sie darüber.

1. Wie heißen die Zeitungen und Zeitschriften bei Ihnen, die skandalöse Nachrichten bringen?

2. Wer liest sie regelmäßig? Was interessiert die Leser? Warum?

Auf den ersten Blick

A „Was in der Zeitung steht“ ist eine Ballade von Reinhard Mey, einem bekannten deutschen Liedermacher. Lesen Sie die Ballade kurz durch und kreuzen Sie alles an, was stimmt.

1. Was sind die Orte, an denen die Ballade spielt?
- ☐ zu Hause
- ☐ im Büro
- ☐ in der U-Bahnstation

2. Die Hauptfigur ist
- ☐ ein Mann, der für eine Zeitung arbeitet.
- ☐ ein Mann, dessen Name nicht genannt wird.
- ☐ ein Mann, der alles glaubt, was in der Zeitung steht.
- ☐ ein Mann, dessen Bild mit der Schlagzeile „Finanzskandal“ in der Zeitung erscheint.

3. Außer der Hauptfigur gibt es noch andere Menschen, die in der Ballade eine aktive Rolle spielen. Wer sind Sie?

☐ die Kollegen

☐ der Chef

☐ die Frau des Mannes

☐ die Kinder des Mannes

☐ ein Zeitungsverkäufer

☐ der Redakteur der Zeitung, der für den Artikel verantwortlich war

☐ der Chef vom Dienst der Zeitung, in der sein Bild gestanden hat

B Welcher Satz wird oft wiederholt?

Was in der Zeitung steht

von Reinhard Mey

Wie jeden Morgen war er pünktlich dran, seine
Kollegen sahen ihn fragend an, „Sag' mal,
hast du noch nicht gesehen, was in der
Zeitung steht?"
5 Er schloß die Türe hinter sich,
neatly   hängte Hut und Mantel in den Schrank fein säuberlich°,
setzte sich, „da wollen wir erst mal sehen,
was in der Zeitung steht."

Und da stand es fett auf Seite zwei
10 „Finanzskandal", sein Bild dabei
und die Schlagzeile „Wie lang das wohl so weitergeht?"
Er las den Text,
und ihm war sofort klar,
mistake, mix-up   eine Verwechslung°, nein, da war kein Wort von wahr,
fabricated   15 aber wie kann so etwas verlogen° sein,
was in der Zeitung steht?

paper   Er starrte auf das Blatt°,
das vor ihm lag,
malicious / blow   es traf ihn wie ein heimtückischer° Schlag°,
20 wie ist das möglich, daß so etwas in der Zeitung steht?
sich … to turn   Das Zimmer ringsherum begann sich zu drehen°,
as blurred   die Zeilen konnte er nur noch verschwommen° sehen.
wehrt … does one defend oneself   Wie wehrt man sich° nur gegen das,
was in der Zeitung steht?

stell … be stolid   25 Die Kollegen sagten, „stell dich einfach stur"°,
staggered   er taumelte° zu seinem Chef über den Flur,
„aber selbstverständlich,
daß jeder hier zu Ihnen steht,
ich glaube, das Beste ist, Sie spannen erst mal aus,
30 ein paar Tage Urlaub, bleiben Sie zu Haus,
Sie wissen ja, die Leute glauben gleich alles,
nur weil es in der Zeitung steht."

Er holte Hut und Mantel, wankte° aus dem Raum,   *swayed*
nein, das war wirklich kalt, das war kein böser Traum,
35 wer denkt sich sowas aus, wie das,
    was in der Zeitung steht?
Er rief den Fahrstuhl°, stieg ein und gleich wieder aus,   *elevator*
nein, er ging doch wohl besser durch das Treppenhaus°.   *stairwell*
Da würde ihn keiner sehen, der wüßte,
40   was in der Zeitung steht.
Er würde durch die Tiefgarage gehen, er war zu Fuß.
Der Pförtner° würde ihn nicht sehen,   *custodian*
der wußte immer ganz genau,
    was in der Zeitung steht.
45 Er stolperte° die Wagenauffahrt° rauf,   *stumbled / driveway*
sah den Rücken des Pförtners,
das Tor war auf,
das klebt wie Pech° an dir,   klebt wie ... *sticks like tar*
das wirst du nie mehr los°,   wirst ... *you will never get rid of*
50   was in der Zeitung steht,
    was in der Zeitung steht,
    was in der Zeitung steht,
    was in der Zeitung steht.

Er eilte° zur U-Bahnstation,   *hurried*
55 jetzt wüßten es die Nachbarn schon,
jetzt war es im ganzen Ort herum,
    was in der Zeitung steht.
Solange die Kinder in der Schule waren,
solange würden sie es vielleicht nicht erfahren°,   *find out*
60 aber irgendwer hat ihnen längst erzählt,
    was in der Zeitung steht.

Er wich den Leuten auf dem Bahnsteig aus°,   wich ... aus *avoided*
ihm schien, die Blicke, alle richteten sich nur auf ihn,
der Mann im Kiosk da, der wußte Wort für Wort,
65   was in der Zeitung steht.
Wie eine Welle° war es, die über ihm zusammenschlug°,   *wave / crashed down*
wie die Erlösung° kam der Vorortszug°,   *deliverance / suburban train*
du wirst nie mehr ganz frei, das hängt dir ewig an,
    was in der Zeitung steht.

70 „Was wollen Sie eigentlich?" fragte der Redakteur°,   *editor*
„Verantwortung°, Mann, wenn ich das schon hör',   *responsibility*
die Leute müssen halt nicht gleich alles glauben,
nur weil es in der Zeitung steht."
„Na, schön, so eine Verwechslung kann schon mal passieren,
75 da kannst du noch so sorgfältig° recherchieren°.   *carefully / research*
Mann, was glauben Sie, was Tag für Tag für ein Unfug°   *nonsense*
in der Zeitung steht?"

„Ja", sagte der Chef vom Dienst, „das ist wirklich zu dumm,
aber ehrlich°, man bringt sich doch nicht gleich um°,   *honestly* / bringt ... *doesn't go and kill oneself*
80 nur weil mal aus Versehen°   aus ... *by mistake*
    was in der Zeitung steht."
Die Gegendarstellung° erschien am Abend schon,   *retraction, corrected version*
fünf Zeilen mit dem Bedauern° der Redaktion,   *regret*
aber Hand aufs Herz, wer liest, was so klein
85 in der Zeitung steht?

Zum Text

Lesen Sie die Ballade nun genauer durch und machen Sie die folgenden Aufgaben.

A Was sind die Tatsachen? Bringen Sie die folgenden Sätze in die richtige Reihenfolge.

_____ Der Mann eilt zur U-Bahnstation, wo er sich vor den Zug wirft.

_____ In der Zeitung sieht er sein Bild neben der Schlagzeile „Finanzskandal".

_____ Später liest man ganz klein in der Zeitung, dass der Bericht über den Mann ein Irrtum war.

_____ Ein Mann kommt wie immer pünktlich ins Büro zur Arbeit und liest die Zeitung.

_____ Sein Chef gibt ihm ein paar Tage Urlaub und schickt ihn nach Hause.

_____ Kein Wort ist wahr, was über ihn in der Zeitung steht.

B Was macht den Text „Was in der Zeitung steht" zu einer Ballade? Welche der folgenden Punkte treffen auf diese Ballade zu? Geben Sie Beispiele aus dem Text. Eine Ballade …

☐ ist ein Lied mit mehreren Strophen.

☐ erzählt eine Geschichte.

☐ berichtet oft ein tragisches Geschehen.

☐ behandelt Themen aus der Geschichte oder dem Alltag einfacher Menschen.

☐ ist meistens gereimt.

☐ enthält einen Kehrreim (Zeilen, die sich wiederholen).

☐ zeigt oft Rede und Gegenrede (Konflikte zwischen Menschen).

C Wie reagieren die folgenden Personen in der Ballade auf die falsche Information in der Zeitung?

1. der Mann, über den Falsches in der Zeitung steht
2. die Kollegen
3. der Chef des Mannes
4. der Redakteur der Zeitung, in der der skandalöse Bericht mit Bild steht
5. der Chef vom Dienst der Zeitung

D **Vom Lied zum Zeitungsartikel.** Verwandeln Sie das Lied in einen Zeitungsartikel.

Schritt 1: Benutzen Sie das Raster unten und machen Sie sich Notizen zu dem Vorfall (*incident*) im Lied.

Wer:	Wann:
Wo:	Wie:
Was:	Warum:

Schritt 2: Bringen Sie Ihre Notizen in die richtige Reihenfolge. Wenn Sie wollen, können Sie mehr Details hinzufügen (*add*).

Schritt 3: Benutzen Sie Ihre Notizen, um den Zeitungsartikel zu schreiben.

Zu guter Letzt

Globale und lokale Probleme

Diskutieren Sie im Plenum einen Vorschlag zur Lösung eines globalen oder lokalen Problems.

Schritt 1: Das Thema. Wählen Sie ein Thema oder Problem aus der Liste mit globalen Problemen auf S. 408 oder ein aktuelles Thema an Ihrer Universität oder in Ihrer Stadt.

BEISPIELE: Armut
Verkehr in der Innenstadt
Umweltverschmutzung
Arbeitslosigkeit
Ausländerfeindlichkeit
Klimawandel
Rassismus
Krieg

Schritt 2: Die Lösung. Formulieren Sie eine mögliche Lösung des Problems. Sie brauchen nicht unbedingt alle mit dieser Lösung einverstanden (*in agreement*) zu sein.

BEISPIEL: Umweltverschmutzung →
Die Benzinsteuern sollen drastisch erhöht werden.

Schritt 3: Dafür oder dagegen? Entscheiden Sie sich, ob Sie dafür oder dagegen sind. Schreiben Sie drei Argumente, um Ihre Meinung auszudrücken.

Schritt 4: Redemittel. Wie führen Sie Ihre Argumente ein? Wählen Sie mindestens drei Redemittel aus der Liste auf S. 409, um Ihre Argumente einzuleiten.

BEISPIELE: ich bin der Meinung
meiner Meinung nach
ich halte ... für ...
ich bin dafür
ich bin dagegen

Schritt 5: Die Klasse wählt eine/n Diskussionsmoderator/in, um die Diskussion zu leiten. Zwei Klassenmitglieder führen Protokoll (*take notes*).

Schritt 6: Diskutieren Sie über die vorgeschlagene Lösung im Plenum. Hier sind einige Redemittel, die dem/der Moderator/in behilflich sein können.

Wir sind hier, um das Thema _____ zu besprechen.	*We are here to discuss the topic _____.*
Wer möchte etwas dazu sagen?	*Who would like to say something about that?*
Einer nach dem anderen bitte!	*Please take turns!*
Wir müssen die Diskussion jetzt zu Ende führen.	*We have to bring the discussion to a close now.*

Schritt 7: Jeder bekommt eine Kopie des Protokolls, um damit eine Zusammenfassung der Diskussion zu schreiben.

Wortschatz

Weltweite Probleme	World Problems
die **Arbeitslosigkeit**	unemployment
die **Armut**	poverty
die **Ausländerfeindlichkeit**	xenophobia, hatred directed toward foreigners
die **Drogensucht**	drug addiction
die **Gewalttätigkeit, -en**	(act of) violence
der **Hunger**	hunger, famine
die **Korruption**	corruption
die **Krankheit, -en**	illness, disease, ailment
der **Krieg, -e**	war
das **Menschenrecht, -e**	human right (*usu. plural*)
der/die **Obdachlose** (*decl. adj.*)	homeless (person)
die **Obdachlosigkeit**	homelessness
der **Rassismus**	racism
der **Rechtsextremismus**	right-wing extremism
der **Terrorismus**	terrorism
die **Umweltverschmutzung**	environmental pollution
die **Verletzung, -en**	injury, violation
die **Welt**	world, earth

Umwelt	Environment
der **Abfall, ⸚e**	waste, garbage, trash, litter
die **Dose, -n**	(tin or aluminum) can; jar
die **Flasche, -n**	bottle
die **Wegwerfflasche, -n**	nonrecyclable bottle
die **Getränkedose, -n**	beverage can
der **Klimawandel**	climate change
der **Lärm**	noise
die **Plastiktüte, -n**	plastic bag
die **Sammelstelle, -n**	recycling center
der **Umweltschutz**	environmental protection
das **Verkehrsmittel, -**	vehicle, means of transportation
die **Verpackung, -en**	packaging, wrapping
das **Windrad, ⸚er**	wind power generator

Sonstige Substantive	Other Nouns
das **Arzneimittel, -**	medication
der **Ausländer, -** / die **Ausländerin, -nen**	foreigner
der **Bürger, -** / die **Bürgerin, -nen**	citizen
die **Demonstration, -en**	demonstration
die **Droge, -n**	drug; medicine
die **Forschung, -en**	research
der **Fortschritt, -e**	progress
Fortschritte machen	to make progress

die **Gefahr, -en**	danger
die **Lösung, -en**	solution
die **Meinung, -en**	opinion
ich bin der Meinung …	I'm of the opinion …
meiner Meinung nach …	in my opinion …
der **Politiker, -** / die **Politikerin, -nen**	politician
die **Regierung, -en**	government
die **Steuer, -n**	tax

Verben	Verbs
ab • stimmen	to take a vote
sich etwas an • schaffen	to purchase or acquire something
behandeln	to deal with
betreffen (betrifft), betraf, betroffen	to affect
ein • führen	to introduce
sich engagieren	to get involved
entwickeln	to develop
fördern	to promote
halten für (hält), hielt, gehalten	to consider, think
isolieren	to isolate; to insulate
lösen	to solve
meinen	to think, be of the opinion
schaffen, schuf, geschaffen	to create
schützen	to protect
sich Sorgen machen um (etwas)	to worry about (something)
teil • nehmen an (+ *dat.*) **(nimmt teil), nahm teil, teilgenommen**	to participate (in)
(sich) trennen	to separate
um • schulen	to retrain
unterbrechen (unterbricht), unterbrach, unterbrochen	to interrupt
verbieten, verbot, verboten	to prohibit, forbid
verbrauchen	to consume
verbreiten	to spread, disseminate
vermeiden, vermied, vermieden	to avoid
vermindern	to decrease, lessen
verwenden	to use, apply
vor • ziehen, zog vor, vorgezogen	to prefer
wählen	to vote, elect; to choose

Adjektive und Adverbien	Adjectives and Adverbs	Andere Ausdrücke	Other Expressions
global	global	außerdem	besides, in addition
möglich	possible, possibly	Ich bin dafür.	I'm in favor of it.
öffentlich	public	Ich bin dagegen.	I'm against it.
sauber	clean	im Grunde genommen	basically
streng	strict(ly)	So ein Unsinn!	Nonsense!
übertrieben	exaggerated		
umweltfreundlich	environmentally friendly		
vertraut	familiar		

Das kann ich nun!

1. Nennen Sie fünf globale Probleme.

2. Welche Substantive assoziieren Sie mit den Verben? (Mehrere Antworten sind möglich.)

   a. an Demonstrationen   _____ entwickeln
   b. die Umwelt   _____ einführen
   c. Plastiktüten   _____ schützen
   d. Obdachlosigkeit   _____ fördern
   e. Fußgängerzonen   _____ vermindern
   f. Recyclingprogramme   _____ verbieten
   g. Umweltschutz   _____ teilnehmen
   h. Alternativenergie   _____ einrichten

3. Nennen Sie zwei oder drei Sachen, die man in Ihrer Stadt tut oder die Sie persönlich machen, um die Umwelt zu schützen.

4. Sie diskutieren mit einem Bekannten über Klimawandel. Wie sagt man folgende Ausdrücke auf Deutsch?
   a. *In my opinion . . .*
   b. *I think it is exaggerated . . .*
   c. *I agree with you that . . .*
   d. *I am against that.*

5. Bilden Sie nun vier Sätze mit den Ausdrücken aus Übung 4, in denen Sie etwas über Klimawandel aussagen.

6. Drücken Sie die folgenden Sätze im Passiv aus.
   a. Man muss die Umwelt schützen.
   b. Kann man Klimawandel verhindern?
   c. Man darf Altbatterien nicht in den Abfall werfen.

7. Ergänzen Sie die folgenden Sätze im Passiv.
   a. In Deutschland _____ viele Zeitungen gelesen.
   b. Letztes Jahr _____ Millionen Digitalkameras gekauft _____.
   c. In der Schweiz _____ in 17 Kantonen Deutsch gesprochen.
   d. Handytelefonieren in Bus and Bahn soll verboten _____.
   e. Mozart _____ in Salzburg geboren.

8. Ergänzen Sie die fehlenden Endungen.
   a. Im kommen_____ Sommer mache ich ein Praktikum im Umweltschutz.
   b. Die steigen_____ Klimaerwärmung ist ein globales Problem.
   c. Die Studenten demonstrierten wegen wachsen_____ Arbeitslosigkeit nach dem Studium.

Landeskunde zum Mitnehmen

Welcome to **Landeskunde zum Mitnehmen.** The title says it all: *Culture to Go.* This section will deepen your understanding of cultural issues in German-speaking countries in a unique way: not just by having you read texts and gather information but by engaging you in activities focusing on the cultures of Germany, Austria, and Switzerland. Each of the six topics opens with a short introduction, followed by activities that further your knowledge. At the end of each topic there is a culminating activity. In some cases, you will work with other students to complete the tasks. It is important that you first try to do the activities without consulting outside resources. Rely on your previous knowledge as well as your world knowledge and clues from the activities themselves in order to complete the exercises. At other times you will have to do extra research at the library or online. The activity at the end of each topic will allow you to regroup the information you have in a new way and perhaps present it to the class. Remember: **Landeskunde zum Mitnehmen** is just that: **zum Mitnehmen.** It should be cultural knowledge you take with you. **Viel Spaß!**

Inhalt

Was wissen Sie über die Geografie Deutschlands, Österreichs und der Schweiz? In welchem Teil Deutschlands liegt Berlin? Wie nennt man die Länder in der Schweiz? Kennen Sie eine Stadt in Österreich? In den folgenden Aktivitäten lernen Sie mehr über die Geografie der deutschsprachigen Länder.

A Wie nennt man das?

In Deutschland und Österreich nennt man die Staaten _____, aber in der Schweiz nennt man sie _____. Die offiziellen Abkürzungen für diese Länder sind A für _____, CH (Confoederatio Helvetica) für _____ und D für _____.

B Deutschland, Österreich oder die Schweiz?

Tragen Sie die Namen der Bundesländer oder Kantone ein.

a. _____   f. _____

b. _____   g. _____

c. _____   h. _____

d. _____   i. _____

e. _____   j. _____

Brandenburg   Schwyz

Kärnten   Thüringen

Baden-Württemberg   Wallis

Burgenland   Graubünden

Oberösterreich   Schleswig-Holstein

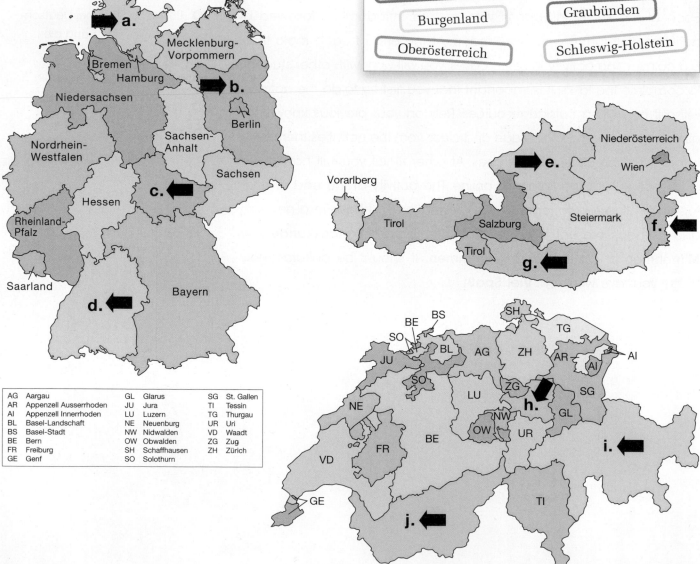

AG	Aargau	GL	Glarus	SG	St. Gallen
AR	Appenzell Ausserrhoden	JU	Jura	TI	Tessin
AI	Appenzell Innerrhoden	LU	Luzern	TG	Thurgau
BL	Basel-Landschaft	NE	Neuenburg	UR	Uri
BS	Basel-Stadt	NW	Nidwalden	VD	Waadt
BE	Bern	OW	Obwalden	ZG	Zug
FR	Freiburg	SH	Schaffhausen	ZH	Zürich
GE	Genf	SO	Solothurn		

C Wo ist das?

Suchen Sie Information über die Bundesländer und Kantone, um die Antworten zu finden.

1. Das Ruhrgebiet befindet sich in diesem Bundesstaat. (Nordrhein-Westfalen / Thüringen)

2. Der Name dieses Kantons stammt von einem Heiligen (*saint*), der ein Kloster gegründet (*founded*) hat. (Schaffhausen / Sankt Gallen)

3. Dieses Bundesland grenzt an (*borders on*) Slowenien. (Salzburg / Steiermark)

4. Es ist das zweitgrößte Bundesland Deutschlands mit der Hauptstadt Hannover. (Hessen / Niedersachsen)

5. So heißt ein Kanton und gleichzeitig (*simultaneously*) die Hauptstadt des Kantons. (Aargau / Schwyz)

6. Alte Hansestädte wie Stralsund, Rostock, und Greifswald befinden sich in diesem Bundesland. (Mecklenburg-Vorpommern / Sachsen)

7. Es ist das größte Bundesland Österreichs. (Wien / Niederösterreich)

D Drei Hauptstädte

Was trifft auf welche Hauptstadt zu? Schreiben Sie entweder B für Berlin, W für Wien oder BE für Bern.

_____ Der berühmte Vergnügungspark „Der Prater" befindet sich hier.

_____ Diese Stadt trug früher als römische Siedlung den Namen „Brenodurum".

_____ Das Symbol dieser Stadt ist der Bär.

_____ Diese Stadt ist eine der vier offiziellen Sitze der Vereinten Nationen (UNO).

_____ Die Olympischen Spiele fanden 1936 hier statt.

_____ Der Stephansdom ist ein Symbol von dieser Stadt.

_____ 1961 wurde die Mauer hier gebaut.

_____ Diese Stadt wurde 1191 von Herzog Berchtold V. von Zähringen gegründet.

E Forschungsprojekt

Wählen Sie eine Stadt, ein Bundesland, oder einen Kanton und schreiben Sie die Geschichte in tabellarischer Form. Die Geschichte sollte wenigstens 12 wichtige Ereignisse nennen, von der Gründung bis auf den heutigen Tag.

Das Riesenrad im Prater von Wien

Stephansdom in Wien

Bern in der Schweiz

Das Ende des Zweiten Weltkriegs in Europa im Mai 1945 bedeutete für Deutschland den totalen Zusammenbruch, aber auch die Hoffnung auf einen neuen Anfang. Man sprach damals von diesem Neuanfang als „Stunde null" (*zero hour*).

Trümmerfrauen bei der Arbeit

Das zerbombte Reichstaggebäude in Berlin

A Der Weg zur deutschen Einigung

Verbinden Sie Daten mit den Ereignissen im Kasten unten.

23. Mai 1949

7. Oktober 1949

13. August 1961

20. Juni 1991

9. November 1989

3. Oktober 1990

Fall der Mauer

Gründung der Bundesrepublik Deutschland (BRD)

Gründung der Deutschen Demokratischen Republik (DDR)

Bau der Mauer in Berlin

Wiedervereinigung Deutschlands

Berlin wird wieder Hauptstadt und Regierungssitz

B Finden Sie zu jedem Bild (a.–d.) die passende Beschreibung unten.

a.

b.

c.

d.

_____ Berliner feiern die Öffnung der Mauer im November 1989.

_____ Der deutsche Bundestag tagt (*meets*) am 1. Mai 1999 zum ersten Mal im neuen Reichstagsgebäude in Berlin.

_____ Der Bau der Mauer in Berlin schließt die letzte offene Grenze zwischen Ost- und Westdeutschland.

_____ Konrad Adenauer war der erste Bundeskanzler der Bundesrepublik Deutschland.

C Stichwörter

Identifizieren Sie die folgenden Begriffe, die für die Entwicklung Deutschlands nach dem Zweiten Weltkrieg von Bedeutung waren.

1. der Marshallplan

2. der Eiserne Vorhang

3. die Luftbrücke

4. die D-Mark

5. das Wirtschaftswunder

6. die Wende

D Fragen zum Weiterforschen!

Schreiben Sie einen kurzen Bericht über eins der folgenden Themen.

1. Wer baute die Mauer in Berlin, und warum?

2. Wer zeigte seine Solidarität mit Berlin, indem er den Berlinern zurief: „Ich bin ein Berliner!"?

3. „Wir sind das Volk." So riefen die Menschen in Leipzig und vielen Orten der DDR im Jahre 1989. Was wollten sie damit erreichen?

E Ein kleines Quiz

Bilden Sie mehrere Gruppen. Machen Sie mithilfe der Informationen in „Kleine Chronik deutscher Geschichte" ein Quiz. Das Format bleibt jeder Gruppe überlassen. Es könnte z.B. eine Quizshow oder ein Wortratespiel sein oder eine Serie von Fragen, die Sie gemeinsam entwickeln. Die anderen Gruppen übernehmen die Rolle der Teilnehmer.

Der Weg nach Europa

Nach dem Zweiten Weltkrieg beschlossen einige europäische Länder, internationale Konflikte in Zukunft durch Zusammenarbeit und Gemeinschaft zu lösen anstatt durch Gewalt. Dies begann mit der wirtschaftlichen Zusammenarbeit von sechs Staaten, die 1957 die Europäische Wirtschaftsgemeinschaft (EWG) gründeten. Die Europäische Union (EU) wurde dann 1993 durch den Maastrichter Vertrag gegründet. Dieser Vertrag bahnte den Weg zur weiteren europäischen Integration.

Die Mitgliedstaaten planten in vielen Bereichen zusammenzuarbeiten, z.B. in Sicherheitspolitik, Justiz und Wirtschaft. Eine gemeinsame Währung, der Euro, wurde am 1. Januar 1999 eingeführt. Allerdings begannen die Länder erst am 1. Januar 2002, den Euro im täglichen Gebrauch zu benutzen.

Belgien, Dänemark, Deutschland, Frankreich, Griechenland, Großbritannien, Irland, Italien Luxemburg, die Niederlande, Portugal und Spanien waren die ersten Mitgliedstaaten der Europäischen Union. Finnland, Österreich und Schweden traten der Union 1995 bei. Inzwischen gibt es 27 Mitgliedstaaten. Allerdings gehören nur 16 davon zu der sogenannten Eurozone, das heißt Ländern, die den Euro eingeführt haben.

F Europa, Europa

Beantworten Sie die folgenden Fragen. Für die Antworten zu einigen Fragen müssen Sie weiter forschen.

1. Was war der ursprüngliche Zweck (*purpose*) der Europäischen Union?

2. Wann wurde der Euro im täglichen Gebrauch eingeführt?

3. Finden Sie die Namen einiger Mitgliedstaaten, die der EU nach 2000 beitraten.

4. Welche Länder der EU haben den Euro als Zahlungsmittel nicht eingeführt?

Politische Systeme: Deutschland, Österreich und die Schweiz

Bundesrepublik Deutschland

Die Bundesrepublik Deutschland ist laut ihrem Grundgesetz (*basic law*) ein demokratisch sozialer Bundesstaat, eine parlamentarische Demokratie. Das Parlament der Bundesregierung heißt Bundestag. Der Bundestag besteht aus Abgeordneten (*representatives*), die alle vier Jahre von den Bürgern gewählt werden. Es gibt zur Zeit (2010) fünf Parteien, die im deutschen Bundestag vertreten sind. Die wichtigste Rolle in der Regierung hat der Bundeskanzler oder, wie zur Zeit, die Bundeskanzlerin.

Die Schweiz

Die Schweiz ist ein moderner Bundesstaat mit einem System der direkten Demokratie. Das bedeutet, dass Schweizer Bürger jährlich an Volksabstimmungen (*elections*) teilnehmen. Jedes Jahr werden ein neuer Bundespräsident und ein neuer Bundeskanzler gewählt. Die Regierung der Schweiz besteht aus einem Multiparteiensystem. Die vier größten Parteien haben eine Koalition gebildet.

Österreich

Österreich ist eine parlamentarische Demokratie mit Kanzler und Präsident. Es gibt über 700 registrierte Parteien. Aber nur vier Parteien haben genügend Wahlstimmen (*votes*) bekommen, um einen Sitz im Parlament zu bekommen.

A **Testen Sie Ihr Wissen mithilfe der Information oben.**

1. Die österreichische Regierung ist eine parlamentarische _____.

2. Der _____ ist das Parlament Deutschlands.

3. Alle _____ Jahre wählen die Deutschen die Abgeordneten für den Bundestag.

4. Die Schweiz ist ein moderner _____ mit einem System der direkten _____.

5. Die Abgeordneten im deutschen Bundestag repräsentieren die _____, für die die Deutschen gewählt haben.

6. Österreich hat auch einen _____ und einen _____.

7. Die Bundeskanzlerin Deutschlands (im Jahr 2010) heißt _____.

B **Parteien im deutschen Bundestag**

Hier sehen Sie die Logos von sechs deutschen Parteien. Vier Logos nennen nur die ersten Buchstaben, die für den Namen der Partei stehen (z. B. CDU, SPD). Versuchen Sie mithilfe der Wörter im Kasten die vollen Namen der Parteien zusammenzusetzen. Einige Wörter kommen zweimal vor.

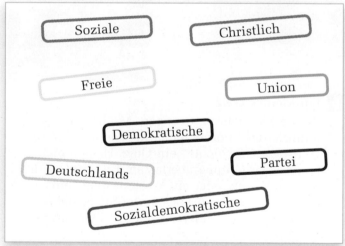

C Sitzverteilung im Bundestag

Schauen Sie sich die Grafik mit der Sitzverteilung im 17. Deutschen Bundestag an.

1. Zwei Parteien bilden eine Koalition. Welche?

2. Welche Partei/Parteien hat/haben die meisten Sitze?

3. Welche Partei hat die wenigsten Sitze?

4. Wie heißt die Partei mit 146 Sitzen im Bundestag?

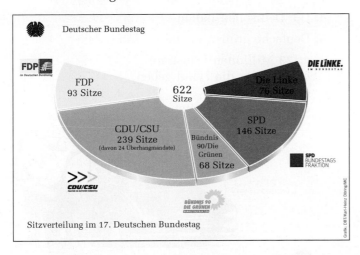

Sitzverteilung im 17. Deutschen Bundestag

D Politische Parteien in Österreich und der Schweiz

Hier sind die Abkürzungen für einige wichtige Parteien in Österreich und der Schweiz. Suchen Sie die vollen Namen dieser Parteien im Internet.

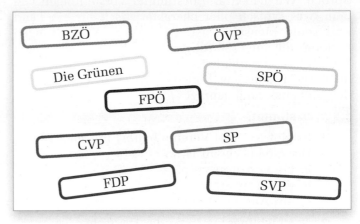

E Eine Debatte

Arbeiten Sie zu dritt. Wählen Sie eine der Parteien aus **Aktivität B** und debattieren Sie über ein Thema, das die Partei vertritt. Suchen Sie drei Argumente für oder gegen das Thema und präsentieren Sie sie der Klasse.

F Wofür stehen diese Parteien?

Unten sehen Sie einige Slogans für die deutschen Parteien. Welche Aussage passt wahrscheinlich zu welcher Partei? Begründen Sie Ihre Wahl.

„Andere Länder, andere Sitten", so heißt ein deutscher Spruch. Wir haben alle bestimmte Vorstellungen von dem, was typisch oder charakteristisch für ein Land und seine Menschen ist. Aber diese Vorstellungen basieren oft auf Erfahrungen (*experiences*) oder auch Vorurteilen, die nicht stimmen, oder nicht mehr stimmen. Die Lebensgewohnheiten unserer Zeit sind von der Globalisierung geprägt (*formed*).

A Was stimmt?

1. Es gibt 550 000 Vereine (*clubs*) in Deutschland. Der größte Verein ist ...
   a. ein Gesangsverein.
   b. ein Turnverein.
   c. ein Automobilclub.

2. Das Lieblingsspielzeug der Deutschen ist ...
   a. das Motorrad.
   b. der Fußball.
   c. das Auto.

3. Die Deutschen haben 23 Millionen davon.
   a. Haustiere.
   b. Kinder
   c. Freunde

4. Wovon essen die Deutschen jedes Jahr 87 Kilo?
   a. Fleisch
   b. Kartoffeln
   c. Brot/Brötchen

5. Deutsche, die miteinander bekannt (*acquainted*) sind, grüßen sich, indem sie ...
   a. einander die Hand geben.
   b. mit dem Kopf nicken.
   c. sich einen Kuss auf die Wange geben

B Die Antworten

Verbinden Sie die passenden Satzteile miteinander, um die Antworten für **Aktivität A** zu finden.

1. Die Deutschen essen jedes Jahr

2. Das Lieblingsspielzeug der Deutschen ist

3. Der größte Verein Deutschlands ist

4. Die Deutschen halten

5. Deutsche grüßen einander, indem sie

   a. 23 Millionen Haustiere.
   b. einander die Hand geben.
   c. das Auto.
   d. 87 Kilo Brot/Brötchen.
   e. ein Automobilclub.

C Andere Länder, andere Sitten

Sie sind um 19 Uhr zum Abendessen bei deutschen Freunden eingeladen. Was erwartet der Gastgeber / die Gastgeberin im Allgemeinen (*generally*)? Was ist üblich (*customary*)? Kreuzen Sie an.

	In Deutschland	In Ihrem Heimatland
1. Man erscheint um 18.45 Uhr.	☐	☐
2. Man steht pünktlich auf die Minute an der Haustür.	☐	☐
3. Es ist akzeptabel, 15–30 Minuten später anzukommen.	☐	☐
4. Man bringt gewöhnlich Blumen mit.	☐	☐
5. Man grüßt alle Leute, Gastgeber und Gäste, indem man ihnen die Hand schüttelt.	☐	☐
6. Am Esstisch sind beide Hände immer auf dem Tisch.	☐	☐

D Diskutieren Sie!

Welche der Lebensgewohnheiten oder Tatsachen auf Seite 438 kennen Sie auch in Ihrem Heimatland? Was ist bei Ihnen anders? Was hat Sie überrascht?

E Typische Redensarten

Hier sind einige typische Redensarten. Was, glauben Sie, ist die Bedeutung?

1. Mein Bruder lebt auf großem Fuß!
   a. Mein Bruder hat große Füße.
   b. Mein Bruder hat zwei verschiedene Füße.
   c. Mein Bruder gibt viel Geld für teure Sachen aus.

2. Lass die Finger davon!
   a. Das ist eine gute Idee.
   b. Tu das nicht!
   c. Das ist nicht richtig.

3. Was du sagst, hat weder Hand noch Fuß.
   a. Was du sagst, stimmt immer.
   b. Was du sagst macht keinen Sinn.
   c. Was du sagst ist ganz unwichtig.

4. Wir sind Feuer und Flamme!
   a. Hilfe! Es brennt im Haus.
   b. Es ist hier sehr heiß.
   c. Wir sind ganz enthusiastisch.

5. Er hat wirklich einen Vogel!
   a. Vögel sind sein Hobby.
   b. Er ist verrückt (*nuts*)!
   c. Er ist krank.

F Ein Sketch

Arbeiten Sie zu zweit oder dritt. Wählen Sie eine der Redensarten oben und machen Sie einen kurzen Sketch darüber. Erfinden Sie eine Situation, wobei Sie diese Redensart mindestens zweimal verwenden. Jede Person spielt eine Rolle. Spielen Sie den Sketch der Klasse vor.

G Zungenbrecher (*Tongue Twisters*)

Mit Zungenbrechern kann man Deutsch lernen und üben. Hier sind vier Zungenbrecher. Was bedeuten diese Zungenbrecher? Üben Sie sie zu dritt. Wer in der Gruppe kann sie am schnellsten und am genauesten sagen? Können Sie noch andere Zungenbrecher finden?

1. Esel essen Nesseln nicht, Nesseln essen Esel nicht.

2. Jedes Jahr im Juli essen Jana und Julia Johannisbeeren.

3. Zwischen zwei Zwetschgenzweigen sitzen zwei zwitschernde Schwalben.

4. Auf dem Rasen rasen rasche Ratten, rasche Ratten rasen auf dem Rasen.

Die deutsche Sprache ist reich an bildlichen (*figurative*) Ausdrücken und Redensarten (*idioms*). Sie beleben die Sprache. Es ist durchaus üblich, diese Ausdrücke und Redensarten in der Umgangssprache in der Familie und unter Freunden zu verwenden.

Der Mann hat einen Vogel!

H Ein Zungenbrecher als Volkslied

Der folgende Zungenbrecher ist ein bekanntes, volkstümliches Lied aus Bayern. Versuchen Sie den Text auszusprechen und beantworten Sie die Fragen.

> Heut' kommt der Hans zu mir, freut sich die Lies.
> Ob er aber über Oberammergau
> oder aber über Unterammergau
> oder aber überhaupt nicht kommt,
> ist nicht gewiss.

1. Wer soll wen besuchen?

2. Was ist nicht gewiss?

3. Sind Oberammergau und Unterammergau wirkliche oder fiktive Orte?

Die Märchen der Brüder Jacob und Wilhelm Grimm sind weltbekannt, aber schon vor ihnen gab es Märchensammler. Märchenbücher wie das *Pentamerone* in Italien und die Sammlungen von Charles Perrault aus Frankreich waren Vorbilder für viele deutsche Märchen. Die Brüder haben hauptsächlich Märchen aus mündlicher Tradition in ganz Deutschland gesammelt. Der erste Band der Sammlung, *Kinder- und Hausmärchen*, erschien 1812 und der zweite Band 1815.

A **Was stimmt?**

Was wissen Sie schon über deutsche Märchen?

Wilhelm und Jacob Grimm

	Das stimmt	Das stimmt nicht
1. Das Volksmärchen wurde im 19. Jahrhundert populär.	☐	☐
2. Die Brüder Grimm haben die Märchen selbst geschrieben.	☐	☐
3. Die Brüder Grimm hatten Hilfe von anderen Leuten, die Geschichten niedergeschrieben und ihnen zugeschickt haben.	☐	☐
4. Jacob und Wilhelm Grimm waren Professoren.	☐	☐
5. Ein Märchen beginnt oft mit „Es war einmal ... ".	☐	☐

B **Märchen der Brüder Grimm**

Welche Märchen der Brüder Grimm kennen Sie? Nennen Sie drei.

C **Märchenrätsel**

Kombinieren Sie die Elemente unten, um die Titel von einigen bekannten Märchen zusammenzustellen.

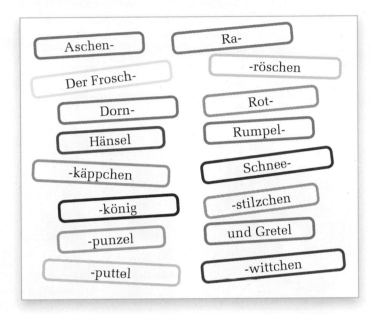

Aschen-

Ra-

Der Frosch-

-röschen

Dorn-

Rot-

Hänsel

Rumpel-

-käppchen

Schnee-

-könig

-stilzchen

-punzel

und Gretel

-puttel

-wittchen

D **Wie heißen diese Märchen in Ihrer Sprache?**

1.

2.

3.

4.

E **Woher stammt das?**

Hier sind einige Sätze aus verschiedenen Märchen. Aus welchem Märchen stammt der Text?

1. „Da musste es (das Mädchen) von Morgen bis Abend schwere Arbeit tun, früh vor Tag aufstehn, Wasser tragen, Feuer anmachen, kochen und waschen."

2. „Als sie mitten in den Wald gekommen waren, sprach der Vater: ‚Nun sammelt Holz, ihr Kinder, ich will ein Feuer anmachen, damit ihr nicht friert.'"

3. „Es wunderte sich, dass die Türe aufstand, und wie es in die Stube trat, so kam es ihm so seltsam darin vor, dass es dachte: Ei, du mein Gott, wie ängstlich wird mir's heute zumut, und bin sonst so gern bei der Großmutter!"

F **Märchencharakteristiken**

Was ist typisch für Märchen? Kreuzen Sie an!

☐ Die meisten Märchen sind pessimistisch.

☐ Die Zeit ist unbestimmt.

☐ Ein Held / eine Heldin hat ein Problem und löst es auf glückliche Weise.

☐ Ein Märchen enthält immer eine Lehre.

☐ Die Natur spielt im Märchen keine Rolle.

☐ Tiere und Dinge sprechen im Märchen.

☐ Es gibt viel Wiederholung.

☐ Es gibt viel Wunderbares im Alltag.

G **Spiel**

„Wie heißt das Märchen?" Lesen Sie ein Grimmsches Märchen und erzählen Sie es der Klasse in 7 bis 10 Sätzen. Die Klasse soll dann sagen, wie das Märchen heißt.

Mythen und Sagen

Viele Landschaften und Orte in Deutschland, Österreich und der Schweiz sind mit Mythen und Sagen verbunden, die bis auf den heutigen Tag von Bedeutung sind und von den Menschen, die dort leben, gefeiert und weitererzählt werden.

A **Welcher Text passt zu welchem Bild?**

1. Der Brocken ist ein Berg im Harz, der oft im Nebel steht. Er wurde schon 1540 _____ genannt.

2. _____ war ein sagenhafter Freiheitskämpfer im 13./14. Jahrhundert in der Schweiz. Er schoss angeblich einen Apfel vom Kopf seines Sohnes.

3. _____ ist der Name eines steilen Felsens im Rhein und einer schönen Jungfrau, die vom Felsen herab den Schiffern ein Lied sang, bis ihre Schiffe am Felsen zerschellten und sie im Wasser den Tod fanden.

4. Im Jahre 1284 folgten die Kinder der Stadt Hameln einem _____, der auf einer Flöte spielte. Die Kinder verschwanden auf immer.

5. Mitten im Rhein bei der Stadt Bingen steht _____, wo angeblich im 10. Jahrhundert ein grausamer Erzbischof von Mäusen getötet wurde.

6. In der Stadt Köln gab es lange Zeit _____, die bei Nacht alle Arbeit für die Menschen machten, bis jemand sie bei der Arbeit sah. Von da an erschienen sie nicht mehr.

7. Die Donau bei der Stadt Wien ist Schauplatz der Sage vom _____, das junge Fischer durch ihre liebliche Stimme zu sich ins Wasser lockte.

Sagen

Sagen sind ursprünglich einfache Volkserzählungen, die mündlich überliefert wurden. Sie verbinden oft Elemente der Magie und des Wunderbaren mit Naturereignissen, historischen Ereignissen, oder Gestalten aus der Geschichte eines Landes, einer Region oder eines Ortes.

a. Lorelei

b. Binger Mäuseturm

c. Hexentanzplatz auf dem Brocken

d. Rattenfänger zu Hameln

e. Wilhelm Tell

f. Heinzelmännchen zu Köln

g. Donauweibchen

B Ergänzen sie die Tabelle mit Information aus den Kurzbeschreibungen der Sagen.

Sage	Historische/ mythische Gestalt	Magie/ wunderbare Tat	Historische Zeit	Ort
Lorelei	die Lorelei	singt	—	Felsen am Rhein
Mäuseturm				
Hexentanzplatz				
Rattenfänger				
Wilhelm Tell				
Heinzelmännchen				
Donauweibchen				

C Vertiefen Sie!

Wählen Sie eine dieser Mythen und Sagen und suchen Sie weitere Information. Gibt es historische Beweise (*evidence*) für die Sage? Welche Rolle spielen diese Mythen und Sagen heute?

D Und bei Ihnen?

Welche Mythen und Sagen gibt es in Ihrer Heimatgegend? Was sind die Themen? Berichten Sie über eine lokale Mythe oder Sage Ihrer Heimat.

Das folgende Gedicht von Heinrich Heine aus dem Jahr 1824 ist zu einem der populärsten deutschen Volkslieder geworden.

COMBING HER LONG GOLDEN HAIR WITH A COMB OF RED GOLD

Loreley
von Heinrich Heine

Ich weiß nicht, was soll es bedeuten,
Daß ich so traurig bin;
Ein Märchen aus alten Zeiten,
Das kommt mir nicht aus dem Sinn.

Die Luft ist kühl und es dunkelt,
Und ruhig fließt der Rhein;
Der Gipfel des Berges funkelt
Im Abendsonnenschein.

Die schönste Jungfrau sitzet
Dort oben wunderbar,
Ihr goldnes Geschmeide blitzet,
Sie kämmt ihr goldnes Haar.

Sie kämmt es mit goldnem Kamme,
Und singt ein Lied dabey;
Das hat eine wundersame,
Gewaltige Melodey.

Den Schiffer, im kleinen Schiffe,
Ergreift es mit wildem Weh;
Er schaut nicht die Felsenriffe,
Er schaut nur hinauf in die Höh'.

Ich glaube, die Wellen verschlingen
Am Ende Schiffer und Kahn;
Und das hat mit ihrem Singen
Die Loreley getan.

Einführung

Aktivität 13 Hin und her°: Wie ist die Postleitzahl?   *back and forth*

This is the first of many activities in which you will exchange information with a partner. Take turns asking each other for the postal codes of the persons living in the cities below.

BEISPIEL: **S1:** Wie ist Bettinas Postleitzahl in Hamburg?

S2: D-21220. Wie ist Peters Postleitzahl in Salzburg?

Bettina	D-21220	Hamburg
Peter		Salzburg
Mathias	CH-8046	Zürich
Kathrin		Dresden
Susanne	A-1010	Wien
Felix		Berlin
Marion	FL-9490	Vaduz
Michael		Eisenach

Kapitel 2

Aktivität 8 Hin und her: Machen sie das gern?

Find out what the following people like to do or don't like to do by asking your partner.

BEISPIEL: **S1:** Was macht Denise gern?

S2: Sie reist gern. Was macht Thomas nicht gern?

S1: Er fährt nicht gern Auto.

	Gern	Nicht gern
Thomas		
Denise	reisen	kochen
Niko	eissen	kartenspilen
Anja	laufen	Bier trinken
Sie	music	putzen
Ihr Partner / Ihre Partnerin	↓	↓

Kapitel 3

relationships

Aktivität 7 Hin und her: Verwandtschaften°

Ask a partner questions about Bernd's family. How is each person related to Bernd?

BEISPIEL: **S1:** Wie ist Gisela mit Bernd verwandt?

S2: Gisela ist Bernds Tante.

S1: Wie alt ist sie denn?

S2: Sie ist 53.

S1: Wann hat sie Geburtstag?

S2: Im Februar.

Person	Verwandtschaft	Alter	Geburtstag
Gisela	Tante	53	Februar
Alexandra			
Christoph	Schwager	36	Dezember
Andreas			
Sabine	Kusine	19	August

Kapitel 4

Aktivität 5 Hin und her: Zwei Stundenpläne

Schritt 1: Milan und Frank sind 18 Jahre alt und gehen aufs Gymnasium (*secondary school*).

Vergleichen Sie ihre Stundenpläne. Welche Fächer haben sie gemeinsam (*together*)?

BEISPIEL: S1: Welchen Kurs hat Milan montags um acht?

S2: Montags um acht hat Milan Physik. Welchen Kurs hat Frank um acht?

S1: Montags um acht hat Frank Französisch.

Schritt 2: Milan und Frank möchten Tennis spielen. Wann ist die beste Zeit? Wann haben sie beide frei?

Zeit	Montag	Dienstag	Mittwoch	Donnerstag	Freitag
8.00–8.45	Physik	Musik	Deutsch	Erdkunde	Mathe
8.50–9.35	Physik	Mathe	Deutsch	Musik	
Pause					
9.50–10.35	Bio-Chemie	Sport	Englisch	Französisch	iVFö
10.40–11.25	Deutsch	Sport	Chemie	Religion	Bio-Chemie
11.45–12.30	Englisch	iVFö	Erdkunde	Englisch	Religion
12.35–13.20	Mathe		Musik	Englisch	
13.20–14.30	Mittagspause				
14.35–15.20	Chemie	Französisch	Bio-Chemie	Handball	Französisch
15.25–16.10	Französisch		Bio-Chemie		

Milans Stundenplan

Kapitel 6

Übung 16 Hin und her: Warum nicht?

Fragen Sie Ihren Partner / Ihre Partnerin, warum die folgenden Leute nicht da waren.

BEISPIEL: **S1:** Warum war Andreas gestern Vormittag nicht in der Vorlesung?

S2: Er hatte keine Lust.

Person	Wann	Wo	Warum
Andreas	gestern Vormittag	in der Vorlesung	keine Lust haben
Anke			arbeiten müssen
Frank	gestern Abend	auf der Party	
Yeliz			schlafen wollen
Mario	Samstag	im Café	
Ihr Partner / Ihre Partnerin			

Kapitel 7

Übung 9 Hin und her: Wochenende und Freizeit

Wer hat was gemacht? Arbeiten Sie zu zweit.

BEISPIEL: **S1:** Was hat Dagmar gemacht?

S2: Sie ist zum Kegelclub gegangen.

Wer	Was
Dagmar	zum Kegelclub gehen
Thomas	
Jürgen	zu Hause bleiben und nur faulenzen
Stefanie	
Susanne	mit Freunden in die Stadt fahren
Felix und Sabine	
die Kinder	schwimmen gehen

Kapitel 8

Aktivität 8 Hin und her: Meine Routine — deine Routine

Jeder hat eine andere Routine. Was machen diese Leute und in welcher Reihenfolge? Machen Sie es auch so?

BEISPIEL: **S1:** Was macht Alexander morgens?

S2: Zuerst rasiert er sich und putzt sich die Zähne. Dann kämmt er sich. Danach setzt er sich an den Tisch und frühstückt.

Wer	Was er/sie morgens macht
Alexander	zuerst / sich rasieren / sich die Zähne putzen dann / sich kämmen danach / sich an den Tisch setzen / frühstücken
Elke	zuerst / sich anziehen dann / sich die Zähne putzen danach / sich kämmen
Tilo	
Kamal	zuerst / sich das Gesicht waschen dann / frühstücken danach / sich rasieren / sich anziehen
Sie	zuerst / ? dann / ? danach / ?
Ihr Partner / Ihre Partnerin	zuerst / ? dann / ? danach / ?

Kapitel 9

unfamiliar

Aktivität 6 Hin und her: In einer fremden° Stadt

Sie sind in einer fremden Stadt. Fragen Sie nach dem Weg. Benutzen Sie die Tabelle unten.

BEISPIEL: **S1:** Ist das Landesmuseum weit von hier?

S2: Es ist sechs Kilometer von hier, bei der Universität.

S1: Wie komme ich am besten dahin?

S2: Nehmen Sie die Buslinie 7, am Rathaus.

Wohin?	Wie weit?	Wo?	Wie?
Landesmuseum	6 km	bei der Universität	Buslinie 7, am Rathaus
Bahnhof			
Post	nicht weit	in der Nähe vom Bahnhof	zu Fuß
Schloss			
Opernhaus	ganz in der Nähe	rechts um die Ecke	zu Fuß, die Poststraße entlang

Übung 14 Hin und her: Was gibt es hier?

Fragen Sie einen Partner / eine Partnerin nach den fehlenden Informationen.

BEISPIEL: **S1:** Was gibt es beim Gasthof zum Bären?

S2: Warme Küche.

S1: Was gibt es sonst noch?

S2: Bayerische Spezialitäten.

Wo?	Was?	Was sonst noch?
Gasthof zum Bären	Küche / warm	Spezialitäten / bayerisch
Gasthof Adlersberg		
Gasthaus Schneiderwirt	Hausmusik / originell	Gästezimmer / rustikal
Hotel Luitpold		
Restaurant Ökogarten	Gerichte / vegetarisch	Bier / alkoholfrei

Kapitel 10

Aktivität 3 Hin und her: Was nehmen sie mit?

Wohin fahren diese Leute im Urlaub? Was nehmen sie mit? Und warum?
Ergänzen Sie die Informationen.

BEISPIEL: **S1:** Wohin fährt Angelika Meier in Urlaub?

S2: Sie fährt in die Türkei.

S1: Warum fährt sie in die Türkei?

S2: Weil …

S1: Was nimmt sie mit?

S2: Sie nimmt …

Personen	Wohin?	Warum?	Was nimmt er/sie mit?
Angelika Meier	in die Türkei	sich am Strand erholen	Buch, Sonnenbrille, Badesachen
Peter Bayer	auf die Insel Rügen	Windsurfen gehen	Sonnenschutzmittel, Badehose
Roland Metz			
Sabine Graf	nach Griechenland	eine Studienreise machen	Reiseführer, Wörterbuch, Kamera

Übung 3 Hin und her: Wie war der Urlaub?

Herr Ignaz Huber aus München war drei Wochen im Urlaub in Norddeutschland. Er war zwei Tage in Hamburg, eine Woche in Cuxhaven und
nicht ganz zwei Wochen auf der Insel Sylt. Stellen Sie Ihrem Partner / Ihrer
Partnerin Fragen über Herrn Hubers Urlaub. Benutzen Sie den Superlativ.

BEISPIEL: **S1:** Wo war es am wärmsten?

S2: Am wärmsten war es in Cuxhaven.

	In Hamburg	In Cuxhaven	Auf der Insel Sylt
1. *Wo war es (kalt/warm)?*	20°C	25°C	15°C
2. *Wo waren die Hotelpreise (günstig/teuer)?*			
3. *Wo hat es (viel) geregnet?*	zwei Tage	einen Tag	fünf Tage
4. *Wo war das Hotelpersonal (freundlich)?*			
5. *Wo war der Strand (schön)?*	kein Strand	sehr sauber, angenehm	zu windig
6. *Wo hat das Essen (gut) geschmeckt?*			

Kapitel 11

Aktivität 3 Hin und her: Wer macht was, und warum?

Ergänzen Sie die Informationen.

BEISPIEL: **S1:** Was macht Corinna Eichhorn?

S2: Sie ist Sozialarbeiterin.

S1: Warum macht sie das?

S2: Weil …

Name	Beruf	Warum?
Corinna Eichhorn	Sozialarbeiterin	Menschen helfen
Karsten Becker	Bibliothekar	sich für Bücher interessieren
Erika Lentz		
Alex Böhmer	Informatiker	mit Computern arbeiten

famous **Aktivität 6** Hin und her: Berühmte° Personen

Diese berühmten Menschen, die alle einen Beruf ausübten, hatten auch andere Interessen. Ergänzen Sie die Informationen.

BEISPIEL: **S1:** Was war Martin Luther von Beruf?

S2: Er war Priester.

S1: Was für andere Interessen hatte er?

S2: Er interessierte sich für Literatur, Musik und die deutsche Sprache.

Name	Beruf	Interessen
Martin Luther	Priester	Literatur, Musik, die deutsche Sprache
Käthe Kollwitz		
Bertha von Suttner	Schriftstellerin	die europäische Friedensbewegung (*peace movement*)
Rainer Werner Fassbinder		
Marlene Dietrich	Schauspielerin	Ski fahren
Willi Brandt		

Kapitel 12

Aktivität 6 Hin und her: Eine neue Wohnung

Diese Leute haben entweder eine neue Wohnung oder ein neues Haus gekauft. Wer hat was gekauft? Wie viele Stockwerke gibt es? Wie groß ist das Wohnzimmer? Wie viele WCs oder Badezimmer gibt es?

BEISPIEL: **S1:** Was für eine Wohnung hat Bettina Neuendorf gekauft?

   S2: Eine Eigentumswohnung.

   S1: Wie viele Stockwerke hat die Wohnung?

   S2: Eins.

   S1: Und wie viele Schlafzimmer? …

Person	Typ	Stockwerke	Schlafzimmer	Wohnzimmer	WC/BAD
Bettina Neuendorf	Eigentums- wohnung	eins	eins, aber auch ein kleines Gästezimmer	mit Esszimmer kombiniert 30 Quadratmeter	eins
Uwe und Marion Baumgärtner	Haus	zwei	drei: Elternschlaf- zimmer, Kinder- schlafzimmer, Gästezimmer	sehr groß mit Balkon 37 Quadratmeter	zwei Badezim- mer: eins im Dachgeschoss und eins im Erdgeschoss
Sven Kersten					
Carola Schubärth	Haus	eins	zwei: ein Schlaf- zimmer ist Arbeitszimmer	klein 25 Quadratmeter	ein Bad

Kapitel 13

Aktivität 3 Hin und her: Wie informieren sie sich?

Wie informieren sich diese Personen? Was lesen sie zur Unterhaltung? Stellen Sie Fragen an Ihren Partner / Ihre Partnerin.

BEISPIEL: **S1:** Was sieht Martin gern im Fernsehen? Was liest er oft?

S2: Er _____.

Person	Fernsehshows	Zeitungen und Zeitschriften
Martin	Talkshows und Dokumentarfilme	*die Zeit*
Stephanie	klassische Spielfilme und Komödien	*der Spiegel*
Patrick		
Kristin	Sportsendungen, Krimi-Serien wie „Die Rosenheim-Cops"	die *Süddeutsche Zeitung* und *Brigitte*
Mein Partner / Meine Partnerin		

Aktivität 10 Hin und her: Erfindungen durch die Jahrhunderte

Sie möchten erfahren, wer was, und wann, erfunden hat. Arbeiten Sie zu zweit.

BEISPIELE: **S1:** Wer hat _____ erfunden?

S2: _____.

S1: Wann hat er/sie es erfunden?

S2: (Im Jahre) _____.

oder: **S1:** Was hat _____ erfunden?

S2: Er/Sie hat _____ erfunden.

S1: In welchem Jahr?

S2: (Im Jahre) _____.

Person	Erfindung	Datum
Johannes Gutenberg	der Buchdruck mit beweglichen Lettern (*movable type*)	um 1450
Daniel Gabriel Fahrenheit	das Alkoholthermometer	1709
	das Fahrrad (Draisine)	
Herta Heuwer	Currywurst	1949
Gottlieb Daimler		
	der Dieselmotor	
Wilhelm Conrad Röntgen	Röntgenstrahlen (*X-rays*)	1895
Melitta Bentz		1908

Kapitel 14

Aktivität 1 Hin und her: Probleme und Lösungen

Stellen Sie Ihrem Partner / Ihrer Partnerin Fragen zu den folgenden Problemen, um herauszufinden, welche möglichen Lösungen es gibt.

BEISPIEL: S1: Was kann man gegen Krieg tun?

S2: Man kann an Antikriegsdemonstrationen teilnehmen.

Probleme	Mögliche Lösungen
Krieg	an Antikriegsdemonstrationen teilnehmen
Inflation	die Ausgaben der Regierung kontrollieren
Drogensucht	
Umweltverschmutzung	alternative Energiequellen (*energy sources*) entwickeln
Verletzung der Menschenrechte	
Obdachlosigkeit	neue Wohnungen bauen
Arbeitslosigkeit	

Übung 6 Hin und her: Zwei umweltbewusste Städte

In zwei Städten, Altstadt und Neustadt, wird für eine bessere Umwelt gesorgt.

BEISPIEL: S1: Was ist in Altstadt zuerst gemacht worden?

S2: Zuerst sind die Bürger über Umweltschutz informiert worden. Und in Neustadt?

S1: Zuerst sind …

	Altstadt	Neustadt
zuerst	Bürger über Umweltschutz informieren	
dann	neue Passivhäuser am Stadtrand bauen	
danach	Autos aus der Innenstadt verbannen	
schließlich	energiesparende Busse kaufen	
zuletzt	ein großes Umweltfest in der Innenstadt feiern	

Appendix **B**
Grammar Tables

1. Personal Pronouns

	Singular					Plural		
Nominative	ich	du / Sie	er	sie	es	wir	ihr / Sie	sie
Accusative	mich	dich / Sie	ihn	sie	es	uns	euch / Sie	sie
Dative	mir	dir / Ihnen	ihm	ihr	ihm	uns	euch / Ihnen	ihnen

2. Definite Articles

	Singular			Plural
	Masculine	*Neuter*	*Feminine*	*All genders*
Nominative	der	das	die	die
Accusative	den	das	die	die
Dative	dem	dem	der	den
Genitive	des	des	der	der

Words declined like the definite article: **jeder, dieser, welcher**

3. Indefinite Articles and **kein**

	Singular			Plural
	Masculine	*Neuter*	*Feminine*	*All genders*
Nominative	(k)ein	(k)ein	(k)eine	keine
Accusative	(k)einen	(k)ein	(k)eine	keine
Dative	(k)einem	(k)einem	(k)einer	keinen
Genitive	(k)eines	(k)eines	(k)einer	keiner

Words declined like the indefinite article: all possessive adjectives (**mein, dein, sein, ihr, unser, euer, Ihr**)

4. Relative and Demonstrative Pronouns

	Singular			Plural
	Masculine	*Neuter*	*Feminine*	*All genders*
Nominative	der	das	die	die
Accusative	den	das	die	die
Dative	dem	dem	der	denen
Genitive	dessen	dessen	deren	deren

5. Summary of Adjective Endings

Adjectives After a Definite Article

	Singular			Plural
	Masculine	Neuter	Feminine	All Genders
Nom.	-e	-e	-e	-en
Acc.	-en	-e	-e	-en
Dat.	-en	-en	-en	-en
Gen.	-en	-en	-en	-en

Adjectives After an Indefinite Article

	Singular			Plural
	Masculine	Neuter	Feminine	All Genders
Nom.	-er	-es	-e	-en
Acc.	-en	-es	-e	-en
Dat.	-en	-en	-en	-en
Gen.	-en	-en	-en	-en

Adjectives without a Preceding Article

	Singular			Plural
	Masculine	Neuter	Feminine	All Genders
Nom.	-er	-es	-e	-e
Acc.	-en	-es	-e	-e
Dat.	-em	-em	-er	-en
Gen.	-en	-en	-er	-er

6. Conjugation of Verbs

In the charts that follow, the pronoun **Sie** (*you*) is listed with the third-person plural **sie** (*they*).

Present Tense

	Auxiliary Verbs			Regular		Vowel Change		Irregular
	sein	**haben**	**werden**	**fragen**	**finden**	**geben**	**fahren**	**wissen**
ich	bin	habe	werde	frage	finde	gebe	fahre	weiß
du	bist	hast	wirst	fragst	findest	gibst	fährst	weißt
er/sie/es	ist	hat	wird	fragt	findet	gibt	fährt	weiß
wir	sind	haben	werden	fragen	finden	geben	fahren	wissen
ihr	seid	habt	werdet	fragt	findet	gebt	fahrt	wisst
sie/Sie	sind	haben	werden	fragen	finden	geben	fahren	wissen

Simple Past Tense

	Auxiliary Verbs			Weak	Strong		Mixed
	sein	**haben**	**werden**	**fragen**	**geben**	**fahren**	**wissen**
ich	war	hatte	wurde	fragte	gab	fuhr	wusste
du	warst	hattest	wurdest	fragtest	gabst	fuhrst	wusstest
er/sie/es	war	hatte	wurde	fragte	gab	fuhr	wusste
wir	waren	hatten	wurden	fragten	gaben	fuhren	wussten
ihr	wart	hattet	wurdet	fragtet	gabt	fuhrt	wusstet
sie/Sie	waren	hatten	wurden	fragten	gaben	fuhren	wussten

Present Perfect Tense

	sein		haben		geben		fahren	
ich	bin		habe		habe		bin	
du	bist		hast		hast		bist	
er/sie/es	ist	} gewesen	hat	} gehabt	hat	} gegeben	ist	} gefahren
wir	sind		haben		haben		sind	
ihr	seid		habt		habt		seid	
sie/Sie	sind		haben		haben		sind	

Past Perfect Tense

	sein		haben		geben		fahren	
ich	war		hatte		hatte		war	
du	warst		hattest		hattest		warst	
er/sie/es	war	} gewesen	hatte	} gehabt	hatte	} gegeben	war	} gefahren
wir	waren		hatten		hatten		waren	
ihr	wart		hattet		hattet		wart	
sie/Sie	waren		hatten		hatten		waren	

Future Tense

	geben
ich	werde
du	wirst
er/sie/es	wird
wir	werden } geben
ihr	werdet
sie/Sie	werden

Subjunctive

Present Tense: Subjunctive I (Indirect Discourse Subjunctive)

	sein	haben	werden	fahren	wissen
ich	sei	—	—	—	wisse
du	sei(e)st	habest	—	—	—
er/sie/es	sei	habe	werde	fahre	wisse
wir	seien	—	—	—	—
ihr	sei(e)t	habet	—	—	—
sie/Sie	seien	—	—	—	—

For those forms left blank in the chart above, the subjunctive II forms are preferred in indirect discourse.

Present Tense: Subjunctive II

	fragen	sein	haben	werden	fahren	wissen
ich	fragte	wäre	hätte	würde	führe	wüsste
du	fragtest	wär(e)st	hättest	würdest	führ(e)st	wüsstest
er/sie/es	fragte	wäre	hätte	würde	führe	wüsste
wir	fragten	wären	hätten	würden	führen	wüssten
ihr	fragtet	wär(e)t	hättet	würdet	führ(e)t	wüsstet
sie/Sie	fragten	wären	hätten	würden	führen	wüssten

Past Tense: Subjunctive I (Indirect Discourse)

	fahren	wissen
ich	sei	—
du	sei(e)st	habest
er/sie/es	sei	habe
wir	seien } gefahren	— } gewusst
ihr	sei(e)t	habet
sie/Sie	sei(e)n	—

Past Tense: Subjunctive II

	sein		geben		fahren	
ich	wäre		hätte		wäre	
du	wär(e)st		hättest		wär(e)st	
er/sie/es	wäre	} gewesen	hätte	} gegeben	wäre	} gefahren
wir	wären		hätten		wären	
ihr	wär(e)t		hättet		wär(e)t	
sie/Sie	wären		hätten		wären	

Passive Voice

	einladen		
	Present	*Simple Past*	*Present Perfect*
ich	werde	wurde	bin
du	wirst	wurdest	bist
er/sie/es	wird } eingeladen	wurde } eingeladen	ist } eingeladen worden
wir	werden	wurden	sind
ihr	werdet	wurdet	seid
sie/Sie	werden	wurden	sind

Imperative

	sein	geben	fahren	arbeiten
Familiar Singular	sei	gib	fahr	arbeite
Familiar Plural	seid	gebt	fahrt	arbeitet
Formal	seien Sie	geben Sie	fahren Sie	arbeiten Sie

7. Principal Parts of Strong and Mixed Verbs

The following is a list of the most important strong and mixed verbs that are used in this book. Included in this list are the modal auxiliaries. Since the principal parts of compound verbs follow the forms of the base verb, compound verbs are generally not included, except for a few high-frequency compound verbs whose base verb is not commonly used. Thus you will find **anfangen** and **einladen** listed, but not **zurückkommen** or **ausgehen**.

Infinitive	(3rd Pers. Sg. Present)	Simple Past	Past Participle	Meaning
anbieten		bot an	angeboten	*to offer*
anfangen	(fängt an)	fing an	angefangen	*to begin*
backen		backte	gebacken	*to bake*
beginnen		begann	begonnen	*to begin*
begreifen		begriff	begriffen	*to comprehend*
beißen		biss	gebissen	*to bite*
bitten		bat	gebeten	*to ask, beg*
bleiben		blieb	(ist) geblieben	*to stay*
bringen		brachte	gebracht	*to bring*
denken		dachte	gedacht	*to think*
dürfen	(darf)	durfte	gedurft	*to be allowed to*
einladen	(lädt ein)	lud ein	eingeladen	*to invite*
empfehlen	(empfiehlt)	empfahl	empfohlen	*to recommend*
entscheiden		entschied	entschieden	*to decide*
essen	(isst)	aß	gegessen	*to eat*
fahren	(fährt)	fuhr	(ist) gefahren	*to drive*
fallen	(fällt)	fiel	(ist) gefallen	*to fall*
finden		fand	gefunden	*to find*
fliegen		flog	(ist) geflogen	*to fly*
geben	(gibt)	gab	gegeben	*to give*
gefallen	(gefällt)	gefiel	gefallen	*to like; to please*
gehen		ging	(ist) gegangen	*to go*
genießen		genoss	genossen	*to enjoy*
geschehen	(geschieht)	geschah	(ist) geschehen	*to happen*
gewinnen		gewann	gewonnen	*to win*
haben	(hat)	hatte	gehabt	*to have*
halten	(hält)	hielt	gehalten	*to hold; to stop*
hängen		hing	gehangen	*to hang*
heißen		hieß	geheißen	*to be called*
helfen	(hilft)	half	geholfen	*to help*
kennen		kannte	gekannt	*to know*
kommen		kam	(ist) gekommen	*to come*
können	(kann)	konnte	gekonnt	*can; to be able to*
lassen	(lässt)	ließ	gelassen	*to let; to allow (to)*
laufen	(läuft)	lief	(ist) gelaufen	*to run*
leihen		lieh	geliehen	*to lend; to borrow*
lesen	(liest)	las	gelesen	*to read*
liegen		lag	gelegen	*to lie*
mögen	(mag)	mochte	gemocht	*to like (to)*
müssen	(muss)	musste	gemusst	*must; to have to*
nehmen	(nimmt)	nahm	genommen	*to take*
nennen		nannte	genannt	*to name*
raten	(rät)	riet	geraten	*to advise*

Infinitive	(3rd Pers. Sg. Present)	Simple Past	Past Participle	Meaning
reiten		ritt	(ist) geritten	*to ride*
scheinen		schien	geschienen	*to seem; to shine*
schlafen	(schläft)	schlief	geschlafen	*to sleep*
schließen		schloss	geschlossen	*to close*
schreiben		schrieb	geschrieben	*to write*
schwimmen		schwamm	(ist) geschwommen	*to swim*
sehen	(sieht)	sah	gesehen	*to see*
sein	(ist)	war	(ist) gewesen	*to be*
singen		sang	gesungen	*to sing*
sitzen		saß	gesessen	*to sit*
sollen	(soll)	sollte	gesollt	*should, ought to; to be supposed to*
sprechen	(spricht)	sprach	gesprochen	*to speak*
stehen		stand	gestanden	*to stand*
steigen		stieg	ist gestiegen	*to rise; to climb*
sterben	(stirbt)	starb	(ist) gestorben	*to die*
tragen	(trägt)	trug	getragen	*to carry; to wear*
treffen	(trifft)	traf	getroffen	*to meet*
trinken		trank	getrunken	*to drink*
tun		tat	getan	*to do*
umsteigen		stieg um	(ist) umgestiegen	*to change; to transfer*
vergessen	(vergisst)	vergaß	vergessen	*to forget*
vergleichen		verglich	verglichen	*to compare*
verlieren		verlor	verloren	*to lose*
wachsen	(wächst)	wuchs	(ist) gewachsen	*to grow*
waschen	(wäscht)	wusch	gewaschen	*to wash*
werden	(wird)	wurde	(ist) geworden	*to become*
wissen	(weiß)	wusste	gewusst	*to know*
wollen	(will)	wollte	gewollt	*to want (to)*
ziehen		zog	(ist/hat) gezogen	*to move; to pull*

Vocabulary
German–English

This vocabulary contains the German words as used in various contexts in this text, with the following exceptions: (1) compound words whose meaning can be easily guessed from their component parts; (2) most identical or very close cognates that are not part of the active vocabulary. (Frequently used cognates are, however, included so that students can verify their gender.)

Active vocabulary in the end-of-chapter **Wortschatz** lists is indicated by the number of the chapter in which it first appears. The letter E refers to the introductory chapter, **Einführung.**

The following abbreviations are used:

acc. accusative
adj. adjective
adv. adverb
coll. colloquial
coord. conj. coordinating conjunction
dat. dative

decl. adj. declined adjective
form. formal
gen. genitive
indef. pron. indefinite pronoun
inform. informal

-(e)n *masc.* masculine noun ending in **-n** or **-en** in all cases but the nominative singular
pl. plural
sg. singular
subord. conj. subordinating conjunction

A

ab (+ *dat.*) from; as of (12); **ab 1. Juni (ab erstem Juni)** as of June 1st (12)

ab und zu now and then, occasionally (8)

abdrehen (dreht ab) to turn off

der Abend (-e) evening (4); **am Abend** in the evening, at night; **gestern Abend** last night; **guten Abend** good evening (E); **der Heilige Abend** Christmas Eve (3); **heute Abend** this evening (1); **morgen Abend** tomorrow evening (4)

das Abendessen (-) evening meal (5); dinner, supper; **zum Abendessen** for dinner, supper

abends in the evening, evenings (4)

das Abenteuer (-) adventure

aber (*coord. conj.*) but (1); however

abfahren (fährt ab), fuhr ab, ist abgefahren to depart, leave (10)

die Abfahrt (-en) departure (10)

der Abfall (¨e) waste, garbage, trash, litter (14)

die Abfallwirtschaft waste management

abfliegen (fliegt ab), flog ab, ist abgeflogen to depart, leave (by plane)

abgeben (gibt ab), gab ab, abgegeben to drop off, turn in (8)

der/die Abgeordnete (*decl. adj.*) member of parliament

abholen (holt ab) to pick up (*from a place*) (4)

das Abi (-s) (*coll.*) = **das Abitur**

das Abitur (-e) *examination at the end of* **Gymnasium** (11)

der Abiturient (-en *masc.***) (-en) / die Abiturientin (-nen)** *graduate of the* **Gymnasium,** *person who has passed the* **Abitur**

die Abkürzung (-en) abbreviation

ablehnen (lehnt ab) to decline

das Abo(nnement) (-s) subscription (13)

abonnieren to subscribe (13)

abreisen (reist ab), ist abgereist to depart, leave (on a trip) (9)

der Absatz (¨e) paragraph

abschalten (schaltet ab) to shut down, turn off

abschicken (schickt ab) to send off, mail

der Abschied (-e) farewell

der Abschluss (¨e) completion; degree (11)

der Abschnitt (-e) section; phase

der Absender (-) sender

absolut absolute(ly)

abspielen (spielt ab) to play

die Abstammung origin, heritage

absteigen (steigt ab), stieg ab, ist abgestiegen to dismount, get off

abstimmen (stimmt ab) to take a vote (14)

die Abstimmung vote; coordination

der Absturz (¨e) fall; crash

das Abteil (-e) compartment

(sich) abwechseln (wechselt ab) to alternate, take turns

abwechslungsreich varied, diverse (11)

das Accessoire (-s) accessory

ach oh; **Ach so!** I see!

acht eight (E)

achte eighth (3)

achten auf (+ *acc.*) to pay attention to, watch (8)

die Achtung attention

achtzehn eighteen (E)

achtzehnte eighteenth

achtzig eighty (E)

die Action action

der Adel nobility

das Adjektiv (-e) adjective

der Adler, - eagle

das Adrenalin adrenaline

die Adresse (-n) address (E)

das Adverb (-ien) adverb

das Aerobic aerobics

afghanisch Afghan

(das) Afghanistan Afghanistan

(das) Afrika Africa

afrikanisch African

das Aggregat (-e) set; setting

aggressiv aggressive

agieren to play one's part

(das) Ägypten Egypt

ah ah; **Ah so!** I see! I get it!

ähnlich similar(ly)

die Ähnlichkeit (-en) similarity

die Ahnung: Keine Ahnung! (I have) no idea!

das Aids AIDS

die Akademie (-n) academy

akkurat precise(ly), exact(ly)

der Akkusativ accusative case

der Akrobat (-en *masc.***) (-en) / die Akrobatin (-nen)** acrobat

die Aktie (-n) stock

die Aktion (-en) (political) action

aktiv active(ly) (10); **sportlich aktiv** active in sports (10)

die Aktivität (-en) activity

aktuell current, topical (13); **Aktuelles** current events (13)

akzentuieren to accentuate; **deutsch-akzentuiert** German-accented

akzeptabel acceptable, acceptably

der Alkohol alcohol (8)

alkoholfrei nonalcoholic (6)

das Alkoholthermometer (-) alcohol thermometer

all all; **vor allem** above all

alle (*pl.*) all (2); every **alle zwei Jahre** every two years; **aller** of all

die Allee, -n avenue

allein alone

allerdings however; to be sure

allerlei all kinds of (things)

alles everything (10); **Alles Gute!** All the best! (3); **Alles klar.** I get it., Everything is clear. (E)

Allgäuer (*adj.*) of/from Allgäu

allgemein general; **im Allgemeinen** in general

der Alltag everyday routine; workday

alltäglich everyday, ordinary

die Alpen (*pl.*) the Alps

alphabetisch alphabetical(ly)

als (*subord. conj.*) as; when (10); than (7);

also thus, therefore; so; well

alt (**älter, ältest-**) old (1); **Alt-** used

das Alter(-) age

die Altstadt ("e) old part of town

am = an dem; am ersten Mai on May first (3); **am Montag** on Monday (3); **möchte am liebsten** would like (to do) most (4)

der Amateurfunker (-) / die Amateurfunkerin (-nen) amateur radio operator

(das) Amerika America

der Amerikaner (-) / die Amerikanerin (-nen) American (*person*) (1)

amerikanisch American

die Amischen (*pl.*) Amish (*people*)

die Ampel (-n) traffic light (9)

das Amt ("er) bureau, agency

amüsant amusing, entertaining

an (+ *acc./dat.*) at; near; on; onto; to (6); **an deiner Stelle** if I were you, (if I were) in your place (12); **an der Ecke** at the corner (9)

die Analyse (-n) analysis

analysieren to analyze

anbieten (bietet an), bot an, angeboten to offer

anbrennen (brennt an), brannte an, angebrannt to burn

anbringen (bringt an), brachte an, angebracht to put up, install

ander- different, other; **am anderen Morgen** the next morning; **der/die/das andere** (*decl. adj.*) the other one, different one; **(et)was anderes** something else

andererseits on the other hand

anders different(ly), in another way; **jemand anders** somebody else

anderswo elsewhere, somewhere/anywhere else

die Änderung (-en) change

anerkennen, erkannte an, anerkannt to recognize, acknowledge

der Anfang ("e) beginning, start

anfangen (fängt an), fing an, angefangen to begin, start (4)

der Anfänger (-) / die Anfängerin (-nen) beginner

anfangs at first

anfordern (fordert an) to request, order

anführen (führt an) to lead; to give, quote

die Angabe (-n) statement, information; **persönliche Angaben** personal information

angeben (gibt an), gab an, angegeben to state, declare, give

angeblich alleged (ly)

das Angebot (-e) (special) offer; selection (10)

angehen (geht an), ging an, angegangen to tackle, take on

die Angelegenheit (-en) matter, issue, affair

angeln to fish (7)

die Angelrute (-n) fishing rod

angenehm pleasant(ly) (7)

der/die Angestellte (*decl. adj.*) employee

angewandt applied

die Anglistik (study of) English language and literature

die Angst ("e) fear (12); **Angst haben (vor + *dat.*)** to be afraid (of) (12)

ängstlich anxious(ly)

angucken (guckt an) (*coll.*) to look at; **sich** (*dat.*) **etwas angucken** (*coll.*) to look at something

der Anhang ("e) appendix; attachment

(sich) anhören (hört an) to listen to

der Ankauf purchase; **An- und Verkauf** buying and selling

ankommen (kommt an), kam an, ist angekommen to arrive (9)

ankreuzen (kreuzt an) to mark; to check off

die Ankunft ("e) arrival (10)

anlegen (legt an) to put on; to put down, lay out

anmachen (macht an) to turn on; to light (a fire)

das Anmeldeformular (-e) registration form (9)

(sich) anmelden (meldet an) to check in, register (9)

anmieten (mietet an) to rent

annehmen (nimmt an), nahm an, angenommen to accept, take

anno: pro anno per year, annual(ly)

anprobieren (probiert an), anprobiert to try on (5)

anregen (regt an) to prompt, stimulate

die Anreise (-n) journey to a place; arrival

der Anruf (-e) (telephone) call

der Anrufbeantworter (-) answering machine (13)

anrufen (ruft an), rief an, angerufen to call up (on the phone) (4); **sich anrufen** to call one another

ans = an das

die Ansage (-n) announcement

der Ansager (-) / die Ansagerin (-nen) announcer

(sich) etwas anschaffen (schafft an) to purchase something, acquire something (14)

anschalten (schaltet an) to turn on

anschauen (schaut an) to look at; **sich** (*dat.*) **etwas anschauen** to look at, watch (13)

der Anschlag ("e) attack

der Anschlagzettel (-) notice, bulletin

anschließend afterward

der Anschluss ("e) connection (10)

die Anschrift (-en) address

ansehen (sieht an), sah an, angesehen to watch; **sich** (*dat.*) **etwas ansehen** to watch, look at (13)

das Ansehen prestige (11)

die Ansicht (-en) view

anstehend upcoming, waiting to be done

anstrengend tiring, strenuous (8)

die Anthropologie anthropology

antideutsch anti-German

die Antikriegsdemonstration (-en) antiwar demonstration

das Antiquariat secondhand bookshop; **modernes Antiquariat** shop or department selling remaindered books

die Antwort (-en) answer

antworten (auf + *acc.*) to answer (to)

die Anzeige (-n) (newspaper) advertisement

anziehen (zieht an), zog an, angezogen to put on; **sich anziehen** to get dressed (8)

der Anzug ("e) suit (5)

der Apfel (") apple (5)

das Apfelmus applesauce (6)

der Apfelrotkohl *dish containing apples and red cabbage*

der Apfelstrudel (-) apple strudel, apple pastry (6)

die Apotheke (-n) pharmacy (5)

der Apparat (-e) set, appliance (*such as TV or telephone*) (9); **sich am Apparat melden** to answer the telephone

das Appartement (-s) one-room apartment

der Appetit (-e) appetite; **Guten Appetit!** Enjoy your meal!

der Applaus (-e) applause

(der) April April (3)

das Aquarium (Aquarien) aquarium

das Äquivalent (-e) equivalent

(das) Arabien Arabia

arabisch (*adj.*) Arab(ian), Arabic

die Arbeit (-en) work; job; assignment; paper (8)

arbeiten to work (1)

der Arbeiter (-) / die Arbeiterin (-nen) worker, laborer

der Arbeitgeber (-) / die Arbeitgeberin (-nen) employer (11)

der Arbeitnehmer (-) / die Arbeitnehmerin (-nen) employee

das Arbeitsamt ("er) employment office (11)

arbeitsfrei off from work

die Arbeitslage (-n) employment situation

der Arbeitslohn ("e) wage(s)

arbeitslos unemployed

die Arbeitslosigkeit unemployment (14)

das Arbeitsmittel (-) material(s); tool

der Arbeitsplatz ("e) workplace; position (11)

die Arbeitsvermittlung (-en) employment agency

das Arbeitszimmer (-) workroom, study (2)

der Architekt (-en *masc.*) (-en) / die Architektin (-nen) architect

die Architektur (-en) architecture

(das) Argentinien Argentina

ärgerlich annoyed, angry; annoying, vexing

ärgern to annoy; **sich ärgern (über + *acc.*)** to be annoyed (about) (12)

das Argument (-e) argument

arm poor

der Arm (-e) arm (8)

die Armee (-n) armed forces

die Armen (*pl.*) poor people

die Armut poverty (14)

arrangieren to arrange

die Art (-en) kind, type; manner

der Artikel (-) article; item

das Arzneimittel (-) medication (14)

der Arzt ("e) / die Ärztin (-nen) physician, doctor (8)

der Aspekt (-e) aspect

das Aspirin aspirin

assistieren to assist

die Assoziation (-en) association

assoziieren to associate

der AStA = Allgemeiner Studentenausschuss students' union

der Astronaut (-en *masc.***) (-en) / die Astronautin (-nen)** astronaut

die Atmosphäre (-n) atmosphere

die Atomkraft nuclear power

der Atomstreit nuclear conflict

ätzend corrosive; caustic

au ouch

die Aubergine (-n) eggplant

auch also, too (E)

die Aue (-n) meadow

auf (+ *acc./dat.***)** on, upon; on top of; at (6); onto; to; **auf Deutsch** in German (E); **auf jeden Fall** in any case (13); **auf welchen Namen?** under what name? (9); **auf Wiederhören** good-bye (*on the phone*) (9); **auf Wiedersehen** good-bye (E)

aufbauen (baut auf) to set up

aufbleiben, blieb auf, ist aufgeblieben to stay up

der Aufenthalt (-e) stay; layover (9)

auffallen (fällt auf), fiel auf, ist aufgefallen to stand out, be conspicuous

die Aufforderung (-en) request

die Aufgabe (-n) task; exercise

der Aufgussbeutel (-) tea bag

aufheben, hob auf, aufgehoben to pick up; to keep

aufhören (mit + *dat.***) (hört auf)** to end, quit, stop (doing something)

aufklären (über + *acc.***) (klärt auf)** to inform (about)

der Auflauf (¨-e) casserole (6)

aufmachen (macht auf) to open

aufnehmen (nimmt auf), nahm auf, aufgenommen to record (*on tape, video, etc.*) (13); to receive

aufpassen (passt auf) to pay attention

aufräumen (räumt auf) to clean up, straighten up (*a room*) (4)

aufregend exciting

aufs = auf das

der Aufsatz (¨-e) essay

der Aufschnitt cold cuts (5)

aufschreiben (schreibt auf), schrieb auf, aufgeschrieben to write down

der Aufstand (¨-e) rebellion, uprising

aufstehen (steht auf), stand auf, ist aufgestanden to get up; stand up (4)

aufstellen (stellt auf) to set up

der Auftrag (¨-e) task, assignment

der Auftritt (-e) appearance (*on stage*)

aufwachen (wacht auf), ist aufgewacht to wake up (4)

aufwachsen (wächst auf), wuchs auf, ist aufgewachsen to grow up

der Aufzug (¨-e) elevator (9)

das Auge (-n) eye (8)

(der) August August (3)

aus (+ *dat.***)** from; out of; (made) of (5); **Ich komme aus . . .** I'm from . . . (E)

ausbauen (baut aus) to convert (*a room or building*)

die Ausbildung (-en) (career) training (11)

der Ausbildungsberuf (-e) career requiring an apprenticeship

ausbrechen (bricht aus), brach aus, ausgebrochen to break out

die Ausbreitung spread

sich (*dat.***) etwas ausdenken (denkt aus), dachte aus, ausgedacht** to think something through

der Ausdruck (¨-e) expression

ausdrucken (druckt aus) to print out

ausdrücken (drückt aus) to express

auseinander apart

der Ausflug (¨-e) excursion

die Ausflugsfahrt (-en) excursion (*by car, bus, etc.*)

ausfüllen (füllt aus) to fill out (9)

die Ausgabe (-n) expense (12)

ausgeben (gibt aus), gab aus, ausgegeben to spend (*money*) (12)

ausgehen (geht aus), ging aus, ist ausgegangen to go out (4)

ausgerechnet of all things

ausgezeichnet excellent (E)

ausgleiten (gleitet aus), glitt aus, ist ausgeglitten to slip and fall

die Ausgrabung (-en) excavation

aushalten (hält aus), hielt aus, ausgehalten to endure

auskommen (kommt aus), kam aus, ist ausgekommen to make ends meet, get by with (*money*)

die Auskunft (¨-e) information (10)

das Ausland (*sg. only***)** foreign countries (11); **im Ausland** abroad (11)

der Ausländer (-) / die Ausländerin (-nen) foreigner (14)

die Ausländerfeindlichkeit xenophobia, hatred toward foreigners (14)

ausländisch foreign

ausleihen (leiht aus), lieh aus, ausgeliehen to borrow; to lend

die Ausnahme (-n) exception

auspacken (packt aus) to unpack

die Ausrede (-n) excuse

ausreichend sufficient(ly), enough

ausrufen (ruft aus), rief aus, ausgerufen to call out

sich ausruhen (ruht aus) to rest

die Ausrüstung (-en) equipment

die Aussage (-n) statement

aussagen (sagt aus) to say, express

ausschalten (schaltet aus) to turn off

ausschneiden (schneidet aus), schnitt aus, ausgeschnitten to cut out

aussehen (sieht aus), sah aus, ausgesehen to look, appear

die Außenpolitik foreign politics; foreign policy

der Außentermin (-e) outside engagement

außer (+ *dat.***)** except for, besides

außerdem besides, in addition (14)

außerhalb (+ *gen.***)** outside of (9)

(sich) äußern to express (oneself)

die Aussicht (-en) view, prospect

ausspannen (spannt aus) to rest, relax, take a break

die Aussprache (-n) pronunciation; discussion, talk

ausstatten (stattet aus) to equip, furnish

die Ausstellung (-en) exhibition

ausstreichen (streicht aus), strich aus, ausgestrichen to cross out, strike through

sich (*dat.***) (et)was aussuchen (sucht aus)** to select, find, choose something (13)

austauschen (tauscht aus) to trade, exchange

der Austauschschüler (-) / die Austauschschülerin (-nen) exchange student (*high school*)

(das) Australien Australia

ausüben (übt aus) to practice, exercise, do

auswählen (wählt aus) to choose, select

auswärts outwards; away from home

der Ausweis (-e) ID card

die Auszeit (-en) time-out

ausziehen (zieht aus), zog aus, ist ausgezogen to move out; **sich (** *acc.***) ausziehen** to get undressed (8); **sich (** *dat.***) etwas ausziehen** to take something off (*clothing etc.*)

der/die Auszubildende (*decl. adj.***)** trainee, apprentice

das Auto (-s) car, auto (2)

die Autobahn (-en) highway

der Autofahrer (-) / die Autofahrerin (-nen) (automobile) driver

das Automobil (-e) automobile, car

der Autor (-en) / die Autorin (-nen) author

Autostop: per Autostop reisen to hitchhike (10)

der/die Azubi (-s) = der/die Auszubildende

B

die Babywäsche baby clothes

der Bach (¨-e) stream

der Bäcker (-) / die Bäckerin (-nen) baker

die Bäckerei (-en) bakery (5)

das Bäckerhandwerk bakery trade

die Backwaren (*pl.***)** baked goods

das Bad (¨-er) bath; bathroom (2); spa

der Badeanzug (¨-e) bathing suit (5)

die Badehose (-n) swim trunks (5)

die Bademoden (*pl.***)** beachwear

baden to bathe

(das) Baden-Württemberg Baden-Württemberg (*German state*)

die Badesachen (*pl.***)** beach accessories

das Badezimmer (-) bathroom (2)

das BAföG = Bundesausbildungsförderungsgesetz government financial aid for students

die Bahn (-en) train; railway (10)

der Bahnhof (¨-e) train station (9)

der Bahnsteig (-e) (train) platform (10)

die Bakterie (-n) bacterium

bald soon (12); **möglichst bald** as soon as possible

der Balkon (-e) balcony (2)

der Ball ("-e) ball

die Ballade (-n) ballad

das Ballett (-e) ballet (4)

die Banane (-n) banana (5)

der Band ("-e) volume (*book*)

die Band (-s) band, musical group

die Bande (-n) gang, mob

die Bank ("-e) bench

die Bank (-en) bank (*financial institution*) (9)

die Bankkauffrau (-en) (female) bank administrator

der Bankkaufmann (Bankkaufleute) (male) bank administrator

die Bankleitzahl (-en) bank routing number

bar in cash

die Bar (-s) bar

der Bär (-en masc.) (-en) bear

das Bargeld cash (10)

der Baron (-e) / die Baronin (-nen) baron / baroness

der Baseball baseball

basieren auf (+ *dat.*) to be based on

das Basilikum basil

basteln to tinker, make things by hand

die Batterie (-n) battery

der Bau (Bauten) building; construction

der Bauch ("-e) belly, abdomen, stomach (8)

der Bauchredner (-) / die Bauchrednerin (-nen) ventriloquist

die Bauchschmerzen (*pl.*) bellyache, stomachache

bauen to build (12)

der Bauer (-n masc.) (-n) / die Bäuerin (-nen) farmer

das Bauernhaus ("-er) farmhouse (12)

der Bauernhof ("-e) farm

der Baum ("-e) tree

der Baumast ("-e) tree branch, bough

die Baumwolle cotton

der Bausparvertrag ("-e) building loan contract

bayerisch (*adj.*) Bavarian

(das) Bayern Bavaria

Bayreuther (*adj.*) of/from Bayreuth (*a town in Bavaria*)

bayrisch (*adj.*) Bavarian

der Beamte (decl. adj.) / die Beamtin (-nen) agent; government employee

beantworten to answer

bearbeiten to work on, deal with

der Becher (-) glass, cup

das Bedauern regret

bedeuten to mean, signify; **Was bedeutet … ?** What does . . . mean? (E)

die Bedeutung (-en) meaning, significance

bedienen to serve

die Bedienung service (6)

das Bedienungsgeld service charge

sich beeilen to hurry (up) (8)

beeindrucken to impress

beenden to complete, finish, end

sich befassen mit (+ *dat.*) to occupy oneself with

das Befinden health, well-being

sich befinden, befand, befunden to be

befolgen to follow, obey

befragen to question

der Beginn start, beginning

beginnen, begann, begonnen to begin, start

die Begegnung (-en) meeting, encounter

begeistert enthusiastic(ally)

begreifen, begriff, begriffen to understand, comprehend

begründen to give reasons for

der Begründer (-) / die Begründerin (-nen) founder

die Begrüßung (-en) greeting

behandeln to treat, deal with (14)

behaupten to claim, assert (13)

behilflich helpful

bei (+ *dat.*) at; near; with (5); at the place of

beide (*pl.*) both

der Beifahrersitz (-e) passenger seat

beifügen (fügt bei) to add; to enclose

beige beige (5)

die Beilage (-n) side dish (6)

beim = bei dem

das Bein (-e) leg (8)

das Beispiel (-e) example; **zum Beispiel** for example

beißen, biss, gebissen to bite

bekannt acquainted, known; well-known; **bekannt werden** to get acquainted

der/die Bekannte (decl. adj.) acquaintance

bekennen, bekannte, bekannt to admit, confess

die Bekleidung clothing, attire

bekommen, bekam, bekommen to receive, get (6); **Was bekommen Sie?** What will you have? (6)

belasten to burden

beleben to animate, liven up

(das) Belgien Belgium (E)

der Belgier (-) / die Belgierin (-nen) Belgian (*person*)

beliebt popular (7)

die Bemerkung (-en) remark, comment

beneiden to envy

benennen, benannte, benant to name

benutzbar usable

benutzen to use

der Benutzerausweis (-e) user ID

die Benutzung use

das Benzin gasoline (12)

bequem comfortable, comfortably (2)

die Beratung (-en) advising; consultation

berechenbar predictable

der Bereich (-e) area, field

bereit sein to be ready, be willing

bereits already

der Berg (-e) mountain (7)

das Bergsteigen mountain climbing

die Bergwanderung (-en) hike in the mountains

der Bericht (-e) report (13)

berichten to report, narrate (13)

Berliner (*adj.*) of/from Berlin

der Berliner (-) / die Berlinerin (-nen) person from Berlin

der Beruf (-e) profession, occupation (1); **Was sind Sie von Beruf?** What do you do for a living? (1)

beruflich professional(ly), on business

der Berufsberater (-) / die Berufsberaterin (-nen) employment counselor (11)

das Berufsleben professional life, working life (11)

der/die Berufstätige (decl. adj.) working person

die Berufswahl (-en) career choice

berühmt famous

sich beschäftigen mit (+ *dat.*) to occupy oneself with (11)

beschreiben, beschrieb, beschrieben to describe

die Beschreibung (-en) description

die Beschwerde (-n) complaint

sich beschweren (über + *acc.*) to complain (about) (9)

der Besen (-) broom

der Besenstiel (-e) broomstick

besetzen to occupy; **besetzt** occupied, taken (6); **Hier ist besetzt.** This place is taken. (6)

besichtigen to view, see

besitzen, besaß, besessen to own, possess (11)

der Besitzer (-) / die Besitzerin (-nen) owner

besonder- special, particular; **etwas/nichts Besonderes** something/nothing special

besonders especially, particularly (8); **nicht besonders gut** not especially well (E)

besprechen (bespricht), besprach, besprochen to discuss, talk about

die Besprechung (-en) discussion; conference

besser better

die Besserung: Gute Besserung! Get well soon! (8)

best- best; **am besten** (the) best; **Wie komme ich am besten dahin?** What's the best way to get there? (9)

bestehen, bestand, bestanden to pass (an exam); **bestehen aus** (+ *dat.*) to consist of

bestellen to order (6); to reserve

die Bestellung (-en) order; reservation

bestens excellently, to the highest level

bestimmen to determine, decide

bestimmt (*adj.*) particular, certain; (*adv.*) no doubt; definitely (1)

der Besuch (-e) visit; visitors; **zu Besuch kommen** to come for a visit

besuchen to visit (1)

der Besucher (-) / die Besucherin (-nen) visitor, guest

der Betrag ("-e) sum, amount

betragen (beträgt), betrug, betragen to amount to, come to; **die Miete beträgt …** the rent comes to . . .

betreffen (betrifft), betraf, betroffen to concern; to affect (14)

betreiben, betrieb, betrieben to drive; to run (*a business, etc.*)

betreten (betritt), betrat, betreten to enter

die Betriebswirtschaft business management

das Bett (-en) bed (2)

die Bettwäsche linens (9)

der Beutel (-) bag

die Bevölkerung (-en) population

bevor (*subord. conj.*) before (10)

bewaffnet armed

(sich) bewegen to move, move about

beweglich movable

der Beweis (-e) proof, evidence

sich bewerben (um + acc.) (bewirbt), bewarb, beworben to apply (for) (11)

der Bewerber (-) / die Bewerberin (-nen) applicant

die Bewerbung (-en) application (11)

das Bewerbungsformular (-e) application form (11)

bewerten to evaluate

die Bewertung (-en) evaluation, assessment

der Bewohner (-) / die Bewohnerin (-nen) resident, tenant

bewölkt cloudy, overcast (7)

bewundern to admire

bewusst conscious, aware

bezahlen to pay

die Bezahlung (-en) payment

bezeichnen als to call, describe as

die Bezeichnung (-en) label, term

sich beziehen auf (+ acc.), bezog, bezogen to refer to

die Beziehung (-en) relationship; affair

die Beziehungskiste (-n) (*coll.*) difficult relationship

der Bezug: mit Bezug auf (+ acc.) with reference to

bezweifeln to doubt

die Bibel (-n) Bible

die Bibliothek (-en) library (4)

der Bibliothekar (-e) / die Bibliothekarin (-nen) librarian (11)

das Bier (-e) beer (5)

der Bierdeckel (-) beer coaster

der Biergarten (¨) beer garden (*restaurant*) (6)

der Bierkeller (-) *type of restaurant where beer is served*

der Bierkrug (¨e) beer stein, beer mug

bieten, bot, geboten to offer, present

das Biken (motor)biking

der Bikini (-s) bikini, two-piece bathing suit

das Bild (-er) picture

bilden to form

bildlich pictorial(ly)

das Billard (-e) billiards

billig inexpensive(ly), cheap(ly) (2)

die Billiguhr (-en) cheap watch

bin am; **Ich bin ...** I am ... (E)

binden, band, gebunden to tie (up)

Binger (*adj.*) of/from Bingen

Bio- organic, natural

die Biochemie biochemistry

die Biografie (-n) biography

der Bioladen (¨) natural-foods store (5)

das Biolebensmittel (-) organic food (8)

die Biologie biology

biologisch biological(ly)

der Biotechnologe (-n masc.) (-n) / die Biotechnologin (-nen) biotechnician

bis (+ acc.) until (6); to, up to; **bis (um) fünf Uhr** until five o'clock (6); **bis zum/zur** (+ dat.) to, as far as (9); **von zwei bis drei Uhr** from two to three o'clock (6)

bisher so far, up to now

ein bisschen a little (bit); somewhat

bist are (*2nd person inform. sg.*); **du bist** you are

das Bistro (-s) bistro

bitte please; you're welcome (E); **bitte schön** you're welcome; please; **bitte sehr** you're welcome; please; **Wie bitte?** Pardon? What did you say? (E); **Würden Sie bitte ... ?** Would you please . . . ? (9)

bitten, bat, gebeten to ask; **bitten um** (+ acc.) to ask for, request (12)

bizarr bizarre

blasen (bläst), blies, geblasen to blow

die Blasmusik brass-band music

das Blatt (¨er) leaf; sheet (of paper)

blau blue (5)

blauweiß blue and white

das Blei (-e) lead

bleiben, blieb, ist geblieben to stay, remain (1)

der Bleigurt (-e) lead belt

der Bleistift (-e) pencil (12)

der Blick (-e) look, glance; view

blitzen to flash (7); **Es blitzt.** There's lightning. (7)

blockweise in blocks

blöd stupid (13); **Das ist mir zu blöd.** I think that's really stupid. (13)

bloggen to blog, keep an online journal (7)

blond blond (e)

die Blondine (-n) blonde woman

bloß merely; only

blühen to blossom

die Blume (-n) flower

der Blumenkohl cauliflower (5)

die Bluse (-n) blouse (5)

der BMW (-s) (Bayerische Motoren Werke) BMW automobile

die Bockwurst (¨e) *type of German sausage*

der Boden (¨) floor of a room; ground

das Bodybuilding bodybuilding; **Bodybuilding machen** to do bodybuilding, do weight training (7)

das Bogenschießen archery

die Bohne (-n) bean (6); **grüne Bohne** green bean, string bean

böig gusty; squally

(das) Bolivien Bolivia

das Boot (-e) boat

der Bootsführer (-) / die Bootsführerin (-nen) boat guide

die Börse (-n) stock exchange (13)

böse angry, mad; angrily; mean; bad

(das) Bosnien Bosnia

der Boss (-e) (*coll.*) boss

die Boutique (-n) boutique, trendy shop

das Bowling bowling

die Box (-en) stereo speaker

der Brandstifter (-) arsonist

brasilianisch (*adj.*) Brazilian

(das) Brasilien Brazil

braten (brät), briet, gebraten to fry; to roast

die Bratkartoffeln (*pl.*) fried potatoes (6)

die Bratwurst (¨e) *type of German sausage*

brauchen to need (2)

das Brauhaus (¨er) brewery

braun brown (5)

bräunen to tan

die BRD = Bundesrepublik Deutschland

brechen (bricht), brach, gebrochen to break

die Bremse (-n) brake

brennen, brannte, gebrannt to burn

die Brennnesselsuppe stinging nettle soup

das Brett (-er) board; **das Schwarze Brett** bulletin board

das Brevier (-e) breviary

die Brezel (-n) pretzel (6)

das Bridge bridge (*card game*)

der Brief (-e) letter (7)

der Brieffreund (-e) / die Brieffreundin (-nen) pen pal

die Briefmarke (-n) postage stamp (7)

der Briefträger (-) / die Briefträgerin (-nen) mail carrier

die Brille (-n) (pair of) eyeglasses (5)

bringen, brachte, gebracht to bring (7)

der Brite (-n masc.) (-n) / die Britin (-nen) Briton, British person

britisch (*adj.*) British

der Brokkoli broccoli (5)

das Brot (-e) (loaf of) bread (5)

das Brötchen (-) bread roll (5)

die Brücke (-n) bridge

der Bruder (¨) brother (3)

der Brunch (-[e]s) brunch

der Brunnen (-) spring, well; fountain

die Brust (¨e) breast; chest (8)

das Buch (¨er) book (1)

der Buchdruck letterpress printing

buchen to book (a trip) (10)

die Bücherei (-en) library

das Bücherregal (-e) bookcase, bookshelf (2)

die Büchertasche (-n) bookbag

die Buchhandlung (-en) bookshop

der Buchstabe (-n masc.) (-n) letter (of the alphabet)

buchstabieren to spell

die Buchung (-en) booking, reservation

das Budget (-s) budget

das Büffet (-s) buffet

die **Bühne (-n)** stage

die **Bühnenanweisung (-en)** stage direction

das **Bühnenbild (-er)** stage decoration

der **Bühnentext (-e)** script (for a stage play)

bummeln, ist gebummelt to stroll

Bundes- federal

das **Bundesausbildungsförderungsgesetz (BAföG)** *government financial aid for students*

der **Bundeskanzler (-) / die Bundeskanzlerin (-nen)** (German or Austrian) chancellor

das **Bundesland ("er)** German state

das **Bundesministerium (Bundesministerien)** federal ministry

die **Bundesrepublik** federal republic; die **Bundesrepublik Deutschland (BRD)** Federal Republic of Germany

der **Bundesstaat (-en)** federal state; state (of the USA)

der **Bundestag** federal German parliament

bündig concise, succinct

das **Bungeejumping** bungee jumping

bunt colorful

die **Burg (-en)** fortress, castle

der **Bürger (-) / die Bürgerin (-nen)** citizen (14)

das **Bürgerhaus ("-er)** (bourgeois) town house

die **Bürgerinitiative (-n)** citizens' group; grassroots movement

der **Bürgerkrieg (-e)** civil war

der **Bürgermeister (-) / die Bürgermeisterin (-nen)** mayor

das **Büro (-s)** office (11)

die **Bürokauffrau (-en)** (female) office administrator

der **Bürokaufmann ("-er)** (male) office administrator

die **Bürokratie (-n)** bureaucracy

der **Bus (-se)** bus (10)

die **Bushaltestelle (-n)** bus stop

die **Butter** butter (5)

der **Button (-s)** button

bzw. = beziehungsweise respectively; or

C

ca. = circa, zirka approximately, about

das **Cabrio (-s)** convertible

das **Café (-s)** café (6)

die **Cafeteria (Cafeterien)** cafeteria

das **Camp (-s)** camp

campen to camp

das **Camping** camping

der **Campingplatz ("-e)** campground

der **Campus (-)** (school) campus

der **Cartoon (-s)** cartoon

das **Casino (-s)** casino

die **CD (-s)** CD, compact disc

der **CD-Spieler (-)** CD player (2)

das **Cello (-s)** cello

Celsius centigrade

der **Cent (-[s])** cent

die **Cerealien** (*pl.*) cereal

CH (= Confoederatio Helvetica) *official name of Switzerland*

der **Champignon (-s)** mushroom

die **Chance (-n)** chance; opportunity

der **Chaot (-en** *masc.*) **(-en)** scatterbrain; anarchist

chaotisch chaotic

der **Charakter (-e)** character, personality

charakterisieren to characterize

die **Charakteristik (-en)** characteristic

charakteristisch characteristic

chatten to chat (online)

checken to check

die **Checkliste (-n)** checklist

der **Chef (-s) / die Chefin (-nen)** manager, boss, head (11)

die **Chemie** chemistry

die **Chemikalie (-n)** chemical

der **Chemiker (-) / die Chemikerin (-nen)** chemist

chemisch chemical

CHF = der Schweizer Franken Swiss Franc

(das) China China

chinesisch (*adj.*) Chinese

der **Chor ("-e)** choir, chorus

christlich (*adj.*) Christian

(der) Christus Christ

die **Chronik (-en)** chronicle

chronisch chronic(ally)

die **Chronologie (-n)** chronology

circa = zirka approximately, about

der **Clan (-s)** clan

die **Clique (-n)** clique

der **Clou (-s)** (*coll.*) main point, highlight

der **Clown (-s) / die Clownin (-nen)** clown

der **Club = der Klub**

der **Cocktail (-s)** cocktail

die **Cola (-s)** cola

das **Comicheft (-e)** comic book

der **Computer (-)** computer (2)

der **Computeranschluss ("-e)** computer connection (2)

das **Computerspiel (-e)** computer game; **Computerspiele spielen** to play computer games (1)

der **Container (-)** recycling bin

die **Cordhose (-n)** (pair of) corduroy pants

die **Cornflakes** (*pl.*) cornflakes; cereal

(das) Costa Rica Costa Rica

der **Couchtisch (-e)** coffee table (2)

die **Couleur (-s)** shade, persuasion; sort

der **Coupon (-s)** coupon

der **Cousin (-s)** male cousin

die **Cousine (-n) = Kusine** female cousin (3)

der **Cowboy (-s)** cowboy

die **Creme (-s)** cream

die **Crew (-s)** crew, team

der **Crouton (-s)** crouton

die **Currywurst ("-e)** *sausage served with curry powder and ketchup*

der **Cutter (-) / die Cutterin (-nen)** film editor

die **Cyberkriminalität** cybercrime

D

da there (2); here; (*subord. conj.*) since; **da drüben** over there (6)

dabei with that; in that context; **dabei sein** to be present, take part

dabeihaben (hat dabei) to have with one

dabeistehen (steht dabei), stand dabei, dabeigestanden to stand by

das **Dach ("-er)** roof (12)

das **Dachgeschoss (-e)** top floor, attic (12)

die **Dachwohnung (-en)** attic apartment

dafür for that; **Ich bin dafür.** I'm in favor of it. (14)

dagegen against that; on the other hand; **Ich bin dagegen.** I'm against it. (14)

daher from there; for that reason, therefore

dahin there (to that place); **Wie komme ich am besten dahin?** What's the best way to get there? (9)

dahinter behind that

damals formerly; at that time, (back) then

die **Dame (-n)** lady; **meine Damen und Herren** ladies and gentlemen

die **Damenkonfektion (-en)** ladies' wear

die **Damenwäsche** lingerie, ladies' undergarments

damit with that; (*subord. conj.*) so that

danach after that; afterward

daneben next to that

(das) Dänemark Denmark (E)

der **Dank** thanks; **Gott sei Dank** thank God; **Vielen Dank!** Many thanks! (6)

danke thanks (E); **danke, gut** fine, thanks (E); **danke schön** thank you very much (E); **danke sehr** thanks a lot (1); **nein danke** no, thank you

danken (+ *dat.*) to thank (5); **Nichts zu danken.** No thanks necessary; Don't mention it. (8)

dann then

daran on that; at that; to that; **es liegt daran, dass ...** it is because . . .

darauf on that; for that; to that

darin in that; in there

das **Darlehen (-)** loan

darstellen (stellt dar) to portray, depict

darüber above that; about that

darunter under that; among them

das that, this; the; **Das ist ...** This is . . . (E)

dass (*subord. conj.*) that (8)

dasselbe the same

der **Dativ** dative case

das **Datum (Daten)** date; **Welches Datum ist heute/morgen?** What is today's/tomorrow's date? (3)

dauern to last; to take (*time*) (7)

davon of that; about that; of them

davonlassen (lässt davon), ließ davon, davongelassen: die Finger davonlassen (*coll.*) to steer clear of it

davor before that; in front of that

dazu to that; for that; in addition to that

dazugeben (gibt dazu), gab dazu, dazugegeben to add

dazugehören (gehört dazu) to belong to that/them

dazwischen between them; during that

die DDR = Deutsche Demokratische Republik German Democratic Republic

die Debatte (-n) debate

debattieren to debate

das Debüt (-s) debut

die Decke (-n) ceiling; blanket, cover

der Deckel (-) lid

decken to cover; **den Tisch decken** to set the table

definitiv definitive(ly)

dein your (*inform. sg.*) (3)

die Delikatesse (-n) delicacy

die Demokratie (-n) democracy

demokratisch democratic(ally)

die Demonstration (-en) demonstration, rally (14)

demonstrieren to demonstrate

denken, dachte, gedacht to think; **denken an** (+ *acc.*) to think about/of (12)

der Denker (-) / die Denkerin (-nen) thinker

das Denkmal (ˇer) monument

denn (*coord. conj.*) for, because (7); then; (*particle used in questions to express interest*); **Was ist denn los?** What's the matter? (2)

die Deponie (-n) garbage dump

deprimiert depressed (8)

der, die, das the; that one; who, which

derselbe the same

deshalb therefore, for that reason (8)

der Designer (-) / die Designerin (-nen) designer

das Dessin (-s) design, pattern

desto: je ... desto ... the . . . the . . .

deswegen because of that (12)

das Detail (-s) detail

detailliert detailed

der Detektivroman (-e) detective novel

deutsch (*adj.*) German

(das) Deutsch German (language) (1); **auf Deutsch** in German (E)

der/die Deutsche (*decl. adj.*) German (person)

die Deutsche Demokratische Republik (DDR) German Democratic Republic (GDR)

die Deutsche Mark (DM) (-) German mark

(das) Deutschland Germany (E); **die Bundesrepublik Deutschland (BRD)** Federal Republic of Germany (FRG)

deutschsprachig German-speaking

(der) Dezember December (3)

d.h. = das heißt that is, i.e. (8)

der Dialekt (-e) dialect

die Dialektik dialectics

der Dialog (-e) dialogue

dich you (*inform. sg. acc.*) (3); **grüß dich** hello, hi (*among friends and family*) (E)

der Dichter (-) / die Dichterin (-nen) poet

dichtmachen (macht dicht) (*coll.*) to close, shut (down)

dick fat; **dick machen** to be fattening

die the

der Dieb (-e) / die Diebin (-nen) thief

die Diele (-n) front hall (12)

der Dienst (-e) service; duty

(der) Dienstag Tuesday (3)

dienstags Tuesdays, on Tuesday(s) (4)

dieselbe the same

der Dieselmotor (-en) diesel engine

dieser, diese, dies(es) this (2)

diesmal this time

digital digital(ly)

die Digitalkamera (-s) digital camera (13)

die Diktatur (-en) dictatorship

das Dilemma (-s) dilemma

der Dilettant (-en *masc.*) (-en) / die Dilettantin (-nen) dilettante

dilettantisch amateurish(ly)

der Dill dill (*herb*)

das Ding (-e) thing, object

die Dinkelflocke (-n) spelt flake

der Diplomat (-en *masc.*) (-en) / die Diplomatin (-nen) diplomat

dir (to/for) you (*inform. sg. dat.*) (5); **Was fehlt dir?** What's the matter? (8); **Wie geht's dir?** How are you? (*inform.*) (E)

direkt direct(ly); (*coll.*) really

der Dirigent (-en *masc.*) (-en) / die Dirigentin (-nen) (orchestra) conductor

die Disco (-s) disco, dance club (4); **in die Disco gehen** to go clubbing (4)

die Diskussion (-en) discussion

diskutieren über (+ *acc.*) to discuss (1); to debate

die D-Mark = die Deutsche Mark

doch still, nevertheless; (*intensifying particle used with imperatives*) (4)

das Dokument (-e) document (13)

der Dokumentarfilm (-e) documentary film (13)

der Dollar (-[s]) dollar

der Dolmetscher (-) / die Dolmetscherin (-nen) interpreter (11)

die Dolomiten (*pl.*) the Dolomites

der Dom (-e) cathedral

die Donau Danube (*river*)

das Donauweibchen (-) Danube mermaid

donnern to thunder (7); **Es donnert.** It's thundering. (7)

(der) Donnerstag Thursday (3)

donnerstags Thursdays, on Thursday(s) (4)

das Donnerwetter: (zum) Donnerwetter! (*exclamation of anger or annoyance*)

das Doppelzimmer (-) double room, room with two beds (9)

das Dorf (ˇer) village

dort there

die Dose (-n) (tin or aluminum) can; jar (14); box

downloaden (downloadet), downgeloadet to download

das Drachenfliegen kite flying

die Draisine (-n) dandy-horse (*predecessor of the bicycle*)

das Drama (Dramen) drama

dran = daran; dran sein to have (one's) turn

drastisch drastic(ally)

draußen outside (7)

die Dreharbeiten (*pl.*) shooting of a film

(sich) drehen to turn, spin

drei three (E)

dreihundert three hundred (E)

dreimal three times (7)

der Dreimonatszeitraum (ˇe) three-month period

dreisprachig trilingual

dreißig thirty (E)

dreißigjährig: der Dreißigjährige Krieg the Thirty Years' War

dreitausend three thousand (E)

dreizehn thirteen (E)

dreizehnte thirteenth (3)

Dresdner (*adj.*) of/from Dresden (*city in eastern Germany*)

drin = darin (*coll.*) inside

dringend urgent(ly) (2)

drinnen inside (7)

dritt: zu dritt as a threesome (10)

dritte third (3)

ein Drittel a third

die Droge (-n) drug; medicine (14)

die Drogensucht drug addiction (14)

die Drogerie (-n) drugstore (*toiletries and sundries*) (5)

drüben, da drüben over there (6); on the other side

drucken to print (13)

das Drücken pressure

der Drucker (-) printer (13)

drum = darum (*coll.*) therefore

du you (*inform. sg.*) (1)

dudeln to toot

der Duft (ˇe) aroma, fragrance

dumm dumb, stupid

die Dummheit (-en) stupidity

dunkel dark (2)

dunkeln to grow dark

dünn thin; slender, skinny

durch (+ *acc.*) through (3); by, by means of

durcharbeiten (arbeitet durch) to work through

durchaus absolutely

das Durcheinander confusion; commotion

durchgehend continuous(ly)

durchlesen (liest durch), las durch, durchgelesen to read through

durchs = durch das

der Durchschnitt (-e) average; **im Durchschnitt** on average

durchschnittlich on average (12)

durchstreichen (streicht durch), strich durch, durchgestrichen to cross out, strike through

dürfen (darf), durfte, gedurft to be permitted to; may (4), **Hier darf man nicht parken.** You may not park here. (4); **Was darf's sein?** What will you have?

der Durst thirst; **Durst haben** to be thirsty (2)

die Dusche (-n) shower, shower bath (9)

(sich) duschen to take a shower (8)

duzen to address with **du** (*informally*)

die DVD (-s) DVD

der DVD-Spieler (-) DVD player (2)

dynamisch dynamic(ally)

E

eben just; simply

echt genuine(ly); (*coll.*) really (1)

die Ecke (-n) corner (9); **an der Ecke** at the corner (9)

egal: Das ist mir egal. I don't care. (5)

eher rather, sooner

die Ehre (-n) honor; **zu Ehren** (+ *gen.*) in honor of

ehren to honor

ehrlich honest

das Ei (-er) egg (5)

die Eiche (-n) oak tree

die Eierbox (-en) egg carton

der Eierlikör egg liqueur

eigen (*adj.*) own (12)

die Eigenregie one's own control

die Eigenschaft (-en) characteristic (11); trait

eigentlich actual(ly), real(ly)

die Eigentumswohnung (-en) condominium

eilen to hurry

ein, eine a(n); one; **Es ist eins. / Es ist ein Uhr.** It's one o'clock. (4); **was für ein …** what kind of a . . . (11)

einander one another, each other

einbegriffen included

einbiegen (biegt ein), bog ein, ist eingebogen to turn, make a turn (9)

einbringen (bringt ein), brachte ein, eingebracht to bring in, yield

einer, eine, eines one (of several)

einfach simple, simply; one-way (*ticket*) (10)

einfallen (fällt ein), fiel ein, ist eingefallen: etwas fällt mir ein something occurs to me

der Einfluss (¨e) influence

einführen (führt ein) to introduce (14)

die Einführung (-en) introduction

der Eingang (¨e) entrance, entryway (12)

eingedeutscht Germanized

eingeschränkt limited

die Einheit (-en) unity; unit

einholen (holt ein) to catch up with

einhundert one hundred (E)

einig united; in agreement

einige (*pl.*) several, some

einiges several things

der Einkauf (¨e) purchase

einkaufen (kauft ein) to shop (4); **einkaufen gehen** to go shopping (4)

das Einkaufszentrum (Einkaufszentren) shopping center

der Einkaufszettel (-) shopping list

das Einkommen income (11)

einladen (lädt ein), lud ein, eingeladen to invite (4)

die Einladung (-en) invitation

sich einlassen auf (+ *acc.*) **(lässt ein), ließ ein, eingelassen** to get involved with

einleiten (leitet ein) to introduce

einmal once (7); **einmal die Woche** once a week (7); **einmal im Monat / Jahr** once a month/year (7)

der Einmal-Fotoapparat (-e) disposable camera

einmalig unique

der Einmalrasierer (-) disposable razor

die Einnahmen (*pl.*) income (12)

einnehmen (nimmt ein), nahm ein, eingenommen to take (*medicine*)

einordnen (ordnet ein) to put in order; to classify, categorize

die Einreise (-n) entry (*into a country*)

einrichten (richtet ein) to furnish, equip (12)

die Einrichtung (-en) furnishings

eins (*numeral*) one (E); **Es ist eins.** It's one (o'clock). (4)

einschlafen (schläft ein), schlief ein, ist eingeschlafen to fall asleep (4)

einsenden, sandte ein, eingesandt to send in

einsetzen (setzt ein) to insert

einsparen (spart ein) to save, conserve

einsteigen (steigt ein), stieg ein, ist eingestiegen to board, get into (*a vehicle*) (10)

eintausend one thousand (E)

der Eintritt (-e) entrance; admission

einverstanden sein (mit + *dat.*) to agree (with), be in agreement (with)

der Einwanderer (-) / die Einwanderin (-nen) immigrant

die Einwanderung (-en) immigration

die Einwegflasche (-n) nonreturnable bottle

der Einwohner (-) / die Einwohnerin (-nen) resident, inhabitant

das Einwohnermeldeamt (¨er) *government office for registration of residents*

die Einzelheit (-en) detail, particular

einzeln individual; scattered

der Einzelunterricht (-e) one-on-one teaching

das Einzelzimmer (-) single room, room with one bed (9)

einziehen in (+ *acc.*) **(zieht ein), zog ein, ist eingezogen** to move in(to) (12)

das Eis ice cream; ice (5)

der Eisbecher (-) dish of ice cream (6)

die Eiscreme ice cream

eisern (made of) iron

der Eiskaffee (-s) iced coffee (mixed with ice cream and topped with whipped cream)

das Eisstadion (Eisstadien) ice-skating rink (7)

die Elbe Elbe (River)

die Elblandschaft (-en) landscape of the Elbe River region

das Elbsandsteingebiet *sandstone region along the Elbe River*

das Elbufer (-) bank of the Elbe

der Elefant (-en *masc.*) **(-en)** elephant

elegant elegant(ly)

die Elektrizität electricity

das Elektrogerät (-e) electrical appliance

der Elektroinstallateur (-e) / die Elektroinstallateurin (-nen) electrician

die Elektronik electronics

der Elektroniker (-) / die Elektronikerin (-nen) electronics engineer

das Element (-e) element

elf eleven (E)

elfmal eleven times

elfte eleventh (3)

eliminieren to eliminate

der Ell(en)bogen (-) elbow (8)

(das) Elsass Alsace

die Eltern (*pl.*) parents (3)

die E-Mail (-s) e-mail (13)

die Emission (-en) emission

der Emmentaler Käse Emmental cheese

der Empfang (¨e) reception

empfangen (empfängt), empfing, empfangen to receive (13)

der Empfänger (-) / die Empfängerin (-nen) recipient

empfänglich receptive, susceptible

empfehlen (empfiehlt), empfahl, empfohlen to recommend (5)

die Empfehlung (-en) recommendation

Emser (*adj.*) of/from Bad Ems (*town in western Germany*)

das Ende (-n) end; **am Ende** at the end, in the end; **Ende April** at the end of April; **zu Ende** to completion

enden to end

endlich finally, at last

die Endung (-en) ending

die Energie (-n) energy

energiesparend energy-saving

eng narrow, tight

sich engagieren (für + *acc.*) to get involved (with), become committed (to) (14)

engagiert committed

(das) England England

englisch (*adj.*) English

(das) Englisch English (language); **auf Englisch** in English

englischsprechend English-speaking

der Enkel (-) grandson (3)

die Enkelin (-nen) granddaughter (3)

das Enkelkind (-er) grandchild

enorm enormous(ly)

das Ensemble (-s) ensemble

entdecken to discover

entfernt von (+ *dat.*) away from

enthalten (enthält), enthielt, enthalten to contain, include; **im Preis enthalten** included in the price (9)

enthusiastisch enthusiastic(ally)

entlanggehen (geht entlang), ging entlang, ist entlanggegangen to go along, walk along (9)

entnervt unnerved

(sich) entscheiden, entschied, entschieden to decide

die Entscheidung (-en) decision

sich entschließen, entschloss, entschlossen to decide (13)

entschuldigen to excuse (6); **Entschuldigen Sie!** Excuse me! (6)

die Entschuldigung (-en) apology, excuse; **Entschuldigung.** Excuse me. (9)

der Entsorger (-) / die Entsorgerin (-nen) (toxic) waste disposal worker

die Entsorgungsplanung waste disposal planning

sich entspannen to relax, take a rest (8)

entsprechend corresponding

entweder ... oder either . . . or (8)

entwerfen (entwirft), entwarf, entworfen to design, draw up (11)

entwickeln to develop (14)

die Entwicklung (-en) development (11)

das Entwicklungsland (¨er) developing country

entzündlich flammable

er he; it (1)

die Erdbeere (-n) strawberry (5)

die Erde Earth

das Erdgeschoss (-e) ground floor (9)

die Erdkunde geography

die Erdwärme geothermal energy

das Ereignis (-se) event

erfahren (erfährt), erfuhr, erfahren to find out, learn; to experience

die Erfahrung (-en) experience

erfinden, erfand, erfunden to invent (13)

der Erfinder (-) / die Erfinderin (-nen) inventor

erfinderisch inventive

die Erfindung (-en) invention (13)

der Erfolg (-e) success (11); **Erfolg haben** to be successful (11)

erfolgreich successful(ly) (11)

erforschen to research

erfragen to inquire, ask for; to ascertain

erfüllen to fulfill

ergänzen to complete; to add to

die Ergänzung (-en) completion; addition

das Ergebnis (-se) result

ergreifen, ergriff, ergriffen to seize, grasp

erhalten (erhält), erhielt, erhalten to get, receive

erhöhen to raise, increase

die Erhöhung (-en) raising, increase

sich erholen to get well, recover (8)

die Erholung rest and recuperation

erinnern an (+ acc.) to remind of; **sich erinnern an** (+ acc.) to remember

die Erinnerung (-en) memory; remembrance

sich erkälten to catch a cold (8)

die Erkältung (-en) cold (8)

erkennen, erkannte, erkannt to recognize

erklären to explain

die Erklärung (-en) explanation

sich erkundigen to seek information, inquire

erlauben to allow, permit (9)

erleben to experience (10)

das Erlebnis (-se) experience, event

erledigen to deal with, finish

erleiden, erlitt, erlitten to suffer

erlernbar learnable

die Erlösung (-en) redemption, salvation

die Ernährung food; nutrition (12)

erneuerbar renewable

ernst serious(ly) (1)

der Ernst seriousness

erobern to conquer

eröffnen to open

die Eröffnung (-en) opening

erraten (errät), erriet, erraten to guess

erreichbar reachable

erreichen to reach

errichten to build, put up

erscheinen, erschien, ist erschienen to appear

erst only, not until

erste first (3); **ab erstem Juni** as of June 1st (12); **am ersten Mai** on May first (3); **der erste Mai** May first (3); **der erste Stock** second floor (10); **erster Klasse fahren** to travel first class (10); **zum ersten Mal** for the first time

erstellen to build; to draw up

erstmals (adv.) for the first time

erstöbern to browse

das Erstsemester (-) first-semester student; freshman

ertönen, ist ertönt to sound, ring out

das Erwachen awakening

erwachsen (adj.) grown-up

erwähnen to mention

die Erwähnung (-en) mention

die Erwärmung warming, increase in temperature

erwarten to expect; to wait for

die Erwartung (-en) expectation

der Erwerb acquisition, purchase

erwerben (erwirbt), erwarb, erworben to acquire, buy

erwünscht desired; desirable

erzählen to tell, narrate

der Erzähler (-) / die Erzählerin (-nen) narrator

die Erzählung (-en) story; narration

der Erzbischof (¨e) archbishop

erzeugen to produce, generate

es it (1, 3); **es gibt ...** (+ acc.) there is/are . . . (3); **Es ist eins. / Es ist ein Uhr.** It's one o'clock. (4); **Es regnet.** It's raining. (7) **Es tut mir leid.** I'm sorry; **Wie geht es dir? / Wie geht's dir?** How are you? (inform.) (E); **Wie geht es Ihnen?** How are you? (form.) (E); **Wie wäre es mit ... ?** How about . . . ? (13)

der Espresso (-s) espresso (coffee)

essen (isst), aß, gegessen to eat (1)

das Essen (-) food; meal; eating (1); **zum Essen** for dinner

die Essgewohnheit (-en) eating habit

der Essig vinegar

der Esstisch (-e) dining room table

das Esszimmer (-) dining room (2)

(das) Estland Estonia

etablieren to establish

die Etage (-n) floor, story (12)

das Etikett (-en) label

etwa approximately, about

etwas something; (adv.) somewhat, a little (2); **etwas anderes** something different; **etwas Neues** something new; **Hast du etwas Geld?** Do you have some money?

euch you (inform. pl. acc.) (3); (to/for) you (inform. pl. dat.) (5)

euer, eure your (inform. pl.) (3)

der Euro (-[s]) euro (monetary unit) (2)

(das) Europa Europe

europäisch (adj.) European; **die Europäische Union (EU)** European Union

der Euroscheck (-s) type of personal check used in Europe

eventuell possible; possibly, perhaps

ewig eternal(ly); constant(ly)

das Examen (-) examination

existieren to exist

exotisch exotic(ally)

experimentieren to experiment

der Experte (-n masc.) (-n) / die Expertin (-nen) expert

explodieren to explode

exportieren to export

extra extra

exzellent excellent(ly)

exzentrisch eccentric(ally) (1)

F

die Fabrik (-en) factory

die Facette (-n) facet

das Fach (¨er) subject, field of study

der Facharzt (¨e) / die Fachärztin (-nen) specialist (physician)

das Fachgeschäft (-e) specialty store

die Fachhochschule (-n) technical college

die Fachschule (-n) technical school

die Fähigkeit (-en) ability, skill

fahren (fährt), fuhr, ist gefahren to drive, ride; **erster/zweiter Klasse fahren** to travel first/second class (10); **Fahrrad/Rad fahren** to ride a bicycle (1, 7); **Ski fahren** to ski

der Fahrer (-) / die Fahrerin (-nen) driver

die Fahrkarte (-n) ticket (for train or bus) (10)

der Fahrkartenschalter (-) ticket window (10)

der Fahrplan (¨e) (train or bus) schedule (10)

das Fahrrad (¨er) bicycle (1); **Fahrrad fahren** to ride a bicycle (1)

der Fahrradverleih (-e) bicycle rental company

der Fahrstuhl (¨e) elevator

die Fahrt (-en) trip; ride

fair fair(ly)

der Fall (¨e) case; fall; **auf jeden Fall** in any case (13)

fallen (fällt), fiel, ist gefallen to fall (7)

falls (subord. conj.) if; in case

falsch false(ly), wrong(ly), incorrect(ly)

die Familie (-n) family (3)

das Familienfest (-e) family celebration (3)

das Familienmitglied (-er) family member

die Familienplanung family planning

der Familienstand marital status

der Fan (-s) fan, enthusiast

fangen (fängt), fing, gefangen to catch

die Fantasie (-n) fantasy

fantasievoll imaginative(ly)

fantastisch fantastic(ally) (1)

die Farbe (-n) color (5)

die Farm (-en) farm

(der) Fasching Mardi Gras (*southern Germany and Austria*) (3)

das Fass ("er) barrel, vat; **vom Fass** on tap, draft (6)

fast almost (8)

das Fast Food fast food

faszinierend fascinating

faul lazy, lazily (1)

faulenzen to be lazy, lie around (7)

das Fax (-e) fax

das Faxgerät (-e) fax machine (13)

(der) Februar February (3)

fehlen to be missing; to lack; to need; **Was fehlt Ihnen/dir?** What's the matter? (8)

fehlend missing

der Fehler (-) mistake, error

der Feierabend (-e) end of the workday; **am Feierabend** after work

feiern to celebrate (3)

der Feiertag (-e) holiday

fein fine, delicate; all right; **fein säuberlich** nice(ly) and neat(ly)

der Feldherr (-n *masc.*) **(-en)** military commander

der Felsen (-) rock, cliff

das Felsengebilde (-) rock shape

das Felsenriff (-e) rocky reef

die Felsmalerei (-en) rock painting

der Fenchel-Anis-Kümmel Tee fennel-anise-caraway tea

das Fenster (-) window (2)

die Fensterbank ("e) windowsill

die Ferien (*pl.*) vacation

fern far

fernsehen (sieht fern), sah fern, ferngesehen to watch television (4)

das Fernsehen television; watching television (4); **im Fernsehen** on television

der Fernseher (-) TV set (2)

das Fernsehprogramm (-e) TV program, TV schedule

der Ferrari Ferrari (automobile)

fertig finished, done; ready

das Fest (-e) festival; party, feast

sich festlegen (legt fest) to commit oneself

das Festspiel (-e) festival production

feststellen (stellt fest) to establish

festverzinslich fixed-interest

die Fete (-n) (*coll.*) party

fett fat; greasy; in boldface

das Feuer (-) fire

die Feuerwehr (-en) fire department

das Feuerwerk (-e) fireworks

die FH = Fachhochschule

das Fieber fever (8)

fiktiv fictitious

das Filet (-s) filet

der Film (-e) film, movie (4)

der Filter (-) filter

der Finanzbeamte (*decl. adj.*) / **die Finanzbeamtin (-nen)** tax official

die Finanzdienstleistung financial service

die Finanzen (*pl.*) finance(s)

finanziell financial(ly)

finanzieren to finance

finden, fand, gefunden to find; to think (1); **Ich finde ...** I think . . . ; **Wie findest du ... ?** How do you like . . . ? What do you think of . . . ? (1)

der Finderlohn ("-e) finder's reward

findig resourceful

der Finger (-) finger (8)

(das) Finnland Finland

die Firma (Firmen) firm, company (11)

der Fisch (-e) fish

fischen to fish (for)

der Fischer (-) / **die Fischerin (-nen)** fisherman/fisherwoman

fit fit, in shape (8); **sich fit halten (hält), hielt, gehalten** to keep fit, stay in shape (8)

die Fitness fitness (8)

der Fitnessberater (-) / **die Fitnessberaterin (-nen)** fitness consultant, personal trainer

das Fitnesscenter (-) fitness center; gym (4)

die Flamme (-n) flame

die Flasche (-n) bottle (14)

die Flaschenpost message in a bottle

das Fleisch meat (5)

fleißig industrious(ly), diligent(ly), hardworking (1)

flexibel flexible, flexibly

die Flexibilität flexibility

fliegen, flog, ist geflogen to fly (7)

fliehen, floh, ist geflohen to flee

fließen, floss, ist geflossen to flow

fließend fluent(ly)

der Flohmarkt ("-e) flea market

die Flöte (-n) flute

flüchten, ist geflüchtet to flee

der Flug ("-e) flight

der Flugbegleiter (-) / **die Flugbegleiterin (-nen)** flight attendant

der Flügel (-) wing

der Flughafen (") airport

das Flüglein (-) little wing

das Flugzeug (-e) airplane (10)

der Flur (-e) hallway (12); **für den ganzen Flur** for the whole floor

der Fluss ("-e) river (7)

flüstern to whisper

der Föhn (-e) hair dryer (9)

folgen (+ *dat.*), **ist gefolgt** to follow; **folgend** following

fordern to demand

fördern to promote (14)

die Form (-en) form, shape

das Format (-e) format

das Formular (-e) form (*paper to be filled out*)

formulieren to formulate

forschen to do research (13)

der Forscher (-) / **die Forscherin (-nen)** researcher

die Forschung (-en) research (14)

das Forsthaus ("er) forester's house

sich fortbilden (bildet fort) to continue one's education

der Fortschritt (-e) progress (14); **Fortschritte machen** to make progress (14)

das Foto (-s) photograph (2)

der Fotoapparat (-e) camera

der Fotograf (-en *masc.*) **(-en)** / **die Fotografin (-nen)** photographer

die Fotografie photography

fotografieren to photograph

das Fotografieren taking photographs

das Foyer (-s) foyer

die Frage (-n) question; **eine Frage stellen** to ask a question; **Ich habe eine Frage.** I have a question. (E)

der Fragebogen (-) questionnaire

fragen to ask (2); **fragen nach** (+ *dat.*) to ask about; **nach dem Weg fragen** to ask for directions (9)

fragend questioning(ly)

der (Schweizer) Franken (-) (Swiss) franc

Frankfurter (*adj.*) of/from Frankfurt

(das) Frankreich France (E)

der Franzose (-n *masc.*) **(-n)** / **die Französin (-nen)** French person

französisch (*adj.*) French

(das) Französisch French (language)

(die) Frau (-en) Mrs., Ms.; woman (E); wife (3)

frei free(ly) (2); vacant, available, unoccupied; **Ist hier noch frei?** Is this seat available? (6)

das Freibad ("er) outdoor swimming pool (7)

Freien: im Freien outdoors (11)

die Freiheit (-en) freedom

der Freiheitskämpfer (-) / **die Freiheitskämpferin (-nen)** freedom fighter

freilich admittedly; of course

(der) Freitag Friday (3)

freitags Fridays, on Friday(s) (4)

die Freizeit free time (7)

die Freizeitbeschäftigung (-en) leisure activity

fremd strange; unknown; foreign

der/die Fremde (*decl. adj.*) stranger

der Fremdenführer (-) / **die Fremdenführerin (-nen)** tour guide

die Fremdsprache (-n) foreign language

freuen to please; **sich freuen auf** (+ *acc.*) to look forward to (12); **sich freuen über** (+ *acc.*) to be glad about (12); **Freut mich.** Pleased to meet you. (E)

der Freund (-e) / **die Freundin (-nen)** friend (1); boyfriend/girlfriend

freundlich friendly (1)

der Friede (-n *masc.*) (*also* **der Frieden**) peace

die Friedensbewegung (-en) peace movement

frieren, fror, gefroren to freeze

das Frisbee (-s) Frisbee

frisch fresh(ly) (5)

der Friseur (-e) / die Friseurin (-nen) hairdresser, barber

der Friseursalon (-s) beauty salon; barber shop

frittieren to deep-fry

froh glad, happy

fröhlich cheerful(ly)

der Frosch (¨e) frog

die Frucht (¨e) fruit

früh early (4); **morgen früh** tomorrow morning (4)

früher earlier; once; used to (*do, be, etc.*) (7)

das Frühjahr (-e) spring (*season*) (7)

der Frühling (-e) spring (*season*) (7)

frühmorgens early in the morning

das Frühstück (-e) breakfast (5); **zum Frühstück** for breakfast

frühstücken to eat breakfast (4)

der Frühstücker (-) / die Frühstückerin (-nen) breakfast eater

die Frühstücksnische (-n) breakfast nook (12)

der Frühstücksraum (¨e) breakfast room (9)

(sich) fühlen to feel (8); **sich wohl fühlen** to feel well (8)

führen to lead, guide, conduct; to carry (*merchandise*); **ein Gespräch führen** to have a conversation; **Protokoll führen** to make a transcript, keep the minutes

der Führerschein (-e) driver's license

die Führung (-en) management; guide, lead; tour

füllen to fill; to fill in

fünf five (E)

fünfte fifth (3)

fünfzehn fifteen (E)

das Fünfzeilenformat (-e) five-line format

fünfzig fifty (E)

funkeln to sparkle

funktionieren to work, function (9)

für (+ *acc.*) for (3); **was für (ein)** what kind of (a) (11)

furchtbar terrible, terribly

fürchterlich horrible, horribly

fürs = für das

der Fürst (-en *masc.*) **(-en) / die Fürstin (-nen)** prince/princess

der Fuß (¨e) foot (8); **auf großem Fuß leben** to live in style; **zu Fuß gehen, ging, ist gegangen** to walk, go on foot (8)

der Fußball (¨e) soccer; soccer ball (7); **Fußball spielen** to play soccer (7)

der Fußballplatz (¨e) soccer field

der Fußballtrainer (-) / die Fußballtrainerin (-nen) soccer coach

die Fußballweltmeisterschaft (-en) world soccer championship, World Cup

der Fußgänger (-) / die Fußgängerin (-nen) pedestrian

die Fußgängerzone (-n) pedestrian zone (9)

G

die Gabel (-n) fork (6)

der Gang (¨e) course (*of a meal*)

ganz complete(ly), total(ly), entire(ly) (12); quite, very, really (1); **ganz toll** really great

gar even; **gar kein(e)** not any; **gar nicht** not at all; **gar nichts** nothing at all

die Garage (-n) garage (2)

die Garantie (-n) guarantee

garantieren to guarantee

die Garderobe (-n) wardrobe; closet (12)

die Gardine (-n) curtain, drapes

der Garten (¨) garden; yard (2)

der Gärtner (-) / die Gärtnerin (-nen) gardener

der Gast (¨e) guest

das Gästehaus (¨er) guesthouse

die Gasteltern (*pl.*) host parents

das Gästezimmer (-) guest room (12)

die Gastfamilie (-n) host family

gastfreundlich hospitable

die Gastfreundschaft hospitality

der Gastgeber (-) / die Gastgeberin (-nen) host/hostess

das Gasthaus (¨er) restaurant; inn

der Gasthof (¨e) hotel; restaurant; inn

die Gastronomie gastronomy

die Gaststätte (-n) full-service restaurant (6)

das Gebäude (-) building

geben (gibt), gab, gegeben to give (3); to put; **es gibt** there is/are (3); **eine Party geben** to have a party, throw a party; **Rat geben** to advise

geboren born; **geboren werden** to be born; **ich bin geboren** I was born (1)

der Gebrauch use

gebrauchen to use

gebraucht used

die Gebühr (-en) fee

gebührend proper(ly), fitting(ly)

die Gebühreneinzugszentrale (-n) fee collection office

der Geburtsort (-e) birthplace (1)

der Geburtstag (-e) birthday, date of birth (1); **Herzlichen Glückwunsch zum Geburtstag!** Happy birthday! (3); **Wann hast du Geburtstag?** When is your birthday? (3)

die Geburtstagsfeier (-n) birthday celebration

der Gedanke (-n *masc.*) **(-n)** thought; **sich über etwas** (*acc.*) **Gedanken machen** to think about something, to ponder something

das Gedicht (-e) poem

geeignet suitable, appropriate

die Gefahr (-en) danger (14)

gefährden to endanger

gefährlich dangerous(ly) (10)

gefallen (+ *dat.*) **(gefällt), gefiel, gefallen** to be pleasing (5); **Wie gefällt Ihnen … ?** How do you like … ? (5)

der Gefallen (-) favor; **einen Gefallen tun** to do a favor

das Gefängnis (-se) prison, jail

das Geflügel poultry

gefroren frozen (5)

das Gefühl (-e) feeling; emotion

gegen (+ *acc.*) against; around, about (+ *time*) (3, 6); **(so) gegen fünf Uhr** around five o'clock (6)

die Gegend (-en) area, region

die Gegendarstellung (-en) opposing view

der Gegensatz (¨e) contrast

gegenseitig mutual(ly); reciprocal(ly)

der Gegenstand (¨e) object

das Gegenteil (-e) opposite

gegenüber von (+ *dat.*) across from (9)

die Gegenwart present (time)

das Gehalt (¨er) salary (11)

gehen, ging, ist gegangen to go (1); **einkaufen gehen** to go shopping (4); **Geht's gut?** Are you doing well? (E); **Na, wie geht's?** How are you? (*casual*) (E); **spazieren gehen** to go for a walk (4); **Wie geht es Ihnen?** How are you? (*form.*) (E); **Wie geht's (dir)?** How are you? (*inform.*) (E); **zu Fuß gehen** to walk, go on foot (8)

gehoben upper; elevated

gehören (+ *dat.*) to belong to (*a person*) (5); **gehören zu** (+ *dat.*) to be a part of

die Geige (-n) violin

geistig mental, intellectual

gelangen in (+ *acc.*)**, ist gelangt** to come into, get into

gelb yellow (5)

das Geld money (2)

die Geldanlage (-n) investment

gelegen situated, located; **zentral gelegen** centrally located (2)

die Gelegenheit (-en) opportunity (11); occasion

gelegentlich occasional(ly)

gelten (+ *dat.*) **(gilt), galt, gegolten** to be valid; **gelten als** to be considered as

gemein common; **gemein haben** to have in common

die Gemeinde (-n) community

gemeinsam common; in common; together

die Gemeinschaft (-en) community; group

gemischt mixed

das Gemüse vegetable(s) (5)

der Gemüsestand (¨e) vegetable stand

gemütlich cozy, cozily (4); comfortable, comfortably; leisurely

die Gemütlichkeit comfort; informality

genau exact(ly) (2); meticulous(ly)

genauso just/exactly as (7); **genauso … wie** just/exactly as . . . as

die Generation (-en) generation

genießen, genoss, genossen to enjoy, savor, relish

der Genießer (-) / die Genießerin (-nen) connoisseur

der Genitiv (-e) genitive case

genug enough, sufficient(ly)

genügend enough, sufficient(ly)

geöffnet open (6)

die Geografie geography

geografisch geographical(ly)

der Geoökologe (-n *masc.***) (-n) / die Geoökologin (-nen)** geo-ecologist

die Geoökologie geo-ecology

das Gepäck luggage (9)

die Gepäckaufbewahrung baggage check (10)

gerade just, exactly (2); straight

geradeaus straight ahead (9); **immer geradeaus** (keep on going) straight ahead (9)

das Gerät (-e) appliance, device (12)

geräuchert smoked

das Gericht (-e) dish (*of prepared food*) (6); (*judicial*) court

germanisch Germanic, Teutonic

die Germanistik German studies

gern(e) (lieber, liebst-) gladly (1); **gern** (*+ verb*) to like (*doing something*) (1); **gern haben** to like (*a person or thing*) (2); **ich hätte gern** I would like to have

das Gesamtbild (-er) overall view, big picture

die Gesamtschule (-n) German secondary school

die Gesangsstunde (-n) singing lesson

der Gesangsverein (-e) choral society

das Geschäft (-e) store, shop; business

die Geschäftsfrau (-en) businesswoman (11)

die Geschäftsleute (*pl.***)** businesspeople

der Geschäftsmann (Geschäftsleute) businessman (11)

geschehen (geschieht), geschah, ist geschehen to happen

das Geschehen (-) event

gescheit intelligent, bright; sensible, decent (13); **nichts Gescheites** nothing decent (13)

das Geschenk (-e) present, gift (3)

die Geschichte (-n) story; history

das Geschirr dishes

der Geschirrspüler (-) dishwasher

geschlossen closed (6)

das Geschmeide (-) jewelry

die Geschwindigkeitsbegrenzung (-en) speed limit

die Geschwister (*pl.***)** brothers and sisters, siblings (3)

die Gesellschaft (-en) society

das Gesetz (-e) law

gesetzlich legal(ly)

das Gesicht (-er) face (8)

das Gespräch (-e) conversation

die Gestalt (-en) figure

gestern yesterday (7); **gestern Abend** yesterday evening; **gestern Vormittag** yesterday morning

gestreift striped (5)

gestresst (*adj.***)** under stress

gesund healthy, healthful; well (8)

die Gesundheit health (8)

gesundheitsbewusst health-conscious(ly)

gesundheitsschädlich unhealthy, unhealthily

das Gesundheitswesen health-care system

das Getränk (-e) beverage, drink (5)

die Getränkedose (-n) beverage can (14)

der Getränkeladen (¨) beverage store (5)

das Getreide (-) cereal, grain

getrennt separate(ly) (6)

die Gewalt violence, force; power, dominion

die Gewaltbereitschaft readiness for violence

gewaltig mighty, mightily

die Gewalttätigkeit (-en) (act of) violence (14)

das Gewicht (-e) weight

gewinnen, gewann, gewonnen to win

das Gewinnsparen profit saving

gewiss certain(ly)

das Gewitter (-) thunderstorm (7)

die Gewohnheit (-en) habit

der Gewohnheitsmensch (-en *masc.***) (-en)** creature of habit

gewöhnlich usual(ly) (4)

die Gewürzgurke (-n) pickle, pickled gherkin

die GEZ = Gebühreneinzugszentrale

das Gift (-e) poison

giftfrei nontoxic

der Giftstoff (-e) toxic substance

der Gipfel (-) peak, summit

das Girokonto (Girokonten) checking account

die Gitarre (-n) guitar

der Gitarrist (-en *masc.***) (-en) / die Gitarristin (-nen)** guitarist

das Gitter (-) bars; **hinter Gitter(n)** (*coll.*) behind bars

glänzend shiny; excellent(ly)

das Glas (¨er) glass

der Glasmacher (-) / die Glasmacherin (-nen) glassmaker

glauben to believe (5); **Ich glaube dir nicht.** I don't believe you.

gleich right away, immediately (8); same; **gleich da drüben** right over there

gleichzeitig simultaneous(ly)

das Gleis (-e) track (10); platform

global global(ly) (14)

die Globalisierung globalization

der Globus (Globen) globe

das Glöckchen (-) little bell

das Glockenspiel (-e) chimes, glockenspiel

das Glück fortune, luck; happiness; **Viel Glück!** Good luck! (1)

glücklich happy, happily

der Glückwunsch (¨e) congratulations; **Herzlichen Glückwunsch zum Geburtstag!** Happy birthday! (3)

GmbH = Gesellschaft mit beschränkter Haftung corporation

das Gold gold

golden golden

der Goldfisch (-e) goldfish

der Goldgräber (-) gold digger

die Goldmedaille (-n) gold medal

(das) Golf golf

googeln to Google, use the Google search engine

der Gorilla (-s) gorilla

der Gott (¨er) God; god; **Gott sei Dank** thank God; **grüß Gott** hello (*in southern Germany and Austria*)

der Gourmet (-s) gourmet

graben (gräbt), grub, gegraben to dig

der Grad (-e) degree (7); **35 Grad** 35 degrees (7)

der Graf (-en *masc.***) (-en) / die Gräfin (-nen)** count/countess

die Grafik (-en) drawing

das Gramm (-e) gram

die Grammatik (-en) grammar; grammar book

das Gras (¨er) grass

gratulieren (*+ dat.***)** to congratulate (3); **Ich gratuliere!** Congratulations!

grau gray (5)

graugetigert with gray stripes

grausam cruel(ly)

die Grenze (-n) border, boundary

grenzen an (*+ acc.***)** to border on

(das) Griechenland Greece

griechisch (*adj.***)** Greek

der Grill (-s) grill, barbecue (6)

grillen to grill, barbecue

der Grillteller (-) grill platter

grimmsch of/by the Brothers Grimm

die Grippe flu (8)

groß big, large (2); tall (1); great

(das) Großbritannien Great Britain

die Größe (-n) size (5); height

die Großeltern (*pl.***)** grandparents (3)

die Großmutter (¨) grandmother (3)

der Großraumwagen (-) rail car without compartments

größtenteils for the most part

der Großvater (¨) grandfather (3)

das Großväterchen (-) (*coll.*) little old man

großzügig generous(ly)

grün green (5)

der Grund (¨e) reason; ground; **im Grunde genommen** basically (14)

gründen to found, establish

die Grundform (-en) basic form

die Grundgangart (-en) basic pace

das Grundgesetz (-e) basic law, constitution

der Grundlsee *lake in Austria*

der Grundpreis (-e) base price

der Grundriss (-e) outline; layout; blueprint

die Grundschule (-n) primary school (11)

die Gründung (-en) founding, establishment

das Grüne (*decl. adj.***)** green, greenery; **im Grünen** in the country; **ins Grüne fahren** to drive out to the country

die Gruppe (-n) group

der Gruß (¨e) greeting (12); **herzliche Grüße** kind regards; **viele Grüße** best wishes (12)

(sich) grüßen to say hello (to one another); **grüß dich** hello, hi (*among friends and family*) (E); **grüß Gott** hello (*in southern Germany and Austria*)

die Grütze: rote Grütze *dessert made of red berries*

(das) Guatemala Guatemala

gucken (*coll.*) to look

das Gulasch (-e) goulash

gültig valid

günstig convenient(ly); favorable, favorably (9); reasonable (in price); **günstig liegen** to be conveniently located (9)

die Gurke (-n) cucumber (5)

der Gurt (-e) strap; seatbelt

der Gürtel (-) belt (5)

gut (besser, best-) good, well (1); **Alles Gute!** All the best! (3); **danke, gut** fine, thanks (E); **Er tanzt gut.** He dances well. (1); **Es geht mir gut.** I am fine; **Geht's gut?** Are you doing well? (E); **Gute Besserung!** Get well soon! (8); **gute Nacht** good night (E); **guten Abend** good evening (E); **guten Morgen** good morning (E); **guten Tag** hello, good day (E); **Mach's gut.** Take care, so long. (*inform.*) (E); **nicht besonders gut** not particularly well (E); **sehr gut** very well; fine; good (E); **zu guter Letzt** in the end, at long last

das Gymnasium (Gymnasien) secondary school (*leading to university*) (11)

die Gymnastik gymnastics

H

das Haar (-e) hair (8)

haben (hat), hatte, gehabt to have (2); **Angst haben (vor + *dat.*)** to be afraid (of) (12); **Durst haben** to be thirsty (2); **Erfolg haben** to be successful (11); **gern haben** to like (*a person or thing*) (2); **Hunger haben** to be hungry (2); **Ich habe eine Frage.** I have a question. (E) **Ich hätte gern ...** I would like to have . . . ; **Lust haben** to feel like (*doing something*) (2); **recht haben** to be correct (2); **Wann hast du Geburtstag?** When is your birthday? (3); **Zeit haben** to have time (2)

der Hackbraten (-) meatloaf

der Hafen (") harbor, port

der Hagel hail (7)

das Hähnchen (-) chicken (5)

der Haken (-) hook

halb half (4); **halb zwei** half past one, one-thirty (4)

halbfest semisoft

die Halbpension accommodation with two meals per day included

die Hälfte (-n) half

der Halfter (-) halter

das Hallenbad (¨er) indoor swimming pool (7)

hallo hello (*among friends and family*) (E)

die Halogenlampe (-n) halogen lamp

der Hals (¨e) neck; throat (8)

das Halsband (¨er) (animal) collar

die Halsschmerzen (*pl.*) sore throat (8)

halt (*particle*) just

haltbar having a long shelf life

halten (hält), hielt, gehalten to hold, keep; to stop; **sich fit halten** to keep fit, stay in shape (8); **halten für (+ *acc.*)** to hold; to consider, think (14); **halten von (+ *dat.*)** to think of; **ein Referat halten** to give a paper

die Haltestelle (-n) (bus or streetcar) stop (9)

die Haltung (-en) posture, stance; attitude

Hamburger (*adj.*) of/from Hamburg

der Hamburger (-) hamburger

Hamelner (*adj.*) of/from Hamelin

der Hamster (-) hamster

die Hand (¨e) hand (8)

der Handel sales, trade (11)

handeln to act; **sich handeln um (+ *acc.*)** to be about; **handeln von (+ *dat.*)** to deal with, be about (13); **Wovon handelt es?** What's it about? (13)

das Handgepäck carry-on luggage (10)

der Händler (-) / die Händlerin (-nen) vendor, trader

die Handlung (-en) plot, action

der Handschuh (-e) glove (10)

die Handtasche (-n) handbag

das Handtuch (¨er) towel

handwerklich as a craftsman/craftswoman

das Handy (-s) cell phone (2)

hängen, hängte, gehängt to hang (up), put up (6)

hängen, hing, gehangen to hang, be hanging (6)

die Hansestadt (¨e) Hanseatic city

hart hard; severe(ly)

der Harz Harz Mountains

das Häschen (-) bunny, little rabbit (*term of endearment*)

hassen to hate

hässlich ugly (2)

der Hauch (-e) breath; wind; whiff

hauen, haute, gehauen to beat

häufig frequent(ly), often

Haupt- main, major, central (*used in compound words*)

das Hauptfach (¨er) major subject

die Hauptfigur (-en) main character, protagonist

das Hauptgericht (-e) main dish, entrée (6)

hauptsächlich mainly, mostly

die Hauptschule (-n) junior high school

das Hauptseminar (-e) advanced seminar

die Hauptstadt (¨e) capital (city)

das Haus (¨er) house (2); **nach Haus(e) gehen** to go home (5); **zu Haus(e)** at home (5)

die Hausarbeit (-en) housework; homework

die Hausaufgabe (-n) homework

der Hausbewohner (-) / die Hausbewohnerin (-nen) tenant

die Hausfrau (-en) homemaker, housewife

die Hausfrauensauce (-n) homemade sauce

hausgemacht homemade

der Haushalt (-e) household (12); budget

die Haushaltswaren (*pl.*) household utensils

das Hausmacher-Vesper (-) homemade snack

der Hausmann (¨er) house husband, stay-at-home husband

die Hausmusik music performed at home

die Hausnummer (-n) street address (number) (E)

der Hausschuh (-e) slipper (5)

das Haustier (-e) pet

die Haustür (-en) front door

die Haut (¨e) skin

die Hautcreme (-s) skin cream

heben, hob, gehoben to lift

das Hefeweizen *unfiltered wheat beer*

das Heft (-e) notebook (12); **das Comic-Heft (-e)** comic book

heikel awkward, delicate

das Heilbad (¨er) spa

der/die Heilige (*decl. adj.*) saint

der Heilige Abend Christmas Eve (3); **am Heiligen Abend** on Christmas Eve

das Heilmittel (-) remedy

die Heimat (-en) homeland, hometown

der Heimatverein (-e) local history society

der Heimcomputer home computer

heimisch domestic, native

heimtückisch treacherous

heimwerken to work on do-it-yourself home projects

das Heinzelmännchen (-) brownie, elf

heiraten to marry, get married (3)

heiß hot (7)

heißen, hieß, geheißen to be called, be named (1); **das heißt (d.h.)** that is, i.e. (8); **Ich heiße ...** My name is . . . (E); **Wie heißen Sie?** What's your name? (*form.*) (E); **Wie heißt ... ?** What's the name of . . . ? (E); **Wie heißt du?** What's your name? (*inform.*) (E)

der Heißluftballon (-s) hot air balloon

heiter pleasant, fair, bright (7)

heizen to heat

die Heizung (-en) heating (12)

die Heizwärme warmth from a heater

das Hektar (-e) hectare (= 2.471 acres)

hektisch hectic(ally)

der Held (-en *masc.*) **(-en) / die Heldin (-nen)** hero/heroine

helfen (+ *dat.*) (hilft), half, geholfen to help (5)

hell light, bright(ly) (2)

das Hemd (-en) shirt (5)

her this way; here; **hin und her** back and forth

herausfinden (findet heraus), fand heraus, herausgefunden to find out

herausfordern (fordert heraus) to challenge (11)

die Herausforderung (-en) challenge

der Herbst (-e) autumn, fall (7)

hereinkommen (kommt herein), kam herein, ist hereingekommen to come inside

herhaben (hat her), hatte her, hergehabt (*coll.*): **Wo hast du die gute Wurst her?** Where did you get that good sausage?

herkommen (kommt her), kam her, ist hergekommen to come here; to come from

herkömmlich conventional, traditional

der Herr (-n *masc.*) **(-en)** Mr.; gentleman (E); **meine Damen und Herren** ladies and gentlemen

der Herrenartikel (-) men's accessory

die Herrenkonfektion men's ready-to-wear clothing

herrlich wonderful(ly), magnificent(ly)

Herrnhuter (*adj.*) of/from Herrnhut (*town in eastern Germany*)

herstellen (stellt her) to produce, manufacture (11)

der Hersteller (-) producer, manufacturer

herum: um ... herum around (*a place*)

herumfahren (um + *acc.***) (fährt herum), fuhr herum, ist herumgefahren** to drive around

herumgehen (um + *acc.***) (geht herum), ging herum, ist herumgegangen** to go around, walk around

herumtönen (tönt herum) to resound

herunterladen (lädt herunter), lud herunter, heruntergeladen to download

das Herz (*gen.* **-ens,** *dat.* **-en) (-en)** heart

die Herzensdame (-n) woman in one's heart

herzlich cordial(ly); **herzlich willkommen** welcome (E); **Herzlichen Glückwunsch zum Geburtstag!** Happy birthday! (3)

(das) Hessen Hesse (*a German state*)

heute today (1); **heute Abend** this evening (1); **heute Morgen** this morning (4); **heute Nachmittag** this afternoon (4); **Welches Datum ist heute?** What is today's date? (3)

heutig (*adj.*) today's

heutzutage nowadays

die Hexe (-n) witch

hi (*coll.*) hi (E)

hier here (1); **Ist hier noch frei?** Is this seat available? (6)

die Hilfe help, assistance

die Hilfsorganisation (-en) aid organization

das Hilfsverb (-en) helping verb, auxiliary verb

der Himmel (-) sky (7); heaven

hin (to) there, thither; **hin und her** back and forth; **hin und zurück** round-trip (10); **vor sich hin** to oneself

hinaufschauen (schaut hinauf) to look up

hinfahren (fährt hin), fuhr hin, ist hingefahren to go there, drive there, ride there

hingehen (geht hin), ging hin, ist hingegangen to go there

hinlegen (legt hin) to lay down; **sich hinlegen** to lie down (8)

sich hinsetzen (setzt hin) to sit down (8)

hinstecken (steckt hin) to stick (in), put (in)

hinten in the back

hinter (+ *acc./dat.*) behind, in back of (6)

hinterher afterward

hinterherlaufen (+ *dat***) (läuft hinterher), lief hinterher, ist hinterhergelaufen** to run behind, run after)

hinterlassen (hinterlässt), hinterließ, hinterlassen to leave behind; leave (*e.g., a message*) (13)

hinunterstürzen (stürzt hinunter) to throw down; to gulp down

der Hinweis (-e) tip, clue

hinzufügen (fügt hinzu) to add

historisch historical(ly)

der Hit (-s) hit

das HIV (= humanes Immundefizienzvirus) HIV

das Hobby (-s) hobby (1)

hoch (hoh-) (höher, höchst-) high(ly) (2); tall

das Hoch high-pressure system (*weather*)

das Hochdeutsch High German, standard German language

hochgemut cheerful(ly)

die Hochschule (-n) university, college

der Hochschullehrer (-) / die Hochschullehrerin (-nen) university instructor (1)

die Hochschulreife college qualification

die Höchstgeschwindigkeit (-en) maximum speed, speed limit

die Hochzeit (-en) wedding (3)

der Hof (¨e) farm; court

das Hofbräuhaus famous beer hall in Munich

hoffen to hope (5)

hoffentlich hopefully; I/we/let's hope (6)

die Hoffnung (-en) hope

höflich polite(ly)

die Höhe (-n) height; **in die Höhe** upward

der Höhepunkt (-e) climax, peak; highlight

holen to get, fetch

(das) Holland Holland

holländisch (*adj.*) Dutch

der Höllenlärm hellish noise

das Holz wood

der Holzhammer (-) (wooden) mallet

der Holzpantoffel (-n) wooden shoe, clog

die Holzreserve (-n) lumber reserve

der Holzzaun (¨e) wooden fence

die Homepage (-s) home page

der Hometrainer (-) home exercise equipment

homöopathisch homeopathic

der Honig honey

die Honignote (-n) touch of honey

hören to hear, listen to (1)

der Hörer (-) / die Hörerin (-nen) listener

das Horoskop (-e) horoscope (13)

der Horrorfilm (-e) horror film

der Hörtext (-e) listening text

die Hose (-n) (pair of) pants, trousers (5)

das Hotel (-s) hotel (9)

das Huhn (¨er) chicken

die Hühnersuppe (-n) chicken soup

die Humanmedizin human medicine

der Humor (-e) humor, sense of humor

humorvoll full of humor, humorous(ly)

der Hund (-e) dog (3) **/ die Hündin (-nen)** female dog

hundert one hundred (E)

hundsmiserabel (*coll.*) sick as a dog (8)

der Hunger hunger; famine (14) **Hunger haben** to be hungry (2)

hungern to go hungry, starve

husten to cough

der Husten (-) cough, coughing (8)

das Hustenbonbon (-s) cough drop

der Hut (¨e) hat (5)

die Hütte (-n) hut, cabin

die Hysterie (-n) hysteria

I

der ICE (= Intercityexpresszug) intercity express train

ich I (1); **ich bin ... geboren** I was born . . . (1)

ideal ideal(ly)

die Idee (-n) idea

identifizieren to identify

identisch identical(ly)

das Idyll (-e) idyllic setting

idyllisch idyllic(ally)

ihm (to/for) him/it (*dat.*) (5)

ihn him; it (*acc.*) (3)

Ihnen (to/for) you (*dat., form.*); **Was fehlt Ihnen?** What's the matter? (8); **Wie gefällt Ihnen ...?** How do you like . . . ? (5); **Wie geht es Ihnen?** How are you? (*form.*) (E)

ihnen (to/for) them (*dat.*) (5)

Ihr your (*form.*) (3)

ihr you (*inform. pl.*) (1); her, its; their (3); (to/for) her/it (*dat.*) (5)

illegal illegal(ly)

im = in dem; im Freien outdoors (11); **im Grunde genommen** basically (14); **im Januar** in January (3); **im Kaufhaus** at the department store

der Imbiss (-e) fast-food stand (6)

immer always (1); **immer geradeaus** (keep on going) straight ahead (9) **immer noch** still

die Immobilien (*pl.*) real estate

der Imperativ (-e) imperative verb form

der Imperativsatz (¨e) imperative clause

das Imperfekt (-e) imperfect tense, simple past

in (+ *acc./dat.*) in/into; inside; to (*a place*) (6); **in der Mitte (der Stadt)** in the center (of the city) (9); **in der Nähe (des Bahnhofs)** near (the train station) (9); **in die Disco gehen** to go clubbing (4); **in die Oper gehen** to go to the opera (4); **in zwei Tagen** in two days (6)

indem (*subord. conj.*) while, as

der Indianer (-) / die Indianerin (-nen) American Indian (*person*)

indirekt indirect(ly)

indisch (*adj.*) Indian, of/from/pertaining to India

individuell individual(ly)

die Industrie (-n) industry

der Infinitiv (-e) infinitive verb form

die Inflation (-en) inflation

das Info (-s) (*coll.*) info(rmation)

die Informatik computer science

der Informatiker (-) / die Informatikerin (-nen) computer scientist (11)

die Information (-en) information

(sich) informieren (über + *acc.***)** to inform (oneself) (about) (8)

der Ingenieur (-e) / die Ingenieurin (-nen) engineer

der Inhaber (-) / die Inhaberin (-nen) proprietor; holder

die Initiative (-n) initiative

inkl. = inklusive

inklusive inclusive; included

das Inland (*sg. only*) home country (13); **im Inland und Ausland** at home and abroad (13)

das Inlineskaten inline skating

inmitten (+ *gen.*) in the midst of

der Innenarchitekt (-en *masc.***) (-en) / die Innenarchitektin (-nen)** interior designer

die Innenpolitik internal politics; domestic policy

die Innenstadt (¨e) downtown, city center (9)

innerhalb (+ *gen.*) within, inside of (9)

innovativ innovative(ly)

ins = in das; ins Kino gehen to go to the movies (4); **ins Theater gehen** to go to the theater (4)

die Insel (-n) island

insgesamt altogether, in total (10)

das Institut (-e) institute

das Instrument (-e) instrument

der/die Intellektuelle (*decl. adj.*) intellectual

intelligent intelligent(ly)

intensiv intense(ly); intensive(ly)

die Interaktion (-en) interaction

interessant interesting (1)

das Interesse (-n) interest (1)

interessieren to interest; **sich interessieren für** (+ *acc.*) to be interested in (11)

interessiert (an + *dat.***)** interested (in)

international international(ly)

das Internet Internet (13); **im Internet surfen** to surf the Internet (1)

der Internetzugang Internet access (9)

die Interpretation (-en) interpretation

der Inter-Treff-Club (-s) club for meeting one another

das Interview (-s) interview

interviewen to interview

investieren to invest

der Investmentfonds (-) investment fund

inzwischen in the meantime, meanwhile

der Iran Iran

irgendwer (*coll.*) somebody

irgendwo somewhere

(das) Irland Ireland

irritieren to irritate

der Irrtum (¨er) error

isolieren to isolate; to insulate (14)

(das) Israel Israel

ist is; **Das ist …** This is … (E)

(das) Italien Italy (E)

der Italiener (-) / die Italienerin (-nen) Italian (person)

italienisch (*adj.*) Italian

(das) Italienisch Italian (language)

die ivFö = individuelle Förderung study hall

J

ja yes (E); of course

die Jacke (-n) jacket (5)

das Jahr (-e) year (1); **dieses Jahr** this year; **einmal im Jahr** once a year (7); **im Jahr(e) …** in the year … ; **jedes Jahr** every year; **letztes Jahr** last year; **mit 10 Jahren** at age 10; **nächstes Jahr** next year (1); **die 90er Jahre** the nineties; **seit zwei Jahren** for two years (6)

die Jahreszeit (-en) season

das Jahrhundert (-e) century

-jährig: 12-jährig (*adj.*) twelve-year-(old), twelve years old; **der/die 12-Jährige** (*decl. adj.*) twelve-year-old (person)

jährlich annual(ly)

(der) Jänner January (*Austrian*)

(der) Januar January (3); **im Januar** in January (3)

(das) Japan Japan

der Japaner (-) / die Japanerin (-nen) Japanese person

der Jazz jazz

je ever; every, each; **je** (+ *comparative*) … **desto** (+ *comparative*) … the … the …

je (*interjection*): **oh je** oh dear

die Jeans (*pl.*) jeans (5)

jeder, jede, jedes each, every (5); everybody; **auf jeden Fall** in any case (13); **jeden Abend** every evening; **jeden Morgen** every morning; **jeden Tag** every day (7); **jedes Jahr** every year

jederzeit (at) any time

jedoch however, but

der Jeep (-s) jeep

jemand somebody, someone

Jenaer (*adj.*) of/from Jena (*a town in central Germany*)

jetzig current, present

jetzt now (1)

jeweils each time, in each case

der Job (-s) (temporary) job

jobben to work (at a temporary job) (12)

jobbenderweise with respect to working at a temporary job

joggen to jog (7)

der Jogger (-) / die Joggerin (-nen) jogger

der Jogginganzug (¨e) tracksuit, jogging outfit

der Joghurt yogurt (5)

der Joghurtbecher (-) carton of yogurt

die Joghurtvariante (-n) variety of yogurt

das Journal (-e) journal

der Journalist (-en *masc.***) (-en) / die Journalistin (-nen)** journalist (1)

der Jude (-n *masc.***) (-n) / die Jüdin (-nen)** Jew, Jewish person

jüdisch Jewish

die Jugend youth; young people

das Jugendgästehaus (¨er) (type of) youth hostel

die Jugendherberge (-n) youth hostel (9)

der/die Jugendliche (*decl. adj.*) young person; teenager

(der) Juli July (3)

jung young (10)

der Junge (-n *masc.***) (-n)** boy (2)

die Jungfrau (-en) virgin, maiden

(der) Juni June (3)

(die) Jura (*pl.*) law (*as a subject of study*)

die Justiz justice

K

das Kabarett (-s) cabaret

das Kabel (-) cable

der Kabelanschluss (¨e) cable TV connection (13)

das Kabinett (-e) cabinet

der Kaffee (-s) coffee

der Käfig (-e) cage

der Kahn (¨e) rowboat

(das) Kairo Cairo

der Kaiser (-) / die Kaiserin (-nen) emperor/empress

der Kaiserschmarren broken-up pancake sprinkled with powdered sugar and raisins

der Kajak (-s) kayak

die Kalbsleberwurst (¨e) veal liver sausage

der Kalender (-) calendar (3)

(das) Kalifornien California

die Kalorie (-n) calorie

kalt (kälter, kältest-) cold (7)

die Kamera (-s) camera (10)

der Kamillentee chamomile tea

der Kamm (¨e) comb

(sich) kämmen to comb (one's hair) (8)

die Kammermusik chamber music

das Kammerspiel (-e) chamber drama

(das) Kanada Canada

der Kanadier (-) / die Kanadierin (-nen) Canadian (person)

der Kanarienvogel (¨) canary

die Kanarischen Inseln (*pl.*) Canary Islands

der Kandidat (-en *masc.***) (-en) / die Kandidatin (-nen)** candidate

der Kanton (-e) canton (*division of Switzerland*)

die Kanu (-s) canoe

kapieren (*coll.*) to get, understand

das Kapital capital

die Kapitalanlage (-n) investment of capital

der Kapitalismus capitalism

der Kapitän (-e) captain

das Kapitel (-) chapter

kaputt broken (9)

der Karamell caramel

die Karibik the Caribbean

kariert checkered, plaid (5)

(der) Karneval Mardi Gras (*Rhineland*) (3)

(das) Kärnten Carinthia (*Austrian state*)

die Karotte (-n) carrot (5)

die Karriere (-n) career; **Karriere machen** to be successful in a career

die Karte (-n) card (7); ticket; chart; map; **Karten spielen** to play cards (1)

die Kartoffel (-n) potato (5)

die Kartoffelchips (*pl.*) potato chips

der Kartoffelkloß (¨e) potato dumpling

der Kartoffelspieß (-e) *potatoes (and other ingredients) roasted on a spit*

der Käse (-) cheese (5)

die Kasse (-n) cash register; check-out (5)

der Kassenbon (-s) receipt

der Kassenzettel (-) receipt

der Kassierer (-) / die Kassiererin (-nen) cashier

der Kasten (¨) box

das Kastenweißbrot (-e) *white bread baked in a square loaf pan*

der Katamaran (-e) catamaran

die Kategorie (-n) category

der Kater (-) tomcat, male cat

katholisch Catholic

die Katze (-n) cat (12)

der Kauf (¨e) purchase; buying, purchasing

kaufen to buy (2)

die Kauffrau (-en) saleswoman (11)

das Kaufhaus (¨er) department store (2); **im Kaufhaus** at the department store

die Kaufleute (*pl.*) salespeople (11)

der Kaufmann (Kaufleute) salesman (11)

kaum hardly, scarcely (8)

der Kaviar (-e) caviar

kegeln to bowl

der Kegler (-) / die Keglerin (-nen) bowler

der Kehrreim (-e) refrain

kein, keine no, none, not any (2); **kein(e) … mehr** no more … ; **noch kein(e)** no … yet

der Keks (-e) cookie (5)

der Keller (-) cellar, basement

der Kellner (-) / die Kellnerin (-nen) waiter, waitress; server (6)

kennen, kannte, gekannt to know, be acquainted with (*a person or thing*) (3)

kennenlernen (lernt kennen) to meet, get to know

die Kenntnis (-se) knowledge

der Kern (-e) core; nucleus; seed, kernel

die Kernenergie nuclear energy

die Kernfusion nuclear fusion

die Kerze (-n) candle

der Ketchup (-s) ketchup

der Kettenbrief (-e) chain letter

das Kfz = das Kraftfahrzeug (-e) motor vehicle

das Kickboxen kickboxing

Kieler (*adj.*) of/from Kiel (*city in northern Germany*)

das Kilo (-s) = Kilogramm (-e) kilogram

der Kilometer (-) kilometer

das Kind (-er) child; **als Kind** as a child

der Kindergarten (¨) nursery school, preschool

der Kindergärtner (-) / die Kindergärtnerin (-nen) preschool teacher

die Kinderkonfektion (-en) children's wear

die Kindheit childhood

kindisch childish(ly)

das Kinn (-e) chin (8)

das Kino (-s) cinema, (movie) theater (4); **ins Kino gehen** to go to the movies (4)

der Kiosk (-e) kiosk

die Kirche (-n) church (9)

der Kirchhof (¨e) churchyard; graveyard, cemetery

der Kirchturm (¨e) church steeple

die Kirmes (-sen) fair

kitschig kitschy

die Kiwi (-s) kiwi (fruit)

die Klamotte (-n) duds, rags (*slang for clothes*)

klar clear; of course; **Alles klar.** Everything is clear., I get it. (E); **na klar** absolutely (E); but of course, you bet

die Klasse (-n) class; classroom; **erster/zweiter Klasse fahren (fährt), fuhr, ist gefahren** to travel first/second class (10)

der Klassiker (-) classic

klassisch classic; classical(ly)

die Klausur (-en) examination

das Klavier (-e) piano

die Klavierstunde (-n) piano lesson

kleben to stick, adhere

das Kleid (-er) dress (5)

die Kleider (*pl.*) clothes

der Kleiderschrank (¨e) wardrobe; clothes closet (2)

die Kleidung clothing, clothes

klein small, little (2)

das Kleingeld (small) change

die Kleinkinderbetreuung child care

der Klettergarten (¨) climbing garden

klettern, ist geklettert to climb

der Klick (-s) click

klicken to click

der Klient (-en *masc.*) **(-en) / die Klientin (-nen)** client

das Klima climate

klimaschädlich harmful to the climate

der Klimawandel climate change (14)

klingeln to ring

klingen, klang, geklungen to sound (8); **Du klingst so deprimiert.** You sound so depressed. (8)

die Klinik (-en) hospital; clinic

klopfen to knock

das Kloster (¨) monastery; convent

klotzen (*coll.*) to show off

der Klub (-s) club

klug smart, intelligent(ly)

km = Kilometer

die Knackwurst (¨e) *type of German sausage*

knallen to slam, bang

knapp just about, barely

knauserig (*coll.*) stingy

knausern (*coll.*) to be stingy

die Kneipe (-n) pub, bar (6)

der Kneipenbummel (-) pub-crawl, bar-hopping

das Knie (-) knee (8)

der Knoblauch garlic

die Knolle (-n) tuber

knurren to growl

der Knusperjoghurt crunchy yogurt

die Koalition (-en) coalition

die Kobra (-s) cobra

der Koch (¨e) / die Köchin (-nen) cook, chef

kochen to cook (1); to boil; **gekochtes Ei** boiled egg

die Kochnische (-n) kitchen nook

der Koffer (-) suitcase (5)

der Kollege (-n *masc.*) **(-n) / die Kollegin (-nen)** colleague, co-worker

(das) Köln Cologne (*city in western Germany*)

Kölner (*adj.*) of/from Cologne

die Kombination (-en) combination

kombinieren to combine

der Komfort (-s) comfort

komisch funny, funnily; strange(ly)

kommen, kam, ist gekommen to come (1); **Ich komme aus …** I'm from . . . (E); **Wie komme ich am besten dahin?** What's the best way to get there? (9); **Woher kommen Sie?** (*form.*) / **Woher kommst du?** (*inform.*) Where are you from? (E)

kommend coming, next

der Kommilitone (-n *masc.*) **(-n) / die Kommilitonin (-nen)** fellow student

der Kommissar (-e) detective inspector; commissioner

die Kommode (-n) dresser (2)

die Kommune (-n) commune

die Kommunikation (-en) communication

das Kommunikationswesen communications

kommunikativ communicative(ly)

die Komödie (-n) comedy (4)

der Komparativ (-e) comparative

komplett complete(ly)

komplex (*adj.*) complex

das Kompliment (-e) compliment

der Komplize (-n *masc.*) **(-n) / die Komplizin (-nen)** accomplice

kompliziert complicated (1)

komponieren to compose

der Komponist (-en *masc.*) **(-en) / die Komponistin (-nen)** composer

das Kompositum (Komposita) compound word

der Kompost (-e) compost

kompostieren to compost

die Kondition (-en) condition

die Konditorei (-en) pastry shop (5)

die Konferenz (-en) conference

der Kongress (-e) congress, convention

der König (-e) / die Königin (-nen) king/queen

die Konjunktion (-en) conjunction

konkret concrete(ly)

können (kann), konnte, gekonnt to be able to; can (4); to know how to

der Könner (-) / die Könnerin (-nen) one who can, expert

konservativ conservative(ly) (1)

der Konstrukteur (-e) / die Konstrukteurin (-nen) technical designer

der Konsum consumption

der Konsument (-en *masc.*) **(-en) / die Konsumentin (-nen)** consumer

der Kontakt (-e) contact (11)

kontaktfreudig outgoing (11)

der Kontext (-e) context

das Konto (Konten) account

der Kontrast (-e) contrast

die Kontrolle (-n) control

kontrollieren to control

die Konversation (-en) conversation

konzentrieren to concentrate

das Konzert (-e) concert (4); **ins Konzert gehen** to go to a concert (4)

(das) Kopenhagen Copenhagen

der Kopf (¨e) head (8)

das Köpfchen (-): kluges Köpfchen clever little person

der Kopfsalat (-e) lettuce

die Kopfschmerzen (pl.) headache (8)

die Kopie (-n) copy

der Korb (¨e) basket

(das) Korfu Corfu

das Korn (¨er) grain, kernel

der Körper (-) body

körperlich physical(ly)

der Körperteil (-e) body part (8)

die Korrektur (-en) correction, revision

korrespondieren to correspond

korrigieren to correct

die Korruption (-en) corruption (14)

(das) Korsika Corsica

die Kosmetik cosmetics

die Kost food

kostbar precious

kosten to cost (2)

die Kosten (pl.) cost, expense

kostenlos free of charge

das Kostüm (-e) costume; fancy dress

der Krach loud noise

die Kraft (¨e) power, strength

kräftig strong(ly), powerful(ly)

krank sick, ill (8)

das Krankenhaus (¨er) hospital

die Krankenkasse (-n) health insurance company

der Krankenpfleger (-) / die Krankenpflegerin (-nen) / die Krankenschwester (-n) nurse (8)

die Krankenversicherung (-en) health insurance

die Krankheit (-en) illness, disease, ailment (14)

krass blatant(ly), crass(ly)

das Kraut (¨er) herb

der Kräutertee herbal tea (8)

die Krawatte (-n) necktie (5)

kreativ creative(ly)

die Kreativität creativity

die Kreditkarte (-n) credit card (9)

Krefelder (adj.) of/from Krefeld (a town in Western Germany)

die Kreuzung (-en) intersection (9)

das Kreuzworträtsel (-) crossword puzzle; **Kreuzworträtsel machen** to do crossword puzzles (1)

der Krieg (-e) war (14)

der Krimi (-s) crime/detective/mystery story, film, or TV show (4)

die Kriminalität criminality

der Kriminologe (-n masc.) (-n) / die Kriminologin (-nen) criminologist

die Krise (-n) crisis

das Kriterium (Kriterien) criterion

der Kritiker (-) / die Kritikerin (-nen) critic

kritisch critical(ly)

kritisieren to criticize

die Kröte (-n) toad; **Kröten schlucken (coll.)** to make unpleasant compromises

die Küche (-n) kitchen (2); cuisine, food (6)

der Kuchen (-) cake (5)

der Kuckuck (-e) cuckoo

der Ku'damm = Kurfürstendamm famous shopping street in Berlin

der Kugelschreiber (-) ballpoint pen (12)

kühl cool(ly) (7)

der Kühlschrank (¨e) refrigerator (9)

kulinarisch culinary

die Kultur (-en) culture

kulturell cultural(ly)

die Kulturwissenschaften (pl.) cultural sciences, arts and humanities

kümmern to concern

der Kunde (-n masc.) (-n) / die Kundin (-nen) customer (2)

die Kundenbetreuung customer service (11)

künftig future; in the future

die Kunst (¨e) art

der Kunstbetrachter (-) / die Kunstbetrachterin (-nen) art viewer

das Kunstgebilde (-) art object

die Kunsthalle (-n) art museum, exhibition hall

der Künstler (-) / die Künstlerin (-nen) artist (11)

künstlerisch artistic(ally)

die Kur (-en) health cure, treatment (at a spa)

der Kurort (-e) health spa, resort

der Kurs (-e) course

kurz (kürzer, kürzest-) short, brief(ly), for a short time (7)

die Kürze: in Kürze soon, shortly

kurzfristig short-term

die Kurzgeschichte (-n) short story

kürzlich recently

die Kusine (-n) = Cousine female cousin (3)

das Küsschen (-): ein dickes Küsschen a big kiss

die Küste (-n) coast

L

das Labor (-s) laboratory

der Laborant (-en masc.) (-en) / die Laborantin (-nen) laboratory technician

das Labskaus type of beef stew eaten with a fried egg

lächeln to smile

lachen to laugh

der Lachs (-e) salmon

laden (lädt), lud, geladen to load

der Laden (¨) store, shop (5)

das Ladenschlussgesetz (-e) law regulating store-closing times

die Lage (-n) location (9); situation

das Lager (-) camp

lala: so lala (coll.) OK, so-so (E)

das Lamm (¨er) lamb

die Lampe (-n) lamp (2)

das Land (¨er) country; nation, land; **auf dem Land(e)** in the countryside

das Landei (-er) farm egg

landen, hat/ist gelandet to land

die Landeskunde regional studies

die Landkarte (-n) map

die Landschaft (-en) landscape (10); scenery

die Landwirtschaft agriculture

lang (länger, längst-) long (7)

lange long (temporal); **wie lange** (for) how long

die Langeweile boredom

langsam slow(ly) (10); **Langsamer, bitte.** Slower, please. (E)

längst (adv.) long since, a long time ago

langweilig boring (1)

der Laptop (-s) laptop (computer)

der Lärm noise (14)

lassen (lässt), ließ, gelassen to leave (behind); to let (6); to have something done; **Lass uns (doch) ...** Let's . . . (6)

die Lastschrift (-en) debit

(das) Lateinamerika Latin America

lateinisch (adj.) Latin

der Lauch (-e) leek

der Lauf (¨e) course; **im Laufe der Zeit** over the course of time

laufen (läuft), lief, ist gelaufen to run, jog (2); to walk; **der Film läuft im ...** the film is playing at . . . ; **Schlittschuh laufen** to ice-skate (7)

der Laufschritt (-e): im Laufschritt at a running pace

laut loud(ly) (10); **(+ dat.)** according to

der Lautsprecher (-) (stereo) speaker

leben to live

das Leben life (11)

lebending lively

der Lebenslauf (¨e) résumé (11); **tabellarischer Lebenslauf** résumé in outline form

das Lebensmittel (-) food, groceries

der Lebensraum (¨e) habitat

der Leberkäs Bavarian-style meatloaf (6)

die Leberknödelsuppe liver dumpling soup

lecker tasty, delicious

das Leder (-) leather

die Lederwaren (pl.) leather goods

ledig unmarried, single

leer empty

legen to lay, put (in a lying position) (6); **sich legen** to lie down (8)

die Lehre (-n) apprenticeship; lesson

der Lehrer (-) / die Lehrerin (-nen) teacher (E)

der Lehrling (-e) apprentice, trainee

die Leibesübungen (pl.) physical education

die Leiche (-n) corpse

leicht easy, easily; light(ly)

leiden an (+ *dat.*), **litt, gelitten** to suffer from

das Leiden (-) suffering

die Leidenschaft (-en) passion

leider unfortunately (3)

leidtun (+ *dat.*) **(tut leid), tat leid, leidgetan** (*impersonal*) to be sorry **Das tut mir leid.** I'm sorry. (9)

leihen, lieh, geliehen to lend; to borrow

Leipziger (*adj.*) of/from Leipzig

leise quiet(ly); softly

die Leistung (-en) accomplishment; performance (11)

der Leitartikel (-) lead article

leiten to lead

der Leiter (-) / **die Leiterin** (-nen) leader, director

die Lektion (-en) lesson

die Lektüre (-n) reading (material)

lernen to learn; to study (1)

die Lernmittel (*pl.*) school supplies

das Leseexemplar (-e) copy of a book

lesen (**liest**), **las, gelesen** to read (1, 2)

der Leser (-) / **die Leserin** (-nen) reader

die Leserschaft readers, readership

das Lesestück (-e) reading selection

die Letter (-n) piece of type (used in printing)

letzt- last; **letzte Nacht** last night; **letzte Woche** last week; **letztes Jahr** last year; **zum letzten Mal** for the last time

Letzt: zu guter Letzt in the end

die Leute (*pl.*) people (2)

liberal liberal(ly)

das Licht (-er) light

lieb kind; dear **alles Liebe** all my love (*at end of letter*)

die Liebe (-n) love

lieben to love

lieber (+ *verb*) rather, preferably; **möchte lieber** would rather (4)

lieblich charming(ly)

der Liebling (-e) darling; **Lieblings-** favorite (*first component of compound nouns*)

am liebsten (+ *verb*) the best, the most; **möchte am liebsten** would like (to do) most (4)

(das) Liechtenstein Liechtenstein (E)

das Lied (-er) song

der Liedermacher (-) / **die Liedermacherin** (-nen) (folk) songwriter

liegen, lag, gelegen to lie; to be located (6); **es liegt daran, dass …** it is because . . . ; **günstig liegen** to be conveniently located (9)

liegen bleiben (**bleibt liegen**), **blieb liegen, ist liegen geblieben** to stay down

die Liegewiese (-n) sunbathing lawn

lila purple, violet (5)

die Limonade (-n) lemonade; any flavored soda, soft drink

die Linde (-n) linden tree; **Unter den Linden** *major street in Berlin*

die Linguistik linguistics

die Linie (-n) line; **in erster Linie** first and foremost

link- left, left-hand; **auf der linken Seite** on the left side

links (on the) left (9); **nach links** to the left (9)

die Liste (-n) list

der Liter (-) liter

literarisch literary

die Literatur (-en) literature

locken to lure

sich lockern to relax, loosen

der Löffel (-) spoon (6)

logisch logical(ly)

der Lohn (¨e) pay, wage(s)

lokal local(ly)

das Lokal (-e) restaurant, pub, bar (6)

die Lokalität (-en) locality

die Lokalnachrichten (*pl.*) local news (13)

die Lokomotive (-n) locomotive

los loose; off; **Was ist denn los?** What's the matter? (2)

löschen to delete

lösen to solve (14)

losgehen (**geht los**), **ging los, ist losgegangen** to start

loslegen (**legt los**) (*coll.*) to start, let rip

die Lösung (-en) solution (14)

loswerden (**wird los**), **wurde los, ist losgeworden** (*coll.*) to get rid of

die Lotterie (-n) lottery

das Lotto (-s) lottery

der Löwe (-n *masc.*) (-n) lion

die Lücke (-n) gap, space, blank

die Luft (¨e) air (8)

luftig airy

die Luftverschmutzung air pollution

die Lüge (-n) lie, falsehood

lügen, log, gelogen to lie, tell a falsehood

der Lügenbaron lying baron (*Münchhausen*)

die Lunge (-n) lung

Lust haben to feel like (*doing something*) (2)

lustig cheerful(ly); fun-loving (1); funny, funnily

das Lustspiel (-e) comedy

(das) Luxemburg Luxembourg (E)

die Luxusjacht (-en) luxury yacht

(das) Luzern Lucerne (*in Switzerland*)

M

machen to make; to do (1); **Das macht nichts.** That doesn't matter. (8); **Das macht Spaß.** That's fun. (1); **das macht …** that comes to . . . (5) **Fortschritte machen** to make progress (14); **Kreuzworträtsel machen** to do crossword puzzles (1); **Mach schnell!** Hurry up!; **Mach's gut.** Take care, so long (*inform.*) (E); **ein Praktikum machen** to do an internship (1); **sich Sorgen machen um** (+ *acc.*) to worry about (14); **Urlaub machen** to go on vacation (8); **Was machst du gern?** What do you like to do?

die Macht (¨e) power

mächtig powerful(ly)

das Mädchen (-) girl

das Magazin (-e) magazine

der Magen (¨) stomach

die Magermilch skim milk

die Magie magic

das Magisterstudium study toward a master's degree

die Mahlzeit (-en) meal

(der) Mai May (3); **der erste Mai** May first (3); **am ersten Mai** on May first (3)

die Mail (-s) e-mail

mailen to e-mail

der Mais corn, maize (6)

mal = einmal once; just; (*softening particle used with imperatives*) (4); **-mal** time(s); **noch mal** again, once again; **sag mal** tell me (1); **schau mal** look

das Mal (-e) time; **zum ersten Mal** for the first time

malen to paint (7)

der Maler (-) / **die Malerin** (-nen) painter

(das) Mallorca Majorca

man (*indef. pron.*) one; you; they; people (4); **Hier darf man nicht parken.** You may not park here. (4); **Wie sagt man … auf Deutsch?** How do you say . . . in German? (E)

der Manager (-) / **die Managerin** (-nen) manager

mancher, manche, manches some; **manch ein(e)** many a; **manches Mal** many a time

manchmal sometimes (8)

die Mandarine (-n) mandarin orange

der Mangel (¨) lack

die Mango (-s) mango

der Mann (¨er) man (1); husband (3)

männlich masculine, male

die Mannschaft (-en) team

der Mantel (¨) (over)coat (5)

das Marathon (-s) marathon

das Märchen (-) fairy tale

marineblau navy blue

die Mark (-) mark (*former German currency*); **die D-Mark (Deutsche Mark)** German mark

die Markenbutter best butter

das Marketing marketing

markieren to mark

der Markt (¨e) (open-air) market, marketplace (5); **auf dem Markt** at the market

der Marktplatz (¨e) market square

die Marmelade (-n) jam

(das) Marokko Morocco

der Mars Mars

(der) März March (3)

die Masche (-n) (*coll.*) trick

die Maschine (-n) machine

der Maschinenbau mechanical engineering

die Maske (-n) mask

die Massage (-n) massage

die Masse (-n) mass

die Massenemigration (-en) mass emigration

die Massenvernichtungswaffe (-n) weapon of mass destruction

mäßig moderate(ly)

das Material (-ien) material

die Mathe (*coll.*) math

die Mathematik mathematics

das Matjesfilet (-s) herring filet

der Matjeshering (-e) young, slightly salted herring

das Matterhorn (mountain in the Swiss Alps)

die Mauer (-n) wall

die Maus (¨e) mouse (also as term of endearment)

maximal maximum

der MDR = Mitteldeutscher Rundfunk broadcasting company in Germany

der Mechaniker (-) / die Mechanikerin (-nen) mechanic (11)

der Mechatroniker (-) / die Mechatronikerin (-nen) mechatronician

(das) Mecklenburg-Vorpommern one of the German states

die Medien (pl.) media

das Medikament (-e) medicine, medication (5)

die Meditation (-en) meditation

meditieren to meditate

die Medizin (field of) medicine

medizinisch medical(ly)

das Meer (-e) sea; ocean (7); **am Meer** at the seaside

die Meeresfrüchte (pl.) seafood

mehr more; **immer mehr** more and more; **kein(e) … mehr** no more; **nicht mehr** not anymore; **nie mehr** never again

das Mehrbettzimmer (-) room with several beds

mehrere (pl.) several

die Mehrfachnennungen (pl.) multiple mentions

die Mehrfachsteckdose (-n) electric power strip

mehrmals often, several times, on several occasions

die Mehrweg-Eierbox (-en) recyclable egg carton

die Mehrwertsteuer (-n) value-added tax; national sales tax

die Mehrzweckhalle (-n) multipurpose hall

mein my (3)

meinen to mean; to think, be of the opinion (14); **Was meinen Sie?** (form.) / **Was meinst du?** (inform.) What do you think?

die Meinung (-en) opinion (14); **ich bin der Meinung …** I'm of the opinion . . . (14); **meiner Meinung nach …** in my opinion . . . (14)

meist mostly

meist- most; **am meisten** (the) most

meistens mostly (8)

der Meister (-) / die Meisterin (-nen) master; champion

sich melden to answer (phone) (13); **Niemand meldet sich.** No one is answering. (13)

die Melodie (-n) melody

der Mennonit (-en masc.**) (-en) / die Mennonitin (-nen)** Mennonite

die Mensa (-s) student cafeteria (1)

der Mensch (-en masc.**) (-en)** human being, person (2)

das Menschenrecht (-e) human right (usually pl.) (14)

menschlich human

das Menü (-s) menu

der Mercedes (-) Mercedes (automobile)

merken to notice, observe

das Merkmal (-e) feature, characteristic

merkwürdig strange(ly); remarkable, remarkably

das Messer (-) knife (6)

die Messung (-en) measurement

das Metall (-e) metal

der Meteorologe (-n masc.**) (-n) / die Meteorologin (-nen)** meteorologist

der/das Meter (-) meter

der Metzger (-) / die Metzgerin (-nen) butcher

die Metzgerei (-en) butcher shop (5)

(das) Mexiko Mexico

mich me (acc.) (3); **Freut mich.** Pleased to meet you. (E)

das Mietangebot (-e) rental offer

die Miete (-n) rent (2)

mieten to rent (from someone) (12)

der Mieter (-) / die Mieterin (-nen) renter

das Mietgesuch (-e) rental request

das Mietshaus (¨er) apartment building

der Mietwagen (-) rental car

der Mikrowellenherd (-e) microwave oven (12)

die Milch milk (5)

mildgesäuert mildly soured

der Milliardär (-e) / die Milliardärin (-nen) billionaire

die Milliarde (-n) billion (1,000,000,000)

der Milliliter (-) milliliter, one thousandth of a liter

die Million (-en) million

der Millionär (-e) / die Millionärin (-nen) millionaire

mindestens at least (8)

der Mindestlohn (¨e) minimum wage

das Mineral (-ien) mineral

die Mineralstofftablette (-n) mineral salt tablet

der Minidialog (-e) mini-dialogue

das Minigolf miniature golf (game)

minimalistisch minimalistic(ally)

der Minister (-) / die Ministerin (-nen) (government) minister

die Minute (-n) minute (4)

mir (to/for) me (dat.) (5); **Das ist mir zu blöd.** I think that's really stupid. (13); **Mir ist schlecht.** I'm sick to my stomach (8)

die Mischung (-en) mixture

mit (+ dat.) with; by means of (5); **Wie wäre es mit … ?** How about . . . ? (13); **Willst du mit?** (coll.) Do you want to come along?

der Mitarbeiter (-) / die Mitarbeiterin (-nen) co-worker, colleague; employee (11)

der Mitbewohner (-) / die Mitbewohnerin (-nen) roommate (2)

mitbringen (bringt mit), brachte mit, mitgebracht to bring along

miteinander together, with one another

die Mitfahrgelegenheit (-en) ride-sharing opportunity

mitgehen (geht mit), ging mit, ist mitgegangen to come along, go along

das Mitglied (-er) member

mithelfen (hilft mit), half mit, mitgeholfen to help, lend a hand

mithilfe (+ gen.) with the help of

mitkommen (kommt mit), kam mit, ist mitgekommen to come along (4)

mitmachen (macht mit) to join in

mitnehmen (nimmt mit), nahm mit, mitgenommen to take along (5); **zum Mitnehmen** (food) to go; take-out (6)

mitprägen (prägt mit) to influence

mitspielen (spielt mit) to play along

der Mitstudent (-en masc.**) (-en) / die Mitstudentin (-nen)** fellow student

der Mittag (-e) noon (4); **heute Mittag** today at noon

das Mittagessen (-) midday meal; lunch (5)

mittags at noon (4)

die Mitte (-n) middle, center (9); **in der Mitte (der Stadt)** in the center (of the city) (9)

das Mittel (-) means, method

das Mittelalter Middle Ages

mittelalterlich medieval

die Mittelklasse (-n) middle class

mittelmäßig mediocre, indifferent(ly)

das Mittelmeer Mediterranean Sea

der Mittelpunkt (-e) center

der Mittelwesten Midwest (USA)

mitten in the midst; **mitten im Dorf** in the middle of the village

die Mitternacht midnight; **um Mitternacht** at midnight (3)

mittler- middle; **die mittlere Reife** high school diploma (not sufficient for university studies)

(der) Mittwoch Wednesday (3)

mittwochs Wednesdays, on Wednesday(s) (4)

mitunter sometimes

die Mitwohnzentrale (-n) shared housing agency

der Mix (-e) mix

die Möbel (pl.) furniture (2)

möbliert furnished (2)

möchte would like to (4); **ich möchte (gern)** I would like; **möchte am liebsten** would like (to do) most (4); **möchte lieber** would rather (4)

das Modalverb (-en) modal verb

die Mode (-n) fashion

das Modell (-e) example, model

der/das Modem (-s) modem

der Moderator (-en) / die Moderatorin (-nen) presenter, moderator

modern modern, in a modern manner

modisch fashionable, fashionably

mögen (mag), mochte, gemocht to care for; to like (4); **ich möchte (gern)** I would like; **Wo mag das sein?** Where can that be?

möglich possible, possibly (14)

die Möglichkeit (-en) possibility, opportunity (10)

möglichst as . . . as possible

der Moment (-e) moment; **im Moment** at the moment; **Moment (mal)** just a moment

momentan (at) present

der Monat (-e) month; **einmal im Monat** once a month (7)

monatlich monthly (12)

(der) Montag Monday (3); **am Montag** on Monday (3)

montags Mondays, on Monday(s) (4)

morgen tomorrow (3); **morgen Abend** tomorrow evening (4); **morgen früh** tomorrow morning (4); **morgen Nachmittag** tomorrow afternoon; **morgen Vormittag** tomorrow morning; **Welches Datum ist morgen?** What is tomorrow's date? (3)

der Morgen (-) morning (4); **am Morgen** in the morning; **(guten) Morgen** good morning (E); **heute Morgen** this morning (4); **jeden Morgen** every morning

morgendlich (*adj.*) morning

morgens in the morning, mornings (4)

das Motiv (-e) motive; motif

motivieren to motivate

der Motor (-en) motor, engine

das Motorrad (¨er) motorcycle (2); **Motorrad fahren** to ride a motorcycle

das Mountainbike (-s) mountain bike

das Mountainbiking mountain biking

der Mozzarella mozzarella (cheese)

müde tired (8)

die Mühle (-n) mill

der Müll trash, garbage (12)

die Müllabfuhr garbage collection

der Mülleimer (-) garbage can

das Multiparteiensystem (-e) multi-party system

der Multivitaminsaft (¨e) multivitamin juice

(das) München Munich

Münchner (*adj.*) of/from Munich

der Mund (¨er) mouth (8)

mündlich oral(ly), verbal(ly)

munter cheerful(ly)

das Museum (Museen) museum (9)

das Musical (-s) musical

die Musik music (1)

die Musikalien (*pl.*) sheet music

der Musikant (-en *masc.***) (-en) / die Musikantin (-nen)** musician, music maker

der Musiker (-) / die Musikerin (-nen) (professional) musician

der Musikfreund (-e) / die Musikfreundin (-nen) music lover

musizieren to make music, play an instrument

der Muskel (-n) muscle (8)

das Müsli (-) granola; cereal (5)

der Müsli-Raspler (-) / die Müsli-Rasplerin (-nen) granola-cruncher

müssen (muss), musste, gemusst to have to; must (4)

das Muster (-) pattern, model, example; **nach dem Muster** according to the example

der Mut courage

die Mutter (¨) mother (3)

mütterlicherseits on the mother's side

die Muttersprache (-n) mother tongue, native language

der Muttertag Mother's Day (3)

die Mutti (-s) mommy, mom

die Mütze (-n) cap (5)

Mwst. = Mehrwertsteuer

der Mythos (Mythen) myth

N

na well; so; **na ja** oh well; **na klar** absolutely (E); but of course; you bet; **Na und?** So what? (13); **Na, wie geht's?** How are you? (*casual*) (E)

nach (+ *dat.*) after (4, 6); to (*place name*) (5); according to; **Es ist Viertel nach zwei.** It's a quarter after two. (4); **fünf nach zwei** five after two (4); **meiner Meinung nach ...** in my opinion . . . (14); **nach dem Befinden fragen** to ask about someone's well-being; **nach dem Weg fragen** to ask for directions (9); **nach Dienstag** after Tuesday (6); **nach Hause** (to) home (5); **nach links/rechts** to the left/right (9); **nach oben** above, upstairs (*directional*) (12); **nach unten** below, downstairs (*directional*) (12)

der Nachbar (-n *masc.***) (-n) / die Nachbarin (-nen)** neighbor

nachdem (*subord. conj.*) after (10)

nachdenken (über + acc.) (denkt nach), dachte nach, nachgedacht to think (about), ponder (over) (11)

nacherzählen (erzählt nach) to retell

nachher afterward

nachkommen (kommt nach), kam nach, ist nachgekommen to come later, follow

der Nachmittag (-e) afternoon (4); **am Nachmittag** in the afternoon; **heute Nachmittag** this afternoon (4); **morgen Nachmittag** tomorrow afternoon

nachmittags in the afternoon, afternoons (4)

der Nachname (gen. -ns, acc./dat. -n) (-n) family name, surname (1)

die Nachricht (-en) message; **die Nachrichten** (*pl.*) news (13)

der Nachrichtensprecher (-) / die Nachrichtensprecherin (-nen) news anchor

nachsehen, sah nach, nachgesehen to check, look up

die Nachspeise (-n) dessert (6)

nächst- next, following; closest, nearest; **am nächsten Tag** on the next day; **nächstes Jahr** next year

die Nacht (¨e) night (4); **gute Nacht** good night (E); **letzte Nacht** last night

der Nachteil (-e) disadvantage

der Nachtisch (-e) dessert (6)

nächtlich nocturnal, during the night

nachts at night, nights (4)

das Nachtskaten nighttime skating

der Nachttisch (-e) nightstand (2)

das Nackensteak (-s) neck steak

nah (näher, nächst-) close by, near

die Nähe vicinity (9); **in der Nähe (des Bahnhofs)** near (the train station) (9)

die Naherholung (-en) vacationing nearby

die Nahrung nutrition; food

das Nahrungsmittel (-) food

der Name (gen. -ns, acc./dat. -n) (-n) name (1); **auf den Namen ... hören** to answer to the name . . . ; **Auf welchen Namen?** Under what name? (9); **Mein Name ist ...** My name is . . . (E); **Wie ist Ihr/dein Name?** What is your name? (*form./inform.*) (E)

nämlich namely, that is to say (3)

nanu now what

die Nase (-n) nose (8)

die Nation (-en) nation; **die Vereinten Nationen** United Nations

national national(ly)

die Natur (-en) nature (10)

die Naturfaser (-n) natural fiber

die Naturkraft (¨e) natural energy

die Naturkunde nature study

natürlich natural(ly); of course (1)

naturnah close to nature

der Naturschutz nature conservation

die Naturwissenschaft (-en) natural science

die Navelorange (-n) navel orange

das Navi (-s) = das Navigationssystem (-e) navigation system, GPS (10)

'ne = eine

das Neandertal valley near Düsseldorf

der Nebel fog (7)

neben (+ *acc./dat.*) next to, beside (6)

die Nebenarbeit (-en) side job

nebenbei on the side

nebeneinander next to each other

die Nebenkosten (*pl.*) utilities; extra costs (12)

der Nebensatz (¨e) subordinate clause

der Nebentisch (-e) adjacent table

neblig foggy (7)

der Neffe (-n *masc.***) (-n)** nephew (3)

negativ negative(ly)

nehmen (nimmt), nahm, genommen to take (5); **im Grunde genommen** basically (14); **Platz nehmen** to take a seat; **zu etwas** (*dat.*) **Stellung nehmen** to take a stand on something

neidisch envious(ly)

nein no (E)

nennen, nannte, genannt to name, call

(das) Nepal Nepal

der Nerv (-en) nerve

nerven (*coll.*) to irritate, get on one's nerves

nett nice(ly) (1); pleasant(ly)

das Netz (-e) net; network

neu new(ly) (3); **nichts Neues** nothing new

der Neubau (Neubauten) modern building (12)

neuerdings recently

das Neujahr New Year's Day (3)

neun nine (E)

neunte ninth (3)

neunzehn nineteen (E)

neunzig ninety (E)

(das) Neuschottland Nova Scotia

(das) Neuseeland New Zealand

die Neustadt (¨e) new part of town

neutral neutral(ly)

(das) Nicaragua Nicaragua

nicht not (1); **Das weiß ich nicht.** I don't know.
(E); **Ich verstehe das nicht.** I don't
understand. (E); **nicht besonders gut** not
particularly well (E); **nicht mehr** no longer;
noch nicht not yet; **nicht wahr?** isn't that so?

die Nichte (-n) niece (3)

**der Nichtraucher (-) / die Nichtraucherin
(-nen)** nonsmoker (2)

nichts nothing (2); **Das macht nichts.** That
doesn't matter. (8); **gar nichts** nothing at all;
nichts Gescheites nothing decent (13);
nichts Neues nothing new; **Nichts zu
danken.** No thanks necessary; Don't
mention it. (8)

der Nichtskönner (-) incompetent person

das Nichtstun inactivity, doing nothing

nicken to nod

nie never (1); **nie mehr** never again

die Niederlande (pl.) the Netherlands (E)

**der Niederländer (-) / die Niederländerin
(-nen)** Dutch person

(das) Niederösterreich Lower Austria (Austrian
state)

(das) Niedersachsen Lower Saxony (German
state)

**niederschreiben (schreibt nieder), schrieb
nieder, niedergeschrieben** to write down

niedrig low (2)

niemand nobody; **Niemand meldet sich.** No
one is answering. (13)

noch still; yet (2); **Ist hier noch frei?** Is this seat
available? (6); **noch (ein)mal** once more;
noch mehr even more; **noch nicht** not yet;
Sonst noch (et)was? Anything else?;
weder ... noch neither . . . nor

das Nomen (-) noun

der Nominativ (-e) nominative case

Nord (without article) north

der Norden north; **im Norden** in the north

nördlich (von + dat.**)** north (of)

Nordost (without article) northeast

nordöstlich (von + dat.**)** northeast (of)

(das) Nordrhein-Westfalen North Rhine-
Westphalia (German state)

die Nordsee North Sea

Nordwest (without article) northwest

normal normal(ly)

normalerweise normally, usually

(das) Norwegen Norway

das Notebook (-s) notebook computer (13)

der Notgroschen (-) savings for a rainy day

notieren to write down

nötig necessary (5); urgent(ly)

die Notiz (-en) note; **sich Notizen machen** to
take notes

(der) November November (3)

die Nudel (-n) noodle (6)

null zero (E)

das Numero (-s) number (no.)

die Nummer (-n) number

nummerieren to number

das Nummernschild (-er) license plate

nun now

nur only (2); **nicht nur** not only

(das) Nürnberg Nuremberg

Nürnberger (adj.) of/from Nuremberg

nützen to be of use

der Nutzer (-) / die Nutzerin (-nen) user

nützlich useful(ly)

O

ob (subord. conj.) if, whether (or not) (8)

der/die Obdachlose (decl. adj.) homeless
person (14)

die Obdachlosigkeit homelessness (14)

oben at the top; above; upstairs (12); **nach
oben** above, upstairs (directional) (12)

ober upper

der Ober (-) waiter (6)

das Objekt (-e) object

das Obst fruit (5)

der Obst- und Gemüsestand ("e) fruit
and vegetable stand (5)

obwohl (subord. conj.) although, even though

der Ochs (-en masc.**) (-en)** ox

oder (coord. conj.) or (7); **entweder ... oder**
either . . . or (8)

offen open

die Offenheit openness, candor

öffentlich public(ly) (14); **öffentliche
Verkehrsmittel** (pl.) means of public
transportation

offiziell official(ly)

der Offizier (-e) / die Offizierin (-nen) officer

offline offline

öffnen to open

die Öffnung (-en) opening

oft often (1)

öfters now and then

oh oh; **oh je!** oh, dear!

ohne (+ acc.) without (3)

das Ohr (-en) ear (8)

der Ökogarten (") organic garden

das Oktett (-e) octet

(der) Oktober October (3)

die Olive (-n) olive (6)

die Olympischen Spiele (pl.) Olympic Games

die Oma (-s) (coll.) grandma (3)

die Omi (-s) (coll.) granny

der Onkel (-) uncle (3)

online online

der Opa (-s) (coll.) grandpa (3)

die Oper (-n) opera (4); **in die Oper gehen** to
go to the opera (4)

die Optik optics

optimal optimal(ly)

orange (adj.) orange (color) (5)

die Orange (-n) orange

das Orchester (-) orchester

die Ordinalzahl (-en) ordinal number

ordnen to arrange

die Ordnung order

die Organisation (-en) organization

organisch organic(ally)

organisieren to organize

der Orientteppich (-e) oriental rug

original original(ly)

das Original (-e) original

originell original, in an original fashion;
inventive(ly), unique(ly)

der Ort (-e) place; locality; location

die Ortschaft (-en) town, village

Ost (without article) east

das Ostblockland ("er) country in the
Eastern Bloc

der Osten east; **im Osten** in the east

der Osterhase (-n masc.**) (-n)** Easter bunny

(das) Ostern Easter (3)

(das) Österreich Austria (E)

österreichisch (adj.) Austrian

die Ostsee Baltic Sea

das Outsourcing outsourcing

das Ozonloch ("er) hole in the ozone layer

die Ozonschicht (-en) ozone layer

P

das Paar (-e) pair

ein paar a few, a couple of; **ein paar Mal** a
couple of times

packen to pack (10)

die Packung (-en) package; box

die Pädagogik pedagogy

das Paket (-e) package, packet

**der Palästinenser (-) / die Palästinenserin
(-nen)** Palestinian (person)

die Panne (-n) breakdown; flat tire

der Papa (-s) dad, daddy

das Papier (-e) paper (12)

der Papierkorb ("e) wastepaper basket (2)

die Papierlaterne (-n) paper lantern

die Paprika bell pepper (6)

das Paradies (-e) paradise

das Paragliding paragliding

das Parfüm (-s) perfume

die Parfümerie (-n) perfumery; perfume store

der Park (-s) park

parken to park; **Hier darf man nicht parken.** You
may not park here. (4)

das Parkhaus ("er) parking structure

der Parkplatz ("e) parking space; parking lot (9)

das Parkverbot: hier ist Parkverbot no parking
here

das Parlament (-e) parliament

parlamentarisch parliamentary

die Partei (-en) (political) party

das Partizip (-ien) participle; **das Partizip Perfekt**
past participle; **das Partizip Präsens** present
participle

der Partner (-) / die Partnerin (-nen) partner

die Party (-s) party (3); **eine Party geben** to
throw a party, have a party

der Pass ("e) passport; pass

der Passant (-en masc.**) (-en) / die Passantin
(-nen)** passerby (9)

passen (+ *dat.*) to match; to fit (5); **passen zu** (+ *dat.*) to be suitable for

passend fitting, suitable

das Passfoto (-s) passport photo

passieren, ist passiert to happen (7)

das Passiv (-e) passive voice (of a verb)

das Passivhaus (¨er) passive (low-energy) house

die Pasta pasta

die Pastille (-n) pastille

der Patient (-en *masc.*) **(-en) / die Patientin (-nen)** patient

die Pauke (-n) kettledrum

das Pauschalangebot (-e) package tour offer

die Pause (-n) pause, break

pausenlos continuous(ly), without interruption

der Pazifik Pacific Ocean

das Pech pitch; bad luck; **So ein Pech!** What a shame! What bad luck! (8)

der Pelz (-e) fur

pendeln, ist gependelt to commute

der Pendler (-) / die Pendlerin (-nen) commuter

penibel over-meticulous(ly)

(das) Pennsylvanien Pennsylvania

die Pension (-en) small family-run hotel; bed and breakfast (9)

per via; by way of; **per Autostop reisen** to hitchhike (10)

perfekt perfect

das Perfekt present perfect tense; **das Partizip Perfekt** past participle

die Person (-en) person; **pro Person** per person (10)

das Personal personnel, staff

der Personalausweis (-e) (personal) ID card (10)

das Personalpronomen (-) personal pronoun

der Personenkraftwagen (Pkw) (-) automobile, car

persönlich personal(ly)

pessimistisch pessimistic(ally)

das Pestizid (-e) pesticide

der Pfad (-e) path; **der Trimm-Pfad (-e)** parcourse, jogging path

die Pfanne (-n) pan (6)

der Pfannkuchen (-) pancake

der Pfeffer pepper (5)

der Pfennig (-e) penny (*former German monetary unit*)

das Pferd (-e) horse

das Pferderennen (-) horse race

das Pfifferling chanterelle mushroom

pfiffig clever(ly); stylish(ly)

der Pfirsich (-e) peach

die Pflanze (-n) plant

pflanzen to plant

pflanzlich (*adj.*) plant, vegetable

pflegen to look after, care for; maintain

die Pflicht (-en) duty

der Pförtner (-) / die Pförtnerin (-nen) porter, doorkeeper

das Pfund (-e) pound; 500 grams

das Phantom (-e) phantom

philadelphisch of / from Philadelphia

die Philharmonie (-n) philharmonic (orchestra)

die Philosophie philosophy

die Physik physics

physikalisch relating to physics

der Physiker (-) / die Physikerin (-nen) physicist

das Picknick (-s) picnic

der Pilot (-en *masc.*) **(-en) / die Pilotin (-nen)** pilot

das Pils (-) Pilsner beer

(das) Pilsen Plzeň (*town in the Czech Republic*)

das Pilsener (-) Pilsner beer (6)

der Pilz (-e) mushroom

die Pipeline (-s) pipeline

die Pistole (-n) pistol, revolver

die Pizza (-s) pizza

die Pizzeria (-s) pizzeria

der Pkw = Personenkraftwagen

das Plakat (-e) poster, placard

der Plan (¨e) plan (4)

planen to plan (3)

der Planet (-en *masc.*) **(-en)** planet

das Plasmamonitor (-en) plasma screen

das Plastik plastic

der Plastikbeutel (-) plastic bag

die Plastiktüte (-n) plastic bag (14)

die Plattform (-en) platform

der Platz (¨e) place; seat (6); room, space; plaza, square; **Platz nehmen** to take a seat

die Platzkarte (-n) place card, seat reservation card (10)

plaudern to chat

pleite (*coll.*) broke, out of money (12)

das Plenum: im Plenum all together

plötzlich sudden(ly); unexpected(ly)

der Plural (-e) plural

plus plus

das Podcast (-s) podcast

die Poesie poetry

(das) Polen Poland (E)

die Politik politics (13)

der Politiker (-) / die Politikerin (-nen) politician (14)

politisch political(ly)

die Politologie political science

die Polizei police; police station (9)

der Polizist (-en *masc.*) **(-en) / die Polizistin (-nen)** police officer

das Polohemd (-en) polo shirt

der Polyester polyester

die Pommes (frites) (*pl.*) French fries (6)

die Popmusik pop music

populär popular(ly)

der Porree (-s) leek

der Porsche (-) Porsche (*automobile*)

die Portion (-en) portion; helping, serving

das Porträt (-s) portrait

(das) Portugal Portugal

(das) Portugiesisch Portuguese (language)

das Porzellan porcelain, china

die Posaune (-n) trombone

die Position (-en) position

positiv positive(ly)

der Possessivartikel (-) possessive adjective

die Post mail; postal system; (*pl.* **Postämter**) post office (9)

das Postamt (¨er) post office (9)

das Poster (-) poster (2)

die Postleitzahl (-en) postal code (E)

potentiell potential(ly)

das Präfix (-e) prefix

(das) Prag Prague

prägen to impress; to shape

das Praktikum (Praktika) internship (1); **ein Praktikum machen** to do an internship (1)

praktisch practical(ly) (1)

prall full(y); intense(ly)

die Präposition (-en) preposition

präsentieren to present

die Präsentation (-en) presentation

der Präsident (-en *masc.*) **(-en) / die Präsidentin (-nen)** president

präzis precise(ly)

der Preis (-e) price, cost (9); prize; **im Preis enthalten** included in the price (9)

preiswert inexpensive(ly), bargain (2); **recht preiswert** quite inexpensive, reasonable (2)

die Presse press (*newspapers, etc.*)

pressen to press, squeeze

das Prestige prestige

der Priester (-) / die Priesterin (-nen) priest

prima great, super (E)

der Prinz (-en *masc.*) **(-en) / die Prinzessin (-nen)** prince/princess

privat private(ly)

pro per; **pro Person** per person (10); **pro Woche** per week (4)

das Problem (-e) problem (2)

problemlos without any problem

das Produkt (-e) product

die Produktion (-en) production

produzieren to produce

professionell professional(ly)

der Professor (-en) / die Professorin (-nen) professor (1)

der Profi (-s) (*coll.*) pro(fessional)

das Profil (-e) profile

das Programm (-e) program; TV station, channel (13); **im ersten Programm** on channel 1

programmieren to program

progressiv progressive(ly)

das Projekt (-e) project

promenieren to promenade

prominent prominent(ly)

die Prominenz prominent people, socialites

das Pronomen (-) pronoun

der Prospekt (-e) brochure

der Protest (-e) protest

das Protokoll (-e) transcript, minutes; **Protokoll führen** to make a transcript, take the minutes

provozieren to provoke

das Prozent (-e) percent

der Prozess (-e) process; legal case

die Prüfung (-en) test, exam

der Psychologe (-n *masc.***) (-n) / die Psychologin (-nen)** psychologist (11)

die Psychologie psychology

der Psychothriller (-) psycho-thriller (*movie, etc.*)

der Pudding (-e) pudding

pudern to powder

der Pullover (-) pullover sweater (5)

der Pump: auf Pump (*coll.*) on credit

der Punkt (-e) point

pünktlich punctual(ly), on time

punkto: in punkto (+ *gen.*) regarding

die Pute (-n) turkey (hen)

das Putenmedaillon (-s) turkey medallion, small slice of turkey

der Putenspieß (-e) turkey kebab, turkey on a skewer

putzen to polish, clean; **sich** (*dat.*) **die Zähne putzen** to brush one's teeth (8)

Q

der/das Quadratmeter (-) square meter

der Quäker (-) / die Quäkerin (-nen) Quaker

die Qualifikation (-en) qualification

qualifizieren to qualify

die Qualität (-en) quality

der Quark curd cheese (*German-style yogurt cheese*)

das Quartal (-e) (academic) quarter

der Quatsch (*coll.*) nonsense; **So ein Quatsch!** Nonsense!

die Quelle (-n) source

die Quittung (-en) receipt

das Quiz (-) quiz

der Quizmaster (-) quizmaster, host of a quiz show

R

der Rabatt (-e) discount

das Rad (¨er) wheel; bicycle; **Rad fahren (fährt Rad), fuhr Rad, ist Rad gefahren** to bicycle, ride a bike (7)

der Radfahrer (-) / die Radfahrerin (-nen) bicyclist

radikal radical(ly)

das Radio (-s) radio (2); **im Radio** on the radio

der Radius (Radien) radius

das Rafting rafting

der Rahmen (-) frame

ran = heran: rangehen (geht ran), ging ran, ist rangegangen (*coll.*) to go up, get closer

der Rand (¨er) edge, border

rangieren to be placed

die Rapmusik rap music

rappelvoll (*coll.*) crazily full

der Rappen (-) (Swiss) centime

rar rare, scarce

die Rasiercreme (-s) shaving cream (5)

sich rasieren to shave (8)

der Rassismus racism (14)

rassistisch (*adj.*) racist

der Raster (-) grid

der Rat advice (8); **Rat geben** to give advice

raten (rät), riet, geraten to guess; to advise

das Ratespiel (-e) guessing game

das Rathaus (¨er) city hall (9)

(das) Rätoromanisch Rhaeto-Romance (language)

der Ratschlag (¨e) piece of advice

das Rätsel (-) riddle; puzzle

der Rattenfänger (-) ratcatcher; **der Rattenfänger von Hameln** the Pied Piper of Hameln

der Räuber (-) / die Räuberin (-nen) robber

rauchen to smoke (8)

rauf = herauf: raufstolpern (stolpert rauf), ist raufgestolpert (*coll.*) to stumble up

der Raum (¨e) room; space

raus = heraus (*adv.*) out

rausgehen (geht raus), ging raus, ist rausgegangen (*coll.*) to go out

reagieren to react

die Reaktion (-en) reaction

die Realität (-en) reality

die Realoberschule (-n) secondary school with a curriculum emphasizing mathematics and science

die Realschule (-n) secondary school with a commercially oriented curriculum

das Rebland (¨er) wine country

recherchieren to research, investigate

die Rechnung (-en) bill (6)

recht quite, rather (2); **recht preiswert** quite inexpensive, reasonable (2)

recht- right, right-hand; **auf der rechten Seite** on the right-hand side

das Recht (-e) right; law

recht haben (hat recht) to be correct (2)

rechts (on the) right (9); **nach rechts** to the right (9)

der Rechtsanwalt (¨e) / die Rechtsanwältin (-nen) attorney, lawyer (11)

der Rechtsextremismus right-wing extremism (14)

rechtzeitig in time, on time

recyceln to recycle

das Recycling recycling

der Redakteur (-e) / die Redakteurin (-nen) chief editor

die Redaktion (-en) editorial staff

die Rede (-n) speech; **indirekte Rede** indirect discourse

das Redemittel (-) speaking resources

reden to talk (about)

die Redensart (-en) expression, saying

reduzieren to reduce

das Referat (-e) paper, report; **ein Referat halten (hält), hielt, gehalten** to give a paper/report

der Referent (-en *masc.***) (-en) / die Referentin (-nen)** speaker; advisor, expert

reflexiv reflexive(ly)

die Reformation Reformation

das Regal (-e) shelf (2)

die Regel (-n) rule

regelmäßig regular(ly) (8)

regeln to regulate, control

der Regen rain (7)

der Regenschauer (-) rain shower (7)

der Regenschirm (-e) umbrella (7)

die Regierung (-en) government (14); administration

die Region (-en) region

regional regional(ly)

der Regisseur (-e) / die Regisseurin (-nen) (film) director

registrieren to register

regnen to rain (7); **Es regnet.** It's raining. (7)

regnerisch rainy (7)

der Reibekuchen (-) pancake made of grated potatoes

reich rich(ly)

reichhaltig extensive; abundant

das Reichstagsgebäude German Parliament Building

der Reifen (-) tire

die Reihenfolge (-n) sequence, order

reimen to rhyme

rein = herein (*adv.*) in

der Reis rice (6)

die Reise (-n) trip, journey (10)

die Reiseapotheke (-n) portable first-aid kit

das Reisebüro (-s) travel agency (10)

der Reiseführer (-) travel guide (book) (10)

reisen, ist gereist to travel (1); **per Autostop reisen** to hitchhike (10)

das Reisen traveling

der Reisepass (¨e) passport (9)

der Reiseprospekt (-e) travel brochure (10)

der Reisescheck (-s) traveler's check (10)

der Reisetermin (-e) date of travel

reiten, ritt, ist geritten to ride (on horseback) (7)

die Reitführung riding instruction

das Reitprogramm (-e) riding program

die Reitschule (-n) riding school

die Rekordschulden (*pl.*) record deficit

relativ relative(ly)

relevant relevant

die Religion (-en) religion

religiös religious(ly)

die Renaissance Renaissance (period)

die Rendite (-n) yield on an investment

renommiert renowned

die Renovierung (-en) renovation

die Rentenversicherung pension insurance

der Rentner (-) / die Rentnerin (-nen) retiree

die Reparatur (-en) repair (12)

die Reparaturwerkstatt (¨e) repair shop

reparieren to repair (9)

der Report (-e) report

die Reportage (-n) report

der Reporter (-) / die Reporterin (-nen) reporter

repräsentieren to represent

die Reproduktion (-en) reproduction

die Republik (-en) republic

das Requisit (-en) prop

reservieren to book, reserve (7)

die Reservierung (-en) reservation

der Rest (-e) remainder

das Restaurant (-s) restaurant (6)

das Resultat (-e) result

retten to save, rescue

die Rettungsleitstelle (-n) control room for rescue operations

revidieren to revise

das Revier (-e) province, region; preserve

die Revolution (-en) revolution

der Revolutionär (-e) / die Revolutionärin (-nen) revolutionary

das Revue-Musical (-s) musical revue

das Rezept (-e) recipe; prescription

die Rezeption reception desk (9)

der Rhein Rhine (River)

rheinisch Rhenish, of the Rhine River

(die) Rheinland-Pfalz Rhineland-Palatinate (German state)

der Rhythmus (Rhythmen) rhythm

sich richten auf (+ acc.) to be directed at

die Richtgeschwindigkeit (-en) recommended maximum speed

richtig correct(ly), right(ly)

die Richtigkeit correctness, accuracy

die Richtung (-en) direction

der Riese (-n masc.) (-n) giant

der Riester-Vertrag ("-e) type of old-age pension

das Riff (-e) reef

das Rind (-er) cow, bull, head of cattle

das Rinderfilet (-s) beef filet

die Rinderroulade (-n) beef roulade

das Rindfleisch beef (5)

der Ring (-e) ring

rings: rings um (+ acc.) all around

ringsherum all around

ringsum all around

das Ritual (-e) ritual

die Robbe (-n) seal

der Rock ("-e) skirt (5)

der Rock / die Rockmusik rock music

das Rodeo (-s) rodeo

die Rohstoffknappheit shortage of raw materials

die Rolle (-n) role

das Rollenspiel (-e) role-play

das Rollerbladen rollerblading

der Roman (-e) novel

die Romanistik (study of) Romance languages and literatures

die Romantik romanticism

romantisch romantic(ally) (1)

die Römerzeit Roman era

römisch (adj.) Roman

die Röntgenstrahlen (pl.) X-rays

die Rösti (Swiss) thinly sliced fried potatoes

rot red (5); rote Grütze dessert made of red berries

die Routine (-n) routine

die Rubrik (-en) category, section; column

der Rücken (-) back (8)

die Rückenschmerzen (pl.) backache

der Rucksack ("-e) backpack (5)

rudern, ist gerudert to row

rufen, rief, gerufen to call (out), shout

die Ruhe quiet; calm(ness); rest

der Ruhetag (-e) day that a business is closed (6)

ruhig quiet(ly) (1); calm(ly)

das Rührei (-er) scrambled egg

das Ruhrgebiet Ruhr (urban area in western Germany)

der Rum (-s) rum

(das) Rumänien Romania

rund round; around; rund um (+ acc.) all around

die Rundfahrt (-en) tour

der Rundfunk radio; broadcasting

die Rundfunkanstalt (-en) broadcasting corporation; radio station

rundum all around

runterladen (coll.) = herunterladen

(das) Russland Russia

rustikal rustic

S

die Sache (-n) thing, object; matter

(das) Sachsen Saxony (German state)

sächsisch (adj.) Saxon

die Safari (-s) safari

der Saft ("-e) juice (5)

die Sage (-n) legend

sagen to say, tell (1); sag mal tell me (1); Wie sagt man … auf Deutsch? How do you say . . . in German? (E)

sagenhaft legendary

die Sahara Sahara (Desert)

die Sahne cream; whipped cream (6)

das Sakko (-s) man's jacket, sport coat (5)

der Salat (-e) salad; lettuce (6)

das Salatbuquette (-s) side salad

das Salz salt (5)

salzen, salzte, gesalzen to salt

sammeln to collect (7); to gather sich sammeln to gather, come together

die Sammelstelle (-n) recycling center (14)

der Sammler (-) / die Sammlerin (-nen) collector

die Sammlung (-en) collection

(der) Samstag Saturday (3)

samstags Saturdays, on Saturday(s) (4)

(das) San Franzisko San Francisco

der Sand (-e) sand

die Sandale (-n) sandal

der Sänger (-) / die Sängerin (-nen) singer

der Satelliten-Empfänger (-) satellite receiver (13)

das Satellitenprogramm (-e) satellite TV program(ming)

der Satz ("-e) sentence

die Satzklammer (-n) sentence frame

der Satzteil (-e) part of a sentence, clause

sauber clean(ly) (14)

säuberlich neat(ly)

die Sauce = die Soße

sauer sour; saurer Regen acid rain

das Sauerkraut sauerkraut, pickled cabbage (6)

die Sauna (-s) sauna

säuseln to murmur

die S-Bahn (-en) (= Schnellbahn) suburban railway

(das) Schach chess; Schach spielen to play chess (7)

schade too bad

schaden to harm

der Schaden ("-) damage, injury

der Schadstoff (-e) harmful substance

schaffen, schuf, geschaffen to create (14)

schaffen, schaffte, geschafft to manage to do; sich schaffen to busy oneself

der Schafskäse sheep's milk cheese

der Schal (-s) scarf (5)

der Schalter (-) counter; window; switch

scharf sharp; spicy

der Schatz ("-e) treasure; mein Schatz my darling

das Schaubild (-er) diagram

schauen (auf + acc.) to look (at/to); Fernsehen schauen to watch TV; Schau mal! Look!

der Schauer (-) (rain) shower

der Schauplatz ("-e) scene

der Schauspieler (-) / die Schauspielerin (-nen) actor/actress (11)

der Scheck (-s) check

scheiden, schied, geschieden to separate

der Schein (-e) banknote, bill, piece of paper money

scheinen, schien, geschienen to shine; to seem, appear (13); Die Sonne scheint. The sun is shining. (7)

scheitern, ist gescheitert to fail

schenken to give (as a gift) (5)

schick stylish(ly) (5)

schicken to send (1); SMS schicken to send text messages

schießen, schoss, geschossen to shoot

das Schiff (-e) ship (10)

der Schiffer (-) / die Schifferin (-nen) boatman/boatwoman

das Schild (-er) sign, road sign

schimpfen to scold; to grumble, curse

der Schinken (-) ham (5)

das Schlachtfeld (-er) battlefield

der Schlaf sleep

schlafen (schläft), schlief, geschlafen to sleep (2)

der Schlafsack ("-e) sleeping bag

das Schlafzimmer (-) bedroom (2)

der Schlag ("-e) blow, punch, slap

die Schlagcreme whipped cream

schlagen (schlägt), schlug, geschlagen to beat, strike

schlagkräftig powerful(ly)

die Schlagzeile (-n) headline (13)

das Schlagzeug (-e) (set of) drums; percussion instruments

schlank slender

der **Service** service; service department

servieren to serve

die **Serviette (-n)** napkin (6)

der **Sessel (-)** armchair (2)

setzen to set; to put (*in a sitting position*) (6); **sich setzen** to sit down (8)

die **Seuche (-n)** epidemic

der **Sex** sex

das **Shampoo (-s)** shampoo

shoppen to shop

die **Shorts** (*pl.*) shorts

die **Show (-s)** show

der **Shrimp (-s)** shrimp

sich oneself, yourself (*form.*), himself, herself, itself, themselves

sicher safe(ly) (10); sure(ly), certain(ly) (5)

die **Sicherheit** security, safety

sichern to make secure

Sie you (*form. sg./pl.*) (1, 3)

sie she; it; they (1); her; it; them (*acc.*) (3)

sieben seven (E)

sieb(en)te seventh (3)

siebzehn seventeen (E)

siebzig seventy (E)

siedeln to settle

die **Siedlung (-en)** settlement

(das) **Silvester** New Year's Eve (3)

sind (we/they/you [*form.*]) are

singen, sang, gesungen to sing

der **Sinn (-e)** sense; mind

sinnvoll sensible, sensibly

die **Sitte (-n)** custom, tradition

die **Situation (-en)** situation

der **Sitz (-e)** seat

sitzen, saß, gesessen to sit, be (sitting) (6)

der **Sitznachbar (-n** *masc.*) **(-n) /** die **Sitznachbarin (-nen)** person seated nearby

(das) **Sizilien** Sicily

der **Skandal (-e)** scandal

skandalös scandalous(ly)

der **Skater (-) /** die **Skaterin (-nen)** skater

das **Skeetschießen** skeet shooting

skeptisch skeptical(ly)

Ski fahren (fährt), fuhr, ist gefahren to ski

der **Skifahrer (-) /** die **Skifahrerin (-nen)** skier

das **Skilaufen** skiing

die **Skizze (-n)** sketch

die **Sklaverei** slavery

die **Skulptur (-en)** sculpture

die **Slowakei** Slovakia (E)

(das) **Slowenien** Slovenia (E)

SMS schicken to send text messages

so so (2); like that; **so ein(e)** such a; **So ein Pech!** What a shame! What bad luck! (8); **So ein Unsinn!** Nonsense! (14); **(so) gegen fünf Uhr** around five o'clock (6); **so lala** (*coll.*) OK, so-so (E); **so was** something like that; **so weit** so far; **so ... wie** as . . . as (7)

sobald (*subord. conj.*) as soon as

die **Socke (-n)** sock (5)

das **Sofa (-s)** sofa (2)

sofort immediately (9)

die **Software (-s)** (piece of) software

sogar even (8)

sogenannt so-called

der **Sohn ("e)** son (3)

solange (*subord. conj.*) as long as

die **Solaranlage (-n)** solar energy system

die **Solarenergie** solar energy

die **Solarzelle (-n)** solar cell

solch such

der **Soldat (-en** *masc.*) **(-en) /** die **Soldatin (-nen)** soldier

die **Solidarität** solidarity

der **Solist (-en** *masc.*) **(-en) /** die **Solistin (-nen)** soloist

sollen (soll), sollte, gesollt to be supposed to; shall; ought to; should (4); to be said to be

somit with that, thus

der **Sommer (-)** summer (7)

sommerlich (*adj, adv.*) summer(y)

die **Sommerzeit (-en)** daylight savings time

der **Sonderabfall ("e)** toxic waste

die **Sonderaktion (-en)** special (sales) offer

das **Sonderangebot (-e)** special offer

sonderbar strange(ly)

sondern (*coord. conj.*) but, rather (7)

(der) **Sonnabend** Saturday (3)

sonnabends Saturdays, on Saturday(s) (4)

die **Sonne (-n)** sun (7); **Die Sonne scheint.** The sun is shining. (7)

die **Sonnenbrille (-n)** (pair of) sunglasses

der **Sonnenschein** sunshine (7)

das **Sonnenschutzmittel (-)** suntan lotion, sunscreen (10)

sonnig sunny (7)

(der) **Sonntag** Sunday (3)

sonntags Sundays, on Sunday(s) (4)

sonst otherwise; else; other than that

Sonstiges other items, miscellaneous

die **Sorge (-n)** worry; **sich Sorgen machen um** (+ *acc.*) to worry about (14)

sorgen für (+ *acc.*) to take care of, look after

sorgfältig careful(ly)

die **Sorte (-n)** kind, sort

sortieren to sort

die **Soße (-n)** sauce; gravy

sowie as well as

sowieso anyway

sozial social(ly)

der **Sozialarbeiter (-) /** die **Sozialarbeiterin (-nen)** social worker

die **Sozialbauwohnung (-en)** low-income housing

der **Sozialismus** socialism

der **Soziologe (-n** *masc.*) **(-n) /** die **Soziologin (-nen)** sociologist

die **Soziologie** sociology

die **Spalte (-n)** (printed) column; slice

das **Spanferkel (-)** roasted suckling pig

(das) **Spanien** Spain

spanisch (*adj.*) Spanish

(das) **Spanisch** Spanish (language)

spannend exciting(ly), suspenseful(ly) (4)

das **Sparbuch ("er)** (savings) passbook

sparen to save, conserve (12)

die **Sparkasse (-n)** savings bank

das **Sparkonto (Sparkonten)** savings account (12)

der **Sparpreis (-e)** discount price

sparsam thrifty, economical(ly) (12)

das **Sparschwein (-e)** piggy bank

das **Sparverhalten** savings behavior

der **Spaß ("e)** fun (1); **Das macht Spaß.** That's fun. (1); **Spaß haben** to have fun; **Spaßmachen** to be fun; **Viel Spaß!** Have fun! (1)

spät late (4); **Wie spät ist es?** What time is it? (4)

spätestens at the latest (12)

die **Spätzle, Spätzli** (*pl.*) a kind of noodles

spazieren gehen (geht spazieren), ging spazieren, ist spazieren gegangen to go for a walk (4)

der **Spaziergang ("e)** walk, stroll

der **Speck** bacon (6)

die **Speckbohnen** (*pl.*) beans with bacon

speichern to store, save (13)

die **Speise (-n)** food; dish (of prepared food) (6)

die **Speisekarte (-n)** menu (6)

spektakulär spectacular(ly)

spekulieren to speculate

spenden to donate, contribute

der **Spender (-) /** die **Spenderin (-nen)** donor, contributor

das **Spezial (-s)** special

die **Spezialität (-en)** specialty

speziell special(ly)

die **Spezies (-)** species

spezifisch specific(ally)

der **Spiegel (-)** mirror

das **Spiegelbild (-er)** reflection

das **Spiegelei (-er)** fried egg (sunny-side up) (6)

das **Spiel (-e)** game; play

spielen to play (1)

spielend (*adv.*) without effort, easily

der **Spieler (-) /** die **Spielerin (-nen)** player; **der CD-Spieler (-)** CD player

der **Spielfilm (-e)** feature film, movie (13)

die **Spielkarte (-n)** playing card (7)

der **Spielplatz ("e)** playground

das **Spielzeug (-e)** toy

die **Spinne (-n)** spider

spitze (*coll.*) marvelous(ly)

die **Spitze (-n)** tip; (pointed) top

spontan spontaneous(ly)

der **Sport** (*pl.* **Sportarten**) sports, sport (7); **Sport treiben, trieb, getrieben** to play sports (7)

die **Sportanlage (-n)** sports field

die **Sporthalle (-n)** gymnasium, sports arena (7)

das **Sportkabriolett (-s)** sports convertible

sportlich athletic(ally) (1); **sportlich aktiv** active in sports (10)

der **Sportplatz ("e)** athletic field (7)

schlapp weak, worn out (8)

schlau clever(ly)

schlecht bad(ly), poor(ly) (E); **Mir ist schlecht.** I feel bad; I'm sick to my stomach. (8)

der Schlegel (-) mallet

der Schlemmer (-) / die Schlemmerin (-nen) gourmet

schließen, schloss, geschlossen to close; **schließen (aus + *dat.*)** to conclude (from)

das Schließfach ("er) locker

schließlich finally, in the end

die Schließung (-en) closing

schlimm bad

der Schlips (-e) necktie (5)

der Schlittschuh (-e) ice skate; **Schlittschuh laufen (läuft), lief, ist gelaufen** to ice-skate (7)

das Schloss ("er) castle, palace (9)

der Schluckauf hiccup(s)

schlucken to swallow (8)

der Schluss ("e) end, conclusion

der Schlüssel (-) key (9)

schmecken (+ *dat.*) to taste (good) (5); **schmecken nach (+ *dat.*)** to taste of

schmeißen, schmiss, geschmissen to hurl, fling

schmelzen (schmilzt), schmolz, geschmolzen to melt

der Schmerz (-en) pain (8)

der Schmuck jewelry

schmutzig dirty (12)

das Schnäppchen (-) (*coll.*) bargain

die Schnecke (-n) snail

der Schnee snow (7)

schneiden, schnitt, geschnitten to cut

schneien to snow (7); **Es schneit.** It's snowing. (7)

schnell fast, quick(ly) (10); **Mach schnell!** (*inform.*)/ **Machen Sie schnell!** (*form.*) Hurry up!

der Schnittkäse hard cheese

der Schnittlauch chives

das Schnitzel (-) cutlet; **das Wiener Schnitzel** breaded veal cutlet

der Schnupfen nasal congestion; head cold (8)

der Schnupperkurs (-e) introductory course

der Schokoeisbecher (-) dish of chocolate ice cream

die Schokolade (-n) chocolate

schon already (2); yet

schön nice(ly), beautiful(ly) (2); **bitte schön** please; you're welcome; **danke schön** thank you very much (E)

schonen to protect

der Schornsteinfeger (-) / die Schornsteinfegerin (-nen) chimney sweep

der Schrank ("e) cupboard; closet; wardrobe

schrecklich horrible, horribly

schreiben, schrieb, geschrieben to write (2); **Wie schreibt man ... ?** How do you write . . . ? (E)

der Schreibtisch (-e) desk (2)

die Schreibwaren (*pl.*) stationery goods

die Schrift (-en) script; text

schriftlich written, in writing

der Schriftsteller (-) / die Schriftstellerin (-nen) writer, author

der Schritt (-e) step

die Schublade (-n) drawer

der Schuh (-e) shoe (5)

der Schulabgänger (-) / die Schulabgängerin (-nen) school graduate

der Schulabschluss ("e) graduation, completion of school

die Schulden (*pl.*) debts; **Schulden machen** to go into debt

die Schule (-n) school; **in die Schule gehen, ging, ist gegangen** to go to school; **zur Schule gehen, ging, ist gegangen** to go to school

der Schüler (-) / die Schülerin (-nen) pupil, student in primary or secondary school

die Schulter (-n) shoulder (8)

die Schupfnudeln (*pl.*) potato noodles

der Schuss ("e) shot; **eine (Berliner) Weiße mit Schuss** *light, fizzy beer served with raspberry syrup*

schütteln to shake

der Schütze (-n *masc.*) (-n) /die Schützin (-nen) marksman/markswoman

schützen to protect (14)

(das) Schwaben Swabia (*region in southwestern Germany*)

schwäbisch (*adj.*) Swabian

schwach weak(ly); gentle, gently

der Schwager (") / die Schwägerin (-nen) brother-in-law (3) / sister-in-law (3)

der Schwank ("e) comic tale, farce

der Schwarm ("e) swarm; heartthrob, idol

schwarz black (5); **das Schwarze Brett** bulletin board

das Schwarzbrot dark brown rye bread

schwarzhaarig dark-haired

der Schwarzwald Black Forest

(das) Schweden Sweden

das Schwein (-e) pig

der Schweinebraten (-) pork roast (6)

das Schweinefleisch pork (5)

das Schweinemedaillon (-s) pork medallion, small slice of pork

die Schweinshaxe (-n) pork knuckle

das Schweinskotelett (-s) pork cutlet

die Schweiz Switzerland (E); **aus der Schweiz** from Switzerland; **in die Schweiz** to Switzerland

Schweizer (*adj.*) of/from Switzerland; **der Schweizer Franken (-)** Swiss franc

der Schweizer (-) / die Schweizerin (-nen) Swiss person

schwer heavy, heavily; difficult, with difficulty

die Schwester (-n) sister (3)

die Schwiegermutter (") mother-in-law

der Schwiegervater (") father-in-law

schwierig difficult, with difficulty

die Schwierigkeit (-en) difficulty

das Schwimmbad ("er) swimming pool (7)

schwimmen, schwamm, ist geschwommen to swim (2)

die Schwimmflosse (-n) flipper

sich schwingen, schwang, geschwungen to swing oneself, jump

schwitzen to sweat

schwül muggy, humid (7)

der Schwung: voll Schwung full of zest

sechs six (E)

sechsmal six times

sechste sixth (3)

sechzehn sixteen (E)

sechzig sixty (E)

der See (-n) lake (7)

die See (-n) sea, ocean

das Seemannspfännchen (-) *fried seafood dish*

das Segelboot (-e) sailboat

die Segelflotte (-n) fleet of sailboats

der Segelkurs (-e) sailing course (instruction)

segeln to sail (7)

sehen (sieht), sah, gesehen to see (2)

sehenswert worth seeing

die Sehenswürdigkeit (-en) (tourist) attraction

sehr very (1); very much; **bitte sehr** you're welcome; **danke sehr** thanks a lot (1); **sehr gut** very well; fine; good (E)

seid (you [*inform. pl.*]) are

die Seidenbluse (-n) silk blouse

die Seife (-n) soap

sein (ist), war, gewesen to be (1)

sein his, its (3)

seit (+ *dat.*) since; (+ *time*) for (5, 6); (*subord. conj.*) since; **seit zwei Jahren** for two years (6)

die Seite (-n) side; page

der Sekretär (-e) / die Sekretärin (-nen) secretary

die Sekte (-n) sect

die Sekunde (-n) second (4)

selb- (*adj.*) same

selber self (my-, your-, him-, her-, *etc.*)

selbst self (my-, your-, him-, her-, *etc.*)

selbstbewusst self-assured (11)

das Selbstbewusstsein self-confidence

selbstständig independent(ly) (11)

selbstversorgend self-sufficient(ly)

die Selbstversorgung self-sufficiency

selbstverständlich natural(ly), of course (5)

die Selbstverteidigung self-defense

selten rare(ly) (2), seldom

seltsam strange(ly)

das Semester (-) semester (1)

das Seminar (-e) seminar

die Seminararbeit (-en) seminar paper

senden, sandte, gesandt to send

senden, sendete, gesendet to broadcast

der Sender (-) broadcaster

die Sendung (-en) broadcast, TV or radio program (13)

der Senf mustard (6)

die Sensation (-en) sensation

sensationell sensational(ly)

sensibel sensitive(ly)

(der) September September (3)

die Serie (-n) series

can, to be able to können (kann), konnte, gekonnt (4)

cap die Mütze (-n) (5)

car das Auto (-s) (2); **der** Wagen (-) (7)

card die Karte (-n) (7); **credit card** die Kreditkarte (-n) (9); **ID card** der Personalausweis (-e) (10); **to play cards** Karten spielen (1); **playing card** die Spielkarte (-n) (7); **report card** das Zeugnis (-se) (11); **seat reservation card** die Platzkarte (-n) (10)

care: I don't care. Das ist mir egal. (5); **Take care.** Mach's gut. (*inform.*) (E)

to care for mögen (mag), mochte, gemocht (4)

career training die Ausbildung (11)

carpet der Teppich (-e) (2)

carpeting (wall-to-wall) der Teppichboden (¨) (12)

carrot die Karotte (-n) (5)

to carry tragen (trägt), trug, getragen (5)

carry-on luggage das Handgepäck (10)

case: in any case auf jeden Fall (13)

cash das Bargeld (10); **cash register** die Kasse (-n) (5)

cashier die Kasse (-n) (5)

casserole der Auflauf (¨e) (6)

castle das Schloss (¨er) (9)

cat die Katze (-n) (12)

to catch a cold sich erkälten (8)

cauliflower der Blumenkohl (5)

CD player der CD-Spieler (-) (2)

to celebrate feiern (3)

cell phone das Handy (-s) (2)

center die Mitte (9); **center (of town)** das Zentrum (Zentren) (9); **in the center (of the city)** in der Mitte (der Stadt) (9); **recycling center** die Sammelstelle (-n) (14)

centrally located zentral gelegen (2)

cereal das Müsli (-) (5)

chair der Stuhl (¨e) (2)

to challenge herausfordern (fordert heraus) (11)

change: climate change der Klimawandel (14)

to change (*trains*) umsteigen (steigt um), stieg um, ist umgestiegen (10)

channel (*TV*) das Programm (-e) (13)

characteristic die Eigenschaft (-en) (11)

cheap(ly) billig (2)

check der Scheck (-s); **baggage check** die Gepäckaufbewahrung (10); **traveler's check** der Reisescheck (-s) (10)

to check in (*hotel*) sich anmelden (meldet an) (9)

check-out die Kasse (-n) (5)

cheerful lustig (1)

cheese der Käse (5)

chess: to play chess Schach spielen (7)

chest die Brust (¨e) (8)

chicken das Hähnchen (-) (5)

chin das Kinn (-e) (8)

to choose wählen (14); **to choose something** sich (*dat.*) etwas aussuchen (sucht aus) (13)

Christmas das Weihnachten (3); **Christmas Eve** der Heilige Abend (3); **Christmas tree** der Weihnachtsbaum (¨e) (3)

church die Kirche (-n) (9)

cinema das Kino (-s) (4)

citizen der Bürger (-) / die Bürgerin (-nen) (14)

city die Stadt (¨e) (E); **city hall** das Rathaus (¨er) (9); **in the center of the city** in der Mitte der Stadt (9)

to claim behaupten (13)

class: to travel first/second class erster/zweiter Klasse fahren (fährt), fuhr, ist gefahren (10)

clean sauber (14)

to clean up aufräumen (räumt auf) (4)

cleaner: vacuum cleaner der Staubsauger (-) (12)

clear: Everything is clear. Alles klar. (E)

climate change der Klimawandel (14)

clock die Uhr (-en) (2); **alarm clock** der Wecker (-) (2); **It's one o'clock** Es ist eins. / Es ist ein Uhr. (4)

closed geschlossen (6); **day that a business is closed** der Ruhetag (-e) (6)

closet die Garderobe (-n) (12); **clothes closet** der Kleiderschrank (¨e) (2)

clothes dryer der Wäschetrockner (-) (12)

clothing: article of clothing das Kleidungsstück (-e) (5)

cloud die Wolke (-n) (7)

cloudless wolkenlos (7)

cloudy bewölkt (7)

club der Verein (-e) (7); **dance club** die Disco (-s) (4)

clubbing: to go clubbing in die Disco gehen, ging, ist gegangen (4)

coat der Mantel (¨) (5); **sport coat** das Sakko (-s) (5)

code: postal code die Postleitzahl (-en) (E)

coffee der Kaffee; **coffee table** der Couchtisch (-e) (2); **a cup of coffee** eine Tasse Kaffee (4)

cold (*adj.*) kalt (kälter, kältest-) (7)

cold die Erkältung (-en) (8); **head cold** der Schnupfen (8); **to catch a cold** sich erkälten (8)

cold cuts der Aufschnitt (5)

colleague der Mitarbeiter (-) / die Mitarbeiterin (-nen) (11)

to collect sammeln (7)

color die Farbe (-n) (5)

to comb (one's hair) sich kämmen (8)

to come kommen, kam, ist gekommen (1); **to come along** mitkommen (kommt mit), kam mit, ist mitgekommen (4); **to come back** zurückkommen (kommt zurück), kam zurück, ist zurückgekommen (4); **to come by** vorbeikommen (kommt vorbei), kam vorbei, ist vorbeigekommen (4); **that comes to** das macht (5)

comedy die Komödie (-n) (4)

comfortable, comfortably bequem (2)

company die Firma (Firmen) (11)

to compare vergleichen, verglich, verglichen (12)

to complain about sich beschweren über (+ *acc.*) (9)

complete(ly) ganz (12)

completion (*of training or school*) der Abschluss (¨e) (11)

complicated kompliziert (1)

computer der Computer (-) (2); **computer connection** der Computeranschluss (¨e) (2); **computer scientist** der Informatiker (-) / die Informatikerin (-nen) (11); **notebook computer** das Notebook (-s) (13); **to play computer games** Computerspiele spielen (1)

concert das Konzert (-e) (4); **to go to a concert** ins Konzert gehen (4)

congestion: nasal congestion der Schnupfen (8)

to congratulate gratulieren (+ *dat.*) (3)

connection der Anschluss (¨e) (10); **cable TV connection** der Kabelanschluss (¨e) (13); **computer connection** der Computeranschluss (¨e) (2)

conservative konservativ (1)

to consider halten (für + *acc.*) (hält), hielt, gehalten (14)

to consume verbrauchen (14)

contact der Kontakt (-e) (11)

convenient(ly) günstig (9); **to be conveniently located** günstig liegen, lag, gelegen (9)

to converse sich unterhalten (unterhält), unterhielt, unterhalten (13)

to cook kochen (1)

cookie der Keks (-e) (5)

cool kühl (7)

corn der Mais (6)

corner die Ecke (-n) (9); **at the corner** an der Ecke (9)

correct: to be correct recht haben (hat recht) (2)

corruption die Korruption (14)

cost der Preis (-e) (9); **extra costs** die Nebenkosten (*pl.*) (12)

to cost kosten (2)

cough, coughing der Husten (8)

counselor: employment counselor der Berufsberater (-) / die Berufsberaterin (-nen) (11)

country das Land (¨er); **foreign countries** das Ausland (*sg. only*) (11); **home country** das Inland (*sg. only*) (13)

course: of course natürlich (1); selbstverständlich (5)

court: tennis court der Tennisplatz (¨e) (7)

cousin (*female*) die Cousine (-n); die Kusine (-n) (3); (*male*) der Vetter (-n) (3)

co-worker der Mitarbeiter (-) / die Mitarbeiterin (-nen) (11)

cozy, cozily gemütlich (4)

crazy verrückt (8)

cream die Sahne (6); **dish of ice cream** der Eisbecher (-) (6); **ice cream** das Eis (5); **shaving cream** die Rasiercreme (-s) (5); **whipped cream** die Sahne (6)

to create schaffen, schuf, geschaffen (14)

credit card die Kreditkarte (-n) (9)

crime film or book der Krimi (-s) (4)

crossword: to do crossword puzzles Kreuzworträtsel machen (1)

crowded voll (6)

cucumber die Gurke (-n) (5)

cuisine die Küche (6)

cup die Tasse (-n) (4); **a cup of coffee** eine Tasse Kaffee (4)

current aktuell (13); **current events** Aktuelles (13)

customer der Kunde (-n *masc.*) (-n) / die Kundin (-nen) (2); **customer service** die Kunden-betreuung (11)

cutlet das Schnitzel (-) (5)

Czech Republic Tschechien (E)

D

daily täglich (6)

to dance tanzen (1); **He dances well.** Er tanzt gut. (1)

dance club die Disco (4)

danger die Gefahr (-en) (14)

dangerous(ly) gefährlich (10)

dark dunkel (2)

date das Datum (Daten); **date of birth** der Geburtstag (-e) (1); **What is today's/ tomorrow's date?** Welches Datum ist heute/ morgen? (3)

daughter die Tochter (¨) (3)

day der Tag (-e) (2); **day of the week** der Wochentag (-e) (3); **day that a business is closed** der Ruhetag (-e) (6); **every day** jeden Tag (7); **good day** (guten) Tag (E); **in two days** in zwei Tagen (6); **time of day** die Tageszeit (-en) (4); **two days ago** vor zwei Tagen (6)

to deal with (*be about*) handeln von (+ *dat.*) (13); (*treat, take care of*) behandeln (14)

December (der) Dezember (3)

decent gescheit (13); **nothing decent** nichts Gescheites (13)

to decide sich entschließen, entschloss, entschlossen (13)

to decrease vermindern (14)

definitely bestimmt (1)

degree (*school*) der Abschluss (¨e) (11); (*temperature*) der Grad (-e) (7); **35 degrees** 35 Grad (7)

demonstration die Demonstration (-en) (14)

Denmark (das) Dänemark (E)

dentist der Zahnarzt (¨e) / die Zahnärztin (-nen) (11)

to depart abreisen (reist ab), ist abgereist (9); abfahren (fährt ab), fuhr ab, ist abgefahren (10)

department store das Kaufhaus (¨er) (2)

departure die Abfahrt (-en) (10)

depressed deprimiert (8); **You sound so depressed.** Du klingst so deprimiert. (8)

to deserve verdienen (11)

to design entwerfen (entwirft), entwarf, entworfen (11)

desk der Schreibtisch (-e) (2); **reception desk** die Rezeption (9)

dessert die Nachspeise (-n) (6); der Nachtisch (-e) (6)

detective film or book der Krimi (-s) (4)

to develop entwickeln (14)

development die Entwicklung (-en) (11)

device das Gerät (-e) (12)

digital camera die Digitalkamera (-s) (13)

diligent fleißig (1)

dining room das Esszimmer (-) (2)

directions: to ask someone for directions jemanden nach dem Weg fragen (9)

dirty schmutzig (12)

to discuss diskutieren (1)

disco die Disco (-s) (4)

disease die Krankheit (-en) (14)

dish (*of prepared food*) das Gericht (-e) (6); die Speise (-n) (6); **dish of ice cream** der Eisbecher (-) (6); **main dish** das Hauptgericht (-e) (6); **side dish** die Beilage (-n) (6)

dishwasher die Spülmaschine (-n) (12)

to disseminate verbreiten (14)

to dive tauchen (7)

diverse abwechslungsreich (11)

to do machen (1); tun (tut), tat, getan (8); unternehmen (unternimmt), unternahm, unternommen (10); **Are you doing well?** Geht's gut? (E); **to do an internship** ein Praktikum machen (1); **to do body-building** Bodybuilding machen (7); **to do crossword puzzles** Kreuzworträtsel machen (1); **to do research** forschen (13); **to do weight training** Bodybuilding machen (7); **to do without** verzichten auf (+ *acc.*) (12); **What do you do for a living?** Was sind Sie von Beruf? (1)

doctor der Arzt (¨e) / die Ärztin (-nen) (8)

document das Dokument (-e) (13)

documentary (film) der Dokumentarfilm (-e) (13)

documentation die Unterlagen (*pl.*) (11)

dog der Hund (-e) (3); **sick as a dog** (*coll.*) hundsmiserabel (8)

door die Tür (-en) (2)

dormitory das Studentenwohnheim (-e) (2)

double room das Doppelzimmer (-) (9)

doubt: no doubt bestimmt (1)

down: to lie down sich (hin)legen (legt hin) (8); **to sit down** sich (hin)setzen (setzt hin) (8)

downstairs unten; (*directional*) nach unten (12)

downtown die Innenstadt (¨e) (9)

draft vom Fass (6)

drama (*stage*) das Theaterstück (-e) (4)

to draw zeichnen (7)

drawing die Zeichnung (-en) (12)

dress das Kleid (-er) (5)

dressed: to get dressed sich anziehen (zieht an), zog an, angezogen (8)

dresser die Kommode (-n) (2)

drink das Getränk (-e) (5)

to drink trinken, trank, getrunken (2)

to drive fahren (fährt), fuhr, ist gefahren (1)

to drop off abgeben (gibt ab), gab ab, abgegeben (8)

drug die Droge (-n) (14); **drug addiction** die Drogensucht (14)

drugstore (*toiletries and sundries*) die Drogerie (-n) (5)

dryer: clothes dryer der Wäschetrockner (-) (12); **hair dryer** der Föhn (-e) (9)

during während (+ *gen.*) (9)

DVD player der DVD-Spieler (-) (2)

E

each jeder, jede, jedes (5)

ear das Ohr (-en) (8)

early früh (4); **earlier** früher (7)

to earn verdienen (11)

earth die Welt (14)

Easter (das) Ostern (3)

to eat essen (isst), aß, gegessen (1); **to eat breakfast** frühstücken (4)

eating das Essen (1)

eccentric exzentrisch (1)

economy die Wirtschaft (13)

egg das Ei (-er) (5); **fried egg** das Spiegelei (-er) (6)

eight acht (E)

eighteen achtzehn (E)

eighth achte (3)

eighty achtzig (E)

either . . . or entweder ... oder (8)

elbow der Ell(en)bogen (-) (8)

to elect wählen (14)

electricity der Strom (12)

elevator der Aufzug (¨e) (9)

eleven elf (E)

eleventh elfte (3)

e-mail die E-Mail (-s) (13)

to employ beschäftigen (11)

employee der Mitarbeiter (-) / die Mitarbeiterin (-nen) (11)

employer der Arbeitgeber (-) / die Arbeitgeberin (-nen) (11)

employment: employment counselor der Berufsberater (-) / die Berufsberaterin (-nen) (11); **employment office** das Arbeitsamt (¨er) (11)

to entertain oneself sich unterhalten (unterhält), unterhielt, unterhalten (13)

entertaining unterhaltsam (13)

entertainment die Unterhaltung (13); **for entertainment** zur Unterhaltung (13)

entire(ly) ganz (12)

entrance der Eingang (¨e) (12)

environment die Umwelt (14)

environmental: environmental pollution die Umweltverschmutzung (14); **environmental protection** der Umweltschutz (14); **environmentally friendly** umweltfreundlich (14)

to equip einrichten (richtet ein) (12)

especially besonders (8)

euro das Euro (-[s]) (2)

even sogar (8)

evening der Abend (-e) (4); **evening meal** das Abendessen (-) (5); **good evening** guten Abend (E); **in the evening, evenings** abends (4); **this evening** heute Abend (1); **tomorrow evening** morgen Abend (4)

event: current events Aktuelles (13)

every jeder, jede, jedes (5); **every day** jeden Tag (7)

everything alles (10); **Everything is clear.** Alles klar. (E)

exact(ly) genau (2); **exactly** gerade (2); **exactly as . . . as** genauso … wie (7)

exaggerated übertrieben (14)

examination (at the end of Gymnasium) das Abitur (-e) (11)

to examine untersuchen, untersucht (11)

excellent ausgezeichnet (E)

to exchange umtauschen (tauscht um) (5)

exciting spannend (4)

to excuse entschuldigen (6); **Excuse me!** Entschuldigen Sie! (6), Entschuldigung! (9)

expense die Ausgabe (-n) (12)

expensive(ly) teuer (2)

to experience erleben (10)

extra costs die Nebenkosten (pl.) (12)

extremism: right-wing extremism der Rechtsextremismus (14)

eye das Auge (-n) (8)

eyeglasses die Brille (-n) (5)

F

face das Gesicht (-er) (8)

fair (weather) heiter (7)

fairly (rather) ziemlich (5)

fall (autumn) der Herbst (-e) (7)

to fall fallen (fällt), fiel, ist gefallen (7); **to fall asleep** einschlafen (schläft ein), schlief ein, ist eingeschlafen (4)

familiar vertraut (14)

family die Familie (-n) (3); **family gathering** das Familienfest (-e) (3); **family name** der Nachname (gen. -ns, acc./dat. -n) (-n) (1); **family tree** der Stammbaum (¨-e) (3); **small family-run hotel** die Pension (-en) (9)

famine der Hunger (14)

fantastic fantastisch (1)

far weit (9); **as far as** bis zum/zur (9); **far (away) from . . .** weit (weg) von … (2)

farmhouse das Bauernhaus (¨-er) (12)

fast schnell (10)

fast-food stand der Imbiss (-e) (6)

father der Vater (¨-) (3)

favor: I'm in favor of it. Ich bin dafür. (14)

favorable günstig (9)

fax machine das Faxgerät (-e) (13)

fear die Angst (¨-e) (12)

feature film der Spielfilm (-e) (13)

February (der) Februar (3)

to feel (well) sich (wohl) fühlen (8); **to feel like** (doing something) Lust haben (hat Lust) (2)

fees (tuition) die Studiengebühren (pl.) (12)

female cousin die Cousine (-n) / die Kusine (-n) (3)

fever das Fieber (8)

few wenig (8)

field: athletic field der Sportplatz (¨-e) (7)

fifteen fünfzehn (E)

fifth fünfte (3)

fifty fünfzig (E)

to fill out ausfüllen (füllt aus) (9)

film der Film (-e) (4); **feature film** der Spielfilm (-e) (13)

to find finden, fand, gefunden (1); **to find something** sich (dat.) etwas aussuchen (sucht aus) (13)

fine sehr gut (E); **fine, thanks** danke, gut (E)

finger der Finger (-) (8)

firm die Firma (Firmen) (11)

first erste (3); (at first) zuerst (9); **first name** der Vorname (gen. -ns, acc./dat. -n) (-n) (1); **May first** der erste Mai (3); **on May first** am ersten Mai (3)

to fish angeln (7)

fit (adj.) fit (8); **to keep fit** sich fit halten (hält), hielt, gehalten (8)

to fit passen (+ dat.) (5)

fitness die Fitness (8)

five fünf (E)

to flash blitzen (7)

floor der Stock (pl. Stockwerke) (9); die Etage (-n) (12); **ground floor** das Erdgeschoss (-e) (9); **top floor** das Dachgeschoss (-e) (12)

flu die Grippe (8)

to fly fliegen, flog, ist geflogen (7)

fog der Nebel (7)

foggy neblig (7)

food das Essen (-) (1); die Küche (6); die Ernährung (12); **food to go** zum Mitnehmen (6); **natural-foods store** der Bioladen (¨-) (5); **organic foods** die Biolebensmittel (pl.) (8)

foot der Fuß (¨-e) (8); **to go on foot** zu Fuß gehen, ging, ist gegangen (8)

for für (+ acc.) (3); (+ time) seit (+ dat.) (5, 6); zu (+ dat.) (5); (coord. conj.) denn (7); **for two years** seit zwei Jahren (6)

to forbid verbieten, verbot, verboten (14)

foreign countries das Ausland (sg. only) (11)

foreigner der Ausländer (-) / die Ausländerin (-nen) (14); **hatred directed toward foreigners** die Ausländerfeindlichkeit (14)

forest der Wald (¨-er) (7)

to forget vergessen (vergisst), vergaß, vergessen (10)

fork die Gabel (-n) (6)

form das Formular (-e); **application form** das Bewerbungsformular (-e) (11); **registration form** das Anmeldeformular (-e) (9)

forty vierzig (E)

forward: to look forward to sich freuen auf (+ acc.) (12)

four vier (E)

foursome: as a foursome zu viert (10)

fourteen vierzehn (E)

fourth vierte (3)

France (das) Frankreich (E)

free(ly) frei (2)

free time die Freizeit (7)

French fries die Pommes frites (pl.) (6)

fresh(ly) frisch (5)

Friday (der) Freitag (3); **Fridays, on Friday(s)** freitags (4)

fried: fried egg das Spiegelei (-er) (6); **fried potatoes** die Bratkartoffeln (pl.) (6)

friend der Freund (-e) / die Freundin (-nen) (1)

friendly freundlich (1); **environmentally friendly** umweltfreundlich (14)

fries: French fries die Pommes frites (pl.) (6)

from aus (+ dat.) (5); von (+ dat.) (5, 6); ab (+ dat.) (12); **across from** gegenüber von (+ dat.) (9); **far (away) from . . .** weit (weg) von … (2); **from two to three o'clock** von zwei bis drei Uhr (6); **from where** woher (1); **I'm from . . .** Ich komme aus … (E); **Where are you from?** Woher kommen Sie? (form.) / Woher kommst du? (inform.) (E)

front: front hall die Diele (-n) (12); **in front of** vor (+ acc./dat.) (6)

frozen gefroren (5)

fruit das Obst (5); **fruit and vegetable stand** der Obst- und Gemüsestand (¨-e) (5)

full voll (6)

full-service restaurant die Gaststätte (-n) (6)

fun der Spaß (¨-e) (1); **have fun!** viel Spaß! (1); **That's fun.** Das macht Spaß. (1)

to function funktionieren (9)

fun-loving lustig (1)

to furnish einrichten (richtet ein) (12)

furnished möbliert (2)

furniture die Möbel (pl.) (2)

future die Zukunft (11)

G

game das Spiel (-e); **to play computer games** Computerspiele spielen (1)

garage die Garage (-n) (2)

garbage der Müll (12); der Abfall (¨-e) (14)

garden der Garten (¨-) (2); **beer garden** der Biergarten (¨-) (6)

gasoline das Benzin (12)

gathering: family gathering das Familienfest (-e) (3)

generator: wind power generator das Windrad (¨-er) (14)

gentleman der Herr (-n masc.) (-en) (E)

German deutsch; (language) (das) Deutsch (1); **How do you say . . . in German?** Wie sagt man … auf Deutsch? (E)

Germany (das) Deutschland (E)

to get (receive) bekommen, bekam, bekommen (6); **What's the best way to get there?** Wie komme ich am besten dahin? (9)

to get dressed sich anziehen (zieht an), zog an, angezogen (8)

to get into (a vehicle) einsteigen (steigt ein), stieg ein, ist eingestiegen (10)

to get involved sich engagieren (14)

to get undressed sich ausziehen (zieht aus), zog aus, ausgezogen (8)

to get up aufstehen (steht auf), stand auf, ist aufgestanden (4)

to get well sich erholen (8); **Get well soon!** Gute Besserung! (8)

gift das Geschenk (-e) (3)

to give geben (gibt), gab, gegeben (3); (*as a gift*) schenken (5); (*drop off, turn in*) abgeben (gibt ab), gab ab, abgegeben (8)

given name der Vorname (*gen.* -ns, *acc./dat.* -n) (-n) (1)

glad: to be glad about sich freuen über (+ *acc.*) (12)

gladly gern (1)

glasses (eyeglasses) die Brille (-n) (5)

global global (14)

glove der Handschuh (-e) (10)

to go gehen, ging, ist gegangen (1); **(food) to go** zum Mitnehmen (6); **to go clubbing** in die Disco gehen (4); **to go for a walk** spazieren gehen (geht spazieren) (4); **to go on a trip** verreisen, ist verreist (10); **to go on foot** zu Fuß gehen (8); **to go on vacation** Urlaub machen (8); **to go out** ausgehen (geht aus), ging aus, ist ausgegangen (4); **to go shopping** einkaufen gehen (geht einkaufen) (4); **to go to a concert** ins Konzert gehen (4); **to go to the movies** ins Kino gehen (4); **to go to the opera** in die Oper gehen (4); **to go to the theater** ins Theater gehen (4)

good sehr gut (E); gut (1); **good day** (guten) Tag (E); **good evening** guten Abend (E); **good luck!** viel Glück! (1); **good morning** (guten) Morgen (E); **good night** gute Nacht (E); **to look good** (*on a person*) stehen (+ *dat.*), stand, gestanden (5); **to taste good** schmecken (+ *dat.*) (5)

good-bye (auf) Wiedersehen (E); (*on telephone*) auf Wiederhören! (9)

government die Regierung (-en) (14)

GPS das Navi (-s), das Navigationssystem (-e) (10)

granddaughter die Enkelin (-nen) (3)

grandfather der Großvater (¨) (3)

grandma die Oma (-s) (3)

grandmother die Großmutter (¨) (3)

grandpa der Opa (-s) (3)

grandparents die Großeltern (*pl.*) (3)

grandson der Enkel (-) (3)

granola das Müsli (-) (5)

grape die Traube (-n) (5)

graphic artist der Zeichner (-) / die Zeichnerin (-nen) (11)

gray grau (5)

great prima (E); **great!** ganz toll! (1)

green grün (5)

greeting der Gruß (¨e) (12)

grill der Grill (-s) (6)

ground floor das Erdgeschoss (-e) (9)

guest room das Gästezimmer (-) (12)

guide: travel guide (book) der Reiseführer (-) (10)

gym das Fitnesscenter (-) (4)

H

hail der Hagel (7)

hair das Haar (-e) (8); **hair dryer** der Föhn (-e) (9)

half halb (4); **half past one** halb zwei (4)

hall: city hall das Rathaus (¨er) (9); **front hall** die Diele (-n) (12)

hallway der Flur (-e) (12)

ham der Schinken (-) (5)

hand die Hand (¨e) (8)

handbag die Tasche (-n) (5)

to hang (*something*) hängen (6); **to hang, be hanging** hängen, hing, gehangen (6)

to happen passieren, ist passiert (7)

happy glücklich; **Happy birthday!** Herzlichen Glückwunsch zum Geburtstag! (3)

hardly kaum (8)

hardworking fleißig (1)

hat der Hut (¨e) (5)

hatred directed toward foreigners die Ausländerfeindlichkeit (14)

to have haben (hat), hatte, gehabt (2); **have fun!** viel Spaß! (1); **to have time** Zeit haben (hat Zeit) (2); **to have to** müssen (muss), musste, gemusst (4); **I have a question.** Ich habe eine Frage. (E); **What will you have?** Was bekommen Sie? (6)

he er (1)

head der Kopf (¨e) (8); (*boss*) der Chef (-s) / die Chefin (-nen) (11); **head cold** der Schnupfen (8)

headache die Kopfschmerzen (*pl.*) (8)

headline die Schlagzeile (-n) (13)

health die Gesundheit (8)

healthful, healthy gesund (8)

to hear hören (1)

heat, heating system die Heizung (12)

hello grüß dich (*inform.*) (E); (guten) Tag (E); hallo (*among friends and family*) (E)

to help helfen (+ *dat.*) (hilft), half, geholfen (5)

help-wanted ad das Stellenangebot (-e) (11)

her ihr (3); sie (*acc.*) (3); **(to/for) her** ihr (*dat.*) (5)

herbal tea der Kräutertee (8)

here hier (1)

hi grüß dich (*inform.*) (E); hi (E)

high(ly) hoch (hoh-) (2)

to hike wandern, ist gewandert (1)

hiking trail der Wanderweg (-e) (10)

him ihn (*acc.*) (3); **(to/for) him** ihm (*dat.*) (5)

his sein (3)

to hitchhike per Autostop reisen, ist gereist (10)

hobby das Hobby (-s) (1)

to hold halten (hält), hielt, gehalten (14)

home (to home) nach Hause (5); **at home** zu Hause (5); **at home and abroad** im Inland und Ausland (13); **home country** das Inland (*sg. only*) (13)

homeless person der/die Obdachlose (*decl. adj.*) (14)

homelessness die Obdachlosigkeit (14)

to hope hoffen (5); **I hope** hoffentlich (6)

horoscope das Horoskop (-e) (13)

horseback: to ride on horseback reiten, ritt, ist geritten (7)

hostel: youth hostel die Jugendherberge (-n) (9)

hot heiß (7)

hotel das Hotel (-s) (9); **small family-run hotel** die Pension (-en) (9)

hour die Stunde (-n) (4); **office hour** die Sprechstunde (-n) (8)

house das Haus (¨er) (2)

household der Haushalt (-e) (12)

houseplant die Zimmerpflanze (-n) (2)

housing: shared housing die Wohngemeinschaft (-en) / die WG (-s) (2)

how wie (1); **How about . . . ?** Wie wäre es mit … ? (13); **How are you?** Na, wie geht's? (*casual*) / Wie geht's (dir)? (*inform.*) / Wie geht es Ihnen? (*form.*) (E); **How do you like . . . ?** Wie findest du … ? (1); Wie gefällt Ihnen … ? (5); **How do you say . . . in German?** Wie sagt man … auf Deutsch? (E); **How do you write . . . ?** Wie schreibt man … ? (E)

human (being) der Mensch (-en *masc.*) (-en) (2); **human right** das Menschenrecht (-e) (14)

humid schwül (7)

hundred (ein)hundert (E)

Hungary Ungarn (E)

hunger der Hunger (14)

hungry: to be hungry Hunger haben (hat Hunger) (2)

to hurry up sich beeilen (8)

to hurt wehtun (+ *dat.*) (tut weh), tat weh, wehgetan (8); **That hurts.** Das tut mir weh. (8)

husband der Mann (¨er) (3)

I

I ich (1); **I am** Ich bin… (E); **I don't care.** Das ist mir egal. (5); **I don't know.** Das weiß ich nicht. (E); **I'm from . . .** Ich komme aus … (E); **I think that's really stupid!** Das ist mir zu blöd. (13); **I was born** ich bin geboren (1)

ice, ice cream das Eis (5); **dish of ice cream** der Eisbecher (-) (6)

to ice-skate Schlittschuh laufen (läuft Schlittschuh), lief Schlittschuh, ist Schlittschuh gelaufen (7)

ice-skating rink das Eisstadion (Eisstadien) (7)

ID card der Personalausweis (-e) (10)

i.e. d.h. (= das heißt) (8)

if (*subord. conj.*) wenn (8); **if I were you** an deiner Stelle (12)

ill krank (8)

illness die Krankheit (-en) (14)

to imagine sich (*dat.*) vorstellen (stellt vor) (11)

immediately gleich (8), sofort (9)

important wichtig (3)

impractical unpraktisch (1)

in in (+ *acc./dat.*) (6); **in addition** außerdem (14); **in any case** auf jeden Fall (13); **in back of** hinter (+ *acc./dat.*) (6); **in front of** vor (+ *acc./dat.*) (6); **in January** im Januar (3); **in shape** fit (8); **in spite of** trotz (+ *gen.*) (9); **in the afternoon** nachmittags (4); **in the evening** abends (4); **in the morning** morgens (4); **in two days** in zwei Tagen (6); **to keep in shape** sich fit halten (hält), hielt, gehalten (8)

offer das Angebot (-e) (10); **job offer** das Stellenangebot (-e) (11)

office das Büro (-s) (11); **employment office** das Arbeitsamt (¨er) (11); **office hour** die Sprechstunde (-n) (8); **post office** die Post (*pl.* Postämter) (9)

often oft (1)

OK so lala (E)

old alt (älter, ältest-) (1)

olive die Olive (-n) (6)

on an (+ *acc./dat.*) (6); auf (+ *acc./dat.*) (6); **on account of** wegen (+ *gen.*) (9); **on average** durchschnittlich (12); **on May first** am ersten Mai (3); **on Monday** am Montag (3); **on Monday(s)** montags (4); **on tap** vom Fass (6); **on top of** auf (+ *acc./dat.*) (6)

once einmal (7); früher (7); **once a month/year** einmal im Monat/Jahr (7); **once a week** einmal die Woche (7)

one eins (E); (*indef. pron.*) man (4); **half past one, one-thirty** halb zwei (4); **It's one o'clock** Es ist eins. / Es ist ein Uhr. (4)

one-way (ticket) einfach (10)

onion die Zwiebel (-n) (6)

only nur (2)

open geöffnet (6)

open-air market der Markt (¨e) (5)

opera die Oper (-n) (4); **to go to the opera** in die Oper gehen (4)

opinion die Meinung (-en) (14); **to be of the opinion** meinen (14); **I'm of the opinion . . .** ich bin der Meinung … (14); **in my opinion . . .** meiner Meinung nach … (14)

opportunity die Möglichkeit (-en) (10); die Gelegenheit (-en) (11)

or (*coord. conj.*) oder (7); **either . . . or** entweder … oder (8)

orange (*adj.*) orange (5)

to order bestellen (6)

organic foods die Biolebensmittel (*pl.*) (8)

ought to sollen (soll), sollte, gesollt (4)

our unser (3)

out of aus (+ *dat.*) (5); **out of money** (*coll.*) pleite (12)

outdoor swimming pool das Freibad (¨er) (7)

outdoors im Freien (11)

outgoing kontaktfreudig (11)

outside draußen (7); **outside of** außerhalb (+ *gen.*) (9)

oven: microwave oven der Mikrowellenherd (-e) (12)

over über (+ *acc./dat.*) (6); **over there** da drüben (6); **left over** übrig (12)

overcast bewölkt (7)

overnight stay die Übernachtung (-en) (9); **to stay overnight** übernachten (9)

own (*adj.*) eigen (12)

to own besitzen, besaß, besessen (11)

P

to pack packen (10)

packaging die Verpackung (-en) (14)

pains die Schmerzen (*pl.*) (8)

to paint malen (7)

pair of eyeglasses die Brille (-n) (5)

palace das Schloss (¨er) (9)

pan die Pfanne (-n) (6)

pants die Hose (-n) (5)

paper das Papier (-e) (12); (*report*) die Arbeit (-en) (8); **papers** (*documents*) die Unterlagen (*pl.*) (11); **toilet paper** das Toilettenpapier (5)

Pardon? Wie bitte? (E)

parents die Eltern (*pl.*) (3)

to park parken; **You may not park here.** Hier darf man nicht parken. (4)

parking lot, parking space der Parkplatz (¨e) (9)

part der/das Teil (-e); **part of the body** der Körperteil (-e) (8)

to participate (in) teilnehmen (an + *dat.*) (nimmt teil), nahm teil, teilgenommen (14)

particularly besonders; **not particularly well** nicht besonders gut (E)

party die Party (-s) (3)

passerby der Passant (-en *masc.*) (-en) / die Passantin (-nen) (9)

passport der Reisepass (¨e) (9)

past: half past one halb zwei (4)

pastry shop die Konditorei (-en) (5)

path der Weg (-e) (9)

patio die Terrasse (-n) (2)

to pay zahlen (5); **to pay attention to** achten auf (+ *acc.*) (8)

pedestrian zone die Fußgängerzone (-n) (9)

pen: ballpoint pen der Kugelschreiber (-) (12)

pencil der Bleistift (-e) (12)

people die Leute (*pl.*) (2); (*indef. pron.*) man (4)

pepper der Pfeffer (5); **bell pepper** die Paprika (6)

per pro; **per person** pro Person (10); **per week** pro Woche (4)

performance die Leistung (11)

perhaps vielleicht (1)

periodical die Zeitschrift (-en) (13)

to permit erlauben (9)

permitted: to be permitted to dürfen (darf), durfte, gedurft (4)

person der Mensch (-en *masc.*) (-en) (2); **per person** pro Person (10)

pharmacy die Apotheke (-n) (5)

phone das Telefon (-e) (2); **cell phone** das Handy (-s) (2); **to talk on the phone** telefonieren (1)

photograph das Foto (-s) (2)

physician der Arzt (¨e) / die Ärztin (-nen) (8)

to pick up (*from a place*) abholen (holt ab) (4)

Pilsner beer das Pilsener (-) (6)

place der Platz (¨e) (6); **(if I were) in your place** an deiner Stelle (12); **place of residence** der Wohnort (-e) (1); **This place is taken.** Hier ist besetzt. (6)

to place (*in a standing position*) stellen (6); **to place inside** stecken (6)

plaid kariert (5)

plan der Plan (¨e) (4)

to plan planen (3); **to plan** (*to do*) vorhaben (hat vor), hatte vor, vorgehabt (4); **to plan to** wollen (will), wollte, gewollt (4)

plastic bag die Plastiktüte (-n) (14)

plate der Teller (-) (6)

platform (*train*) der Bahnsteig (-e) (10)

play (*theater*) das Theaterstück (-e) (4)

to play spielen (1); **to play cards** Karten spielen (1); **to play chess** Schach spielen (7); **to play computer games** Computerspiele spielen (1); **to play soccer** Fußball spielen (7); **to play sports** Sport treiben, trieb, getrieben (7); **to play tennis** Tennis spielen (7)

player: CD player der CD-Spieler (-) (2); **DVD player** der DVD-Spieler (-) (2)

playing card die Spielkarte (-n) (7)

pleasant angenehm (7)

please bitte (E); **Slower, please.** Langsamer, bitte. (E); **Would you please . . . ?** Würden Sie bitte … ? (9)

pleased: Pleased to meet you. Freut mich. (E)

pleasing: to be pleasing to gefallen (+ *dat.*) (gefällt), gefiel, gefallen (5)

Poland (das) Polen (E)

police, police station die Polizei (9)

politician der Politiker (-) / die Politikerin (-nen) (14)

politics die Politik (13)

pollution: environmental pollution die Umweltverschmutzung (14)

pool: swimming pool das Schwimmbad (¨er) (7); **indoor swimming pool** das Hallenbad (¨er) (7); **outdoor swimming pool** das Freibad (¨er) (7)

poor(ly) schlecht (E)

popular beliebt (7)

pork das Schweinefleisch (5); **pork roast** der Schweinebraten (-) (6)

position der Arbeitsplatz (¨e) (11); die Stelle (-n) (11); die Tätigkeit (-en) (11)

to possess besitzen, besaß, besessen (11)

possibility die Möglichkeit (-en) (10)

possible, possibly möglich (14)

post office die Post (*pl.* Postämter) (9)

postage stamp die Briefmarke (-n) (7)

postal code die Postleitzahl (-en) (E)

poster das Poster (-) (2)

potato die Kartoffel (-n) (5); **fried potatoes** die Bratkartoffeln (*pl.*) (6)

poverty die Armut (14)

practical praktisch (1)

to prefer vorziehen (zieht vor), zog vor, vorgezogen (14)

to prepare (for) sich vorbereiten (auf + *acc.*) (bereitet vor) (11)

to prescribe verschreiben, verschrieb, verschrieben (8)

present das Geschenk (-e) (3)

prestige das Ansehen (11)

pretzel die Brezel (-n) (6)

price der Preis (-e) (9); **included in the price** im Preis enthalten (9)

primary school die Grundschule (-n) (11)

to print drucken (13)

printer der Drucker (-) (13)

probably wahrscheinlich (11); wohl (11)

problem das Problem (-e) (2)

to produce herstellen (stellt her) (11)

profession der Beruf (-e) (1)

professional life das Berufsleben (11)

professor der Professor (-en) / die Professorin (-nen) (1)

program das Programm (-e) (13); **TV or radio program** die Sendung (-en) (13)

progress der Fortschritt (-e) (14); **to make progress** Fortschritte machen (14)

to prohibit verbieten, verbot, verboten (14)

to promote fördern (14)

to propose vorschlagen (schlägt vor), schlug vor, vorgeschlagen (10)

to protect schützen (14); **environmental protection** der Umweltschutz (14)

psychologist der Psychologe (-n *masc.*) (-n) / die Psychologin (-nen) (11)

pub die Kneipe (-n) (6); das Lokal (-e) (6); das Wirtshaus (¨er) (6)

public öffentlich (14)

pullover sweater der Pullover (-) (5)

to purchase something sich (*dat.*) etwas anschaffen (schafft an) (14)

purple lila (5)

purse die Tasche (-n) (5)

to put (*in a lying position*) legen (6); (*in a sitting position*) setzen (6); (*inside*) stecken (6); (*in a standing position*) stellen (6)

puzzle: to do crossword puzzles Kreuzworträtsel machen (1)

Q

quarter das Viertel (-) (4); **It's a quarter after/to two.** Es ist Viertel nach/vor zwei. (4)

question die Frage (-n); **I have a question.** Ich habe eine Frage. (E)

quick(ly) schnell (10); **to read quickly** überfliegen, überflog, überflogen (13)

quiet ruhig (1)

quite ganz (1); recht (2); **quite inexpensive** recht preiswert (2)

R

racism der Rassismus (14)

radio das Radio (-s) (2); **radio program** die Sendung (-en) (13)

railway die Bahn (-en) (10)

rain der Regen (7)

to rain regnen (7); **It's raining.** Es regnet. (7)

rain shower der Regenschauer (-) (7)

rainy regnerisch (7)

rare(ly) selten (2)

rather recht (2); ziemlich (5); (*coord. conj.*) sondern (7); **would rather** möchte lieber (4)

to read lesen (liest), las, gelesen (1, 2); **to read quickly** überfliegen, überflog, überflogen (13)

really echt (*coll.*) (1); ganz (1); wirklich (1)

reasonable (*in price*) preiswert (2)

to receive empfangen (empfängt), empfing, empfangen (13)

receiver: satellite receiver der Satelliten-Empfänger (-) (13)

reception desk die Rezeption (9)

to recommend empfehlen (empfiehlt), empfahl, empfohlen (5)

recommendation (*from a former employer*) das Zeugnis (-se) (11)

to record (*e.g., on video*) aufnehmen (nimmt auf), nahm auf, aufgenommen (13)

recorder: video recorder der Videorekorder (-) (2)

to recover sich erholen (8)

recycling center die Sammelstelle (-n) (14)

red rot (5)

refrigerator der Kühlschrank (¨e) (9)

register: cash register die Kasse (-n) (5)

to register sich anmelden (meldet an) (9)

registration form das Anmeldeformular (-e) (9)

regular(ly) regelmäßig (8)

related to verwandt mit (3)

to relax sich entspannen (8)

to remain bleiben, blieb, ist geblieben (1)

rent die Miete (-n) (2)

to rent (*from someone*) mieten (12); **to rent out** (*to someone*) vermieten (12)

repair die Reparatur (-en) (12)

to repair reparieren (9)

report der Bericht (-e) (13); **report card** das Zeugnis (-se) (11); **weather report** der Wetterbericht (-e) (7)

to report berichten (13)

to request bitten um (+ *acc.*), bat, gebeten (12)

research die Forschung (-en) (14)

research: to do research forschen (13)

reservation: seat reservation card die Platzkarte (-n) (10)

to reserve reservieren (7)

to reside wohnen (1)

residence: place of residence der Wohnort (-e) (1)

responsible verantwortlich (11)

restaurant das Restaurant (-s) (6); das Lokal (-e) (6); **full-service restaurant** die Gaststätte (-n) (6)

résumé der Lebenslauf (¨e) (11)

to retrain umschulen (schult um) (14)

to return zurückkommen (kommt zurück), kam zurück, ist zurückgekommen (4)

rice der Reis (6)

to ride fahren (fährt), fuhr, ist gefahren (1); **to ride a bike** Fahrrad/Rad fahren (fährt Fahrrad/Rad) (1, 7); **to ride on horseback** reiten, ritt, ist geritten (7)

right rechts (9); **to the right** nach rechts (9)

right das Recht (-e); **human right** das Menschenrecht (-e) (14)

right-wing extremism der Rechtsextremismus (14)

rink: ice-skating rink das Eisstadion (Eisstadien) (7)

river der Fluss (¨e) (7)

road der Weg (-e) (9)

roast: pork roast der Schweinebraten (-) (6)

roll das Brötchen (-) (5)

romantic romantisch (1)

roof das Dach (¨er) (12)

room das Zimmer (-) (2); **breakfast room** der Frühstücksraum (¨e) (9); **dining room** das Esszimmer (-) (2); **guest room** das Gästezimmer (-) (12); **living room** das Wohnzimmer (-) (2); **room with one bed** das Einzelzimmer (-) (9); **room with two beds** das Doppelzimmer (-) (9)

roommate der Mitbewohner (-) / die Mitbewohnerin (-nen) (2)

round-trip hin und zurück (10)

rug der Teppich (-e) (2)

to run laufen (läuft), lief, ist gelaufen (2)

S

safe(ly) sicher (10)

to sail segeln (7)

salad der Salat (-e) (6)

salary das Gehalt (¨er) (11)

sales der Handel (11); der Verkauf (11)

salesman der Kaufmann (*pl.* Kaufleute) (11)

salesperson der Verkäufer (-) / die Verkäuferin (-nen) (2)

saleswoman die Kauffrau (-en) (11)

salt das Salz (5)

satellite receiver der Satelliten-Empfänger (-) (13)

Saturday (der) Samstag (3); (der) Sonnabend (3); **Saturdays, on Saturday(s)** samstags (4); sonnabends (4)

sauerkraut das Sauerkraut (6)

sausage die Wurst (¨e) (5); **white sausage** die Weißwurst (¨e) (6)

to save (*conserve*) sparen (12); (*store*) speichern (13)

savings account das Sparkonto (Sparkonten) (12)

to say sagen (1); **How do you say . . . in German?** Wie sagt man ... auf Deutsch? (E); **that is to say** nämlich (3); **What did you say?** Wie bitte? (E)

scarcely kaum (8)

scarf der Schal (-s) (5)

schedule der Fahrplan (¨e) (10)

school die Schule (-n); **primary school** die Grundschule (-n) (11); **secondary school** das Gymnasium (Gymnasien) (11)

scientist: computer scientist der Informatiker (-) / die Informatikerin (-nen) (11)

sea das Meer (-e) (7)

season die Jahreszeit (-en) (7)

seat der Platz (¨e) (6); **Is this seat available?** Ist hier noch frei? (6); **seat reservation card** die Platzkarte (-n) (10)

second (*adj.*) zweite (3)

second die Sekunde (-n) (4)

secondary school das Gymnasium (Gymnasien) (11)

to see sehen (sieht), sah, gesehen (2)

to seem scheinen, schien, geschienen (13)

to select something sich (*dat.*) etwas aussuchen (sucht aus) (13)

selection das Angebot (-e) (10)

self-assured selbstbewusst (11)

semester das Semester (-) (1)

to send schicken (1)

sensible gescheit (13)

to separate (sich) trennen (14)

separate(ly) getrennt (6)

September (der) September (3)

serious ernst (1)

server der Kellner (-) / die Kellnerin (-nen) (6)

service die Bedienung (6); **customer service** die Kundenbetreuung (11)

set (*TV, telephone, camera, etc.*) der Apparat (-e) (9)

to set setzen (6)

seven sieben (E)

seventeen siebzehn (E)

seventh sieb(en)te (3)

seventy siebzig (E)

shame: What a shame! So ein Pech! (8)

shape: in shape fit (8); **to keep in shape** sich fit halten (hält), hielt, gehalten (8)

shared housing die Wohngemeinschaft (-en) / die WG (-s) (2)

to shave sich rasieren (8)

shaving cream die Rasiercreme (-s) (5)

she sie (1)

shelf das Regal (-e) (2)

to shine scheinen, schien, geschienen; **The sun is shining.** Die Sonne scheint. (7)

ship das Schiff (-e) (10)

shirt das Hemd (-en) (5); **T-shirt** das T-Shirt (-s) (5)

shoe der Schuh (-e) (5); **tennis shoe** der Tennisschuh (-e) (5)

shop das Geschäft (-e) (5); **butcher shop** die Metzgerei (-en) (5); **pastry shop** die Konditorei (-en) (5)

to shop einkaufen (kauft ein) (4)

shopping: to go shopping einkaufen gehen (geht einkaufen), ging einkaufen, ist einkaufen gegangen (4)

short kurz (kürzer, kürzest-) (7)

should, to be supposed to sollen (soll), sollte, gesollt (4)

shoulder die Schulter (-n) (8)

to show zeigen (5)

shower die Dusche (-n) (9); **rain shower** der Regenschauer (-) (7)

to shower sich duschen (8)

siblings die Geschwister (*pl.*) (3)

sick krank (8); **sick as a dog** (*coll.*) hundsmiserabel (8); **I'm sick to my stomach.** Mir ist schlecht. (8)

side dish die Beilage (-n) (6)

simple einfach (10)

since seit (+ *dat.*) (5, 6)

single room das Einzelzimmer (-) (9)

sister die Schwester (-n) (3)

sister-in-law die Schwägerin (-nen) (3)

to sit sitzen, saß, gesessen (6); **to sit down** sich (hin)setzen (setzt hin) (8)

six sechs (E)

sixteen sechzehn (E)

sixth sechste (3)

sixty sechzig (E)

size die Größe (-n) (5)

to skate: to ice-skate Schlittschuh laufen (läuft Schlittschuh), lief Schlittschuh, ist Schlittschuh gelaufen (7)

to skim (a text) überfliegen, überflog, überflogen (13)

skirt der Rock (¨e) (5)

sky der Himmel (7)

to sleep schlafen (schläft), schlief, geschlafen (2)

slipper der Hausschuh (-e) (5)

Slovakia die Slowakei (E)

Slovenia (das) Slowenien (E)

slow(ly) langsam (10); **Slower, please.** Langsamer, bitte. (E)

small klein (2)

to smoke rauchen (8)

snow der Schnee (7)

to snow schneien (7); **It's snowing.** Es schneit. (7)

so so (2); **So long.** Mach's gut. (*inform.*) (E); tschüss (*inform.*) (E); **So what?** Na und? (13)

soccer, soccer ball der Fußball (¨e) (7); **to play soccer** Fußball spielen (7)

sock die Socke (-n) (5)

sofa das Sofa (-s) (2)

solution die Lösung (-en) (14)

to solve lösen (14)

something etwas (2)

sometimes manchmal (8)

somewhat etwas (2); ziemlich (5)

son der Sohn (¨e) (3)

soon bald (12); **Get well soon!** Gute Besserung! (8)

sorry: I'm sorry. Das tut mir leid. (9)

so-so so lala (E)

to sound klingen, klang, geklungen (8); **You sound so depressed.** Du klingst so deprimiert. (8)

soup die Suppe (-n) (6)

space: parking space der Parkplatz (¨e) (9)

to speak sprechen (spricht), sprach, gesprochen (2)

special offer das Angebot (-e) (10)

to spend (*money*) ausgeben (gibt aus), gab aus, ausgegeben (12); (*time*) verbringen, verbrachte, verbracht (7)

spite: in spite of trotz (+ *gen.*) (9)

spoon der Löffel (-) (6)

sport, sports der Sport (*pl.* Sportarten) (7); **active in sports** sportlich aktiv (10); **to play sports**

Sport treiben, trieb, getrieben (7); **sport coat** der/das Sakko (-s) (5); **sports arena** die Sporthalle (-n) (7)

to spread verbreiten (14)

spring (*season*) das Frühjahr (-e), der Frühling (-e) (7)

stadium das Stadion (Stadien) (7)

staircase die Treppe (-n) (12)

stamp: postage stamp die Briefmarke (-n) (7)

stand der Stand (¨e); **fast-food stand** der Imbiss (-e) (6); **fruit and vegetable stand** der Obst- und Gemüsestand (¨e) (5)

to stand stehen, stand, gestanden (6); **to stand up** (*get up*) aufstehen (steht auf), stand auf, ist aufgestanden (4); **to stand up** (*put in a standing position*) stellen (6)

station (*TV or radio*) das Programm (-e) (13); **police station** die Polizei (9); **train station** der Bahnhof (¨e) (9)

stay der Aufenthalt (-e) (9); **overnight stay** die Übernachtung (-en) (9)

to stay bleiben, blieb, ist geblieben (1); **to stay overnight** übernachten (9)

stereo die Stereoanlage (-n) (2)

still (*yet*) noch (2)

stock market die Börse (-n) (13)

stomach der Bauch (¨e) (8); **I'm sick to my stomach.** Mir ist schlecht. (8)

stop: bus stop die Haltestelle (-n) (9)

store das Geschäft (-e) (5); der Laden (¨) (5); **beverage store** der Getränkeladen (¨) (5); **department store** das Kaufhaus (¨er) (2); **natural-foods store** der Bioladen (¨) (5); **toiletries and sundries store** die Drogerie (-n) (5)

to store speichern (13)

story (*level*) der Stock (*pl.* Stockwerke) (9); die Etage (-n) (12)

straight ahead geradeaus (9)

to straighten up aufräumen (räumt auf) (4)

strawberry die Erdbeere (-n) (5)

street die Straße (-n) (E); **street address** die Hausnummer (-n) (E)

strenuous anstrengend (8)

stress der Stress (8)

stressful stressig (1)

to stretch sich strecken (8)

strict(ly) streng (14)

striped gestreift (5)

strong stark (stärker, stärkst-) (7)

strudel: apple strudel der Apfelstrudel (-) (6)

student der Student (-en *masc.*) (-en) / die Studentin (-nen) (1); **student cafeteria** die Mensa (-s) (1)

study (*room*) das Arbeitszimmer (-) (2)

to study (*at university*) studieren (1); (*for an exam*) lernen (1)

stupid blöd (13); **I think that's really stupid.** Das ist mir zu blöd. (13)

stylish(ly) schick (5)

to subscribe abonnieren (13)

subscription das Abo(nnement) (-s) (13)

success der Erfolg (-e) (11)

successful(ly) erfolgreich (11); **to be successful** Erfolg haben (11)

sugar der Zucker (5)

to suggest vorschlagen (schlägt vor), schlug vor, vorgeschlagen (10)

suit der Anzug (¨e) (5); **bathing suit** der Badeanzug (¨e) (5)

suitcase der Koffer (-) (5)

summer der Sommer (-) (7)

sun die Sonne (7); **The sun is shining.** Die Sonne scheint. (7)

Sunday (der) Sonntag (3); **Sundays, on Sunday(s)** sonntags (4)

sunny sonnig (7)

sunscreen das Sonnenschutzmittel (10)

sunshine der Sonnenschein (7)

suntan lotion das Sonnenschutzmittel (10)

super prima (E); **super!** (coll.) (ganz) toll! (1)

supermarket der Supermarkt (¨e) (5)

to support unterstützen, unterstützt (12)

supposed: to be supposed to sollen (soll), sollte, gesollt (4)

sure(ly) sicher (5)

to surf surfen (1); **to surf the Internet** im Internet surfen (1)

surname der Nachname (gen. -ns, acc./dat. -n) (-n) (1)

suspenseful spannend (4)

to swallow schlucken (8)

sweater: pullover sweater der Pullover (-) (5)

to swim schwimmen, schwamm, ist geschwommen (2)

swim trunks die Badehose (-n) (5)

swimming pool das Schwimmbad (¨er) (7); **indoor swimming pool** das Hallenbad (¨er) (7); **outdoor swimming pool** das Freibad (¨er) (7)

Switzerland die Schweiz (E)

T

table der Tisch (-e) (2)

table: coffee table der Couchtisch (-e) (2)

to take nehmen (nimmt), nahm, genommen (5); **to take** (time) dauern (7); **to take a vote** abstimmen (stimmt ab) (14); **to take along** mitnehmen (nimmt mit), nahm mit, mitgenommen (5); **Take care.** Mach's gut. (inform.) (E); **take-out** zum Mitnehmen (6)

taken besetzt (6); **This place is taken.** Hier ist besetzt. (6)

to talk on the phone telefonieren (1)

tall groß (1)

tap: on tap vom Fass (6)

to taste (good) schmecken (+ dat.) (5)

tax die Steuer (-n) (14)

taxicab das Taxi (-s) (10)

tea der Tee (5); **herbal tea** der Kräutertee (8)

teacher der Lehrer (-) / die Lehrerin (-nen) (E)

technique die Technik (-en) (11)

technology die Technik (-en) (11)

telephone das Telefon (-e) (2); **telephone number** die Telefonnummer (-n) (E); **to talk on the telephone** telefonieren (1)

television (set) der Fernseher (-) (2); **to watch television** fernsehen (sieht fern), sah fern, ferngesehen (4); **watching television** das Fernsehen (4)

to tell sagen (1); **tell me** sag mal (1)

temperature die Temperatur (-en) (7)

ten zehn (E)

tender(ly) zart (5)

tennis das Tennis; **to play tennis** Tennis spielen (7); **tennis court** der Tennisplatz (¨e) (7); **tennis shoe** der Tennisschuh (-e) (5);

tent das Zelt (-e) (10)

tenth zehnte (3)

terrace die Terrasse (-n) (2)

terrorism der Terrorismus (14)

than als (7)

to thank danken (+ dat.) (5); **thank you very much** danke schön (E)

thanks danke (E); **fine, thanks** danke, gut (E); **Many thanks!** Vielen Dank! (6); **No thanks necessary.** Nichts zu danken. (8); **thanks a lot** danke sehr (1)

that das; (subord. conj.) dass (8); **that comes to** das macht (5); **That doesn't matter.** Das macht nichts. (8); **that is** d.h. (= das heißt) (8); **that is to say** nämlich (3); **That's fun.** Das macht Spaß. (1)

the der, die, das

theater das Theater (-) (4); **to go to the theater** ins Theater gehen (4); **movie theater** das Kino (-s) (4)

their ihr (3)

them sie (acc.) (3); **(to/for) them** ihnen (dat.) (5)

then: now and then ab und zu (8)

there da (2); **over there** da drüben (6); **there is/are** es gibt (3); **What's the best way to get there?** Wie komme ich am besten dahin? (9)

therefore deshalb (8)

they sie (1); (indef. pron.) man (4)

to think (about/of) denken (an + acc.), dachte, gedacht (12); **I think that's really stupid.** Das ist mir zu blöd. (13); **to think (about)** nachdenken (über + acc.) (denkt nach), dachte nach, nachgedacht (11); **to think** (be of the opinion) meinen (14); **to think** (consider) halten (für + acc.) (hält), hielt, gehalten (14); **to think over** sich überlegen, überlegt (10); **What do you think of . . . ?** Wie findest du … ? (1)

third dritte (3)

thirsty: to be thirsty Durst haben (hat Durst) (2)

thirteen dreizehn (E)

thirteenth dreizehnte (3)

thirty dreißig (E)

this dieser, diese, dies(es) (2); **this afternoon** heute Nachmittag (4); **this evening** heute Abend (1); **This is . . .** Das ist … (E); **this morning** heute Morgen (4)

thousand (ein)tausend (E)

three drei (E); **three times** dreimal (7)

threesome: as a threesome zu dritt (10)

thrifty sparsam (12)

throat der Hals (¨e) (8); **sore throat** die Halsschmerzen (pl.) (8)

through durch (+ acc.) (3)

to thunder donnern (7); **It's thundering.** Es donnert. (7)

thunderstorm das Gewitter (-) (7)

Thursday (der) Donnerstag (3); **Thursdays, on Thursday(s)** donnerstags (4)

ticket (bus or train) die Fahrkarte (-n) (10); **ticket window** der Fahrkartenschalter (-) (10)

time die Zeit (-en) (2); **At what time?** Um wie viel Uhr? (4); **to have time** Zeit haben (hat Zeit) (2); **to spend time** Zeit verbringen, verbrachte, verbracht (7); **three times** dreimal (7); **time of day** die Tageszeit (-eh) (4); **What time is it?** Wie spät ist es? / Wie viel Uhr ist es? (4)

tin can die Dose (-n) (14)

tired müde (8)

tiring anstrengend (8)

to nach (+ dat.) (5); zu (+ dat.) (5); (a place) in (+ acc.) (6); **five to two** fünf vor zwei (4); **It's a quarter to two.** Es ist Viertel vor zwei. (4); **to (as far as)** bis zum/zur (9); **(to) home** nach Hause (5); **to the left/right** nach links/ rechts (9); **to where** wohin (5)

today heute (1); **What is today's date?** Welches Datum ist heute? (3)

toe die Zehe (-n) (8)

together zusammen

toilet das WC (-s) (9); **toilet paper** das Toilettenpapier (5)

toiletries and sundries store die Drogerie (-n) (5)

tomato die Tomate (-n) (5)

tomorrow morgen (3); **tomorrow evening** morgen Abend (4); **tomorrow morning** morgen früh (4); **What is tomorrow's date?** Welches Datum ist morgen? (3)

too (also) auch (E)

tooth der Zahn (¨e); **to brush one's teeth** sich die Zähne putzen (8)

toothpaste die Zahnpasta (Zahnpasten) (5)

top: on top of auf (+ acc./dat.) (6); **top floor** das Dachgeschoss (-e) (12)

topical aktuell (13)

total insgesamt (10); **total(ly)** ganz (12)

tourist der Tourist (-en masc.) (-en) / die Touristin (-nen) (9)

town die Stadt (¨e) (E); **center of town** das Zentrum (Zentren) (9)

track das Gleis (-e) (10)

trade der Handel (11)

tradition die Tradition (-en) (3)

traffic light die Ampel (-n) (9)

tragedy die Tragödie (-n) (4)

trail: hiking trail der Wanderweg (-e) (10)

train der Zug (¨e) (10); (railway) die Bahn (-en) (10); **train platform** der Bahnsteig (-e) (10); **train station** der Bahnhof (¨e) (9)

training die Ausbildung (11); **to do weight training** Bodybuilding machen (7)

transcript das Zeugnis (-se) (11)

to transfer (trains) umsteigen (steigt um), stieg um, ist umgestiegen (10)

to translate übersetzen, übersetzt (11)

transportation: means of transportation das Verkehrsmittel (-) (14)

trash der Müll (12); der Abfall ("e) (14)

travel: travel agency das Reisebüro (-s) (10); **travel brochure** der Reiseprospekt (-e) (10); **travel guide (book)** der Reiseführer (-) (10)

to travel reisen, ist gereist (1); **to travel first/second class** erster/zweiter Klasse fahren (fährt), fuhr, ist gefahren (10)

traveler's check der Reisescheck (-s) (10)

tree der Baum ("e); **Christmas tree** der Weihnachtsbaum ("e) (3); **family tree** der Stammbaum ("e) (3)

trip die Reise (-n) (10); **to go on a trip** verreisen, ist verreist (10)

trousers die Hose (-n) (5)

trunks: swim trunks die Badehose (-n) (5)

to try versuchen (8); **to try on** anprobieren (probiert an) (5)

T-shirt das T-Shirt (-s) (5)

Tuesday (der) Dienstag (3); **Tuesdays, on Tuesday(s)** dienstags (4)

tuition die Studiengebühren (pl.) (12)

turkey der Truthahn ("e) (5)

to turn einbiegen (biegt ein), bog ein, ist eingebogen (9)

TV das Fernsehen; **cable TV connection** der Kabelanschluss ("e) (13); **TV channel** das Programm (-e) (13); **TV program** die Sendung (-en) (13); **TV set** der Fernseher (-) (2)

twelfth zwölfte (3)

twelve zwölf (E)

twentieth zwanzigste (3)

twenty zwanzig (E)

twice zweimal (7)

two zwei (E)

twosome: as a twosome zu zweit (10)

U

ugly hässlich (2)

umbrella der Regenschirm (-e) (7)

uncle der Onkel (-) (3)

under unter (+ acc./dat.) (6); **Under what name?** Auf welchen Namen? (9)

to understand verstehen, verstand, verstanden; **I don't understand.** Ich verstehe das nicht. (E)

to undertake unternehmen (unternimmt), unternahm, unternommen (10)

undressed: to get undressed sich ausziehen (zieht aus), zog aus, ausgezogen (8)

unemployment die Arbeitslosigkeit (14)

unfortunately leider (3)

unfriendly unfreundlich (1)

unfurnished unmöbliert (2)

university die Universität (-en) (1); **university instructor** der Hochschullehrer (-) / die Hochschullehrerin (-nen) (1); **university lecture** die Vorlesung (-en) (4)

unlikable unsympathisch (1)

until bis (um) (+ acc.) (6); **until five o'clock** bis (um) fünf Uhr (6)

upstairs oben; (directional) nach oben (12)

urgent(ly) dringend (2)

us uns (acc.) (3); **(to/for) us** uns (dat.) (5)

to use verwenden (14)

used to (do, be, etc.) früher (7)

usual(ly) gewöhnlich (4)

utilities die Nebenkosten (pl.) (12)

V

vacation: to go on vacation Urlaub machen (8)

vacuum cleaner der Staubsauger (-) (12)

Valentine's Day der Valentinstag (3)

varied abwechslungsreich (11)

VCR der Videorekorder (-) (2)

vegetable das Gemüse (5); **fruit and vegetable stand** der Obst- und Gemüsestand ("e) (5)

vegetarian vegetarisch (6)

vehicle das Verkehrsmittel (-) (14)

very ganz (1); sehr (1); **thank you very much** danke schön (E); **very well** sehr gut (E)

vicinity die Nähe (9); die Umgebung (-en) (12)

video(tape) das Video (-s) (2); **video camera** die Videokamera (-s) (13); **video recorder** der Videorekorder (-) (2)

violation die Verletzung (-en) (14)

violence die Gewalttätigkeit (14)

to visit besuchen (1)

vote: to take a vote abstimmen (stimmt ab) (14)

to vote wählen (14)

W

to wait warten (6)

waiter der Kellner (-) (6); der Ober (-) (6)

waitress die Kellnerin (-nen) (6)

to wake up aufwachen (wacht auf) (4)

to walk zu Fuß gehen, ging, ist gegangen (8); **to go for a walk** spazieren gehen (geht spazieren), ging spazieren, ist spazieren gegangen (4); **to walk along** entlanggehen (geht entlang), ging entlang, ist entlanggegangen (9)

wall die Wand ("e) (2)

wall-to-wall carpeting der Teppichboden (") (12)

to want to wollen (will), wollte, gewollt (4)

war der Krieg (-e) (14)

wardrobe die Garderobe (-n) (12)

warm warm (wärmer, wärmst-) (7)

to wash (oneself) sich waschen (wäscht), wusch, gewaschen (8)

washing machine die Waschmaschine (-n) (12)

waste der Abfall ("e) (14)

wastepaper basket der Papierkorb ("e) (2)

to watch something sich (dat.) etwas anschauen (schaut an) (13); sich (dat.) etwas ansehen (sieht an), sah an, angesehen; **to watch television** fernsehen (sieht fern), sah fern, ferngesehen (4); **watching television** das Fernsehen (4)

water das Wasser (5); **mineral water** der Sprudel (6)

way der Weg (-e) (9); **by the way** übrigens (9); **What's the best way to get there?** Wie komme ich am besten dahin? (9)

we wir (1)

weak schlapp (8)

to wear tragen (trägt), trug, getragen (5)

weather das Wetter (7); **weather report** der Wetterbericht (-e) (7)

website die Website (-s) (11)

wedding die Hochzeit (-en) (3)

Wednesday (der) Mittwoch (3); **Wednesdays, on Wednesday(s)** mittwochs (4)

week die Woche (-n) (4); **day of the week** der Wochentag (-e) (3); **once a week** einmal die Woche (7); **per week** pro Woche (4)

weekend das Wochenende (-n) (4)

weight training: to do weight training Bodybuilding machen (7)

welcome herzlich willkommen (E); **you're welcome** bitte (E)

well gut (1); (healthy) gesund (8); **Are you doing well?** Geht's gut? (E); **to feel well** sich wohl fühlen (8); **to get well** sich erholen (8) **Get well soon!** Gute Besserung! (8); **He dances well.** Er tanzt gut. (1); **not particularly well** nicht besonders gut (E); **very well** sehr gut (E)

were: if I were you an deiner Stelle (12)

what was (1); **At what time?** Um wie viel Uhr? (4); **So what?** Na und? (13); **Under what name?** Auf welchen Namen? (9); **What a shame! What bad luck!** So ein Pech! (8); **What did you say?** Wie bitte? (E); **What do you do for a living?** Was sind Sie von Beruf? (1); **What do you think of . . . ?** Wie findest du … ? (1); **What does . . . mean?** Was bedeutet … ? (E); **What is . . . ?** Wie ist … ? (E); **What is the name of . . . ?** Wie heißt … ? (E); **What is today's/tomorrow's date?** Welches Datum ist heute/morgen? (3); **what kind of (a)** was für (ein) (11); **What time is it?** Wie spät ist es? / Wie viel Uhr ist es? (4); **What will you have?** Was bekommen Sie? (6); **What's it about?** Wovon handelt es? (13); **What's the best way to get there?** Wie komme ich am besten dahin? (9); **What's the matter?** Was ist denn los? (2); Was fehlt Ihnen/dir? (8); **What's your name?** Wie heißen Sie? (form.) / Wie heißt du? (inform.) (E); Wie ist Ihr Name? (form.) / Wie ist dein Name? (inform.) (E)

when (adv.) wann (1); (subord. conj.) wenn (8); (subord. conj.) als (10); **When is your birthday?** Wann hast du Geburtstag? (3)

where wo (1); **from where** woher (1); **(to) where** wohin (5); **Where are you from?** Woher kommen Sie? (form.) / Woher kommst du? (inform.) (E)

whether (subord. conj.) ob (8)

which welcher, welche, welches (2)

while (subord. conj.) während (9)

whipped cream die Sahne (6)

white weiß (5); **white sausage** die Weißwurst ("e) (6)

who wer (1)

whom wen (acc.); **(to/for) whom** wem (dat.) (5)

why warum (2)

wife die Frau (-en) (3)

wind der Wind (-e) (7); **wind power generator** das Windrad (¨er) (14)

window das Fenster (-) (2); **ticket window** der Fahrkartenschalter (-) (10)

windy windig (7)

wine der Wein (-e) (6)

winter der Winter (-) (7)

wish: best wishes viele Grüße (12)

to wish wünschen (3)

with mit (+ *dat.*) (5); bei (+ *dat.*) (5)

within innerhalb (+ *gen.*) (9)

without ohne (+ *acc.*) (3); **to do without** verzichten auf (+ *acc.*) (12)

woman die Frau (-en) (E)

work die Arbeit (-en) (8)

to work arbeiten (1); (*at a temporary job*) jobben (12); (*function*) funktionieren (9)

workplace der Arbeitsplatz (¨e) (11)

workroom das Arbeitszimmer (-) (2)

world die Welt (14)

worn out schlapp (8)

to worry about sich Sorgen machen um (+ *acc.*) (14)

would: would like to möchte (4); **would like (to do) most** möchte am liebsten (4); **would rather** möchte lieber (4); **Would you please . . . ?** Würden Sie bitte … ? (9)

wrapping die Verpackung (-en) (14)

to write schreiben, schrieb, geschrieben (2); **How do you write . . . ?** Wie schreibt man … ? (E)

X

xenophobia die Ausländerfeindlichkeit (14)

Y

yard der Garten (¨) (2)

year das Jahr (-e) (1); **for two years** seit zwei Jahren (6); **next year** nächstes Jahr (1); **once a year** einmal im Jahr (7)

yellow gelb (5)

yes ja (E)

yesterday gestern (7)

yet noch (2)

yogurt der Joghurt (5)

you du (*inform. sg.*), ihr (*inform. pl.*), Sie (*form. sg./pl.*) (1); dich (*inform. sg. acc.*), euch (*inform. pl. acc.*), Sie (*form. sg./pl. acc.*) (3); dir (*inform. sg. dat.*), euch (*inform. pl. dat.*), Ihnen (*form. sg./pl. dat.*) (5); (*indef. pron.*) man (4); **You may not park here.** Hier darf man nicht parken. (4); **you're welcome** bitte (E)

young jung (jünger, jüngst-) (10)

your dein (*inform. sg.*), euer (*inform. pl.*), Ihr (*form. sg./pl.*) (3)

youth hostel die Jugendherberge (-n) (9)

Z

zero null (E)

zone: pedestrian zone die Fußgängerzone (-n) (9)

zoo der Tierpark (-s) (9)

Index

The index is followed by a list of major topics. **Landeskunde-Info** categories are listed under the heading **Culture;** vocabulary items are grouped by category under **Vocabulary;** reading titles are listed under **Readings;** and Video locations are listed under **Videoclips.**

Note: *LI* = **Landeskunde-Info;** *SI* = **Sprach-Info**

Vocabulary

Credits

Photos

Einführung Opener: © Laurence Mouton/Getty Images; p. 2 (top): © Ausserhofer/Joker/Ullstein/The Image Works; p. 2 (bottom): © Michael Gottschalk/ddp images/Ullstein Bild; p. 3: © Halfdark/Getty Images; p. 6: Courtesy of Monica Clyde.

Chapter 1 Opener: © Klemmer/Caro/Ullstein Bild/The Image Works; p. 21: © Pando Hall/Getty Images; p. 22 (top): © Brigitte Sporrer/Getty Images; p. 22 (middle): © Dimitri Vervitsiotis/Getty Images; p. 22 (bottom): © Ayse Yavas/Keystone/Corbis; p. 30: Courtesy of Robert Di Donato; p. 35: © imagebroker/Alamy.

Chapter 2 Opener: © Spiegl/Ullstein Bild/The Image Works; p. 59: © Michael Gottschalk/ddp images; p. 60 (top left): © AKG Images; p. 60 (top right): © Dave & Les Jacobs/Getty Images; p. 60 (bottom): © Meissner/Ullstein Bild/The Image Works; p. 62: © Manfred Witt/Visum/The Image Works; p. 66: © Martin Leissl/Visum/The Image Works.

Chapter 3 Opener: © Cultura/Alamy; p. 83 (photo): © Svea Ingwersen; p. 83 (camera): © Bartomeu Amengual/AGE Fotostock; p. 90 (top): © Schmied-Helga Lade Fotoagentur/Peter Arnold/Photolibrary; p. 90 (bottom): © BAV-Helga Lade Fotoagentur/Peter Arnold/Photolibrary; p. 91, 95 (both), 98: Courtesy of Monica Clyde; p. 103: © Archiv für Kunst und Geschichte, Berlin/AKG Images; p. 105: © Wodicka/Ullstein Bild/The Granger Collection; p. 106: Courtesy of Monica Clyde; p. 110 (all): © Archiv für Kunst und Geschichte, Berlin/AKG Images; p. 111 (left): © Bilderdienst Süddeutscher Verlag, München/The Granger Collection; p. 111 (right): © Archiv für Kunst und Geschichte, Berlin/AKG Images.

Chapter 4 Opener: © Ecopix - Ullstein Bild/The Granger Collection; p. 122 (top): © H. & D. Zielske/Getty Images; p. 122 (bottom): © Ullstein Bild/ Lieberenz/Photolibrary; p. 131, 134: Courtesy of Monica Clyde.

Chapter 5 Opener: © Adam Jones/DanitaDelimont.com; p. 156, 166, 168: Courtesy of Monica Clyde.

Chapter 6 Opener: © Carsten Koall/Visum/The Image Works; p. 177 (cafe): Courtesy of Robert Di Donato; p. 177 (hotel): © Fishman/Ullstein Bild/The Granger Collection; p. 177 (Wurst): © Ilona Studre/Ullstein Bild/The Granger Collection; p. 177 (restaurant): © Lengemann/Ullstein Bild/The Granger Collection; p. 179: © Robert Wallis/Corbis; p. 182 (bottom): © Brinckmann/Ullstein Bild/The Granger Collection; p. 182 (top left): © Kujath/Ullstein Bild/The Granger Collection; p. 182 (top right): © Springer-Pics/Ullstein Bild/The Granger Collection; p. 186: Courtesy of Monica Clyde; p. 188: © Gerig/Ullstein Bild/The Image Works; p. 191: Courtesy of Monica Clyde; p. 204 (top): Art © 2010 Artists Rights Society (ARS), NY/VG Bild Kunst, Bonn. Photo © AKG London; p. 204 (middle): © 2010 Artists Rights Society (ARS), NY/VG Bild Kunst, Bonn; p. 204 (bottom): Art © 2010 Artists Rights Society (ARS), NY/VG Bild Kunst, Bonn. Photo © AKG London; p. 205: "Der Leser" by Jiri Georg Dokoupil.

Chapter 7 Opener: © Ed Kashi/Corbis; p. 207: © Globus; p. 212 (top left): © Julie Marcotte/Stock Boston; p. 212 (bottom left): © Fridmar Dann/eStock; p. 212 (top right): Courtesy of Monica Clyde; p. 212 (bottom right): © David Ulmer/Stock Boston; p. 216: Courtesy of the Luelsdorf family; p. 218: © Ulrike Welsch/PhotoEdit; p. 222: © Syracuse Newspapers/Marilu Lopez-Fretts/The Image Works; p. 223: Courtesy of Monica Clyde; p. 228: Courtesy of the Luelsdorf family; p. 230: © Globus; p. 231: © Topham/The Image Works.

Chapter 8 Opener: © Ullstein Bild/ ThomasRosenthal.de/Photolibrary; p. 236 (top): © Michael P. Gadomski/Photo Researchers; p. 236 (middle): © Teich/CaroUllstein Bild/The Granger Collection; p. 236 (bottom): © Photodisc; p. 240: © dpa; p. 241: © Wodicka/Ullstein Bild/The Granger Collection; p. 246: © Marco Urban/Süddeutsche Zeitung Photo/The Image Works; p. 250: Courtesy of Monica Clyde; p. 253: © Medium/Ullstein Bild/The Granger Collection.

Chapter 9 Opener: Courtesy of Robert Di Donato; p. 264: © David Crausby/Alamy; p. 267: © INTERFOTO/Alamy; p. 270: © Lange/Ullstein Bild/The Granger Collection; p. 276: Courtesy of Monica Clyde; p. 277: © Rico Hofmann/Visum/The Image Works; p. 279: Courtesy of Monica Clyde; p. 280: © Shaun Egan/Getty Images; p. 281: © Jochen Kallhardt/BlueBox; p. 288 (top): © Helga Lade/Peter Arnold/Photolibrary; p. 288 (bottom left): © Helga Lade/Peter Arnold/Photolibrary; p. 288 (bottom right): © Hartmann/Ullstein Bild/The Granger Collection; p. 289: Michael Wolgemut and Wilhelm Pleydenwurff, Nuremberg Chronicle.

Chapter 10 Opener: © Arco Images GmbH/Alamy; p. 294: © Werner Otto/AGE Fotostock; p. 296: © Karl-Heinz Haenel/Corbis; p. 297: Courtesy of Monica Clyde; p. 304: © Merlen/The Granger Collection; p. 308 (top): © Ulrike Welsch/PhotoEdit; p. 308 (bottom): © Wolfgang Steche/Visum/The Image Works; p. 314: © Pixtal/AGE Fotostock; p. 315: © Digital Vision.

Chapter 11 Opener: © Sven Doering/Visum/The Image Works; p. 321, 323: © Globus; p. 327: © Helga Lade/Peter Arnold/Photolibrary; p. 330: © David Young-Wolff/PhotoEdit; p. 342: © Pusija/Ullstein Bild/The Image Works.

Realia

Readings

46 "Dialog" by Nasrin Siege from *Texte dagegen*, Silvia Bartholl (Hrsg.), 1993 Beltz Verlag, Weinheim und Basel Programm Beltz & Gelberg, Weinheim; *106* Excerpts from „Wie feierst du deinen großen Tag?" by Kristina Dörnenburg, *JUMA* 2/2004, www.juma.de; *168* "Die Obstverkäuferin" by Leonhard Thoma from *Das Idealpaar*, Editorial Idiomas, © by Leonard Thoma, Barcelona, Spain, 2007. © Editorial idiomas, Madrid, Spain, 2007; *199* Ekkehard Müller, "Die Soße" © Gebühr; *231* Bertolt Brecht, "Vergnügungen" from *Gesammelte Werke* by Bertolt Brecht © Suhrkamp Verlag, Frankfurt am Main, 1967. Used by permission; *255–256* Text: Monika Hillemacher, adapted from "Sage mir, was du isst..." UNICUM, April 2005. Used by permission of Monika Hillemacher; Illustrations: © Sabine Kühn, www.sabinekuehn.de; *283* "Die Gitarre des Herrn Hatunoglu" by Heinrich Hannover from *Als der Clown die Grippe hatte.* Copyright © 1992 by Rowohlt Taschenbuch Verlag GmbH, Reinbek bei Hamburg; *343* Used courtesy of *Die Zeit; 344* Courtesy of www.jungeseiten.de—Everything young people need to know: A project of Jugend-Stiftung Baden-Wuerttemberg; *374* www.jungeseiten.de: Everything young people need to know: a Project of Jugend-Stiftung Baden-Wuerttemberg. Used by permission; *402* Adapted excerpts from „Gute Freunde im Netz" by Kerstin Kohlenberg, *Die Zeit*, No. 41/2005; *424* "Was in der Zeitung steht" by Reinhard Mey *Alle meine Lieder*, Maikäfor Musik Verlagsgesellschaft, Berlin.